Richard W

Richard Woodman is well
Drinkwater series, ten other se
and a work on sea-power in the Napoleonic Wars. He first became fascinated with the Arctic campaign when he sailed with survivors of PQ17. With *Malta Convoys* (published in 2000) he continued his study of British maritime services in the Second World War.

Born in London in 1944, Richard Woodman spent over thirty years at sea and has extensive experience of command and operational planning. He now writes full-time and is a regular contributor to *Lloyd's List*.

Other books by the author

THE DRINKWATER NOVELS

An Eye of the Fleet
A King's Cutter
A Brig of War
The Bomb Vessel
The Corvette
1805
Baltic Mission
In Distant Waters
A Private Revenge
Under False Colours
The Flying Squadron
Beneath the Aurora
The Shadow of the Eagle
Ebb Tide

OTHER NOVELS

Voyage East
Wager
The Darkening Sea
Endangered Species
Waterfront
Under Sail
The Accident
Act of Terror
The Captain of the *Caryatid*
The Cruise of the Commissioner
The Guineaman

NON-FICTION

Keepers of the Sea
View from the Sea
The History of the Ship
The Victory of Seapower, 1806–1814
The Story of Sail (with Veres László)
Malta Convoys

The Arctic Convoys

1941–1945

RICHARD WOODMAN

John Murray

First published in 1994 by John Murray (Publishers)
A division of Hodder Headline

Trade paperback edition 1995

This paperback edition 2004

1 3 5 7 9 10 8 6 4 2

A CIP catalogue record for this title is available from the British Library

ISBN 0-7195-6617 7

Typeset in Adobe Palatino

Printed and bound in Great Britain by Clays Ltd, St Ives plc

John Murray (Publishers)
338 Euston Road
London
NW1 3BH

For all who served in the Arctic,
1941–1945

A useful chapter in naval history and tactics could be written on the defence of convoys, by which it might perhaps be made manifest, that a determined bearing, accompanied by a certain degree of force, and a vigorous resolution to exert that force to the utmost, would, in most cases, save the greater part of the convoy, even against powerful odds.

Captain Basil Hall RN (1788–1844)

Contents

Illustrations

MAPS

The author and publishers would like to thank the following for permission to reproduce photographs:

Plates 1, 13, 14 and 16, C. Keen; 2, 10, 12, 18, 19, 21, 22, 23, 24, 27, 28, 29, 30, 31 and 34, the Trustees of the Imperial War Museum; 3, W.A. Wood; 4 and 5, World Ship Society; 6, 7, 9, 11, 25 and 26, J. Hawkins; 8, D. Craig; 15, C. Elles; 17, Mrs Keeble; 20, H. Robinson; 32 and 33, Trustees of the Fleet Air Arm Museum.

Foreword

by Admiral of the Fleet Lord Lewin

IN THE HISTORY of the Second World War, the term 'Arctic Convoys' conjures up an image of endurance against great odds, of battles fought in the Arctic night in which ice, snow and high winds added to the horrors of war. It was indeed conditions in the Arctic which set the convoys to northern Russia apart from other theatres of war. In all some thirty ships were forced to turn back because of bad weather. In winter seamen fought a continual battle against gales and ice in almost perpetual darkness; in summer the sun rarely set and there was no respite from the threat or reality of attack.

The exceptional conditions in the Arctic seas and the fate of one convoy, PQ17, have combined to give the impression that the Arctic convoys were competing against overwhelming odds. PQ17 was instructed to scatter by direct order from the First Sea Lord in Whitehall in the belief that it was about to be struck by the great German battleship, the *Tirpitz*: as a result, twenty-nine ships of that ill-fated convoy were sunk by air and submarine attack, and only ten got through. In fact, the Arctic convoys were amazingly successful. Of a total of 40 outward convoys comprising 811 ships, only 58 were sunk. Those that got through delivered great quantities of tanks, aircraft, ammunition and other essential war material which made a significant contribution to Russia's role in the war.

In this book, Richard Woodman describes the course of each Arctic convoy, and sets these maritime operations in the context of the political and military pressures of the time. Based on thorough and meticulous research, his account provides an extraordinarily vivid and accurate picture of the conduct of the convoys and of the conditions that men faced in these high latitudes.

Most of us who served in the Royal Navy during the war had experience of convoy and watched, often with sinking hearts, often with frustration that we could not do more, as the merchant ships in our charge were hit by bomb or torpedo. From that experience was born an admiration and respect for our merchant seamen that the years can never dim.

Lewin of Greenwich

Preface

TO A GENERATION of Britons now in middle age, the Soviet Union was the bogyman of the Cold War in whose shadow they grew up and raised their children. Then, half a century after the start of the Second World War, the immense empire bequeathed by Stalin collapsed: the 'domino theory' was reversed.

This astonishing shift in world politics provokes a re-examination of our relationship with the Russian people who, we realize, achieved this dramatic revolution and have always existed behind the façade of Communism, and in particular a review of the contribution made by Great Britain and the United States to the Red Army's part in the Allied victory over Hitler's Wehrmacht. The purpose of this book is, therefore, concerned with the enormous task of convoying cargoes through the Arctic Ocean to North Russia. Without the logistical support of tanks, aircraft, transport vehicles, guns, ammunition, chemicals, rubber, aluminium and much else besides, Stalin's forces could not have rolled up the Nazi armies on the Eastern front and pursued them deep into the heart of the Fatherland. Much of Russia's armoury was destroyed in the first weeks of the German invasion and although production rose to meet the demands of war, it was insufficient. To contain the enemy and then assume the offensive required weaponry and *matériel* from her allies, Great Britain and the United States. Most of these reinforcements came from the latter, though they were carried in merchant ships of several Allied nations.

Largely unappreciated at the time and the target of Stalin's personal prejudice, these convoys were a magnificent achievement, 'attempting the impossible', according to the Royal Navy's distinguished historian Sir Michael Lewis. The defensive tactic of the convoy was used first to sustain a hard-pressed ally in the field, later as a vital component of a mighty strategic offensive. These battles of supply, more than an offshoot of the Battle of the Atlantic, were fought in the most inhospitable waters where the heavy ships of the Kriegsmarine lurked amid the Wagnerian grandeur of the Norwegian fiords, maintaining the classic threat of a 'fleet in being', tying down Britain's Home Fleet and making every Russia-bound convoy a potential political as well as military disaster. Despite Hitler's neurotic mismanagement of his surface fleet, great ships like the *Tirpitz* and the *Scharnhorst* remained a potent threat until they had been annihilated, the one by the bombers of the Royal Air Force, the other by the guns of the Royal Navy.

Escort of these Russian convoys was a British responsibility. The Royal Navy provided covering forces with the capital ships of the Home Fleet, cruisers, and close and ocean escorts. Later the 'Woolworth' or escort aircraft-carrier gave local air support, while the fleet and escort destroyers, sloops and minesweepers all played their part in a gradual build-up of naval support. Less glamorous and often inadequate extempore solutions – armed trawlers, merchant anti-aircraft 'cruisers' and merchant ships armed with a catapult-launched fighter aircraft (CAM ships) – played their part in the early years; and the plucky vessels of the Ocean Rescue Service were vital later in maintaining the morale of merchant seamen.

Of all the Allies, Russia gained most from the defeat of Germany and, in the light of immediate post-war events, the support of Anglo-American Arctic convoys may have seemed a hollow triumph, part of the enormous and profligate waste of war. The ultimate success of these convoys was only achieved at a price. Merchant ship sinkings were considerable and, in particular, the destruction of convoy PQ17 cast a long shadow over the relationship between Britain's Royal and Merchant Navies. Losses in escorting warships, too, were high, for in addition to the German surface ships, the Arctic Ocean concealed the waiting U-boats and the cloudy Arctic skies the Luftwaffe.

None of these horrors matched the intense cold and misery of the polar seas. It is the theatre of this campaign that has left its indelible imprint upon its veterans, not the players. By an irony of geography, the conditions making the 'impossible' a task worth attempting originate half a world away.

The warm water of the Gulf Stream uncoils itself from the Gulf of Mexico, passes Key West at the southern tip of Florida and turns north-east, becoming the North Atlantic Drift, to wash against the western shores of the British Isles. Together with its associated tropical maritime air mass, it generates the wet, warm and windy weather characteristic of the British climate.

The pelagic current flows on, past the Shetlands, the Faeroes and Iceland, degenerating in both temperature and vigour, but carrying still a residual, comparative warmth as it passes the coast of Norway and rounds the North Cape.

Encountering the high-pressure air mass and ice cap of the high Arctic, its less dense waters resist the incursion of the eutrophic polar sea. The colder water slides beneath the warmer, forming layers of differing densities, relinquishing its surface ice to the melting influence of the remnant current in summer, remorselessly cooling it, narrowing its navigable width in winter and finally exhausting it off the mouth of the Kola Inlet, a little to the south-east of the North Cape and leading to the Russian port of Murmansk. Only during the brief weeks of the boreal summer does the Gulf Stream maintain its supremacy further east, extending navigation from the Barents to the Kara Sea, and opening the narrow Gourlo into the White Sea and the Dvina River, permitting ships to reach Archangel.

This monstrously slow, yet readily perceptible encounter in the sea is matched in the air above. The less dense residue of tropical air battles vainly with the cold high-pressure winds sliding southwards from the North Pole. This collision is fomented by the spinning of the earth, causing intense depressions which spawn gales of exceptional violence. These in turn generate huge waves, or seas as seamen call them, which, though they are above freezing as they break, when dashed into spray rapidly turn to ice in the freezing air. Ships caught in such gales pitch and roll, shipping 'green' water which, where it falls upon cold steel, rapidly forms rime, building moment by moment into heavy, obstinate encrustations of thick ice. In these conditions not only does the keeping of a watch become an ordeal of unimaginable misery, and the moving parts of deck machinery and weapons seize solid, but the top weight caused by this accumulation of ice adds to the seaman's ultimate horror: the risk of capsize.

A ship is designed to be inherently stable. In the case of merchant ships loading and discharging cargoes, this is not immutable, but is carefully controlled by her officers, often to fine limits as, in quest of profit or, in war, the maximizing of her capacity, the ship is loaded to her marks. As a voyage progresses and she consumes the oil or coal in her bunkers, she removes bottom weight, so that her stability is constantly reducing and is always a factor at the forefront of her master's mind.

In a few hours of heavy weather in an Arctic gale the fine balance between metacentric heights, righting levers and heeling moments can be destroyed. Gun barrels, aerials, wires and guard-rails, derricks, masts, ladders, winches and boat davits all gather the pernicious accretions of black ice which, unless attacked with axes and steam hoses, will cause disaster.

It is this cold men remember most; either the damp misery of bulkheads running with condensation, the chill miasma penetrating every nook and cranny of the ship; or the bitter Arctic cold that froze the same condensation solid, turned exhaled breath to rime, and spray to ice. There was no comfort to be had anywhere in such weather, though the larger ships were less violent in their motion than the smaller. The sparse 'Arctic clothing' issued from official 'slops' was largely ineffective and the 'comforts' knitted lovingly by anonymous donors at home were often insufficient. The warmest a man could get was in his bunk or hammock, fully clothed, and from which being turned out was an act of petty cruelty. Tobacco and hot, sweet cocoa, or 'kye', sustained the body, while a grim gallows humour sustained the spirit.

'Who the hell are you?' asked a destroyer commander as, coming on to the bridge one black night, he bumped into a figure on his bridge.

'I'm the port lookout, sir, and there's nothing to report . . .'

The captain, being of a poetic bent, recognized a first line and later declaimed:

> I'm the port lookout and there's nothing to report,
> Unless I spoke the truth, sir, and told you what I thought,
> It's a fucking awful night, sir, and my nose is running cruel,
> And it's my confirmed belief, sir, that you're a bloody fool!

And yet the region can bear a serene face, a calm, cold and clear beauty in which temperature inversions cause mirages and visibility may exceed thirty miles. The air stream predominating from the south-west, which manifests itself in areas of low pressure and the gales of depressions, is a stark contrast to the high pressure of the polar regions, and these two weather systems fight constantly for mastery over the climatic conditions of the Arctic Ocean. Transition from one to another can be swift, the shifts in barometric pressure abrupt, and while a fog may mar the perfection of a summer's day, winter or summer, the Arctic can produce memorable wonders. One former destroyer lieutenant recalled that 'the sound of the ship surging through ice as she rose and fell to a gentle swell was like the tinkling of glass', while a merchant ship's master remembered 'the sight of the aurora undulating across the sky like the curtains of a great theatre'.

But the ice was omnipresent, even when out of sight. In winter the pack edged south, sometimes within eighty miles of the North Cape, narrowing the strip of navigable water, forcing convoys south, closer to the enemy airfields. Even in summer, as the ice broke up and allowed the convoys to detour northwards, round Bear Island towards Novaya Zemlya, the presence of bergs, of pancake ice and the almost submerged growlers added their dangerous presence to the passage. 'You could smell it in the air, that peculiar, dank smell borne on a north wind and which prevails in those far northern waters.'

Yet even the ice could impress, as a young gunner on a rescue ship discovered. 'One wonderful sight was the "birth" of an iceberg. A tremendous crack of noise and the enormous shift of ice. It was several hundred yards long and created a wave that we had to turn into [to avoid swamping].'

Ships encounter special problems navigating in the polar seas. A magnetic compass forsakes the familiar, comforting horizontal plane expected of it, and tries to dip down towards the vast mass of iron which forms the earth's magnetic pole. The normally more precise and less variable gyro compass does the opposite and, in seeking a polar star, tilts upwards. Even the projection of the chart is different from that used elsewhere on the earth's surface. Atmospheric depressions cause overcast, and mist, fog and ice brume obscure the horizon, depriving the navigator of the use of his sextant, almanac and chronometer. Often ships ran on dead reckoning, or DR, an amalgam of course, speed and an assumed distance, with estimated values for leeway thrown in for good measure, a mixture of inspiration and guesswork over which no two navigators ever agree. Frequently ships, whether naval or merchantmen, simply got lost, particularly those separated from a convoy or proceeding alone. Such stragglers or single ships were extremely vulnerable to U-boat attack. When torpedoed, they sank in a sea seldom above 4°C, so that their people had little chance of survival and, even when rescued and wrapped in blankets, continued to lose core heat from the remorseless effects of the then misunderstood condition now known as hypothermia.

For most, though, the implacable indifference of the weather and the technical difficulties were at least comprehensible, the traditional foes of the seafarer, to be feared in a general sense and fought with the resources of morale, experience and leadership. The malice of the enemy was a different matter and in the face of it the cloak of winter was something of a comfort. For in that season in the Arctic, as the earth's axis tilts away from the sun, there is a four-month period when the sun fails to rise at all, noon being characterized by a twilight gloom. This was the season Admiral of the Fleet Sir Dudley Pound, Britain's First Sea Lord, favoured for passing convoys through the Barents Sea. But during the weeks of high summer the sun never sets in polar latitudes, and even when it dips ten or twelve degrees below the horizon, twilight prevails. Such endless days, beautiful though they might be, exposed a convoy to the vigilance of the enemy's long-range reconnaissance aircraft quartering the ocean. Furthermore, an Arctic fog, or sea-smoke, where cold air condenses when passing over the surface of a sea a few degrees warmer, produces sudden, dense fogs which hug the wavetops. In these conditions, the navigation of a convoy became a matter of the lookouts' eyes straining after the fog buoys towed by every ship and designed to throw up a conspicuous plume of water astern of her, facilitating the station-keeping of the next ship in the column. The anxiety of worried navigators on their blinded bridges was not matched in the clear skies above, where the masts of the convoy might protrude above the writhing tendrils of vapour and mark the plodding progress of the target to searching eyes above.

At least the winter, awful though it was, brought them real obscurity. It was then, they thought, that luck might lie with them, not the enemy: it was the time to go. Peter Gillingham, the young chaplain of the 17th Destroyer Flotilla, expressed this feeling of foreboding and inevitable commitment as well as an overwhelming sense of being the hunted quarry:

> When the sun sinks daily lower and slacks her heat and light,
> When in far off Arctic regions, grows the long, perpetual night,
> Where Aurora Borealis mocks the frozen seaman's plight,
> The season's opening . . .
>
> Farewell the quiet hours around the safely shackled ship,
> Farewell the gay companionship, the merry jest and quip,
> And farewell too the softer joys of eye and cheek and lip,
> The season's opened . . .

This philosophic view was not shared by all. Such unimaginable conditions that challenge the descriptive powers of the historian had their own effect upon the morale of the young men forced to go to war in these high latitudes. To say that they adopted the traditional recourse of the seaman, black humour, a foul vocabulary or a religious tendency, is a gross over-simplification, though a superficial judge might consider this tripartite claim justified. Most afterwards admitted a modest determination; they had 'just got on with the job', and for that it did not matter which ensign they sailed under, only that they ran their cargo or their convoy through to its destination.

Such an achievement stands on its own merits, whether set against the other momentous events of the Second World War or the long chronicle of maritime history. Obscured by the great struggle in the Atlantic, the Arctic campaign seems worthy of re-examination, particularly from the British point of view, for it was one of the final manifestations of our sea-power. In attempting a book about 'the Kola Run' I have been mindful of the different characteristics of ships, each of which was unique to the men in her, and of the men themselves, many of whom were still in their teens or early twenties. Space has limited the degree to which I have been able to quote individuals directly from the mass of correspondence I have received; however, I have made an effort to reflect the views of the many veterans whom I have met or with whom I have exchanged letters and telephone calls. I am profoundly grateful to all of them, and to the descendants of some of those who did not survive, for permission to use papers or photographs: a list of acknowledgements appears at the end of the book.

It has been a paramount consideration to produce a book which, insofar as I am capable of so doing, reflects the reality of this long naval campaign as well as the wider influences upon it and its implications. In the whole history of maritime war, no theatre has been as demanding or as rigorous as the Arctic.

I have avoided the interruption of the text with footnotes, and have confined myself to general notes on each chapter, together with a select bibliography at the end of the book. Where British naval officers are concerned, I have appended only initials indicating them as belonging to either of the Reserves and I have omitted all decorations for clarity. I have also retained older, contemporary forms of names, more familiar to British and American readers, most notably Spitzbergen for Svalbard, Bear Island for Bjørnøya and Vaenga for Severomorsk.

In an area where longitude changes rapidly and shifts of time zones are further confused by the Arctic's extremes of darkness or daylight, I have kept times to simple twenty-four-hour notation applicable to the local time of the event and, where possible, have indicated the seasonal and meteorological conditions in the text.

During the course of my researches I have predictably come across a number of inconsistencies. Where possible I have reconciled these according to what, in my judgement, seemed the best available information. If I have further perpetuated errors, and for those other omissions or mistakes which must form an integral part of any human undertaking, I ask forgiveness.

Richard Woodman
Harwich, 1993

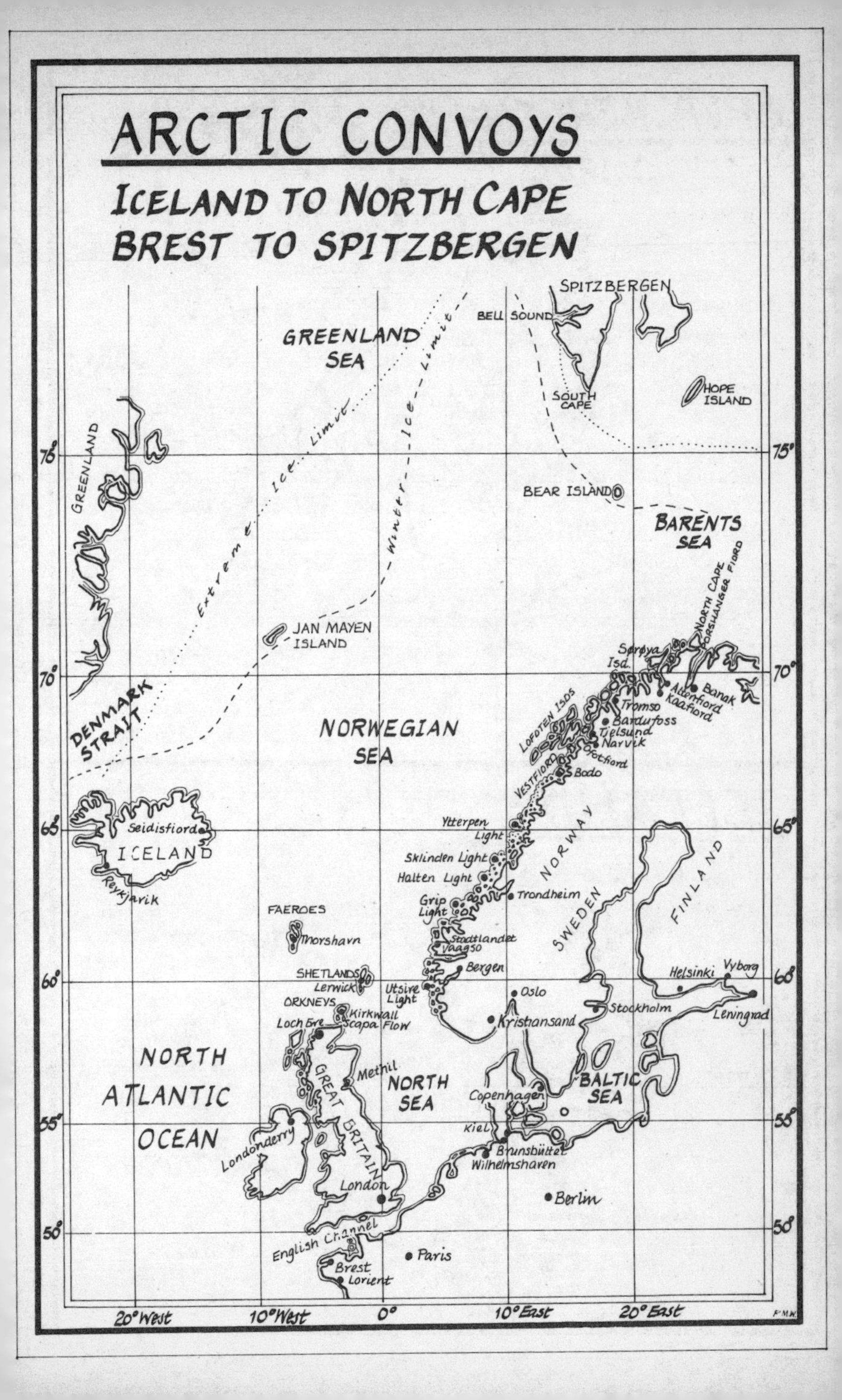

ARCTIC CONVOYS
ICELAND TO NORTH CAPE
BREST TO SPITZBERGEN
SPITZBERGEN
BELL SOUND
GREENLAND SEA
SOUTH CAPE
HOPE ISLAND
GREENLAND
Extreme Ice Limit
Winter Ice Limit
BEAR ISLAND
BARENTS SEA
NORTH CAPE
PORSANGER FIORD
JAN MAYEN ISLAND
Sørøya Isd.
DENMARK STRAIT
NORWEGIAN SEA
LOFOTEN ISDS
Tromso
Altenfiord
Kaafiord
Banak
Bardufoss
Tjelsund
Narvik
Ofotfiord
Bodo
VESTFIORD
Ytterpen Light
Sklinden Light
Halten Light
Grip Light
Trondheim
NORWAY
SWEDEN
FINLAND
Seidisfiord
ICELAND
Reykjavik
FAEROES
Thorshavn
Stadtlandet
Vaagso
Bergen
SHETLANDS
Lerwick
ORKNEYS
Kirkwall
Scapa Flow
Loch Ewe
Utsire Light
Oslo
Helsinki
Vyborg
Leningrad
Stockholm
Kristiansand
NORTH ATLANTIC OCEAN
GREAT BRITAIN
Methil
NORTH SEA
Copenhagen
BALTIC SEA
Kiel
Brunsbüttel
Wilhelmshaven
Londonderry
London
Berlin
English Channel
Paris
Brest
Lorient
75°
70°
65°
60°
55°
50°
20° West
10° West
0°
10° East
20° East

SPITZBERGEN
(SVALBARD)
80° North
NORTH EAST LAND
SPITZBERGEN
NORTH FIORD
SASSEN FIORD
TEMPLE BAY
BARENTS ISLAND
ICEFIORD
COAL BAY
ADVENT BAY
Barentsburg
EDGE ISLAND
AXEL SOUND
LOWE SOUND
BELL SOUND
STOR FIORD
HORN SOUND
HOPE ISLAND
SOUTH CAPE
15° East

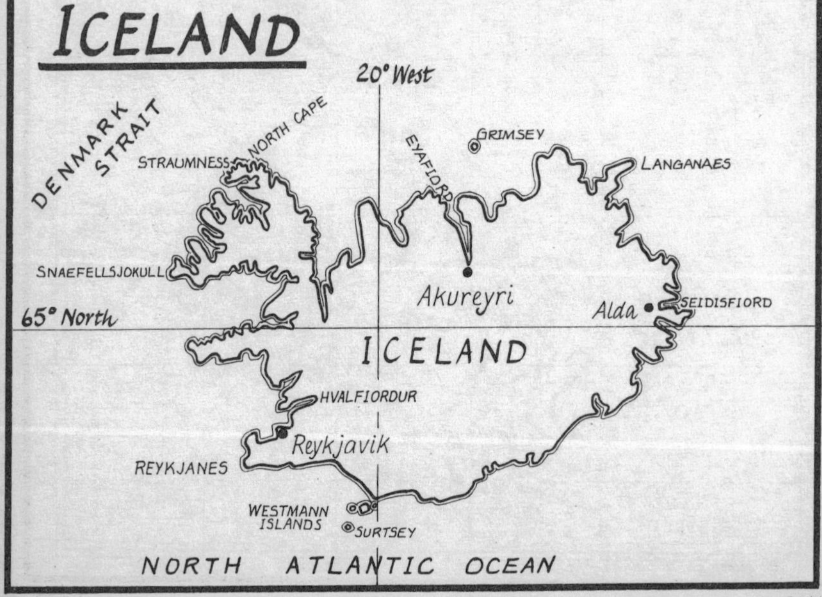
ICELAND
20° West
DENMARK STRAIT
NORTH CAPE
GRIMSEY
EYAFIORD
STRAUMNESS
LANGANAES
SNAEFELLSJOKULL
Akureyri
Alda
SEIDISFIORD
65° North
ICELAND
HVALFIORDUR
Reykjavik
REYKJANES
WESTMANN ISLANDS
SURTSEY
NORTH ATLANTIC OCEAN
R.M.W.

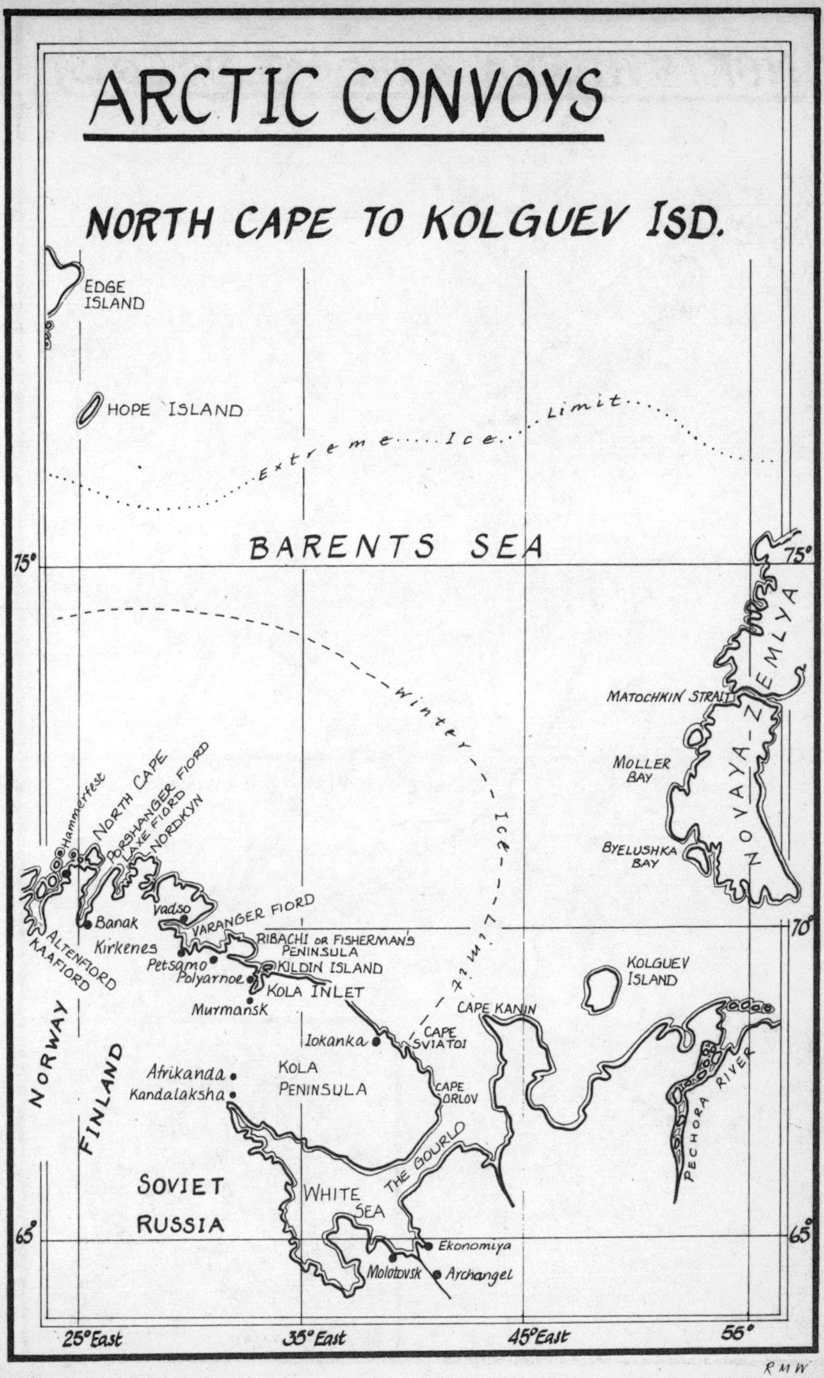

ARCTIC CONVOYS

NORTH CAPE TO KOLGUEV ISD.

EDGE ISLAND
HOPE ISLAND
extreme....Ice....Limit
BARENTS SEA
75°
75°
winter — Ice — Limit
MATOCHKIN STRAIT
NOVAYA-ZEMLYA
MOLLER BAY
BYELUSHKA BAY
Hammerfest
NORTH CAPE
PORSHANGER FIORD
LAXE FIORD
NORDKYN
Vadso
VARANGER FIORD
Banak
ALTENFIORD
KAAFIORD
Kirkenes
Petsamo
RIBACHI OR FISHERMAN'S PENINSULA
KILDIN ISLAND
Polyarnoe
KOLA INLET
Murmansk
70°
KOLGUEV ISLAND
CAPE KANIN
CAPE SVIATOI
Iokanka
NORWAY
FINLAND
Afrikanda
Kandalaksha
KOLA PENINSULA
CAPE ORLOV
PECHORA RIVER
THE GOURLO
SOVIET RUSSIA
WHITE SEA
65°
65°
Ekonomiya
Molotovsk
Archangel
25° East
35° East
45° East
55°
RMW

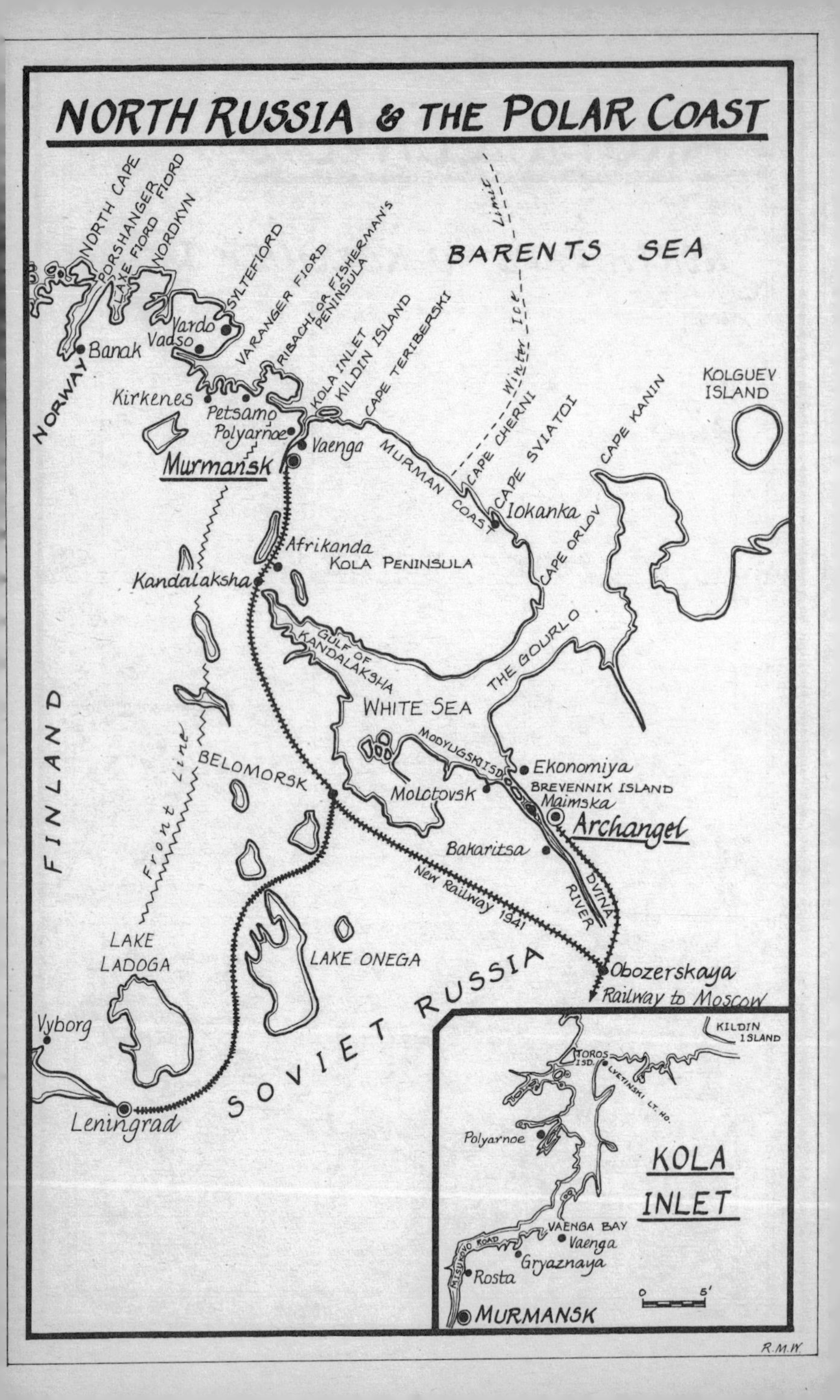
NORTH RUSSIA & THE POLAR COAST
BARENTS SEA
Winter Ice Limit
NORTH CAPE
PORSHANGER FIORD
LAXE FIORD
NORDKYN
SYLTEFIORD
VARANGER FIORD
RIBACHI OR FISHERMAN'S PENINSULA
KOLA INLET
KILDIN ISLAND
CAPE TERIBERSKI
Vardo
Vadso
Banak
NORWAY
Kirkenes
Petsamo
Polyarnoe
Vaenga
Murmansk
MURMAN COAST
CAPE CHERNI
CAPE SVIATOI
Iokanka
CAPE KANIN
KOLGUEV ISLAND
CAPE ORLOV
Afrikanda
KOLA PENINSULA
Kandalaksha
GULF OF KANDALAKSHA
THE GOURLO
WHITE SEA
MODYUGSKI ISD
Ekonomiya
BREVENNIK ISLAND
Maimska
Molotovsk
Archangel
Bakaritsa
DVINA RIVER
FINLAND
Front Line
BELOMORSK
New Railway 1941
Obozerskaya
Railway to Moscow
LAKE LADOGA
LAKE ONEGA
SOVIET RUSSIA
Vyborg
Leningrad
KILDIN ISLAND
TOROS ISD.
LYETINSKI LT. HO.
Polyarnoe
KOLA INLET
VAENGA BAY
Vaenga
MISUKOVO ROAD
Gryaznaya
Rosta
0 5'
MURMANSK
R.M.W.

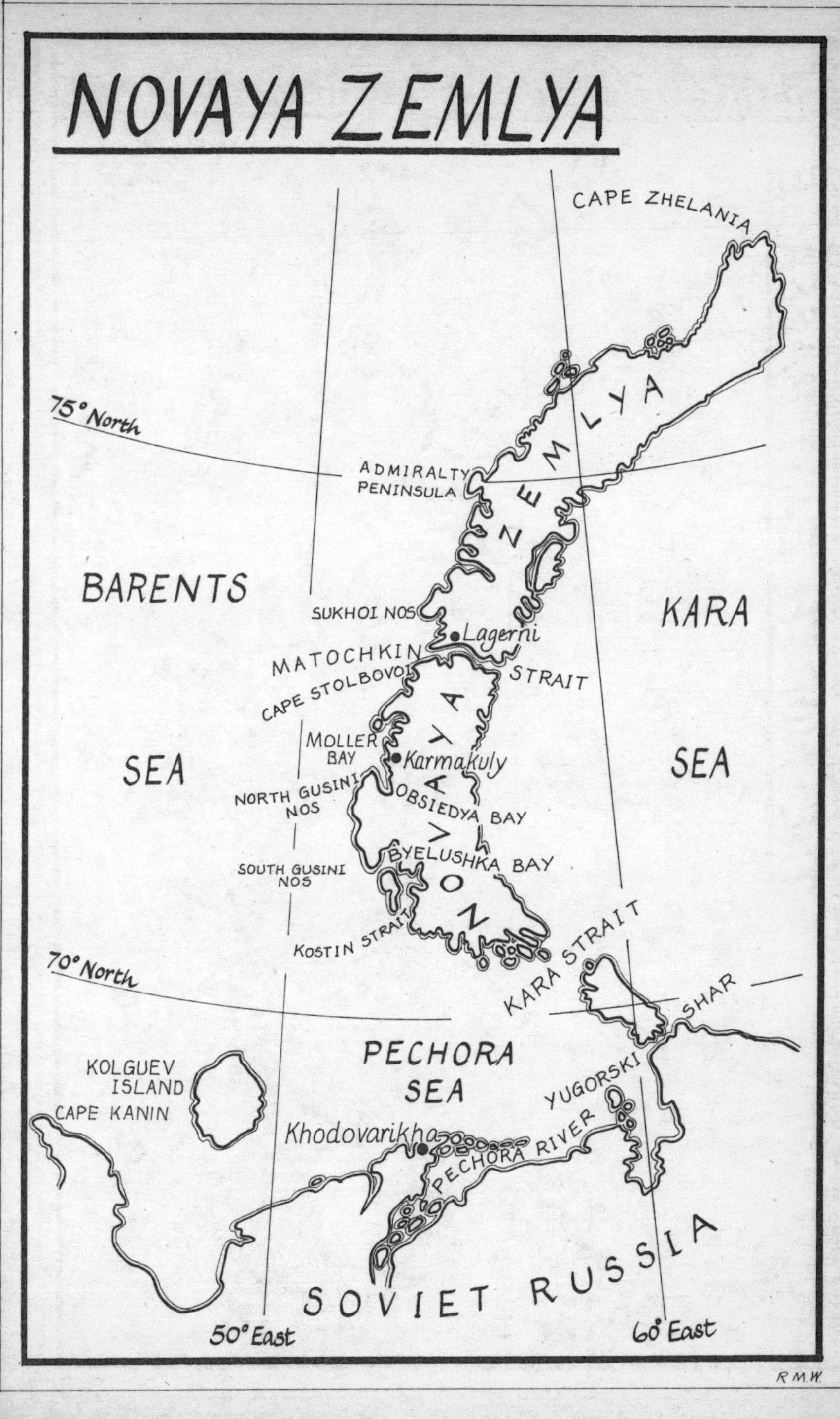

NOVAYA ZEMLYA

CAPE ZHELANIA
ZEMLYA
75° North
ADMIRALTY
PENINSULA
BARENTS
SEA
KARA
SEA
SUKHOI NOS
Lagerni
MATOCHKIN
STRAIT
CAPE STOLBOVOI
MOLLER
BAY
Karmakuly
NOVAYA
NORTH GUSINI
NOS
OBSIEDYA BAY
BYELUSHKA BAY
SOUTH GUSINI
NOS
KOSTIN STRAIT
KARA STRAIT
70° North
SHAR
PECHORA
SEA
YUGORSKI
KOLGUEV
ISLAND
CAPE KANIN
Khodovarikha
PECHORA RIVER
SOVIET RUSSIA
50° East
60° East

R.M.W.

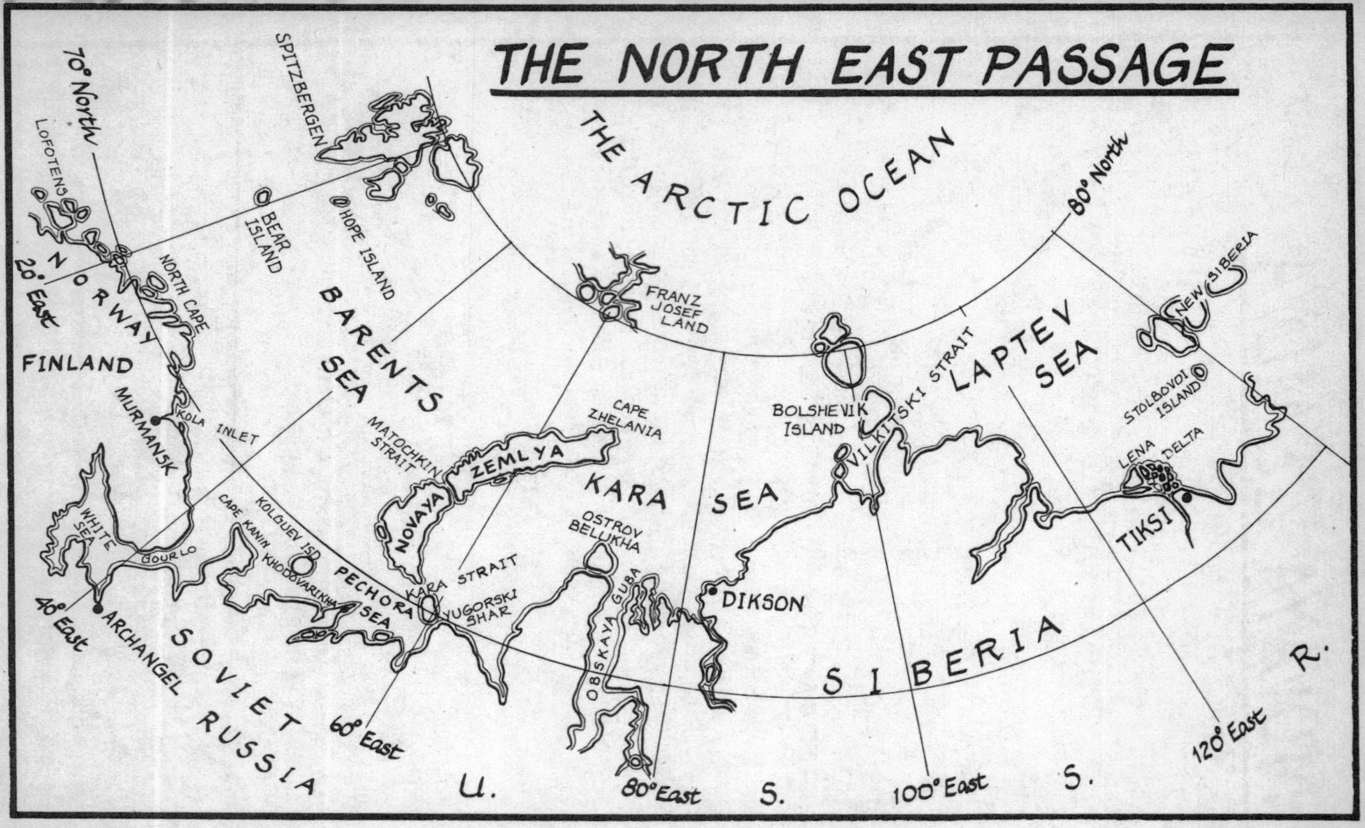
THE NORTH EAST PASSAGE
THE ARCTIC OCEAN
70° North
80° North
20° East
40° East
60° East
80° East
100° East
120° East
LOFOTENS
SPITZBERGEN
BEAR ISLAND
HOPE ISLAND
NORWAY
NORTH CAPE
FINLAND
MURMANSK
KOLA INLET
BARENTS SEA
WHITE SEA
GOURLO
ARCHANGEL
CAPE KANIN
KOLGUEV ISD
KHODOVARIKHA
PECHORA SEA
SOVIET RUSSIA
MATOCHKIN STRAIT
NOVAYA ZEMLYA
CAPE ZHELANIA
FRANZ JOSEF LAND
KARA STRAIT
YUGORSKI SHAR
KARA SEA
OSTROV BELUKHA
OBSKAYA GUBA
DIKSON
BOLSHEVIK ISLAND
VILKITSKI STRAIT
LAPTEV SEA
STOLBOVOI ISLAND
NEW SIBERIA
LENA DELTA
TIKSI
SIBERIA
U. S. S. R.
R.M.W.

1

'The world will hold its breath'

AT 03.15 ON the morning of 22 June 1941, the darkness of the night was broken by a flickering of light. A few seconds later the insistent croaking of frogs in the reed-beds of the River Bug, where the storming parties of the German Wehrmacht lurked expectantly, was obliterated by the concussion of distant artillery. Shells from more than 7,000 guns whined overhead and the explosions of their detonations thundered and flashed on the far bank to the east. The bombardment began Operation Barbarossa, the German invasion of Soviet Russia. Advance troops started to cross the Bug on a 500-mile front by every method military cunning could devise. Over an hour earlier Heinkel bombers of the Luftwaffe had dropped mines in the waters of the Black Sea and the Baltic. Other aircraft went into action at first light, bombing and strafing ahead of the advancing columns, destroying roads, tanks and fuel dumps. Most significantly, by noon, the Luftwaffe had eliminated over 1,000 Russian aircraft, most of them on the ground. Their own loss was trifling. A German officer likened it to throwing stones at glasshouses. 'When Operation Barbarossa is launched,' Adolf Hitler had boasted, 'the world will hold its breath.'

In fact the world had been holding its breath since learning of the astonishing German-Soviet non-aggression pact agreed in late August 1939 by their respective foreign ministers, Ribbentrop and Molotov. Though alarmed by the openly declared territorial ambitions of Germany, Stalin's overtures to Britain and France had for some time remained inconclusive. Mutual suspicion clouded all negotiations: the Western powers feared the Communist 'infection'; the Russians, wholly antipathetic to the Fascist Axis, had a yet deeper aversion to an alliance with the traditional enemy of Marxism, the capitalist and imperialist governments in Paris and London. Russian policy was highly subjective, centralized in the person of the Soviet leader, Josef Stalin, a man as ruthless as Hitler, but with a greater cunning. The expedient solution of an accommodation with Hitler would buy time, and Ribbentrop and Molotov swiftly concluded their pact under the very noses of the Anglo-French mission still in Moscow.

When in September 1939 the German army invaded Poland from the west, the Red Army did likewise from the east, recovering territory lost to the Poles under Marshal Pilsudski in 1920 but also, and more significantly, increasing Russian-held territory for the traditional strategy of defence in depth against the day when this might become necessary. Similar reasons were given for the annexation of Lithuania, Latvia and Estonia in 1940. Like Germany and in marked contrast to the Western democracies, Soviet Russia had been preparing for war for many years,[1] spurred on by the doctrine of world revolution. The Red Army regarded a major European war as likely from about 1932, with this crystallizing into 'absolute certainty' by the time Hitler became Reichskanzler.[2] Ironically, the military and naval limitations imposed on Germany in 1919 by the Treaty of Versailles had created a hothouse of debate within a small, almost intimate, officer corps. As early as 1922 the German Ambassador to Moscow, Count Brockdorff-Rantzau, had engineered an agreement known as Rapallo-Politik allowing officers of the then Reichswehr to conduct military studies and experiments in Russia, beyond the supervising restrictions of the Inter-Allied Military Control. Here Soviet and German officers exchanged views and while the Reichswehr was incapable of deploying massed tank formations such as the Red Army displayed at the Kiev manœuvres of 1935, the advent of National Socialism gave Germany the dynamic to convert theory to practice, to build an economy based on an armaments industry and to field at the Mecklenburg manœuvres of 1937 the first Nazi tank squadrons, forerunners of the Panzer divisions. Similar expansion of the German airforce took place and further 'experimentation' in land, sea and air warfare followed during the Spanish Civil War. The German reoccupation of the industrial Rhineland in 1936 increased Germany's war potential, and the Fascist alliance with Mussolini's Italy created the power bloc from which the coming war was to be waged. As the decade drew to its close the annexation of Austria and Czechoslovakia resulted in the acquisition of enormous war booty, and the coercion and formation of vassal states in the Balkans secured reserves of fighting manpower as well as assets such as the Ploesti oilfields of Romania.[3]

Nor had the Russians been idle. The victorious emergence of the Bolsheviks after the revolutions of 1917 and the ensuing civil war led to years of strenuous restructuring of the exhausted Russian economy. It was not until the end of the 1920s that the production of coal, iron and steel reached the output of 1913. The tank formations which the Germans observed and then emulated were constructed by industrial plants initially set up with the aid of foreign advisers. Americans helped organize mass production of motor vehicles, Germans that of aircraft. As Marshal Voroshilov, the People's Commissar for Defence, said of it in *Pravda* in March 1933, the First Five Year Plan (1929–33) laid 'excellent foundations on which to build all the technical appliances for modern warfare'.

As the political differences between the ideologies of Soviet Russia and Nazi Germany widened, the *rapprochement* between the military professionals withered and died. They met as opponents on the 'experimental' battlefields of Spain; the rupture seemed complete, the battlelines drawn, until the revival of mutual military expedience in the Ribbentrop-Molotov accord. Neither of the contracting powers regarded the pact as anything other than temporary. For the Germans, as they planned the invasion of France immediately after the suppression of Poland, it removed the fear of fighting on two fronts; for the Russians it bought time in which to step up military production and the opportunity to gain defensive territory without German interference. As the Germans invaded Poland, the Russians followed, driving a salient beyond Lvov to protect the Ukraine, aware that they were vulnerable not only if Germany chose later to seize the Ukraine for the wealth of its resources, but also because the area nurtured a politically unreliable separatist movement based on Lvov.

Stalin also wished to protect the seaward approaches to Leningrad and in November 1939 commenced the Winter War with Finland. This hard-fought, bitter campaign was a pyrrhic victory for the Russians. They lost an estimated 200,000 men, 700 aircraft and 1,600 tanks. Marshal Semyon Timoshenko was appointed to rectify the defects in the Red Army exposed by its mauling at the hands of the outnumbered Finns. He had little time to replace the aeroplanes and tanks before Hitler pounced. For their part, the Finns, unsupported by the Western powers in their hour of need and driven into the Axis camp by 1941, retained their independence despite the loss of Vyborg and territory in the north. Stalin had achieved his objectives at a cost: Vyborg protected Leningrad; the narrow northern buffer covered the Arctic port of Murmansk.

Operation Barbarossa was planned for May 1941. Norway, Denmark, the Low Countries and France had already fallen. Although the British had extricated the men of their expeditionary force at Dunkirk, it had been at the expense of their equipment. They too were short of the means with which to wage effective war. Fortunately, the resources of the Royal Air Force staved off a German invasion by defeating the Luftwaffe's air offensive in the summer of 1940 in what came to be called the Battle of Britain. Nevertheless, Britain was subjected to increasingly heavy bombing raids while German U-boats from the French Biscay ports now had access to the Atlantic trade routes to attack with ease her immense seaborne trade. Augmented by the demands of war and, in these early months, inadequately escorted, Britain's merchant shipping was vulnerable to attack by both submarine and surface raider. The latter could now move almost undetected in the Norwegian fiords and break out into the Atlantic at will.

Shelving plans for invading Britain, Hitler began to transfer his Panzer divisions across Europe. The Soviet Union, home of the despised Slavs and seed-bed of the hated Communist creed, was the real enemy; Russia was the declared ground upon which the victorious Reich would expand and consolidate its 1,000-year rule. But Hitler was compelled to delay his attack in the east and to divert troops to Yugoslavia, Greece and North Africa. The pro-British Serbian majority in Yugoslavia had refused to submit quietly to Hitler's hegemony and their suppression cost Germany valuable time. Moreover, his Italian ally's military operations had badly miscarried. Mussolini's invasion of Greece was held up by ferocious resistance. The Wehrmacht and the Luftwaffe were ordered to retrieve the situation and save the Italians from defeat. The Greek campaign was complicated by the intervention of British, Australian and New Zealand troops under Britain's treaty obligations, but these were eventually driven south, to be withdrawn by the ships of the Royal Navy. Meanwhile, the British in North Africa, though poorly equipped, defeated the Italians and proved stubborn and difficult to evict. Resources involved in the fight for the Western Desert were to impinge on the campaign on the Eastern front by diverting German arms to North Africa and affecting the flow of Allied supplies to Russia.

Not only did these unintended campaigns cost the Germans time and the disruption of their logistical arrangements for the transfer of troops to the line of the Bug, they also began to turn public opinion in the United States in favour of the Allies. Shocked by the arrogance of Hitler's actions, a growing awareness of the true situation in Europe began to spread in America.

These delays and the early onset of the Russian winter cost the Germans their political and military objectives. Despite their early tactical successes, eventually they were to lose the campaign and, in the Russian counter-attack, combined with the Allied invasion of Normandy, the war in Europe. But in the first few days of the invasion of Russia the German officer's euphoric reference to the destruction of glasshouses seemed justified. Despite earlier Russian efforts to secure territory for defence in depth, standing orders designed to preserve the non-aggression pact were confirmed to incredulous field commanders now confronted by a full-scale invasion. In an excessively centralized command structure, local initiative was paralysed and so, it seemed, was Stalin. Although the Soviet leader had himself warned that a spring offensive by the Germans was likely, it had been his policy to adhere strictly to the terms of the Ribbentrop-Molotov pact. Russia supplied Germany with grain and oil up to the very day of invasion and Russian reconnaissance flights were inhibited by standing orders intended to avoid provocation. The object of all this was to buy Stalin time. The impressive tanks of the 1935 manœuvres had become obsolete and many were defective; more had been lost in Finland and only a quarter of the most modern were serviceable. Manpower was spread too thinly; the Red Army's 170 divisions in the west were largely unsupported after fanning out to garrison the areas of Poland occupied in 1939. Most important of all, despite Timoshenko's reforms, Stalin had compromised the Red Army and destroyed its command structure by 'purging' 35,000 officers *pour encourager les autres*. This policy only served to weaken the morale of the remainder.

Stalin's apparent paralysis at the moment of invasion is curious. He had ignored many warnings: Germans in the Soviet Union sent their families home; in January, in a Berlin cinema, an American commercial attaché had been given details of Barbarossa by an anti-Nazi and this warning was eventually passed to Moscow; the Soviet agent Richard Sorge sounded a strident warning from Tokyo; and informative German radio traffic transmitted via the Enigma encrypting device was intercepted and decoded by the British at Bletchley Park. This 'Ultra' intelligence confirmed other indications garnered by the British and on 10 June, Sir Alexander Cadogan, Permanent Under-Secretary at the Foreign Office, told Maisky, the Russian Ambassador in London, that Churchill 'asks you urgently to communicate all these data to the Soviet Government'. On 18 June the anti-Nazi 'Lucy' spy-ring based in Lucerne, in Switzerland, which consisted of a German, a Swiss, an Englishman and a Russian, fed the Kremlin with detailed plans for Barbarossa (and continued to inform the Soviets of German troop movements, plans and positions for the entire Russian campaign). Simultaneous with the 'Lucy' warning, a German deserter revealed the date of an attack as Sunday, 22 June. He too was ignored.

But Stalin, as well as being callous and crafty, was also ignorant. He chose not to act upon these warnings, despite his own misgivings, blinding himself to the flood of evidence with the characteristic impenetrable detachment and self-conceit which had enabled him to gain immense power and to wield it with a terrifying disregard of all reason. Whether or not he had a nervous breakdown at this time, or deliberately retreated into a world of self-delusion, it is impossible to say, but when the blow came it stupefied him, confronting him personally with a challenging reality perhaps hitherto unimagined. Whatever the true reasons, the cost to the Soviet war apparatus by the end of that fateful Sunday was the loss of 1,500 Russian aircraft on the ground and 322 in the air; in addition, 3 Russian divisions were unaccounted for. This was but a foretaste of what was to follow.

By the end of June the German High Command was celebrating the success of Barbarossa. The tanks of Guderian's Panzer Group 2 and Hoth's Panzer Group 3 had trapped three Russian armies and the Germans were advancing along the whole of the vast front. Only one fact was beginning to emerge to suggest it would not simply be a matter of breaking glass: although surrounded and taken prisoner in enormous numbers, even against hopeless odds individual Russian soldiers refused to submit. They fought, Hitler wrote to Mussolini, with a 'stupid fanaticism' and 'the primitive brutality' of animals. The Wehrmacht's losses began to mount ominously. In the opening weeks of Barbarossa they reached 100,000, more than the total of all other campaigns since the war had begun.

Stalin's paralysis did not last long. A fortnight after Barbarossa had been launched, a new Russian Stavka, or High Command, had been formed. Voroshilov, Timoshenko and Budenny were appointed to command the right, centre and left of the line. With savage and intimidating brutality, Stalin had those of the old front-line commanders who had survived shot, thus providing the cause of the Russian disaster for public consumption. Throughout the Red Army, political orthodoxy was more important than military ability, and defeat was perceived as treachery; there were political commissars on hand to interfere with field operations and make a nightmare reality of this fear, even in the face of the enemy. But the paranoid insecurity of Communist control, which was a legacy of revolution, civil war and minority power, now disappeared beneath an emerging patriotism. This was brilliantly exploited by Stalin who emerged publicly from his cataleptic state on 3 July to broadcast to a people hitherto treated as traitors unless submitting to his will. With all the fulsome fraternity of Marxist rhetoric, he addressed his 'comrades, citizens, brothers and sisters', announced 'a patriotic war' and called for a scorched-earth policy which would result in 'freedom for our Motherland'. He reawoke the powerful, demotic image of Mother Russia, revived historical memories of the great struggle against Napoleon's Grande Armée and invoked the deep feelings of the Russian people for their country. Patriotism of the most self-abnegating sort was to characterize the spirit of the Russians in the coming struggle with the Germans, replacing to a large degree the fear of extreme coercion, and ironically elevating Josef Stalin to the ancient, Tsarist status of 'Little Father'.

The Russian people's 'passionate defence of their native soil', Churchill commented later, 'while the struggle lasted, made amends for all'.

For Winston Churchill, Prime Minister and his own Minister of Defence, the period of Britain's standing alone with little beyond the moral support of the American President Roosevelt behind the vital Lease-Lend Act had ended. But having the Soviet Union, if not exactly as an ally, then at least as a co-enemy of the Third Reich, was cold comfort. Churchill had no love for Communists and had marked 'the stony composure' with which the Russian government had regarded events in France in 1940 'and our vain efforts in 1941 to create a front in the Balkans'. Furthermore, the Soviets had given economic and material aid to the Germans. The Arctic port of Murmansk, preserved from the Finns, was nevertheless used as a fuelling port by German ships. From the White Sea the commerce raider *Komet* had been assisted by Russian ice-breakers to break out into the Pacific through the Kara Sea and North East Passage.

From the moment of invasion, Churchill complained, the Soviet Union's 'first impulse and lasting policy was to demand all possible succour from Great Britain and her Empire . . . They did not hesitate to appeal in urgent and strident terms to harassed and struggling Britain to send them the munitions of which her armies were so short.' For Stalin the continuing Anglo-German fighting in North Africa was a sideshow. The British were apparently doing nothing. He comprehended little of the war at sea, an ignorant and infuriating disinterest he was to exhibit during the whole of the maritime Arctic campaign that he now expected Churchill to open. Moreover his demands went beyond this embattled island: the Soviet government, Churchill recounts, 'urged the United States to divert to them the largest quantities of the supplies on which we were counting, and above all, even in the summer of 1941, they clamoured for British landings in Europe regardless of risk and cost, to establish a second front'. Second Front graffiti appeared all over Britain as the indigenous Communist party executed a conspicuous volte-face, but herein lay the core of Stalin's objectives insofar as the West was concerned: the relief of a diversionary front and material aid, in that order. If the British were too cowardly and wanted stiffening, the Russians could send an army corps or two to spearhead the landing, an outraged Churchill recorded, well knowing that even with this help the landing was quite beyond the resources at his disposal.[4] Material aid, however, was a possibility.

On the evening of the German invasion, Churchill broadcast a message pledging all possible assistance to the Soviet Union against the common enemy. Apart from an abbreviated reprinting by way of acknowledgement in *Pravda* and a diplomatic request for the reception of a military mission, there was only an 'oppressive' silence from the Kremlin. On 7 July Churchill took the initiative and wrote to Stalin; he also instructed the British Ambassador, Sir Stafford Cripps, to open negotiations for a treaty of mutual aid and alliance. It was not until 18 July that Maisky delivered his master's reply. Stalin suggested that the military situation of both the Soviet Union and Great Britain would be 'considerably improved' by the opening of a front against 'Hitlerite Germany' in northern France and 'in the north – the Arctic'.

Despite the presence of the bulk of the German army in Russia, not inconsiderable forces remained in the occupied countries of the west. Forty divisions were in France alone where the formidable defences of the Atlantic Wall had already been a year in the building and on which vast numbers of Russians served as slave labour. The only area of coast where Churchill thought local air superiority might be achieved was the Pas de Calais, the most heavily defended and inaccessible. In explaining this to Stalin, Churchill revealed his greatest worry of the entire war: 'The Battle of the Atlantic, on which our life depends, and the movement of all our convoys in the teeth of the U-boat and Focke-Wulf blockade, strains our naval resources, *great though they be*, to the utmost limit [author's italics].'[5]

Without huge ground forces and total control of the air, the invasion of France was impossible. What Stalin had in mind in the Arctic was 'easier . . . Here . . . would be necessary only naval and air operations'. What was thought easy by Stalin and what was being considered by Churchill, was seen by the First Sea Lord, Admiral Sir Dudley Pound, as the most hazardous of operations, especially in the summer. The proposition was 'most unsound', he argued, 'with the dice loaded against us in every direction'.

Nevertheless, Churchill, aware that Stalin might make a separate peace (as we now know he tried to, offering Hitler the Ukraine), decided to go ahead. Russia must be kept in the war against Germany, otherwise the world would never breathe again.

2

To the edge of the earth

ON 1 AUGUST 1941 the fast mine-laying cruiser HMS *Adventure* arrived at the Russian part of Archangel with a consignment of war materials including mines. As a gesture of solidarity her arrival in the White Sea was timely, but she was not a convoy and, according to Admiral Golovko of the Soviet Northern Fleet, her mines were 'quite valueless'. This was not a promising start, though it was to characterize the dog-in-the-manger attitude of Soviet officialdom.[1] Nevertheless, between 10 and 15 September four Russian destroyers laid these supposedly useless objects on the seabed off the Fisherman's Peninsula in two mine barrages.

The establishment of a regular convoy schedule was not a matter arranged at a moment's notice. With winter approaching, the regular route would terminate not at Archangel, but at Murmansk on the Kola Inlet, a port built in 1915 with British aid for the supply of the Tsar's armies and which took its name from a local dialect: in the Saami tongue, Murmansk meant 'the edge of the earth'.

Faced with Churchill's orders, Admiral Tovey, the Commander-in-Chief of Britain's Home Fleet, was the officer directly responsible for the complex arrangements now being put in train. In order to establish what facilities existed in North Russia, in mid-July Tovey had dispatched Rear-Admirals Vian and Miles to confer with Golovko and discuss such matters as the arrangements for the discharge of loaded merchant ships, the refuelling of escorts and the provision of local support, particularly air cover. Vian and Miles flew to Polyarnoe, the Soviet Northern Fleet headquarters near the entrance to the Kola Inlet. Vian was an opinionated officer and did not impress Golovko who preferred Miles, a fortunate circumstance for Miles was to go on to Moscow as head of the British Military Mission there.

Golovko himself impressed Rear-Admiral Burrough, who was to meet him later in the year, as

> clever, far-seeing and probably ruthless . . . possessing the ability to weigh up a situation very rapidly, but definitely a man of the people. A rough diamond, quite unpolished and with poorish table manners. Rather scruffy but surprisingly well read. Very keen to co-operate and undoubtedly a capable man. I found him likeable, friendly and frank.

Vian reported back to Tovey: he was not encouraging. Murmansk was only a few minutes flying time from the hostile air-base at Petsamo. It had suffered badly from bombing and most of its population had been evacuated. Anti-aircraft defences were sparse and port facilities minimal. The largest crane was incapable of handling tanks. However, the enemy had failed to capture the town and although they cut the railway line to Leningrad, the Russians laid new track between Belomorsk and Obozerskaya to link up with the Archangel-to-Moscow line.

Whilst the wooden wharves of Polyarnoe lay in a deep, narrow, well-protected *guba*, or fiord, Murmansk, further up the Kola Inlet, had few berths and several of these had been damaged by bombing. Thus merchant ships would be obliged to wait at anchor in Vaenga Bay where the holding ground was poor and they would be exposed to air attack. A naval dry dock and repair shops existed nearby at Rosta, but neither coal nor oil bunkers were readily available. In short, convoys would be faced with more problems than simply the violence of the enemy or the inclemency of the weather. Effort would have to be expended in helping the Russians strengthen the port and improve the facilities; and some sort of British naval presence would have to be established ashore to assist liaison. Tovey was not heartened, for he shared the First Sea Lord's profound misgivings. Churchill's orders, however, were imperative.[2]

Faced with Stalin's demands and concerned about events in the Western Desert as well as the Far East, Churchill consulted Roosevelt. The American President was worried that in attempting too much, Britain might 'lose all'. At the same time as

Tovey sent Vian to Polyarnoe, Roosevelt dispatched his own envoy, Harry Hopkins, to London where, with members of the American Military Mission, he conferred with Churchill before going on to Moscow. A conference was also arranged between Churchill and Roosevelt, to be held secretly at sea in a bay off the Newfoundland coast. Hopkins returned from Russia to join Churchill on Britain's newest but ill-fated battleship, HMS *Prince of Wales*, for the Atlantic crossing. *Prince of Wales* made her rendezvous with the USS *Augusta* in Placentia Bay on the morning of 9 August 1941. The cordial relations established by correspondence and telephone between the British Prime Minister and the United States President were now firmly cemented by personal contact.

If the consequences of this meeting were momentous for the future of the world in laying the foundations for the post-war United Nations they were especially so for Russia herself, for she was to emerge as a world super-power only four years later. As a result of the meeting President Roosevelt affirmed the support of American industry for Britain and Russia, and he and Churchill cabled Stalin on 12 August to assure the Soviet Premier that the Western Allies 'were co-operating to provide you with the very maximum of supplies you most urgently need'. Churchill also summoned Lord Beaverbrook and asked him to endeavour to increase American manufacturing production by every means in his power and to 'cope with the painful splitting of supplies between Great Britain and Russia which was desirable and also inevitable'.[3] Churchill was to agonize over this point, particularly as Stalin was never to accept anything other than the superior claim of the Soviet Union, even though this deferred any chance of the opening of the second front he so continuously harped upon. To Attlee, the Deputy Prime Minister left in London, Churchill summarized Russia 'as a welcome guest at a hungry table'.

Nevertheless, Churchill was pleased with the outcome of the conference. A joint declaration of intent had been made, supplies of war material were to be stepped up and, in addition to Lease-Lend, the Americans agreed to assume responsibility for the escort of convoys from their own coast to the Iceland area, thus relieving pressure on British shipping and providing cover where British escorts had been unable to, due to lack of fuel capacity. Returning to Scapa Flow, the *Prince of Wales* passed dramatically through a convoy of seventy-three merchantmen in mid-Atlantic.

Beaverbrook returned to London from the United States at the end of August after helping to stimulate a 'stupendous increase in production'. Nevertheless, the division of this invigorated source of supply was to the British military chiefs 'like flaying off pieces of their skin' for the benefit of an ally who was 'surly, snarling, grasping and so lately indifferent' to Britain's survival, for an impatient Stalin increased his demands as von Rundstedt's Army Group thrust southwards towards the Ukraine, his ambassador presenting these on 4 September. Churchill angrily brushed aside Maisky's protests that the British were not doing enough by pointing out Russia's former indifference and pact with the Germans. In fact, he insisted, a very great deal was being done, but it could not produce instant results. Churchill's tough line mollified Maisky as he went on to explain the intention of doubling the capacity of the existing railway line through Persia between Basra and the Caspian. Supply trains were to increase from 2 to 20 a day; 48 locomotives and 400 railway trucks were already at sea and by October 1941 a small number of tanks would begin to travel north via this route. No large flow was predicted via the Persian Gulf until the following year and the plans for production then in hand would not yield significant results until 1943.

This was not what Stalin wanted to hear. The Germans had taken Novgorod and laid siege to Leningrad on 4 September, the day Maisky called on Churchill. In typical fashion he claimed that what he was already receiving was inadequate. As the Germans first used the gas chambers of Auschwitz on Russian prisoners-of-war and Kiev submitted along with a quarter of a million Russian soldiers on the 19th, he belittled the Hawker Hurricane fighters of the latest mark sent to North Russia and asked for 30,000 tons of aluminium plus a *monthly* quota of 400 aircraft and 500 tanks.

These early cargoes in the first convoys were either directly from British production or from American Lease-Lend supplies already allocated for British purposes. Churchill promised one half of the next month's total from British sources, hoping the rest could be managed from the United States. He also dismissed Stalin's mention of payment, doubtless divining Stalin's desire not to be beholden to the West, and suggested that the *matériel* be supplied 'upon the same basis of comradeship as the American Lease-Lend Bill, of which no account is kept in money'. Disregarding preposterous demands that twenty or thirty British divisions be sent to North Russia, Churchill firmly stated that any precipitate action, 'however well meant, leading only to costly fiascos would be no help to anyone but Hitler'. Meanwhile arrangements were made for 5,000 tons of aluminium to be shipped from Canada, followed by 2,000 tons a month. This would be sent via Vladivostok unless the Russians favoured the Persian Gulf. Threats of Japanese disruption of the Far East route had been countered by threats from Stalin, though the Russian leader avoided declaring war on Japan until after the dropping of the atomic bomb on Nagasaki in August 1945, and then chiefly to seize the Kurile Islands.

To co-ordinate the long-term delivery of supplies and enable an integrated strategic policy to be developed with the Russians, an Anglo-American Supply Mission led jointly by Beaverbrook and Averell Harriman proceeded to Scapa Flow. Ferried out by the destroyer *Offa*, they embarked aboard the cruiser *London* waiting at anchor. Among the Mission were officials of the British military staff and aircraft production, and a bevy of American military officers plus a representative of the United States motor manufacturing industry. The Arctic weather was seductively fine and *London* arrived at Archangel on 27 September where a Russian destroyer came alongside and Admiral Popov met the Mission. A witness recorded that Popov slipped and fell on the deck.[4]

In Moscow the Mission was received coldly. Nevertheless, as a consequence, Churchill asked for an increase in American output and Roosevelt undertook to supply 1,200 tanks monthly to Britain and Russia between July 1942 and the following January. Thereafter 2,000 tanks plus a further 3,600 front-line aircraft would be sent in addition to those already promised. A protocol was signed and the atmosphere thawed, though Stalin's reproaches continued to be insulting and his demands preposterous.

On receiving Beaverbrook's cabled report, on 6 October 1941, Churchill signalled to Stalin his intention of initiating a regular ten-day schedule of convoys sailing from Iceland. One was already on the way and would arrive at Archangel on or about 12 October; another would leave on the same day, another on the 22nd. As a precautionary measure to prevent a German invasion after the seizure of Norway, Iceland had been occupied by British and Canadian forces in May 1940. It was here, in the exposed and miserable anchorage of Hvalfiordur outside Reykjavik, that British, American, Dutch, Panamanian, Belgian, Norwegian and Russian merchant ships were to assemble and form up in convoy, deeply laden with aircraft, tanks, trucks, bren-gun carriers, anti-aircraft and anti-tank guns, ammunition, chemicals, several million pairs of boots, tin, wool, jute, lead and rubber.

The United States Navy, already ordered by Roosevelt to shoot on sight any Axis ship attacking a convoy in waters under American protection, suffered its first casualty on 16 October when the USS *Kearney* reached Iceland after being torpedoed. On the 31st a second destroyer was torpedoed off Iceland. USS *Reuben James* was not so lucky and sank.

As the first convoys left Iceland, on 21 October 1941, General von Bock, halted in his advance by Hitler while a Panzer corps was diverted south to assist von Rundstedt, resumed his advance on Moscow. On 19 October, Stalin issued an Order of the Day: 'Moscow will be defended to the last.'

By re-routeing commodities already earmarked in Britain, by raiding home stocks and negotiating with the Americans in response to the Kremlin's peremptory demands, the British war machine adapted to co-operation with its new ally. To the men and women toiling in the British munitions plants and factories and on the docks, the ultimate destination of their labour had hitherto not been of much significance. The Phoney War had ended in Dunkirk and there had not subsequently been much to raise the public spirit, only a grim determination to uphold it. But many now embraced the Russian alliance fervently, ignorant of the true nature of Stalinism and believing in the ultimate victory of Socialism over Fascism. It was an expression of aspirations that grew steadily, and culminated in the rejection of Churchill as a peacetime prime minister with the return of a Labour government in the first post-war general election. This sentiment found increasing expression on the lower decks of many Royal Naval warships, filled as they were with 'hostilities only' conscripts; officers were generally less enthusiastic. On the British merchant ships now being alloted the task of conveying these vast quantities of goods to the edge of the earth, the reaction was more complex.

At the inception of the Arctic campaign the burden of providing merchant ships fell upon the British Ministry of War Transport (MOWT). It mustered the resources of what the press and propagandists were pleased to call the 'Merchant Navy'. No such thing actually existed; it was a courtesy title given to a huge collection of ships of which ownership was vested in a variety of companies whose standards represented the whole spectrum of corporate responsibility from a pure and ruthless capitalist exploitation to a benign paternalism which fostered its own assumptions of élitism. Amongst the former might be included a score of small shipping interests based in Cardiff or upon the banks of the Tyne, whose masters, officers and engineers were paid according to the bare minimum scale stipulated by the Board of Trade, with Lascars on deck and Sudanese firemen in the boiler room; among the latter were the prestigious liners of the Cunard-White Star Line and the Peninsular and Oriental Steam Navigation Company, whose officers dined like viceroys and whose crews were subject to social gradations on a truly imperial scale which embraced the Hindu caste system with enthusiasm.

While these British merchant seamen were all subject to the surveyors of Lloyds or the Board of Trade, and their officers and engineers all held certificates of competency issued by the latter, there was no common denominator between ships of different owners. Although their crews were governed by minimum scales of pay and provisions, the hard-lying, 'pound and pint' go-anywhere tramps were a sharp contrast to the multi-menued passenger liners on the glamorous passenger 'runs'. And although all, including new-built war tonnage, now came under the general overall direction of the MOWT, and thus assumed more closely the character of a 'navy', this was not seen as being of any advantage to their crews, as for more than any other section of the civilian population, war was a monstrous intrusion on their lives.[5]

At the outbreak of war Great Britain was emerging from a depression. Thousands of tons of British shipping, mostly of the speculative, tramp-ship type, were laid up for want of cargoes. When the demands of war were able to fill their holds, they remained immobilized for lack of crews. As the demand for officers and men increased, many of these men, so recently laid off, sought employment on ships which offered meals of more than a basic fare and wages over the disreputable levels which the government had set at just above subsistence. Faced with this problem the newly formed MOWT began the direction of seafaring labour by forming the 'pool' system and stopped the crocodile tears of frustrated patriotism shed by the tramp-ship owners who bewailed the lack of manpower. While many officers with commissions in the Royal Naval Reserve went off to man the corvettes and small escort vessels of the Royal Navy,[6] the bridges and engine rooms of merchant ships were filled with men whose age in any other profession would have debarred them from military service. Fifteen-year-old deck boys and sixteen-year-old apprentice and radio officers lay at one end of a scale which uprooted pensioned men in their seventies at the other. Propaganda made much of their willingness to return to the colours, but by November 1941, when convoys to Russia were well-established, *The Times* succinctly stated the emerging truth: 'in the sustained endurance of our . . . merchant seaman lies our hope of victory'. That endurance was only put in perspective long after the war by Douglas Marshall, MP for Bodmin, when the lack of escort vessels was being debated in the House of Commons. 'It is true that the Merchant Navy gets through,' he said, 'but they get through only at a terrible self-sacrifice and a terrible loss of life.' In percentage terms it was to be proportionally greater than *any* of the three armed services.

This was the more remarkable because merchant seamen lacked the long tradition of the Royal Navy. There were, of course, company traditions, but the mercantile marine had no cohesive *esprit de corps* comparable with that of the Senior Service. The ramrod stiffening of the Royal Navy was enshrined in its most sacred signal, not 'England expects . . .' but what in Nelson's day was known as 'No. 16', and decoded bore the cryptic order to 'engage the enemy more closely'. It was born of a time far older than the age of Nelson, derived from a distant past when the distinction between Royal and mercantile sailors was blurred, and the Crown sought its fighting seamen from the ranks of its entrepreneurial adventurers. The purpose of the fighting tradition was to imbue the men of the Royal Navy, particularly the commissioned officers, with selflessness in time of battle. It was uncompromising, amoral and very effective. It was a means to an end which afterwards could be called heroic, even if its implementation had been tragic. It whipped in the lax, spurred the over-cautious; it gave the British Royal Navy that self-confessed 'air of conscious superiority' which allowed it to survive the many disasters which it was now to endure, for this was not a tradition of the past, but a living force.

It was thus that Fegen of the *Jervis Bay* and Kennedy of the *Rawalpindi* took their armed merchant cruisers, apologetic warships at best, against superior odds; thus had the *Bismarck* been sunk in grim retaliation for the loss of the *Hood*; and thus did the tiny destroyer *Glowworm* ram the heavy cruiser *Hipper* in the ill-fated Norwegian campaign, to the astonishment of the watching German officers.

More prosaically, being part of such a tradition sustained men in the long hours of apprehensive boredom which characterized wartime service. Such an expectation maintained the gallows humour of the naval seaman in his rolling and pitching escort as it danced its desperate dido in the teeth of an Arctic gale; it reconciled him to his washed-out accommodation, brought strength to a body numbed with fatigue and cold, and comfort to an individual submerged in the awful misery of war.

No such tradition supported the merchant sailor. He was continually a victim of economic conditions, his employment erratic, his future uncertain. Irrespective of his rank, he was unsupported by the team-spirit prevalent in a well-run warship. The regulation of the pool system often broke his company loyalty if he had any, and while he understood his part in the Allied war effort well enough, for the mere sight of a large convoy bore that in on even the dullest perception, different, more pragmatic fears than disgrace or cowardice nibbled at *his* morale. He was conscious of not being well treated, of being undervalued, perceptions given substance by the general unpreparedness of the Royal Navy to protect him adequately, and by the fact that at the beginning of the war his pay stopped the day his ship was sunk. Time spent fighting for his life on a float or a lifeboat was an unpaid excursion. He had the ignoble privilege of dying unemployed and though this injustice was later rectified, the fact that it had occurred at all left its mark. In short he was aware that he sailed under the red duster while the navy sailed under the white ensign, and despite the propaganda, he continued to behave very largely as he had always done. Morale in merchant ships, glossed over at the time and largely unexamined since, was occasionally uncertain enough to cause concern in high places, though it should be emphasized that most participants got on with the job in hand. In the Arctic that alone produced heroes.

Now, in the late summer of 1941, at the height of the Battle of the Atlantic and the commencement of a new maritime campaign, the two services, the one imbued with the weight of an immense tradition, the other a neglected, civilian arm of a rickety economy, were to act as one. Naval officers were surprised that when merchant ships were sunk and survivors picked up, the ratings often owed their officers no obedience, failing to understand the contractual nature of discipline on board merchant ships;

similarly, because merchant ships carried much smaller crews than warships, losses were often trivialized. True, merchant ships carried among their crews hard-bitten, rough and thoroughly disreputable characters, hardly surprising given the harsh circumstances of a merchant seaman's existence; true, too, that many companies employed Indian, Chinese, Sudanese and Somali ratings, men whose contribution to the Allied victory is rarely recorded because they occupied the lowest rungs of imperial social status, but none of these circumstances warranted the shameful gap between the Royal and the Merchant Navies.

Perceptive naval officers recognized the dangers of this breach. Captain Jack Broome, whose escort group operated in the Arctic and who was to be personally touched by it, wrote afterwards, 'for years we had turned up our snobbish noses and maintained that the Merchant Navy was something to be seen and not heard . . . It was entirely our fault that they thought that we thought we were some superior form of sea life.' One detects a ruefulness in Broome's hindsight; many of his escorts were officered by the professional merchant seamen of the Royal Naval Reserve. A rear-admiral recalled from retirement, as so many were to serve as convoy commodores aboard merchant ships, saw things from a slightly different angle: 'The men sailing under the Red Duster felt that they were the only real sailors and the sailors who manned our warships were a bunch of softies . . . the blunt fact was that they preferred to have as little contact with us as possible . . . For a dyed-in-the-wool RN officer like myself it was a difficult task to get to know these merchant seamen . . . a gulf seemed to separate the officers and men of the two services.'[7]

It is important to make these distinctions, for the gulf existed and the Arctic convoys were to provide a catalyst which bred its own tragic consequence in a widening of this difference, which affected the British Merchant Navy for a very long time.

Despite Roosevelt's pledge to help the British war effort and the President's commitment to escort convoys in the Western Atlantic made at the Placentia Bay conference, among the personnel of the United States Navy there was little enthusiasm for actively joining the fight against Fascism. But after the sinking of USS *Kearney* and USS *Reuben James*, and the entry of the United States fully into the war following the Japanese attack on Pearl Harbor in December 1941, America committed vast quantities of aid to Russia in its own vessels. It also began a crash building programme which was to prove a spectacular example of international co-operation and produce the Liberty ship.

To replace severe shipping losses emergency war-building programmes were instituted by the British MOWT based on a 'standard' design by Joseph L. Thompson's shipyard at Sunderland in northern England. Thompsons had modernized and planned for expansion during the depression and in 1935 built the coal-burning SS *Embassage* for Hall Brothers of Newcastle upon Tyne. This prototype ship grossed 9,300 tons and was followed by twenty-four others. Faced with crippling losses in the Atlantic and elsewhere, the design was taken up by the MOWT. The first 'standard ship' to be built under the Ministry's aegis was the SS *Empire Liberty* which, like all war-built tonnage, was put under the management of an established shipping company, in this case R. Chapman and Co. of Newcastle upon Tyne.

Modifications and adaptations of the 'standard ship' concept went into production on both sides of the Atlantic and its most innovative exponent was Henry Kaiser, an American engineer specializing in prefabrication and mass production who had been involved with the building of the San Francisco harbour bridge and the Grand Coolee, Hoover and Shasta dams. Kaiser was assisted by Cyril Thompson, son of J.L. Thompson's chairman, who went on to help extend production in Canada.

Kaiser developed the technique of prefabricated construction and shipyard assembly from components manufactured by companies dispersed right across the United States. The first of Kaiser's ships was launched on 7 September 1941 at the Bethlehem Fairfield Yard, Baltimore, and commissioned three weeks later. She was called the *Patrick Henry*, establishing a tradition that identified Liberty ships by their names. Those named after prominent American citizens were US-built and manned. Some 200 of them, manned by the British, were prefixed *Sam* . . . They were distinguished by being oil-fired with midships accommodation and funnel. Indeed their name owed nothing to their transatlantic origin, though it was popularly assumed to refer to Uncle Sam, but to the bureaucratic terminology of the British MOWT who denominated them as 'superstructure aft of midships types'.

By contrast, Canadian-built ships had 'split' accommodation and asymmetrical derrick-sampson posts serving the hatch between the bridge and the funnel housing, a misalignment intended to confuse attacking U-boats. Those named after *Parks* were

Canadian-crewed, while the *Forts* were Canadian-built and British-crewed. Standard ships built in Britain, together with special ships and enemy captures, were prefixed *Empire* and apart from the configuration of the superstructure were all basically similar.

Though the average was 42 days per ship, the fastest building achieved was that of the *Robert G. Peary*, launched from the No. 2 Yard of the Permanente Metals Corporation of Richmond, California, on 12 November 1942, 4 days and 15½ hours after the keel was laid. The vessel was fitted out and ready for sea 3 days later. Despite early problems with weld failure and President Roosevelt's description of them as 'dreadful-looking objects', they could lift 10,500 deadweight tons and steam at 11 knots; many lasted long after the end of the war. More important to their crews, they were armed with a 4-inch low-angle gun to drive off surface attack and an anti-aircraft defence system comprising a 12-pounder, Oerlikons, Bofors and PAC rockets (which climbed into the sky trailing wires, intended to bring down attacking aircraft). These ships were to feature conspicuously in the convoys to North Russia.[8]

Churchill was at pains to impress upon Stalin the fact that he could guarantee the provision of the promised munitions 'at the point of production' only, partly to underline the likelihood of losses in passage, but also to encourage the participation of Russian merchant ships. These, when they materialized, behaved with the utmost gallantry, as will be seen in due course, but not in the numbers Churchill hoped as Dönitz's U-boats and the Kriegsmarine's commerce raiders continued to decimate merchant shipping. Many flag-of-convenience ships, chiefly Panamanian, were chartered in, though most of these were actually American-owned.

Fortunately for the Allied war effort there was another source of shipping, that of the Norwegian merchant marine. On 7 June 1940 Norway fell to the invading Germans. An abortive Anglo-French attempt to intervene resulted in severe losses for the Royal Navy, including that of the aircraft-carrier *Glorious*. King Haakon, Crown Prince Olav and the Norwegian government escaped aboard the British cruiser *Devonshire*; almost immediately, the government-in-exile transmitted a radio message to all Norwegian merchant ships on the high seas effectively taking over management from London and integrating their merchant fleet with the British. An invaluable contribution was thus received in the acquisition of 233 tankers and over 600 general cargo vessels, most of which were of a higher quality than their British counterparts. They were, Churchill wrote, 'worth a million soldiers'. Surplus Norwegian seamen were drafted into British-built corvettes, destroyers and submarines. Deficiencies in technicians were made up with Britons, who also fulfilled liaison and signals functions. To all intents and purposes these ships and men became 'naturalized' for the duration, operating with Western Approaches Command in northern waters under overall British control. As all Norwegian naval officers had to have served in merchant ships, there was no social distinction between the two arms and the protective instinct between them was inviolable.[9]

The convoy system operating in the North Atlantic and now transferred to the Arctic was, by the autumn of 1941, well established. The assembled merchant ships steamed in a formation of short columns on a wide front to frustrate U-boat attack. Control of the merchant ships *en masse* was vested in a convoy commodore, often a retired rear-admiral or, more usually in the case of Arctic convoys, a Captain RNR. He flew a blue-crossed white pendant and in large convoys might be supported by experienced masters in other ships acting as vice- and rear-commodores, ready to take over if the commodore's ship was sunk. The commodore was not in command of the ship he was stationed on, but merely took passage for the duration of the convoy in the capacity of a flag-officer. He had a small, peripatetic signals staff who were permanently attached to him and normally comprised a yeoman, usually a regular petty officer, assisted by two or three visual signalling ratings who were engaged for 'hostilities only'. They transferred from ship to ship taking their own signal lamps, semaphore flags, telescopes and code-books in a weighted bag. It was a commendably simple and effective command structure, governing, as it did, such a mass of war *matériel*.

The commodore was responsible for alterations of speed, course and zigzag pattern, and it was his duty to liaise with the escort commander, usually a much younger and more junior regular naval officer than himself; the escort commander had overall responsibility for the 'safe and timely arrival of the convoy'. This dual command worked well in practice. Prior to departure, the merchant ship-masters and their radio officers attended a pre-sailing conference to ensure that all concerned with the management, safe conduct and passage of the convoy were adequately informed and instructed on the operation as a whole. As the campaign grew in intensity the composition of the escort escalated, but it was always with the close escort commander that the commodore and his mercantile associates worked and to whom they looked for support and defence in extremity. The complexities of grand strategy, of the distant support of cruiser squadrons and the battle fleet whom the ship-masters would rarely see, were explained by a senior naval staff officer. The intended route, steaming order, convoy speed and special signals would be revealed; expected enemy submarine concentrations would be explained and the location of 'friendly' minefields disclosed. A meteorological officer would give the most up-to-date prognosis of the weather likely to be met, and the composition of the escort and various rendezvous and fuelling points for the warships would be enumerated. This would be largely a matter of boosting morale, because once the convoy was at sea, maintaining radio silence at least until attacked and even then, and lacking the frequencies of the tactical naval networks, the personnel aboard the merchantmen were ignorant of what exactly was happening around them. Then questions would be invited and disposed of and last-minute defects confessed. Finally the conference would break up with the customary warning of the dangers of making smoke and straggling.

Returning to their ships the masters, Britons, Americans, Norwegians, Dutchmen, Greeks, Poles and Russians, some the hastily promoted products of war, others fitter for the vegetable patch and retirement than the grey wastes of the Arctic Ocean, nevertheless reflected by their very presence the complexity of the convoy system. It was blessed with the successes of historical precedent, but it was also an expedient device intended to supply troops at a distant front, and as a consequence it drew upon itself the attention of the enemy as a target in its own right.

3

Undertaking the impossible

THE DECISION TO supply Russia posed immediate problems for the Royal Navy. Overstretched in the Atlantic, the Admiralty had to find the resources to open a new convoy route through even more inhospitable seas.

At the outbreak of war Great Britain was desperately short of anti-submarine escort vessels. Although new construction was stepped up, fifty elderly escort destroyers were acquired from the United States under Lease-Lend arrangements and the conversion of equally ancient British fleet destroyers to long-range escorts (LREs) was taken in hand, the German navy gained enormous strategic advantages from direct access to the Atlantic after the defeat of France and Norway in the summer of 1940.

Thus, as the Battle of the Atlantic approached its long, wearying crisis, the additional burden of organizing and protecting convoys to North Russia fell upon a heavily committed and inadequate British navy. Britain was already reaping the rewards of neglecting anti-submarine measures in the inter-war years and the shortage of escorts was resulting in ever-increasing losses of the unfortunate and ill-protected merchant ships upon which the nation depended.

At the end of the First World War British prestige remained enshrined in her navy, as it had done throughout the preceding century. Distant-water cruises by its heavy ships, known as 'showing the flag', were carried out to keep the world mindful of this. Possession of battleships, lineal descendants of Nelson's *Victory* and her wooden sisters, was still considered the yardstick by which naval puissance was measured. Heavily armoured and gunned, they were designed to bring to battle and crush an enemy squadron. To lure an opponent into action the similarly gunned, but lighter armoured battlecruiser had been developed. Battlecruisers were the most glamorous and beautiful heavy warships ever built; but the type was flawed and had proved appallingly vulnerable at Jutland in 1916 when outgunned by the Kaiser's High Seas Fleet. They were to prove equally useless under the guns of the resurgent Kriegsmarine and the bombs of the Japanese airforce. They and their heavier sisters nevertheless continued to dominate naval thinking and the efforts of the ill-fated League of Nations to prevent a naval arms race between the wars had sought, with only partial success, to curb their size. The big gun dominated the naval consciousness at the expense of antisubmarine weapons. Capital ships were excessively costly and were preserved at the expense of convoy escorts. Technical improvements also outran the ability of the navy to incorporate them practically, a situation well understood by the inhabitants of the lower deck who rechristened the *Repulse* and *Renown*, the *Repair* and *Refit*.[1]

Even more prominent in the worldwide role of showing the flag were the long-range cruisers. Lighter armed and armoured than capital ships, with guns of 6- or 8-inch calibre upon which depended their classification as light or heavy cruisers, they were fast and seaworthy ships. Capable of either commerce-raiding themselves or hunting enemy raiders, they achieved the first major naval success of the war by Christmas 1939 with the engagement of the *Graf Spee* off the River Plate. Cruisers were also deployed with a major fleet or in support of convoys and in this latter role they were to play a crucial part in the Arctic. The war was to produce some hybrid 'cruisers'. Passenger liners armed with obsolete 6-inch guns and taken under naval command acted as armed merchant cruisers (AMCs), smaller merchant ships were armed with lighter calibre, high-angle weapons as anti-aircraft ships, and a number of regular cruisers were similarly modified or completed. They, too, were to be found in the Arctic.

While cruisers could operate singly or in small, mutually supportive squadrons, the heavier capital ships, including the increasingly important aircraft-carriers, required 'screening' from submarine attack by fast, light escorts known as destroyers, which had been called into existence a generation earlier to counter the threat of the surface-delivered torpedo. Originally known as torpedo-boat destroyers, the name had contracted as their role became less specific and the submarine threat increased. These small vessels, dedicated to capital-ship protection, had become 'fleet destroyers'. They were prestigious commands for ambitious young regular career officers. In addition to protecting the fabulously expensive battleships from enemy torpedo attack, destroyers were themselves lethal torpedo carriers, a function they were to demonstrate with good effect in the Barents Sea, but many of them were deficient in effective anti-aircraft armament. The most modern fleet destroyers operated with the Home Fleet from its base at Scapa Flow, in the Orkney Islands, but their attachment to Admiral Tovey's capital ships was maintained at the expense of proper protection of the Atlantic convoys.[2]

The demands of convoys to North Russia, however, were to disrupt this somewhat cosy routine, for the complex task of defending the Arctic convoys fell upon the Home Fleet directly, as distinct from the Western Approaches Command which was based at Liverpool and was responsible for the Atlantic sea lanes. Later in the campaign this distinction became blurred, and Western Approaches ships were 'lent' to protect Arctic convoys, coming under the operational control of the Commander-in-Chief Home Fleet. As time passed it became a task which demanded the deployment of all these classes of ship, together with British and Allied submarines and minor warships of the exiled navies of occupied countries, most notably the Poles, Norwegians and Free French who operated as Royal Naval units.

The chief danger to convoys throughout the war were the enemy's submarines. Despite the proximity of German airbases and anchorages for heavy ships, the U-boat remained the primary threat in the Arctic as elsewhere.

The danger of submarine warfare had been readily appreciated as long ago as 1917, when food stocks in the United Kingdom had been reduced to six weeks' supply by the interdiction of imports, and the British High Command had already resigned itself to defeat. The German collapse, however, came first and, significantly, it was on land. The U-boat, in the words of one British admiral, was 'foiled rather than defeated' while the British Admiralty remained at its 'wit's end as to how to deal with these submarines'.

In that same year of 1917 the Anglo-French Allied Submarine Detection Investigation Committee was set up to determine a countermeasure to the submarine. In due course it gave its initials to the acronym used for the echo-locating device it fostered, asdic, better known today as sonar, first used in 1918. It was announced that 'never again would the submarine be the threat it had been', a piece of conceit swiftly dispelled by Otto Kretschmer's tactic of surfacing *inside* a convoy at night and torpedoing selected merchant ships as they steamed past.

This unimaginative misunderstanding of the Kriegsmarine's tactics was compounded by other false assumptions. It was thought the Geneva Convention would be observed by the Germans, that lone merchant vessels would be stopped, told not to transmit radio signals and their crews ordered to abandon ship. To cope with this possibility and give merchant ships a fighting chance of escape, the Admiralty prided itself on arming in short order 1,000 merchantmen with obsolete but usable 4-inch guns. This, and the fact that British merchant ship-masters objected to being ordered to leave their ships without transmitting the triple-S signal indicating attack by submarine or 'having a crack at the Hun', gave Hitler the 'provocation' he needed to order unrestricted submarine warfare: there would be no warnings and merchant ships would be sunk on sight, usually by torpedo, a fact that wanted no proof, for the liner *Athenia* had been 'mistakenly' sunk in this manner within hours of the outbreak of war.

The architect of the German submarine offensive was Karl Dönitz, one of the thwarted U-boat commanders of 1918. Though angry at the sinking of the *Athenia*, he reacted to these supposed inconsistencies of mercantile practice in November 1940 by issuing Standing Order 154: 'Rescue no one and take no one with you. Have no care for the ship's boats . . . we must be hard in this war . . .' Although there are a number of recorded instances where U-boat commanders disobeyed this order and rendered assistance, this was no more nor less than concurrence with the dictum of Britain's Admiral 'Jackie' Fisher who developed the 'all big gun' ship in 1906. Fisher believed that 'the essence of war is violence, and moderation in war is imbecility'. Imbecility or not, Dönitz's order jettisoned the Hague Convention's Prize Laws and total war was declared at sea.

While asdic sought to locate and hunt submerged U-boats, attack, or more usually counter-attack, was achieved with the depth-charge. Developed originally at the end of the First World War, this cheap explosive device contained 300 pounds of Amatol hydrostatically fused by the launching crew to fire at a pre-set depth. Dropped over the stern or thrown sideways, attack could only be pressed *after* the attacker had passed over the target. Accuracy of echo-location by asdic diminished rapidly in the final approach, definition suffering from lack of vertical discrimination and hence of depth data, and became useless in the short but crucial last moments of an attack. Although asdic improved throughout the war, conditions in the Arctic sometimes baffled and deflected it. The layers of differing density, which resulted from the collision of the residue of the tropical Gulf Stream and the chill waters of the melting ice-cap in which bergs slowly dissolved, could provide hiding places for a U-boat occasionally as impenetrable as a brick wall, reflecting the sound emission. And while forward-firing weapons such as Hedgehog and later Squid marked advances in the anti-submarine war, it was the co-ordinated attacks of groups of ships combined with air superiority which proved decisive in defeating the U-boats. In the early days poverty of these resources was, in Pound's words, to load the dice heavily in the enemy's favour, particularly on the Russian run where the lack of local air cover could only be overcome by the presence of aircraft-carriers.[3]

The events leading up to the Munich crisis of 1938, the subsequent months of uneasy peace and the so-called Phoney War bought Britain some valuable time. For the Germans too, despite their vast rearmament programme, this period was useful.

The winter manœuvres of 1938–9 led Admiral Karl Dönitz to submit to the head of the Kriegsmarine, Grossadmiral Erich Raeder, a requirement for 300 *Unterseebooten*. Whilst Hitler had surprised Raeder in May 1938 by telling him that Britain was a potential enemy, he had also reassured him that he did not anticipate hostilities until about 1943, by which time this formidable establishment of submarines would be available. In December 1938 Hitler had increased his submarine building programme, begun clandestinely in the Netherlands, 'in response' to Soviet naval construction. Tied to the provisions of an escape clause in the Anglo-German Naval Treaty, Britain was compelled to agree, sanctioning an increase in the building of heavy cruisers to match Russian output.[4]

Such cynical manœuvring on the part of the Nazi government began to alarm the British Admiralty. It launched a crash building programme of anti-submarine vessels capable of being produced quickly and simply in commercial shipyards. Responding to a basic design derived from a whale-catcher submitted by the Smith's Dock Company of Middlesbrough on the River Tees, the Admiralty ordered the Flower-class corvettes, borrowing the generic term from the French navy of the Napoleonic era. Powered by triple-expansion steam reciprocating engines they were capable of only 15 knots but possessed the twin virtues of endurance and seaworthiness. In the wake of these simple little ships another old term was revived, that of the frigate (whose role had been usurped and name subsumed in the nineteenth century by the cruiser). Several frigate classes followed the corvettes into the war against the U-boat in the Atlantic and Arctic Oceans, joining the too few sloops which a neglectful Admiralty had considered sufficient by way of anti-submarine investment in the 1930s.

A second, faster escort with the emphasis on anti-aircraft armament went into production shortly after the outbreak of war. The Hunt-class destroyer could turn in an excess of 20 knots in good conditions, but did not possess the range of the LRE conversions of the First World War V and W classes, nor the speed of the pure-bred 'fleet' destroyers. This lack of endurance was to present a problem to Tovey who had to arrange either refuelling, or a substitute system of anti-aircraft defence, for whereas the war in the Atlantic was against the U-boat, the new campaign to which Churchill had committed Pound and Tovey confronted them with two other significant threats: the Luftwaffe's aircraft and surface intervention by heavy cruisers and capital ships of the Kriegsmarine. All these considerations omitted the problems confronting both men and ships in the appalling conditions prevailing in the Arctic seas.

The German occupation of Norway brought much of the convoy route within range of German air-strikes from Bardufoss and Banak. In addition, as Vian reported to the C-in-C, both the Kola Inlet and the White Sea ports were within range of aircraft flying from the Finnish airbase of Petsamo. Junkers Ju87 and Ju88 bombers and torpedo-carrying Heinkel He 111s could be called up almost at will as soon as the long-range Blohm and Voss or Focke-Wulf reconnaissance planes had located each convoy.

In the thinking of both the German High Command and the British Admiralty a belief persisted that total destruction of a convoy could best be achieved by the surface-raiding capital ship. As long as the Germans maintained a handful of heavy ships in the grim fastnesses of the Norwegian fiords capable of intercepting a Russia-bound convoy or breaking out to strike at a transatlantic one, Britain was obliged to maintain a disproportionately high number of ships on preventative patrol or instant readiness to respond.

Their Lordships were justifiably apprehensive. As well as the spell cast by the big gun, the Germans had a long history of intelligent commerce raiding. They built ships well able to achieve this aim, essential if they were to defeat Britain which was in 1939, for all her maritime inadequacies, still the world's major naval power.

In the First World War both submarines and converted merchant ships proved very effective commerce raiders, forcing shipowners to submit to a return to the defensive tactic of the convoy used during the days of sail. The British shipowner's reluctance to send his ships in convoy was at least partly due to his disregard for losses which, under the prevailing system of compensation, were highly profitable.[5] But the planners of the Nazis' Kriegsmarine needed capital ships, those manifest symbols of intimidation deployable in peacetime. The deliberations of German naval strategists in the 1930s resulted in violent controversies. No submariner took an active part in these deliberations, despite Dönitz's demands, and the conclusions laid before the Führer offered him a choice of plans. The first emphasized submarines, armed merchant commerce raiders and the heavily armed, diesel-engined, long-range heavy cruisers which the British had perceptively nicknamed 'pocket battleships' because of their six 11-inch guns.[6] It was a cheap, practicable proposition, a guerilla plan with no grandiose pretensions to naval parity with Britain, but possessing tremendous potential to harm her. The second choice offered to Hitler was for a battle-fleet, potentially rivalling that of Britain and a very real threat to her sea-power, but slow and expensive to implement. Hitler, reassuring Grossadmiral Raeder that there was plenty of time, chose the latter: he was immensely susceptible to the majestic sight of a great warship. As a consequence the six-year Z-plan went into secret and priority production.

It was to be impractical in its entirety, ruined by Hitler's impatience, but in detail the careful design and the desire to out-Herod Herod produced heavy ships of a very superior class, ships which could deliver and moreover *absorb* an immense amount of punishment. The chief outcome of the Z-plan, insofar as it affected the Arctic campaign, was the building of the battleships *Tirpitz* and *Scharnhorst*. The experience of destroying the former's sister ship, the *Bismarck*, in the spring of 1941, sounded a cautionary note in Whitehall and was to invest Admiralty policy in respect of Arctic convoy defence with a healthy respect for the effectiveness of German ship design. There appeared still to be that superior difference in the quality of German ships which had caused Beatty to lament something was 'wrong with our bloody ships', as his battlecruisers exploded about him at Jutland.[7]

The consequences of a German capital ship getting at a convoy had been demonstrated in October 1940 when the *Admiral Scheer* attacked convoy HX84 inbound from Halifax, Nova Scotia. The sole and inadequate escort, the armed merchant cruiser *Jervis Bay*, sacrificed herself as the convoy scattered. Nevertheless, the *Scheer* sank five of the thirty-seven ships, and in ordering the convoy to scatter, a precedent had been set which was to have more fateful results later in the Arctic. But Captain Fogarty Fegen of the *Jervis Bay* demonstrated the one thing the Kriegsmarine could not destroy, just as Captain Hans Langsdorff's scuttling of the *Graf Spee* demonstrated the Kriegsmarine had yet to acquire it: the fighting tradition of the Royal Navy.[8]

Nevertheless, such a threat, even if only of a single ship such as the mighty *Tirpitz*, compelled Tovey to hold a superiority of equally heavy ships in Scapa Flow; to operate 'Black' and 'White' cruiser patrols in the Denmark Strait and the Iceland–Faeroes–Shetland gaps, together with submarine patrols along the Norwegian coast; and to operate radar stations in Allied occupied Iceland and maintain a huge mine barrage across the Norwegian Sea. Provision had to be made to cover each individual outward and homeward convoy with the battle-fleet; to provide local cruiser support, an ocean and a close escort, in fact to employ the whole range of the naval armament in forcing these supplies through to North Russia for four years. The complexities of this task, the scheduling, routeing and assembly of convoys, the arrangements for fuelling escorts, appointing rendezvous points, collecting and collating ice reports and liaising with the Americans, all required massive staff support and co-ordination of a high degree. Nor was the task confined to the Royal Navy, for it was also necessary for the Royal Air Force to carry out air reconnaissance of the deeply indented Norwegian fiords and to maintain contact with agents of the Norwegian resistance.

Both First Sea Lord and Commander-in-Chief, whose flagship when at her buoy in Scapa Flow was in direct telephone communication with London, had therefore a triple problem, worthy of the trident they naturally assumed was theirs to wield: defence against submarine-launched torpedoes, against aerial bombing and air-borne torpedoes, and against the guns of surface ships operating out of the Norwegian fiords.

As the campaign progressed, increasingly powerful escorts were provided in fits and starts, eventually reaching an approximate ratio of one warship to every merchant ship, a measure of the value of the lumbering hulls that rolled and pitched across the top of the world. This is a point not to be missed, a point Dönitz perfectly understood as he pressed his U-boats to greater and greater self-sacrifice in the final defence of the Fatherland, desperately trying to remedy the awful cost of Hitler's tyrannical impatience. The victory gained by perhaps a single torpedo, even at the cost of the U-boat that fired it, was worthwhile. A 10,000-ton Liberty ship sunk thus in the Arctic represented a very real success, for to destroy in action on the Eastern front the contents of her holds and 'tween decks – the crated fighters, the tanks, guns, vehicles and ammunition which gave the Red Army a proportion of its mobility and firepower – was vastly more complicated, expensive and doubtful a matter. It meant, too, a measure of relief for the Wehrmacht as the invader became the pursued, while the mauling of an entire convoy was the equivalent of a major land victory.

Upon Sir Dudley Pound, the burden of supplying the Russians fell particularly heavily. The First Sea Lord was compelled to bow under the fearsome pressure Churchill was capable of exerting upon his commanders, although both he and Tovey protested the folly of attempting to maintain a year-round schedule of convoy sailings, 'particularly in summer'. Churchill had initially set this at ten-day intervals, ignoring the admirals' assessment that the operation was 'fundamentally unsound', and despite the fact that the option of supply via the Persian Gulf, though longer and exposed to considerable risk, was, on balance, safer. The Arctic Ocean was a unique and terrible theatre for war.

4

'Now there is no end to our troubles'

ON 12 JULY 1941 as a consequence of Churchill's reaction to Stalin's requests for assistance, the C-in-C Home Fleet, Admiral Tovey, was ordered to form a striking force to work in the far north in support of the Russians. Sir John Tovey had distinguished himself in destroyers at Jutland and had become one of the Royal Navy's most popular fighting admirals, second-in-command to Cunningham in the Mediterranean. His appointment to the Home Fleet, however, was to bring him into conflict with Churchill, many of whose schemes Tovey regarded as hare-brained, foolhardy and ill-conceived. In so far as operations in the Arctic were concerned, Tovey was opposed to them, agreeing with Admiral Pound. Thus Churchill thought him 'negative' with 'an unenterprising attitude of mind'. Much of Tovey's obstinacy was due to a very real appreciation of Arctic conditions and the practical burdens of his new job. He was forthright in his criticism of Coastal Command's poverty of new aircraft, early realizing the immense importance of air cover in the Atlantic, and was well aware of the deficiencies of his ships, in particular of the brand-new King George V class of battleships, which were markedly inferior to the heavy German ships they were supposed to intercept. Tovey considered Churchill's ideas to be 'based upon expediency . . . without any real governing policy', and while admirable as a war leader, 'as a strategist and tactician [he] is liable to be most dangerous . . .'[1]

Tovey was a deeply religious man, possessed of great strength of character and fearlessness. He inspired loyalty and affection and was imbued with a very real 'goodness'. But the active employment of the Mediterranean was to be denied him in the bleak north. The pursuit of the *Bismarck* was flawed and its attendant disastrous loss of the *Hood* and the questionable readiness of the *Prince of Wales* were circumstances which seem to have robbed him of some of his dash, for a commander-in-chief is denied the catharsis of action and has to rely upon his subordinate admirals. Moreover, the coming months were to involve the Royal Navy in the most crippling losses in its long history and this undoubtedly had an effect on the morale of those charged with its stewardship, even one with the personal qualities of Sir 'Jack' Tovey.

Tovey's command was seen as the source of all reinforcement. *Prince of Wales* and *Repulse* left his charge for their disastrous sinking off Malaya and later, as we shall see, the Home Fleet was depleted to cover the invasion of North Africa. Whilst Tovey was not opposed to offensive operations against western Norway, the Admiralty's order of 12 July to form a new striking force for Arctic waters did not meet with his approval. In this he was overridden by the political necessity of being active in support of the Russians while the machinery and resources for regular convoy sailings were mustered.

British naval operations in the Arctic commenced with several incursions into the Barents Sea coincident with the delivery of mines made by the *Adventure*. The first, Operation EF, was in response to Russian requests for attacks to be made on German coastal shipping sailing between Kirkenes and the former Finnish port of Petsamo, centre of a nickel-producing region.

Rear-Admiral W.F. Wake-Walker in the cruiser HMS *Devonshire*, with HMS *Suffolk* and the carriers *Victorious* and *Furious* escorted by six destroyers, sailed from Scapa Flow on 23 July to refuel at Iceland. It was intended that this squadron should make a wide sweep to the north, well out of range, it was thought, of aircraft based in Norway. British caution on account of the supposed strength of the Luftwaffe in Norway was groundless, for much of the enemy's air forces had been diverted to the Russian front at the time, but the element of surprise was lost when the squadron was sighted by long-range enemy air reconnaissance on the 30th.

Cheated of their primary objective, for no coastal shipping was sighted offshore, the carriers' aircraft were flown off to strike the secondary targets, the ports' installations. German fighters and anti-aircraft fire over Kirkenes destroyed eleven of the twenty ageing Swordfish torpedo-bombers flown off from the new aircraft-carrier HMS *Victorious*. Encountering less resistance at Petsamo, the aircraft from *Furious* found the harbour empty. Wake-Walker's bruised and frustrated force returned to Scapa Flow after raiding Tromso.

Admiral Tovey, probably aware that the mines delivered by HMS *Adventure* had been deployed, consoled himself with the consideration that 'the Russians were most appreciative' of them despite Golovko's complaints that they were useless. HMS *Adventure* had accompanied Wake-Walker's squadron, then broken away to the eastwards under the cover of the cruiser *Shropshire* and the destroyer *Anthony*. Arriving on 1 August, she left Archangel on the 4th and returned alone.

Meanwhile, Rear-Admiral Vian had returned from his mission to Murmansk with Rear-Admiral Miles and reported the deficiencies of the Kola Inlet generally, the inadequacies of the Russian air defences at Polyarnoe in particular, and the doubtful value of attacks on enemy shipping in the vicinity of the North Cape, confirming Tovey's misgivings. Vian was next instructed to take a close look at the western coast of Spitzbergen which, it was thought, being largely ice-free might be suitable as a base. Vian accordingly hoisted his flag in the cruiser *Nigeria* and, taking a second, the *Aurora*, and two destroyers in company, sailed from Iceland on 27 July. Spitzbergen had the merit of distance from the German airfields, but otherwise its very remoteness argued against it, being 450 miles north of Norway. Despite being Norwegian territory, the simple camp provided for the Russian miners who worked the coal seams constituted the sum of its installations, and the immense practical difficulties of setting up any sort of depot outweighed the somewhat illusory advantages so primitive a base detached from the Russian mainland could afford the Royal Navy. Spitzbergen was later used as both a fuelling rendezvous and a meteorological station, ironically by both sides simultaneously, but as a forward base it had no value. An aggressive commander, Vian now made two attempts to close the Norwegian coast but, lacking air cover, these were prudently aborted when the squadron was discovered by long-range enemy aircraft and Vian returned to Scapa Flow.

As the first convoy to Russia assembled at Hvalfiordur in Iceland, Vian was ordered back to Spitzbergen to evacuate the Russian coal-miners and Norwegian personnel stationed there.

The squadron which sailed on 19 August consisted of HM cruisers *Aurora* and *Nigeria*, the destroyers *Icarus, Tartar, Anthony, Antelope* and *Eclipse*, the oiler *Oligarch* and the liner *Empress of Canada* with Canadian troops on board. The invading force landed at Barentsburg and wrecked the coal mines before embarking 2,000 Russian miners. The *Empress of Canada* and *Nigeria* then ran on to Archangel to disembark their passengers there before rejoining *Aurora* off Barentsburg on 1 September.

Meanwhile Vian's supplementary orders to destroy enemy shipping were effectively achieved by the co-operation of the Norwegian military governor, a naval lieutenant, who maintained the illusion that all was well, luring three colliers by radio which, being seized in the time-honoured fashion, were sent in as prizes, along with a whaler, a tug, an ice-breaker and two fishing boats. The Canadian troops re-embarked on 2 September and left the following day, bringing with them 800 Norwegian colonists. The prizes and troopship were escorted by the destroyers.

Vian now took his two cruisers *Aurora* and *Nigeria* south towards the Norwegian coast again where, in the early hours of 7 August, they discovered a small German convoy off Porshanger, just east of the North Cape. In thick weather and a gale, at very short range, Vian engaged and sank the elderly training minelayer *Bremse*, but the two troopships she was escorting, the *Barcelona* and the *Trautenfels*, with 1,500 soldiers embarked, succeeded in escaping. Vian arrived back in Scapa Flow on 10 September with *Nigeria's* bow mysteriously damaged. This was at first thought to have been caused by her having run down the sinking *Bremse*, but post-war analysis suggests she may have struck a mine during the action.[2]

While these incursions were taking place, the convoy at Hvalfiordur had sailed on 21 August 1941. Code-named Dervish and arriving at its destination of Archangel ten days later, it was unimpressively small, consisting of only six merchant ships, several of which were 'very ancient', under the direction of Captain J.C.K. Dowding RNR as Commodore. The ships of Operation Dervish were loaded with some of the raw materials desperately needed by the Russians, principally wool, rubber and tin. On board the elderly *Llanstephan Castle* were two journalists and the artist Feliks Topolski, evidence of Churchill's astute mastery of propaganda. The other British ships were the *Lancastrian Prince,*

New Westminster City, Esneh and *Trehata*, with the fleet oiler *Aldersdale* and the Dutch freighter *Alchiba*. The escorts comprised the ocean minesweepers *Halcyon, Salamander* and *Harrier*, which possessed an anti-submarine capability and were destined to be stationed in North Russia; the destroyers *Electra, Active* and *Impulsive*; and the anti-submarine trawlers *Hamlet, Macbeth* and *Ophelia*. Concurrent with the arrival of the Dervish convoy, the ageing aircraft-carrier *Argus*, loaded with two dozen Hurricanes of No. 151 Wing of the Royal Air Force, was dispatched to Russia in an operation somewhat grandiosely code-named Strength. *Argus* was supported by HMS *Shropshire* and the destroyers *Matabele, Punjabi* and *Somali*, aboard all of which RAF personnel were accommodated.

A further fifteen crated Hurricanes had been stowed in the holds of the Dervish vessels and were intended to replace some of the Soviet airforce's catastrophic losses. These Hurricanes were to protect Murmansk, Archangel and Polyarnoe. When within range of the Russian airfield at Vaenga the operational fighters were flown off from *Argus* and landed safely. The remainder, unloaded at Archangel and assembled with Russian assistance, had joined them by 12 September.

In addition to these escorts, Admiral Tovey provided a covering force to the various raids consisting of HMS *Victorious*, the cruisers *Devonshire* and *Suffolk*, and the destroyers *Inglefield, Eclipse* and *Escapade*. The purpose of this covering force was to intercept and pin down any intervention by surface units of the Kriegsmarine based in Norway.

With the dispatch of the Dervish convoy, operations in the Arctic took on a new character. The dashing raids of Wake-Walker and Vian were to be replaced by the ploddingly serious business of convoy and convoy support. As the Arctic days shortened and as the dwindling hours of daylight progressively frustrated German aerial reconnaissance, the increasing cold and incidence of bad weather, the problems of fuelling the smaller ships, of keeping all units habitable and the warships in fighting trim, began to occupy the minds of those involved. Tovey's concern in respect of bombing attacks initially proved groundless for the Luftwaffe had too many aircraft engaged to the south-east, but this respite was merely temporary and his fears were shortly to be justified in full. Tovey had also to provide reinforcements elsewhere, principally the Mediterranean, but some support was forthcoming from the Americans who in August assumed the responsibility of garrisoning Iceland.

Of the logistical problems that faced the Arctic convoys, that of refuelling was the most critical, while the paucity of facilities of any kind for both naval and mercantile personnel at journey's end posed a serious threat to morale. The Royal Navy had been used to the luxury of worldwide fuelling stations in Britain's far-flung colonies. Techniques for refuelling at sea were rudimentary (though practised in the Arctic) and only truly perfected at the end of the war by the British fleet operating in the Pacific with the United States Navy. Little regard had been paid in British warship design to the ability of a ship to remain at sea for long periods, a quality known as endurance or range. It was a problem that bedevilled many destroyers, including the new Hunts, and even Great Britain's latest battleships, the King George V class, were deficient in this respect. Only the cruisers possessed real range and acted as milch-cows to smaller vessels, though the extempore conversions of elderly destroyers helped. The corvettes and anti-submarine trawlers possessed adequate fuel stocks. As for facilities for personnel, provisions were made for naval sailors, but there were none for merchant seamen at the beginning. They gradually improved, though at a scandalously slow pace.

While Tovey's staff, the planners of the Admiralty Trade Division, the Ministry of War Transport and the Ministry of Supply concerned themselves with ships, cargoes, times of arrival, anchorages, fuelling, crewing and the multitudinous details vital to the assembly of a single convoy, the Commander-in-Chief worried about his resources as well as his opponents.

In addition to his ships, Tovey had to hand the aircraft of Coastal Command. Inadequate and obsolescent though many of them were, their commander, Air Chief Marshal Sir Frederic Bowhill, had started his career at sea in the Merchant Navy and perfectly understood maritime war.[3] Bowhill commanded from Northwood, near London. At Pitreavie, close to the naval base at Rosyth in eastern Scotland, lay Coastal Command's Combined Area Headquarters, manned by a joint naval and air staff, which provided air reconnaissance and anti-submarine patrols. American-supplied Catalina flying boats flew from Sullom Voe in northern Shetland, and from Reykjavik, but their respective ranges did not extend much beyond the Lofotens or Jan Mayen

Island. In July the Commander-in-Chief had also dispatched the submarines *Tigris* and *Trident* to operate from Kola, and others were to follow, largely to encourage and support Russian operations against shipping along the polar coast of occupied Norway.

Following the conference Vian had had with Golovko before his first Spitzbergen operation, Tovey divided the convoy route into two, expecting additional Russian air, surface and submarine support east of Bear Island as the convoy closed the Murman coast. In this expectation he was disappointed; Russian destroyers gave excellent anti-aircraft cover when available, but they lacked weatherliness and were poor sea-boats; Russian air support was not often forthcoming; and co-operation with Russian submarines proved difficult. Moreover, with von Bock concentrating against Moscow, Churchill now insisted on a punishing schedule: 'we intend to run a continuous cycle of convoys, leaving every ten days . . . counting on Archangel to handle the main bulk of deliveries', Churchill assured Stalin in early October. This was one of those hare-brained schemes Tovey justifiably criticized. Archangel was iced up during the winter; with a minimal escort of one cruiser and two destroyers per convoy the Commander-in-Chief must allocate four cruisers and eight destroyers if the ten-day schedule was to be met. Tovey and the Admiralty planners had been aiming at a forty-day cycle. Perhaps Churchill dissembled, perhaps it was a political decision rather than a practical one, a commitment designed to keep Russia in the war no matter the difficulties of implementation it posed to his naval chiefs and based on Beaverbrook's assessment of Stalin's attitude at this difficult juncture when Russia might have wavered.

But the failure of his allies to keep to this schedule and their inability to deliver the promised quotas due to losses on passage were seen by Stalin as sabotage. Stalin's ignorance of the true nature of what his allies were attempting is breathtaking. Evidently succumbing to the myth of the superiority of Communism, he believed that Soviet ice-breakers could keep open the Dvina and the ports of the White Sea throughout the year. This attitude infected the whole official Soviet appreciation of the Anglo-American effort at this stage and coloured the reception awaiting the incoming ships on the Dvina and at Kola.

With the Germans now laying siege to Leningrad (the 890-day siege had begun with the seizure of the outer defences on 20

August), Hitler was preoccupied by the campaign in the Ukraine and the resumption of the advance on Moscow. Nevertheless, although stubborn Russian resistance in the Rybachi peninsula had pinned Dietl down, the Führer reiterated that German strategy in this area was to be dedicated to the severance of the Murmansk railway in the following year and the security of the nickel mines of Petsamo. Hitler's appraisal of British intentions expressed in his 36th Directive of 22 September 1941 was that 'the English will deploy strong air forces around Murmansk . . . and that they will send as much war material as possible . . .' In October's 37th Directive he laid particular stress on the need for close co-operation between the Luftwaffe and the Kriegsmarine to prevent this. As set out in his 21st Directive which initiated Barbarossa, the German navy was to regard as its primary target operations against England.

Hitler's obsession with an amphibious British assault against Norway meant he regarded the polar coast as a 'decisive area'.[4] In this he was partly right, for British sea-power, dented though it was to be, was indeed decisive, not in striking at Norway, but in outflanking it and succouring the Russians. Ironically, however, Hitler's fear compelled Raeder to concentrate his heavy ships in Norwegian waters, thus posing a perpetual and very real threat to Arctic operations. The Royal Navy and the Kriegsmarine had already joined combat in the region in the operations during and following the seizure of Norway. British losses had been heavy, the aircraft-carrier *Glorious* and attendant destroyers having been sunk by the guns of the *Scharnhorst* and the *Gneisenau*, but the sheer size of the Royal Navy continued to feed Hitler's paranoia.[5]

The German naval command structure in Norway was cumbersome but demands some explanation in the light of subsequent events. German naval orders emanated from the Supreme Naval Staff in Berlin, the Seekriegsleitung. Operations in the Arctic were directed from Naval Group North headquarters at Kiel (Admiral Boehm). A subordinate command for Norway was based at Oslo with three detached flag-officers responsible for minesweeping, coastal defences, patrols and minelaying on the west, north and polar coasts. The direction of main fleet units and U-boats in the area bypassed the Admiral Commanding Norway, and passed to the Flag Officer Northern Waters at Narvik who in turn commanded the Flag Officer Battle Group, who took the ships to sea. This cumbersome arrangement existed until March 1943 when Naval Group North assumed the title of Admiral Commanding the

Fleet upon the abolition of the Flag Officer Northern Waters. In May 1944, Naval Group North was itself abolished and power was vested in Naval Command Norway.

In addition to fleet units and U-boats, the Flag Officer Northern Waters (Narvik) also directed aircraft allocated to the Kriegsmarine for tactical purposes and these were drawn from Luftflotte 5, the air-fleet based in occupied Denmark and Norway. The Norwegian section was divided into three with headquarters at Kirkenes, Trondheim/Stavanger and Bardufoss. Only at Kirkenes, where the Flag Officer Polar Coast was based, were the German navy and airforce in close touch. The constant rivalry between these two armed services dashed Hitler's hopes of their co-operation. It was aggravated by Reichsmarschall Herman Goering's intimacy with Hitler, in marked contrast to Raeder's apolitical professionalism but total lack of influence. The Luftwaffe was never to realize its potential in the Arctic and its deficiency in torpedo-bombers was, as we shall see, a decisive factor in its failure to obtain air superiority. As it had lost the Battle of Britain to the Royal Air Force, so the Luftwaffe was to lose the Arctic campaign to the Royal Navy. What small number of purely German naval aircraft there were in Norway, some Heinkel He115 seaplanes, were themselves under the Air Commander and intelligence swapping suffered as a consequence.

Despite his appreciation of the Arctic situation in the autumn of 1941, Hitler was confident of the success of Operation Taifun against Moscow, 'the last, the great, battle of the year'. German hopes of a Russian collapse were high. The Royal Navy, the mighty force which Hitler's premature war had challenged so recklessly, had achieved little, while the Wehrmacht, with the exception of Dietl's mountain units, carried all before it and the achievements of the Kriegsmarine, 'our little navy', were by no means to be despised. Of the High Command, only Raeder seems to have appreciated the long-term significance of Dietl's failure to take Murmansk in the first heady days of Barbarossa.

Pinned down though he was, General Dietl was supported by Flieger Korps V comprising 230 aircraft which continued to attack Murmansk. On Dietl's seaward flank the light units of the Kriegsmarine were stationed in Norwegian Arctic ports, on the polar coast. These consisted of five T-class 'torpedo-boats' (a misnomer, as they were the equivalent of British sloops, and not to be confused with E-boats, the German motor torpedo-boat), minesweepers and patrol craft to protect the coastal trade associated with nickel production. Dönitz had U-boats operating in the Norwegian Sea, but Raeder's big ships had yet to concentrate. The battleships *Scharnhorst* and *Gneisenau* with the heavy cruiser *Prinz Eugen* were still at Brest. The *Lützow* was undergoing repairs at Kiel after being torpedoed by HM Submarine *Spearfish* during the Norwegian campaign. Other units were in the Baltic, among them the *Tirpitz*, undergoing trials.

On 28 September 1941, the same day that Beaverbrook and Harriman arrived in Moscow to draw up the Moscow Protocol promising the Soviet Union British and American supplies and finalizing Stalin's 'shopping list', Convoy PQ1, named after the initials of Commander Philip Quellyn Roberts, a planning officer in the Admiralty, sailed from Hvalfiordur. It consisted of eleven ships under the overall direction of Captain D. Ridley, the Commodore and Master of the SS *Atlantic*. Other British ships taking part were the *Blairnevis, Elna II, Harmonic, Gemstone, Lorca* and *River Afton*, together with the fleet oiler *Black Ranger*, while the Panamanian-flagged *Capira* and *North King* and the Belgian *Ville d'Anvers* completed the complement. *Gemstone*'s crew refused to sail without additional blankets which were found for them. Among the cargoes borne were 20 tanks and 193 fighters. The close escort throughout was provided by the cruiser *Suffolk*, the destroyer *Impulsive* and the ocean minesweepers *Britomart, Leda, Hussar* and *Gossamer*, relocating, like their sisters sent earlier, to the Kola Inlet. Other destroyers were present at different stages of the voyage. *North King*'s engines broke down, but her engineers succeeded in effecting repairs in difficult conditions. Thereafter convoy and escorts passed an uneventful twilit passage, arriving at Archangel on 11 October, a day early.

Simultaneously on the 28th, Dowding with the returning Dervish ships, additional Russian ships and the oiler *Black Ranger* (which with the destroyer *Anthony* had transferred from the outward PQ1), left Archangel and arrived at Scapa on 9 October. The participating Russian ships were the *Sevaples, Sukhona, Alma Ata, Budenny, Mossovet, Rodina* and *Starii Bolshevik*, of which we shall hear more. *Mossovet* and *Sukhona* straggled, but arrived safely.

Having delivered Hurricane fighters and RAF personnel to Russia, Dowding's commodore ship, the Union Castle liner *Llanstephan Castle*, together with other ships in convoy evacuated large numbers of Polish soldiers who had escaped the German invasion of their homeland and had no great love for the Russian camp.

Convoy QP1 was covered by the cruisers *London* and *Shropshire*, the destroyers *Electra* and *Active*, and the trawlers *Macbeth, Hamlet, Celia* and *Ophelia*, the latter ending up at Akureyri under tow from the *Active*. *Shropshire*'s captain wrote: 'Generally it was a pleasure to act as ocean escort to such a well-mannered convoy and credit is due to the Russian Masters, probably none of whom had been in a convoy before'. Meanwhile the destroyers *Norman* and *Anthony* embarked a Trades Union Congress delegation and conveyed them to Russia, arriving on 12 October. Awaiting their departure on the 27th, the destroyers returned the trade unionists to Scapa on 2 November, an exercise in liaison which was intended to spur factory output throughout Britain's industrial heartland and to improve relations with the Russian authorities.

These first convoys were small, their cargoes mainly made up of the war material Churchill had promised from British sources. Some of this had suffered damage from poor storage, particularly that loaded at Glasgow. In order to cover the homeward convoys and afford mine countermeasures, Tovey built up a locally based flotilla of ocean-going minesweepers at Kola. Fluctuating in number, there were usually five or six of these Halcyon-class ships possessing, as well as their minesweeping gear, an armament and a speed comparable with Flower-class corvettes and a very effective anti-submarine capability. Moreover, being specialized vessels, they were commonly commanded by regular officers. They were supported by a fleet oiler, initially the *Aldersdale* (later chartered tonnage was used), independent of Russian resources, which remained on station to refuel naval units, particularly the incoming destroyers. It was the beginning of a considerable British presence. Several Polyarnoe-based Russian destroyers were also available to help run the convoys through the dangerous funnel of the Kola approaches.

Homeward escort usually comprised one destroyer and two of these minesweepers, reinforced by anti-submarine trawlers. These were coal-burners, designed for Arctic conditions with adequate endurance. They were commanded by their skippers, elevated to the rank of Skipper RNR, and manned by their peacetime crews, an exceptionally tough breed of men inured to the moods and caprice of the Barents Sea and who were supplemented with an anti-submarine team of volunteer reservists specially trained for the work, making up in enthusiasm what they initially lacked in experience. Both the trawlers and their crews, fishermen and reservists alike, proved more potent than their appearance suggested.

These dispositions were those Tovey strove for, inadequate though he considered them to be. The convoys usually left their assembly point and met the escort at sea. In the case of ships leaving Hvalfiordur, the rendezvous was north of Iceland, the warships usually using Seidisfiord on Iceland's east coast as their own meeting-place.

Further cover was given these early convoys by a second cruiser at sea to the west of Bear Island. As has already been mentioned, air support was only local, Coastal Command Squadrons 330 and 269 operating from Iceland, though anti-U-boat patrols from Sullom Voe flying along the Norwegian coast assisted.

The six ships of PQ2 assembled at Scapa Flow and sailed on 17 October. The *Harpalion, Hartlebury, Queen City, Orient City, Temple Arch* and *Empire Baffin* were all British; the through escort consisted of HM Cruiser *Norfolk*, the destroyers *Icarus* and *Eclipse*, and the minesweepers *Bramble, Seagull* and *Speedy*. PQ2 arrived at Archangel without loss on the 31st.

Norfolk, Eclipse and *Icarus* departed Archangel with the returning dozen ships of QP2 on 2 November. The British merchantmen were joined by the Russian ships *Ijora, Stepan Khalturin* and *Chernyshevski*, with the trawlers *Celia* and *Windermere* seeing them safely into Kirkwall in the Orkneys on the 17th.

By this time of the year the sun rises increasingly briefly north of the Arctic circle, a phenomenon which persists until the winter solstice. Admiral Raeder appreciated both the fact that these conditions favoured the passage of convoys and that 'the British realize the vital importance of the sea route off the Arctic coast for supply of the German forces'. The lack of British raids against *German* coastal convoys worried him and in daily expectation of their materializing, he complained to Hitler of the lack of Luftwaffe reconnaissance flights.

Equally anxious, though for a different reason, Admiral Tovey was unable to stop the homeward QP2. However, he did prevent the sailing of PQ3 from Hvalfiordur both because of the need to effect repairs to weather damage sustained by his destroyers and because he had received intelligence reports that a sortie by *Tirpitz* and *Admiral Scheer* was expected.

In fact it was not until 13 November that Raeder suggested this to Hitler, but a lack of boiler oil and the fear of the *Tirpitz* sharing the fate of her sister ship, the *Bismarck*, made Hitler veto the suggestion for the time being, though he agreed to the *Admiral Scheer* moving into northern waters, for there was no restriction on the availability of diesel oil. Raeder also strengthened naval forces on the polar coast, relieving the T-class torpedo 'boats' with five Beitzen-class destroyers, powerfully armed with five 5-inch guns and eight 21-inch torpedo tubes, but which suffered badly from defective high-pressure water-tube boilers that supplied steam to their geared turbines. In addition, Dönitz was instructed to maintain a patrol strength of three U-boats on station.

Tovey dispatched the delayed convoy of eight merchant vessels on the 9th. Though one, the *Briarwood*, turned back due to ice damage, escorted by the trawler *Hamlet*, on the 28th the Russians were treated to the sight of fifteen merchant ships coming into the River Dvina. Among these were the British ships *Cape Corso*, *Cape Race*, *Trekieve*, *San Ambrosio* and *Wanstead*, and the Panamanians *Cocle* and *El Capitan*. *Cape Corso* straggled, but arrived independently. With them were the faster ships of PQ4, the *Budenny*, *Mossovet*, *Sukhona*, *Alma Ata*, *Empire Meteor*, *Rodina*, *Eulima* and *Dan-y-Bryn*, which had left 'the whale's haven' on the 17th and had caught up. PQ3 was escorted by the cruiser *Kenya* with HM destroyers *Bedouin* and *Intrepid* and two trawlers, though only *Macbeth* had continued through to Archangel. PQ4 was covered by the cruiser *Berwick*, the destroyers *Offa* and *Onslow* and the trawlers *Bute* and *Stella Capella*. While waiting to join PQ3, anchored at Seidisfiord with General Gromov and a Russian military mission on board, HMS *Kenya* and her destroyers had flown the Soviet flag in honour of the anniversary of the October Revolution, a gesture much appreciated by Gromov and his staff.

This co-operation extended to a short Anglo-Russian operation when Rear-Admiral Burrough in *Kenya*, with *Bedouin* and *Intrepid*, took under his command the Russian destroyers *Gromki* and *Gremyashchi* for a brief bombardment of enemy batteries at Vardo. On 25 November 1941 Golovko wrote to Burrough, 'I wish you to understand . . . my heartiest gratitude and full satisfaction with the operation.'

The homeward QP3 of ten ships sailed on 27 November and although two, the *Arcos* and *Kuzbass*, turned back, six British ships reached Seidisfiord on 7 December. Two remaining Russian ships, the *Revolutsioner* and *Andre Marti*, proceeded direct to Kirkwall under the escort of HMS *Gossamer* and *Hussar*. QP3' s attendant cruiser was *Kenya*, with the destroyers *Bedouin* and *Intrepid*.

The same day that QP3 sailed from Archangel and exactly ten days after the departure of PQ4, convoy PQ5 left Hvalfiordur. The *Briarwood, Trehata, Chulmleigh, St Clears* and *Empire Stevenson* were accompanied by the Russian ships *Petrovski* and *Komiles*. HMS *Kent*, later reinforced by *Sheffield*, with a shuttle of minesweepers formed the escort. Incorrect data passed by the Home Fleet staff to the *Onslow, Offa* and *Oribi* had the three destroyers searching vainly along the ice-edge for six anxious days until sighting the convoy's smoke rising in the still Arctic air. The seven ships forced the passage of the Gourlo, the narrow strait into the White Sea, with the assistance of Russian ice-breakers. PQ6, which left Hvalfiordur on 8 December, initially escorted by the trawlers *Hugh Walpole, Cape Argona* and *Stella Capella*, had worse luck and was too late to reach Archangel. It likewise had had two ships turn back. One was the rescue ship *Zamalek*, the other the SS *Harmatris*.

At 5,395 tons, the *Harmatris* was typical of the ships participating in these early convoys. Coal-burning, with a bunker capacity sufficient to cross the Pacific and quite capable of making North Russia and back at 8 knots, she was owned by J. and C. Harrison of London. Her master, 47-year-old Captain R.W. Brundle, had brought her independently to the rendezvous at Iceland. Brundle had a crew of 46, including 7 DEMS gunners to man the 4-inch low-angle gun on her poop, a 20-mm Hispano cannon, 5 Lewis machine guns and 2 twin Marlins. The *Harmatris* was loaded with 8,000 tons of military stores which included vehicles and ammunition. Merchant ships' armaments were manned by naval ratings known as DEMS (an acronym for Defensively Armed Merchant Ships). These men were supplemented by soldiers from the Maritime Royal Artillery (MRA) and formed the nucleus of a ship's gun crew, training up merchant seamen as additional hands. They usually messed with the engineers and were led by a petty officer or NCO. American merchant ships' guns were served by a 'naval guard', usually led by an ensign, roughly the equivalent of a British midshipman.

Soon after leaving Iceland the convoy was overtaken by a south-westerly gale which developed into a storm. In the darkness and low visibility, the *Harmatris* fell behind the convoy and

Brundle prudently hove to, to minimize damage to his ship and her cargo. Two days out, on the 10th, it was noticed from the bridge that water on the deck above No. 4 'tween deck was vaporizing to steam. Men were mustered, the corner of the hatch was exposed and a hatch board cautiously lifted. In the gloom below, a burning lorry was loose, slamming around as the ship laboured, breaking open bales and cases which then ignited. In the hold beneath the 'tween deck, ten tons of cordite and a quantity of small arms ammunition were stowed. Brundle ordered the space steam-smothered through the ship's fixed installation, but this was ineffective. The Mate, Mr G. Masterman, then entered the hatch wearing the vessel's sole smoke helmet and dragging a hose. Eventually overcome by smoke, he was relieved by Chief Steward Peart whose gallant efforts failed to stop the fire. Brundle was compelled to break radio silence and transmit an SOS. In response the rescue ship *Zamalek* turned back to assist.

Meanwhile Brundle and Peart spelled each other through the night until they finally succeeded in dowsing the fire. *Zamalek* was thus relieved of her duty to stand by and proceeded to Iceland. Aboard the tramp other cargo then came adrift and an exhausted Brundle received permission from the now distant Commodore to turn back and make for the Clyde, as Hvalfiordur was dead to windward and lacked any facilities. *Harmatris* spent Christmas in Glasgow, left on Boxing Day, and again reached Hvalfiordur on New Year's Day, 1942. She was to prove a dogged survivor.

There had been other ships making this passage in early December. In the first week many of the RAF personnel transported to Russia during Operation Strength returned home in the cruisers *Berwick* and *Kenya* and the destroyers *Intrepid* and *Offa*, having handed over their Hurricane fighters. *Onslow* and *Oribi* had left twenty-four hours earlier. They thus evaded the appalling weather the *Berwick*, *Kenya* and company now ran into, in which even the cruisers suffered upper-deck damage from the heavy seas.

The following week the *Kent* carried the British Foreign Secretary, Anthony Eden, Ambassador Maisky and their staffs to Murmansk. At their meeting with Stalin in Moscow, the Soviet leader pressed for more munitions and British recognition of Russia's annexation of Latvia, Lithuania and Estonia. The Wehrmacht was within twenty-five miles of Red Square and Leningrad invested, but the Red Army had begun to counter-attack and had that very week recaptured Tikhvin. The Germans were also confronted by the Russian's greatest ally: 'General Winter'. 'We have seriously underestimated the Russians,' Guderian, doyen of Panzer officers, wrote to his wife, 'the extent of the country and the treachery of the climate . . . This is the revenge of reality'.

As Brundle and his crew toiled to fight the fire in No. 4 'tween deck of the SS *Harmatris*, the cruiser *Edinburgh* arrived at Seidisfiord to bunker. Three days earlier, anchored at Scapa Flow, the watching of a film had been interrupted by a highly significant order: 'Commence hostilities against Japan forthwith.'

Although this might have seemed a somewhat tall order from the Orkney Islands, the Japanese bombing of Pearl Harbor was to have a marked and almost immediate impact on the convoys to North Russia, namely vastly to increase the amount of cargo shipped there, and to involve American merchant ships in the composition of the convoys. For the remainder of the PQ series of convoys, the rendezvous point would be Iceland.

Edinburgh was delayed by the same gale which separated *Harmartis* from her convoy and found Seidisfiord bleak, with snow on the surrounding hills and more falling as she bunkered, though Alda, the little town on the shore, 'looked like a Christmas card picture'. Here they received more news, 'about the worst news we have had about the sea this war' – the *Prince of Wales* and *Repulse* had been sunk off Malaya.

At 16.00, ship's time, *Edinburgh* weighed, her crew exchanging snowballs with that of the oiler and, in company with two destroyers, *Echo* and *Escapade*, headed north. The wind had dropped; it was cold, calm and 'quite pleasant'.

The following afternoon the three warships fell in with PQ6 under the sole escort of His Majesty's Trawler *Hugh Walpole*. The Panamanian ships *El Oceano* (a tanker) and *Mount Evans* accompanied four British merchantmen, *Explorer, Empire Mavis, El Mirlo* and *Elona*, the latter of which was the Commodore, and the Russian vessel *Dekabrist*.

Explorer, a cargo liner owned by T. and J. Harrison of Liverpool, rather than Harrisons of London who owned the *Harmatris*, had sailed in a small convoy from Loch Ewe on 20 November, having loaded a military cargo in her home port. On passage, her crew had been issued with the standard Arctic clothing which included a fur-lined duffle coat, two pairs of heavy woollen long johns, a white submariner's polo-necked jersey, thick mittens and heavy sea-boot stockings. Such largesse was viewed with suspicion, recalled one crew member: 'This was certainly not the type of behaviour we were accustomed to from shipowners, especially Harrisons,' whose funnel colours, a red band between two white, were colloquially referred to as 'two of fat and one of lean'. Another benefit of war for these seamen was that their pay had been raised from £8 to £24 per month, the difference being 'danger money'. Like *Harmatris, Explorer* bore DEMS ratings, though some of her crew had undergone basic gunnery training at HMS *President*, the RNR training ship which still lies on the Thames Embankment. At Hvalfiordur *Explorer* loaded transhipped cargo, an experience which resulted in two of her crew getting frost-bitten hands.

The following day, station-keeping was somewhat erratic, but the weather remained fine and clear with the temperature near freezing. On Saturday, 13 December 1941, when north of the 72nd parallel, 'after the faint light of dawn and/or dusk had filtered into the sky', *Edinburgh* detached from the convoy for a gunnery exercise, firing at her own star-shells. 'The Oerlikons' yellow tracers, turning to red, looked very gay in the half-light,' one of the cruiser's officers wrote in his journal. Total darkness sent the cruiser at high speed back to the convoy, which had reached its most northerly point, 73° 44′, 300 miles west of Bear Island, where it was treated to the spectacle of the aurora borealis. A young officer recorded:

> The argument about whether the northern lights are coloured was dramatically settled . . . A streak of purple flame appeared faintly in the distance and, shooting this way and that, gradually approached . . . It grew in brightness and colour until like a great flaming dragon, contorting itself fantastically, it shot in a series of convolutions around the sky. It was quite terrifying[ly] . . . close and violent and was such an intense red light [it] played on the ship, illuminating it like a red searchlight.

Exercises on the merchant ships were less dramatic, though no less purposeful. Aboard *Explorer* the four-handed deck watch, increased by one from its peacetime establishment, rotated the tasks of helmsman, lookout and two in the gun-pits. The day-workers, men not on watch, spent their time on the constant and unenviable task of clearing ice. There were four of them, a pathetic number compared with the large working parties *Edinburgh* could muster for the same task.

Oiling *Escapade* the next day, *Edinburgh* experienced difficulties due to the coagulation of cold boiler fuel, for though remaining calm, the temperature had dropped well below freezing as the convoy swung south. A brief crepuscular daylight made a welcome appearance. Regarding the pipeline stretched between the two ships, the upper-deck parties on both the cruiser and the destroyers stamped in the cold as their breath froze on the fur of their duffle-hoods and woollen scarves.

On the 18th, off the Murman coast, news was received aboard *Edinburgh* that two minesweepers from Kola, *Speedy* and *Hazard*, sent out to clear the approaches, had had a brush with German destroyers themselves laying mines. These ships, of the 8th Flotilla under Kapitän Pönitz, were the *Z23*, *Z24*, *Z25* and *Z27*, and they mistook the Halcyon-class sweepers for G-class destroyers. Fortunately, the small British ships escaped in the gloom under a smoke-screen, though the Germans fired star-shell and succeeded in hitting *Speedy*, which was compelled to withdraw to Kola while *Hazard* waited for the convoy. News of the attack brought Captain Cunninghame-Graham in HMS *Kent*, cruiser escort to PQ5, out of Kola with the Russian destroyers *Grozni* and *Sokrushitelni* in an unsuccessful attempt to intercept Pönitz's destroyers. A third minesweeper, HMS *Leda*, which had been sent out to relieve the wounded *Speedy*, was located by *Escapade* and both with *Hazard* rejoined the convoy.

At this juncture, off the entrance to the Gourlo, *Edinburgh*, her two destroyers and the *El Mirlo* and *Dekabrist* detached for the run back along the coast to Murmansk, leaving the minesweepers to see the rest of the convoy into the White Sea port of Molotovsk. The Dvina was already freezing, the homeward ships of QP4 struggling seaward in the wake of the Russian ice-breakers *Stalin* and *Lenin*, but a Russian ice-breaker assisted the *Empire Mavis*, *Mount Evans*, *El Oceano*, *Elona* and *Explorer* to their berths at Molotovsk, where they finally secured on 23 December. In coming in, *Explorer*'s Master had established contact with his pilot through the unusual medium of a common knowledge of Latin.

In Molotovsk these ships were frozen in with their ice-breaker until the following June. Conditions were miserable. Fresh water, washing and toilet facilities all froze and scabies broke out among the crews. Their cargoes were discharged by German prisoners who were grateful for the scraps of food the crew threw over the rail on to the ice, disgusted as they were with the deteriorating provisions. In the end the Russians, hard-pressed themselves, brought yak carcasses alongside on sleighs.

Meanwhile, on the morning of the 20th as they proceeded west to the Kola Inlet in worsening weather and a rising gale, *Edinburgh* lost contact with the *El Mirlo*, which had proved something of a problem ship throughout the passage. *Escapade* had to be sent to search for her while the cruiser left *Echo* to shepherd the fast *Dekabrist* into Murmansk at 18 knots. This was a mistake, for shortly afterwards the sound of gunfire was heard and *Edinburgh* swung round to find the Russian freighter and her escort, whose 4.7-inch guns were not very effective against aircraft, under attack from two low-level Junkers Ju88 bombers. *Dekabrist* had been shaken by a near miss and had two unexploded bombs rattling about on her decks. Furthermore, in working up to full speed, *Echo* had lost two men, washed overboard from their station at A-gun on the forecastle. The appearance of the cruiser and six Russian Hurricanes drove the Ju88s away. Zigzagging in the wake of the Russian ship, cruiser and destroyer finally picked up their pilots at 16.00 on 20 December, anchoring four miles below Murmansk in the Kola Inlet, 'very desolated [*sic*] at its entrance and only a few small fir trees break the snow near Murmansk'.[6]

Ironically, *El Mirlo* had got there before them. Admiral Golovko regarded her arrival with a jaundiced eye. As the Dvina froze, he had noted, 'matters are evidently moving in favour of Murmansk becoming the reception port for the convoys'. It seems that Moscow had yet to approve this, and on Christmas Day, five days after the arrival of the Allied ships of PQ6 and while Captain Brundle's crew celebrated their lucky escape in Glasgow, Golovko wrote in his diary, 'the signs are that cargo vessels will sail into Murmansk. Now there is no end to our troubles.'[7]

5

'A matter of the highest urgency'

By the winter solstice the White Sea was freezing and the approaches to Archangel were blocked. In the Barents Sea the bitterly cold and dense high-pressure polar air asserted itself: calms descended and the sea ran smooth, then bore a sheen as of oil before, quite suddenly, it froze – no more than a skin at first, then thickening between floes and broken pack from last winter's ice fields, solidifying and holding fast the larger icebergs of the far north and the decaying, smooth-humped growlers, so dangerous to ships because they barely broke the surface but lay concealed, as lethal as any reef. The twilight of the daytime darkened to black night by early afternoon and remained thus until mid-morning next day. Overcast skies, snow, squalls and fog compounded this dreary gloom and while occasions of clear skies brought on the magnificent spectacle of the aurora borealis, this almost mystical sight seemed to those whom the caprice of war had sent hither, only a confirmation that man trespassed in these remote and inhospitable seas.

To the ships waiting in Kola over Christmas for news of QP4, which was thought to have left Archangel on 20 December 1941, the sudden cold was only alleviated by the extraordinary, though relative, 'warmth' of a gale, when all became damp and felt paradoxically even chillier and more uncomfortable as maritime air blew in from the west. Weird contrasts abounded, for the low mist of 'arctic smoke' created by air more than 10°C cooler than the sea below it gave the curious impression that the sea itself was gently simmering.

The cruiser *Kent* left on Christmas Day, bearing Eden home

from Moscow. For the *Edinburgh*'s crew shore leave and forays in the ship's boats were the only diversions. Their surroundings were bleak and they envied the native Russians only their fur coats and hats, the *shuba* and *papenka*, seeking to barter for them. Little hostility seems to have been encountered by the naval personnel at this early stage in Anglo-Russian relations. From time to time German aircraft came over and were driven off, while the rumbling sound of distant gunfire reminded the naval personnel that the enemy were little more than thirty miles away.

Meanwhile, at Bush Terminal in Brooklyn, New York, Common Brothers' SS *Waziristan* was the first British ship to load military supplies in the United States for Russia. With two other cargo ships and an escort of two trawlers she diverted from the transatlantic convoy SC60, bound for Reykjavik and the rendezvous in the 'whale's fiord'. Eager to maintain the schedule and with only two ships ready, PQ7A, consisting of the *Waziristan* and the Panamanian-flagged *Cold Harbour*, left Hvalfiordur on Boxing Day escorted by the trawlers *Ophelia* and *Hugh Walpole*. Due to meet the minesweepers *Britomart* and *Salamander* on the departure of the trawlers, the merchantmen missed the rendezvous and proceeded in company unescorted. In the gloom of New Year's Day, somewhere in the grey turbulent wilderness of the Arctic Ocean between Norway's North Cape and Bear Island, the two ships laboured through thick ice in the teeth of an easterly gale which seriously hampered their progress. At 16.00 the frozen lookouts on watch aboard the *Cold Harbour* lost contact with the *Waziristan*, though this was not surprising given the weather conditions, for these merchantmen carried no radar. The two ships struggled on through the heavy seas alone. For all they knew they might have been a thousand miles apart, but they were already in the presence of the enemy. Shortly before seven the next morning the *Waziristan* was struck by a torpedo from *U134* (Oberleutnant Schendel). She sank with the loss of forty-seven men, including ten gunners.

The balance of nine ships forming PQ7B followed. They arrived safely in the Kola Inlet on 11 January 1942, a day ahead of the *Cold Harbour*. While they had been skirting the floes and passing Bear Island, Convoy QP4 struggled to get free of the ice of the White Sea, as the fateful year drew to a close. Japan's provocative attack on Pearl Harbor on 7 December 1941 had brought the United

States of America, with all its vast resources, into what Churchill was later to call the Grand Coalition. Over the New Year period Churchill and Roosevelt conferred in Washington. Their meeting, code-named the Arcadia conference, set up the Combined Chiefs of Staff Committee to co-ordinate the progress of the war. Its most important decision was to defeat Germany before Japan, a decision formally backed up in April 1942 by the resolve to 'keep Russia effectively in the war'. This was to be the mainspring of the Arctic campaign.

In the New Year, too, the coalition's third member, the Soviet Union itself, had begun a counter-attack against the German army. To assist it, a total of fifty merchant ships had reached Archangel and three Murmansk, carrying between them 800 fighters, 750 tanks and 1,400 military vehicles, plus quantities of ammunition and raw materials, all of which had been discharged in Russian ports. However, some disturbing reports of neglect and mismanagement in the reception of these cargoes had reached London. 'Please make sure that our technicians who are going with the tanks and aircraft have full opportunity to hand these weapons over to your men under the best conditions,' Churchill wrote to Stalin. The Russian leader, ever the grudging and graceless recipient, protested that this was being done but that 'tanks, planes and artillery are arriving inefficiently packed, that sometimes parts of the same vehicle are loaded in different ships, [and] that planes, because of the imperfect packing, reach us broken'. Much of Stalin's peevishness was due to Churchill's reluctance to declare formal war on Finland, now reinforced by German arms in considerable numbers. Although Churchill appreciated the vulnerability of the railway line southward from Murmansk in its proximity to the Finnish border, he hedged upon the matter, unwilling to worsen an already delicate situation. Nevertheless, despite this note of diplomatic discord, great things were expected of the new year. In the event it was to prove momentous, in the Arctic as elsewhere.

The thirteen merchant ships and escorting trawlers and minesweepers of QP4 began their homeward passage from the Dvina on 29 December 1941, trailing in the wake of the huge new Russian ice-breakers *Stalin* and *Lenin*. Deprived of aerial reconnaissance, the ice-breakers had followed a false lead, driving into ever-thickening ice. Eventually, they turned south-west, found thinner ice, coaled from one of the ships in convoy, then finally broke out into the open sea beyond the Gourlo.

As soon as this news was flashed to Kola, *Edinburgh* and her attendant destroyers *Echo* and *Escapade* prepared to sail, intent upon a rendezvous with two minesweepers, which had proceeded ahead of the convoy. Snow was falling and it was coming on to blow as they left on 4 January. A certain degree of confusion existed after the delay in extricating the homeward ships from the Gourlo. The cruiser encountered the minesweeper *Hazard*, escorting to Murmansk a merchant ship desperately short of fuel, which was able to signal a bearing of the convoy. At this time, with radar in its infancy and not generally available for navigation, and in the Arctic darkness, the mere location of even a concentration of ships was both hazardous and chancy, and generally owed more to inspiration than precision. Suddenly, 'the moon came out over a glassy sea' – *Edinburgh* and the convoy 'were steaming north as though we had been together for days'. Luck played its part in the mundane events of war as well as the more obviously dramatic.

The homeward QP4, including the recalcitrant *El Mirlo*, now steamed north, seeking the 73rd parallel before the ships swung to the westward; well north, but not as far as the latitude of Bear Island, where U-boats were reported operating. On 8 January 1942 *Edinburgh* was ordered to disperse the convoy and patrol south of the convoy route where she 'encountered nothing but bad weather'.

Edinburgh and her destroyers drove into a furious wind, so strong that it failed to raise a heavy sea but sliced the surface with hurricane force and filled the air with spindrift. This formed thick encrustations of ice on the steelwork of the cruiser's forecastle guard-rails and the guns in A-turret. 'Very picturesque', was one midshipman's laconic record.

The following day, 10 January 1942, the temperature rose above freezing for the first time in three weeks. 'Everything melted and dripped and all the ice disappeared . . . not only that, but the sun rose, the first time for thirty days.'

Edinburgh arrived at Scapa Flow the next day, to be greeted by 180 bags of mail and 'fresh meat, potatoes and fresh vegetables . . . Within half an hour of anchoring we were the centre of a busy swarm of oilers, lighters and drifters,' a tribute to the organization supporting the Home Fleet. 'We even had a calm, warm evening to greet us and everyone felt very glad to be back after thirty-four days, twenty-eight of which were with[in] the Arctic circle.'

Convoy QP4 which had consisted of thirteen ships when it had left Archangel, two of which, *San Ambrosio* and *Eulima*, had put back to Murmansk for lack of fuel, reached Seidisfiord on 16 January 1942 and dispersed. Again there had been no loss.[1]

At this early stage of the Arctic campaign the peripatetic convoy commodore system was not yet in force. One of the British ship-masters was usually nominated to carry out his function. Dowding of the Dervish operation was an exception to this, due to the special nature of that first, almost experimental, convoy.[2] Now, as PQ8 prepared to sail from Hvalfiordur, its Commodore was Captain R.W. Brundle, his broad pendant hoisted on the gallant *Harmatris*. The seven-ship convoy departed on 8 January under the close escort of the Halcyon-class fleet minesweepers *Harrier* (Lieutenant-Commander E.P. Hinton) and *Speedwell*. By 10 January the cold wind had moderated and that night in fine, clear weather they met the ocean escort of the brand-new, all-welded light cruiser *Trinidad* (Captain L.S. Saunders) and HM destroyers *Matabele* and *Somali*, crack ships of the pre-war Tribal class, all of which had come up from Scapa Flow and refuelled at Seidisfiord on the 9th.

In addition to the *Harmatris*, PQ8 was made up of other British ships, the tankers *British Pride* and *British Workman*, the *Dartford* and *Southgate*, the Panamanian *El Amirante*, the Russian *Starii Bolshevik* and, for the first time, an American vessel, the *Larranga*, which was also the Vice-Commodore.

The following day, having reached 73°45′N, the convoy was forced southwards by the ice-field. The calm persisted, with a fierce cold and phenomenal visibility, despite the tedious darkness which was only relieved by the pale daylight of high noon. *Trinidad* frequently withdrew from the convoy itself and Captain Saunders exercised his raw recruits at night action stations. On the afternoon of Saturday, 17 January 1942, as it approached Russian waters, Brundle led the convoy southwards at 8 knots. *Harrier* was zigzagging ahead;. *Trinidad* kept station on *Harmatris*'s starboard bow, with the destroyers disposed a mile distant on either beam; HMS *Speedwell* brought up the rear. A rendezvous with the locally based fleet minesweepers was hampered by fog: *Britomart* and *Salamander* were stuck in Kola, though *Sharpshooter* had sailed and was followed later by *Hazard*. No help was forthcoming from the Russians.

At 19.45 the *Harmatris* loomed in the attack periscope glass of *U454* (Kapitänleutnant B Hackländer), a member of the three-strong Ulan group, the first wolf-pack to be deployed against Arctic convoys. Captain Brundle had just left the bridge for a shave, leaving it to the First Mate, Mr Masterman, and was entering his cabin when a torpedo from *U454* fired from a position on the convoy's starboard bow struck the *Harmatris*'s No. 1 hold. With commendable presence of mind Masterman, seeing the hatchboards and derricks fly upwards, stopped the ship to prevent her driving under as her forward hold filled rapidly. Master and Mate, regarding the wrecked forepart of their ship, sent their crew to boat stations. Incongruously, a large consignment of clothing intended for Polish internees festooned the forward rigging, having been blown upwards. By no less a fluke, the torpedo warheads which No. 1 hold also contained had fallen undetonated through the tramp's ruptured bottom.

From *Trinidad* it looked as though *Harmatris* had struck a mine, although *Matabele* reported hearing a torpedo noise on her hydrophone and *Harrier* detected a speeding object moving towards her. In fact a torpedo had been fired, and had passed under *Harrier*. The two destroyers carried out an inconclusive anti-submarine sweep and *Speedwell* was ordered to drop back and stand by the *Harmatris*, while the convoy plugged past the stricken ship and re-formed under the direction of the Vice-Commodore. About an hour after the first explosion, while Brundle and Masterman assessed the damage and concluded their ship could, and should, be saved, a tremor ran through her and Brundle himself was deceived into thinking they had indeed hit a mine, whereas *U454*, disregarding the presence of the departing destroyers, had in fact boldly sent a second torpedo into the British ship's port side. Fortunately it had failed to detonate, causing the vibration Brundle had sensed.[3] Captain Brundle now signalled *Speedwell* whose commanding officer, Lieutenant-Commander J.J. Youngs RNR, took advantage of the calm and ran alongside to evacuate *Harmatris*'s crew. Brundle, conferring with Williams, suggested the *Speedwell* could tow the freighter in and called for assistance, whereupon a large number of his crew volunteered. After a prodigious effort a towing wire was passed between the two ships. Taking the strain, the minesweeper found she was unable to move the *Harmatris* because the merchantman's starboard anchor, let go with its cable by the impact of the torpedo, had dug into the sea-bed.

It was now approaching 22.00 and aboard *Trinidad*, Captain Saunders, seeing the delay, ordered *Matabele* back to cover the struggling ships as *Sharpshooter* joined the screen from Kola. Finding his presence not required, Commander Stanford swung *Matabele* round and increased speed to zigzag his way back to the convoy.

Meanwhile, the frustrated Hackländer had manœuvred *U454* ahead of the convoy and, seeing the *British Pride* faintly illuminated in the revolving beams of the lighthouse on Cape Teriberski, loosed a salvo of torpedoes which missed the tanker but struck *Matabele* in her magazine. The destroyer disappeared in a sheet of flame and, though many bodies in lifejackets were later picked up, only two Ordinary Seamen, Higgins and Burras, survived from her complement of two hundred men, many being killed by the cold, more by the explosion of the destroyer's own depth-charges, for Higgins estimated that 'between 50 and 60 men left the ship alive'. While Captain Eaton carried out an anti-submarine sweep in *Somali*, *Harrier* had the sad task of recovering the dead from a sea covered with the foul slime of *Matabele*'s fuel oil.

In the aftermath of the explosion, nerves were increasingly strained aboard *Harmatris* and *Speedwell*. It was proving difficult to slip the cable in the intense cold and Brundle and his crew withdrew to the comparative shelter of the minesweeper which circled the wounded freighter all night. Next morning at 06.00, with the two ships alone on the ocean, Brundle and his men returned to find a steam valve had been left cracked open, the boilers were almost dry and the steam pipes leading forward to the windlass had frozen. Nevertheless, the anchor cable was unshackled and slipped to the sea-bed, the wire was reconnected and at 08.00 *Speedwell* again began to tow. The two ships had now been joined by *Sharpshooter* and *Hazard* which had put out earlier from the North Russian base of the 6th Minesweeping Flotilla. Shortly afterwards, in the brief lightening of noon, a German Heinkel He111 half-heartedly attacked at low level but was driven off by gunfire from both the DEMS gunners on *Harmatris* and the AA armaments of the minesweepers. A second plane made a pass, dropped her bombs a mile away and beat a retreat from the hostile reception, a fortunate outcome since Russian air support was not possible 'owing to visibility'.

At about 14.30 a high-pressure steam-pipe aboard the minesweeper burst, badly scalding three men, and Youngs signalled for a Soviet tug which arrived within the hour. *Speedwell* departed at speed to seek medical assistance for her injured men and at 17.00 two further tugs arrived alongside *Harmatris* to help her limp into Murmansk, down by the head with her propeller exposed. She secured to her berth at breakfast time on 20 January, most of her cargo safely delivered following an operation in which the Royal and Merchant Navies had co-operated fully.[4]

At Vaenga *Trinidad* and *Somali* bunkered from a Russian tanker, the company of the Tribal very dispirited after the loss of their 'chummy' ship. *Trinidad*'s marine band was sent over to cheer them up, a circumstance which nearly lost the returning musicians as the cruiser's boats ran into and on to ice-floes in the darkness.

Trinidad dispensed hospitality, comforts and mail to the members of the British naval staff and crews of the 6th Minesweeping Flotilla and British submarines. Finally, just before her departure, the cruiser went alongside and embarked 250 Polish internees whose emotional relief at being released from internment was moving: many were in tears, others knelt and kissed the deck. One, by a quirk of shifting frontiers, had fought on the German side at Jutland. Most of these men afterwards joined the Free Polish Air Force.

During the passage of PQ8, the four ships of QP5, the *Arcos, Dekabrist, Eulima* and *San Ambrosio*, had sailed from Murmansk on 13 January escorted by *Cumberland, Icarus* and *Tartar*. They arrived at Reykjavik on the 24th.

At this time QP6 of six ships prepared to follow under Captain Davitt aboard the *Empire Redshank* as Commodore, covered by *Trinidad* and *Somali* with their Polish passengers. The convoy was sighted briefly by a lone Junkers Ju88 but proceeded unmolested, and the cruiser detached and returned to Scapa prior to carrying out a dismal Patrol Black in the Iceland-Faeroes Gap.

Davitt's charges, the *Aneroid, Chernyshevki, Empire Howard, Empire Activity* and *Reigh Count*, finally arrived at the Tail o' the Bank in the Clyde on 2 February. During the latter part of the passage, on 31 January, the Commodore's ship, *Empire Redshank*, was attacked and damaged by enemy planes.

On the same day QP6 dropped anchor in the Clyde, PQ9 and 10 combined into a ten-ship convoy escorted by Rear-Admiral Wake-Walker's flagship, the cruiser *Nigeria*, supported by the destroyers *Faulknor* and *Intrepid*. The Norwegian armed whalers

Hav and *Shika* also provided close escort and, as was now the custom for all PQ and QP convoys, local anti-submarine and minesweeping support was given by the Halcyon-class sweepers from Kola, in this case *Britomart* and *Sharpshooter*.

The American ship *West Nohno*, four Russians, the *Friedrich Engels, Tblisi, Ijora* and *Revolutsioner*, the Panamanian *El Lago* and the Norwegian tanker *Noreg* joined the *Empire Selwyn, Trevorian* and *Atlantic*. PQ9 had been delayed by intelligence reports of *Tirpitz* moving north up the inshore Norwegian passages known as the Leads, but the combined convoy made up for lost time and arrived unscathed in the Kola Inlet on 10 February. Five days later, the cruiser *Cairo* brought in a British trade delegation.

PQ11, an assembly of thirteen ships gathering at Loch Ewe, sailed on 6 February for Kirkwall, with the Master of the SS *Kingswood* as Commodore. The escort of two minesweepers, *Niger* and *Hussar*, the corvette *Sweetbriar*, two Hunt-class destroyers, *Airedale* and *Middleton*, and three anti-submarine trawlers, *Blackfly, Cape Argona* and *Cape Mariato*, was commanded by Commander A.J. Cubison of *Niger*. The convoy was weather-bound in the Orkneys, not leaving Kirkwall until 14 February, and after the escort had been joined by a second corvette from Iceland, HMS *Oxlip*, the Hunts and trawlers were detached on the 17th, an example of the increasing complexity of convoy escorts which were organized at this level by Robert Burnett, the Rear-Admiral, Home Fleet Destroyers, and his staff.

Both *Sweetbriar* and *Oxlip* were 'on loan' from Western Approaches Command and were due to go back to their Londonderry base on their return from Russia. The latter, a new ship, had had a very bad passage north from her Londonderry base. Her first lieutenant, C.W. Leadbetter, who was later to command her, recalled ruefully that

> it is always unwelcome to those of us who sail in small ships to find ourselves thrust into severe weather before we [have] had adequate time to secure and batten down all openings. This was a lesson I was now to learn in the bitter school of experience. If the work is not done in good time before the bad weather makes it impossible for the men to move around the decks, then it has been left too late.

Leadbetter was a professional seaman of the Reserve, used to the peacetime flying-fish trades of the British India Line, and he writes candidly of the problems encountered in the Arctic on this, the last unmolested PQ convoy:

> *Oxlip* battled her way northwards, swept from end to end by the seas that broke over her forecastle, sending clouds of spray over the bridge. The anchor cables had not been broken, nor sent below, nor the spurling pipes sealed off with cement, and so the cable locker soon became flooded. This water in turn found its way onto the mess-deck and soon it was awash with water swilling madly from side to side as the ship rolled, lifting the newly laid corticene from the deck and carrying with it crockery, bedding, hammocks and kitbags. It spelled chaos and misery for the men, most of whom were too seasick to worry about their discomfort and lay around stupefied.

Sent on a Patrol White in the Denmark Strait, the corvette was ordered to refuel at Seidisfiord before sailing with *Sweetbriar* to rendezvous with PQ11, 'an undistinguished collection of grey-hulled ships low in the water'. These were the Russians *Ashkabad* and *Stepan Khalturin, Barrwhin, City of Flint* (American), *Daldorch* (which carried 300 tons of platinum), *Empire Baffin, Empire Magpie, Hartlebury, Kingswood* (commodore), *Lowther Castle, Makawao* (Honduran), *Marylyn* and *North King* (Panamanian), averaging about 8 knots in the rain, fog and snow which secured them from aerial observation and was ideal for convoy work. Gales threw spray over the ships, freezing the gun-mountings and the depth-charges to their racks, and threatening the stability of the small escorts. As soon as the weather moderated all hands were turned out to clear the ice with steam hoses, shovels and picks. The periods of calm between a succession of gales brought fog which stretched the nerves of the watch-keepers. On the escorts the primitive type 271 radar proved a boon to station-keeping. In his report, *Oxlip*'s captain complimented the Master of the *Kingswood* for his skill in keeping his charges together despite an understandable tendency to straggle in the fog, remarks that were customarily passed on by the Admiralty to the commodore's owners, in this case Constantines of Middlesbrough.

And there were, too, those rare moments of compensation when 'the whole vault of the sky was ablaze with shifting light'. Like the midshipman of the *Edinburgh*, Lieutenant Leadbetter remembers his own sense of wonder at the aurora.[5]

As PQ11 closed the Russian coast the convoy received cover from the local cruiser, HMS *Nigeria*, and on the last day of its passage, 23 February 1942, *Gromki* and *Grozni* joined, after somewhat erratic movements, and the convoy arrived undetected by the enemy. *Oxlip* and *Sweetbriar* were ordered by Rear-Admiral Miles (Senior British Naval Officer, North Russia) to join the assigned minesweepers from the 6th Minesweeping Flotilla based at Kola for the return convoy QP8 which was ready to sail by the 26th.

Meanwhile, QP7 had left Murmansk on the 12th and, passing PQ11, arrived equally safely at Seidisfiord on the 22nd. It consisted of seven veterans of the outward passage with the 'first-timer' *Stalingrad* covered by the escort of PQ9/10, namely *Faulknor* and *Intrepid*. So far in the Arctic, tragic though the losses of ships and men had been, in the grim comparative scale of twentieth-century warfare they were 'acceptable'.

At the same time that Captain Brundle had been celebrating the survival of the *Harmatris* from his first brush with fate in the form of a 'tween deck fire, and Admiral Golovko made his gloomy Christmas entry in his diary, Hitler was preoccupied with an increasing conviction that the British were meditating a landing in northern Norway following two commando raids on Vaagso and the Lofoten Islands. In particular he contemplated the dispositions of his capital ships which, in his post-Christmas 1941 naval conference, he assessed as requiring radical redeployment. Two of these, the battleships *Scharnhorst* and *Gneisenau*, were unfavourably positioned in Brest.[6]

As part of a major offensive launched by the surface forces of the German navy in the spring of 1941, they had scored some notable successes in sinking British merchant ships despite being hampered by orders not to engage superior forces and having to 'run away each time the enemy pointed a heavy gun at them'.[7] By Christmas they were in Brittany, within range of the Royal Air Force. At the end of March 1941 an abortive 100-bomber raid was made on the occupied French port. All the bombs missed their targets, bar one dud, which landed impotently in the bottom of the *Gneisenau*'s dock, but a few days later, at dawn on 6 April, four Beaufort torpedo-bombers made a raid and one, flown by Flying Officer Campbell, with a crew of three sergeants, pressed home an attack on the *Gneisenau* against furious anti-aircraft flak. Undaunted, Campbell flew directly towards the German capital ship which was now out of dock and lying in the inner basin. He launched his torpedo at point-blank range an instant before his plane was shot to pieces and he and his crew were killed. The torpedo blew the stern off the battleship and she was returned to dry dock where, five nights later, she sustained four direct hits from further bombs.

Grossadmiral Raeder attributed Campbell's success to a lucky hit. After a lifetime believing in the overwhelming puissance of capital ships, Raeder's faith in them remained inviolate: a few weeks later the mighty *Bismarck* succumbed to the overwhelming numerical superiority of the Royal Navy. Her consort, the heavy cruiser *Prinz Eugen*, escaped the same fate, only to become mewed up with the *Scharnhorst* and *Gneisenau* in Brest. By mid-summer 1941 all three had been hit by bombs and were under almost constant remedial repair. They diverted a great deal of labour and materials away from the maintenance of Dönitz's submarines and, contrary to conventional naval wisdom, Dönitz did *not* consider these heavy ships indispensable to the Atlantic campaign.

In mid-November, Raeder had reported to Hitler the readiness of the three ships for a further sortie into the Atlantic. Barely listening to his naval chief, Hitler had asked, 'Is it possible to bring the ships home by a surprise break-back through the English Channel?'

Impressed by British naval power and obsessed with the vulnerability of Norway, Hitler now returned to the theme at the end of December 1941. If it could not be done, Hitler said, the ships should be paid off and their guns and crews should be sent to defend the Norwegian coast. There was also the question of the newly worked-up *Tirpitz*, just then completing her trials in the Baltic. What was to be done with her? The Führer's petulance sent Raeder back to his staff for a further tactical assessment and at the next naval conference on 12 January 1942 at the Wolfsschanze headquarters in East Prussia two fateful decisions were made, one concerning the new battleship, the other the relocation of the Brest squadron to Norway.

Confirming the Führer's plan for a withdrawal eastwards up the English Channel, Vizeadmiral Ciliax, C-in-C Battleships, expressed the opinion that the boldness of the plan possessed the great merit of maximum surprise and was the best chance of saving the ships for more useful work. Raeder thought otherwise but was overruled. Consequently, on the foggy evening of 11 February 1942, a day after the combined convoys PQ9 and 10 arrived unscathed in the Kola Inlet, Ciliax led his squadron to sea for Operation Cerberus.

Covered by the Luftwaffe and supported by Konteradmiral 'Achmed' Bey's destroyers, a host of small craft and a series of measures designed to throw the British surveillance systems off balance, Ciliax's squadron passed the Straits of Dover in daylight where they came under desultory gunfire and a gallant but suicidal attack by Swordfish torpedo-bombers from Manston in north Kent. The humiliation of the British on their own hitherto undisputed doorstep was complete, and made worse by the knowledge that the enemy could, and very likely would, attempt such a bold dash. *The Times* of 14 February claimed that 'nothing more mortifying to the pride of sea-power has happened in home waters since the seventeenth century'. The shame and dismay felt by the British public remains to this day a memorable nadir in national fortunes. 'Where was the Royal Navy?' was a question on everyone's lips.[8]

But off the Belgian coast the German squadron's good fortune began to run out: both battlecruisers set off mines, though they struggled into German naval bases. Two weeks later the *Gneisenau* was bombed again and effectively put out of the war. Nevertheless, the 'lucky' *Prinz Eugen* survived and so too did the *Scharnhorst*, yet to play her full and final part in the Arctic war.[9]

The significance of the dramatic break-out from Brest in so far as the Arctic campaign was concerned lay not so much in its eventual consequence off the North Cape, but in the fact that it constituted the first movement of a defensive strategy for Norway, marking the end of that period of 'acceptable' loss on the Kola Run. Hitler's belief that a British invasion of northern Norway was imminent may have been incorrect, but his desire to protect the route along the Norwegian coast by which the Third Reich's vital supplies of Swedish iron ore came meant he sought to concentrate the capital ships of the Kriegsmarine in northern waters. Almost unwittingly Hitler had escalated the naval war in the Arctic and in doing so confronted Admiral Tovey with an increase in the demands made on the Home Fleet at a time when the Royal Navy had suffered an unparalleled series of losses. By his defensive policy of escape, Hitler had enabled the *Scharnhorst*, *Gneisenau* and *Prinz Eugen* to assume that most potent unknown factor in maritime war, a fleet in being.

Although the Germans had not yet fully appreciated the importance of the northern convoy route, at the same time that Hitler had ordered Raeder to study the possibility of the Channel 'break-back', he had also discussed the advantages of sending *Tirpitz* north. Stocks of boiler fuel remained low at 156,000 tons, but Hitler felt such a move would compel the British to maintain a strong force in home waters which would prevent reinforcement of the Mediterranean and the Indian Ocean, deter the feared interdiction of the iron ore trade and provide opportunities for attacks on the convoy route between Britain and North Russia. This, Hitler realized, was increasingly important. Indeed his anger at the fact that mounting Russian counter-attacks had thrown the German army on the defensive had already resulted in his removal of General Brauchitsch from his post as Commander-in-Chief. He had assumed the supreme command himself. Pending a final decision, Raeder had ordered the *Tirpitz* to move from the Baltic to the naval base at Wilhelmshaven, by way of the Kiel canal, to avoid detection.

On 12 January 1942 Hitler, in addition to initiating the break-out from Brest, also approved the move of the *Tirpitz* from the River Jahde to Trondheim. On the night of the 14/15 January Kapitän Karl Topp conned the magnificent new 43,000-ton battleship clear of the Helgoland Bight and headed north with an escort of four destroyers. His ship was almost 800 feet long with a main armament of eight 15-inch guns and a complement of 2,400 men. She carried a secondary armament of a dozen 5.9-inch dual-purpose guns and a massive battery of anti-aircraft artillery of varying calibres, as well as eight torpedo tubes and six Arado aircraft. She was, moreover, capable of an impressive all-weather speed of 30 knots.

Tirpitz arrived off Trondheim on the 16th, undetected by the British for some days. Only her absence from Wilhelmshaven was noted, by aerial reconnaissance on the 17th. It was this that had delayed the sailing of PQ9 from Iceland, for it was initially feared that the *Bismarck*'s sister ship had broken out into the Atlantic. Far from it; she had obeyed Hitler's dictum that 'every [surface] ship not stationed in Norway is in the wrong place'.

Both Pound and Tovey had long apprehended such an enemy move. Tovey had also taken precautions against an Atlantic break-out by maintaining a cruiser in the Denmark Strait on Patrol White, with a battleship and two American cruisers in support at Hvalfiordur, and the laying of an extensive though imperfect minefield across the Iceland-Faeroes gap which was itself watched over by aircraft of Coastal Command and ships on Patrol Black.

Churchill, too, was clear about the malign influence of the *Tirpitz* when finally, on the 23rd, the questing reconnaissance aeroplanes located her lying in the Aasfiord, fifteen miles east of Trondheim, protected by camouflage and anti-torpedo netting. He wrote to the Chiefs of Staff urging them to draw up plans for air attacks to be mounted upon her by both shore-based and carrier-borne aircraft to achieve

> the destruction or even the crippling of this ship . . . The entire naval situation throughout the world would be altered . . . The whole strategy of the war turns at this period on this ship which is holding four times the number of British capital ships paralysed, to say nothing of the two new American battleships retained in the Atlantic. I regard the matter as of the highest urgency and importance.[10]

But the Aasfiord was steep-sided and narrow, and the German battleship lay parallel to its banks, which made it difficult for carrier-launched torpedo attacks to succeed. Four nights later, on 29 January 1942, a long-range raid was made by sixteen bombers without effect. The consequent preoccupation of Coastal Command with this target undoubtedly had its doleful effect in the Channel a fortnight later.

If there had been a lack of British naval activity whilst the Brest squadron steamed up the Channel, the same could not be said of the Norwegian Sea. On 19 February 1942, the *Tirpitz* was seen under way. British air patrols were stepped up, submarines were ordered off the Norwegian coast and Admiral Tovey sailed from Hvalfiordur and set course for Tromso, his anxiety increased by the knowledge that the departure of a large troop convoy from the Clyde was imminent.

On the morning of the following day, the 20th, a British aircraft located the *Admiral Scheer* and *Prinz Eugen* with three destroyers steering north at speed from the Dutch coast. Beaufort torpedo-bombers were sent that afternoon to attack the German squadron off Utsire light, midway between Stavanger and Bergen. Bad weather and a short reversal of course by the Germans resulted in loss of contact and the ships had anchored in Griumstad fiord near Bergen by mid-afternoon. Meanwhile Admiral Tovey, anticipating the continued northward movement of the enemy squadron through the Inner Leads in the shelter of the islands dotting the Norwegian coast, abandoned his move against Tromso and sent the cruiser *Berwick* with four destroyers to cover the aircraft-carrier *Victorious* south-east towards Stadlandet, following himself in the battleship *King George V* with the remainder of his force. Snow, heavy weather and a consequent lack of visibility ruined the chances of the aircraft striking the German ships, but the submarine *Trident* (Commander G.M. Sladen), off the southern entrance to the Trondheim approach, torpedoed the *Prinz Eugen* at 06.00 on the 23rd. For a time the heavy cruiser lay stopped in the water, but her wound was not fatal and she followed the *Scheer* into the Aasfiord late that night.

Although not unscathed, the German attempt to concentrate a number of heavy units in northern waters had been successful enough to worry the Commander-in-Chief of the Home Fleet, whose concern for the long, outflanked passage of the Russia-bound convoys could only intensify as the days lengthened and before there had been any significant retreat of the ice to the north. His representations regarding these increasing risks fell upon deaf ears. Whilst Sir Dudley Pound was sympathetic, Churchill was adamant. The political rationale was overwhelming; the risks were acceptable.

During February 1942, while the Germans attempted to effect the establishment of their northern battle-fleet, the 10th Cruiser Squadron under Rear-Admiral Burrough (known as CS10) in HMS *Nigeria* had been covering the area between Bear Island and the Kola Inlet. Its commander constantly urged the Russian naval authorities at Polyarnoe to mount anti-submarine patrols in their own waters and to afford air cover to the convoys to avoid any repetition of the loss of the *Matabele* and damage to the *Harmatris*. This, Tovey believed, was the least an ally could do and was well within Russian capabilities. Meanwhile his overall appreciation of the increasing dangers to the convoys was that their passage could be divided into two. East of Bear Island attacks by aircraft and U-boats were inevitable, while between Bear Island and Jan Mayen Island, intervention by surface units was more likely. In order to make the best use of his own resources and cover the Jan Mayen-Bear Island gap, Tovey requested that the next convoys, both outward and homeward, should sail on the same day. Accordingly QP8, comprising fifteen veteran ships which were ready to sail, was held in Kola for four days and left on 1 March 1942, just as the eighteen ships comprising PQ12 departed from Iceland, the first to be covered by the main strength of the

Home Fleet. Coastal Command stepped up its patrols over the Trondheim area and long-range Liberators flew north-east from Iceland, but it was a German plane which scored the first success, a Focke-Wulf Condor, which spotted PQ12 at about noon on the 5th, some seventy miles south-east of Jan Mayen. It was a large convoy consisting of the Russian ships *Kiev, Belomorcanal, Dneprostroi* and *Sevaples*; the Panamanians *Artigas, Bateau, El Coston, Ballot, Capulin, El Occidente* and *Stone Street*; and the British merchantmen *Empire Byron, Temple Arch, Llandaff* (Commodore, Captain H.T. Hudson RNR), *Navarino, Lancaster Castle, Earlston* and *Beaconstreet*. The latter was a fleet oiler, loaded with boiler oil to be pumped into tanks at Polyarnoe for the locally based minesweepers.

Then, at 17.00 on the evening of the following day, 6 March, it was once again HM Submarine *Trident* that observed the counter-move by the Kriegsmarine. Unfortunately, the submarine was too far away to make a report and it was left to Lieutenant R.P. Raikes of the *Seawolf*, which had just relieved the Free French submarine *Minerve*, to make contact. Raikes dived to avoid detection by the 'wave-hopping' flying boats which preceded the enemy departure, but not before he had seen faint smoke and the upperworks of 'a large enemy warship' off Trondheim, heading north. He surfaced at 19.40, timing his report 18.01, and transmitted this intelligence to the Admiralty.

Fresh from his Channel adventure, Vizeadmiral Otto Ciliax had arrived in Trondheim, joined Kapitän Karl Topp and hoisted his flag aboard the *Tirpitz*. Taking the destroyers *Paul Jacobi, Friedrich Ihn, Hermann Schoemann* and *Z25* under his command, he had left the Aasfiord at 11.00 that morning. His quarry was PQ12 and he assumed he had the advantage of surprise.

Professionally cautious in his report, Lieutenant Raikes had his private opinion: 'I was certain in my own mind that it was the *Tirpitz*.'[11]

6

'Ideal weather for carrier aircraft'

As Lieutenant Raikes made his report and alerted the Admiralty to the presence of the German battleship in the Norwegian Sea, PQ12 ran into loose pack-ice. The close escort consisted of the Colony-class 6-inch gun cruiser *Kenya*, two O-class fleet destroyers, HMS *Oribi* and *Offa*, and several Norwegian anti-submarine whalers. *Kenya* had sailed from Hvalfiordur on 3 March as part of a force consisting of the battleship *Duke of York*, the battlecruiser *Renown* and six destroyers under Vice-Admiral A.T.B. Curteis, to join Admiral Tovey in the *King George V* who, with the carrier *Victorious*, the cruiser *Berwick* and six destroyers left Scapa the following day. *Berwick* was capable of only 27 knots and was to have been relieved by *Sheffield*, but the latter was mined and had to be escorted back to Seidisfiord by two of Curteis's destroyers, a situation showing the complexity of Home Fleet dispositions under such circumstances as the presence of German capital ships in northern waters now produced.[1]

Kenya, sent to reinforce PQ12's close escort, had joined the convoy by the evening of 6 March, when the ships encountered the loose pack. One merchant ship, the Russian vessel *Kiev*, had straggled as early as the 3rd, as had some of the whalers, but now attempts to avoid damage to ships not strengthened for navigation in ice only succeeded in breaking up the cohesion of the convoy. One of the two remaining whalers, the *Stefa*, also fell astern, as did the merchant ship *El Occidente*, while HMS *Oribi* suffered considerable ice damage to her bows, affecting her value as a fighting escort.

'After experience with PQ12,' remarked Captain Denny of HMS *Kenya*, 'I would never take a convoy anywhere near ice, accepting almost any other risk in preference.' Captain H.T. Hudson, the Commodore, was similarly concerned and ordered an alteration of course from north-east to south-east in an attempt to break free of the pack. To add to the misery, thick squally weather prevailed and it was not until well into the afternoon of 7 March that the visibility began to clear dramatically, enabling the convoy to resume its course to the north-east.

Admiral Tovey was not informed of Raikes's report until after midnight, at about 00.10 on 7 March. He had to decide whether the *Tirpitz* was attempting a break-out into the Atlantic, or an attack on the two Russian convoys which were now approaching their crossing point. He had also to assess whether *Scheer* was at sea, a division of force which could distract the British and allow either a combination of the two capital ships later, or the break-out of one to attack the North Atlantic convoy routes, while the other decimated a major convoy to the Russians. In fact, due to her inferior speed, no role had been found for the *Scheer*, and the unimaginative, over-cautious nature of German surface naval strategy had discarded another opportunity. Admiral Tovey was denied the comfort of such hindsight. Having been reinforced by Curteis he had continued north-east until the middle of the previous afternoon, then turned for a sweep to the south-west. On receipt of Raikes's relayed intelligence he considered the wisdom of dividing his force, detaching Curteis to cover the convoy while he went in pursuit of *Tirpitz*, but the Admiralty thought the danger from the Luftwaffe operating against surface forces was too risky, and the Commander-in-Chief was constrained to keep his fleet together under the putative umbrella of his carrier's aircraft. Tovey accordingly hauled the combined squadrons round to the north-east again and ordered all ships to have full steam available at daylight, and *Victorious* to have her Fairey Albacores ready to take off at 08.00 the following morning.

Dawn broke to thick weather with drizzle, snow squalls and fog patches, writhing over a lumpy sea. Icing up made flying operations impossible. The first air search was cancelled, though the Home Fleet increased speed and made two alterations of course, one more to the eastward which, unbeknown to both Tovey and Ciliax, converged with the *Tirpitz*, and a second to the northward, which slowed the rate of convergence. Despite the lack of aerial reconnaissance, Admiral Tovey made his dispositions: *Victorious* and *Renown* were to disengage if *Tirpitz* was encountered (he wanted no repeat of the fate of the *Hood*, nor the foolhardy exposure of his one aircraft-carrier), and his senior destroyer officer, Captain H.T. Armstrong in *Onslow*, was to 'be prepared to deliver a close range [torpedo] attack, if sudden contact is made'.

But at about 11.20 a frustrated Tovey again swung the Home Fleet south-west to seek clearer weather and, he believed, to give better cover to QP8 which was erroneously assumed to be to the westward of them. Instead, about a hundred miles to the north-eastward, PQ12 making 8 knots and QP8 seriously delayed by the weather, approached their passing point. It was snowing hard.

Equally thwarted by the poor conditions Vizeadmiral Otto Ciliax, Commander-in-Chief Battleships, and Kapitän Karl Topp were prevented from flying off one of the *Tirpitz*'s Arado seaplanes. Less well-informed than his opponent, Ciliax had had no information since the report of the Focke-Wulf Condor locating PQ12 at noon two days earlier, a flight made in response to intelligence that a number of ships had left Murmansk for the homeward run and that an outward convoy was therefore likely to be at sea. As was usual the Seekriegsleitung, the Supreme Naval Staff, headed by Grossadmiral Raeder, had hamstrung its commander at sea. Ciliax's orders permitted him to engage equal forces *only* if the success of the main task, the destruction of PQ12, warranted it. Under no circumstances was he to risk action with superior forces. Furthermore, if Ciliax believed his own men to be better trained than his enemy, he also knew that his four escorting destroyers, well armed though they were, had sacrificed stability for weight-of-metal, and were consequently poor sea-boats. Their high-pressure steam plants were also proving operationally unreliable and they therefore possessed insufficient endurance for an operation likely to last several days.

Nevertheless, denied his aircraft's eyes, he now dispatched the destroyers on a northward course in line abreast. Shortly afterwards they were ordered to resume a north-westerly sweep which would result in the German force searching on a wide front with the *Tirpitz* on its left, most southerly flank. There were also four U-boats, *U134, U377, U403* and *U584*, deployed across the path of the convoys. Ignorant of the very considerable British force at sea, Ciliax and Topp remained sanguine.

Having missed the laden outward convoy due to an underestimate of the convoy's speed by 2 knots, the German squadron stretched in extended order between thirty and sixty miles to the south of the wake of PQ12, but advancing north-west across the track of QP8.

A further seventy miles west-north-west of *Tirpitz* herself, the Home Fleet was steaming *away* from the two convoys and the enemy, in a desperate search for clear weather and in the mistaken belief that QP8 was already west of it.

It was now QP8 which was in the greater danger, weakly guarded as it was by two ocean minesweepers and two corvettes: *Hazard* (Lieutenant-Commander J.R.A. Seymour, Senior Officer) and *Salamander*, with *Oxlip* and *Sweetbriar*. Seymour had been a worried man since he had left Kola. *Salamander*'s asdic was defective and *Sweetbriar*'s packed up on 3 March; *Oxlip*'s radar had also refused to work.

While a local reinforcement of *Harrier* and *Sharpshooter* together with the Russian destroyers *Gremyashchi* and *Gromki* had seen them clear of Russian waters, the two minesweepers had returned to their lonely northern base and the two Russian warships were more of a hindrance than a help, carrying out independent sweeps, obscuring the *Hazard*'s asdic and then asking permission to detach before reaching the prearranged departure point. Moreover, no reassuring sighting had been made of the supporting cruiser *Nigeria*.

By 3 March QP8 was on its own with its close escort of the two minesweepers and two corvettes. The homeward convoy had weathered one U-boat scare and, in 73°15′N 037°10′E, had altered course to the westward. A calm day was followed by a rising gale during the night which next morning brought several ships to a standstill, including the Commodore's *Empire Selwyn*. The empty, lightly ballasted merchant ships presented a lot of windage, their propellers often thrashing the air as they pitched into the heavy head-sea, with just enough momentum to maintain steerage way, but insufficient to make significant progress. By dawn on the 5th, clear visibility enabled most of the ships to regain their stations, but two vessels, the *Larranga* and the Russian *Ijora*, had vanished. By noon on 6 March, QP8 was lashed and dispersed by a Force 10 storm with seas estimated as being forty feet from trough to crest.

By noon on the 7th, 200 miles south-west of Bear Island, a dozen merchant ships had regained station in good order, and in falling snow the two convoys passed through each other, executing 'a perfect gridiron in visibility of one mile'.[2]

Longitude comparisons made between *Hazard* and *Kenya* revealed a discrepancy of ninety-five miles, a common error in high latitudes where the meridians converge and when no accurate sights have been obtained. Seymour's reckoning had of course been complicated by the adverse effects of the weather and the notorious difficulty of estimating speed of advance in such conditions. On *Kenya*'s advice, he altered course two hours later a little to the southward to avoid the ice which had plagued PQ12. Although the radio traffic indicated 'something big going on somewhere', Seymour had no idea how close he and his charges now came to disaster as the German squadron swept across his bow, for although the *Tirpitz* was about fifty miles ahead of QP8, the nearest German destroyer, *Z25*, was less than a dozen.

Meanwhile PQ12 steamed doggedly eastward and at the same time that afternoon *Kenya* detached at speed to investigate a sighting of distant smoke which, in the perverse and abrupt changes encountered in the Arctic, was discerned thirty miles away. Having confirmed the ship was no threat but a freighter steaming south-west and clearly a straggler from QP8 (probably the *Ijora*), Captain Denny sped back to his own convoy. A little later he received a signal from the Admiralty that enemy surface forces 'may be in vicinity of PQ12'. Denny manœuvred *Kenya* alongside the Commodore and by megaphone advised Captain Hudson of this fact. Hudson ordered PQ12 to 'wheel' to a course of due north. Immediately telegraphists in both PQ12 and QP8 heard a signal from the lone *Ijora* that she was being 'gunned' by a warship. Doubts as to the accuracy of the position broadcast by the *Ijora*, based on his exchange with Seymour and his healthy fear of the ice, caused Denny again to consult with Hudson and also Commander McBeath of the ice-damaged *Oribi* who had lost two men swept overboard from his destroyer's low 'iron deck'.

As a consequence PQ12 swung east-north-east at twilight; just before this Denny sent off his amphibious Walrus aircraft with orders not to be a signpost to the enemy. The Walrus reported nothing approaching the convoy from the south-westward. Finally, an hour after recovering the *Kenya*'s Walrus, PQ12 turned to the north-east as 'it would help the general situation if the convoy was brought gradually nearer to its official track' from which it had been forced by ice.

The *Ijora*'s cry for help was intercepted by the Home Fleet, but her position was unclear and Tovey also received radio bearings of an unidentified and possibly hostile vessel which caused him to alter the Home Fleet's course to the eastward at 17.50 and to the north-east at 20.00. He sent six destroyers under Captain Armstrong to steam further east, then to turn and sweep northwards at 15 knots across what Tovey hoped would be the Germans' line of retreat to their base. In fact *Tirpitz* was 150 miles to the northward. Ciliax too had heard the *Ijora*, knew that she was being shelled by the German destroyer *Friedrich Ihn* and closed her as the Russian ship sank.

By 17.30 the German destroyers had rejoined the flag and were in need of fuel. Ciliax decided to try and replenish them from *Tirpitz*, a bold plan given the prevailing ice, so he turned south, himself now searching for better conditions but to no avail. At 20.30 the *Friedrich Ihn*, now desperately short of oil, was detached to Tromso and the remaining ships headed east, still in pursuit of PQ12: at 04.00 on 8th the *Hermann Schoemann*, *Paul Jacobi* and *Z25* were also sent off to bunker, and *Tirpitz* continued to the eastward alone.

Further south, Captain Armstrong's destroyers, *Onslow*, *Punjabi*, *Fury*, *Ashanti*, *Echo* and *Eclipse*, had discovered nothing and were themselves short of fuel. Accordingly, at 08.00 on the 8th they proceeded to Seidisfiord, leaving only HMS *Lookout* with the battle-fleet as the C-in-C had been obliged to send the *Intrepid* and *Icarus* to bunker at Seidisfiord at 20.00 the previous evening. Tovey was now steaming roughly south-west at 24 knots, having concluded at midnight that the enemy had eluded him. His intention was to collect some destroyers, for without them he himself was vulnerable to U-boats. QP8 was then steaming parallel at 9 knots, seventy miles away on his starboard beam.

About 240 miles to the north-east *Tirpitz* sped east, with PQ12 roughly 100 miles to the north-north-west of her. Both battleship and convoy were diverging until at 07.00, renewing his search for the convoy, Ciliax ordered a sharp alteration of course to the north. At 10.45, the German flagship was astride the convoy route in position 73°23′N 020°09′E and Ciliax now shrewdly turned to a course of west-south-west, zigzagging to cover as broad a front as possible, guessing quite rightly that he was now east of PQ12. The *Tirpitz* passed about fifty-five miles south of Bear Island and again posed an acute threat to PQ12 since she lay between the convoy and its destination.

The east-bound, outward convoy had plodded on, heading north-east towards Bear Island, and at daylight on the 8th, thanks to the intelligence received at the Admiralty from the Ultra decrypters at Bletchley Park, PQ12 was ordered to head north of Bear Island, to open up the distance between itself and the enemy battleship.

Captain Denny remained apprehensive about the ice, the vulnerability of his thinly plated destroyers and the cohesion of the convoy. Consultation with Captain Hudson resulted in the two men disregarding the Admiralty's order. At noon PQ12 turned south-east again, skirting the ice-field and steaming in weather that alternated between snow squalls and phenomenal visibility, a circumstance that only emphasized the difficulty of playing this immense game of blind man's buff. Notwithstanding this Nelsonian disobedience, PQ12 avoided interception by *Tirpitz*.

At 17.00 the convoy's lookouts sighted Bear Island forty miles away to the north-east and the dull gleam of more ice extending ahead of them which they took three hours to work round. Anxiety for *Oribi* caused Denny to detach the damaged destroyer and she proceeded independently, reaching Murmansk on the 10th. Although convoy and predator were now moving on almost diametrically opposite courses, PQ12 was only about 110 miles away from *Tirpitz* at 18.00 when Ciliax, having sighted nothing and unaware of how close he had got to PQ12, gave up and turned south, intending to return to the Vestfiord. PQ12 continued to edge round the ice and was protected from aerial detection by 'exceptionally thick and persistent sea-smoke rising many feet into the air'. Breaking free of the ice-field, the bulk of the convoy arrived safely at Murmansk on the 12th.

In his report, Commodore Hudson remarked that 'many of the Merchant Masters expressed concern that they heard the BBC announce that a valuable cargo was on its way to Russia . . .' But a more significant complaint emanated from Murmansk where it was 'conceded that all the American [stowed] cargoes are landed in a much better condition than the British cargoes'. This was due to bad ballasting and poor securing and packing arrangements. The former, consisting in British ports of putting all heavy weights low in a ship, made her 'stiff' and subject to violent rolling; the latter caused wire lashings to cut through packing and damage the light fabric of the disassembled aircraft. Hudson concluded that 'most of the British vessels . . . seemed to be suffering from the same sort of bad stevedoring which not only causes damage to the cargo but also is a severe strain on the ships and the remedy only requires just a little extra time and a very little extra trouble'. Such damage was to give Stalin grounds to complain of the condition of some *matériel* then arriving in Russia.

Four merchant ships had straggled from PQ12 during its passage, the *Bateau* early on, the *Kiev* on the 3rd, *El Occidente* on encountering the ice on the 6th, and the *Sevaples* as they broke out of the ice on the 11th. One of the escorting anti-submarine whalers, the *Stefa*, had lost contact on the 6th. *Kiev* and *El Occidente* reached Iokanka unmolested on the 10th and *Sevaples* sighted and joined forces with the *Stefa* which, on the 13th, shot down an aircraft trying to bomb the merchant ship. Ironically, despite the presence of a German battle squadron and a wolfpack of four U-boats strung out across the route of PQ12 between Jan Mayen and Bear Island, this was the *only* engagement directly connected with the passage of PQ12. *Bateau* joined PQ13.

Sadly though, there was one tragedy attached to PQ12 that occurred on the day after the entire convoy almost found itself under the heavy guns of the *Tirpitz*. Two more Norwegian whalers had been sent on from Iceland in support of the convoy and one of these, the *Shera*, capsized on 9 March without having located PQ12. Only three of her crew survived, Lieutenant Hansen RNR, Ordinary Seaman Harris and Steward Phillips, to be rescued by her consort, the *Svega*, which reached Murmansk independently on the 11th, unaware that PQ12 had been dodging far to the northwards.

This was not, however, the end of the affair, for Admiral Tovey and Vizeadmiral Ciliax were, so to speak, still in the ring. The Home Fleet had spent most of the 8th steaming nervously southwest without its destroyer screen, a situation which understandably Tovey found worrying. The Admiralty intelligence that the *Tirpitz* was still in the far north caused the Commander-in-Chief to reverse his course at 18.20 and to break radio silence. He informed the Admiralty he was operating without anti-submarine protection and that his move north would, he thought, drive *Tirpitz* south, where the light forces of the Home Fleet could dog and wound her, as they had done her sister, the *Bismarck*. The Admiral also requested that the Admiralty control these cruisers and destroyers for he was having difficulty communicating with them and was less well informed as to their whereabouts than London.

The Admiralty had already relieved the cruisers *London* and *Kent* from their Patrol White in the Denmark Strait with three American ships, and *Kent* had been briefly sighted proceeding east by the escorts of QP8. The *Trinidad* and *Liverpool* were also ordered out of Seidisfiord with the refuelled destroyers *Echo*, *Fury* and *Punjabi*. The four cruisers took up stations in pairs 200 miles east and south of Jan Mayen, ready to refuel all available destroyers which were being hurriedly concentrated at Iceland, Scapa Flow, Rosyth and Loch Ewe.

Further Ultra decrypts had alerted the Admiralty in London to the fact that the *Tirpitz* was steaming south. The advantage was now passing to the British Home Fleet, hitherto cheated of even the 'near misses' achieved twice by the German squadron. At 02.40 on 9 March 1942 the Home Fleet altered course to east-south-east, heading for the Lofoten Islands (which the retiring *Tirpitz* would have to double to the south to make the Vestfiord), and increased speed to 26 knots. Once again the order was transmitted to *Victorious* to ready her Albacores for use at daylight.

Daylight in the Norwegian Sea brought a sudden clearing of the weather, with white cirrus mare's tails high in a limpid blue sky. Observing this from the foretop of the *Tirpitz*, the battleship's second gunnery officer, Kapitänleutnant Albrecht Schnarke, thought it 'ideal weather for carrier aircraft'. It was an apprehension he shared with his captain and flag officer on the bridge below. The *B-Dienst* radio intercept detachment on board the German capital ship had alerted Topp and Ciliax to the fact that a British battle-group, including an aircraft-carrier, were searching for them.[3]

The distance between the two protagonists was too great for Tovey's aircraft to strike his enemy at dawn, but at 06.40 six reconnoitring Albacores were flown off from *Victorious*, followed fifty minutes later by a striking group of a dozen more armed with torpedoes. Designed as an improvement on the Fairey Swordfish, the popular though archaic 'Stringbag', the heavier Albacore was a contrastingly unpopular aircraft and as slow and unwieldy as its predecessor. Moreover, due to the rapid expansion of the Fleet Air Arm and the consequent dilution by semi-trained crews, *Victorious*'s squadron lacked any form of intensive training while its commander had only just taken over his team.

Nevertheless, a heartened Admiral Tovey signalled Captain Bovell, expressing the rising mood of optimism on his flagship's bridge: 'a wonderful chance which may achieve most valuable results. God be with you.'

Between these two air launches, shortly before 7 o'clock, *Tirpitz* had met the first of *her* anti-submarine screen, the now refuelled destroyer *Friedrich Ihn*. An hour later a questing Albacore located the two ships eighty miles east of the Home Fleet, both proceeding south at high speed. A few minutes after the Albacore made contact, Chief Petty Officer Finselberger, at an after anti-aircraft position aboard *Tirpitz*, spotted the shadowing plane and all the battleship's formidable array of anti-aircraft weaponry, sixteen twin 10.5-cm guns, sixteen 3.7-cm twin flak cannon, and forty-eight machine guns of lesser calibre were made ready. Ciliax flew off an Arado seaplane in an attempt to gain a little local air cover, then turned for the coast with an alteration of course to east which would, with *Tirpitz*'s superior speed, open out her distance from the Home Fleet. The observer in the trailing Albacore wrongly reported this alteration as being to the north-east, an error which, with the loss of surprise, now conspired to rob Admiral Tovey of any chance of victory.

At 08.42 the torpedo-armed Albacores sighted their quarry to the south-eastwards in the direction of the rising sun. So slow were they and so fast was the battleship that with the combined effect of the wind they overhauled their target at a mere 30 knots. The squadron commander ordered his aircraft to climb into cloud cover, hoping to get ahead of the *Tirpitz*, but as they overflew the battleship and the *Friedrick Ihn*, a rent in the clouds exposed them to flak. Nevertheless, the Albacores split into sub-flights which attacked immediately.

The Germans acknowledged the gallantry and determination of the British pilots, despite the shortcomings of their training and their lack of experience. The barrage of fire put up by the German ships, especially the *Tirpitz* herself, was terrific.

For their part, the first sub-flight of Albacores released their torpedoes at long range on the *Tirpitz*'s port bow but at too fine an angle for them to hit the racing ship. With great skill and coolness, Topp put his helm over to port and combed the approaching torpedo tracks. The second sub-flight attacked from the starboard quarter with the same lack of success. The third and fourth also approached on the starboard side, but were delayed due to the difficulties of manœuvring ahead of the speeding ship. Topp applied counter helm, which reduced the angle of approach of their torpedoes, and *Tirpitz* succeeded in evading them all. Two of these Albacores were shot down and, though more were thought by the Germans to have been hit, so intense was their fire, these were the only losses. The British planes had themselves fired machine guns at the grey superstructure as they had roared past.

It was a bitter disappointment. The attack, made from leeward and from astern, had robbed the Albacores of any tactical advantage to be gained from a high rate of speed of attack. As the biplanes headed back for the carrier, the unscathed *Tirpitz* was racing unopposed for the Vestfiord.[4]

When he reported the encounter to Hitler, Grossadmiral Raeder remarked upon the 'resolute attacks' of the British and the escape of the *Tirpitz* 'thanks partly to skilful evasive action, but above all to sheer good luck'. This was a clear snipe at the failure of the Luftwaffe to come to the support of the harried warship, though one Heinkel He115 had flown over the *Tirpitz* twenty minutes after the attackers withdrew. Raeder was adamant that the destruction of British aircraft-carriers was essential if his heavy ships were to operate successfully against the convoys, and it was these, rather than the feared invasion of Norway, which now became the prime target for German naval strategy in the far north.

But this element of 'sheer good luck', though it might demonstrate the shortcomings of the Luftwaffe, did nothing but reinforce the caution with which the German High Command regulated all the operations of their capital ships. Equally, the overwhelming importance of the Russian convoys was now borne in upon Berlin, a cause, it was thought, of the energy of the Russian counterattacks outside Moscow. Hitler ordered the interdiction of the supply line by every means possible and to this end the resumption of work on the aircraft-carrier *Graf Zeppelin* and the conversion of the cruiser *Seydlitz* and the liner *Potsdam* to auxiliary carriers.

There is yet a postscript to this frustrating chapter of missed opportunities. Having recovered the surviving aircraft in the late forenoon of 9 March, the Home Fleet turned west, away from any retaliation the Luftwaffe might seek to mete out. There was little the *Victorious*'s aircraft could do in penetrating Norwegian airspace beyond inviting the attention of the superior machines of the Luftwaffe; indeed, when heavy Blohm and Voss reconnaissance aircraft began shadowing the Home Fleet, no Fulmar fighters were flown off on the assumption that they would be ineffective.

At 15.45 the Home Fleet was subject to a weak and unsuccessful attack by three Junkers Ju88 bombers, one of which dropped its bombs close to *Victorious*. Had these aircraft been torpedo-bombers history might have been different, but just as the presence of the *Tirpitz* kept heavy units of the Royal Navy from reinforcing the distant squadrons in the Far East, so Allied pressure in the Mediterranean had depleted the Luftwaffe's strength in Norway.

Three hours after the retreat of the German bombers, the destroyers *Faulknor*, *Eskimo*, *Bedouin* and *Tartar* joined the Commander-in-Chief who, though he had meditated an air raid on the Norwegian coast, now withdrew towards Scapa Flow. A further eight fleet and Hunt-class destroyers arrived to increase the capital ships' cover. These, the *Javelin*, *Inconstant*, *Verdun*, *Lancaster*, *Ledbury*, *Grove*, *Woolston* and *Wells*, were a measure of the Admiralty's efforts in earlier concentrating the maximum number of destroyers in the vain hope of hitting the *Tirpitz*. The Home Fleet reached Orkney on the night of 10 March 1942, leaving the field to Coastal Command who sent bombers in an attempt to hit the *Tirpitz* before she again hid in the fastnesses of the fiords. But by the time Admiral Tovey received his first detachment of destroyers, the *Tirpitz* had safely reached Narvik.

The British Admiralty, on the advice of the exiled Norwegian government combined with reports by the Resistance, gambled on one last chance to seal the fate of the German battleship when she moved south to her base in Aasfiord. The number of British submarines on patrol was stepped up in the approaches to Trondheim, and a flotilla of destroyers led by Captain Scott-Moncrieff in the leader *Faulknor*, and composed of the *Fury*, *Intrepid*, *Icarus*, *Bedouin*, *Eskimo* and *Tartar*, slipped out of Scapa on the evening of the 11th and arrived off the Ytterpen light at 01.30 on the 13th. Meanwhile the patrolling submarines were to the southward, *Uredd* off the Sklinden lighthouse, *Junon*, *Seawolf* and *Trident* off the Halten lighthouse, and *Sealion* off the Grip light.[5] They were exhorted by the Commander-in-Chief Submarines to stick with their tedious task but, when *Tirpitz* steamed south with her five escorting destroyers in wind and snow on the afternoon of the 13th, Scott-Moncrieff's force had long gone; and though *Trident*'s hydrophones were filled with the noise of passing ships, those on board were unable to distinguish the battleship from her attendants. These were actively firing depth-charges to keep enemy submarines at a distance and the German squadron reached Trondheim unscathed. When the weather cleared again, on 18 March, air reconnaissance showed the *Tirpitz* back in Aasfiord.

Both before the operation and in the assessments afterwards, Admiral Tovey adhered to his original plan that the cover of the convoys should be undertaken by a detachment of the Home Fleet under his second-in-command, Vice-Admiral Curteis, while he with his flagship and carrier, screened by destroyers, attempted the annihilation of either *Tirpitz* or any other heavy German units that might make a sortie. The First Sea Lord firmly disagreed, maintaining that it was essential for its own defence that the Home Fleet remained massed together. Moreover, Sir Dudley Pound had the benefit of the Ultra decrypts to guide him, information that, but for the perversity of the weather, might have sealed the *Tirpitz*'s fate. Tovey disliked this distant control of his units, even when, as proved the case in the operation of 6–13 March 1942, he had to request Admiralty direction of his destroyers and light cruisers. Pound was not to forget this element of the war in the Arctic, and there is now little doubt that it was to have a malign influence in the coming months.

Tovey, God-fearing man though he was, was nevertheless a naval commander-in-chief and expressed the opinion of his profession when he stated that the destruction of the *Tirpitz* was 'of incomparably greater importance to the conduct of the war than the safety of any convoy'.

It is doubtful if any of the men sailing in the merchant ships and escorts of the remaining PQ and QP convoys to be dispatched that year would have agreed with him but, like Pound's assumption of the superiority of the Admiralty's intelligence overview, Tovey's opinion as to the pre-eminent need to remove the menace of heavy ships, even at some risk, was part of the perception of admirals.

One element of Tovey's debate with the Admiralty concerned

the area in which the capital ships should operate to cover the Russian convoys, in particular how far east they should proceed before German air attacks seriously compromised them. Generally speaking this was agreed as being limited to the longitude of Bear Island, but the reader can decide to what effect such distant cover truly afforded protection to the convoys as their importance became apparent to the enemy. The Admiralty did, however, insist that cover for the convoys was paramount, and Tovey's disappointment at failing to nail the *Tirpitz* can be readily imagined. Air cover was, as we shall see, the key to this theatre as elsewhere, but Tovey was largely denied it, the Fairey Albacores and Swordfish being charismatic but inferior aircraft.

Admiral Tovey was undisputably right in one thing; far the greatest threat to the convoys, he wrote, was that of U-boats and aircraft for which British defences were 'quite inadequate'. This was an assessment of ominous prescience.

7

'Baptism of fire'

HIS MAJESTY'S CRUISER *Trinidad* bunkered at Seidisfiord on the night of 21 March 1942 and sailed next day, a Sunday, to rendezvous with convoy PQ13 which had left Loch Ewe on the 10th and Reykjavik on the 20th. After the ship's company had attended Divine Service, Captain Saunders broadcast to his men explaining that the cruiser's duty had changed from patrols to convoy cover. 'We now have to escort a . . . most important convoy through to Russia; running the gauntlet between Bear Island and North Cape, over which the enemy patrol with superior forces. We can almost certainly expect to meet their ships, U-boats and planes, and many of you will receive your baptism of fire.'

PQ13 consisted of twenty-one ships of several nationalities. The Polish flag was represented by *Tobruk*, the Panamanian by *Gallant Fox*, *Raceland*, *El Estero*, *Ballot* and *Bateau*, the Honduran by *Mana*. Britain's red ensign was worn by *Empire Ranger*, *Empire Cowper*, *Empire Starlight*, *Induna*, *Scottish American*, *Harpalion*, *Lars Kruse* (possibly a chartered Swedish ship), and *New Westminster City*, and the stars and bars of the United States flew over *Effingham*, *Eldena*, *Mormacmar* and *Dunboyne*. The Commodore, Captain D.A. Casey RNR, was embarked with his small staff in the *River Afton*, a ship like others in PQ13 destined to figure more than once in these Arctic convoys. The British tanker *Scottish American* acted as escort oiler.

Once again Admiral Tovey strove to synchronize the sailings of the outward and homeward convoys, though QP9 was delayed a day by the reported presence of U-boats in the approaches to Kola, that most vulnerable leg of the route where Russian air and surface cover would, it had been vainly hoped, be at its most effective. Nevertheless the delay was not significant and nineteen discharged ships left on 21 March. Daylight hours were increasing: enemy aerial reconnaissance would therefore be more effective and some form of surface intervention could be expected.

To this end Admiral Tovey made it clear that he required his escorting forces to shadow and maintain contact with any such superior force as might operate against the passage of the convoys to 'enable them to be brought to action by our heavier forces or submarines'. Tovey's anxiety was due not only to the lost opportunity of bringing *Tirpitz* to battle, but also to reports that the heavy cruiser *Hipper* was being moved to Trondheim. In fact she made a passage from Brunsbüttel, on the Elbe, and anchored near the *Tirpitz* on the 21st. In addition to the air and surface threat there was always that of the U-boats. For all of these possibilities the Commander-in-Chief's staff planned.

His vice-admiral, Curteis, was to cover the western route in *King George V* with a second battleship, the newly commissioned *Duke of York*, the battlecruiser *Renown*, the carrier *Victorious* and the cruisers *Edinburgh* and *Kent* screened by eleven fleet destroyers. The *Trinidad* was to provide close cover to PQ13 together with two destroyers, *Fury* (Lieutenant-Commander C.H. Campbell, Senior Officer) and *Eclipse* (Lieutenant-Commander E. Mack), which joined off Iceland just prior to *Trinidad*. The Hunt-class destroyer *Lamerton* and the trawlers *Blackfly* and *Paynter* had accompanied PQ13 from Reykjavik, together with ex-Norwegian whalers *Sulla, Sumba* and *Silja,* which were to transfer to the Soviet navy in an attempt to beef up the local minesweeping force. *Lamerton* and the fleet oiler *Oligarch* formed an independent Force Q, sailing with the convoy but only temporarily a part of it.

As for QP9, under Captain Hudson, late Commodore of PQ12, it was covered west of Bear Island by the cruising *Nigeria* and had an ocean escort of the minesweepers *Sharpshooter* (Lieutenant-Commander Lampen) and *Britomart* and the destroyer *Offa*. Additional local support was given by five minesweepers led by *Harrier*, two Russian destroyers and the damaged *Oribi*. These saw QP9 two days into its homeward passage, until the early hours of the 23rd, though one of the Russian destroyers lost contact some time earlier. Little more was achieved by the cruiser *Kenya*, intended to be performing the equivalent role of *Trinidad*, which left Kola on the 22nd and failed to locate the convoy. She did, however, succeed in carrying home ten tons of bullion.[1]

Despite the meticulous planning by the C-in-C's staff, the co-ordination and execution of this complex series of movements could not take account of the one great variable. For while Admiral Tovey and his officers could make informed and expert assessments of the German reaction, they were powerless against the weather and it was now the season of the equinox.

On 23 March QP9 ran into a severe south-westerly gale with heavy snowstorms. Mercifully the convoy hung together. As the weather abated on the evening of the 24th, lookouts aboard *Sharpshooter* spotted a surfaced U-boat in a dusky break between snow showers. Lampen immediately altered course towards her, increased speed and succeeded in ramming and sinking *U655* before she had time to dive. *Sharpshooter* was damaged and Lampen handed the convoy over to Lieutenant-Commander Ewing of *Offa* and proceeded independently. Both the minesweeper and the convoy reached their destinations without further event, though the Russian freighter *Pravda* straggled. Such, however, was not the fate of the outward, laden PQ13.

PQ13 was on the far side of the depression which generated the severe gale experienced by QP9, and was destined to experience the full fury of an Arctic storm. Initially a strong south-westerly had enhanced the convoy's progress. Shortly after midday on the 23rd, when abeam and 120 miles south-east of Jan Mayen, PQ13 was re-routed due east, an Ultra decrypt having alerted the Admiralty to a waiting patrol line of Dönitz's U-boats. During this unscheduled leg HMS *Lamerton* and the oiler *Oligarch* detached for an ocean rendezvous to refuel the eleven destroyers in Curteis's squadron.

Ten hours later, at noon the next day, 24 March, in 69°20′N 000°20′E, the convoy course was resumed to the north-eastward, heading for the waypoint off Bear Island. PQ13 was now several miles nearer than planned to the German airfield at Bardufoss, between Narvik and Tromso. Nevertheless, the convoy was forty miles ahead of schedule and making almost 9 knots. When PQ13 resumed its course, leaving Force Q in its wake, Vice-Admiral Curteis was on a similar course, but 250 miles astern.

In conformity with standard practice, *Trinidad* drew off for the night to the south and east of the convoy and in the long hours of darkness the wind veered to the north-east and rapidly increased. In the short, wide-fronted columns of merchantmen, station-keeping became a nightmare as the deeply laden ships pitched into the heavy seas that now drove at them from ahead. Spray filled the air, reducing visibility, and the wallowing, laden merchantmen increasingly took spray and green water aboard as the sea state worsened. The cold air froze what failed to sluice out through the clanging washports into heavy encrustations of ice on decks, upperworks, masts, rigging, aerials and guns. At noon on the 25th the full gale was beginning to disrupt the good order of the convoy. Maintaining a proper lookout became difficult, threatening station-keeping; masters and mates were constrained to con their vessels from one huge crest to the next, to nurse their charges and thus minimize damage to ship and cargo. It was all standard seamanship, but it played havoc with the fragile cohesion of a convoy. Nor did the escorts fare much better. The whalers and trawlers bucked and rolled appallingly, their hard-bitten crews swearing in their own time-honoured tradition and navigating by instinct rather than science. But on the destroyers the seasick misery of 'hostilities only' ratings and ex-yachtsmen volunteer reserve officers beggared description. This was a sodden baptism far worse than one of fire, for in seasickness there are two stages, the first an apprehension of death, the second a longing for eternal stillness. Below decks the accommodation became a shambles of water and loose gear, and men kept exposed at 'cruising stations' discovered a nadir of discomfort only emphasized by the lack of hot food. 'Kye', the Royal Navy's cocoa, and corned beef sandwiches alone maintained the fragile unity of body and soul.

The disintegration of the convoy concerned Captain Saunders of the *Trinidad* and on the evening of the 25th he reluctantly broke radio silence, aware of Admiral Tovey's strict injunctions not to do so, but anxious that the Commander-in-Chief, the Admiralty and the Senior British Naval Officer, North Russia, Rear-Admiral R.H. Bevan, should know the situation. He also broadcast to the merchantmen a rendezvous position south of Bear Island for the 27th. This was a considerable risk but not a foolhardy one, for he knew full well that a scattered convoy offered the enemy easy pickings as it sought the Murman coast.[2]

But at dawn on the 27th the convoy was nowhere near the rendezvous. The gale had blown unabated for a day and a half and PQ13 was widely scattered, labouring under ice and plunging through a heavy swell. The previous afternoon *Induna*, in company with *Empire Starlight*, *Ballot* and the whaler *Silja*, had beaten off an attack by a solitary German aircraft, possible credit for a 'kill' going to her DEMS gunners. This group of ships, later collecting the *Effingham*, *Dunboyne* and *Mana*, became the eastern concentration of the convoy. Meanwhile, far to the south-west and with no prospect of affording the convoy any cover if surface forces did attack, Vice-Admiral Curteis had turned back to Scapa, *Victorious* and *Tartar* both having sustained damage.

During 27 March the weather continued foul with low visibility, overcast skies and a freezing wind. The day was barely one minute old when the warships received the first of three messages from the Admiralty indicating the possibility of surface attack. For Lieutenant-Commander Campbell, the ocean escort's senior officer aboard *Fury*, the first priority was to round up the merchant ships but, shortly before noon, his destroyer's radio operators intercepted a frantic plea from the whaler *Sumba* that she was fifty miles north-east of Bear Island, incapable of making headway and desperately short of fuel. A quick-witted operator obtained a radio-bearing of the transmission and Campbell turned to a course of west-south-west, locating the *Sumba* at 16.00, her dead reckoning miles adrift. The *Fury* spent the next four and three-quarter hours hove to with the *Sumba* greedily guzzling boiler oil from a hose trailed astern, a pair of sitting ducks for any U-boat commander in the vicinity. The anxiety these short-ranged whale-catchers caused those responsible for them was eloquently conveyed by Campbell in his report. *Sumba*'s lack of endurance combined with her need to break radio silence was nothing short of 'a menace'.

Almost equally paralysed, PQ13's Commodore, Captain Casey aboard the *River Afton*, found his ship unable to make headway or point her bow closer than sixty degrees off the wind. In these circumstances the *River Afton* drew inexorably closer to the Lofoten Islands until noon, when the gradual moderation of the wind permitted her to make headway and she proceeded to Kola alone.

During the height of the gale, Rear-Admiral H.M. Burrough in the independently cruising *Nigeria* was about 100 miles south-west of Bear Island where *Trinidad* came up with her. The latter cruiser appears to have caught sight of the *Empire Ranger* the previous evening, then lost contact, but *Trinidad* had located two merchant ships by 22.00 on the 27th, one of which was the tramp *Harpalion*, owned by J. and C. Harrison of London. The second destroyer, HMS *Eclipse*, had also succeeded in finding one merchant ship and they remained in company while a group of five more vessels huddled together to the southward of the questing escorts, but well north of the isolated *River Afton*. The remaining ships straggled in groups.

By 08.30 the following morning, the 28th, the weather had greatly improved, being clear and sunny. During the night Captain Saunders had ordered an increase in speed; HMS *Trinidad* swept eastwards and the cruiser now found the *Empire Ranger* eighty miles north of the North Cape, the most advanced ship of the disrupted convoy. Saunders then reversed his course, anxious to join forces with the two destroyers in view of the Admiralty's appraisal of imminent surface attack.

Some forty miles astern, the cluster of six merchant ships, a whaler and a trawler (the *Induna*, *Empire Starlight*, *Ballot*, *Dunboyne*, *Effingham* and *Mana* with the whaler *Silja* and trawler *Blackfly*) had formed up in an 'eastern' group; thirty-five miles west of them were *Fury* and *Harpalion*; a further sixty miles behind lagged *Eclipse* with the trawler *Paynter*, the whaler *Sumba* and another group of six merchant vessels which included the tanker, *Scottish American*. Having proceeded as far west as *Fury* and *Harpalion*, *Trinidad* swung round to the eastwards at 11.25. All that was then known of the remaining merchantmen and one whaler was that they were still straggling. Eighty minutes earlier lookouts on the cruiser had spotted a Blohm and Voss BV138 reconnaissance seaplane, and an ineffective, long-range anti-aircraft barrage had been thrown up to no effect. Impudently the German aircrew flashed 'your shots are falling short'.[3]

A response from the Luftwaffe could confidently be expected, for the groups of ships had one thing in common – they were all well within range of Banak, the nearer ships no more than 150 miles. As for the surface threat, this too was materializing, though not from heavy ships, for the position of the convoy and the chronic shortage of fuel prevented effective intervention from the capital ships in far-off Trondheim. Admiral Hubert Schmundt, 'Admiral Arctic', ordered three of the large Narvik-class destroyers stationed at Kirkenes to sail, and at 13.30 the *Z24* and *Z25* left to intercept the convoy under the command of Kapitän Pönitz in *Z26*. With a main armament of 5.9-inch guns, torpedoes, and a reputed speed of over 35 knots they were a match for the 6-inch guns of the slower Colony-class *Trinidad*.[4]

The first affected by what was to develop into a running battle was the anti-submarine trawler *Paynter*, which was attacked from the air at 11.27. The 'eastern' group with *Silja* and *Blackfly* was twice dive-bombed by Junkers Ju88s of Luftflotte 5. Near misses affected *Mana* and the Panamanian-registered SS *Ballot*, which was so shaken that burst pipes threatened to immobilize her and preparations to abandon ship were made as she lost steam and dropped astern, losing touch with *Induna*. Her Master decided to reduce the numbers of his crew and sent sixteen men off to *Silja* in a lifeboat. Subsequently, however, she made port under her own steam. Those sent off to the whaler for safety were to find they had drawn the short straw.

The radar operators aboard *Trinidad* had been making intermittent transmissions to try and locate the scattered ships of the convoy. Then, at 13.15, the scanners picked up a lone aircraft which dived out of the cloud and dropped three bombs close to the cruiser. An hour later a short, sharp and persistent attack was made by more Junkers dive-bombers, but to little effect, though the near misses were close and shook the racing cruiser, damaging her main radio transmitters. *Trinidad*'s anti-aircraft fire was tremendous and Captain Saunders handled his ship skilfully, taking her into patches of mist at high speed to confuse his attackers. As this first wave of Ju88s withdrew, *Harpalion* reported being bombed; she too escaped serious damage, but the convoy had already sustained its first loss. The straggler *Raceland* had been bombed shortly after noon as she steamed east alone, not far from the position where, four days earlier, *Sharpshooter* had rammed *U655*.

Then, at 19.30, in the last of the day's twilight, *Empire Ranger* was sunk by bombers far to the eastward. She too was alone in latitude 72°13'N, having reached the longitude of 032°10'E, not far from that of the Kola Inlet. Her distress signal was picked up and the *Blackfly* was dispatched to search this area for survivors. Arriving next day she found nothing. Lieutenant Hughes was not to know that Pönitz's destroyers had already beaten him to it.

The German destroyers had steamed north until only a few miles east of the last position of the *Empire Ranger*. Pönitz had then turned west and deployed his ships into line abreast, three miles apart and steaming at 15 knots. It was already dark and bitterly cold. As the lookouts peered around the horizon through their Zeiss binoculars moisture streamed from their eyes and froze on their cheeks.

Ahead of the German ships the survivors from the *Empire Ranger* huddled miserably in their lifeboats, struck through with the piercing cold. At 22.45 they were spotted by the lookouts in the German destroyers, which stopped and picked them up as prisoners-of-war.

Resuming their westward progress, half an hour after midnight Pönitz's ships ran across the straggling Panamanian *Bateau* and, Pönitz having ordered her crew to abandon ship, *Z26* sank her by torpedo and gunfire. Again, the survivors were rescued and from them intelligence was gleaned as to the position, plight and escort of the convoy, the latter perhaps deliberately exaggerated as being two cruisers and four destroyers. Pönitz lingered in the area while this operation and its sequel took place, and then turned south-east at 25 knots, thinking he was too far north. At 05.30, having sighted nothing further, the three German destroyers began steaming north for three hours, almost on the meridian of the Kola Inlet.

Meanwhile, during the early part of the night, *Trinidad* and *Fury* had cruised in company to the southward of the mid-point between the two main groups of PQ13, hoping to cover both from interception by enemy surface forces by virtue of the cruiser's radar. This was south of Position Tango (72°25′N 030°00′E), a waypoint on the convoy route and the rendezvous for reinforcements expected from Vaenga Bay at 08.00 that morning, 29 March.

At 02.00 both ships headed east-north-east, to close both the eastern group and the rendezvous. Suddenly, shortly after 04.00 as the sun rose, *Trinidad*'s lookouts spotted something on the surface to starboard about four miles distant. Haze made identification difficult but it was thought to be a surfaced U-boat and the cruiser opened fire, checking after three salvoes as further deliberation on the bridge inclined to the view that it might have been a lifeboat from the *Empire Ranger* under sail. The 'lifeboat' submerged and Saunders swung away to the west, just as his reinforcements, consisting of *Oribi* and the Russian destroyers *Sokrushitelni* and *Gremyashchi*, arrived.

The cruiser and four destroyers continued west to locate *Eclipse* and her charges and almost immediately discovered debris on the sea from the *Empire Ranger*, together with four well-provisioned but empty lifeboats. At 06.30 HMS *Eclipse* was sighted, supported by *Paynter* and *Sumba*, and now escorting eight merchantmen. These were the *Eldena, El Estero, Empire Cowper, Gallant Fox, New Westminster City, Mormacmar, Scottish American* and *Tobruk*. The two Russians were attached to the escort and *Oribi* was ordered to sweep twenty miles astern to round up any strays before joining the screen.

Saunders then again turned east and, with *Fury* in his wake, increased speed to 20 knots, set a course of east by south and resumed his interrupted search for the eastern group.

This group, centred on *Silja* and consisting of the *Dunboyne, Effingham, Empire Starlight, Induna* and *Mana*, had run into heavy ice during the night. It had already been reduced by the loss of the *Ballot* straggling astern in the aftermath of the air attacks, and the ice now added further difficulties. Moreover the whaler was running desperately short of fuel and was gallantly taken in tow by the *Induna*, to which the sixteen men from the SS *Ballot* had transferred by crossing an ice-floe to avoid overcrowding the little *Silja*. The complement of the *Induna* was now sixty-six souls.

Aboard *Empire Starlight*, a 10,000-ton tramp built on government account in Hong Kong and being managed by the tramping firm of Ropner's, an ordeal was just beginning. Captain Stein had a crew of thirteen British deck and engineer officers, fifty-one Chinese seamen, greasers, cooks and stewards, and fourteen DEMS gunners. Like the others in this eastern group they had already been shadowed and later attacked by Junkers bombers. Now a blizzard of heavy snow and the additional hazard of ice complicated life further. The open pack grew denser and Stein watched helplessly as the *Induna*, having got *Silja* in tow, found herself almost fast in the ice. The ships now backed and filled and Stein drove a lead through which the other ships followed. The blizzard had rendered visibility negligible, but after four hours all except *Induna* and the helpless *Silja* had broken clear away to the south-east to close with their destination. By next morning they had been joined by *Blackfly*, which had been searching unsuccessfully for signs of the *Empire Ranger* until 06.00.[5]

Leaving the *Empire Ranger*'s emptied lifeboats to puzzle

Captain Saunders and his officers at first light, Pönitz's destroyers had now doubled back and by 08.30 lay athwart the convoy's route. The *Silja*'s eastern group had evaded them and were astern of the destroyers as they turned away from them, increased speed to 17 knots and swept due westwards.

Twenty-five miles south of them the *Harpalion* ploughed to the eastwards, but directly ahead lay *Trinidad* and *Fury*, steaming at 20 knots on a reciprocal course to locate *Silja* and her consorts, neatly placed between the marauding Germans and the remaining eight 'western' ships of the convoy under the cover of *Eclipse*, *Oribi* and the two Russians.[6]

As the two groups of warships rapidly closed, the fine almost cloudless morning gave way to an overcast scud and a rising breeze. The extreme visibility of early daylight quickly grew murky, with swirls of mist rolling down from the ice edge. The cold seemed worse to the men whose cruising stations left them exposed on the upper decks. Had conditions not been fine earlier and had Captain Saunders been unable to identify *Oribi* and her Russian allies at dawn, the echoes appearing on *Trinidad*'s radar displays and first observed by the duty operator, Able Seaman J. Anderson, might have misled him, for the rendezvous had actually taken place four hours early. Discovered to the eastward at 6½ miles, the echoes were confirmed at 08.45 at 4½ miles as three ships. Already at cruising stations, the ship's company of *Trinidad* now closed up to action stations. The ranges and bearings were passed below to the transmitting station situated low in the ship and between two bunker tanks. Here the twenty-one-man crew, including the marine bandsmen, processed the information which controlled the training and elevation of the cruiser's armament, computing the offset angles which allowed for the relative motion of the engaging ship and her target. The accuracy of a warship's fire depended upon the speed and accuracy with which this information was updated. Confirmation that the guns bore on the correct bearings and angles of elevation was revealed by 'gun-ready' alarms based on the latest data: the guns could then be fired.

Four minutes later, at 08.49, in latitude 71°21′N, longitude 033°32′E, the silhouettes of three 'foreign' destroyers were glimpsed emerging from the mist. Leading Signalman Jordan had only flashed two letters of the British challenge when Captain Saunders acted. 'Fortunately,' he later reported, 'I had already located the

Russian destroyers and I was able to open fire without challenging at the leading destroyer at 08.51.'

On the signal bridge the signalmen hoisted the time-honoured flag signal: 'enemy in sight'. In a matter of seconds this enemy destroyer, *Z26*, had both returned fire, two shells striking the base of *Trinidad*'s Y-turret, and been hit amidships. *Trinidad* then shifted target to the second destroyer which was thought to have been hit, and both she and *Z26* turned away to the north-west. Immediately, fearing a torpedo attack, Captain Saunders ordered a cease-fire as the destroyers vanished in the mist. He swung *Trinidad* hard a-starboard to comb the tracks of the approaching torpedoes and two were seen to overtake the cruiser and pass down her port side.

Saunders continued his starboard swing, steadied briefly on a heading of due north and regained radar contact with *Z26* at four miles. Water poured into the cruiser through a shell-hole as she listed under full helm while the damage-control parties fought to gain the upper hand, aided by the cruiser steadying on a new course. Now almost reversing his previous heading, Captain Saunders drove down towards the enemy on a slightly converging line, with both ships running roughly north-westwards. *Fury* turned in the cruiser's wake while *Z24* and *Z25* diverged wildly from their wounded leader in the mistaken belief that the British ships had also fired torpedoes. After turning north-east, they made off erratically to the northwards to vanish in grey swirls of snow that fell from the low fractus. It was now 09.00 on 29 March, no more than nine minutes since the engagement had begun.

Seventeen minutes later, having worked up to 30 knots, the outline of the damaged *Z26*, blurred by dense clouds of black smoke, became distinguishable from the murk, fine on the cruiser's port bow as the pursuing *Trinidad* overhauled her. Altering course slightly to starboard to bring all his guns to bear, Saunders made to cross the destroyer's stern and opened fire at a range of 1½ miles, simultaneously preparing his port torpedo tubes.

Z26 made a series of continuous and violent zigzags to avoid the British shells plunging into the sea around her, though she seemed incapable of retaliating with either her 5.9-inch guns or her torpedoes, and had clearly lost any advantage of speed. The situation of the German vessel now appeared desperate and her destruction assured as *Trinidad* loomed on her starboard beam, port torpedo tubes trained on her quarry. As she crossed the enemy's wake, the British cruiser passed through a number of German seamen, some already dead, but all in their lifejackets, who had been blown overboard from their exposed positions at the enemy destroyer's after guns and torpedo tubes. Above their bobbing heads their ship laid its own pall of black smoke.

There now occurred one of those ironies which abound in war. It was later described by Admiral Tovey, with masterly understatement, as 'cruel hard luck'.

Upon attempting to fire his triple port torpedo tubes at 09.22, Lieutenant-Commander Dent, *Trinidad*'s torpedo officer, loosed the first, then hesitated a moment to improve the angle of attack just forward of the cruiser's port beam. Upon firing again, Dent discovered that his weapons had frozen in their tubes and that the approved measures to ensure that this could not happen were ineffective in such conditions. He was about to become the unknowing victim of an even greater irony, for the first torpedo broke surface a cable from the ship. It was spotted and Captain Saunders once again put his helm over, remarking with a cool prescience that 'it looks remarkably like one of ours'.

Later discovery of a fragment of the torpedo confirmed this and the explanation was claimed to be a failure of the gyro-controlled direction system, though an officer high in the ship's forebridge at the air defence control position opined that a salvo of *Trinidad*'s own shells landing short just ahead of the torpedo's track may have toppled the gyro and reversed its course. Nevertheless, the disaster was as unique as it was unpredictable. At 09.24 HMS *Trinidad* torpedoed herself.

With an impacting roar the rogue weapon struck on the port side below the bridge, rupturing the wing bunker tanks, flooding the marines' mess deck and almost cutting off all the men in the transmitting station below. Four escaped before the armoured hatch fell and broke the back of the fifth. Almost simultaneously the bulkhead separating the compartment from the breached oil tank gave way and the seventeen men remaining below were drowned in the filth of heavy fuel oil.

Water poured into the forward boiler room and in the darkness, amid super-heated steam escaping from fractured mains, men were scalded in their fight to abandon the space. The ship rapidly listed to port as she slowed; steering and command were shifted to the after emergency position, orders being relayed from the compass platform by a chain of men. As if shaking off her malfunctioning member, the combined effect of the explosion and the list caused the port torpedo tube mounting to be first torn from the deck and then jettisoned over the side. Torpedoman Bowditch, sitting at the controls, escaped only by the quickest of thinking as the cruiser swung to port and dropped out of the fight. For the time being, *Z26* had had the luckiest of escapes.

Seeing the explosion under his enemy's bridge, Pönitz ordered *Z26* turned to the south-west, hoping to escape. But breaking away from her position astern of the now listing cruiser, HM Destroyer *Fury* appeared in hot pursuit, though in the constantly swirling snow showers she had barely yet seen the German destroyer.

Both the pursued *Z26* and pursuing *Fury* were now heading towards HMS *Eclipse*, the two Russian escorts and the *Oribi* with the western detachment of PQ13. In the rough sea, mist and snow squalls, a degree of confusion was inevitable; radar could not distinguish friend from foe, and the noise of the *Trinidad*'s cannonade had caused *Eclipse*'s commanding officer, Lieutenant-Commander Mack, to increase speed and zigzag furiously around the convoy. Suddenly, to the north-north-east the grey shape of a warship loomed out of the mist. Those on *Eclipse*'s bridge took her for *Trinidad* and held their fire; one of the Russian destroyers, the *Sokrushitelni*, was less cautious and briefly opened fire before realizing her error. Then, at about 09.30 and right ahead of *Eclipse*, *Fury* broke clear of the mist and snow, a high bow wave curling back from her stem as her turbines spun at maximum revolutions. 'For some minutes,' Mack recorded, as friend and foe strove to identify each other, 'chaos reigned in the destroyer screen.'

Fury impetuously loosed off two salvoes before recognition took place. Fortunately these did no damage and Campbell, having located the second part of the convoy *Fury* had once been in charge of, now swung his ship round to stand by the beleaguered *Trinidad*. Mack also decided to use his initiative and, 'as there seemed altogether too many destroyers round the convoy', put his helm hard a-port and went in pursuit of the briefly glimpsed ship which had passed north of them, still believing it to be *Trinidad*, of whose self-inflicted torpedoing he as yet knew nothing. In an exchange with Commander J.E.H. McBeath of *Oribi* on the TBS system, Mack announced his intention of joining the cruiser.[7] He also knew from an earlier signal from *Trinidad* that there was a damaged enemy destroyer in the offing, which 'might be worth beating up'.

At about 15 knots *Eclipse* now took up the pursuit of *Z26*, picking her up on her radar at two miles, fine on her port bow. It was not until 09.50, when no more than half a mile away, that she could be dimly made out from the *Eclipse*'s exposed bridge and it was still a few minutes before the correct identification of an enemy Narvik-class destroyer was made. Aboard *Z26* a similar mistake was made – she flashed the German challenge at *Eclipse* on the assumption that she was either *Z24* or *Z25*.

In swirling snow the two ships now fought a running action. The German's fire was intermittent and largely ineffective after the damage inflicted by *Trinidad*, but she made smoke and increased speed in an effort to shake off her tormentor, zigzagging in an attempt to spoil the *Eclipse*'s gunlaying and to get in the occasional shot from her undamaged forward turrets. Aboard the British destroyer, A-gun, situated on the forecastle, was frozen and useless and Mack had to work up on his enemy's exposed quarter and sheer away in order to open the arcs of his after guns. The two ships twisted and turned, Mack clinging on to the astern position and avoiding the heavy punishment he knew the German's 5.9-inch bow guns could inflict.

Spray swept over *Eclipse*'s main armament and bridge, freezing instantly on the cold steel; the gun platforms were lethally slippery and the gun wells full of water, slush and ice. Moreover, the use of binoculars by bridge and director personnel was almost impossible. The snow still occasionally obscured the target, but a slick of oil from *Z26* enabled Mack to retain contact. A degree of confusion existed internally too, for the Gunner (T), in charge of *Eclipse*'s torpedo tubes, loosed off three torpedoes in the mistaken belief that his communications with the bridge had broken down.

Despite these difficulties, over the next half hour, *Eclipse* succeeded in hitting *Z26* with six 4.7-inch shells. One was seen to cause an explosion in an after cordite store while another struck her in her boiler room. *Z26*'s stern sank progressively lower in the water as she developed a port list and lost speed. At about 10.22 *Z26* lay stopped and Mack ranged up to fire his remaining torpedo, having passed close south of the stationary destroyer which had turned in a lazy circle as she finally lost way. *Eclipse* herself was damaged, having sustained two hits aft which had injured several men when ready use ammunition exploded.

Then, quite suddenly, two miles to starboard, *Z24* and *Z25* were seen approaching to succour their consort. They had first retired northwards and then looped south-west towards the sound of gunfire, homing on their harried leader and passing close to the westward of the stricken *Trinidad* and the *Fury* as they cast about for *Z26*. Now they had found her and, with an inferior and solitary enemy lying between them and their sister ship, they opened fire with their heavy calibre armament just as the snow squalls ceased, rent aside like a gigantic curtain with that abrupt change in conditions that characterizes the weather in the Barents Sea. Mack's reaction was instinctive; he rang on full speed and headed north-west, following the retreating snow squalls. German shells again hit *Eclipse* as she retaliated with her after guns. She was hit twice aft and holed forward from two shells which burst under the flare of her bow. She also had her main aerials shot away before, at 10.35, she was mercifully hidden by snow.

The German destroyers did not follow her, but stood by the sinking *Z26* whose stern was now awash. At 10.50 *Z26* capsized and plunged to the sea-bed. Having picked up her survivors, *Z24* and *Z25* made for Kirkenes at speed, arriving safely that evening.

Mack now swung east; damage assessment aboard *Eclipse* revealed one man killed and a dozen wounded, nine severely from the explosion of ammunition. The remainder of her crew were exhausted and the ship lacked fuel and was in a generally unseaworthy state, being particularly tender and lacking stability. At this critical moment, *Eclipse* drove out of the snow and discovered a surfaced U-boat two cables distant on her port bow. Surprise was mutual and, though the U-boat loosed two torpedoes before Mack had time to open fire, he succeeded in hauling hard-a-port, combed their tracks and attempted to reach the U-boat before she crash-dived, saturating the area with depth-charges before abandoning the hunt.

Having failed to receive a signal sent by *Trinidad* ordering *Eclipse* to stand by the cruiser and form an anti-submarine screen, Mack made independently for the Kola Inlet where he arrived next day, 30 March, with only forty tons of fuel remaining. Later he received the approbation of the Commander-in-Chief for his conduct.

The local Royal Naval detachment base in the Kola Inlet had sent out the minesweepers *Harrier*, *Gossamer*, *Hussar* and *Speedwell* (not a corvette) the previous day, the 28th, to cover the southward leg by which the incoming convoys approached Kola from the north. *Harrier* had orders to search for the *Empire Ranger*'s boats, not knowing they had been located, albeit empty. The minesweepers also had orders to look out for the *River Afton* and the *Empire Cowper* both of which had naval personnel on board who, for some reason, were *personae non gratae* with the Russians, and to remove them from the merchant ships on which they were travelling as supernumeraries.[8]

Whilst on passage towards the convoy, *Hussar* and *Gossamer* both sighted a surfaced U-boat which crash-dived and evaded them before they could attack. They went on with *Speedwell* to reinforce the screen round the western remnant of the convoy. Meanwhile Commander Jay of *Harrier* was acquainted with the fact that the *Trinidad* had been torpedoed and altered course towards her.

The cruiser, with *Fury* in attendance, had been limping south-east at 6 knots since 09.45 on the 29th. It was her best speed in view of the strain on her bulkheads. The small arms magazines had been flooded and the several fires extinguished or brought under control. There remained no lights except a battery circuit which mercifully illuminated the sick bay – now an overcrowded casualty clearing station. Efforts had been made to serve hot drinks and some form of food to the hungry and tired ship's company, who had nevertheless cheered the welcome sight of *Fury* coming back to circle them and ward off any prowling U-boats.

As the western group of merchant ships drew level with *Trinidad*, *Oribi* was ordered to join the cruiser and augment *Fury*'s anti-submarine screen. She later sighted a surfaced U-boat through a patch in the mist and both destroyers attacked with depth-charges after she crash-dived. *Fury* was duly credited with the destruction of *U585* (Lohse), though the U-boat was actually lost later in a minefield.

The further reinforcement of *Harrier* arrived during the afternoon and, by dint of much pumping and the transfer of fuel, *Trinidad*'s list was greatly reduced, and her speed increased to 12 knots. Later, the wind died and the sky cleared as salt in the boiler-feed water brought the ship almost to a stop. A full moon and brilliant aurora further worked on the nerves of men exhausted with the business of saving their ship. Now she lay silent, a perfect target. *Oribi* and *Fury* circled, picking up asdic contacts, and laid deterrent patterns of depth-charges, driving off a U-boat.

A signal was now sent to the Senior British Naval Officer, North Russia, Rear-Admiral R.H. Bevan, requesting tugs and air cover, for *Trinidad* was only seventy miles from the Kola Inlet. Two hours later, her engine-room staff having drained off the salt water, the *Trinidad*'s speed had been worked up to 7 knots.

By now, however, the wind was rising again; *Trinidad* soon laboured slowly southwards in a northerly gale and on one occasion broached beam on to the wind and heavy sea. It was necessary to go astern to draw the cruiser's stern into the wind and then continue ahead on the correct course, for she would handle no other way without greater power. At 09.30 on 30 March, HMS *Trinidad* entered the Kola Inlet under her own steam and, though tugs were in attendance, she came to her anchor off the dry dock at Rosta without assistance. *Fury* then anchored in company while *Oribi* returned to sea.

The major naval unit was now safe. Convoy PQ13 had yet to make port.

The western group under the escort of the minesweepers and the Russian destroyers was rejoined by *Oribi* and although subjected to a half-hearted attack by German aircraft off the entrance to the Kola Inlet, entered and anchored. One of the merchant ships, the *Tobruk*, claimed to have shot down two aircraft in this attack, but this was unconfirmed. Ironically this ship was shortly after bombed and sunk while at anchor.

The eastern group had, with the exception of the *Induna* and *Silja*, got clear of the ice during the afternoon of the 29th. At 09.30 the following morning the *Effingham* was torpedoed and sunk by *U435* (Strelow), one of the four U-boats awaiting the approaching ships north of Kildin Island. The remaining ships arrived safely at Kola later that day, followed by Commodore Casey in the *River Afton*, which had been unmanœuvrable in the gale of the 24th, but had successfully evaded a pursuing surfaced U-boat during her lone voyage to Murmansk.

Two hours before *Effingham* was hit, the gallant *Induna* also sank. Her master and crew had, with great difficulty, reconnected the tow with the *Silja* which had parted in the ice, and finally drew into clear water at about 15.00 on the 29th. The bad weather that had so hampered *Trinidad* now parted the tow and, despite a search in driving squalls of snow, contact with the whaler was lost. *Induna* put about and headed south for her destination. At 07.30

on 30 March, she was hit by a torpedo from *U435* which struck in No. 5 hatch, containing gasoline. In the chaos which followed, barbed-wire rolls were blown into the fire, preventing men stationed or accommodated aft from reaching the boats. Many men, some from the *Ballot*, scantily clad and barefoot, dived overboard. Others were horribly burned. On the boat deck, the starboard lifeboat was lowered by a party under the Second Mate, Mr Rowlands, while the Chief Mate had difficulties getting the port boat away from the ship's side. Eventually most of the survivors, including some of *Ballot*'s crew, were embarked as Strelow brought his boat to the surface and put a second torpedo into No. 4 hold. The *Induna* settled rapidly by the stern, lifting her bow high out of the water while escaping steam, internal explosions and the roar of the inrush of water filled the air, drowning the cries of the remaining men as they strove to get clear of the ship. *U435* then submerged and the overloaded boats were left alone on the windswept seas. There followed an ordeal of extreme privation which lasted four days. The boats soon lost touch, but both headed south under sail. Second Mate Rowlands's boat was largely manned by firemen and greasers from both ships, several of whom were burned or scalded and all of whom were inadequately clothed for the exposed conditions in which they now found themselves. Hypothermia quickly set in, some of the men having taken whisky in the mistaken belief then prevalent that it helped survival. Seven men died the first night. The others endured the wracking pain of frostbite. Although the boat was adequately stored, the fresh water was frozen solid. By dawn on 1 April, two more men had perished and the remainder were so weak that jettisoning the bodies was only accomplished with difficulty. By the time a greaser and steward died quietly later in the day, no one had the strength or control over their limbs to lift them over the side. As dawn broke on the 2nd, four more men succumbed. With only seventeen left alive, Rowlands did not think the rest had much chance of survival. Shortly before dark, however, they finally made out Cape Sviatoi lighthouse,* marking the eastern entrance to the Kola Inlet, and soon afterwards they were overflown by Russian fighters. By 20.00 a Russian minesweeper had arrived and the unfortunate and prostrate men were, with a rough solicitude,

*Several capes with this name exist on the Russian coast. A second lies at the entrance to the White Sea.

hauled on board in rope slings, for they were immobilized by the cold. Once aboard they were stripped, wrapped in thick woollen coats and given hot coffee and vodka. On their way back the minesweeper ran across the port lifeboat with nine men in it. One man, a badly burned and then frostbitten Canadian fireman and coal trimmer from the *Ballot* named Auger, survived until picked up. His stoicism had been inspirational to the men in the Mate's boat: his last words were, 'We made it.' Two more men died later in hospital. Of the *Induna*'s sixty-six men only twenty-four survived, six of them intact. The others lost limbs.

The *Oribi*, still searching the approaches for stragglers, found the drifting *Silja* late on the 30th and she was finally brought in under tow by *Harrier*.

The confused and complex saga of PQ13 was over, but its lessons were yet to be analysed and its aftermath had yet to be played out.[9]

8

'Just a process of attrition'

THE PASSAGE OF PQ13 could hardly be acclaimed a success: almost 30,000 tons of Allied merchant shipping had been sunk, more than a quarter of the convoy. There is a rather pathetic note of disclaimer in the Admiralty's assessment of these losses as being 'stragglers', an implicit inference that somehow it was the fault of the merchant ships that they had been lost, whereas two of the five had been part of the eastern group which had re-formed after dispersal by the weather and had received no close escort for the remainder of the passage. This assumption tended to blind the Admiralty to the dangers of scattering a convoy, either by order or by act of God.

Although the convoy action had demonstrated a great deal of the Royal Navy's fighting spirit, and individual ships had behaved with great gallantry, it had done little to demonstrate its fighting sense. Moreover the 'distant' units of the Home Fleet were no support whatsoever, whereas its destroyers might have been sent north to refuel from *Nigeria* and assist the hard-pressed escorts in rounding up the convoy. Poor *Trinidad* had suffered grievously from her self-inflicted wound and it was cold comfort that both sides experienced serious technical defects in their torpedoes, to which the extreme low temperatures of the Arctic only added a further complication. Now the cruiser was in a foreign dry dock of limited means belonging to a grudging ally, subject to promises that steel for repairs would arrive 'tomorrow' and, like Alice, finding out that tomorrow never came. The fortuitous discovery of a torpedo trigger fragment among debris in A-boiler room confirmed Captain Saunders's intuition. The unlucky cruiser had indeed torpedoed herself. The subsequent enquiry at Plymouth cleared the ship, but made the disquieting discovery that the low-temperature lubricants were ineffective.

Later experience and the received wisdom of the Admiralty would suggest that there could never be too many destroyers around a convoy even if the prospect of 'beating up' an enemy was tempting, and doubly so if 'the convoy' was but a fragment of the whole. It was an unfortunate, though not entirely unfounded, consequence of PQ13 that the merchant seamen began to doubt the total commitment of the Royal Navy to their protection. If *Trinidad*'s company cheered the appearance of *Fury* there were a number of men aboard the merchant ships who afterwards wondered why she had not stuck to her original task.[1]

Nevertheless, *Trinidad* had made port and the PQ13/QP9 operation had accounted for several aircraft, two U-boats and one Narvik-class destroyer. The fate of the latter made the German Seekriegsleitung even more cautious in its employment of surface forces, though an appreciation by Admiral Tovey accurately predicted that the enemy was 'determined to do everything in his power to stop this traffic'. Correctly judging that the response of the Kriegsmarine's heavy ships would be 'reluctant', the Commander-in-Chief was aware that enemy intervention would concentrate on the use of the U-boat and aircraft, formidable enough in themselves. Hitler, preparing a counter-attack against the resurgent Russians, ordered Luftwaffe reinforcements to Norway and in April the strength of the German air forces began building up.

Tovey requested the Russians to increase their submarine patrols in the Barents Sea and to step up their destroyer contribution to the last leg of the convoy route. His and Sir Dudley Pound's representations that the convoys should be suspended during the weeks of twenty-four-hour daylight that were fast approaching were dismissed by Churchill. The Russians must, at all costs, be kept in the field. Political expedience overrode naval wisdom. Tovey consequently drew increasingly heavily on escorts from the Western Approaches Command.

The dispositions for the next pair of convoys were similar to those for the last. The heavy cruiser *Norfolk* would patrol south-west of Bear Island; heavy cover would be provided by the *King George V*, *Duke of York*, *Victorious*, *Kent* and eight destroyers.

PQ14 consisted of twenty-five merchant ships under a variety of flags. The British contingent were the *Empire Howard, Briarwood, Cape Corso, Dan-y-Bryn, Trehata* and *El Mirlo*, the tankers *Athel Templar, British Corporal* and *Hopemount*, the heavy lift ship *Empire Bard* and the fleet oiler *Aldersdale*, most of them already veterans of the run. The ten ships flying the stars and stripes were the *Hegira, Ironclad, Mormacrio, Seattle Spirit, West Gotomska, City of Joliet, Francis Scott Key, Minotaur, West Cheswald*, and *Yaka*. The hammer and sickle flew over the sterns of the *Arcos* and *Sukhona*, the Dutch tricolour on the *Pieter de Hoogh* and the red, white and blue of Panama on the Greek-owned *Exterminator*. The Commodore, Captain E. Rees RNR, was aboard the SS *Empire Howard* (Captain Downie) and they all sailed from Reykjavik on 8 April 1942, having come up from Oban. At the other end of the run, QP10 of eighteen discharged ships under Captain Casey, aboard *Temple Arch*, left Murmansk on the 10th. QP10 was made up of returning vessels from PQ12 and some of those from PQ13, many of them loaded with timber as a homeward freight.

PQ14 had as initial local escort the minesweepers *Hebe* and *Speedy* with the anti-submarine trawlers *Chiltern* and *Northern Wave*, and the Hunt *Wilton*. The convoy made for the rendezvous 120 miles south-south-west of Jan Mayen where Rear-Admiral S.S. Bonham-Carter flying his flag in HMS *Edinburgh*, the destroyers *Bulldog* (Senior Officer, Commander M. Richmond), *Beagle, Beverley, Forester, Foresight* and *Amazon*, the British corvettes *Campanula, Oxlip, Saxifrage* and *Snowflake*, and the trawlers *Lord Austin* and *Lord Middleton* were to have joined them on the 11th. The usual distant cover was provided by heavy units of the Home Fleet.[2]

During the night prior to making this junction the convoy ran into heavy ice consisting of growlers from which it proved impossible to extricate themselves due to dense fog. Sixteen ships were separated from the convoy and the two minesweepers *Hebe* and *Speedy* were so damaged that they were unable to continue the voyage and put back to Hvalfiordur on the 13th with the majority of the disabled merchantmen. Only the *Empire Howard, Briarwood, Treharta, Dan-y-Bryn, Yaka* and *West Cheswald*, and the tankers *Athel Templar* and *Hopemount* carried on. The latter, with 12,000 tons of diesel, boiler and lubricating oil aboard, was holed in the forepeak and had damaged her propeller on a growler.

Despite this she was considered fit to carry on. Six others, the *City of Joliet, Ironclad, Mormacrio, Francis Scott Key, Minotaur* and *West Gotomska,* continued independently until they met QP10, when they joined that convoy and returned to Iceland.

Early on 15 April a Blohm and Voss flying boat discovered the remnant convoy and was then relieved by a Condor which droned round the horizon sending out its homing signals. Later that day the first air attack by Junkers Ju88 bombers of KG 30 arrived and attacks continued throughout the rest of the day. 'They were not particularly effective,' the Chief Officer of the *Hopemount* recalled.

Things were different on the 16th. Continuous high-level and dive-bombing attacks were made by Ju88s and were combined with intense submarine attacks in a series of co-ordinated waves. 'It was a process of attrition as they tried to pick us off. Sometimes the bombers attacked so low that the escorts used to fire, hoping the shells exploding on the water would send up shock-waves and water to disrupt the attacks.'

U-boat torpedoes were another matter for the men on the merchant ships as they plodded doggedly along the appointed tracks of the carefully formulated zigzag pattern, closed up in two short columns. 'The water was so gin-clear you could see the two red and white bands on the torpedoes. They passed right across the bow . . . I can see them now.'

For defensive armament the tanker *Hopemount* carried two large guns, an HA/LA 4-inch and a Japanese 4.7-inch of 1914 vintage, plus Lewis guns on the after accommodation and Oerlikons, all manned by a detachment of DEMS naval gunners and soldiers from the Royal Marine Regiment of Artillery. The *Hopemount*'s remaining armament of Hotchkiss machine guns was tended by the ship's company and cleaned by the apprentices, one of whom was a mere 16. These guns were very unpopular: 'They had dreadful canvas ammunition belts which jammed.'[3]

During the intense battle of the 16th the convoy suffered its only loss in the torpedoing of the Commodore's ship, the *Empire Howard,* which was hit by two or three torpedoes from *U403* (Kapitänleutnant Clausen). The first struck the 1941-built ship in the boiler room and a second was believed to have hit the engine room, killing all on watch below. A few seconds later another hit the after holds, where her cargo of ammunition exploded, instantly cutting the ship in two. Observers watched as her 'tween deck cargo of army trucks fell from her port side into the sea.

Of her total complement of fifty-four, about forty men jumped overboard but, at that moment, the counter-attacking trawler *Northern Wave* dropped depth-charges in the vicinity. Many of those in the water died horribly of broken bones and ruptured organs as a result. The remainder were dragged semi-conscious aboard the second trawler, the *Lord Middleton*. Of the eighteen rescued, only nine lived, including Captain Downie who afterwards ascribed their survival in the freezing sea to the oil from the ship's ruptured bunker tanks which covered them. Captain Rees was not among the saved, though several saw him in the water.

Captain W.H. Lawrence, Vice-Commodore and Master of the *Briarwood*, now took over the duty. The *Briarwood* had become a veteran of the run. At the beginning of PQ3 she had had to turn back due to ice damage. The combined services of Admiralty divers and the ingenuity of her crew had patched her up with cement boxes and she had left again with PQ5. During the passage of PQ14 she was to account for two German aircraft.[4]

Activity on Friday, 17 April 1942, began at 04.30 with the arrival of the *Sokrushitelni* and *Gremyashchi* which, having escorted QP10 to longitude 30°E, transferred to PQ14. Shortly before 05.00 the first Ju88s were overhead and *Briarwood* succeeded in achieving the first of her two 'kills'. The attack developed without success and by now visibility was decreasing. At 07.50 HMS *Bulldog* swung to attack an asdic contact and reported an unconfirmed sinking. The torpedoes fired by this U-boat, probably *U376*, found no target as the convoy zigzagged. More torpedo tracks were sighted at 10.07 and *Bulldog* made a second counter-attack, but no further air strikes were forthcoming as patchy visibility again closed in.

Aware that German destroyers had sallied from Kirkenes to attack QP10 on 12 and 13 April, a further alarm at 02.00 on the 18th caused Bonham-Carter to order Captain Faulkner to take *Edinburgh* out of the convoy. Perversely, the visibility had cleared again as, with spectacular panache, she hoisted battle ensigns and drew away to the westward where the horizon was broken by the jagged outlines of the upperworks of a line of enemy destroyers hull-down. These, the *Hermann Schoemann*, *Z24* and *Z25*, turned away and vanished, as unsuccessful against PQ14 as they had been against QP10.[5]

Later, when a combined surface, submarine and air attack was expected, dense fog 'saved the convoy's bacon'. Enemy aircraft could be heard low overhead and those aboard *Hopemount* were anxious lest 'the greenhorn and trigger-happy Yanks gave our position away'. As the weather cleared again *Niger, Harrier, Hussar* and *Gossamer* joined from QP10. On the final run in to Kola a strong gale from the north-west sprang up.

Finally, on 19 April, the ships of PQ14 arrived off Kildin Island and entered the inlet. Their troubles were far from over, however, for they, and the remaining undischarged ships of PQ13, were to suffer further the attentions of the Luftwaffe.

Despite the tragic loss of only one ship, the co-ordinated intensity of the combined aerial and submarine attacks led Rear-Admiral Bonham-Carter to sound a cautionary note in his report to Whitehall. Notwithstanding so large an escort for so small a number of merchant ships, the Admiral was concerned that 'with no hours of darkness, continually under air observation for the last four days, submarines concentrating in the bottlenecks, torpedo attack to be expected, our destroyers unable to carry out a proper hunt or search owing to the oil situation, serious losses must be expected in every convoy'.

As his battered charges entered Kola they steamed past *Edinburgh* where Bonham-Carter had hoisted the plain-language message in the international code of signals: 'Well done.' Such small courtesies made him widely respected among merchant seafarers, for he was a master of the informal meeting and devoid of condescension.

'One of the things about being in the Merchant Navy', one tanker officer reminisced fifty years later, 'was that you were treated like children.' Not even the simplest and most obvious intelligence was vouchsafed – a situation quite incomprehensible to the American merchant seamen. As for the British, for whom the barriers of class were more tangible: 'We were kept in the dark. It was most unsettling.'

It was also an atmosphere in which mistrust could flourish.

QP10, which had left Murmansk on 10 April escorted by the cruiser *Liverpool*, the destroyers *Oribi, Punjabi, Fury, Eclipse* and *Marne*, the minesweeper *Speedwell* and the trawlers *Paynter* and *Blackfly*, consisted of sixteen ships under Commodore Casey. The now customary local escort of British sweepers and Russian destroyers saw them on their way.[6]

The convoy was attacked immediately after its departure by aircraft and U-boats in a sustained action which lasted until the ships reached Bear Island three days later, when the enemy switched its attention to PQ14, in the knowledge that a departure from Kola indicated a laden inward convoy from Iceland. The escort fought off both threats and the merchant ships augmented the anti-aircraft barrage, but on 11 April the *Empire Cowper* was bombed and sunk by a Junkers Ju88 of KG30.

On the next day, *U435* (Strelow), having vainly attacked *Punjabi*, succeeded in evading the escorts and torpedoed the Russian ship *Kiev* and the Panamanian *El Occidente*. The *Harpalion* was badly damaged in the air attacks on the 13th and became unmanageable due to the loss of her rudder. She was reluctantly sunk by the gunfire of the escort. Dense fog followed by a westerly gale later that day forced the enemy to withdraw and, although a shadowing aircraft regained contact on the 14th, the Germans were now preparing their assault on PQ14.

QP10, though it lost four ships totalling 24,481 tons, had by its combined efforts succeeded in shooting down six enemy planes and damaging a seventh. It had, moreover, avoided contact with the destroyers from Kirkenes which had put to sea on two occasions in quest of it, but which had been deterred by ice and the weather. The remaining ships, except the *Stone Street* damaged by near misses, arrived at Reykjavik on 21 April.

The tanker *Hopemount*'s cargo was not intended directly for the Russian war effort. Her duty was to relieve the exhausted tanker sent to Vaenga in the autumn of 1941 as fleet supply ship. Her boiler oil was destined for the escorts and she also carried drums of lubricating oil for the British submarines at Polyarnoe as well as a quantity of diesel oil. She was anchored midstream, off Vyelika Point to the west of Vaenga Bay.

The Kola Inlet, and in particular the exposed anchorage of Vaenga Bay, had taken on the aspect of a naval base. Ashore there was little to see beyond a few huts and the interminable pine forest which concealed the dirt runway of the Russian airstrip where a party of British airmen of the Royal Air Force helped prepare and maintain the Hurricane fighters arriving in the merchant ships. But the waters of the bay were filled with activity. Laden merchant ships lay at anchor awaiting berths. Empty ships awaited convoy. The recuperating destroyers, corvettes and trawlers huddled up alongside the cruiser, their mooring ropes straining as they ranged alongside their larger sister in the gales that swept across the grey waters, causing anxiety among the cruiser's officers as they checked their anchor bearings and recalled their captain's cautions about the poor holding ground.

Only the submarines shared the Russian naval facilities at Polyarnoe at this stage of the war, so the Royal Navy was compelled to make the best of a bleak spot. Not only was it building up its facilities in so far as the suspicions, prevarications and obstructions of the Russians would allow, but, as will be seen, the Ministry of War Transport too was preparing specialized ships to help speed up the discharge of the cargoes so gallantly brought 2,000 miles to an unappreciative ally. One of these, the heavy lift ship *Empire Bard*, had been among the ice-damaged casualties of PQ14.

The biggest problem experienced by the British in North Russia at this stage of the war was the lack of hospital facilities for the increasing numbers of injured and the survivors suffering the foul consequences of exposure. As a temporary solution, the arrival of *Edinburgh* was timely, and her sick-bay became busy treating those whom the overstretched and primitive Russian hospitals could not cope with, dealing as they were with their own wounded from the front line no more than twenty-five miles away.

The Kola Inlet was too near the Finnish airfields to allow ships the comfort of a safe haven, though a watch was maintained on the enemy from the hills, and the international code flag 'L' flown from this observation post warned the ships below to prepare for an attack. The anchored merchant ships had been suffering before the arrival of PQ14.

Already, on the night of 3 April 1942, the *New Westminster City* (Captain Harris), belonging to Reardon-Smith's of Cardiff and a veteran of PQ13, had been hit by four bombs. Her discharge was incomplete and the balance of her cargo of ammunition blew up. Another ship of PQ13, Captain Stein's *Empire Starlight*, berthed at Murmansk, was to undergo a series of attacks which gave the impression that she had become the victim of a peculiar vendetta.

Sustaining damage which started some seams, her discharging had resumed on 4 April when one large bomb burst through the deck and another four exploded round the ship. No. 1 hold was damaged and a fire began in No. 2. Six Russian dockers were killed, eight lorries and three Hurricanes were destroyed and another three were damaged. Meanwhile the ship's own armament had joined the anti-aircraft barrage and the Russians confirmed afterwards that the ship had shot down her attacker.

By the following morning, the 5th, the fire was extinguished and the ship's Chinese crew worked manfully to plug leaks and pump out the bilges. The ship now seemed singled out, for more aircraft attacked her, though without success. On the following day the *Empire Starlight* suffered two air raids and took aboard most of the survivors of the *New Westminster City*. The day after that the ship's discharge was completed. Throughout this period she had maintained her own defence, which had proved excellent for the crew's morale.

Further air raids took place on the 8th and on the next day the *Starlight* steamed out and anchored until the 13th when she returned alongside to load a homeward cargo of pit-props and timber. During this time she sustained daily air attacks. While loading, repair parties continued to prepare the vessel for sea but on the evening of 15 April eight bombs straddled the ship, one dropping into the open No. 2 hatch where it burst, fracturing the bilge line and flooding the hold. The forepeak now filled, fractures in the bulkheads finally split and flooding was progressive through into No. 3 hold and then the engine room. The crew, the survivors and Russian divers attempted to save the ship which had become, to those involved, a symbol of their united struggle against a common foe and called from them exertions of heroic optimism. Softwood plugs, tarpaulins, cement boxes, rags and cotton waste were all pressed into use and, with the exception of No. 2 hold, all leaks were brought under control.

On the 14th, while anchored off, the cargo ship *Lancaster Castle* had been badly bombed and later sunk. Her survivors now joined those of the *New Westminster City* aboard the *Empire Starlight*, where the first signs of strain were developing. No more cargo was loaded and the ship was moved upstream to Michakov, where there ensued seven days of peace in which sleep and work became the rhythms of a normal existence again. Renewed attacks were made on the 23rd, the day the SS *Briarwood* scored her second success against the Luftwaffe. The enemy rediscovered the whereabouts of the *Empire Starlight* and attacked once more, but the successful defence combined with the rest to revive an aggressive spirit. Two raids were beaten off next day with more the following morning. Another high-level bombing raid was made at noon, and another in the evening in which three aircraft kept up a 'criss-cross running attack' in an attempt to confuse the air defence.

The sheer number of near misses and straddling bomb bursts now began to take effect. Underwater plates were buckling and the bulkhead between Nos. 4 and 5 holds was rippled. Nevertheless, one Junkers Ju88 was hit and crashed, restoring *Empire Starlight*'s corporate spirit and bringing her 'bag' to three. On the 24th another straddle was experienced, then the ship was left alone until, on 5 May 1942, coinciding with a considerable access of Luftwaffe strength, the attacks resumed.

Further damage was done on the 6th, when four attacks were repelled, but daily raids now gradually wore the ship's company down. By 17 May the pumps were unable to overcome the influx of water in Nos. 1 and 3 holds. Captain Stein moved his ship to a shallow-water anchorage above the little town. His efforts to get further help from the Russians were to no avail, for they were themselves under great pressure, and his own resources were now running out. On the 18th, 19th and 20th the ship was bombed once daily. On the 21st seven raids opened new wounds. Two attacks occurred daily on the 22nd and 23rd. On the 24th five raids succeeded in damaging the shaft tunnel. At 17.00, during the third raid on the 25th, six bombs straddled the ship. With a roar the bulkhead at the after end of No. 1 hold gave way and it filled from the water already in No. 2. The ship settled by the head.

On 26 May the *Empire Starlight* suffered five attacks. At 11.00 bombs increased the leaks forward and caused water to flood No. 3, then at 17.15 a 'sustained and heavy attack was deliberately aimed at the *Empire Starlight*'. She was set upon by six Ju88s, three four-engined and unidentified bombers and three Ju87 Stuka dive-bombers. Anti-aircraft defence was superb and not one bomb hit its target, but the near miss effect of an estimated forty bombs took its toll. The gallant ship began to settle further by the head and the crew were moved ashore. Almost incredibly they returned the following day to resume salvage operations.

The illusion that the enemy might have found better things to do was shattered on 1 June, when a stick of six bombs burst along her port side and the *Empire Starlight* finally gave up the unequal struggle, though the attacking plane was shot down alongside her.

The crew now took off everything movable and finally abandoned her on 16 June. Of her crew and the men who had finally sought refuge aboard her, a total of seventy-seven, only one became a casualty, a Chinese steward, cruelly killed in an air raid while sheltering ashore.

Few ships were subjected to so much punishment. Her company fought off a persistent enemy with great determination, making super-human efforts to save their own vessel while befriending those who had lost theirs. There is something pathetically inadequate in recording the OBEs awarded to Captain Stein and his chief engineer, Mr Morgan, for few can have claimed to have suffered such attrition in order to win them.

Incredibly the *Empire Starlight* was raised after the war, refitted and resumed trading, a testimony to her builders.[7]

Prodigies of a different kind were being performed at Rosta aboard the battered *Trinidad*. Her damage compelled the Russians to co-operate to the extent of offering the dry dock which she entered on 7 April 1942. Gangs of workers, including women 'liberated' by Communism, toiled alongside the ship's company. First, however, it was necessary to bury the dead, and the twelve bodies were placed on the deck of HMS *Niger* and taken to sea, a duty that, for the rest of the war, occupied one or other of the small flotilla of 'little ships' which attended this lonely outpost.

Russian guards patrolled the quayside and naval and marine guards patrolled the ship. The latter were necessary to stop the pilfering of the indigent Russians. On one occasion they were compelled to fire a volley over the heads of a group of workmen making off with stolen stores through the gaping hole in *Trinidad*'s side. The following day a commissar arrived shepherding a group of children and claimed they were the thieves, saying that 'it was most regrettable that the British should have opened fire on small helpless children'. Senseless, provocative and exasperating incidents like this were characteristic of the official Soviet attitude at the time.

Eventually the ship's company laced the cruiser's gash with morsels of food before daily dumping it on the quayside. The Russians made regular calls on this source of supply, but when the ship's damaged refrigerated spaces were emptied of their contents, the Russians made a determined assault on the tainted carcases under cover of night. One old man who was unable to get away with his booty was shot by the Russian guards, as was another who had stolen a jar of jam. This was to become a familiar theme in the everyday life of those who spent long periods in North Russia, and promoted not a few arguments on the messdecks where the virtues of Communism had, for some time, been of interest to many.

Commander Collet, brushing aside a Commissar's apologies for the drunkenness of a Soviet destroyer officer at a wardroom party, said no offence had been taken and asked the officer back on board. 'That is not possible,' replied the Commissar, 'he was shot this morning.'

Parties visited Murmansk where they found the local people friendly and the children importunate in their demands for chocolate and cigarettes. When the generosity of the visitors had been exhausted they were subjected to the abuse all sailors find in the sad and deprived parts of the world.

'Fuck you, Jack,' they were told, clear evidence that 'our minesweeper crews had obviously been here before us'.

Sleigh rides over the snow and skating on the ice formed lighthearted diversions, though several men suffered from snow-blindness, while the joys of extemporizing latrines for 600 men through holes in the river-ice provided opportunities for crude practical jokes. The inoculation of the entire ship's company against typhoid was not such a laughing matter.

Luckiest were the Walrus crew who, with their aircraft and some fuel, were shipped to the seaplane base at Gryaznaya where an attractive interpreter was provided and from where they flew patrols out into the Barents Sea.

More formal hospitality came in the form of a performance of a Red Army choir who sang in the empty hangar to universal approval. Competitive drinking bouts took place and the officers mounted a reciprocal concert-party. This too was to become a familiar pattern in the dreary months ahead.

The repair of the cruiser was a triumph of organization and improvization, though a multitude of problems had to be solved. A power-source was found in a static, dock-side steam engine which was overseen by an ancient crone; the ship was camouflaged with nets, tarpaulins and quantities of snow and cinders, though during air attacks some of her lighter armament opened up. Most importantly, HMS *Edinburgh* had arrived carrying steel plates for *Trinidad* and a naval constructor, Commander Skinner, to supervise repairs. More had been expected in *Edinburgh* than steel plates; mail and fresh food assume great importance to seamen and these had been anticipated, but instead a consignment of attaché cases and boots arrived, a silly blunder which caused bitter disappointment.

The main problem confronting the constructor and the ship's first lieutenant was not the repair of the shell-plating, now solved by the arrival of the sheet steel and a plentiful supply of rivets and native riveters, but the internal stiffening. Despite a quantity of girders lying about the yard, the only solution the Russians could offer was timber, which was plentiful and which was being loaded in the merchant ships as a homeward cargo. It had been noted, though, that there was an apparently redundant system of railway tracks which led out beyond the yard wall. Without seeking approval, two parties of ratings left the ship, one to cause a diversion by dispensing quantities of chocolate to the sentries, the other armed with oxy-acetylene cutting gear. The requisite stiffening was brought aboard at appropriate moments, welded up, then braced with additional timber and cement.

Trinidad finally hauled out of dock and was anchored on 2 May. Rear-Admiral Bonham-Carter rehoisted his flag on the 5th. In the meantime, PQ15 had arrived.

The threat of the *Tirpitz* and the other heavy ships around Trondheim loomed constantly in the First Sea Lord's mind as the days lengthened. His repeated representations to stop the convoys during the summer failed, due largely to the extreme pressure exerted by President Roosevelt and the commitment of American merchant ships. To these was now added a squadron of the United States Navy consisting of the new 16-inch-gun battleship *Washington*, the carrier *Wasp*, the heavy cruisers *Wichita* and *Tuscaloosa*, and six destroyers. These ships, under Rear-Admiral R.C. Giffen, had arrived at Scapa Flow on 3 April and were attached to the British Home Fleet.

Attempts to neutralize the Germans' own heavy ships had not been successful. On the last day of March, thirty-three Halifax bombers of No. 4 Group had set off to bomb the *Tirpitz*, but bad weather had frustrated them, most failed to find their target, and those that did released their bombs to no good effect. Five planes were shot down. A further seven bombers were lost when raids were repeated on 28 and 29 April. The aircraft were met with a ferocious anti-aircraft barrage and the bomb-layers were deceived by an effective smoke-screen.

Pound persistently addressed the problem of increasing the Russian contribution at the narrow funnel of the final approach to Kola, where the convoys steamed due south, skirting the winter ice-edge. Both U-boat concentrations in this locality and air attacks from the adjacent base at Petsamo were proving increasingly costly as the losses to PQ8 and PQ13 testified. Nor was the security of the Kola Inlet and the anchorage at Vaenga satisfactory. Stalin responded to Churchill's request for increased assistance by stating that 'naval and air forces would do their utmost'.

In fact, during the winter of 1941–2, Russian submarine chasers had laid mines off Petsamo, and Russian and British submarines sank enemy shipping off the polar coast in a series of operations designed to frustrate the coastal trade upon which the Germans depended. Several Russian ships were lost and much was made of these actions by Stalin's propaganda machine, but the Kriegsmarine was not prevented from laying their own mine-barrages, nor from concentrating U-boats in the approaches to Kola and the Gourlo, and Soviet air attacks on German airfields in Finland and Norway were not very effective. Though displaying both *élan* and gallantry, neither the Soviet navy nor its air force ever relieved the British Home Fleet of any appreciable share of the responsibility for the defence of an Arctic convoy.[8]

As April turned into May, a significant decision taken by the German High Command increased the difficulties of the British in their role as protector of the Allied convoys. Bonham-Carter's assessment of the German response to the passage of PQ14 was to be borne out with interest. Hitler's anxiety about the effectiveness of the northern supply route to the Red Army led to a meeting with Raeder at which the Führer stressed the importance of torpedo-bombers. Raeder considered the torpedo a naval weapon, but the Kriegsmarine's torpedo-armed Heinkel 115s were slow seaplanes and easily shot down. The Heinkel He111 had shown itself capable of attacking effectively with two torpedoes and the Ju88 was also found to be adaptable to this role. Although the dislike of Goering for Raeder delayed their deployment, the first adapted machines arrived at Bardufoss on 1 May. These reinforcements, together with a greater concentration of U-boats, were therefore in place for the passages of PQ15 and QP11, both of which sailed at the end of April 1942.

9

'It is beginning to ask too much . . .'

THE STATE OF hostilities in the Arctic was inexorably approaching a crisis. Set against the greater battle of supply across the North Atlantic, itself reaching a climactic intensity, it had assumed for the Western Allies a secondary importance. This is an illusion, a distortion of historical perspective, for it remained an absolute necessity for the success of Russian arms, despite the gradually increasing volume of *matériel* flowing through the Persian Gulf. It was to remain so as long as the war lasted and there was to be no wave of final, overwhelming superiority upon which to coast home to victory as there was in the Atlantic.

German surface naval strength was at its height in the form of a potentially formidable fleet-in-being in the fiords; German U-boat activity was sustained in an area where certain natural advantages favoured the predator; German air supremacy was increasingly possible due to the introduction of the aerial torpedo, about to make its début against PQ15; the long summer days favoured the retention of continuous reconnaissance contact with a convoy and the consequent homing of co-ordinated attacks; and the port of Murmansk and the Kola Inlet were themselves highly vulnerable.

To these must be added the negative factors working against the Allies within their own ranks, chief among which was low morale, but which also included the ineffectiveness of certain weapons, the lack of endurance of some of the escorts, the poor facilities in Russia, both material and moral, and the general attitude of the Soviet ally.

In the Allies' favour, however, were factors of less immediately military significance, but which were likely to tip the final balance. These included the might of American support both in the Arctic and elsewhere, relieving pressure on the Royal Navy in particular; the gradual acceptance by the Admiralty that the commitment of escorting Russian convoys was a matter of increasing burden; a gradual and subtle build-up of reception facilities to smooth the entire operation; and acceptance, at least at the local level in North Russia, of a sense of partnership between the Western Allies and the Soviet state. In addition, although the summer days increased the vulnerability of the convoys, they were able to track further north as the ice-edge retreated, and the opening of the White Sea and the port of Archangel enabled sorely tried men to recover their spirits in a modicum of security.

Finally, the negative elements working within the German side included the ever-growing strength of the Red Army; the shortage of fuel oil for capital ships; and Hitler's obsessive unwillingness to risk his surface vessels, which engendered in his sea-going flag-officers a fear of using their initiative.

Over the next four convoys, PQ15 to 18, and their homeward counterparts, the first of two vital series of battles would be fought at the end of which essential lessons were learned. The tragedy was, they were only learned the hard way.

PQ15 departed from Reykjavik on 26 April and consisted of twenty-five ships, including two ice-breakers, under the direction of the splendidly named Captain H.J. Anchor RNR, whose Commodore's pendant flew from the masthead of the SS *Botavon*. Three innovations accompanied this convoy: a submarine, HMS *Sturgeon*, which was to keep company until reaching the longitude of 5°E; a CAM ship, the *Empire Morn*; and an 'anti-aircraft cruiser', stationed in the body of the convoy to augment the anti-aircraft barrage of the merchant ships.

This latter vessel, HMS *Ulster Queen* (Acting Captain C.K. Adam), was a former Irish Sea mail and passenger packet capable of 18 knots, requisitioned and commissioned under the white ensign as a fighting ship, converted for naval use and fitted with six properly directed high-angle 4-inch guns, four twin 2-pounder anti-aircraft guns and ten 20-mm Oerlikons. Several of these extempore but effective warships were to feature in the next few convoys in an attempt to deal with the growing menace of air attack.

Another such measure was the introduction of the CAM ship, the acronym signifying Catapult Aircraft Merchant ship, intended to knock out the long-range Condor or Blohm and Voss flying boat as soon as it appeared. 'There were some bright ideas incorporated in these ships and it is fair to bet that they did not originate in any of the people who had to sail in them.'[1] A multi-rocket powered catapult was fitted over a merchant ship's forecastle upon which an early Mark 1 Hurricane was kept ready. Exposed to spray, these inadequate machines posed little threat to their long-range enemies. The pilots of these planes had a one-way ticket. If they were lucky, they would ditch or bale out, to be recovered by one of the escorts. If not, a sodden man did not survive long in the icy waters of the Barents Sea. 'It is a job for steady nerves,' a war-time publication blandly stated, 'the catapult aircraft fliers take it all as part of their job.'[2]

A second, crated Hurricane was stowed in the ship's hold, to be gingerly mounted when the ship reached her destination and prepared for the homeward run, but other, much later marks of Hurricanes filled the ships' 'tween decks and no little resentment was caused by the use of the redundant and largely useless aircraft when more efficient machines were being sent to the Russians. It might have been a 'quaint substitute' for what was really required, light aircraft-carriers, but although some successes were scored, the desire to harbour the one vital Hurricane often meant it was not used. Such was to be the fate of the machine aboard the *Empire Morn*.

In addition to the *Ulster Queen*, the *Sturgeon* and the CAM ship, the close escort was comprised of four Halcyon-class minesweepers, of which *Bramble* (Captain J.F.H. Crombie) was the senior officer's ship, and four trawlers which accompanied PQ15 from Reykjavik. The destroyers, the Hunt *Badsworth*, the twelve-year-old *Boadicea*, the elderly LRE *Venomous*, *Matchless*, the Tribal *Somali* and the Norwegian *St Albans*, together with Force Q, joined from Seidisfiord on the 29th. Force Q consisted of the fleet oiler *Gray Ranger* which, with the dedicated Hunt-class destroyer *Ledbury*, represented an attempt to provide fuel for the smaller escorts.

The cruisers *Nigeria*, flying the flag of Rear-Admiral Burrough, and *London* joined on the 30th; heavy distant cover for PQ15 and QP11 was provided by the reinforced Home Fleet in the form of Admiral Tovey's flagship, the *King George V*, the carrier

Victorious, HM Cruiser *Kenya* and the US cruisers *Wichita* and *Tuscaloosa*. Rear-Admiral Robert C. Giffen flew his flag in the battleship *Washington* and the screen of ten destroyers included four Americans. This force left Scapa and was at sea by 28 April, heading to cruise to the southward of the outward and homeward convoy routes.

There was a predominance of American ships in the convoy itself, no less than fifteen of them, *Alcoa Cadet*, *Alcoa Rambler*, *Bayou Chico*, *Expositor*, *Lancaster*, *Paul Luckenbach*, *Topa Topa*, *Deer Lodge*, *Hegira*, *Seattle Spirit*, *Texas*, the *Mormacrio* and *Mormacrey* owned by Moore, Macormack, and the Liberty ships *Zebulon B. Vance* and *Francis Scott Key*.[3] Most of the rest were British regulars – *Cape Corso*, *Cape Race*, *Botavon*, *Southgate*, *Empire Morn*, the heavy lift ship *Empire Bard* and *Jutland*. The balance was made up of the Panamanian *Capira*, the Russian ice-breaker *Krassin* and the Canadian ice-breaker *Montcalm* on delivery to her new Russian owners. Several of these ships had set out with PQ14 and been turned back by the weather. Due to the increasing hours of daylight, it had been found necessary to withdraw the British and Allied submarine patrol line 150 miles off the Norwegian coast to avoid its detection from the air. The loss of these 'eyes of the fleet' from their position off Trondheim conferred an advantage to the Germans only partially mitigated by redeploying them in shifting zones, moving north and east according to the progress of the convoys. As a consequence, their ability to conform to the requirements of the staff officers overseeing the plot in the concrete citadel behind the old Admiralty building in Whitehall was limited. Those on patrol at the end of April, in extended order from south to north, were *Unison* (*P43*, British), *Minerve* (Free French), *Uredd* (Norwegian) and *Jastrzab* (*P551*, Polish). *Sturgeon* was to double back and join the southern end of the line after detaching at longitude 5°E.

PQ15 was 250 miles south-west of Bear Island before being seen by a long-range Condor shortly before midnight on 30 April 1942, some hours after the cruisers joined. Low cloud, with snow squalls and showers at sea level, obscured the laden ships and prevented any attacks developing, although several submarine alarms kept the escorts busy investigating and dropping the occasional pattern of depth-charges. Then, in intense cold, at 22.00 on 1 May, six Ju88s suddenly appeared and dropped bombs in a 'ragged and very poorly executed attack'. The leading aircraft had peeled off and made for *London*, whose gunners succeeded in shooting it down ahead of *Nigeria*. The cruiser 'ground it underfoot'. The remaining planes concentrated on one of the trawlers on the starboard wing before being driven off by the 'volume of fire which was put up by the escort and convoy, who were keeping excellent station.'[4]

This minor triumph had been offset earlier on this May Day by a tragedy which had occurred 350 miles east of Iceland. While with other destroyers providing a screen to Tovey's capital ships, the Tribal-class destroyer *Punjabi* (Commander the Hon. J.M. Waldegrave) ran under the bow of the flagship and was cut in two. The unfortunate accident took place as the combined Anglo-American battle-fleet ran into fog. *King George V* signalled all ships to cease zigzagging forthwith, but this was not received aboard *Punjabi* in time. The sad incident was compounded when the destroyer's fused depth-charges exploded as her stern quickly sank, increasing the damage inflicted to the *King George V*'s bow and killing many of *Punjabi*'s crew. The destroyer's forward section remained afloat for forty minutes, sufficient time for 206 men to be rescued.

Vice-Admiral Curteis arrived from Hvalfiordur in HMS *Duke of York* the following day and Tovey shifted his flag into her, while the *King George V* returned first to Scapa and then to Liverpool for a refit. Curteis returned to Scapa to HMS *Nelson*. It was an inauspicious start for the Royal Navy, which was to suffer grievously in the coming days.

Later on 1 May, Force Q had detached ready to rendezvous and refuel the homeward escort of QP11, which was already on its way west and had been heavily engaged by the enemy. *Sturgeon* had also detached to join the submarine patrol line off the Norwegian coast and at midnight *London* turned away to the west, followed ten hours later by *Nigeria*. Both cruisers then reunited and awaited QP11 in conformity with Admiralty orders that they were not to proceed beyond Bear Island, where the risk of U-boat attack was high. The departure of such formidable ships from the support of PQ15 might have been based on sound principles, but it conveyed a simple message to the polyglot community manning the merchant ships. In the absence of any proper briefing, their sense of exposure was acute, though it was shared equally with the naval seamen aboard the smaller warships of the close escort.

This stand-off by the cruisers was somewhat unnecessary for

by 10.00 on the 2nd QP11 was in sight, coming down from the east-north-east where it had tangled with the ice as well as the enemy. Captain Crombie ordered *Somali* ahead to intercept and she returned, having gleaned by signal lamp from the approaching escorts of QP11 the dismal intelligence of the proximity of ice, U-boats and enemy destroyers and, perhaps worst of all, the appearance of torpedo-bombers.

It was only a matter of minutes before PQ15 felt the omnipresent malice of the enemy. 'The feeling of being shadowed with such efficiency is uncomfortable,' Crombie reported. From then on, until the ice turned them south and a gale blew up to obscure them again, the ships of PQ15 were under constant observation.

Further tragedy occurred later that evening when the Halcyon-class minesweeper *Seagull* (Lieutenant-Commander Pollock) and the Norwegian destroyer *St Albans* (Commander S.V. Storeheil) launched a depth-charge assault on an asdic contact which breached and revealed itself to be not a U-boat but the Polish submarine *Jastrzab*, otherwise *P551*.

Built as *S25* for the United States Navy in 1922, she had been taken over by her Polish crew at the New London Navy Yard in Connecticut in November 1941 and, under the command of Lieutenant-Commander Romanowski, commissioned under the red and white ensign of Poland. After crossing the Atlantic for an expensive refit at Blyth, the *Jastrzab* sailed from her base in Holy Loch on 22 April 1942. With her she took a British naval liaison officer and two signals ratings. Stopping briefly at Lerwick, she proceeded in concert with other submarines for her patrol area 180 miles north-west of Altenfiord. Romanowski was an experienced navigator, who had specialized in the subject and served as navigation officer aboard the Polish submarine *Wilk*, brought from the Baltic to Scapa Flow after the occupation of Poland. The morale of his men was high, a feature shared by all Polish warships operating with the Royal Navy and a circumstance which made the subsequent tragedy the more poignant.

For a week of bad weather the *Jastrzab* thrashed about her patrol area. Sighting an aircraft one afternoon Romanowski dived, only to find his forward hydroplanes had jammed; the elderly submarine ran deep before control could be regained, but the aircraft proved friendly and the submarine later learned she was leaking oil from a bunker tank. Then, at 16.00 on 2 May, while at periscope depth investigating engine noises on the hydrophones, Romanowski spotted a U-boat running on the surface and prepared to make an attack, but again problems of trim cost him the opportunity and he reverted his boat to normal cruising routine until the next alert, three hours later.

The reasons why the Polish submarine encountered units of the escort of PQ15 are somewhat confused. The subsequent enquiry thought *Jastrzab* was as much as 100 miles from her patrol area, though PQ15 had altered course to the southwards at 09.45 that morning to avoid the ice met by QP11 and athwart the convoy's intended track, a course held until the sinking of the *Jastrzab*.

At about 19.45 it was snowing and Romanowski, having detected warships approaching, was able to see them. After studying them for a few moments and consulting the ship recognition book, he announced they were friendly, but altered course and ordered the release of recognition flares to avoid being attacked. The flares broke from the casing and surfaced to release smoke signals.

These were not seen on either the *St Albans* or the *Seagull* and there followed a chaotic few moments as the destroyer and minesweeper made a determined depth-charge attack, the consequences of which were serious. The main circuits were blown and the submarine again lost trim. Seams burst and water was soon pouring into the pressure hull, contaminating the batteries and releasing chlorine: Romanowski blew his tanks and surfaced between his two tormentors.

To the men of the *St Albans* and the *Seagull* 'any submarine was an enemy'. As the *Jastrzab* broke the surface she appeared to be heading towards the Norwegian destroyer and thus her identifying pendant numbers, *P551*, were invisible. However, her torpedo tubes were also laid upon the Norwegian ship and a shot from a secondary 2.7-inch gun was fired at her as Romanowski, seconded by his British liaison officer and signalmen and the duty watch, scrambled up on to the conning tower, whereupon fire was also opened by machine guns from the bridges of both ships. Five people, including the two British ratings, were killed outright and six others, including Romanowski and his liaison officer, were wounded before it was realized aboard *Seagull* that an unfortunate error had occurred. This had been realized aboard *St Albans* and both ships ceased fire and launched boats.

'Thankfully, there were no hard words or feelings afterwards, our own surviving crew clamouring already for a new submarine the minute they climbed on board the *Seagull* . . . and before recovering from the shock of losing the old one,' a crew member recalled. Romanowski, though hit by five bullets, brought his confidential code-books off with him. His ship was sunk by *Seagull*'s 4-inch gun as there was no hope of saving her. The survivors were later transferred to the cruiser *London*.

The enquiry subsequently held aboard the depot ship *Forth* exonerated the commanding officers of all three ships. That the *Jastrzab* was off station merely illustrates the extreme difficulties of navigating in the Arctic, and the whole episode the grim uncertainty of war.[5]

Following this sad and demoralizing event the twilit gloom of the Arctic night closed over the convoy as it headed due east. A cold low mist came and went so that four miles' visibility would close abruptly to less than half, and a sense of desolation gripped the imaginations of the individual men as they tried to keep warm, huddled at their cruising stations or maintaining a lookout. Experience had taught the navy that men could not perform this duty for longer than an hour. The cold, the shifting mist, snow and half-light played tricks on their streaming eyes and it was not unusual for a mesmeric catalepsy to affect lookouts on duty for a longer period, while more serious ophthalmic conditions could also develop.

Radar was supposed not merely to compensate for this physiological human weakness, but also to penetrate fog and snow, and thus extend the range of the outer defences of a convoy, but an hour and a half into 3 May 1942, it too proved fallible, for in a low-level attack approaching echoes were masked by the 'sea-clutter' produced by wave crests in the vicinity of the transmitting ship.[6] The convoy was then in latitude 73°00'N, longitude 019°40'E.

Six enemy aircraft of I Coastal Group 26 approached at wave-top height, sweeping in low on the convoy's advanced right flank. Alarms jangled and men ran to their action stations while those men already on duty furiously laid their weapons as quickly as they could.

The Heinkel He111s were met with a ferocious fire, all the more effective for its late eruption. Three were hit, two being blown out of the sky, the third crashing later, but torpedoes struck Commodore Anchor's *Botavon*, the *Jutland* and the *Cape Corso*. These three British merchantmen quickly sank at a loss of 15,800 registered tons of shipping, though the escorts picked up 137 survivors.

After this action the convoy continued to lumber east. Frequent U-boat sightings and asdic contacts were made but the dash and energy of the escorts, though none succeeded to the extent of sinking a U-boat, deterred the Germans from pressing home an attack. A further bombing raid was made at 22.30, when the convoy, still running along the 73rd parallel, had reached 031°15'E. Junkers Ju88s dropped several bombs, one of which scored a near miss and slightly damaged the trawler *Cape Palliser*, at the cost of one of their number shot down.

The U-boat alarms continued until the evening of 4 May when a south-easterly gale blew up off the Russian mainland, filling the air with snow clouds and concealing the convoy which entered the Kola Inlet under its cover on the evening of 5 May 1942.

If the comparative lack of enemy interest in the laden PQ15 surprised Rear-Admiral Burrough to the extent of his commenting on it, this is explained by their concentration on QP11 and its aftermath, which was a notable German triumph. It is therefore necessary to trace the movements of QP11's thirteen ships, which had left Kola on 28 April 1942.

Once again the Master of the SS *Briarwood*, Captain W.H. Lawrence, acted as Commodore. Commander M. Richmond in the 1930-vintage *Bulldog* was senior officer of the close escort of the equally elderly fleet destroyer *Beagle*, the even older *Amazon* (1926), the newer *Forester* and *Foresight*, and the Town-class ex-American 'four-stacker' *Beverley*. In addition, there were four corvettes (HMS *Oxlip*, *Campanula*, *Snowflake* and *Saxifrage*) and the anti-submarine trawler *Lord Middleton*.

For the first day the usual added support of the locally based minesweepers *Harrier*, *Hussar*, *Niger* and *Gossamer* was available and the Russian destroyers *Sokrushitelni* and *Gremyashchi* were to prove a valuable asset as they accompanied QP11 to the 30th meridian. Finally Rear-Admiral Bonham-Carter, back aboard *Edinburgh*, provided close cover.

Prior to departure the usual convoy conference had assembled. The masters of the *Athel Templar*, *Ballot*, *Dan-y-Bryn*, *Dunboyne*, *Trehata* (British), *Eldena*, *El Estero*, *Gallant Fox*, *Mormacmar*, *West Cheswald* (American), *Stone Street* (Panamanian) and *Tsiolkovsky* (Russian) had been briefed by Lawrence and Richmond; it had been decided that in the event of a surface attack, the corvettes would stay with the convoy as it turned away from the threat, while the destroyers would interpose themselves between the enemy and the convoy.

But at Kirkenes, 'Admiral Arctic', Konteradmiral Schmundt, decided against risking his own destroyers and sent out the seven U-boats of the Strauchritter group. A German reconnaissance plane located the convoy on the 29th, after the local Russian air cover had prematurely vanished.

At 04.30 on 30th, British 'Huff-Duff' radio intercepts in the convoy reported submarine homing signals from *U88*, which was shadowing QP11 and appears to have been the U-boat sighted on the surface astern at 07.30. She was forced by the escorts to dive and made one unsuccessful torpedo attack. Another U-boat seen on the surface ahead compelled an alteration of course and the day was filled with asdic alarms and the crump of depth-charge attacks on the periphery of the convoy which, if they did not hit any U-boats, again kept them at bay. At 17.30 the minesweepers put about for Kola.[7]

Meanwhile Bonham-Carter, alarmed at the extent of U-boat activity round the convoy, had decided to adopt 'night stations' and ordered Captain Faulkner to take *Edinburgh* fifteen miles ahead of the convoy. The unscreened cruiser increased speed to 19 knots and drew ahead, relying on her speed to keep her out of trouble.

Alas, both Kapitänleutnant Seibicke's *U436* and Kapitänleutnant Teichert's *U456* were lying in wait for QP11 on the 73rd parallel in longitude 033°E. Seibicke's salvo of four torpedoes missed *Edinburgh*, but at 16.15 two from *U456*, attacking from her starboard side, struck the cruiser. One entered the forward boiler room, causing extensive flooding; the other hit aft with such devastating effect that it blew the cruiser's stern off, destroyed her rudder, rendered her two inner propeller shafts useless, and folded the quarterdeck back over Y-turret like an opened sardine can.

The duty asdic operator had obtained a response minutes before the attack, but allegedly was told to disregard it by his superiors; the off-duty men had just been piped to tea. Now breached bunker tanks and sea-water were flooding into the ship causing her to slow, list and sink by the head. As men died in the riven hull, Teichert could only watch through his periscope, for he had no more torpedoes to administer the *coup de grâce*, while under her outer screws the battered cruiser attempted to turn and make for Murmansk.

A huge column of white water rising into the air followed by a cloud of black smoke was seen from QP11, preceding the signal confirming that *Edinburgh* had been torpedoed. *Foresight* (Commander J.S. Salter), *Forester* (Lieutenant-Commander G. Huddart) and the two Russian destroyers were detached to assist.

Thus deterred from further interference and short of torpedoes, the two U-boats shadowed and reported the extent of their success, tempting Schmundt to intervene. The Kriegsmarine's stocks of fuel oil were minimal. Consequently an order had been given suspending operations, 'including those by light forces'. However, 'the sole exceptions . . . made necessary by enemy action' gave Schmundt the excuse he needed.

The order might have read 'enemy misfortune'; Schmundt contacted Navy Group North and was permitted to send out Kapitän Schulze-Hinrichs with the *Hermann Schoemann* (Wittig), *Z24* (Salzwedel) and *Z25* (Peters). These ships left Kirkenes at 01.00 on 1 May 1942 and headed north-north-west.

QP11, which had already turned west, parallel with the distant ice-edge, was within 150 miles of Bear Island at 05.40 on 1 May. As the pale, twilit and freezing night turned imperceptibly to daylight, six Ju88s flew in from the south. *Snowflake* turned towards the aircraft and engaged them with her 4-inch, two Lewis guns and her 'Chicago piano', and many of the other ships also opened fire. The attack was unsuccessful, but it did mark what was believed to be the first aerial torpedo attack made against an Arctic convoy, albeit the release of the torpedoes was premature. While this was in progress the Huff-Duff intercepts continued and *Amazon* (Lieutenant-Commander Roper) turned to force a surfaced U-boat to dive.[8]

Steaming at about 8 knots, at 07.15 the convoy made a turn to port to avoid a submarine,and then at 08.40 another to the north-west, which brought the ships into the immediate proximity of the ice. A bitingly cold northerly breeze blew towards them over the floes, bringing snow showers and visibility varying from two to ten miles. The presence of U-boats filled everyone's consciousness and the escort kept closed up, leaving no gaps in the screen for the watching enemy to exploit.

Suddenly, at 13.45, *Snowflake* (Lieutenant-Commander H.G. Chesterman RNR) reported her radar showing three hard echoes to the southward. Then *Beverley* (Commander R.A. Price), screening the advanced left flank, reported the enemy destroyers in sight to the south-west. Immediately Commander Richmond implemented the plan agreed at the conference, ordering the destroyers to form on *Bulldog* and make smoke. The convoy turned away 40 degrees to starboard, the merchant ships releasing smoke floats with the corvettes and trawler closing ranks around them and also making smoke which hung low over the sea in the cold air and was most effective. At about 14.00, as the destroyers drew away astern of *Bulldog*, a submarine was sighted from the convoy and QP11 made a further turn to starboard, an order difficult to execute because of the pall of smoke surrounding the extending line of ships. QP11 then continued to edge into the ice to avoid the falling shot of a series of brief actions to the southward.

Richmond's ships had by now formed line in the order *Bulldog, Beagle, Amazon* and *Beverley*. The enemy destroyers were 5½ miles away, heading for the convoy and swinging to starboard as the British swung to port to open up all their gun arcs. Both sides opened fire at 14.07 and loosed torpedoes, none of which hit immediately; then, after only three minutes, the much heavier armed Germans turned away.[9]

The British fell back on the convoy, which was now working through the drift ice and still suffering U-boat alarms, none of which matured due to the ice and smoke, the presence of the corvettes and the stalwart manœuvring of the merchantmen. The destroyers were still making smoke and *Amazon* had suffered damage to her telegraphs and steering gear, though she remained under emergency control. Sadly, either one of the torpedoes from the German destroyers or a U-boat caught the straggling Russian freighter *Tsiolkovsky*, which had fallen behind the main body. She sank rapidly, but the trawler *Lord Middleton* was sent back for survivors.[10]

Having perhaps taken the measure of theoretically weaker opponents, Schulze-Hinrichs, who had been in command of the aborted sorties against PQ14, now turned and launched a second attack from the south-south-east. Richmond again swung towards them, having detected the renewed threat at 8½ miles. Shortening the range by two miles, both sides re-engaged at 14.40. This second engagement lasted for five minutes before Schulze-Hinrichs again withdrew and the British fell back towards QP11 where Captain Lawrence had received reports of two submarines waiting for the convoy to emerge from the disruptive and dubious cover of the ice.

Richmond was now confronted with what he called 'a nice problem' – how to retain touch with the extended convoy in the ice-leads and yet maintain a degree of freedom to manœuvre, for he could not believe the Germans had given up, suspecting them of wanting a piecemeal destruction of the destroyer screen having first broken its unity. In this he proved correct: the enemy reappeared at 16.00 at a distance of six miles, coming up from the east-south-east.

Fire was immediately exchanged as Richmond again confronted the German ships. Though straddled and suffering splinter damage, *Bulldog* and her consorts thwarted their opponents who, after ten minutes, made off to the southward under smoke.

QP11 was now spread out over seven miles, the ships making their individual way through the ice, a vulnerable target if the British destroyer screen could be outwitted.

Half an hour after disappearing under their own smoke, the corvette *Snowflake* reported the Germans at twelve miles to the south-east on radar. Richmond repeated his tactics. Fire was opened at 16.58 and after seven minutes, neither side having scored hits, Schulze-Hinrichs again withdrew under smoke. His ammunition was now seriously depleted and he had yet to carry out his orders and attack the wounded *Edinburgh*.

At about 17.40 a fifth and final attack was made and aborted. No hits were scored, but some near misses occurred. It was all over in six minutes. Then, under full helm, the German destroyers drew away. This time Richmond pugnaciously pursued them until the hindmost German destroyer vanished in the smoke bank and they made off eastwards. Commander Richmond remained expectantly south and east of the convoy as it banged its way clear of the ice, wondering if he had finally seen the last of the enemy. After three hours he decided he had, and rejoined the convoy as the last of its ships, much to Captain Lawrence's relief, finally extricated themselves from the floes. The reappearance of the British destroyers close to QP11 deterred the two shadowing U-boats from making attacks and by 22.00 the convoy had reformed in good order and was making west at 8½ knots, with the *Amazon* under emergency steering.

Next morning, 2 May, the destroyers attacked an asdic contact, but the claimed 'kill' went unconfirmed. Later a single aircraft made a torpedo attack which failed, following which it circled the convoy. As we have seen, between 10.00 and noon QP11 passed PQ15. Submarine attacks took place on either side of the convoys, but the activity of the escorts again paid off. Later a Heinkel He115 torpedo-carrying seaplane circled QP11 but stood off.

During the forenoon of the 3rd, *Amazon* and *Beverley* detached to refuel and land their wounded, *London* and *Nigeria* were seen to the north, and the remaining destroyers shelled some floating mines. On the 4th a Walrus was sighted. Friendly aircraft were now overhead as the various escorts departed for fuel and at 07.00 on 7 May the last escorts detached for Hvalfiordur and QP11 finally arrived for dispersal at Reykjavik.[11]

Richmond's defence of QP11 is the more remarkable when it is remembered that his force was deprived of the *Foresight* and *Forester* which, with the two Russian destroyers *Gremyashchi* and *Sokrushitelni* following, had gone to the assistance of *Edinburgh* on 30 April.

Teichert's torpedoes had mortally wounded the cruiser. Within her twisted hull the loss of power in the damaged areas plunged everything into darkness as terrified men fought to escape. Watching as *Edinburgh*, recovering slowly from her shock, began her long and ultimately futile struggle to survive, Teichert's satisfaction was tempered only by the knowledge that, had he had at his disposal a further torpedo and an undamaged periscope, he could have finished off his immobilized victim there and then.

Those of the *Edinburgh*'s company who escaped the appalling chaos below now began to assemble on deck where they met Captain Faulkner, coming down from the bridge to survey the damage. 'The Admiral', he said almost abruptly, 'accepts full responsibility.'[12]

Faulkner was now confronted with the problem of saving his ship. Having received his officers' reports and seen things for himself, he and Rear-Admiral Bonham-Carter conferred. There was an additional factor confronting the two men: *Edinburgh* had secured in one of her magazines five tons of Russian bullion, destined for the United States Treasury in part payment for the *matériel* and munitions coming from America. The gold had been loaded at Vaenga from a heavily guarded lighter in the presence of Soviet soldiers and their own marines, which soon put paid to the pretence that the heavy boxes contained ammunition. Crudely stencilled water-painted marks on the boxes were washed off by the sleet falling at the time, dripping red splotches on the slush-covered decks.

'It's going to be a bad trip, Sir,' one labouring rating remarked to an officer, 'this is Russian gold, dripping with blood.'

Something of the accuracy of this lugubrious prophecy must now have struck the shocked company of the cruiser, compounding the bleak task upon which they found themselves in these inhospitable northern waters. Numbed with cold and the extremity of their grim circumstances, learning of the loss of mess-mates and with the cries of the trapped and dying still ringing in their ears, it took a few minutes for order and discipline to reassert themselves, by which time both Admiral and Captain had resolved to save the ship. The convoy was informed of their plight and the four destroyers sent to screen them.

After disaster, only activity can rekindle hope, and in the coming hours *Edinburgh* and her consorts were to be supra-active. Once the watertight doors were shut, it was found possible to steam on the two outer shafts at 8 knots. With 250 miles to go to safety this was encouraging. Steering a course, however, was another matter. With her waterlogged bow seven feet deeper than normal, tons of water washing in and out of the gashed hull and no rudder, the ship was unmanageable.

Conditions on the upper deck were appalling. The ship was listing and was covered with ice, and her after end was a shambles. Nevertheless, it was decided to attempt a tow, an evolution frequently practised in ideal conditions. With great skill Lieutenant-Commander Huddart brought *Forester* in under the cruiser's bow and a line was passed, followed by a heavier towing hawser. The encrustations of ice, however, prevented the slithering men on *Edinburgh* from detaching one of the cruiser's anchors from its cable to add the dead weight of a chain catenary to the tow, so essential to the success of such an operation. As the dead weight of the cruiser gathered way, she turned up into the wind, sheered across the destroyer's stern and parted the wire which whipped back viciously over the decks of both ships. Three further attempts were made but with the same result.

The task was suspended while the destroyers carried out an attack on a U-boat seen on the surface four miles away, and then Commander Salter brought *Foresight* alongside *Edinburgh*'s quarter and passed a line through the destroyer's bull-ring. Acting as a drogue, the *Foresight* was able to keep the flagship on a rough course and the beleaguered squadron proceeded south-eastwards at about 3 knots during the twilit hours of the Arctic night.

At 06.00 on the morning of 1 May 1942 the Russian destroyers *Gremyashchi* and *Sokrushitelni* reported that they were short of fuel and detached. Bonham-Carter, well aware of the presence of a growing number of U-boats encircling his ships, ordered Salter to cast off the tow and join her sister ship in maintaining a screen. Captain Faulkner now had the unenviable task of attempting to steer with the two remaining propellers, a task much theorized about but rarely tried. The cruiser's list and a steady north-north-easterly breeze on her port beam induced a persistent swing to port which it was necessary to counter by frequently going astern, so that any forward progress was maddeningly slow. *Edinburgh*'s 'tortuous track could be seen winding astern, indicated by the [leaking] oil, and occasionally the ship got completely out of control and swept round in a complete circle'.

Despite the difficulties and exposure, the vigorous activity of *Foresight* and *Forester* kept *Edinburgh* immune from attack by enemy submarines for almost a day until Commander Richmond's reports of his own assault by German destroyers were received, at which Bonham-Carter instructed his destroyers to 'take every opportunity to defeat the enemy without taking undue risks to themselves'. This humane order left the hands of the destroyer commanders free, relying upon that unique blend of fighting spirit and common sense which characterized and imbued the Royal Navy's officer corps and was capable of making an often remarkable best of any situation. It demonstrates the degree of confidence existing between these men, faced as they were with a situation of mounting desperation. Bonham-Carter was thinking of the men aboard the cruiser. As for his flagship, he had few illusions: '*Edinburgh* is to proceed wherever the wind permits, probably straight into the wind.'

This spirit of mutual support was evidenced elsewhere. Admiral Bevan, learning of the *Edinburgh*'s plight, had not been idle. At 18.00 that evening, amid swirling snow squalls, with the visibility varying between two and ten miles, the Russian patrol vessel *Rubin* arrived on the scene to be joined at about midnight by a Russian tug and minesweepers from the Kola-based flotilla.[13]

With the tug secured forward and HMS *Gossamer* aft on the port quarter, *Edinburgh* limped south-south-eastwards trailing her oil slick, her anti-submarine screen augmented by the *Harrier* and

Hussar. Above her a cloud of smoke dispersed in the breeze. Spirits began to rise aboard the cruiser as the prospects of success seemed within grasp. The sight of other ships and the appearance of their ally and the coming day infused an air of optimism which spurred her company to greater efforts. But then further reinforcements in the form of the refuelled Russian destroyers failed to materialize and at 06.30 the *Hussar* caught sight of unidentified ships approaching through the snow and opened up with her 4-inch gun. Fire was returned immediately, straddling the tiny sweeper, which fell back towards *Edinburgh*.

Kapitän Schulze-Hinrichs and his three destroyers had finally found their quarry.

The *Hermann Schoemann*, *Z24* and *Z25* had steamed east during the night, intending to attack *Edinburgh* from the north, and therefore upwind, using the snow to cover their approach. In extended line abreast Schulze-Hinrichs would give his ships room to swing and deliver a near simultaneous torpedo attack before retiring into the snow showers and mist. Preparations were made for a long-range attack as the destroyers took up their stations. At 06.00 on 2 May they ran into a large patch of oil. A quarter of an hour later the most westerly destroyer, *Z25*, reported a vessel ahead. Schulze-Hinrichs made a small alteration of course but within twelve minutes the advantage of surprise had been lost and the minesweeper *Hussar*, stationed to the north of *Edinburgh*, had opened fire. Immediately *Harrier*, leading, and *Foresight* and *Forester*, on the cruiser's port and starboard bows respectively, swung round, the destroyers working up to full speed as they headed for the gunflashes.

The German ships were also turning, ready to fire torpedoes, but a snow shower obscured *Edinburgh* from *Z24* and *Z25*, frustrating Salzwedel and Peters. Korvettenkapitän Wittig's *Hermann Schoemann* broke out of the snow, her torpedo crews frantically resetting their mountings to short range, swinging the tubes in the direction of the heavily listing and disabled British cruiser as the destroyer's deck canted under full helm. Suddenly the supine appearance of their target was transformed by the flash, smoke and thunder of her main armament. The shells splashed into the sea astern of the *Schoemann*.

Bonham-Carter ordered the tow cast off the minute the alarm was raised and Faulkner called for full speed. *Edinburgh* went into a series of random and unpredictable circlings, making her difficult to attack, but equally hampering the efforts of B-turret to engage the enemy. She was to turn three times in the next forty minutes, but her second salvo hit the *Hermann Schoemann* with devastating effect, almost stopping the enemy ship dead as the engines and electrical supply were destroyed. It was to Heinrich Wittig 'the worst luck that could possibly have overtaken us'. In self-defence Wittig ordered smoke made. His ship's plight now conditioned the conduct of her consorts.[14]

Meanwhile, *Gossamer* and *Harrier* closed on *Hussar* and *Edinburgh*, 'like young terriers going in and firing when they could', their asdics maintaining their vigil against the enemy below. *Foresight* was in advance of *Forester* and, as *Edinburgh* opened fire, she caught sight of a German destroyer emerging from the snow to the north-east. The British destroyer opened fire. Her target was *Z24* and, as the range closed, Salter swung to the east to open his after gun arcs, describing the enemy as 'playing hide and seek in the snow and their own smoke-screens'. At between 3½ and 4 miles the two British destroyers fired at anything that offered.

Huddart had taken *Forester* more directly towards the glow of gunfire and the dark silhouettes of the enemy flitting in and out of the mist and swirling snow. At 06.50, as Salter was aborting his run to the east and turning back towards the *Edinburgh*, *Forester* swung to launch torpedoes. The weapons had hardly left their tubes with a hiss of compressed air, when the destroyer staggered under the effects of three 5.9-inch shell-hits. The breech was blown off X-gun; No. 1 boiler room, the bridge and B-gun were devastated; and Huddart was among those killed instantly. *Forester* continued to swing to starboard as she lost speed and her dazed company sought to regain control of their ship, fight the fires blazing amidships and assess the extent of the damage. Torpedoes were seen to pass under the ship, fired by *Z24*.

Foresight was now steaming west and the men on her bridge could see their chummy ship listing and on fire. With her remaining A-gun *Forester* was still firing at the equally immobilized *Hermann Schoemann* three miles to the northward, and engaging the others when they made an appearance. Aboard the German destroyer three guns were operational, all laid by hand, and the torpedo officer, Leutnant Hans Temming, was endeavouring to unjam his torpedo tubes. But stopped and incapable of further manœuvre,

Wittig gave orders to destroy secret documents and prepare to blow up the ship while Schulze-Hinrichs, having an emergency short-wave transmitter to hand, passed orders to Salzwedel and Peters. *Z24* and *Z25* turned to interpose themselves between the *Hermann Schoemann* and the enemy, and make smoke. It was shells from *Z25* which had hit *Forester* and she now fired torpedoes at *Edinburgh*, lying beyond the two destroyers.

Meanwhile, to the northward Salter, seeing *Foresight* persistently straddled, steamed west to draw the enemy's fire, an action which greatly heartened *Forester*'s crew, now under the command of Lieutenant Bitmead and fighting to get their destroyer moving again. Having passed between *Forester* and the enemy, Salter turned *Foresight* through 180 degrees and loosed a salvo of torpedoes at the *Hermann Schoemann*, none of which hit. *Foresight* now received the concentrated fire of *Z24* and *Z25*. Increasing speed, she was struck by four shells, one of which knocked No. 3 boiler out of action and, 'in a welter of steam and smoke with only one gun still in action', brought her to a stop.

Z24 was manoeuvring to get alongside the *Schoemann* and take off her crew. In the prevailing sea conditions and with shells from *Edinburgh* further hampering Salzwedel, this proved difficult and several attempts were made before, at 08.15, the two ships came together and most of the sinking destroyer's crew, including the wounded, were taken off. Others had got away on rafts or by boat and, having fitted depth-charges to demolish the ship, the last officers abandoned her. At 08.30 the *Hermann Schoemann* raised her bow into the air in a parody of the Nazi salute and disappeared beneath the sea. The men on the rafts and in the boat cheered.[15]

By this time, however, the Germans had, quite unknowingly, scored their desired success. The torpedoes fired from *Z25*, though they had frequently broken surface on their long run and had been seen from the bridge of the 'eccentrically gyrating' cruiser, struck *Edinburgh* on the port side almost opposite the first wound. It was 07.02. She was now open from side to side and might break in two at any moment. Gradually she lost way, first righting herself and then listing to port. Soon her guns could no longer be laid on the enemy. Bonham-Carter had already ordered *Gossamer* alongside to remove the wounded and the passengers, who were largely Merchant Navy personnel, survivors of vessels sunk on passage to Russia. He now ordered Faulkner to abandon ship.

Having disabled the two destroyers and given *Edinburgh*

her death wound, the tactical advantage now passed to the Germans. They failed to seize it due in part to their complete ignorance of the torpedo strike on the cruiser, but also because of their preoccupation with the sinking of the *Hermann Schoemann*. In fact it was not until Teichert's *U456* returned to base that the Germans became aware of the final sinking of *Edinburgh*. Teichert had taken his boat close to the British cruiser, but deep enough to be out of harm's way. The detonation of *Z25*'s torpedo was heard at 07.02 and then at 08.52 the sounds of a large ship sinking, 'so near that we were frightened she would fall on top of us'. Later Teichert surfaced amid a large oil slick upon which the pith helmets of the cruiser's marine band were discovered.

Although neither *Z24* nor *Z25* pressed an attack against the stationary fleet destroyers, they continued to fire at them as the constantly moving snow showers opened the visibility. The engine-room and boiler-room staff of *Forester* had succeeded in getting steam to her turbines again and at 07.35 she was once more under command. The enemy were now concentrating on *Foresight*. Bitmead, Huddart's successor, worked to the north sufficiently to lay a smoke-screen to protect *Foresight* and the action was broken off. *Z24* and *Z25*, which had been hit in the radio room, having taken off 200 survivors from the *Hermann Schoemann*, withdrew at speed to the north-westwards at 08.20. The sixty men left in rafts and boats were rescued in the early afternoon by Heino Bohmann's *U88*, which had been given their position by Schulze-Hinrichs breaking radio silence on the U-boat frequency.

Edinburgh had finally been abandoned at 08.00. A quarter of an hour later temporary repairs had been effected to *Foresight* and she was under way on her port screw. Rear-Admiral Bonham-Carter, having hoisted his flag aboard *Harrier*, was concerned about the reappearance of the enemy and the slow settling of *Edinburgh*. He had nearly 450 of her men aboard *Gossamer* and about 350 with him aboard *Harrier*, which had attempted to hasten the cruiser's end with her own gunfire and depth-charges but to little effect. The Admiral now ordered Salter to sink the cruiser with his one remaining torpedo and she too slid beneath the Barents Sea to join the *Hermann Schoemann* and to lie there until a later generation could leave her gold undisturbed no longer.

Out of a complement of 760, 57 officers and men had been lost and 23 wounded. That the minesweepers had been able to evacuate so many was due to the quietening of the sea between squalls. The two destroyers had, between them, lost 21 killed and 20 wounded of their ships' companies. Aboard *Foresight* three men from the merchantman *Lancaster Castle* were wounded and the Master, Captain Sloan, was killed.

The laden sweepers, with the *Rubin* and the damaged *Foresight* and *Forester*, now set course for the Kola Inlet. To Bonham-Carter's surprise they arrived unmolested, for he had thought that a bolder enemy would have completely destroyed his force, though the loss of the *Edinburgh* was bad enough. There is some evidence to suggest Schulze-Hinrichs and his officers believed the Halcyon-class minesweepers were destroyers, an understandable mistake given the weather conditions and the boldness of their handling. At 10.20 HMS *Niger*, which had been detached in the night to locate and bring in the refuelled Russian *Gremyashchi* and *Sokrushitelni*, rejoined.

The Russian destroyers did not sail until long after expected and failed to make the rendezvous. Had they been on the scene during the action, there is little doubt that Schulze-Hinrichs could have been driven off and that the *Edinburgh* would have stood a good chance of surviving, at least to reach Vaenga and follow *Trinidad* into the dry dock at Rosta.

The Russians had nevertheless sustained their own losses during this period. Two of the Northern Fleet's submarines, *D2* and *K3*, had attacked German coastal convoys off Kirkenes without success. Then, on 12 May, *K23*, commanded by Kapitan 3 Ranga Potapov but with Kapitan 2 Ranga Gadzhiev on board, was detected by a group of German patrol boats and submarine chasers when approaching a small convoy off the polar coast. Attempting to get away on the surface, *K23* was forced to dive when an aircraft appeared overhead, whereupon the submarine chasers closed on her and, in a group attack, sank her with depth-charges.

More fortunate, *S101* (Kapitan 3 Ranga Vekke) endured a twenty-two-hour attack on 25 May and, though severely damaged, escaped destruction.

When he arrived at Kola on 5 May 1942, Rear-Admiral Bonham-Carter transferred his flag from *Harrier* to the patched-up *Trinidad*. Her dispatch first to Iceland and subsequently to a repair yard in the United States now superseded the priority of the next pair of convoys and she weighed anchor shortly before midnight on 13 May 1942 in 'the grey aura of Arctic night'. A northward movement of German capital ships had been reported from Trondheim, but aerial reconnaissance established that only the *Admiral Scheer* had moved to Narvik and dispositions were made to dissuade her from sallying. These consisted of four cruisers, *Nigeria, Kent, Norfolk* and *Liverpool,* and four destroyers, *Inglefield, Escapade, Onslow* and *Icarus,* under Rear-Admiral Burrough, sent to cruise west of Bear Island; while Admiral Tovey in *Duke of York* with HMS *Victorious* and *London,* and the USS *Tuscaloosa* and *Washington,* with eleven destroyers lay far to the south-west.

With only the after boiler room supplying steam to the turbines, *Trinidad* was nevertheless capable of 20 knots. She was accompanied by the destroyers *Forester* and *Foresight,* both temporarily repaired but still only partially effective, together with *Matchless* and *Somali,* whose commanding officer, Captain J.W. Eaton, was Captain (D).[16]

The promised Russian air cover failed to materialize properly, only three of the expected six Hurricanes and none of the PE3 fighters arriving, a galling snub given the efforts being made to supply the Soviet airforce. German aerial reconnaissance was predictably more thorough, discovering the British ships next day, the 14th, when little more than 100 miles out. Several aircraft were observed circling round, transmitting homing signals, and though several distancing shots were thrown up from the *Trinidad,* it was clear that attack could be expected from both submarines and aircraft. At 11.00 a surfaced U-boat was seen to the northward, where the sea was dotted with ice-floes. Bonham-Carter's force was obliged to haul to the westwards.

In Norway at Banak, Major Bloedorn's KG30 was preparing its Junker Ju88 dive-bombers, and at Bardufoss Colonel Roth's Heinkel He111 torpedo-bombers of KG26 were arming. These units were to be the Luftwaffe's principal weapons against Arctic convoys.

As the sun descended under an overcast sky to hang redly just above the horizon, a light westerly breeze blew over a calm sea. Mist patches confused the lookouts with a varying distance to the sea horizon. The very quietude of the Arctic night lent an air of foreboding to the passage of the mottled grey warships. The cooks left their action stations and a hot meal was whipped up, after which men redonned their white anti-flash gear, adding a macabre and ghostly touch to the appearance of the upper decks. Then a second U-boat was sighted to the north, a third astern to the east.

At 21.00 *Trinidad*'s radar located waves of enemy aircraft coming up from the south and south-south-east at fifteen, thirty and forty miles. More were ranged at sixty miles: indeed, the screen was 'full of aircraft'. The sense of foreboding spread through *Trinidad* like wildfire. In addition to the ship's company and two Russian officials taking passage in the cruiser, *Trinidad* carried surviving merchant seamen, many of them non-European, and survivors from *Edinburgh* and the ill-fated *Jastzrab/P551*. Of the latter most were Poles, but among them the wounded British liaison officer, Morris Hanbury, lay with shattered legs.

At 22.00 the first Ju88 dive-bombers of KG30 appeared, plunging out of the cloud cover, indiscriminately attacking *Trinidad* and the destroyers, and pulling out of their dives at apparently suicidally low altitudes. A furious anti-aircraft barrage was thrown up and, although several near misses exploded alongside the ships and both water and shrapnel fell on their decks, no hits were scored. The drone and Doppler shift of the aircraft engines, the chatter of the light anti-aircraft armament and the thunder of the heavier guns filled the air. Aboard *Trinidad* the guns were fired locally as Captain Saunders took evasive action with port and starboard helm. The cruiser shuddered at every near miss, her roughly welded repairs groaning under the strain. At 22.37 the Junkers aircraft were joined by Heinkel torpedo-bombers of KG26 and the gunners shifted target to the low-level approach of the He111s. This disrupted the first attack, but the German airmen regrouped and attacked again. The destroyers, particularly *Somali* and *Foresight*, so intensified their fire that this attack was not pressed, though any sense of reprieve evaporated as lookouts diligently reported more U-boats gathering on the horizon. Wheeling again, the eight Heinkels came in towards *Trinidad*, releasing their torpedoes which Saunders saw and altered course towards, the deadly machines whirring past on either side. These attacks, though abortive, proved decisive in preoccupying the defenders.

A moment later a lone Ju88 rolled out of the thin cloud above *Trinidad* and dived on the cruiser, releasing her cluster of four bombs. The 'urgent and anguished' cry of the Air Defence Officer instructing the starboard pom-poms to shift target was too late. *Trinidad* was turning to port, evading three torpedoes on her starboard side. Above, the bombs could be clearly seen from the cruiser's bridge, dropping as the Junkers flared out, roared overhead and climbed away.

All four exploded with devastating effect. One missed, but blew up just under the port bridge, ripping off the temporary plates and sending water flooding into the compartments below B-gun, the only mitigation for the ship being a flooding of the magazine rather than the eruption of its stock of cordite shells. A second bomb penetrated the Admiral's sea cabin just below the bridge and went on through several compartments to detonate in the stokers' and petty officers' messdecks with a massive blast that opened the whole of the port side of the ship in the vicinity. Fire broke out in a multitude of places and filled the spaces with smoke and flame. The remaining two bombs also exploded outboard, but so concussively that they checked the progress of the ship and sent splinters through forward compartments, immediately admitting the sea. The secondary blast damage further shook apart the repairs effected at Rosta, rending the wounded ship until her bow began to settle as an immeasurable volume of water rushed into her.

Holed and on fire as she was, Captain Saunders continued to fight his ship as the Heinkels flew round and sought another opening to capitalize on the success of their comrade's audacity. As for the Junkers Ju88, the dilatory fire of the starboard pom-poms had streamed after it across the ship and succeeded in reducing it to a 'streaking fireball', whereupon it fell into the sea to port.

Despite a demoralizing starboard list of 14 degrees and the loss of her forward fire main, telecommunications and engine indicators, *Trinidad* was still capable of 20 knots. Below, the aggravation of smoke and darkness, the juddering of the fractured hull and the noise of shouts and screams made for chaos. The survivors of previous sinkings had been accommodated in canteen and recreation spaces now destroyed. Searing hot air rushed through the alleyways in the seconds following the bomb-strike as the fires gained a hold.

In the hangar the cruiser's Walrus aircraft blazed furiously, obstructing one escape route from the damaged compartments below the bridge. The marines manning B-gun got out by crawling along their gun barrels, but most of their supply parties perished. Although B-gun was toppled at a crazy angle on the edge of a crater, A-gun was still intact and far below, in its magazine, men were trapped by the jamming of the escape hatches. The amplification of the bomb hits below the waterline had been deafening, but the discovery of jammed hatches made the ordeal of the ammunition handlers, stewards in their regular daily duties, truly terrifying. By dint of banging they attracted the attention of those above and were released from their tomb even though the space into which they emerged was on fire. Thus men crawled or were dragged from the forward end of the ship, burned and mutilated.

Meanwhile, fire and damage-control parties struggled to contain the disaster. Counter-flooding reduced the list, but increased the ship's forward trim; lack of water pressure on the fire main and the clouds of dense, choking smoke made suppression of the fires a lost cause. Ready-use ammunition, cooked by the fires below, began exploding on deck.

Individual acts of heroism abounded. Constructor Lieutenant Chatter and a stoker tried to release men they could hear trapped forward, but to no avail. Stoker Petty Officer Shepherd and two other stokers also worked their way forward to flood a compartment as part of the damage limitation. Leaving his men to finish, Shepherd returned to the Engineer's Office to learn that the order to abandon the ship had been given. He coolly went forward again through the damaged area to let his two men know.

Captain Saunders had continued to evade the torpedo attacks which were now pressed with the utmost energy as the German pilots and their aircrews observed the extremity to which they had reduced the *Trinidad*. That none of these yet found its mark attests to the excellence of the barrage thrown up by the cruiser's gunners and the effectiveness of the destroyers' support. By 23.30 the enemy had begun to draw off, exhausted. Saunders was able to reduce speed and stop fanning the flames. It was too late, the cruiser's fuel was on fire, as were the temporary timber shores supporting her structure. The bridge was becoming untenable as fire raged below, funnelling through the superstructure and roaring up the very ladders leading below.

Consulting the Admiral, Saunders ordered the engines stopped and the ship abandoned. Commander Collet passed the word and the muster-point, the ship's quarterdeck. Constructor Commander Skinner, whose presence at Rosta had been intended to save *Trinidad*, was now summoned. Bonham-Carter said, 'Skinner, we have ordered abandon ship, were we right?' to which the smoke-blackened Skinner is alleged to have replied, 'Sir, it would take the whole Glasgow fire brigade to put out that fire.'

One by one *Trinidad*'s guns fell silent as her company gathered aft. An incongruous sight was presented by a signalman busy cycling a wheel-less bicycle to generate power for a signal lamp with which contact was maintained with the escorts as they closed in, forming an anti-submarine screen round the dying cruiser.

Lieutenant-Commander Mowlam edged *Matchless* alongside, skilfully keeping her bow clear of the smoke and flames belching across the ship in the vicinity of the bridge superstructure while small-calibre ammunition blew up in a continuous fusillade. The stretcher cases and walking wounded were transferred over the rails despite the difficulties caused by the list and the movement of the two vessels.

The other destroyers followed in orderly succession. *Trinidad*'s crew were mustered and allocated by the Master-at-Arms, until almost all had been evacuated. Engineer Lieutenant J.G. Boddy refused to leave without his stokers and returned below, an act which earned him a posthumous Albert Medal. Opportunists aboard *Forester* asked that the quarterdeck Oerlikons be transferred and this was swiftly accomplished as the destroyer filled up with her quota of survivors. *Foresight* was next and, although German aircraft were seen circling, they did not intervene. *Somali* now came alongside and a final search was being carried out by the cruiser's first lieutenant and a petty officer, when a Heinkel was seen approaching on the port quarter. Fortunately two men had been covering the evacuation with one of the cruiser's twin after anti-aircraft mountings. The Heinkel made a wave-top approach and the gunners, struggling to aim their gun by hand, succeeded in exploding their shells just beneath it, betwixt wind and water. To huge cheers the aircraft veered away, released its torpedo 'at a crazy angle' and ploughed into the sea.

They were the last shots to be fired from the cruiser. A chain of men led by Commander Collet were assisting the last survivors down the steeply canting deck. To general amusement, the Captain's steward made the leap with Saunders's No. 1 uniform intact on its hanger. Admiral Bonham-Carter preceded Collet, then came Saunders. HMS *Trinidad* was abandoned.

Her midships structure glowing red hot and licked by flame, the heavily listing cruiser belched black smoke through which the midnight sun showed intermittently. From *Somali* Admiral

Bonham-Carter ordered *Matchless* to terminate her ordeal. Three torpedoes thudded into her starboard side and her bow dipped; then she moved forward and downwards with a ponderous acceleration, leaving the watchers on the destroyers mute with emotion. From her signal yard the naval code spelt out her last message to her consorts, 'I am sailing to the westward,' while from her mastheads the white battle ensigns still fluttered. Her stern hung for a moment in a cloud of smoke and steam and then vanished. It was 01.20 on 15 May 1942.[17]

Above, German aircraft still circled.

The destroyers made off towards the north, their speed limited by the boiler damage sustained earlier by *Forester* and *Foresight*. On *Somali*'s deck a small, muffled figure drank tea amongst the ratings, his cuff lace covered by a duffle-coat. 'I hope you won't throw me overboard . . . you see I'm rather a Jonah . . . *Trinidad* is the fifth ship that has gone down under me. I'm Admiral Bonham-Carter.'

They were again attacked by Ju88s. Near misses caused splinters to fly about the destroyers' upper decks, forcing the huddling survivors to dodge about the casing to avoid them, but eventually the enemy was beaten off. Next a rumour flew about, almost as lethal in its way as the circling Junkers, which suggested the emergence of heavy units of the German fleet. It appeared to have substance when the upper works of large ships were sighted and those aboard *Somali* felt the deck cant as the faster Tribal-class destroyer left her older sisters astern in an act of what appeared to be self-immolation. To everybody's relief, the strange warships proved to be Rear-Admiral Burrough's cruiser squadron, HMS *Nigeria, Kent, Norfolk* and *Liverpool*, but their ordeal was not yet over.

A submarine alarm diverted the overloaded *Foresight* to carry out an inconclusive depth-charge attack. Then, though 350 miles from the Norwegian coast, a further group of twenty-five Ju88s dive-bombed the combined force, but with no hits recorded on either side, despite a sustained attack being made.

Two days out from Iceland the cruisers detached to resume their cruising stations for PQ16, though the long-range reconnaissance plane maintained touch until almost within sight of the northern base. From Seidisfiord the refuelled destroyers went on to Scapa where the wounded were transferred to the hospital ships *Amarapura* and *Isle of Jersey*. The fit continued on to the Firth of Clyde and then by train to HMS *Drake*, the Royal Navy's 'stone frigate' at Plymouth. There one or two experienced a degree of heartlessness from those as yet untouched by the harshness of war. One poor man reliving the horrors of his ordeal was diagnosed as suffering from 'an excess of imagination'. Another, hobbling on crutches and with a head bandaged after suffering fractures and burns, was admonished for not wearing a hat.

Apocryphal or not, these stories lived on, passed by the telegraphy that mysteriously unites men undergoing a common experience and aware that their contribution is unrecognized.

That most humane of admirals, Bonham-Carter, was conscious of this cancer and its effect upon men engaged in this northern campaign. He was convinced that until the airfields of Banak, Tromso and Bardufoss were destroyed and there were 'some hours of darkness', the convoys 'should be stopped'. Aware, too, of the political obstacle this advice would founder upon, he knew that a danger existed more insidious than the inevitable increase in German forces opposing them and he did not lack the moral courage to express it to the Commander-in-Chief who was himself, together with the First Sea Lord, opposed to the principle of convoys in summer.

'We in the Navy are paid to do this sort of job,' Bonham-Carter wrote, 'but it is beginning to ask too much of the men of the Merchant Navy. We may be able to avoid bombs and torpedoes with our speed, a six or eight knot ship has not this advantage.'

Just how much was ultimately to be asked of the men of the Allied merchant fleets was not yet clear, but on the same day that *Trinidad* had sunk to the bottom of the Barents Sea, Stukas had attacked Murmansk, damaging a Russian submarine and the American freighter *Yaka*.

10

'Success was beyond expectation'

BONHAM-CARTER'S WARNING carried far less clout than that of Tovey or Pound. Churchill had already made up his mind. Despite the failure of the Russians to supply more than a handful of ships to carry the vast amount of munitions promised by the Western Allies, American pressure to maintain the convoys come what might combined with Churchill's own unwillingness to relax Britain's commitment. He, more than anyone else, was aware of British weaknesses. He perhaps foresaw the end of Empire in the increasing dependence of the war effort upon American economic output, shipping and manpower.

The Americans too perceived this. Indeed, Roosevelt wanted nothing less than for the defeat of Germany to result in the emergence of the United States as a super-power. 'We have made such a tremendous effort to get our supplies going', he wrote to Churchill in late April 1942, 'that to have them blocked except for most compelling reasons seems to me a serious mistake. I realise in talks I have had with Pound this morning and my own naval advisers that the matter is extremely difficult. I do hope . . . you can review again the size of the immediate convoys, so that the stuff now banked up in Iceland can get through.'

In the aftermath of the loss of *Edinburgh*, and with the tragic news of the *Punjabi* just arrived and *Trinidad* penned in at Rosta, Churchill was unable to clear the amount of shipping building up quickly. 'I beg you not to press us beyond our judgement in this operation,' he wrote to Roosevelt on 2 May, 'of which we have not yet been able to measure the full strain. I can assure you, Mr President, we are absolutely extended . . .'

This is Churchill on the defensive, pleading and fending off his ally. There was, moreover, additional pressure from a more sinister quarter: 'I have a request for you,' Stalin wrote bluntly. 'Some ninety steamers loaded with important war materials for the USSR are bottled up at present in Iceland or in the approaches from America . . .'

It was useless to point out to Stalin that, because of the *Tirpitz*, 'every convoy has become a serious fleet operation'. That the presence of a single battleship was a problem to a naval power possessing several in her home waters was incomprehensible to Stalin. Moreover, the Russian leader dismissed British charges that Russian forces were not doing their part with the explanation that the Russian navy was too small and the airforce committed to the main battle fronts. Merchant ships were a subject Stalin knew little of and he concluded his allies had sufficient.

Churchill bowed to these pressures and increased the demands on his own people. 'The Russians are in heavy action,' he explained, 'and will expect us to run the risk and pay the price entailed by our contribution.' He gave orders for the dispatch of the next convoy: it was to be bigger than hitherto. 'The operation is justified if half gets through. Failure on our part to make the attempt would weaken our influence with both our major allies.'

Herein lay the crux of the Arctic campaign.

Aboard the *Ocean Voice*, Commodore N.H. Gale RNR led thirty-six of the log-jammed ships out of Hvalfiordur on Thursday, 21 May 1942. They did not leave unobserved; a German agent in Reykjavik reported their departure. The merchant ships forming convoy PQ16, the largest so far, represented five nations. British ships headed each of the nine columns.[1] The close escort appeared pathetic: the minesweeper *Hazard* and four trawlers, *St Elstan*, *Lady Madeleine*, *Northern Spray* and *Retriever*. The latter, manned by a Free French crew, turned back three days out, unable to keep up. On the 23rd, however, appearances began to change. Andrew Weir's former Bank Line tramp *Alynbank*, now dignified by the white ensign, fitted with radar, armed with high-angle 4-inch, director-controlled guns, pom-poms and Oerlikons, manned by the Royal Navy and commanded by Acting Captain Nash, joined from Seidisfiord. With her came the British corvettes *Honeysuckle*, *Starwort* and *Hyderabad*, and the Free French *Roselys*. Two submarines, the *Trident* and the *Seawolf*, also joined as well as Force Q, the fleet oiler *Black Ranger* and the Hunt-class destroyer *Ledbury*.[2]

The damage inflicted on the German destroyers in northern Norway in the action of 2 May in defence of *Edinburgh* had relieved the Admiralty of the need to risk cruisers too far east: Admiral Burrough was ordered to support the convoy west of Bear Island in *Nigeria*, with the cruisers *Kent, Norfolk* and *Liverpool* and the destroyers *Oribi, Onslow* and *Marne*. The *Nigeria* and her three destroyers plus the destroyers intended as fighting escort to PQ16, *Garland, Volunteer, Achates, Ashanti* and *Martin*, left Seidisfiord on the 23rd and were joined later by the other three cruisers from Hvalfiordur. Their main potential opponent was thought to be the *Admiral Scheer*, transferred to Narvik by 10 May and reinforced on the 26th by the pocket battleship *Lützow*, the tanker *Dithmarschen*, the destroyer *Hans Lody* and the torpedo 'boat' *T7*.

To contain the *Tirpitz*, Admiral Tovey in HMS *Duke of York* was to cruise north-east of Iceland with *Washington* (flagship of Rear-Admiral Giffen), *Wichita, Victorious, London* and thirteen fleet destroyers, nine British and four American. The submarine cover off Norway consisted of five British and three Russian boats. More Soviet support was promised in the form of a 200-bomber offensive against airfields in northern Norway. In fact, only a tenth of this number were forthcoming, in a single attack that took place after the crucial battles around PQ16 had been fought.

Concurrently with the departure of PQ16, the homeward-bound QP12 left Kola that Thursday. Four of the locally based mine-sweepers saw the convoy clear of the land and two Russian destroyers accompanied the ships to the longitude of 30°E. The escort was led by the *Inglefield*, which had gone on to Murmansk after escorting Burrough's cruisers sent to cover *Trinidad*'s ill-fated return passage. As a flotilla leader she was commanded by a full captain, Percy Todd, who was senior officer of the group consisting of the *Escapade*, the old V-class LRE *Venomous, Boadicea*, the Hunt-class *Badsworth* and the Norwegian *St Albans*. Additional support was afforded by four trawlers, *Cape Palliser, Northern Pride, Northern Wave* and *Vizalma*, the anti-aircraft cruiser *Ulster Queen* and the CAM ship *Empire Morn*, which had yet to launch its obsolete Hurricane against the enemy. Its use was to prove the only action attending the return of the fifteen empty merchant ships which, although unhampered by low visibility, were not overflown by enemy aircraft until the 25th. In the forenoon of that day an FW Condor, a Blohm and Voss flying boat and two Junkers Ju88s appeared. Since conditions were favourable and HMS *Boadicea* had been assigned pick-up duty, the *Empire Morn* launched her Hurricane by catapult. Flying Officer John Kendal of the Royal Air Force Volunteer Reserve immediately found he had lost touch with his fighter direction officer, Sub-Lieutenant P.G. Mallett in the CAM ship, as his radio transmitter was faulty, though his receiver was functioning. Moreover, he had also lost sight of his primary target, the BV138, in the cloud. Undaunted, he swooped down on a Ju88 and began a long and dogged chase which culminated in both aircraft flying the length of the convoy. Kendal rocked his Hurricane from one quarter of the enemy plane to the other in a tenacious and perfectly judged attack, firing two long bursts of gunfire before he overshot his quarry. Black smoke began to pour from the engine nacelles of the Junkers. Her aircrew jettisoned their bombs in order to maintain height as the engine failed. Finally, the plane crashed into the sea. By now the Hurricane was short of fuel and the other German aircraft showed no signs of pressing an attack.

Kendal prepared to ditch near *Boadicea*, but the destroyer was approaching a patch of low, rain-bearing cloud and Mallett advised Kendal to select a rear escort. Though he received no acknowledgement, Mallett was gratified to see the Hurricane break out of the cloud and double back to circle over *Badsworth*, while Mallett signalled the change of plan to the senior officer. Kendal now flew a tight, left-hand circuit and waggled his wings to indicate he intended to bale out rather than ditch. Flying east, he turned and, heading for *Badsworth*, climbed to gain height and vanished in the cloud. The sound of the victorious Hurricane's engine cutting out was heard by the hundreds of men now watching from every ship in the convoy. Then the fighter dropped out of the overcast and fell into the sea. A second later the figure of Kendal tumbled down, his parachute unopened. Fifty feet above the sea, the canopy fluttered into life, but it was far too late. Kendal hit the water with the parachute imperfectly extended. A few moments later *Badsworth* signalled *Empire Morn* that the young man had been picked up with fearful injuries. Ten minutes later Kendal was dead. He was buried from the quarterdeck.

There is little doubt that Kendal's action drove off the German reconnaissance and may have delayed the interception of PQ16, for just under three hours later *Boadicea* signalled ships ahead, and these turned out to be the eastbound PQ16.

QP12 continued unmolested and, after passing through extensive fog which prevented any U-boats in the vicinity from making contact, arrived safely in Iceland on 29 May. One ship, unable to maintain convoy speed, had turned back to Kola on the 22nd. The lack of attention the enemy paid to the latter part of QP12's passage was only partly attributable to the thick weather: a major battle was brewing round the laden ships of PQ16, clearly a far more fruitful target.

Burrough's cruiser and destroyer force was located at 19.00 by enemy aircraft and at midnight ran into dense fog. With the thick wraiths of impenetrable vapour complicating the handling of the ships, the fighting escort under Commander R.G. Onslow of *Ashanti* detached while the cruisers headed north-east.

Onslow was accompanied by the *Martin*, *Achates* and *Volunteer*, and the Polish destroyer *Garland* which became separated in the fog and was compelled to rejoin Burrough. Onslow too had trouble in locating the convoy which was itself disrupted and only saved from total confusion by the basic radar sets in the escorts, particularly *Volunteer* and *Hyderabad*.

During Monday, 25 May 1942, the ships blundered about in the fog, sounding 'Course 080°, speed 6 knots' in morse on their sirens. It was not until that evening that some semblance of order was restored, though the fog came and went with a maddening persistence that exhausted lookouts and watch-keepers attempting to keep station. There was no darkness, so the nacreous light was unrelieved, only made more or less oppressive by the density of the vapour.[3]

At about 05.00 the visibility improved somewhat and the cruisers joined company, entering the body of the convoy in pairs between the central columns. Captain Armstrong of the 17th Destroyer Flotilla, in HMS *Onslow*, placed himself under the orders of the close escort's senior officer, Commander Onslow of HMS *Ashanti*, an odd juxtaposition of names.

Onslow from now on bore the heavy responsibility of safeguarding the convoy. It was to be the fate of PQ16 to engage the enemy in a six-day running battle during which time few of those on board, either escorts or escorted, were to get any sleep apart from snatched bouts of cat-napping at action stations. Whenever it was possible for any men to be stood down to cruising stations, that is, second-stage readiness, they slept in full kit, ready to turn out at a moment's notice. Onslow did have one highly secret advantage, a small party of Royal Air Force airmen under a sergeant who were conversant with German and who, armed with high-frequency receivers, were able to monitor the Luftwaffe's air traffic, and thus give forewarning of attack. So acute was this espionage that it was possible to hear the pilots chatting to each other prior to take-off and to obtain some idea of their perception of success by listening to their claims when they returned to Banak and Bardufoss.

The first enemy aircraft appeared at 06.00, an FW Condor, which was fired upon by a destroyer as the convoy zigzagged, though more fog patches occurred and this evasive action was alternately discontinued and resumed as circumstances dictated. Meanwhile the destroyers were topping up with fuel from *Black Ranger*, an operation that was concluded by noon, when Force Q detached.

The homeward bound QP12 was sighted at 14.00, just having lost Kendal, and reported having seen a U-boat earlier. Then, an hour later, a surfaced U-boat was sighted from *Martin* on PQ16's starboard flank. The destroyer dashed off at speed, opening fire on the enemy boat until it crash-dived; depth-charges were dropped but contact had been lost and the destroyer soon resumed her place in the screen.

PQ16 ploughed on to the eastward through a sea ruffled by a moderate breeze, but the eternal daylight dislocated perception and added immeasurably to the fatigue of nervous tension. The sense of impending trouble was emphasized when the Condor was relieved by a huge Blohm and Voss BV168, a lumbering, ugly flying boat which earned the soubriquet 'flying clog' from Allied seamen. The anticipated attack began at 19.10 out of a clear sky.

Despite the provision of the *Alynbank* and the cruisers, PQ16 was not over-endowed with anti-aircraft armament. As the first enemy aircraft were seen coming in from the south the CAM ship *Empire Lawrence* launched her Hurricane. Pilot Officer Hay attacked and set on fire one of the nineteen attacking He111s and damaged a second, but was himself hit by gunfire, believed to have come from an American merchant ship. Hay had already been wounded in the legs and, after ditching ahead of the convoy, was fortunate to be recovered promptly by HMS *Volunteer*.[4]

Several torpedoes were released by enemy aircraft and were seen to be running, but none hit the ships. Dive-bomb attacks made by six Ju88s were little more successful. A near miss shook *Hyderabad* and her ensign was shot through, while another so shook the American merchantman *Carlton* that her main steam supply pipe from her boiler to her engine was fractured. It soon became clear she would have to be towed back to Iceland, for which duty Commander Onslow assigned the trawler *Northern Spray* (Lieutenant G.T. Gilbert RNVR). Both ships earned Onslow's approbation for, despite the difficulties of their task, they reached port safely. PQ16's day closed with an abortive attack by a dozen Ju88s. In addition to Hay's success, the gunfire of PQ16 had been intense and had accounted for two enemy aircraft. Later, the convoy passed through drifting ice, grinding and squealing as it passed down the ships' sides.

Unbeknown to it, the convoy had avoided a wolfpack, but sonar contacts were obtained shortly before 03.00 on the 26th and depth-charges fired. Nevertheless, at 03.05 Kapitänleutnant Bielfeld in *U703* succeeded in torpedoing the hindmost ship in the seventh column, the *Syros*. Nine men were lost, the remainder being picked up by *Hazard* and the trawler *Lady Madeleine*. The escorts counter-attacked, but Burrough, aware of the danger to his cruisers in the centre of a slow convoy so far to the east, broke away with his own destroyer screen and proceeded north at 20 knots to join and support QP12. Once again, whatever the cogent naval justification for this, its effect, particularly upon the Americans and Russians, was unfortunate. The anti-aircraft firepower of the cruisers and additional destroyers had been of significant benefit and their withdrawal was seen, however unjustly, as a retreat. The 'Limey Navy' was not improving its reputation among the more critical of its Allied dependants.

Nevertheless, Burrough's ships were undoubtedly vulnerable and after the dual loss of *Trinidad* and *Edinburgh* the Admiralty was not prepared to risk losing further cruisers. As it was, torpedoes fired from *U436* and *U591* had missed a merchantman and *Ashanti*. Enemy submarines continued to be sighted during the rest of the day, but were chased off by the remaining destroyers. Though they were not to know it, and though U-boats remained in contact transmitting homing signals and causing the destroyers to make attacks on contacts and distant sightings, PQ16 had endured its last successful submarine attack. It was to escape the Luftwaffe less easily. Continuously shadowed, the air attacks on Tuesday, 26 May, began early and, as on the previous day, consisted of Ju88s and He111s. The last attack occurred at about 18.00. Again seven He111 torpedo-bombers of KG26 and eleven Ju88s of KG30 approached, but in the face of a fierce barrage they fell back. A similarly testing but ineffective attack occurred at 03.20 the following morning.[5]

When 100 miles west of Bear Island on the evening of the 26th the convoy had altered course more to the eastward. Then, after the enemy's contact at 03.20 on the 27th, the proximity of heavy pack ice turned PQ16 on to a more south-easterly heading, almost directly for the North Cape and the enemy's airfield at Banak. The weather was fine and clear with thin layers of cloud. A light breeze from the west did no more than ruffle the blue surface of the sea.

The convoy skirted the southern edge of the pack until, by mid-morning, the ships had resumed their easterly track. The alteration had, however, significantly shortened their range from the enemy, who now fell upon the convoy. After intermittent brushes with the air defence, Junkers Ju88s and Heinkel He111s attacked in a well co-ordinated series of waves, making maximum use of the aircraft available, considerably fewer than the confused defenders thought. The main cloud base at 3,000 feet was broken. However, a film of stratus at half that height provided the dive-bombers with good cover and made it difficult to see the descending planes until they were upon their targets.

With the departure of the cruisers and their destroyer screen, only the *Alynbank* and *Martin* possessed the capability of elevating their heavy guns to hit the bombers. The older destroyers and corvettes had to wait until their lighter armament could respond. The ack-ack cruiser *Alynbank* recorded over 100 attacks and at about noon the *Starii Bolshevik* sustained a bomb hit which set her on fire forward. She was carrying explosives and vehicles, and her Russian crew fought the blaze on her forecastle where ready-use ammunition for her forward gun began to explode. The gun itself fell through into the forepeak below.

The ship began to drop astern and the destroyer *Martin*, while under attack from aircraft concentrating on her and the Russian freighter, lowered her whaler with her young surgeon-lieutenant,

Ransome-Wallis, in it. Splashed by near misses, the boat's crew succeeded in reaching the Russian ship. Ransome-Wallis struggled aboard and was able to help withdraw to *Martin* three badly wounded Russians upon whom he later operated. With assistance from the *Roselys* the fire was eventually brought under control and the *Starii Bolshevik*, though spewing smoke for two more days, regained her station in the convoy.

A stick of four bombs now fell close alongside the Polish destroyer *Garland*; one detonated on impact with the water, counter-mining the others. They in turn riddled her entire length with splinters, disabled an Oerlikon and A- and B-guns, and put the forward boiler room out of action. Twenty-five men were killed and forty-three wounded. Smoke floats were ignited on B-gun deck and the ship's radio aerials were brought down. The former were jettisoned, but it was necessary for the trawler *Lady Madeleine* to run alongside as a communication link between the Poles and Onslow in *Ashanti*.

At about 13.10, after a short lull, more aircraft attacked. Two bombs hit the freighter *Alamar* and five minutes later near misses and possible hits set the *Mormacsul* on fire. Both American ships fell astern and the corvette *Starwort* was ordered to stand by them until they both sank at about 13.30. Three Ju88s, flying in V formation, dived on the *Empire Lawrence*, their bombs penetrating No. 2 hold. One passed through the shell plating and exploded, causing the ship to list to port, settle by the head and lose speed as she drew out of line. Her boats were already swung out and the crew waited for the ship to lose way before lowering them into the sea.

Orders had been given that all corvettes and trawlers were to act as rescue ships and the ubiquitous *Lady Madeleine*, accompanied by HMS *Hyderabad*, immediately shaped course for the damaged freighter. Meanwhile, Captain H.S. Darkins and his chief wireless operator burnt the confidential books in the *Empire Lawrence*'s galley and were just emerging as another attack was made on the damaged cargo vessel. Four bombs struck the ship in her engine room, Nos. 4 and 5 holds and her magazine. As the *Lady Madeleine* was drawing alongside, the *Empire Lawrence* split apart and ship and trawler were engulfed in smoke. This cleared to reveal a brief glimpse of the freighter's bow.

The starboard lifeboat was blown clear and capsized while the loaded port boat flew to pieces, with the loss of several men. The

German planes now strafed the settling remains of the ship. Darkins, 'a fearless and extremely good leader', was not seen again. 'All the crew and particularly the [DEMS] gunners,' Second Officer Hulse reported later, 'behaved magnificently throughout, fighting the guns and keeping them supplied with ammunition without the slightest sign of fear or panic.'

Lady Madeleine lowered her boat which was 'extremely well handled and this contributed . . . to the speed at which the survivors were brought on board', mostly from the capsized boat. Another thirty, including Hulse, were picked up by *Hyderabad*, 'single men clinging to small pieces of wreckage which consisted of splintered wood and oil drums'. The rescued 'had all been in the water some time and all complained of the bitter cold.'

The two little ships remained in the area searching until no other survivors were visible, then they turned away to rejoin the convoy. The *Empire Lawrence* had taken 5,000 tons of war material to the bottom of the Barents Sea.

Other ships were damaged in these attacks. Shuddering under the close concussions of near misses, the *Empire Baffin* and the *City of Joliet* were shaken, the latter so badly she was briefly abandoned.

Some amelioration of the convoy's plight was obtained as the ice thinned and Onslow was able to order a course alteration to the north-north-east at 14.35, when the convoy was about eighty miles south-east of Bear Island. Increasing distance and lower cloud would, it was hoped, provide a measure of relief. For a while this indeed seemed to the case.

Following these attacks, some of the survivors rescued by the trawler needed medical attention. In a brilliant piece of seamanship, in a smooth sea and long swell, Commander Thompson laid his destroyer, HMS *Martin*, so close alongside the *Lady Madeleine* that Surgeon-Lieutenant Ransome-Wallis was able to leap across the gap.[6]

'This is a hell of a party!' Lieutenant-Commander Ogden RNVR shouted down from the bridge with the sang-froid considered obligatory in the circumstances. Bundled into Neil Robertson stretchers, the wounded, one of whom had one leg broken grotesquely in six places, were being passed across to *Martin* when another attack by eight Ju88s was made. It was ineffective, but sufficiently disruptive to make the transfer of these unfortunate men hasty and clumsy. *Martin* peeled away from the gallant trawler. She herself was overloaded with survivors, and the smaller escorts succeeded in rescuing 471 officers and men from the 7 ships sunk in the course of PQ16's passage.

By this time *Martin*, in common with all the other ships, was running short of ammunition, for the highly effective barrage was a drain on finite resources. For the moment at least, however, the driving off of the Junkers bombers seemed to confirm the wisdom of Onslow's diversion to the north-north-east.

Alas, the lull was not to last. In brilliant sunshine, just before 20.00, dive-bombing attacks were resumed from the refuelled and rearmed aircraft. As the ships engaged these high targets, waves of torpedo-bombers attacked at low altitude. Witnesses reported that the lack of ammunition was becoming evident; several of the merchant ships were observed to be silent, having run out. Now a pair of bombs hit the *Empire Purcell*'s No. 2 hold and set it on fire, while two near misses exploded alongside. Hatches and beams were blown into the air, the bunker bulkhead collapsed and an avalanche of coal ran into the stokehold. Despite the fact that his gunner was blown from the bridge Oerlikon, Captain Stephenson estimated that his ship expended 'some 3-quarters [*sic*] of a ton' of ammunition on the numerous planes attacking the convoy.

Water was already flooding the engine room through fractured ship's side valves and the duty engineers stopped the main engines. Aware that his cargo of ammunition might explode at any moment, Stephenson ordered his crew to abandon ship. However, the cold had stiffened the ropes so the falls on one boat ran slack, dropping the boat and throwing its occupants into the numbingly cold sea. Six men lost their lives in this incident and two more died in the confusion, but men trapped under the capsized boat were rescued one at a time by Able Seaman William Thomson, whose gallantry was exemplary. Stephenson and three of his officers succeeded in lowering the remaining lifeboat and pulling clear before the *Empire Purcell* blew up with a stunning explosion. The survivors were picked up by the corvette *Hyderabad*.

The *Lowther Castle* was the next to suffer, struck forward by two aerial torpedoes launched by a Heinkel almost beyond the range of any guns. Despite an attempt to comb their tracks, the torpedoes struck the port side of the ship, penetrating No. 2 hold and quickly setting its cargo ablaze. The concussions of the torpedoes had damaged the ship's telemotor and the steering broke down. The Master stopped engines. While the Mate surveyed the damage, the ship settled by the head and the order was given to abandon her.

According to the *Lowther Castle*'s Chief Mate, Mr J.G. Lomas, the horrible explosion of the *Empire Purcell* now affected a few firemen and some difficulty was experienced getting one of the boats launched. One, with the Master, was clumsily let go and threw its occupants into the water. They were all recovered with the exception of the Master, the only casualty. Having settled by the head, the ship paused and, remaining thus, dropped astern where she was first strafed and then further dive-bombed. Lomas and the Third Mate, Mr Ruckledge, were the last to leave her. The survivors were picked up by HMS *Honeysuckle*, their ship burning for eight hours before she exploded astern of the convoy in a huge column of black smoke.

Observing the fate of the *Lowther Castle* as she ran back to pick up twenty-six of the *Empire Purcell*'s survivors, HMS *Hyderabad* was ordered to attempt the transfer of ammunition from the American freighter *John Randolph* to the *Hybert*. A request for more ammunition from the *Pieter de Hoogh* was met with a reassuring 'don't worry' from her escort, but Onslow was seriously concerned about the lack of fire from the newer guns fitted on the American merchant ships and arrangements had been made over the TBS for the *John Randolph* to have boxes of cartridges ready on her after deck. The *John Randolph*, however, was not in her station and, while attempting to locate her amid the action, *Hyderabad* received a request for ammunition from *Ironclad*. With some difficulty the corvette effected these reinforcements, her commanding officer, Lieutenant Hickman RNR, commenting that although the Americans 'had had a very gruelling time . . . their morale was extremely high and all they wanted was . . . another chance to hit back at the enemy'.[7]

Next the Commodore's ship, the *Ocean Voice*, was hit by a bomb which set her on fire and blew a huge hole in her shell plating just above the waterline in way of her forward hold. Fortunately, despite the low swell, there was no wind sea and although Onslow later wrote, 'I had little hope of her survival', he was able to add, 'this gallant ship maintained her station, fought her fire, and with God's help arrived at her destination'.

Due to fire damage to the bridge of the *Ocean Voice*, Commodore Gale was compelled to hand over control of the convoy to the Vice-Commodore, Captain J.T. Hair, Master of the *Empire Selwyn*.

The pluck and sheer guts of those quenching the fires on the *Ocean Voice* and the *Starii Bolshevik*, the coolness of the smaller escorts effecting rescues and transfers while under attack and the eagerness of those under aerial bombardment to fight back are what is expected of men in battle. But Bonham-Carter had identified a darker side to war, a baleful aspect not consonant with glory. The medical men involved occupied a front line of a different kind where the moral effect of comradeship was washed away in exhaustion and fear. Here the individual suddenly perceived his insignificance and loneliness. Aboard *Martin*, for example, Ransome-Wallis was dealing with cases of lost nerve and battle fatigue. Doubtless this tiny, unpopular statistic could be extrapolated to form a small, significant proportion of the men engaged, a true measure of the horrors of this ruthless campaign. It was happening on the warships; Bonham-Carter had alluded to it as it affected merchant seamen. Onslow, however, in his report on the conduct of the *Ocean Voice*, had properly recognized that in battle there could be no distinction between the behaviour of the two services.

There were no more attacks that day. The hastily abandoned *City of Joliet* had been reboarded but was continuing to settle by the head and drop astern. At the time, the loss of the Commodore's ship was considered imminent and the *Garland* was so severely affected that she was ordered to detach and proceed independently.

Having lost a fifth of the convoy three days out from his destination, Onslow was 'far from optimistic'. He issued strict injunctions on the preservation of ammunition and later remarked that 'we were . . . inspired . . . by the parade ground rigidity of the convoy's station-keeping, including *Ocean Voice* and *Starii Bolshevik* who were both billowing smoke from their foreholds'.

Early on the 28th the *City of Joliet* succumbed to her mortal wound and sank, adding to the debris on the seabed. At the same time the injured man with the shattered leg died aboard *Martin*. Her young surgeon continued to toil with the desperately wounded, who included a man with a broken back and another deeply unconscious and requiring brain surgery. It grew colder, ice formed again on the ships' upper works, bergs dotted the sea.

Martin buried her dead, the merchant seaman under a white ensign. To port the *Ocean Voice* and *Starii Bolshevik* continued to smoulder and beyond, on the grey rim of the horizon, the Blohm and Voss flying boat circled relentlessly. The ships ploughed on through a low mist of sea-smoke.

But by the time German air attacks resumed at 21.30 that evening, Onslow's tired escort had been reinforced by the Soviet destroyers *Grozni, Sokrushitelni* and *Kuibishev,* whose anti-aircraft fire-power was impressive and timely, for many of the merchant ships were now completely out of ammunition. This, and the attack made in the early hours of Friday, 29 May, were ineffective despite the presence of Junkers Ju88s and Heinkel He111s. That evening Captain Crombie, commanding the 1st Minesweeping Flotilla based at Kola, joined the convoy in HMS *Bramble* together with *Leda, Seagull, Niger, Hussar* and *Gossamer*. At the time PQ16 was 140 miles north-east of the Kola Inlet. Onslow's ordeal was not yet over.

Crombie was to escort six of the merchant ships bound for Archangel into the White Sea, which was now open to navigation. He also took under his wing the *Martin* and the *Alynbank*, thus depriving Onslow of his best, longest-ranging radar at a time when he knew he had yet to run the gauntlet of U-boat patrols. Onslow was therefore obliged to disperse his remaining escorts to provide an anti-submarine screen at the cost of reducing the ability to throw up effective anti-aircraft fire.

Half an hour before midnight, while the two sections of the divided convoy were still in sight of each other, eighteen Ju88s dived on the Murmansk-bound ships, and fifteen made for the Archangel contingent. Both attacks were beaten off. Crombie's section went unmolested through the Gourlo into the White Sea beyond, while Onslow's charges were attacked three times during the course of 30 May. Fortunately, no ships were hit and for their temerity the enemy paid the price of two Ju88s. The last enemy aeroplane withdrew at 13.00, after which Russian Hurricanes gave air cover. At 16.00, 'reduced in numbers, battered and tired, but still keeping perfect station', Onslow's ships entered the Kola Inlet.

Crombie's division, proceeding in line ahead and led by the *Empire Elgar*, arrived at the estuary of the Dvina the same day, to have the ice-breaker *Stalin* meet them with the pilots off Sozonoya. They began a passage through the ice lasting forty hours. Confined to the narrow lead cut by the *Stalin*, they were assailed by Junkers Ju87 Stukas in a noisy but useless attack. Apart from her small arms, *Martin* was reduced to firing armour-piercing shells, but *Alynbank* justified her conversion to the last and drove off the dive-bombers.

At the end of this attack *Martin*'s magazines were empty and she detached for Vaenga, arriving on the following day. She anchored close to *Volunteer*, who relayed a signal from the King: 'Splice the mainbrace'. Meanwhile the merchant ships passed Archangel proper and, on 1 June, secured alongside at Bakaritsa, a new wharf two miles upstream.

For Onslow the time of assessment had arrived. The defence of PQ16 had been principally against enemy aircraft and, although the performance of *Alynbank*, especially against dive-bombers, had been magnificent, he could not disguise the fact that most of the escorts, including his own crack *Ashanti*, had an inadequate anti-aircraft armament. He was unimpressed with the provision of a single CAM ship, gallant though Hay's counter-attack had been, and, while *Alynbank*'s long-range radar had proved invaluable, a second set aboard *Empire Lawrence* had broken down. So, despite the fact that Onslow's leadership had been unimpeachable, with his ship always at 'the centre of trouble', he was sensible to the fundamental weakness of the escort.[8]

In his report, Onslow recommended greater anti-aircraft capability plus an escort carrier, and whilst noting the splendid humanitarian service of his smaller escorts he called for the provision of rescue ships dedicated to the task of recovering survivors. Onslow knew this could have nothing but a beneficial effect both materially and morally. Among other suggestions, Onslow wanted faster submarines and fire-fighting tugs which could, he thought, have saved the *Empire Purcell*. Finally, he was extremely concerned about the lack of ammunition, recommending that stocks be built up in the same way as fuel oil was being made available at Vaenga.

At her anchorage there, the tanker *Hopemount* was currently attending to this duty. The first of the escorts of PQ16 to arrive alongside her was the badly damaged Polish destroyer *Garland*, which had earned high praise for her fighting spirit. Her wounded and dying had been lying in the alleyways and the *Hopemount*'s Chief Officer went aboard to find the white paintwork marred by bloody lettering. 'They were hard men,' he afterwards recounted, 'they had written in their own blood, LONG LIVE POLAND.'

From a more detached viewpoint Admiral Tovey expressed a deeper satisfaction, a satisfaction enhanced by the reflection that the defence of PQ16 had been achieved entirely by little ships without close heavy cover. Moreover, Richard Onslow, though an officer of great skill and ability, was as a commander comparatively junior. Four-fifths of the convoy had got through 'due to the gallantry, efficiency and tireless zeal of the officers and men of the escorts and to the remarkable courage and determination of those of the merchant ships. No praise can be too high for either.'

To the escorts of PQ16 Tovey sent his 'heartiest congratulations and great admiration for the gallant way they fought their passage through in the face of strong and constant opposition. I sympathise with them in the loss of their fine shipmates.'

And from the Senior British Naval Officer, North Russia, Rear-Admiral Bevan, came the relayed congratulations of both the First Lord of the Admiralty, Mr A.V. Alexander, and the First Sea Lord, Sir Dudley Pound, to 'the officers and men of all Allied Merchants [*sic*] and Allied Forces concerned on their magnificent exploit . . . fighting PQ16 through to North Russia'.[9]

Dönitz's war diary underlines the British High Command's sense of victory: 'My opinion as to the small chances of success for U-boats against convoys during the northern summer . . . has been confirmed by experience with PQ16 . . . This must be accounted a failure when compared with the results of the anti-submarine activity for the boats operating.' The Luftwaffe, Dönitz concluded, had the best chance against convoys in the Arctic summer. In making this admission he was aware that the numbers of Heinkel torpedo-bombers in northern Norway had increased, but he was misled by over-optimistic claims from the German pilots as to their effectiveness, a circumstance all the more curious considering the constant presence of the reconnaissance planes. Depressed he might be, but Dönitz was yet to have his Arctic victory. Tovey, on the other hand, having so persistently warned London of the inherent risks run by the polar convoys, was justifiably proud of PQ16's achievement – the convoy's 'success was beyond expectation'.

11

'It is not enough'

CAPTAIN STUY'S *Pieter de Hoogh* was in the Murmansk-bound portion of PQ16. As his laden ship steamed into the Kola Inlet he passed the Free French corvette *Roselys* and the Polish destroyer *Garland*. The exiled crews of the three ships felt a kinship: their homelands were under German occupation. In mutual recognition, both warships dipped their tattered ensigns to the gallant merchantman, a courteous and chivalrous reversal of the sea's ancient custom.

In the naval code 'the safe and timely arrival of the convoy' meant the discharge of a duty. Relaxing, the young officers of HMS *Martin*, which had doubled back to Vaenga, joked over drinks aboard *Volunteer* until interrupted by an air raid, but for the merchant seamen arrival did not mark the end of their duties. The passage of the convoy had brought them to the ports, anchorages and berths of the Kola Inlet where they were now to be subject to almost constant air attacks as they discharged their cargoes, while the comparative peace of those on the Dvina subjected the Allied merchant seamen to an ordeal of another kind: neglect.

During the course of time, the attitude of the Russian authorities changed and, as a reflection of the hold that the Communist Party had over the populace, so too did the reception given by ordinary Russians. During Christmas 1941, when the *Edinburgh*'s midshipmen were pottering about in their picket boats coping with problems of freezing fuel, things were relatively relaxed, despite the frequent presence of a 'political lieutenant'. Behind its three or four miles of riverside quays, war-ravaged Murmansk was like an encampment of scattered huts, 'interspersed with little groups of larger brick and concrete buildings. The streets, which are large . . . are the haunt of fast lorries which purr silently over the snow.'

Stalin Street was 'flanked by imposing but dilapidated and bomb-damaged buildings of six and ten storeys, a contrast to the lower buildings surrounding it,' one midshipman recorded in his journal, remarking on the lack of purpose of the inhabitants in the Hall of Culture. This

> was like a super-cinema which had been neglected for several years and which on entry appeared full of silent people standing in groups in rooms lit vaguely by single electric lights. The actual cultural activities seemed rather lost in its shadowy depths. But for all its faults, the people seem quite contented and we were moved to jealousy by the opulent appearance of their fur coats and hats.

The naval sailor was never subjected to the humiliations of his mercantile cousin and had the infrastructure of the Royal Navy's apparently infinite resources to ease his situation in the most trying circumstances. Such was the demand for escorts that naval personnel did not stay in Russian waters long, sometimes not even long enough to escort a homeward convoy. Commander Richard Onslow's *Ashanti*, for instance, was required for Operation Pedestal, the resupply of beleaguered Malta, and embarking some 'rather sad and twitchy chaps' from HMS *Edinburgh*, a former junior officer remembered, she sailed for home almost immediately.

For the merchant seaman, it was otherwise. Just as the Soviet government failed to supply merchant ships in the numbers that had been anticipated by the Western Allies, so the Russians were incapable of handling cargo in the quantities in which it now arrived, despite Stalin's constant harping on the subject of delays. Such facilities as existed had suffered grievously from neglect or bomb damage. River frontage had collapsed, rendering berths unusable; only a limited number of cranes were available; and the railway network was under enormous pressure.

Medical help, what there was of it, was equally primitive, and recreational and social diversions were limited. Since the merchant ships remained until their holds were discharged and return cargoes or ballast loaded, their stay in these northern waters could be extensive. It is only fair to say that in no way were the Allied seamen any worse off than the ordinary Russians themselves, privileged party members excepted, but this aura of neglect had its effect on the morale of men used to better things and destined to spend long months in this polar backwater.

The formal Soviet attitude was a barometer of Moscow's perception of the effort of the Western Allies. Usually one of displeasure, it mellowed towards the end of the war, but by that time the British had done more than their fair share to ameliorate conditions, gradually building up what amounted to an extempore naval base of which the *Hopemount* and her successors, anchored at Vaenga with their cargoes of bunker oil for the escorts, were a manifestation.

These 'facilities' were built up round two naval parties, NP100 and NP200 stationed at Murmansk and Archangel respectively, largely British affairs, but with a handful of Americans attached. These formed the staff of the British Admiral commanding in North Russia. While Admiral Miles handled the complexities of naval diplomacy in Moscow, the Senior British Naval Officer, North Russia (SBNONR), was initially Rear-Admiral R.H. Bevan. Bevan's duties included liaising with his Russian counterpart, Admiral Golovko, commander of the Soviet Northern Fleet, and arranging for the co-operation of Russian destroyers; attending to the multifarious wants of the escorts; dealing with the staff work attendant upon the organization of the QP convoys, their composition and commodores; and the allocation of homeward 'berths' for the empty or ballasted merchant ships. It was the duty of his staff officers to initiate the pre-convoy conferences; arrange the signals procedures and radio frequencies; organize intelligence debriefings of the inward ships and briefings on the local situation for the homeward-bound; effect the replenishment of stores and ammunition, fuel and water; and oversee the staff communications ratings – all this under a relentless and disruptive regime of German air raids.

Bevan was succeeded in due course by Rear-Admiral E.R. Archer and he in turn by Rear-Admiral J. Egerton. Initially based at Murmansk, it was 1943 before closer liaison with the Russians could be achieved and the SBNONR shifted to the Red Navy's base at Polyarnoe.

Under the Rear-Admiral's immediate control NP100 handled the radio communications with incoming convoys; allocated anchorages, berths and priorities of cargo discharge; and acted as a relay station for messages from Britain, a duty often complicated by atmospheric distortion in the high Arctic. NP100 also monitored enemy signals and recoded them for onward transmission as part of the overall Allied intelligence-gathering network. Naval detachments, each under its own Senior British Naval Officer of commander's rank, were also stationed at Murmansk and at Vaenga, where there was a hospital and a survivors' camp. These officers and ratings maintained close contact with the merchantmen working cargo at the various berths and quays in the upper inlet. NP200 was a subsidiary detachment sent to work at Archangel while the White Sea was navigable. These naval parties consisted mostly of communications ratings on nine-month postings. However, the Soviet bureaucracy's insistence on visas and failure to understand why men needed relieving and could not serve for the duration, often extended these. Depression, the monotony of the landscape and the slow change of the seasons could combine with the ready availability of one commodity, vodka, to have its sad effect on some men susceptible to this polar cafard.

At the beginning of the war Soviet mistrust prevented any British warships from berthing at Polyarnoe, but the necessity of accepting assistance in the matter of minesweeping and submarine support gradually mellowed the attitude of even a hard-liner like Golovko. Eventually whole destroyer flotillas double-banked along the wooden quays lining the deep water of the narrow *guba*, or fiord.

The British Rear-Admiral commanding in North Russia had under his direct control a handful of Halcyon-class minesweepers whose basic duty of keeping the swept channels clear of German mines was, as we have seen, quickly expanded to providing anti-submarine ocean escorts to considerable effect. They also attended the larger ships that came in, their commanding officers being familiar with the pilotage of the inlet and with the Russian authorities. Their contribution was as great as their duties were multifarious. That such small, unsuitable ships served with distinction in these high, inhospitable latitudes remains a tribute to their crews.

In addition, the British at Polyarnoe had the trawler *Chiltern*, acting as dogsbody to the incoming ships. Having served as escort to PQs 12 and 14, she finally arrived with PQ15 to take up the unglamorous duties of fleet tender. Attempts to transfer a smaller launch were frustrated by enemy action which sank the freighter carrying it. *Chiltern* collected food and stores for the naval parties, ran errands, conveyed the staff officers about the anchorage and had the melancholy duty of conveying the dead to sea for burial. The little ship remained at the Russian naval base under the command of a professional fishing skipper, manned by a succession of crews. One of her telegraphists, A. Thomas, recalls being forbidden to use his transmitter but, with the versatility that the Royal Navy historically displays, learnt enough Russian to maintain contact over the landline to which the trawler was connected when alongside at Polyarnoe.

The immediate staff of the SBNONR consisted of a commander, several staff lieutenants, four interpreters, an engineer, a doctor and two cipher officers who dealt with the wants of incoming ships as best they could. Contact with the Russians was fraught with difficulty. 'The Russian people are charming, it is the system that is the problem,' Archer's flag-lieutenant, Robert Towersey, recalled. 'Anybody who was exceedingly friendly we knew to be suspect. Political commissars [and] the NKVD were everywhere . . . even our telephones were tapped, it was almost impossible to make a telephone call without hearing the tapper talking to his mates or music playing.'

Closest contact with Russians was, perforce, with the interpreters. Since most of these seemed to be attached to the NKVD, they were treated with great suspicion, though Golovko's Chief of Staff, a Captain Rigermen, was 'a real charmer'. Many interpreters were young women, university graduates from Moscow, whose lives appear to have been governed by the twin necessities of thwarting the natural inclinations of young British sea-officers with whom they were forced to liaise and avoiding the taint of fraternization.

A move to provide British interpreters was initiated and the armed services were scoured for likely men hidden in their anonymous ranks. Several university graduates with linguistic abilities were found and sent on a nine-month course, followed by a further two-month conversion course prior to being commissioned into the RNVR. One of these, at 54 possibly the oldest sub-lieutenant in the Royal Navy, having had family connections with the timber trade, needed little tuition: he swore in Russian with impressive fluency and proved a popular success. In the autumn of 1942 these men were dispatched in four destroyers making a run direct to Russia to reinforce the escort of QP14.[1]

As will be seen, the force of the escorts increased as greater resources became available. The close, fighting escort would no longer be entrusted to a mere commander, despite Onslow's success with PQ16, and a rear-admiral sailed in command. At the end of the passage it would become customary for him to be dined by Golovko and to reciprocate this hospitality in turn. For the interpreters such occasions were both busy and boring. 'Each assured the other that sailors could always reach an understanding', Richard Kindersley recalled, 'if only the politicians would not interfere.' The translation of repeated jokes became tedious, though occasional lighter moments occurred, Tolstoyan in their character, as when General Kustov, commanding Red Army units in the locality, offered to bring his horse into the dining-room to show the animal off to Rear-Admiral Louis Hamilton, a man passionately interested in fox-hunting. The horse was finally examined outside and as a consequence the General made mounts available to officers based at Polyarnoe.

Occasionally, British interpreters would sail on the Russian destroyers which reinforced the convoy escorts as far out as 30°E. Close professional relationships with Russian servicemen always raised the question of the second front in conversation, a vexatious issue to both sides, but over-familiarization was largely prevented by mutual suspicion, the presence of the NKVD and differences of culture, class and political opinion. When genuine friendships developed, Stalin's baleful shadow fell upon even this remote region. One Russian liaison officer, having been recommended for a British decoration for his co-operation, was abruptly transferred. Seen later by British officers in Moscow, he turned and bolted when he realized he had been recognized.

A similar fate might await any of the young women who worked as hostesses at the International Club. The demonstration of too much familiarity with their guests could lead to a mysterious disappearance. The Russian authorities were eternally suspicious, particularly of the officers to whom, perhaps, they attributed the vices of their own former Tsarist officer corps. Or perhaps they saw these Britons as representatives of capitalism, enemies of the proletariat, and put them to deliberate and mischievous inconvenience by such ploys as delaying the delivery of firewood on the excuse that none was available, when logs were stockpiled within sight. Other petty irritations seemed to their victims to be deliberately provocative, particularly to those actually stationed in North Russia. One of the worst was interference with mail, until this was discreetly circumvented by the use of diplomatic bags.

By far the most annoying restriction was enforced by the ubiquitous guards who manned every gangway, gate and gunpit. These sentries regarded anyone not obviously Russian with a suspicion engendered by their political masters and further aggravated by ignorance and the language barrier. The constant demand for the showing of passes, and the refusal of passage if there was the slightest doubt about the validity of documents, was an irksome circumstance which exasperated men who felt they were being treated more like enemies. Ironically, such experiences ended many a flirtation with Communism.

Compensations were few and far between. The singing of a Russian naval choir could transform an evening, and it became customary for a naval choir to give concerts aboard the major British warships that came in with the later convoys. But other entertainments attracted as much opprobrium as some ENSA concert parties.

However, a modicum of female society could be enjoyed by British naval officers at the Red Navy Club at Polyarnoe, where ladies serving in the Soviet Navy might be prevailed upon to dance, though their behaviour was always circumspect and unbending. Apart from the liaison staff, almost all attempts to fraternize formally met with only a stiff and perfunctory courtesy; 'a single drink, but nothing more'. There were, nevertheless, exceptions, and some officers found sleeping partners.

It is possible that part of the Russians' mistrust was rooted in memories of British 'intervention' in the turmoil of the Russian civil war which followed the revolution of 1917. British troops had landed and fought on Russian soil; British money and effort had helped found Murmansk as a supply port. But the Soviet authorities did not make any propaganda from this, and a tank captured from the British during this period and displayed at Archangel was discreetly boarded over. Nevertheless, Britain was an imperial power and was, in purely Marxist terms, fundamentally in the camp of the enemy. That she was an ally was a matter of expedience. Had Hitler not launched Barbarossa, the Soviet government would have been delighted to see her overcome in 1940. 'Can't you understand that . . . we are forced into a coalition with a bastard like Churchill', was the hard-line attitude of the Politburo and a reflection of Stalin's thinking.[2]

Entertainment of a rather more impromptu kind occurred in the closing years of the war when the destroyer flotillas berthed at Polyarnoe for their five-day turn-round period. In a release of tension, these ships' companies tended to play the fool. Typical were the ships of the 17th Destroyer Flotilla, 'The Lucky "Os" ', each of which reflected the idiosyncracies of her captain, exuberant and usually junior regular officers whose discretion was conditioned by their *esprit de corps*, not their present grim surroundings. They were held in indiscriminate affection by their even younger crews who forgave them their high jinks as when, for instance, dressed as Red Indians, they paddled out to an anchored cruiser aboard Carley floats, in defiance of the cold.

In October 1944, with five of the class alongside, the commanding officers decided to hold inter-ship sports which, with regattas, were the prescribed naval remedy for flagging morale. The three-legged and sack races were held on the ice with heavy betting laid on. Anyone falling over was heartily kicked back into activity by his shipmates. The Russians believed these men to be under punishment, for with their own strict discipline anything else was incomprehensible.

Yet against these frivolous outbursts there has to be set another mood. Earlier that year, on Good Friday, 7 April, there were six destroyers of the 17th Flotilla, together with a handful of corvettes, alongside at Polyarnoe. The return convoy RA58 was about to sail when the flotilla chaplain, Peter Gillingham, expressed his regret to the Captain (D) that none of the ships' companies could take part in any religious service before departure. Captain J.A. McCoy of HMS *Onslow* thought for a moment then replied, 'Give me half an hour, Padre, and we'll surprise God and the Russians.'

Thirty minutes later all the ships' companies were paraded and marched through the snow to the Red Navy Club where, under the eyes of NKVD officers, they attended a service and heard Gillingham preach.

Gillingham's pastoral care was ensured by rotating him between the destroyers in the flotilla. By convention a naval chaplain can enter any mess in a ship, automatically assuming the rank of his 'parishioner'.

'Come in and sit down, Padre', Gillingham recalled Rear-Admiral Burnett once greeting him, 'you're a bloody Rear-Admiral now!'

On the other hand, a ship's commanding officer does not have this access, except on formal business. Alongside at Polyarnoe, Gillingham frequently found the strain of war telling on the exuberant and dashingly youthful destroyer captains, whose escapades masked a darker aspect. In quiet, reflective moments 'they were rather lonely young men'.

Loneliness, or personal isolation, could be found in more oppressive surroundings such as the crowded wardroom of a warship, particularly among those not inducted from an early age into the hearty brotherhood of the Royal Navy. For those willing to run the gauntlet of innumerable guards and the accompanying ritual of pass-showing, walking provided solace, as Lieutenant Geoffrey Law RNVR of HMS *Palomares* found, in the aftermath of PQ17. Archangel was

> interesting, but the smells and unfriendly people were not attractive . . . Walked out to collective farm. An interesting silage cutter. Very hard workers filling the timber lined pit with coarse wet grass, reeds or weeds. Soon became friendly after a smoke. Prolific wild flowers, catmint, cranesbill. Walked up to higher ground. Bog, very wet. Blackberries of a large size, heather. As the land rises there are birch, silver birch, fir, spruce, savin, rosebay, golden rod . . .

For a country-lover this was consolation after his ordeal, a contrast to the first entries after the remnants of the shattered convoy came in: 'beginning to sleep better . . . the weather when hot is most enervating. When raining, cold and beastly.' But the war was ineluctable: 'Two alarms so I missed my walk. There was much blind gunfire at very little, if anything at all.' Then later he 'walked to a distant village . . . very attractive . . . The flowers in the windows are wonderful – geraniums of most unusual colourings, fuchsias, gloxinias, even roses . . . saw a spotted flycatcher . . .'

Numerous naval ratings enlisted for 'hostilities only' came from the industrial slums of Britain and had understandably left-wing tendencies. To many the idea of personally supporting the Russian Communists against the Fascists appealed strongly. The reality of Uncle Joe's 'workers' paradise' appalled and disillusioned some, while others found that the desperate plight of the indigent Russians only emphasized the need for class struggle, stirred their compassion and reaffirmed their dedication to the socialist cause. However, these men were seamen by accident and their short stay recuperating between convoys left them with vivid glimpses, but little more.

On the other hand, their merchant counterparts were already inured to poverty in all parts of the world, just as they were inured to often dramatic climatic changes, all part and parcel of their workaday life. They were thus conditioned to rubbing along with the dockside community of any port and regarded the Russians, with whom they had to work closely in the discharge of their vital cargoes, with less detachment. A merchant seaman from the *Bolton Castle* wrote after PQ17, when full of an overwhelming sense of failure, 'it was very difficult to understand the ways of the Russian people. They were in a very desperate state and I felt guilty that we were unable to help. I could never forget the great ordeal of the Russian people.'

An officer of a rescue ship wrote of Archangel:

> there was a pathetic market laid out by the roadside, consisting of broken dishes and crockery, bottles, rag dolls . . . We [passed] boarded up shops and burned out buildings. A heavily escorted working party of prisoners passed by. A queue of muffled up women stood outside a closed baker's shop. A small group of mourners shuffled along preceded by a coffin on a two-wheeled hand cart – and silence, a silence you could feel . . . A silence broken only by the loudspeaker suspended at the street intersections – long harangues and martial music. We returned to the ship infinitely depressed, almost ashamed of our smart uniforms amid so much squalor.

After discharging their cargoes, many ships had to wait weeks before joining a homeward convoy. The daily round grew irksome, as a seaman of the *Explorer*, which arrived at Molotovsk with PQ6, described:

> As the days progressed it snowed and the wind was bitter. No one was able to go out in the open unprotected. If one didn't wear gloves and touched metal, the result was lost skin. Our only occupation was keeping the ship clear of ice and snow. It was seldom possible to bath. All the toilets were frozen up . . . One's W.C. was a bucket of snow up on deck . . . At this time scabies became a nuisance and added to our cocktail of complaints. Eventually we had our water rationed and we used to go with our buckets and obtain a supply of warm red water for our ablutions. It was during one of these

> queues that . . . the man in front suddenly accused us of writing home to his wife regarding the size of his rudimentary equipment and impairing his marital relations . . . the poor chap had had a breakdown. Eventually he had to be locked in one of the upper cabins . . .
>
> Our daily food became steadily worse and almost uneatable. The poor old cook became our worst enemy so that every mealtime he used to disappear from the galley and take refuge in his room. As we ran out of stores we replenished from ashore . . . four yak carcasses arriving on a sleigh . . . Under the circumstances we should have considered the Russians generous. The problem was we couldn't leave and they couldn't get rid of us because of the ice.
>
> Christmas Day [1941] duly arrived, a very dull affair. All we got was a tot of rum on the [shipping] company – not that we had much interest in drinking to their health.

Many merchant seafarers of all ranks spent as much time in the ports of North Russia as the naval personnel drafted to NP100, NP200 and their offshoots. Among these were the heavy lift ships designed to enhance the cargo facilities on the Kola Inlet and the Dvina.

With the arrival of PQ16 came the *Empire Elgar*, another specially built heavy lift ship like the *Empire Bard*, mentioned earlier, designed to facilitate the discharge of heavy tanks in the absence of adequate craneage in the Russian ports. Having led the Archangel-bound component of PQ16 into the Dvina, the ship was based there until ice threatened the river, when she transferred to Murmansk to join the *Empire Bard*. A later ship of the same class, the *Empire Buttress*, afterwards relieved them. These ships became part of the ports' installations, lifting tanks directly from the incoming merchant ships and then manœuvring alongside the rickety wooden quays to land them on to railway wagons. They often worked under aerial attack and only a bad raid would halt discharge. During the Arctic winter the necessary provision of deck lights could not be adequately blacked out or masked from the air, a circumstance which only emphasizes the difficulties men laboured under in these high latitudes.

When these raids occurred every available gun opened up. Local anti-aircraft fire was often thought by British observers to be indiscriminate, hitting friend and foe alike, or ineffective, hitting nothing and wasting ammunition. As armaments reached Russia, the defences of Murmansk and its environs gradually improved and less reliance was placed on support from the merchant ships in port.

German successes against docked ships were limited. The harassing and eventual sinking of the *Empire Starlight* on 1 June 1942 and the loss of the *New Westminster City* and *Lancaster Castle* in April have already been described, while on 3 June the American freighter *Steel Worker* struck a magnetic mine and sank in Murmansk Road. Forty-nine years later her engine telegraph was lifted from the wreck. The *Alcoa Cadet* suffered the same fate on the 21st. But it was to be March 1943 before the next ship, the British freighter *Ocean Freedom*, succumbed to air attack at Murmansk, and although other ships were damaged, they carried on trading.

It is in the character of the merchant seafarer to grumble and there were many complaints on many subjects in North Russia. The restriction placed upon movement by Soviet guards has already been mentioned and was harshly applied to merchant seamen who, unlike their officers, generally wore no uniform and thus had little status in Russian eyes. But one or two circumstances provoked real anger, particularly the casual disregard of war material left on the dockside because of inefficient transport. The irony of single CAM ships, mounting obsolete Mark 1 Hurricanes, guarding ships whose holds were stuffed with the latest machines with heavy calibre cannon was not lost on these men. And so when a party of them, enjoying the brief respite of a watch ashore, strayed on to the edge of the airfield at Gryaznaya and found brand-new Hurricanes abandoned unused, they were justifiably upset. Tags still hung in the cockpits marking the machines as passed for active service with the date and initials of the test flight and pilot. Some had clearly been the victims of heavy, careless landings, their undercarriages damaged.

'The Russians did not repair anything,' one naval officer complained. The remark was more despairing than accurate, after the sacrifices which had been made to deliver the material. Certainly there were numerous examples of Soviet profligacy and neglect, but the Russians did repair *some* things, and in the matter of ships did their utmost in difficult circumstances.

The *Hopemount*, it will be remembered, had suffered ice-damage on her way to Murmansk. As she discharged her oil into the bunker tanks of the thirsty escorts, she gradually grew lighter and rose out of the water, and her damaged bow and stern came into view. The sprung plates of the forepeak and bent propeller blades now underwent repair, the former drawn together with long bolts, which eventually cured the leak. For the latter an enormous blow-lamp, shrouded by canvas curtains to contain the heat, was mounted on rickety wooden scaffolding, and the bent propeller blades were brutally beaten back into a semblance of their original configuration by Russian labourers who 'worked like hell', her Chief Officer recalled. 'They didn't get it quite right and we always had a period of critical revs when the ship shook, but it worked.' Indeed, it worked well enough to restore the *Hopemount* to a degree of seaworthiness adequate for yet another arduous passage.

In late July 1942, having discharged her entire cargo, she was relieved of her duty in support of the Royal Navy and chartered to the Soviet government as an oiler to the Russian navy. Escorted by HM minesweepers *Hazard* and *Leda* she proceeded to Molotovsk and loaded a further cargo of oil and then, her crew issued with padded clothing, fur *papenkas* with red stars and the felt boots known as *velinki*, she joined a Russian force including two destroyers and three ice-breakers. The minesweepers *Bramble, Hazard* and *Seagull* with the corvettes *Dianella, Lotus* and *La Malouine* accompanied the Russian ships, which sailed on 29 July. Passing south of Novaya Zemlya the ships entered the Kara Sea where, at the ice-edge, all the warships detached, leaving the convoy and the ice-breakers bound to the eastward to rendezvous in support of the annual westbound convoy from Russian Tartary.

It was early August and shipping movements through the North East Passage were a target of the Kriegsmarine. A specially equipped, very long-range Blohm and Voss BV138 flying boat and the U-boats *U255* and *U435* reconnoitred Spitzbergen, the latter landing a party of meteorologists in what was imaginatively designated Operation Wunderland. Meanwhile *U601* and *U251* were sent into the Kara Sea, followed by the pocket battleship, the *Admiral Scheer*, in pursuit of the Russian ships known to be moving along the north Siberian coast. The *Scheer* passed Cape Zhelania on 16 August and her seaplane located a number of ships, including the *Hopemount* being shepherded by the ice-breakers *Krassin* and *Lenin* in the Vilkitski Strait, between Bolshevik Island and the mainland. However, ice and mist frustrated Kapitän

Meendsen-Bohlken from making an approach. Two days later the *Scheer* came upon the ice-breaker *Aleksandr Sibiryakov*, under the command of Captain Kacharev and famous as the first ship to traverse the North East Passage in 1932. The Russian ship put up a furious defence, but the *Scheer* succeeded in sinking her off Ostrov Belukha with grievous loss of life. On 27 August the *Scheer* attacked the shore installations at Dikson, where the small Russian convoy had been sheltering from her foray into the far north. The German ship inflicted damage on the Soviet patrol ship *Dezhnev* and the freighter *Revolutsioner* (late of PQ16) bearing her cargo eastwards towards Vladivostok. But Meendsen-Bohlken was surprised by heavy shore batteries which struck the *Admiral Scheer* aft, causing casualties, and she withdrew on the 28th, arriving at Narvik on the 30th. Her consort, *U601*, had torpedoed one ship east of Dikson on the 24th.

While the *Scheer* operated in the Kara Sea, west of Novaya Zemlya the Russians lost two tugs, the *Nord* and *Komsomolets*, together with their towed lighters on the 17th, torpedoed by *U209*; and *U255* joined *U209* in shelling the radio stations on Cape Zhelania and at Khodovarikha on the 25th and 28th.

The departure of the *Admiral Scheer* enabled the undamaged Russian ships to proceed east, the *Hopemount* with them. Her master, Captain W.D. Shields, was a sick man, but her Chief Officer assiduously drew observations of the coastline for future pilotage, aware that no other British ship had ever penetrated these forbidden waters. She reached Tiksi Bay in longitude 134°E on 31 August and anchored in company with the other ships. On 16 September the Russian destroyers *Baku*, *Razumny* and *Razyarenny* arrived from Vladivostok and were refuelled. On the 18th, a northerly wind began closing the ice and, with the prospect of more ships arriving from the Pacific diminishing, the *Hopemount* turned about and headed west again, stopping at Dikson on the 26th, short of supplies and with symptoms of scurvy among her crew. The supply convoy reassembled and left Dikson on 6 October, reaching Yugorski Shar on the 11th. Here the *Halcyon*, *Hazard* and *Sharpshooter* arrived to sweep a number of air-laid mines but did not linger as ice was forming rapidly, leaving the *Hopemount* on Trafalgar Day, 21 October. Broken out of encroaching ice by Russian ice-breakers, the weary tanker at last reached open water a month later, on 20 November, slowed by her damaged propeller. She was finally succoured by the minesweepers on 29 November by which time she had reached Iokanka. The food and medical stores supplied by *Bramble* were greatly appreciated and the minesweeper's loss later, in action against the *Hipper*, was sincerely mourned.

The *Hopemount* finally left Russian waters in the return convoy RA51 and arrived at Methil in Scotland on 16 January 1943, where she sustained slight damage in collision. Later she proceeded to the States for full repairs. 'All', reported Captain Shields with routine and rather grudging hyperbole, 'behaved extremely well . . .'

Although something of an aside, the voyage of the *Hopemount* vividly illustrates the uncertain fate that could overtake British merchant seamen. For her Chief Officer it was a dramatic professional challenge, navigating in the Arctic to latitude 84°N being a specialized subject which he, conscious of the unique opportunity offered, was determined to master.

The *Hopemount*'s passage of the northern sea-route was not typical. Other merchantmen, caught in Russian waters and waiting for a homeward convoy, were employed in short coasting voyages, usually laden with timber, while those emptied at the ports of the Kola Inlet with no homeward convoy available were, in the summer months, sent through the Gourlo and the White Sea to Archangel, out of range of the Luftwaffe.

Most merchant seamen, consigned to languish in Soviet ports, remembered above all the lack of any real social life. The recreational facilities at the various ports used by the merchant ships were limited. At Murmansk and Archangel the Intourist Hotels and International Clubs, or 'Interclubs', were the focus for shore leave. Ships berthed at Bakaritsa, opposite Archangel, or at the White Sea port of Molotovsk, on the estuary of the Dvina, were less fortunate, as were those at Economiya, another new, Soviet-built port on the White Sea.

Some men nevertheless broke more than the Arctic ice and not a few actually achieved what most considered impossible, the traditional triumph of Jack ashore, sexual intercourse. Even in these inauspicious surroundings the oldest profession survived. One pathetic woman, 'aged about sixty', stood nightly in a secluded gap in the log-stacks piled on the quay at Archangel to receive her customers. According to her Chief Officer, two of *Hopemount*'s crew contracted gonorrhea. 'Don't know how they managed it. There were girl-soldiers manning the ack-ack batteries alongside the ship at one point, but they refused the chocolates an apprentice offered them. They were very suspicious of us.'

However, another veteran recalled that many Russian women were sexually available, though most were mature married matrons, driven to desperate measures to support children and consumed with loneliness and uncertainty with their menfolk at the front. In their felt boots and muffled in heavy clothing they were not sufficiently attractive to overcome the fastidiousness of many of the younger sailors, but older hands were less scrupulous, reflecting no doubt that life was a chancy business, especially in wartime. Long afterwards a merchant seaman wrote:

> The ladies of Molotovsk mostly inclined to be heavy of limb and feature made even heavier by their clothing . . . and although there were invitations to go home by these ladies after visits to the communal hall, very few, if any, were accepted . . .
>
> However, I would stress how friendly these people were and provided a sharp contrast with the military who were always stand-offish and sullen. In the communal hall we were immediately given vodka on arriving . . . It seemed like a small charge of dynamite . . . The only thing there seemed to be much of was this vodka and money. The children seemed to have bundles of it. I never did find out where they got it from.

Chocolate and cigarettes became the currency of the Western Allies in the ports of the Dvina and the Kola Inlet, with Russian children acting as go-betweens in a multitude of transactions, all of which were of doubtful legality, most harmless and perhaps a few morally reprehensible.

Most, contemplating the temptations of the flesh, remember only these bulkily clad matrons seen in the streets or working on the dockside. More attractive girls were available for chaste dancing at the Interclub, but it was foolish to make passes at them for they were rumoured to be informers. In all probability, the harsh punishments for fraternization deterred these young women from any great friendliness while British perceptions of 'informers' were exaggerated.

We now know the Soviet authorities were concerned about the 'widespread phenomenon' of this so-called 'prostitution' and that although 'thirty girls were sent away from Archangel . . . this made no impression on other[s]'. Such a number reported while the demoralized survivors of PQ17 were awaiting passage home does not seem excessive.

Exceptions, however, prove the rule. It was the DEMS ratings and Maritime Artillerymen who seem to have had the most success in this matter. The Russians were unimpressed by the merchant seamen and their lack of uniform. The gunners, however, wore the garb of fighting men. One DEMS rating scored a notable success and made it to his girl's dormitory though it was very cold and not conducive to sexual ecstasy. When he eventually managed an erection he found the rest of the girls watching his performance.

The DEMS personnel proved themselves invaluable in battle, but aboard merchant ships they occasionally regarded themselves as superior to their merchant counterparts. Maurice Irvin, Chief Officer of the *Empire Elgar*, daily discharging tanks for the Red Army with his ship's heavy lift gear, had an unpleasant encounter with one DEMS petty officer, who flouted Irvin's authority as the *Elgar*'s mate with the sneering comment that he was 'RN, whereas I was *only* a merchant seaman'. Commander Dickson, Bevan's local man-on-the-spot, dressed the DEMS petty officer down, but his was a common and persistent prejudice.

This difference between the 'armed', that is to say, uniformed, services, of which the DEMS ratings were a part, and the civilian merchant seamen was to cause much bitterness. It will be recalled that, before the establishment of the naval parties, a detachment of the Royal Air Force had been sent to North Russia to augment the defences of Murmansk. A wing of Hurricanes had been flown off from *Argus* during the Dervish operation in August/September 1941. Their pilots, who flew in combat over Murmansk, were withdrawn after training Russians to fly their machines, but some remained to train pilots for those that were to follow in the convoys to come.[3]

These airmen, accommodated in the Intourist Hotel, received NAAFI stores and a regular supply of beer, cigarettes and chocolate, the latter two commodities the black-market currency of North Russia.[4] By contrast, notwithstanding their gallant defence of their ships, merchant seamen were mere civilians, entitled only to what the shipowner and the Ministry of War Transport allowed them, and that was little enough. The protest they raised was, in the end, grudgingly acknowledged, but more for the pragmatic reason that such discrimination was having a bad effect on morale than out of any sense of righting a palpable injustice.

Such inequities were bad enough, but worse still was the plight of many of the merchant seamen arriving as survivors without the documentation beloved by the Soviet bureaucracy. Those from the *Empire Lawrence* under the charge of Second Officer Hulse found themselves landed from HMS *Hyderabad* at six in the evening. After six days of almost continuous action stations they were exhausted. They were left to stand on the quayside, cold and hungry, until 10.00 the following forenoon, when a harassed and perplexed British representative of the Ministry of War Transport finally arranged for them to transfer to the holding camp at Vaenga. Here they subsisted on a diet of thin tea and fat pork for a further six days before being shipped aboard the returning vessels of QP13. Hulse himself returned with Commodore Gale aboard the *Empire Selwyn* with survivors of the *Lowther Castle* and the *Empire Purcell*.

After PQ17, related in the next chapter, Archangel was full of survivors who were compelled to subsist on black bread, grass soup and barley, overwhelming the inadequate arrangements made by the British naval authorities. Morale was at a nadir, the full realization of what exactly had happened only slowly permeating even those who had taken part. Fights broke out between the British and Americans, one consisting of some 200 combatants. The Interclub became a mass of depressed individuals, dispirited, broke, without proper clothes or possessions. One evening an American gunner walked in and, rummaging among some scratched and disregarded records lying about, put a Souza march on the hand-wound turntable. At first reluctant, but with an infectious good humour, the British and Americans were drilled for half an hour, the ridiculous exercise re-establishing their good humour and spirits, at least for a while.

Perhaps it was some of the same men who gate-crashed the banquet given by the Russians for the seamen who finally fought the last of the PQ convoys, PQ18, into Archangel. With a quiet dignity each of these bore his meagre meal on a tin tray. Marching to the top table they made the ironic request that their food be added to the feast, for they were tired of such inadequate rations.

For those merchant seamen simply working their ships while they were emptied of their cargoes, the conditions in Murmansk left a lot to be desired. 'There is no hospitality shown towards our men,' reported Captain Stuy of the *Pieter de Hoogh*, 'there are no forms of recreation for them, and apart from this the cost of everything is far beyond their means.' What there was, was cold comfort; Russian beer was 'four roubles a half-pint, looked like lager, tasted of onions and one was enough'.

The plight of the British in Russia was no different from their exiled allies, the Dutch, Norwegians and Poles. The legendary parsimony of British shipowners in the matter of feeding their crews was not noticeably altered by war but was now thrown into stark contrast with that of their more fortunate allies. 'The American survivors did much better than we did', complained a British merchant seaman, 'as they were distributed amongst the American ships . . . but there were too many British survivors to be spread [similarly] amongst the few British ships.'

Not that the condition of the Russians themselves was to be envied. For all their wads of money, the children had little to sell beyond badges and other relatively worthless souvenirs. *Trinidad*'s company had already witnessed the privations endured by the natives of Rosta. Others came across similarly moving sights which left indelible impressions. Len Matthews, Commodore's Yeoman, can never forget 'a gaunt woman attaching herself to a small party of us going to a dinner for the Commodore and myself laid on by the Mayor. She was naturally denied entry and dropped down in front of us and died on the doorstep.' Such events were harrowing in the extreme for the more sensitive observers, but may also explain some of the offhandedness of the Russians to whom these foreigners must, in such circumstances, have been seen to enjoy 'privileges' not available to themselves.

News of events in the outside world was non-existent. Rumours abounded, most of them unfounded and grown in the telling: a CAM-ship pilot was parachuting into the sea when a downed German pilot in his dinghy shot him with a Lüger, was but one such that did the rounds. On the other hand, whilst seamen knew of PQ17, they did not know what had happened. Rumours were inevitable and were not the result of cynical manipulation, but rather of the naturally selective filtration and emphasis of men denied real news, seeing only an influx of survivors each with his own tale to tell and passing on snippets of ill-informed scuttlebutt.

If they did not already possess it, they grew a tough skin, these men, well aware of their low social status, but acquiring a very real pride in their own achievements. They also drew on their grim sense of gallows humour, and needed it, not only to counter the ennui endemic to North Russia, but also to survive the well-meaning if disastrous efforts of those at home to succour these 'heroes' of official propaganda who patently felt themselves regarded as anything but heroic.

The making of woollen 'comforts' for those 'at the front' became almost a cottage industry for women's church groups throughout Britain. One ship's company opened a box of mitts and balaclavas clearly knitted from odds and ends of wool, brilliant with colour and obviously culled from a myriad of sources. With these had come a box of equally unsuitable books. The merchant seamen sat round in a great circle wearing ridiculous head-gear, their hands clad in parrot-coloured finery, attentively listening while one of their number solemnly read them fairy stories!

But the grim purpose of the merchant ships was to bring in their cargoes. Maurice Irvin, Chief Officer of the heavy lift ship *Empire Elgar*, tutored his mixed group of Russian workers led by a man named Ivanov in the operation of the ship's winches. Women as well as men laboured at this task. The *Empire Elgar* herself yielded a Hurricane fighter as deck cargo which, lifted clear of No. 3 hatch, revealed Matilda tanks, landed to the cheers of the assembled workforce. The first, inexpertly driven by a Russian who waved aside the offered assistance of a British sergeant, ploughed deep into the wooden quay, but it was not long before the tanks were rolling on to railway wagons and trundling off to the front. When the ship had discharged her own cargo she ran alongside others with similar loads and transferred them ashore, a process which made her crew part of the dreary scenery. Yet if they watched the departure of the empty returning ships with regret, it was a sentiment tempered by the knowledge that in Archangel they were, at least relatively speaking, safe.

Irvin and his men became regular visitors to the Interclub, forcing their way through the tall, heavy red doors. Here two dances a week with 'specially selected partners' were held and there was the possibility of a film show on Sundays. Thanks to their black-market transactions, the *Elgar*'s crew became comparatively well off and thus popular.

Against the odds, Maurice Irvin formed a touching friendship with a girl called Tanya, who became his regular dancing partner. Both returned across the Dvina from Archangel to Bakaritsa.

> On the ferry she stood near to me until we approached the bank when, after a quick glance round, she squeezed my hand before disappearing into the crowd . . . Each night followed the same routine with furtive contact in the café and on the ferry. Never would I have thought that such an existence would bring happiness but it did.

As the remnants of PQ17 arrived, the surviving ships were directed to Molotovsk and the *Empire Elgar* followed to service them. While Lord Haw-Haw announced the total destruction of the convoy, the men of the *Elgar* played 'Land of Hope and Glory' as each ship came in and spent the succeeding eight weeks discharging what they had brought. It was mid-September before all the ships were emptied, and then those of PQ18 arrived, three of which ran aground and required lightening. Rain and sleet fell almost continuously, precursors of winter, and when at last the *Elgar* followed the lightened freighters upstream to Bakaritsa, her crew had a curious sensation of homecoming.

At the Intourist Hotel that evening, Irvin was greeted by the entire orchestra who stopped playing, stood and bowed before striking up his favourite tune, 'Cymuko', a Georgian love-ballad said to be a favourite of Stalin's. Later, at the Interclub, Tanya greeted him with ill-concealed delight.

At the first sign of the Dvina freezing, the *Empire Elgar* was ordered to Murmansk. Irvin paid a sad and passionate farewell to Tanya. Murmansk was a scene of devastation, the Intourist Hotel a shadow of its Archangel counterpart. 'The place was deserted and the only greeting we got in the dimly lit reception [area] was from a six-foot stuffed black bear.'

During the suspension of convoys after PQ18, the few single ships that made the run kept the *Elgar* employed, but by Christmas, with the re-establishment of convoys, Irvin was surprised and delighted to see old Ivanov and his twin female assistants, linchpins of the discharging gangs at Bakaritsa, on the quayside ready to help unload the newly arrived ships of JW51A.

As has been noted, cargo work usually went on irrespective of air raids and was only occasionally suspended when the raid proved severe. By now Grant and Churchill tanks, twice the weight of the obsolescent Matildas, were arriving in great numbers, and in one raid, with a heavy tank halfway out of a hold, the dockers ran for the shore shelters. Irvin and his female assistant reloaded it, for which action she was afterwards decorated.

Despite the stricken appearance of Murmansk, the barrage now put up by the Russians was impressive. One observer spoke with admiration of a 'perfect box barrage' thrown up by the batteries, others of the Russian sentries' habit of taking pot-shots at German pilots baling out: 'They did not even bother standing up, but fired from wherever they were seated.' A harsh regime awaited those pilots who did succeed in landing and many died of starvation, working on the docksides next to native Russian prisoners. All were kept in conditions of extreme privation.

A British merchant seaman recalled:

> Our rubbish disposal was straight over the side [on to the ice]. This gradually built up and was cleared up by the German prisoners. They were glad enough to do this, as what we considered uneatable was probably, in their terms, a veritable feast. Many times I used to see them being beaten up by their guards using their rifle butts when they tried to salvage any food they came across. During this time we saw a man running away across the ice. Where he thought he was headed for, God only knows, but he didn't get there as he was shot dead in the process.

Cruel though this was, it was understandable, given the atrocities being committed elsewhere in Russia. More difficult to comprehend was the attitude of the Russians to the Allied wounded. Makeshift and primitive hospital facilities were available at Vaenga and large ships, like the cruisers, were co-opted as extempore hospitals while they remained in Russian waters. But this was not long, and though the Russians probably did as much for their Allies as they did for their own wounded, it was inadequate. The Western Allies could not absorb the terrible losses seemingly acceptable to the Russians, particularly among trained seamen. It was, moreover, bad for morale and this delicate, intangible commodity had to be preserved at all costs, particularly after PQ17.

Signs of strain were already evident following PQ16, when the contemplation of even a homeward convoy was not a happy prospect. The crew of one ship refused to sail. This act, seen by the naval authorities as mutiny, pure and simple, was solved by drafting in the unarmed marine survivors of HMS *Edinburgh* to quell it. The fact that the crew was largely Chinese made the rebellion 'explicable' and, presumably, easier to deal with. There is, nevertheless, some evidence to suggest that native British crews were often reluctant to proceed, particularly in the atmosphere that prevailed during the post-PQ17 period. What was mutiny to a naval officer was the recognized withdrawal of labour to a merchant seaman who had a very fine notion of what, even in wartime, constituted his obligations. It was, after all, only a matter of months since the old injustice of his pay being stopped the day his ship was sunk had been done away with, and the rumour that the Royal Navy had deserted a convoy reached some ships with all the exaggeration of oversimplification and misrepresentation.

In the post-PQ17 period, unrest among American survivors also became critical. Many of these men were extremely young and inexperienced, though all were volunteers, many were ineligible for military service. Their complaints about conditions in Russia, a sharp contrast to the comparative luxury of their customary sea-going amenities, were vociferous, exacerbated by uncertainties over their repatriation. They required the intervention of the United States Navy's representative in Archangel, Commander Frankel USN, who dealt capably with these problems with swift common sense.

Incipient mutiny proved easier to quell than did medical problems. The hospital at Vaenga was crude and dirty, its patients often crammed two to a bed, without antiseptics or anaesthetics, in a state of abject misery. At Archangel, survivors of PQ17 were accommodated with the wounded at Sevroles hospital. Immersion foot, frostbite and the consequent amputations formed the principal cases, with the dreadful complication of gangrene if prompt and efficient treatment was neglected. Survivors arriving in Archangel in the summer from the freezing cold of the Barents Sea found the warm mugginess, ideal for the swift corruption of frostbitten tissues, almost unendurable. Mosquitoes were a universal plague, while poor food and often contaminated water aggravated conditions, and a black-market trade in vodka resulted in widespread demoralization.

Murmansk hospital had been partially destroyed by fire after a bombing raid and was no better. Every effort was made to get Allied seamen back to Britain in the warships. On one occasion, in anticipation of repatriation, 116 patients were shipped aboard the *Salamander* to Murmansk, only to find arrangements for their embarkation had not been concluded: they returned to Vaenga.[5] Here they found that those medical stores that did exist had been largely destroyed in an air raid.

While many spoke of the kindness and warm-heartedness of ordinary Russians, relations with the Russian doctors were often strained. Procrastination and excuses based on a refusal to admit shortcomings masked their inability to cope. When a professor of medicine was presented with a pair of rubber gloves from the sick-bay of a rescue ship, he was overcome with gratitude. Drug shortages, the language barrier and the mutual suspicion engendered by wide political and cultural differences occasionally clouded workaday relations. In an extreme case, the Polish wounded from the *Garland* and the *P551* refused to be left in Russian hands.

Top-level representations from Churchill to Stalin produced no improvement. Indeed a demountable hospital and medical unit sent to Russia earlier had been refused and turned back on the grounds that it was not necessary. The Soviet High Command gave their own wounded priority; it was for the Western Allies to remedy what Stalin, like Golovko, considered to be their own shortcomings. And that, in the end, is what happened. The previously rejected medical unit was sent back in October 1942 aboard the cruiser *Argonaut* and the destroyers *Obdurate* and *Intrepid*, greatly improving things.

The Russian attitude to their Western Allies remained complex, although the arrival of PQ18 caused a thaw in the frostiness that had followed the official reception of PQ17 when, after an interview Admiral Stepanov granted Acting Captain Lawford of the anti-aircraft cruiser *Pozarica*, the journalist Godfrey Winn reported Stepanov as totally unsympathetic. 'You should send bigger convoys, and you should provide better means of protection,' Stepanov railed. 'There should be fighter cover the whole way.' Deeply wounding though it was, Russian incomprehension of the true nature of the undertaking or the resources required was something the British became inured to, putting it down to ignorance. But it did not help to know that Stepanov was right or that in the summer of 1942 the Royal Navy did not yet possess the means to provide local fighter cover the whole way. It had rather been hoped the Russians might have achieved a little more in that direction, but the navy had become used to adversity.[6]

Even after the successful arrival of PQ18 in the autumn of that year, Captain Papanin, a liaison officer on Golovko's staff who was an Arctic explorer of distinction and twice a Hero of the Soviet Union, marred his speech thanking Allied seamen at the banquet given in their honour. Unfortunately, perhaps in an attempt at the kind of exhortation Soviet workers were used to, he ended his speech with the words, 'It is not enough; we want more tanks, more planes, quicker discharge!'

The row that ensued was finally smoothed over with the gift of quantities of vodka in jeroboam-sized bottles, but the Russian appetite for arms remained unassuaged. Churchill, too, was still adamant that everything possible should be done to satisfy it, even after the greatest convoy disaster of the war.

12

'A serious fleet operation'

'WE ARE RESOLVED', Churchill telegrammed Stalin on the successful conclusion of PQ16, 'to fight our way through to you with the maximum amount of war materials. On account of *Tirpitz* and other enemy surface ships at Trondheim, the passage of every convoy has become a serious fleet operation. We shall continue to do our utmost'.

At the beginning of December 1941 the German advance had ground to a halt on the outskirts of Moscow, arrested by the onset of winter for which the Wehrmacht was ill-prepared and which was to be the century's worst to date. Thanks to Richard Sorge, their spy in Tokyo, the Russians knew the attack on Pearl Harbor would remove the feared break-out of the battle-hardened Japanese from their puppet state of Manchukuo. They were therefore able to switch thirty divisions of Arctic-trained Siberian troops from the Far Eastern to the European front and on 5 December Marshal Zhukov ordered the Red Army to counter-attack. At his Christmas meeting with Britain's Foreign Secretary, Anthony Eden, Stalin was optimistic about the outcome, for the extraordinary spirit of the Russian soldiers had resulted in a rolling back of the enemy front line, though at a terrible cost in both men and *matériel*.

The Wehrmacht's retreat concentrated the Germans into a series of fortresses and strong points from which the Russians found it difficult to dislodge them. Thus, all along the 1,000-mile front, the counter-offensive faltered, and in the weeks that followed, as the convoys poured their supplies into the ports of North Russia, the struggle of attrition bogged down across this vast battlefield.

Although his generals had failed to take Moscow, in the summer of 1942, having assumed command himself, Hitler announced, 'German arms have achieved a great defensive success'.[1]

By June the German armies had succeeded in investing Sevastopol in the Crimea and had killed or captured many thousands of Russians. Hordes of the latter were sent to build reinforcements to the Atlantic Wall and prevent the Western Allies breaching the security of the Reich with a second front in the west. The German armies occupying the Ukraine were now launched on Operation Blau, a massive drive south and east to seize the vital oilfields of the Caucasus and the industrial centres in the Don valley.

Despite the capture of papers outlining Blau, Stalin insisted they were a ruse and, even as Sevastopol fell, he awaited a renewed offensive on Moscow. But the assumed feint against Voronezh and the Don proved all too real and by the time Stalin realized the extent of his self-deception, Timoshenko's army group on the line of the Donets river was in disarray. It eventually fell back on Stalingrad, with orders to hold the city at all costs. It was against this titanic background that convoy PQ17 prepared to sail from Iceland.

Operations to reinforce Malta had called away from Scapa Flow a considerable portion of the Royal Navy's Home Fleet, interrupting supplies to the Soviet Union at a crucial time in its struggle against German arms. The shortcomings of the internal Russian logistics system notwithstanding, this hiatus contributed to the rapid depletion of armour, artillery and ammunition at the Red Army's disposal, for although 147 tanks were lost during the passage of PQ16, 321 had been discharged in North Russia, along with 124 aircraft and 2,507 vehicles. The consequences of this interruption to the convoys were known to Churchill and, combined with his assurances to Stalin, prompted a resumption of the convoys as soon as the immediate danger to Malta had been averted.[2]

For the British naval staff officers planning the new convoy the danger of attack by German capital ships, particularly the *Tirpitz*, loomed large. Attempts to bomb her in April had failed, and plans to base British torpedo-bombers in North Russia were not completed before the departure of PQ17, though Catalina flying boats of 210 and 240 Squadrons were earmarked for operations based there to supplement intelligence from the Norwegian Resistance.

It was thus hoped to obtain early warning of a sortie by any combination of the *Tirpitz* and *Hipper* from Trondheim, or the *Scheer* and *Lützow* from Narvik. By the end of June the five allocated Catalinas were overflying Altenfiord, near Norway's North Cape, and then making 'cross-over' flights to maintain a watch for German heavy ship movements.

It remained part of the perception of admirals brought up with the tradition of fleet strength based upon capital ships and the big gun, to fear most the intervention of these ships. It was equally inconceivable to these men that the Germans would fail to pursue a policy of total war in Arctic waters and use *every* means at their disposal to interdict supplies, especially at a time when their own land forces were engaged in war *à outrance*.

To Admiral Tovey, Commander-in-Chief, Home Fleet, and the man operationally responsible for Russian convoys, 'the strategical situation . . . was wholly favourable to the enemy'. German capital ships could operate 'close to their own coast, with the support of powerful shore-based air reconnaissance and striking forces and protected . . . by a screen of U-boats . . . Our covering forces . . . . would be without shore-based air support . . . with their destroyers too short of fuel to escort a damaged ship to harbour'. He did not have to point out to the First Sea Lord the implications of endless daylight during the summer months. Pound had already expressed his opinion that summer convoys were 'fundamentally unsound', and that Churchill's punishing schedule was a 'regular millstone round our necks'.[3]

Tovey's answer to attack by heavy German surface ships was to order the convoy to reverse course to the west on the meridian of 10°E, thus luring the predators on to the guns of the so-called 'distant covering force' of the Home Fleet, waiting beyond effective German air cover. In consultations with Pound via the telephone line that ran to his flagship's mooring buoy in Scapa Flow, Tovey expanded upon his plan:

> I hoped that this temporary turn back would either tempt the German heavy ships to pursue, or cause them to return to harbour, or compel them to cruise for an extended period among our submarines, nine of which were concentrated between Bear Island and the Norwegian coast. Three Russian submarines were also in this area. The Admiralty did not approve of this plan . . .

It did, however, approve a reversal of the convoy 'under certain circumstances' though this movement was not to be precisely timed as a ploy, as Tovey wanted, and in the event 'this question did not arise'.

Instead, the First Sea Lord proposed that should the convoy come under attack by heavy ships, it would scatter. Tovey expressed in forthright terms his dismay at Sir Dudley's proposal, protesting that the result would be 'sheer bloody murder'. Pound demurred and the upshot was that the Home Fleet would give the customary distant cover; close cruiser support would supplement the escort to longitude 10°E; and thereafter the escort and the Allied submarine forces would see the convoy through. Tovey suggested splitting the convoy in two, but again the Admiralty disapproved. American munitions were piling up and the Soviet army was in desperate need of them. Thus political and military considerations overrode naval caution. Instead the Rear-Admiral commanding the cruisers would have discretionary orders to proceed beyond Bear Island only if 'the convoy was threatened by the presence of a surface force which the cruiser force could fight'. Moreover, it was 'not intended . . . in any case to go beyond 25° East'.

The Admiralty's consideration for its cruisers was a result of the loss of the *Edinburgh* and *Trinidad* in the Barents Sea, and casualties sustained in other theatres; but as compensation the escort would be a large one, rescue ships would be attached and a dummy convoy would be sailed. Meanwhile, at Scapa Flow, as the Home Fleet waited for its detached units to return from the Mediterranean, His Majesty's ships were honoured by a visit from King George VI. The King conferred with his Commander-in-Chief aboard the *Duke of York*, inspected the ship's company and met Tovey's subordinate rear-admirals, Burnett and Hamilton. The former, to play an active part in later phases of the Arctic campaign, was then Rear-Admiral, Destroyers (RAD), with his headquarters in the depot ship *Tyne* at Scapa; the latter was the commander of the First Cruiser Squadron (CS1), whose ships were soon to cover the ill-fated PQ17. Tovey also presented Rear-Admiral Giffen to the King. Giffen, commanding the United States' Task Force 99, was attached to the British Home Fleet and he too was to be part of Tovey's distant cover to both PQ17 and QP13.

Also to sail in support of PQ17 was Tovey's new second-in-command, Vice-Admiral Sir Bruce Fraser. Before the year was out he was to succeed the Commander-in-Chief. Like Burnett, Fraser's destiny awaited him in the waters of the Barents Sea.

Anchored conspicuously at Scapa among the waiting ships of the Home Fleet was the dummy convoy with which it was intended to feint towards Norway. It consisted of the First Minelaying Squadron and four colliers escorted by the cruisers *Sirius* and *Curacoa*, five destroyers and a handful of trawlers. Operation ES sailed two days after PQ17 and trailed its coat in the Norwegian Sea to simulate a raiding force making for southern Norway. It was not seen by enemy reconnaissance, nor was a repeat of the operation a week later. In both cases the main 'battlefleet sailed . . . and adjusted its course to give the impression of covering the raiding force'. Sadly, the ruse was a dismal failure.

At the time, no one but Tovey and Pound themselves was privy to the division of opinion between them. Other secrets were less easily kept. There was a growing sense among merchant seamen, as well as their naval cousins in the escorts, that they were, to a degree, a form of bait to lure the German capital ships out of their Norwegian lairs. In the mid-summer of 1942 it was a vague, uneasy feeling, grown out of stories of earlier convoys and spiced with cynical black humour and the keen sense of being disregarded pawns. Nevertheless, it was obvious enough to be commented upon by a few perceptive men in influential places, such as Burrough and Bonham-Carter, as we have seen.

Tovey was also aware of it, and this would have fuelled his opposition to the plan to scatter. It was imperative that a convoy stuck together even if, as the Commander-in-Chief planned, the whole force reversed course. In such unity lay strength and self-confidence. Allied merchant ships had proved themselves capable of making a major contribution to their own protection, particularly in the Arctic in the matter of air defence, and had, moreover, repudiated early naval contempt for their station-keeping. Richard Onslow had said of PQ16, 'we were all inspired . . . by the parade-ground rigidity of the convoy's station-keeping'.

Morale is a fragile thing and Tovey knew it to be near breaking-point on some of the merchant ships awaiting convoy in idleness at Iceland. Idleness begets indiscipline and discipline itself was often in short supply, particularly aboard new and hurriedly manned American vessels. Many seamen tuned in to the anti-British broadcasts of Lord Haw-Haw who warned American seamen of the dangers awaiting them in the Barents Sea. Aboard the American-owned *Troubadour*, an ageing, British-built tramp steamer then flying the Panamanian flag after first serving Belgian and Italian owners, was a tough and rebellious crew. The ship had already suffered acts of petty sabotage when her crew learned of America's entry into the war. Composed of an unhappy, polyglot mixture of sea-going drifters and regular professional American seamen earning danger money atop their wages, they were commanded by Captain George Salvesen, a Norwegian, who had been compelled to use his United States Navy armed guard to subdue a mutiny of a score of his crew who refused to take the ship to Russia. Later, in Archangel, after trouble over women, Salvesen again had to lock up some of his men before turning them over to the Russians for imprisonment. He, his officers and the ensign commanding the naval armed guard were later cleared of charges laid against them at an enquiry held by the American War Shipping Administration.

While the merchant ships in Hvalfiordur and the warships in Scapa waited for orders to proceed, the Admiralty received confirmation of its worst fears. The British naval attaché in Stockholm, Captain Henry Denham, had been informed by Swedish intelligence sources that they had intercepted and decoded German landline traffic to northern Norway to such an extent that they had obtained a fleet operations order telexed to Narvik on 14 June.

Denham signalled London with the news:

> Most Immediate. Following is German plan for attack on next Russian convoy: 1. Air reconnaissance to locate eastbound convoy when it reaches Jan Mayen. Bombing attacks from bases in north Norway will then be made. 2. Pocket battleships and six destroyers will move to Altenfiord . . . *Tirpitz* and *Hipper* to Narvik. Naval forces may be expected to operate . . . once convoy has reached five degrees east. Simultaneous attacks when convoy on meridian of Bear Island by two surface groups supported by U-boats and aircraft.

In true Wagnerian manner the operation was coded Rösselsprung, 'The Knight's Move'.[4]

The outcome of the battles then being fought on a front which extended from the Barents Sea to the Caspian were clearly crucial to the German High Command. It was imperative therefore to employ those resources not actively engaged against the Soviet armies in support of the main effort. The most supine arm of the Nazi war-machine was its surface fleet.

After the narrow escape of *Tirpitz* during the passage of PQ12, Raeder, paralysed by the shortage of fuel oil, had withheld his heavy units until he received adequate support, despairing of true co-operation from Goering, despite the huge reinforcement of the Luftwaffe in northern Norway. Instead he had sought a proper naval air arm and had succeeded in persuading Hitler to order the conversion of several large merchant ships to aircraft-carriers and the resumption of work on the *Graf Zeppelin*. However, these were long-term plans that should have been carried out before Hitler committed the Fatherland to war. In the meantime it became of paramount importance to strike decisively at the Russian convoys.

Earlier in the year Hitler had decreed that 'Anglo-American intentions . . . depend on sustaining Russia's ability to hold out by maximum deliveries of war materials'. Germany must, therefore, henceforth impede this, but Hitler added a caveat, his old obsession that an Allied second front might be opened in Norway. Given this circumstance it was an irony that German aircraft failed to locate the dummy operation launched across the Norwegian Sea by the British.

In response to the Führer's directive, the Luftwaffe had, as we have already seen, reinforced their squadrons in Norway. Mustered for the assault on PQ17 were a small number of Heinkel He115 torpedo-armed seaplanes, 103 Junkers Ju88 bombers, 30 Junkers Ju87b Stuka dive-bombers and a large number of reconnaissance aircraft including Ju88s, BV138 flying boats and FW200 Condors. The Heinkel He111 torpedo-bombers had by now been trained to the satisfaction of the commander of the 5th Luftflotte, Colonel-General Stumpff. In addition, German cryptographic interception and analysis were highly efficient and were able to decode signals with a facility almost equal to the Enigma traffic being broken by Ultra at Bletchley Park.

Despite the Luftwaffe's great strength and its numerous reconnaissance planes, co-operation with the Kriegsmarine was only grudgingly offered. This amounted to the usual 'search and locate' operations, followed by the maintenance of close monitoring and the homing of Dönitz's U-boats. However, it could not entertain anything which would compromise its own bombing offensive.

The naval staff regarded this as a rebuff and pointed out that the bombing of PQ16 had been only a limited success. More important, they wanted positive location of British aircraft-carriers whose fighters, for all their shortcomings, had shaken the German High Command by their attack on the *Tirpitz* during the sortie against PQ12. Admiral Rolf Carls, then commanding Navy Group North, could not justify a sortie of the heavy ships without the assurance that they could destroy the convoy and retire without interference from either British carrier-borne aircraft or British battleships. Moreover, this assurance was necessary before Raeder could put the proposition to Hitler and gain the Führer's consent. The Grossadmiral was eager to justify his beloved navy, eager to prove the worth of his ships and men, and could brook no thought of failure to take advantage of an attack through the lack of the Luftwaffe's co-operation.

On 30 May Raeder was in Trondheim where Vizeadmiral Otto Schniewind had relieved the sick Ciliax in command of *Tirpitz* and *Hipper*. Schniewind was in favour of an offensive operation and had put his case to Raeder. Two days later Raeder's representative at Hitler's headquarters, Vizeadmiral Theodor Kranke, informed the Führer that a plan involving a sortie by *Tirpitz* had been drawn up. There were a number of reasons for Raeder's eagerness – the relatively low incidence of fog in June, the prevalence of high pressure calms and good visibility and the assumption of the unmelted position of the ice edge were important, but the most cogent was the allocation of 15,000 tons of crucial fuel oil.

The Knight's Move was to be no mere tip-and-run raid, though it would be conducted by a lightning strike; what was intended, given moderately favourable conditions, was the destruction of a convoy 'down to its very last ship', a localized superiority of overwhelming force which would achieve more in a couple of hours than a wolfpack in as many days, the very guerilla tactics conceived as being the Kriegsmarine's true role. But the lack of guaranteed aerial location of the British aircraft-carriers compromised the use of the *Panzerschiffs Lützow* and *Scheer*, then lying at Narvik with the 8th Destroyer Flotilla; their speed of 28 knots was insufficient to keep them out of trouble and their optical gunnery systems were potentially vulnerable in the fickle conditions of the Arctic.

Nevertheless, a German conference brief was prepared by the naval staff by 9 June and on the 11th, Admiral Arctic, responsible for submarine movements in the area, ordered three U-boats of the Eisteufel group (*U251*, Timm; *U376*, Marks; and *U408*, von Hymmen) to patrol the Denmark Strait with orders to shadow rather than attack the convoy and strike at escorting warships only when positive identification had been made. Schmundt did not want his U-boats torpedoing German warships by mistake.

On 15 June, *U334* (Siemon) put to sea, followed on the 16th by *U657* (Göllnitz) and *U88* (Bohmann), on the 18th by *U457* (Brandenburg), and on the 23rd by *U255* (Reche) and *U456* (Teichert). Bielfeld's *U703* and La Baume's *U355* were also ordered to augment the wolfpack, which lay in wait off Jan Mayen for the next scheduled convoy.

In the meantime, on 14 June, Schniewind's own operational order for Rösselsprung was completed and forwarded to Raeder who laid it before Hitler at Berchtesgaden the following day. Raeder stressed the importance of full co-operation from the Luftwaffe, something only Hitler could initiate, and the excellent prospect of success that the plan offered. Hitler approved moving the German capital ships to the north in conformity with Schniewind's plan but, mindful of Raeder's earlier caution, ordered the British carriers located and bombed by Ju88s 'before any attack is made by our surface ships'. The only concession to this stipulation Raeder could wring out of Hitler was a provision that if the carriers were so far distant that their aircraft were out of range, then the attack could proceed, but even if this was the case, the order to proceed remained 'subject to the Führer's approval'.

This was the beginning of a series of provisos which tied the hands of every flag-officer in the long, complex chain of command from Raeder in Berlin, through Carls at Wilhelmshaven, Kummetz commanding the pocket-battleships then at Narvik, Schmundt as Admiral Arctic also at Narvik, to Otto Schniewind aboard the *Tirpitz* in Trondheim. Nor were the communications of the Luftwaffe in Norway much better, while the liaison between the two services was erratic. But it did not matter; despite Captain Denham's timely warning from Stockholm, despite Tovey's elaborate measures for its cover and protection, PQ17 was doomed. The awesome threat of a fleet in being was to be enough to influence the outcome of events.

The convoy's close escort and cruiser covering force were supplemented by the usual distant cover of heavy ships. Tovey, his flag flying in *Duke of York*, put to sea with Rear-Admiral Giffen aboard the USS *Washington*, Vice-Admiral Fraser aboard the *Victorious*, and Rear-Admiral Burrough aboard the cruiser *Nigeria*. With them steamed a second cruiser, HMS *Cumberland*, and a dozen destroyers.[5]

Tovey took his ships first eastwards, covering the false convoy in the unsuccessful attempt to deceive the enemy, then turned north to take up that ambiguous duty of 'distant cover'. He was probably still mulling over his telephone conversation with Pound, and doubtless regretting the circumstances, in the operation against *Tirpitz* during PQ12, that had compelled him to ask the Admiralty to take over the direction of his destroyers. On 27 June he had received a long and essentially confusing signal which deprived him of freedom of action. 'As Admiralty may be in possession of fuller and earlier information of movements of enemy surface forces . . . it appears necessary for Admiralty to control movements of convoy as far as this may be influenced by movements of enemy surface forces'. Doubtless an allusion to the possibility of superior intelligence gleaned from Ultra decrypts, Pound reserved to himself the authority for the ultimate decision.

The secret instruction acknowledged the possible necessity of reversing the convoy's course, not to lure the enemy striking force under the guns of the Home Fleet, but as an expedient that might be tried if attack came when PQ17 was east of Bear Island. It was also asserted that generally speaking the safety of the convoy from surface ships to the eastwards of Bear Island 'would be dependent on our submarine dispositions'. Moreover, it was not expected that the 'covering force will be placed in a position where it will be subject to heavy air attack unless there is a good chance of bringing *Admiral von Tirpitz* to action'.

Unfortunately, the signal then went on to prohibit Hamilton's cruisers proceeding beyond the meridian of 25°E and to permit all the local commanders, Tovey, Hamilton, Broome and Commodore Dowding, if circumstances arose 'in which the best thing would be for convoy to be dispersed . . . to Russian ports . . . to give this order'.

All this was muddled thinking, unhelpful to those officers at sea bearing a heavy burden of responsibility. The signal did contain one sentence which for Commander Broome outlined 'the policy of the operation' and which, had it been followed, might have achieved the degree of success of PQ16: 'Our primary objective is to get as much of the convoy through as possible and the best way to do this is to keep it moving eastwards even though it is suffering damage'.[6]

A baleful influence was already being felt.

Convoy PQ17 sailed from Hvalfiordur on 27 June 1942. It consisted of thirty-six merchant ships, predominantly American and including a number of war-built Liberty types. The previous day the westbound QP13 had left Archangel, picking up more returning vessels from Murmansk on the 28th. It, too, was composed of thirty-five merchant ships, all veterans of the northern route; they were under Commodore N.H. Gale in *Empire Selwyn*. The usual Russian destroyers and British minesweepers provided local escort before turning back, leaving the ocean escort to HM Destroyers *Inglefield* (Commander P. Todd, Senior Officer), *Intrepid, Achates* and *Volunteer*, the Polish *Garland*, the anti-aircraft ship *Alynbank*, the corvettes *Honeysuckle, Starwort, Hyderabad* and the Free French *Roselys*, the minesweepers *Niger* and *Hussar*, and the trawlers *Lady Madeleine* and *St Elstan*. HM Submarine *Trident* also accompanied the convoy until 1 July. *Inglefield* and *Intrepid* had made a direct run through to Kola from Scapa with spare parts and ammunition for the returning escorts. On the homeward passage they carried some of *Edinburgh*'s survivors; others from the cruiser had volunteered and helped make up the deficit in *Garland*'s crew.[7]

Thick weather prevailed in the Barents Sea and navigation became a matter of dead reckoning. The convoy was reported on 30 June and 2 July, the day on which the two convoys passed, but the Germans were by then concentrating on PQ17. Force Q, the by now familiar fleet oiler with her destroyer, in this case the ice-damaged *Gray Ranger* escorted by HMS *Douglas*, joined company from PQ17 on the afternoon of the 2nd as the two convoys passed.

The following day *Inglefield, Intrepid* and *Garland* were detached on Admiralty orders to sweep southwards in a brief, inconclusive search for the *Tirpitz* which was missing from her moorings, her whereabouts unknown. Their negative report was a small factor in the flawed and fatal decision to be made in distant London the following day.[8]

On the fateful 4 July 1942, as it approached the north coast of

Iceland, obeying an unexpected Admiralty order received late on the evening of the 2nd, QP13 divided. Commodore Gale, with nineteen ships in company, altered course for Loch Ewe and arrived without incident. The remaining sixteen merchantmen, most of them American, continued towards Hvalfiordur with Captain J. Hiss, Master of the *American Robin* of the United States Lines, as Commodore. These ships were escorted by the minesweepers *Niger* (Commander A.J. Cubison, Senior Officer) and *Hussar*, the corvette *Roselys*, and the trawlers *St Elstan* and *Lady Madeleine*. The destroyers *Inglefield* and *Intrepid*, which had remained with the Iceland detachment, departed on the morning of the 7th to refuel at Seidisfiord where they arrived in dense fog.

As Hiss and Cubison approached Straumness, the north-west cape of Iceland, Hiss formed his ships into five columns and they rolled and pitched south-west, with a quartering sea driven by a north-easterly gale. The sky remained overcast, visibility poor; the last astronomical fix was three days old. Considerable doubts were entertained as to the exact position of the convoy. Shortly after 19.00 on the 5th, Cubison signalled Hiss, suggesting reforming in two columns to pass between the ness and the British minefield to the north-west. Hiss had had no prior knowledge of this minefield, since the division of the convoy had not been planned.

At 20.00 Cubison took soundings and estimated his position to be north-east of Straumness; QP13 accordingly altered course to the south-west. Ordering *Hussar* to take station astern of *Niger*, but to remain in sight of the convoy, Cubison went ahead to make a landfall.

At about 22.00 the men on *Niger*'s bridge sighted land one mile distant and signalled an alteration of course to due west. Alas, the 'land' was an iceberg, though in the swirling har this was not realized. Forty minutes later *Niger* strayed into the so-called 'friendly' minefield and blew up with heavy loss of life. Cubison's last act was to signal his mistake to Hiss and recommend a resumption of the south-westerly track. It was too late. Even as Hiss digested this intelligence with the reverberation of *Niger*'s detonation fading, more explosions were erupting around him. Confused, the ships thought themselves victims of U-boat torpedoes, or the shells of a distant raider. The *Hybert*, *Massmar*, *Heffron*, *Exterminator* and *Rodina* were sunk, and the *John Randolph* was mine-damaged. *American Robin* and *Hegira* had detached for Reykjavik.

Whilst ignorance confused the merchantmen, the remaining warships had charts indicating the position of the British minefield. With this knowledge the escorts entered the minefield and rescued those survivors they could. Lieutenant Biggs of HMS *Hussar* had obtained a fix and led the shattered and nervous merchantmen due south and proceeded to Reykjavik, leaving the Free French corvette *Roselys* (Lieutenant de Vaisseau A. Bergeret) to quarter the area for six and a half hours. Bergeret succeeded in rescuing 179 men.

The Admiralty signal which caused the unplanned division of the convoy took no account of the imperfect briefing of the extempore commodore, while the *Niger*'s primitive radar confused Cubison in the matter of a landfall. In the light of the greater tragedy then overwhelming PQ17 in the Barents Sea, the fate of QP13 has been forgotten. Yet tragedy cannot be evaluated in comparative forms; its magnitude is a constant. Perhaps more pertinent, the root cause of QP13's losses was almost identical to what was now happening to PQ17.

Commodore J.C.K. Dowding had led his deeply laden merchantmen out of Reykjavik on 27 June. Because Murmansk had been reduced to a standstill after heavy bombing, all except eight American ships were bound for Archangel; one, the *Richard Bland*, ran aground before the Icelandic coast was cleared. The tug *Adherent* and trawler *Northern Pride* were sent to assist, but the Liberty ship was left behind and PQ17 was reduced to thirty-five ships.

Aerial reconnaissance had reported an early recession of the ice-edge, permitting the ships to pass north of Bear Island and to stretch up into the Arctic Ocean, well away from the Luftwaffe's Norwegian airfields, but in the Denmark Strait the convoy encountered heavy loose ice, and a further ship, the American *Exford*, was too damaged to continue. Breaking radio silence, her master transmitted a series of requests for orders, frustrated by Dowding's silence and potentially betraying the departure of the convoy. Finally the *Exford* turned back, reducing Dowding's charges to thirty-four, plus the fleet oiler *Gray Ranger*. It had originally been intended to pass her and her cargo of boiler oil through to Russia to serve as a fuel depot in North Russia. Unfortunately she too sustained ice-damage, a growler splitting her bow wide enough open for the surge and suck of the sea to pour in and out of her as she rose and fell in the swell. It was clear she would be unable to complete the voyage and it was decided her cargo should be used to top up the escorts. She thus exchanged places with the fleet tanker *Aldersdale*.

Only three minesweepers and four anti-submarine trawlers accompanied the merchant ships from Hvalfiordur until, on 30 June, PQ17 received the reinforcement of the ocean escort, commanded by an experienced and dashing destroyer officer and former submariner, Commander J.E. Broome, in *Keppel*. Broome and his staff had already met the convoy's masters in Hvalfiordur, and he wrote later of their obvious interest and experience. He also recorded that in response to queries about the likelihood of attack by the *Tirpitz*, he had spoken of the opportunity his escort group had had to work out some anti-surface attack tactics using smoke and torpedoes. Elsewhere he complained of the weakness of 'scratch' escorts and the fact that his escort commanders had not all met each other until he summoned them aboard *Keppel* at Seidisfiord.[9]

Nevertheless, on meeting PQ17 at sea, Broome rapidly turned theory into practice, deploying his anti-submarine trawlers at the extreme corners of the convoy box. *Lord Middleton* steamed on the port advanced flank, *Lord Austin* on the starboard, with *Ayrshire* on the port, and *Northern Gem* on the starboard rear flank. Within this outer screen, the destroyers, corvettes and minesweepers formed an inner diamond pattern round the nine columns of merchantmen. *Keppel* led with the Hunt-class destroyer *Wilton* and the ex-American four-stacker *Leamington* on her port and starboard quarters, then the corvettes *Lotus* and *Poppy*, and finally on the port flank *Fury* and on the starboard, *Offa*. *La Malouine* and *Ledbury* were close on the after quarters of the convoy itself, with the three rescue ships in line abreast between them. For the first few days the elderly destroyer 'leader' *Douglas* was attached, but she was not part of the close escort, forming the cover to Force Q. Immediately astern of the centre were stationed two submarines, *P614* and *P615*, then a short line abreast consisting of the ocean minesweeper *Halcyon*, the corvette *Dianella* and the minesweeper *Salamander*. Finally, at the opposite diamond point to *Keppel* was the minesweeper *Britomart*. These ships ringed the convoy at 3,000 yards range, closing in to 1,000 yards when the hoisting of the 'Q' flag signalled imminent air attack.

Just within the outer columns of the convoy itself were stationed the anti-aircraft 'cruisers' *Palomares* and *Pozarica*, former fruit-carriers belonging to the shipping firm of McAndrews. Commodore Dowding was in the *River Afton* (Captain H.W. Charlton), leading the centre column, and within the convoy were the CAM ship *Empire Tide* and the oiler *Aldersdale*.[10]

With these dispositions and the armaments of the merchant ships to help, Broome had ably mixed his ships to provide both anti-submarine and anti-aircraft capability. With the well-armed Liberty ships on the outskirts of the convoy itself, the *Pozarica* and *Palomares* with their relatively sophisticated air-warning radars just within its perimeter, and the three leading destroyers to cover the line of advance, Broome had placed *Offa* and the other Hunt, *Ledbury*, on the starboard side, that from which air attack would most likely come. He had thus maximized his anti-aircraft capability with an effective barrage from ships which would not stray far from their defence stations, though in the event, closing on the convoy allowed torpedo-bombers to get within range of the merchant ships.

Anti-submarine warfare was a different matter; it required the detachment of escorts to hunt and destroy, or at least put down, enemy submarines. Early warning of U-boat attack by both visual and sonic means could be obtained from the trawlers while the dispositions of the corvettes and Halcyon-class minesweepers meant that they could be detached from appropriate sectors of the convoy without significantly weakening the bailiwick.

Finally Broome had his submarines which, with his three fleet destroyers, might have achieved something had a heavy enemy unit appeared, though their surface and submerged speeds made this most unlikely. As will be seen, subsequent actions of small, boldly handled destroyer detachments against heavy ships proved that much could be achieved if this circumstance occurred.

The escort was supplemented by the three rescue ships, the *Zaafaran*, *Zamalek* and *Rathlin*. These ships were fitted with high-frequency radio direction-finders, and could thus combine with the warships to 'fix' the positions of radio transmissions made by U-boats, which allowed Broome to counter-attack before they themselves made their approach.

In the holds of the guarded ships were 297 aircraft, 594 tanks, 4,246 military vehicles, both lorries and gun-carriers, and over 150,000 tons of military stores and general cargo. It was a prodigious amount of *matériel* with which to rearm the Red Army, and for twenty-four hours convoy PQ17 settled down to its routine, purposefully steering north-east at 8 knots through calm seas over which an intermittent mist came and went. It was already very cold.

Along with Broome at the conference in Hvalfiordur had been Rear-Admiral Louis 'Turtle' Hamilton, an advocate of naval air power and an opponent of Churchill's policy of bombing Germany at the expense of air supremacy over the Arctic and Atlantic Oceans. Broome described him as 'a bachelor, wedded to the white ensign, courteous, unflappable and popular'. He was keen on hunting and was no aesthete. 'I can't recall ever having seen him reading a book,' recollected one of his officers aboard his flagship, the cruiser *London*, 'yet one couldn't help serving him loyally.' Addressing the convoy conference he had outlined the proposed cover of the Home Fleet, and in particular his own cruisers, and the possibility of attack by a heavy German squadron. 'Impress upon your men the necessity for strict fire discipline . . . Keep a lookout for torpedo bombers, and be careful not to fire into other ships'.

Hamilton had then returned to Seidisfiord, the narrow inlet dominated by snow-capped mountains whose summits were lost in cloud. Some of the Icelandic houses bore crudely daubed black swastikas on their walls, betraying the sympathies of the occupants. German agents in Iceland had reported the departure of PQ17 and later its escort, a fact confirmed by the reconnaissance flights made overhead by Condors.

Broome's escorts had already refuelled from the fleet oiler stationed in the fiord and sailed to their rendezvous with the merchant ships. Hamilton's squadron prepared to follow. *London*, together with *Norfolk* and the destroyer *Somali*, were now joined by the United States cruisers *Tuscaloosa* and *Wichita*, and the destroyers *Wainwright* and *Rowan* under Rear-Admiral Giffen. The Allied navies exchanged courtesies with dipping ensigns, the notes of the saluting bugles echoing back and forth from the steep slopes of rock and scree rising from the waters of the fiord.

In his operational orders Hamilton had emphasized that 'the primary object is to get PQ17 to Russia, but an object only slightly subsidiary is to provide an opportunity for the enemy's heavy ships to be brought to action by our battlefleet and cruiser covering force'. As for the active part the cruiser force would play in achieving this 'slightly subsidiary' objective, Hamilton's response was classic cruiser strategy: 'It is not my intention to engage any enemy unit which includes *Tirpitz*, who must be shadowed at long range and led to a position at which interception can be achieved by the Commander-in-Chief'.

After a final briefing held at 02.00 on 1 July, Hamilton's Allied cruiser squadron put to sea to cover PQ17 which was by now well on its way. The grey ships cleared the fiord and, forming up, turned north and increased speed. Aboard Giffen's flagship Lieutenant Douglas Fairbanks of the United States Naval Reserve made disparaging observations on the Royal Navy and its technical abilities. 'Its legendary superiority is gone . . . Its present state is a source of wonderment and discussion'. In particular its failure to appreciate or to exploit the advantages of naval aviation had subjected it to 'several unnecessary misfortunes'.

Taking advantage of the calm on the morning of 1 July 1942 as they passed Jan Mayen Island, the destroyers forming Broome's close escort of PQ17 queued in turn to refuel from the oilers. At noon the first U-boats were sighted and driven off, during which radio silence was again broken and the German *B-Dienst* intercepts learned of the convoy's progress. Reche's *U255* and von Hymmen's *U408* maintained contact, however, and *U334* and *U456* were directed to their support. More U-boats, *U251, U355, U657, U88, U457* and *U376,* were grouped in an intercepting cordon further east.

At about 14.00 the ominous drone of a 'Shad' was heard and the ugly, lumbering Blohm and Voss BV138c appeared through the misty veil of cloud. In distant London, in the Submarine Tracking Room at the Admiralty, radio monitoring on 4995 kilocycles intercepted the flying boat transmitting homing signals for the U-boats. Tension in all the ships began to build up in expectation of air attack. A brief alarm occurred when the distant silhouettes of capital ships were made out on the horizon to the eastwards. The trawler *Lord Austin* was detached to investigate and reported the only sighting PQ17 had of Tovey's heavy squadron.

Early on 2 July Force Q detached to fuel the homeward escorts of QP13.[11] The two convoys passed each other the same afternoon in about latitude 73°N, longitude 003°E. QP13 had yet to receive its instruction to divide and all appeared in good order in both convoys, but there were now up to three aircraft shadowing PQ17 and shortly afterwards the whole eastbound convoy wheeled to avoid torpedoes thought to have been fired by *U456* (Teichert), which was abortively counter-attacked by *Fury*, *Wilton*, *Lotus* and *Ayrshire*. Still the shadowing aircraft droned on the rim of the horizon. The weather remained calm and cold, with the occasional mist patch drifting over the steel-blue sea and pockets of colder air in the vicinity of icebergs. A Walrus from Hamilton's distant cruisers overflew the convoy but avoided tangling with the German shadowers. At 18.00 that evening as the USS *Rowan* appeared, the first of Hamilton's squadron to make contact, and closed the *Aldersdale* intent on fuelling, nine Heinkel He115 torpedo-armed seaplanes first circled the convoy and then pressed a 'not very skilful' attack on the *Pozarica* until she opened fire and they shied away. The approaching *Rowan* also erupted with her formidable armament and one of the enemy aircraft was shot down, a shell bursting underneath her. The stricken Heinkel crashed and one of its consorts coolly landed alongside it and rescued its aircrew before withdrawing with the rest. As the sun dipped, but did not set, fog closed about the convoy, concealing the alteration of course to east, towards Bear Island and the Barents Sea, which went unobserved by the shadowing Blohm and Voss.

On the 3rd, a day of fog banks 'with sharp but invisible edges' which gradually cleared during the forenoon, the escorts were occupied with several U-boat alarms. The diversion of the destroyers to drop depth-charges kept them at bay and Broome thought them from the 'second eleven'. After the attack of the previous day the atmosphere remained tensely expectant, a feeling 'more marked', wrote Surgeon-Lieutenant Wilkins of the rescue ship *Rathlin*, 'by lack of sleep and the knowledge that the most dangerous part of the voyage is yet to be encountered'.[12] Some of the men listened to Lord Haw-Haw whose broadcast specifically mentioned by name and threatened the rescue ships *Zamalek* and *Zaafaran*.

Admiral Hamilton, with his cruisers some forty miles away to the north, running parallel to PQ17, maintained contact using the *London*'s Walrus, known with a familiar contempt as a 'shagbat'.

Aware that the Germans could deploy two heavy squadrons, the first made up of the pocket-battleships *Lützow* and *Scheer*, the second the *Tirpitz* and the *Hipper*, Hamilton thought it likely that the enemy would send the latter west towards QP13, thus drawing the might of the Home Fleet away from PQ17 which would then be vulnerable to attack from the *Panzerschiffs*. 'The longer I remained unseen the greater my chance of bringing the pocket-battleships to action', he later reported. Such a force, Hamilton judged, was not of sufficient strength to compel him to refuse battle in accordance with his instructions.

During the afternoon Hamilton closed the convoy and launched *London*'s Walrus aircraft. The BV138 had relocated the convoy and the amphibious Walrus exchanged shots with it as it landed close to *Keppel* with a message for Broome. This was to the effect that air reconnaissance flights from Russia had indicated the ice-edge had receded considerably and Hamilton therefore wanted the convoy to alter course significantly to the northwards, rapidly opening up the distance from Banak, but Broome demurred, making a smaller alteration than Hamilton would have wished, mindful of the injunction to keep the convoy moving east.

The low cloud and fog had frustrated the taking of sights and there was disagreement between the dead-reckoning positions of *London* and *Keppel*. Hamilton thought PQ17 about twenty miles south of its reckoning and a repeat flight was made, compelling Broome to swing PQ17 further north. Air defence was Broome's reponsibility and, while not wishing to appear disobedient, he argued that 'with long endurance shadowers present to home attacking aircraft it seemed to me to make very little difference'. Furthermore the mutual estimated position of the entire convoy agreed with his own.

During these exchanges, with PQ17 passing to the north of Bear Island, the Admiralty signalled that the *Tirpitz*, the *Hipper* and the four destroyers *Karl Galster*, *Friedrich Ihn*, *Hans Lody* and *Theodor Riedel*, together with the torpedo-boats *T7* and *T15*, had left Trondheim. Bad weather had frustrated British air flights over Norway for some days, and that on the afternoon of the 3rd which reported the empty anchorage at Trondheim failed to sight the Narvik ships. In fact Schniewind had left Trondheim on the afternoon of the 2nd, but unbeknown to the British, Kummetz's force, consisting of the *Lützow*, the *Scheer* and the destroyers *Richard Beitzen*, *Z24*, *Z27*, *Z28*, *Z29* and *Z30*, had also slipped north from Narvik. Thereafter, however, disaster struck the Germans, for in negotiating the narrow passage in the Tjelsund as she emerged from Ofotfiord near the Storboen lighthouse in fog, the *Lützow* ran aground. Worse still, uncharted rocks at Altenfiord claimed the *Hans Lody, Theodor Riedel* and *Karl Galster* of Schniewind's force. The Knight's Move was seriously compromised though Schniewind had received reinforcements in the shape of the destroyers *Erich Steinbrinck* and *Friedrich Eckoldt* by the time he arrived in the Altenfiord with *Hipper* and the mighty *Tirpitz*.

Hamilton's squadron had withdrawn again after making contact with PQ17 that afternoon, but at 22.00, having received the Admiralty's message, Hamilton edged south and was sighted and reported by the shadowing aircraft, which gratified him in light of the news from the Admiralty indicating a movement of German ships. He again sent off *London*'s Walrus which landed and had to be taken in tow by the *Lord Middleton*. The amphibious plane had run out of fuel and the convoy once more ran into fog. The Walrus had been fired on by the trawler and *Lotus* as it jettisoned depth-charges prior to touching down, the explosions deceiving the two escorts into thinking her hostile.

As the fog wrapped itself round the convoy, the ships streamed their fog buoys and awaited another white midnight. Above them the shadowing planes lost contact.

In the early hours of 4 July 1942, as the convoy's lookouts saw the fog lift, to hang like a blanket above the mastheads of the ships and reveal the convoy steaming in almost perfect formation, a further Admiralty signal arrived indicating the convoy would be attacked by warships between the 15th and the 30th meridian. This had emanated from Swedish intelligence. The Admiralty also knew from Ultra decrypts that the *Admiral Scheer* had arrived in Altenfiord, and the *Tirpitz*'s departure from Trondheim was confirmed. Everything pointed to a northward movement of German heavy units intent on threatening PQ17 which was now about sixty miles north of Bear Island, midway between the meridians of 15 and 30°E.

Aboard *Palomares*, Signalman Taylor reported what he thought was an aircraft engine overhead. Captain Jauncey was called to the bridge in time to see, through a thinning of the vapour shroud lying above the convoy, a diving Heinkel which released its torpedo before climbing swiftly out of sight. The watch at cruising stations opened up ineffectually with Oerlikons and pom-poms, and, her siren shrieking the six short blasts that alerted neighbouring ships to the fact that *Palomares* was about to make erratic alterations of course, the helm was thrown over and the torpedo sped down the ack-ack cruiser's side, to strike 'a fine Yankee', the Liberty ship *Christopher Newport*. It was 04.52 and the first blood of PQ17 had been drawn. Some of the mixed crew aboard this American merchantman may have panicked, though one gunner was cool enough to attempt to hit the approaching torpedo with his 30-calibre machine guns. The warhead exploded in the engine room, killing the junior engineer and two greasers. The ship quickly lost way, swung round and endangered the adjacent vessels, which detoured past her. The rescue ship *Zamalek* was soon on the scene and forty-seven survivors were 'quickly and efficiently embarked'. Captain Owen Morris of the *Zamalek*, a Welshman of small stature but immense spirit, was surprised at the cheerfulness of the Liberty ship's largely black crew, some of whom arrived aboard in their best shore-going clothes and whose ages varied between 17 and 80. Morris was not happy to see either small arms or baggage coming aboard and vigorously discouraged both. In the event he was right, for *Zamalek* was to be a very crowded little ship in the days ahead.

The *Christopher Newport* did not sink immediately; the *Aldersdale* offered to tow her and the opinion on several ships was that she could and should have been salvaged. But the delay in passing the tow would have rendered the attending ships vulnerable and Broome was constrained to order her destroyed by the accompanying submarine *P614*. The British torpedoes failed to sink her, as did a couple of depth-charges lobbed from *Dianella*. PQ17 steamed on, leaving her afloat.

The solitary attack notwithstanding, the Germans had still not re-established reliable contact with the convoy. It was not until some hours later when the questing Brandenburg in *U457*, alerted by the noise of explosions on his hydrophones, found the derelict *Christopher Newport* and sank her, that they picked up their spoor again. The Liberty ship took with her to the seabed 10,000 tons of war munitions.

As the bitterly cold and windless day passed, the fog lifted from the calm grey sea. Two Blohm and Voss flying boats reappeared aloft. During the forenoon the lookouts and gunners closed up at their stations aboard the British merchantmen were astonished to see the American ships striking their ensigns. In the tension then prevailing, with the mixed and uncertain temper of many of the

American crews a matter of debate aboard British ships, the sight was greeted with momentary alarm, but all was swiftly explained when the tattered Stars and Stripes which had flown during the long weeks since these ships had left their loading ports in the States were replaced with brilliant new ensigns. The British woke up to the fact that in the Yankee calendar, 4 July had a special significance as Independence Day.

Within the cruiser squadron a courteous exchange of signals took place as *Tuscaloosa* and *Wichita* hoisted masthead ensigns in celebration. 'It is a privilege for us all to have you with us,' flashed the message from *London*'s bridge.

'We are particularly happy to be a portion of your command,' replied *Wichita*, 'celebration of this holiday always required large fireworks displays. I trust you will not disappoint us.'

At noon Admiral Hamilton also received a signal from the Admiralty giving him discretionary freedom to go beyond the limiting meridian of 25°E. He welcomed this, conceiving it his duty, as he put it, not to 'divorce' himself from the convoy, but 'from the vague information concerning enemy main forces . . . [to] remain with the convoy as long as possible'. The Admiralty unwisely added that this discretionary instruction was subject to no contrary orders emanating from Tovey. Shortly afterwards, Hamilton received a compromising signal from the Commander-in-Chief himself, who was not in full possession of even the limited facts at the Admiralty's disposal. Tovey ordered Hamilton not to enter the Barents Sea unless positive confirmation that he would *not* meet the *Tirpitz* came from the Admiralty, on the grounds that to allow the cruisers to proceed further east 'was a reversal of the policy agreed between the Admiralty and myself. No information in my possession justified this change.'[13]

Poor Hamilton was now a victim of competing loyalties. He acknowledged Tovey's order evasively, committing his force to the convoy until 22.00 on the 4th and repeated this to the Admiralty, admitting the loss of the *Christopher Newport*. 'I endeavoured to comply with the spirit of both signals,' he wrote later.

It was clear to Hamilton that should surface attack come it would be from the south, the side opposite to that on which he was now stationed. Edging south again the cruisers were in sight of PQ17 at 13.30 and once more the discrepancy in positions was discussed aboard *London*. The squadron navigator,

Lieutenant-Commander Frewen, 'had a lurking, unhappy feeling . . . that we were involved in some misunderstanding about our position'. The convoy was thirty miles south of where Hamilton's staff expected it to be.

Taking station a dozen miles ahead of PQ17, the cruisers zigzagged across its line of advance and at 16.45, after a relatively quiet day with only the droning presence of shadowing aircraft and the occasional half-hearted bombing raid by Ju88s which were driven off easily, Hamilton ordered Broome once more to head to the north-east. The convoy wheeled obediently through a four-point alteration of course. Shadowing the convoy after sinking the *Christopher Newport*, Brandenburg reported the distant cruiser squadron as including a battleship. This, and the fact that anti-submarine air patrols flown from *Wichita* appeared to the observers to be carrier-borne aircraft, deceived the Germans into thinking the British Home Fleet was not far off. Hitler's injunction about neutralizing British carriers before launching Rösselsprung thus prevented the German surface striking force from sailing. The effect of this report was as ironic as it was inaccurate.

Occasional fog banks lay across the surface of the sea, but as evening approached the visibility was clear and a ghostly rank of ice-bergs lay on the horizon against which the cruisers could be seen in jagged silhouette. Overhead a veil of overcast obscured the sky. Alerted by *U457*'s reports, other U-boats were closing in on PQ17. Bohmann's *U88* had manoeuvred to lie in wait ahead of the convoy, submerging to allow the unsuspecting outer escorts to pass overhead and then rising to periscope depth to deliver a salvo from both bow and stern tubes, all of which missed. Heinkel He115s were also homing on the convoy to join the shadowing BV138s and a Ju88 from KG30. For two hours the seaplanes made half-hearted attempts to penetrate the vigorous air defence of the escorts without success. Meanwhile the destroyers from the cruiser squadron dropped back within the convoy to fuel from the *Aldersdale*. At 19.30 the USS *Wainwright* was just arriving to replenish when a stick of bombs exploded on her port bow. Captain Moon of the *Wainwright* aborted his proposed fuelling operation, hauled out alongside *Keppel* and awaited the air attack all now felt to be imminent, for the air was full of the homing tone of shadowing aircraft and U-boats.

The glassy calm through which PQ17 now plodded was particularly helpful to radar surveillance and at 20.20 the alarms were sounded aboard *Palomares* as her operators detected a low-level attack. A few moments later the aircraft were visible in the brilliant afternoon light. This time there was no cautious, testing circling: the twenty-five or more He111s of KG26 and torpedo-armed Ju88s of KG30 flew straight into the attack from astern. Captain Moon, free of the constraints of the assigned escorts, peeled off to starboard and took *Wainwright* towards the enemy. Along with all the other ships, he opened fire at the intruders, swinging his destroyer beam on at 32 knots as he did so. *Wainwright*'s long-range barrage put the British destroyers to shame and was, in Broome's opinion, largely instrumental in thwarting the German attack, though at first the flame and smoke erupting from the American destroyer gave the impression she had herself been hit.

Wainwright's shells struck the Heinkel of Leutnant Kaumeyer, and although the aircrew fired both their torpedoes it was to no effect. Kaumeyer's plane smacked into the water close to HMS *Ledbury*. Apparently demoralized by this, most of the first wave of attackers released their torpedoes prematurely and withdrew in the face of Moon's barrage. The second, though, was pressed with greater vigour and the roaring approach of the low aircraft was met with the vicious stutter of small-calibre ack-ack guns and the louder boom of the larger weapons as warships and merchantmen opened fire.

The leading Heinkel, piloted by Leutnant Hennemann, thundered towards a column interval over *P614* upon which it released a bomb and then banked across the bow of the *Pozarica* with all the panache of a medieval *Landsknecht*, apparently contemptuous of the shell bursts of the ack-ack ship's pom-poms. Behind Hennemann, his comrades levelled at the *William Hooper* which was hit by a torpedo that blew the boiler out of the ship.

Hennemann's plane had been hit by gunfire several times and was now on fire. From the *Aldersdale* men could see into the Heinkel's cockpit, for the aircraft was low, so low in fact that the tracking gunners ignored all warnings and fired into adjacent ships. *Empire Tide* and *Ironclad* were both victims of this incaution. As flames licked about him, Hennemann released his torpedoes. They bounced on the water, disappeared and a few seconds later struck the British freighter *Navarino* which was engulfed in smoke as the weapons detonated. Lowered in haste, her lifeboats slipped their falls and dangled uselessly as her men went over the side into the icy water. Astern of *Navarino*, *Bellingham* hauled out of her line to avoid the settling ship, her gunners leaning over the side as she steamed through the British seamen in the water. One gave the Communist salute and bawled defiantly, 'On to Moscow – see you in Russia!'

Meanwhile the blazing Heinkel hit the water ahead of *Keppel* and, as the *El Capitan* passed, her burning crew could be seen dying in her sinking airframe. The men on deck shouted abuse as the shattered Heinkel sank. One by one the ships in the outer port columns overtook the spot, and by the time the *Troubadour* had gone by, all that remained was a dark swirl of oily water and a curling, ghostly flame. Leutnant Hennemann was posthumously awarded the Knight's Cross, and scarcely a witness in PQ17 was unimpressed with his daring.

After Hennemann's reckless gallantry the attackers faltered. Hamilton's cruisers had turned back and added to the tumultuous barrage. In addition to *Wainwright*, *Offa* claimed an aircraft and many were hit in the crossfire. The attack was driven off with the loss of three aircraft and damage to others. Nevertheless many torpedoes had been dropped, most in haste and fortunately to no effect, though they were conspicuous in the clear water. The air was alive with TBS traffic as watch-keeping officers monitored the trailing streams of bubbles and shouted warnings to neighbouring vessels. *Keppel* dodged one, as did *Bellingham*, and *Donbass* deflected two with gunfire. Shots from *Hoosier* actually exploded one torpedo's warhead; another skimmed the stern of the *Aldersdale* to hit the Russian tanker *Azerbaijan* which disappeared behind a huge sheet of flame, the noise of the explosion unnoticed in the awesome din, only to reappear a second later, venting smoke and steam. Along with the sinking *Navarino* and *William Hooper*, the Russian tanker fell behind.

As the enemy withdrew, the rescue ships moved in quickly to pick up survivors from the two cargo ships which were settling slowly. At the same time, *Zamalek*'s surgeon was just beginning an operation on a survivor wounded in the attack of the 2nd. Commander Broome steamed *Keppel* back through the convoy, encouraging and complimenting his charges. Asking Dowding how he was, the Commodore replied 'Fine'. Broome now ordered *Halcyon* and *Britomart* to sink the *William Hooper* and the *Navarino*, but found the *Azerbaijan*, which had fallen astern and carried linseed not fuel oil, 'holed but happy, capable of nine knots, with the female part of the watch busy [re]hoisting the boats'.

Once it was clear the tanker was not about to sink, most of the Russians remained aboard their ship to repair the damaged pipework in their engine room. One boat, however, was not recovered and its occupants pulled clear of their ship. The *Azerbaijan* was consequently soon making way to regain her station rapidly as *Zamalek* approached this boat-load of 'survivors'.

Captain Morris stopped and embarked them, and with their boat in tow astern, caught up with the Russian tanker. He then slowed down, drew the boat alongside and prepared to return the absent Russians. The master of the *Azerbaijan*, who spoke good English, refused to receive them as they had 'deserted', and Morris was obliged to keep them. With the exception of these wretched Russians, convoy PQ17, pleased with its performance despite its loss, closed ranks and settled down again. HMS *Ledbury* had the closest encounter with the Luftwaffe, picking up Leutnant Kaumeyer and his three aircrew while Broome, taking his destroyer back to her vanward station, wrote, 'My impression on seeing the resolution displayed by the convoy and its escort was that, provided the ammunition lasted, PQ17 could get anywhere.'[14]

Finally, Captain Moon brought the USS *Wainwright* up astern of *Aldersdale* to commence his delayed refuelling.

At the conclusion of the attack Admiral Hamilton, ignored by the Heinkels, was equally pleased. Although several U-boats were in contact (*Ledbury* had sighted seven) they had not intervened and it was clear PQ17 could defend itself very competently from air attack. The convoy was now over 300 miles from Banak and these considerations eased Hamilton's mind as the hour for his planned departure approached. *Wainwright* was rejoining him and he sent *Somali* back to fuel in her turn. The convoy was still steaming north-east, directly away from Bear Island which was 130 miles astern, and he informed Tovey and the Admiralty of PQ17's course and speed, together with her position.[15]

But Hamilton's relief was short-lived. Six hours earlier the Admiralty had intimated further information might be available and this now arrived, warning him of 'the proximity of surface forces'. This was to prove a wholly false assumption and it was not passed directly to Broome, as the Admiralty had promised, though Hamilton now transmitted it by lamp while *Keppel* was regaining station. Shortly afterwards the *Norfolk*'s Walrus was catapulted to fly ahead of the convoy on an ice reconnaissance. Hamilton had probably planned this to be his last act directly contributing to the safe and timely arrival of PQ17. *Tuscaloosa* also had an aircraft airborne to keep the U-boats down. Now the mention of surface forces threw everything back into the melting pot.

The Admiralty's contingency plan for the defence of PQ17 from surface attack in the Barents Sea was, as we have seen, something of an act of faith 'dependent on our submarine dispositions'. Already, on the morning of 3 July 1942, the Flag Officer Submarines had sent a general signal to all submarines operating under Royal Naval control north of the 51st parallel that the estimated position of PQ17 was then such as to render it vulnerable to surface attack. The submarine patrol areas occupied by six Russian boats were intended to maintain a close watch on the Norwegian coast between Vanna and the North Cape. Further offshore in a double cordon lay HM submarines *Sahib, Sturgeon, Unshaken, Unrivalled, Ursula, Tribune, Seawolf* and *Trident* together with the Free French *Minerve*. On the 4th all these boats, plus the two submarines which had set out with the convoy, *P614* and *P615*, were to shift to new positions to the eastward to cover the approach to the Russian coast.

In view of the signal Hamilton now repeated to Broome, the latter ordered the CAM ship *Empire Tide* to prepare her Hurricane to destroy the BV138 shadower and contacted his accompanying submarines, *P614* (Lieutenant Beckley) and *P615* (Lieutenant Newstead), the senior of whom signalled 'in the event of attack by heavy enemy surface forces propose to remain on the surface'. The irrepressible Broome replied, 'So do I!'

As *Norfolk*'s Walrus roared away, a signal arrived on *London*'s bridge. It was simultaneously received by Tovey, 350 miles to the west. It was prefixed *Secret* and *Most Immediate*. It read: *Cruiser force withdraw to westward at high speed*. Timed at 21.11 it could mean only one thing to its recipients: the *Admiral von Tirpitz* was at sea. Combined with the early intimation couched in words pregnant with foreboding of 'the close proximity of surface forces', attack could reasonably be expected to be imminent.

Twelve minutes later a second signal from the Admiralty, addressed to Broome and repeated to Hamilton and Tovey, arrived: *Secret* and *Immediate*. *Owing to threat from surface ships convoy is to disperse and proceed to Russian ports.*

Finally, after a further thirteen minutes, what appeared to be an upgrading of this last was received, to the stunned disbelief of Broome and his officers, to whom it seemed 'like an electric shock'.

Secret. Most Immediate. Admiralty to Escorts of PQ17 (repeated) Commander-in-Chief, CS One. Convoy is to scatter.

These positive and peremptory orders had in their sequence and the escalation of their tone the authority of superior knowledge. They meant only one thing to the naval commanders on the spot: their first assumption was correct and at any moment the *Tirpitz* and her battle-group would appear over the horizon.

The inevitability of this logical interpretation by the men on the spot seems indisputable, even with the wisdom of hindsight.

But this was not what had happened at all.

13

'Sheer bloody murder'

THE TRAGEDY ABOUT to overwhelm convoy PQ17 had its origins in the Admiralty in London. It was known by 14.00 on 3 July that the battleship *Tirpitz* was no longer at her moorings near Trondheim. It was this news which prompted the signal referring to the threat of surface attack and its sequel indicating the possibility of further information being forthcoming. Much was implicit in these messages, almost nothing explicit. Unfortunately, due to an accident to a Catalina, the cross-over reconnaissance flights had been suspended during the vital afternoon of 4 July, but it was deduced as 'tolerably certain' that the *Scheer* and *Lützow* had also left Narvik. In London an uneasy apprehension was growing, a preoccupation which was to prove fatal to PQ17. As Leutnant Hennemann was flying his Heinkel into the storm of gunfire from the convoy, Britain's First Sea Lord, Admiral Sir Dudley Pound, convened an urgent staff meeting.

Recalling it in later years, Sir Henry Moore, Vice-Chief of the Naval Staff and Pound's second-in-command, said,

> We talked for over an hour. Most of the time Admiral Pound sat with his eyes closed, saying nothing. He always did that. He looked asleep, but he always kept an absolute track on what was going on. All the discussion was on the basis that the *Tirpitz* was at sea. I was completely convinced of it. Perhaps some chance remark had planted it in the back of our minds.[1]

If so, it was a fatal implant, and on it was to be based a major naval blunder. During his deliberations, Pound consulted his intelligence staff. He was told by Paymaster-Commander

N.E. Denning that if *Tirpitz* had sailed, London would be in receipt of 'certain indications', an allusion to the Ultra decrypts and agents' reports his department processed. Denning could not confirm whether or not *Tirpitz* was actually at anchor, only that she had not put to sea. He was afterwards to regret that he failed to convince the First Sea Lord on this point, for Pound disregarded his advice; he knew that an operation against PQ17 from the North Cape area would have to sail soon, in fact it was inconceivable that it had not already done so.[2]

Denning's negative evidence (lack of signals traffic to surface ships or to the Eisteufel wolfpack warning them of friendly surface warships at sea) was insufficient to counter-balance Denham's warning from Sweden. Rodger Winn, the brilliantly intuitive head of the Submarine Tracking Room, also advised the First Sea Lord of intense U-boat activity in the vicinity of the convoy. The threat to Hamilton's cruisers was obvious.

As Moore observed, Pound sat in silence, his eyes closed, so that an incredulous junior member remarked he had fallen asleep. He had not. He was no fool, but a man with an immense burden of responsibility. He had faults; he was excessively fearful of delegation, took inadequate rest and was increasingly unfit, suffering from an arthritic hip and the onset of a brain tumour that was to kill him the following year. As he listened to his advisers, all of whom, with the exception of Sir Henry Moore, were opposed to dispersal, he was doubtless considering what he would be doing in Raeder's place with such ships as the Grossadmiral had at his disposal. Those very ships had gone north, that much he knew; there was a plan to attack PQ17, *that* much he knew; and now the fog of war had shrouded intelligence and he had only experience and intuition to guide him.

In Pound's mind the dissolution of the convoy was his only option. It did not matter that by their very nature, Russian convoys were bounded by ice or enemy territory; that they fought their way through a narrowing funnel to their destination; that in the Barents Sea ships swinging south drew nearer the enemy's airbases; that dispersal meant a slow, pre-arranged divergence of a mass of ships which became easier to pick off with every mile they steamed. But it *did* matter to Pound that with Hamilton detaching, it was unfair to devolve such responsibility upon Commander Broome. The Admiralty had arrogated to itself the overall control of the operation, believing it alone possessed sufficient facts to direct it; Sir Dudley was not a man to shirk the consequent obligation fate had laid upon him in his high office.

After a short interval he motioned for a signal pad. Writing upon it, he announced to his staff, 'The convoy is to be dispersed'.

As the signal was taken away to the Registry for logging and transmission, Moore pointed out the dangers of slow dispersal, believing that surface attack warranted the swiftest possible action. He suggested PQ17 should be scattered. 'I meant them to scatter', replied Pound, and so a simple correction was sent as a unique, second signal, giving the men on the spot an entirely false sense of heightening tension and the unequivocal and incontrovertible impression of imminent attack.[3]

As the signal arrived at the Registry it was received by Mrs Sherbrooke whose husband was, later in the war, to find himself in the very situation now thought to be about to overwhelm PQ17. She read the word 'scatter' with dismay. 'We all knew a convoy had to stick together.' That too was what the merchant seamen had been told to do in every pre-convoy conference since the outbreak of war: keep station, do not straggle, maintain convoy speed.

Rear-Admiral Hamilton had obeyed the spirit of his orders to the limit of their elasticity. The Admiralty's signals deprived him of further discretion. He held his easterly course for half an hour while he attempted to recall *Norfolk*'s Walrus, but to no avail; then he swung his squadron round and began to retire in accordance with his orders. To do this he had to cross ahead of the convoy and pass down PQ17's starboard flank.

Broome's duty was less clear. The scatter order meant PQ17 ceased to exist and would degenerate into 'a shambles'. He wrote later of 'a crescendo of priority' which could only mean the Admiralty possessed 'confirmation of overwhelming attack . . . reliable enough to decide that these defenceless merchant ships would stand a better chance on their own. We were all expecting to see either the cruisers open fire or . . . enemy masts appearing over the horizon.'[4]

At about 22.15, 'a very angry' Broome ordered Leading Signalman Elliot to hoist the white pendant with its red cross. It was the visual signal to scatter.

The instructions for this manœuvre were in the convoy manual but had not been stressed at the conference in Hvalfiordur. The procedure was for a fanwise separation, each column inclining outwards at 10° more than its inner neighbour. Individual ships then edged away from their closest companions, suddenly competing for isolation and increasing to full sea speed. Only the centre stood on, then it too broke up, odd-numbered ships edging out to starboard, evens to port. For the moment, however, PQ17 stood on to the eastward.

At the sight of the scatter pendant, HMS *Somali* aborted her fuelling from *Aldersdale* and steamed to rejoin Hamilton's approaching squadron. Signal lamps flashed to and from the various escorts across the convoy as Broome sent 'Join me' to his destroyers, formalizing this as: *All escorts from* Keppel: *all convoy scatter and proceed to Russian ports. Escorts negative destroyers proceed independently to Archangel. Destroyers join* Keppel.

Broome now noted that Dowding aboard *River Afton* had hoisted his repeating signal at the dip, not close up to its yardarm, signifying he acknowledged the message but did not understand it. Since the arrival of the scatter order, Broome had continued to steam east while his destroyers closed up with him. Now he manœuvred *Keppel* alongside the *River Afton* and raised his megaphone, confirming the order verbally to an incredulous Dowding and the *River Afton*'s stunned master, Captain Charlton, who stood next to the Commodore on the bridge.

'Sorry to leave you like this,' Broome hailed, 'goodbye and good luck. It looks like a bloody business.'

Dowding, a captain in the Reserve, replied 'Thank you. Goodbye and good-hunting;' then he and Charlton watched as *Keppel* swung away, and *Leamington, Wilton, Ledbury, Fury* and *Offa* raced up to take station in her wake.

'Maybe Broome knows something,' Dowding remarked to Charlton, and ordered the pendant hoisted close up and then lowered smartly. That downward jerk was the signal to execute the order and with it Commodore Dowding abdicated command. PQ17 ceased to exist. The merchant ships were on their own and the 'bloody business' Broome thought he was about to encounter himself turned out to be awaiting them.

Dowding sent a message to Chief Engineer Miller that he would give him two cigars for some extra knots. The last insouciant remarks about PQ17 had been exchanged. It was the nascent moment of controversy. 'The limey navy', an American commented years later, 'just turned and ran.' And that is how it looked to many who witnessed it, and how many who were not there believed it had been. As Broome had said, PQ17 was to turn into 'a shambles' and became, as Admiral Tovey had predicted, 'sheer bloody murder'.

Hamilton's cruisers were now astern. They had been ahead of the convoy and their hurried approach had looked purposeful. Broome swung after them, taking with him the ex-American four-stacker *Leamington* and the fleet destroyers *Fury* and *Offa*, all of which had torpedoes, plus the two Hunts. The augmentation of such a force to Hamilton's was obvious if a surface threat of the magnitude of *Tirpitz* was to be countered. With PQ17 dissolved, Broome considered it his duty, as the old naval saw has it, 'to steer towards the sound of the guns', or at least towards where the guns might reasonably be expected to be heard. He proposed joining forces with Hamilton; the Rear-Admiral approved and ordered Captain Moon of the *Wainwright* to form all the destroyers now in company into two divisions in anticipation of a battle.

Hamilton's ships 'careered westwards at thirty knots into an Arctic, icy mist, expecting the superstructure of *Tirpitz* and her force to appear over the southern horizon at any minute. Instead we wove our way among . . . icebergs and some very surprised U-boats who had been shadowing the convoy.'[5]

It was the presence of these very U-boats which had prompted the Admiralty to order the Rear-Admiral to withdraw fast, though that was not understood at the time. Hamilton himself knew exactly how his speeding exit would be viewed: 'We were – in the eyes of all who did not know the full story – running away, and at high speed.'

The Anglo-American squadron rapidly opened up the distance between itself and the scattering merchant ships; time passed; no enemy hove in sight and no information came from London. The silence was baffling, ominous even. A creeping, instinctive unease stole over Hamilton, Broome, their staffs and all the naval officers involved. Something was very wrong, but what? Then, five hours after the signal to scatter, the Admiralty finally broke silence: 'It is presumed enemy ships are north of Tromsö but it is not repeat not certain they are at sea.'

The enormity of the Admiralty's misjudgement was now apparent, confirming all the misgivings of worried men swept by a sense of utter desolation, a feeling of defeat without the opportunity of upholding honour. Aboard *Offa* this sense of dishonour was acute and had been prevalent for hours. Captain, First Lieutenant and Navigating Officer all expressed their horror at what they rightly considered to be the abandonment of their duty. When the enemy failed to appear it was seriously suggested that they arrange a 'breakdown'. 'We very nearly did this,' Vice-Admiral W.D. O'Brien, who had been *Offa*'s first lieutenant, recalled years later. 'To this day I blame myself for not pressing this policy more forcefully to my captain . . . Our instinct that we should turn back was right, it was a moment to disobey; there must always be a sense of shame that we did not do so.'[6]

Aboard *London*, Hamilton's flag captain, Captain Servaes, told his admiral that some explanation had to be offered to the crew. His steward, bringing him kye on the bridge, had remarked, 'It's a pity, sir, we had to abandon that convoy', and Servaes knew the buzz was round the whole ship. At 01.15 on the morning of 5 July, before receiving the Admiralty's signal of uncertainty as to the whereabouts of the German heavy ships, Hamilton piped a broadcast to the cruiser's company and signalled it to all the ships in his squadron.

On the American warships the sense of incredulity was perhaps worse, placed as they were under British command. Aboard *Wichita* a special edition of the cruiser's newspaper came out: 'No one can ever accuse us of having a faint heart, nor can anyone say the British lack guts.' It was a damage-limitation exercise of the worst kind, and did very little good. Fairbanks asked, 'Have the British become gun-shy?' It was an unfortunate end to the first Anglo-American naval operation.

Even as Hamilton refuelled his destroyers in the vain hope that he would join Tovey and that the entire Home Fleet would steam east, the air was filling with the distant death cries of sinking merchantmen. In the event it was left to the little corvettes and those bastard warships, the anti-submarine trawlers and ack-ack 'cruisers', to salvage the Royal Navy's honour.[7]

It was Teichert in *U456* who at about midnight reported the withdrawal of Hamilton's augmented squadron. In the succeeding hours Teichert and other shadowing U-boats reported merchant ships heading in odd directions. Air reconnaissance corroborated the appreciation growing among the staff of Admiral Arctic that PQ17 had dispersed. Schmundt's submarine commanders now transmitted a stream of reports including one from *U334* (Siemon) stating that he had fired at the damaged *Navarino* (which had sunk just before his torpedoes struck), and sunk the abandoned *William Hooper*. Neither of these ships had been sunk by the mine-sweepers, as Broome had instructed. As the morning drew on, Schmundt ordered all the Eisteufel boats to operate against the lone and dispersed merchant ships. On their runways at Banak the Heinkels of KG30 were warming up prior to take-off.

Far away in Kiel, Admiral Carls of Navy Group North also learned of the dispersal of PQ17. Conditions now suddenly seemed favourable for Rösselsprung; Carls requested permission to initiate it but Raeder, still worried about British carriers, refused sanction on the 5th. Then, through a gap in low cloud, aerial reconnaissance discovered the Home Fleet moving north-east to cover Hamilton's withdrawal. Tovey's intervention was impossible if the German force moved fast: the threat of carrier-borne aircraft evaporated.

Already at one hour's notice for steam, the German ships at Altenfiord began shortening in their anchor cables as Carls renewed his proposals to Raeder who now requested the Führer's blessing via Kranke. It was not long in coming. Raeder informed Carls who signalled Schniewind in code, but Schniewind had anticipated the order and was already under weigh. The mighty *Tirpitz* slipped out of the Leads accompanied by the *Scheer*, the *Hipper*, seven destroyers and two torpedo-boats. By 15.00 on 6 July they were in the open sea.

The sortie was abortive and almost as demoralizing to the Kriegsmarine as was their own withdrawal to the British. Schniewind was immediately pursued by a preposterous cautionary signal from Raeder in which 'partial success' was held to be more important than 'a total victory involving major expenditure of time'. Had Raeder known that Kapitan 2 Ranga Lunin in the Soviet submarine *K21* had not merely sighted but had also attacked *Tirpitz*, albeit unsuccessfully, he would have recalled the fleet at once. As it was, it was sighted by a British Catalina and HM Submarine *Unshaken* before the High Command got cold feet. U-boats and aircraft were taking such a toll of PQ17, the intervention of the surface ships was superfluous. Nevertheless, the order to turn back was devastating. 'They should have let us make *one* little attack!' an officer raged. Another, aboard the destroyer *Z28*, wrote, 'The mood is bitter enough. Soon one will feel ashamed to be on the active list . . . watching other parts of the armed forces fighting, while we, "the core of the fleet", just sit in harbour.' Referring to the heavy ships he went on to complain that the destroyers had been 'bound to these birds of ill omen with iron chains . . . the ship commanders have now been awaiting action up here for nearly six months. They tore their hair enough the last time, when we let PQ16 get through.' As for Schniewind, he agreed with Kummetz in *Scheer*, who proposed an immediate return to sea, if necessary with only the pocket-battleship, but this was refused. The Admiral was reduced to deploring the lack of offensive spirit, while Kapitän Wagner, the Chief of Naval Operations, cut to the heart of the matter: 'Every operation by our heavy surface forces has been hampered by the Führer's desire to avoid losses and reverses at all costs.'

Rösselsprung had been a damp squib. *Tirpitz* and her great grey sisters returned to the fiords, to be kept held again 'like chained dogs'.

Broome's last instruction to his erstwhile command was, with the exception of his destroyers, 'to proceed independently to Archangel. Submarines remain to attack if enemy approaches before convoy dispersed, then act under orders of Senior Officer.' By his own admission, these orders were 'hurried and inadequate', a fact which, given the circumstances, is unsurprising. Acting Captain Jauncey of the *Palomares* was the senior officer and, having taken *Norfolk*'s Walrus in tow and ordered *Britomart* and *Halcyon* under his lee, he set course accordingly. The corvette *Dianella* remained as escort to the two submarines while *Lotus*, *La Malouine* and *Poppy* set off to the eastward. Lawford of *Pozarica*, a quiet, monosyllabic man who made a deep impression on Godfrey Winn and Geoffrey Law, attempted to re-form part of the convoy with a vestigial escort, but this was refused on the grounds that the scatter order was explicit. This disagreement between the two remaining senior naval officers was unfortunate, but has to be seen in the light of the scanty knowledge then available to them. Used to obeying orders, the principle behind the tactic of scattering was well understood, but Lawford was racked by conscience.

'We can't leave these poor beggars,' he muttered, and turned *Pozarica* north-east towards the ice, gathering up *La Malouine*, *Lotus* and *Poppy* in a loose formation. This anti-submarine support of the ack-ack ships was unpopular aboard the corvettes, whose officers conceived their primary duty to be protecting the merchant ships. On both *Britomart* and *La Malouine* disagreement was passionately voiced.[8]

In fact Lawford considered doing what he could, knowing the combination of ack-ack and anti-submarine vessels provided a core about which he could gather some of the fleeing merchant vessels. He was equally well aware of the damage, both moral and physical, that would occur to these ships and their companies who knew only a tiny fragment of the reasoning, imperfect though it was, that had cast them loose and unprotected into the Arctic Ocean. Notwithstanding these thoughts, he had a duty to preserve his own, invaluable ship, and the pragmatic priority overrode the moral. Lieutenant Hall commanding *Lotus* suggested that they round up those merchant ships close by, but Lawford wavered and in the end reluctantly concluded, 'The order to scatter was to avoid vessels falling into traps', though he did not object to Hall turning back to do what he could. No one aboard *Pozarica*, Lawford included, pretended this was a satisfactory resolution, but it received a spurious approval from an Admiralty signal which now arrived indicating 'most likely time of enemy surface attack now tonight of 5th–6th, or early tomorrow morning, July 6th'. It was as inaccurate as earlier Admiralty assessments, a distant grasping at the straws of misconception.

And so the fateful signals which had detached Broome continued to exert their mischievous influence over the conduct of all the ships. It was not until many hours later that the instinct of self-preservation would bring the luckiest together again.

During the night of the 4th Lawford determined to make for Novaya Zemlya with *La Malouine* and *Poppy*. He also collected the loaded rescue ship *Rathlin*, but next morning the *Bellingham*, when ordered to alter course by Lawford, allegedly to avoid ice, replied 'Go to hell', and proceeded independently. According to sources aboard the American freighter, the anti-aircraft cruiser and her three consorts 'moved away without waiting for us'. Whatever the truth, mistrust was growing among the wandering ships which were mostly seeking some protection from the ice-edge and keeping as far from the hostile coast as possible. The scatter procedure had been followed only so far; in the main all the ships edged north but kept on to the eastward. The prevailing calm, clear weather, interrupted only occasionally by fog and mist banks, kept most of them in sight of one another. Seals and seabirds there were aplenty in the smooth, gently undulating sea and overhead a blue sky spread benignly.

By mid-morning four American merchant ships had re-formed around the *Palomares*, namely *Fairfield City*, *Daniel Morgan*, *Benjamin Harrison* and *John Witherspoon*. These were soon located by Blohm and Voss flying boats and at about 13.00, *Palomares* altered course, instructing the merchantmen to maintain their own headings. Captain Jauncey was also heading for the Matochkin Strait, separating the north and south islands of Novaya Zemlya.[9]

A New Zealander by birth and a barrister by profession, Leo Gradwell was of an independent frame of mind. As a Lieutenant RNVR he commanded the anti-submarine trawler *Ayrshire* and was unenthusiastic about proceeding directly to Archangel. Instead, from his position on PQ17's port quarter, he headed in the opposite direction, north-west, towards the ice-edge, taking with him the *Ironclad* which happened to be scattering on a northerly course. Captain Salvesen of the Panamanian *Troubadour* had similar ideas and had set his ship's head for Hope Island. Gradwell caught sight of her and called her up, delighted to discover she had on board vast quantities of bunker coal which Salvesen was not averse to sharing for a little anti-submarine protection.

Near the ice-edge the next morning the trio of ships encountered another American vessel, the *Silver Sword*; all four edged into the ice, penetrating deep into the embrace of the pack. When he was satisfied, Gradwell ordered their engines stopped and fires damped. Then he sent his second-in-command, Lieutenant Richard Elsden, across the ice to confer with the masters of the three merchant ships. They agreed to clear away the guns of the tanks stowed on deck and to load them as supplementary armament in case of attack. In addition to coal, the *Troubadour* also yielded a part cargo of drums of white paint. Within four hours of this being broached, all the ships had been liberally slopped with the stuff, a camouflage so effective that reconnoitring aircraft were seen to the southward, yet turned in reports that the pack-ice was impenetrable. Here Gradwell sensibly proposed to play possum until the hue and cry had blown over.

But overstrained nerves were epidemic elsewhere in that harried cluster of ships, and where air attack might at least be fought by the merchantmen, submarine attack could not. In the early forenoon of 5 July the lookouts aboard the well-armed and brand-new Liberty ship *Samuel Chase* reported a shadowing U-boat surfaced astern. The enemy was overhauling them, then disappeared after a three-hour chase. An attack seemed imminent. At about 10.30 the ship was stopped and all hands are reported to have taken to the boats, though such conduct was in direct contravention of the United States government's specific instructions to masters in the merchant marine. The expected attack never materialized and after lying on their oars for two hours, the crew reboarded their ship, raised steam and proceeded on their voyage. They were luckier than many to have had only their pride wounded, though the balance of one man's mind was already showing signs of serious disturbance.[10]

Another such incident is alleged to have occurred aboard the *Alcoa Ranger* where, having been circled by an FW200 for some time, a dispute took place on the bridge during which some form of capitulation was discussed as the crew hovered at boat stations. At its conclusion *Alcoa Ranger* seems to have resumed her passage. In the meantime the FW200 had lost interest and had flown off!

More serious, however, was the abandonment of the ancient American freighter *Pan Kraft*. Laden with a mixed cargo and aircraft, she had become derelict in the ice after a high-level bombing attack. Near misses ruptured vital steam pipes and the *Pan Kraft* came to a standstill. As the last boat pulled away, a Ju88 strafed the *Pankraft* with incendiary shells, killing the Second Mate, David Stockton, and setting the derelict ship on fire amid the icefloes.[11] One other man, John L. Carley, was to die of his injuries and be buried at sea from a lifeboat.

As the forenoon had drawn on, the pursuing U-boats fell on their quarry. One of them, Bielfeld's *U703*, made two unsuccessful attacks on the *Empire Byron*, Captain J. Wharton. It was his fifth, stern torpedo that struck the 6,645-ton ship's engine room; a sixth, intended to give the *coup de grâce*, also missed, but the freighter was badly hit. The explosion had flung her deck cargo of army trucks high into the air and damage was widespread; she rapidly began to settle stern first. Not far off, the American ship *Peter Kerr* transmitted an SOS on the British ship's behalf, though she failed to give a position. Meanwhile Bielfeld had brought his U-boat to the surface where the majority of *Empire Byron*'s survivors huddled in the ship's lifeboats. Wharton ordered his officers to take off their epaulettes and, unbetrayed, they avoided capture. Bielfeld took aboard an army officer who had taken passage as an instructor for the new Churchill tanks, an early consignment of which had formed part of the *Byron*'s cargo. One of Bielfeld's officers who had come down on to the U-boat's casing derided the British merchant seamen's efforts at rowing and asked why, if they were not Bolsheviks, they were helping the Russians. Some basic provisions were handed down into the boats, photographs were taken and then *U703* sank beneath the Barents Sea, heading south-east. Bielfeld reported his success: 'Convoy in rout . . . I am following hard.' Eighteen men had perished with the freighter.

Heino Bohmann in *U88* was stalking the *Carlton*, Captain Hansen, loaded with steel, tin, food, oil, tanks and explosives, and which was on a southerly course. The mist and fog patches which alternated with the fine, clear weather gave the ship's company a false sense of security. At about 10.15 Bohmann loosed his torpedoes and the *Carlton* began to sink, a third torpedo running amok among the lowering lifeboats and rafts. Bohmann surfaced, took details of the ship, and disappeared. Although several men were badly burned, Hansen had lost only the three men on watch in the engine room. His men settled down, lashing the rafts and boats together, and confidently awaited the outcome.

In this they were not to be disappointed. Some hours later they were overflown by Heinkel He115s. An hour or so later the returning floatplanes, their torpedo racks empty, re-passed them and one landed alongside. Thereafter a succession of German seaplanes, including a Dornier Do24 rescue aircraft out looking for the crew of a reportedly ditched Heinkel, recovered most of *Carlton*'s crew except seventeen who hoisted the remaining lifeboat's sail and set course for the Murman coast. The rescued seamen were flown into the seaplane base at Billefiord. During the course of their interrogation some of *Carlton*'s crew were persuaded to believe their ship had been sunk by a British submarine alarmed by the *Carlton*'s southerly course, a story lent credibility by rumours said to have been circulated about the ship. This was not all the mischief wrought; the German propaganda machine made much of smiling photographs and fulsome interviews of the relieved American seamen, not only poisoning the minds of the Americans with the fabrication of British perfidy, but also leaking to the British the story that the *Carlton* had surrendered. What the Germans did learn was that the port of Murmansk was badly damaged, and that the *Carlton*'s cargo had included thirty-seven tanks, amongst them six heavy Grant types. Her crew were finally incarcerated in Stalag Marlag-Milag Nord, near Bremen.

After sinking the *Carlton*, Bohmann picked up the trail of other merchant ships from the sightings now being reported by the Luftwaffe. When the four American freighters close to *Palomares* became detached, he closed them as they slipped in and out of fog banks, homing on the signals transmitted by the Blohm and Voss at which the *Daniel Morgan* had defiantly opened fire. *U88* located the *Daniel Morgan* and the *Fairfield City* at the same time as Ju88s of KG30, about 15.00. The Junkers attacked and bombed the *Fairfield City* with heavy loss of life, though three lifeboats got away from the sinking ship and set a weary course due east, towards Novaya Zemlya. The *Daniel Morgan* disappeared to the eastward into the mist as the *Fairfield City* took her cargo of steel and tanks to the seabed.

All three squadrons of KG30 were now airborne, quartering the Barents Sea and homing in on their victims, the airwaves crackling with position reports from gleeful aircrews. Five Ju88s flew out of the sun to attack the fleeing *Daniel Morgan*. Her armed guard, under Lieutenant Morton E. Wolfson USNR, who had been at action stations for more than twenty-four hours, beat off several attacks and managed to shoot down two of their tormentors and damage others. But a near miss split the ship's shell plating in way of Nos. 4 and 5 holds and she took an immediate list; several of the crew panicked and launched lifeboats prematurely. Captain Sullivan manœvred the sinking ship until he had a line aboard a capsized boat and eventually his men were able to take to the three serviceable boats. Three men had died in the panic and one had been killed by bomb blast. As the boats pulled away from the Liberty ship, Bohmann sank her with two torpedoes, surfaced and demanded the name and cargo of their ship from the survivors.

Sullivan told the German his cargo was only 'general cargo–food and leather'. The U-boat then moved away on the surface. The Americans were fortunate in being rescued some hours later by the Russian tanker *Donbass* and, though exhausted and suffering from exposure, the armed guard gallantly volunteered to man one of her guns.

Further west the *Honomu*, loaded with a cargo of food, steel, munitions and tanks, had become the unwitting target of three U-boats, all attacking independently. Even as Siemon loosed his torpedoes from *U334*, a torpedo from Teichert's *U456* struck the freighter's No. 3 hold and she began to settle by the head. A second torpedo then hit No. 4 hold and the thirty-seven surviving crew abandoned her. Both U-boats now surfaced and were joined by *U88*; Teichert ordered the *Honomu*'s master, Captain Frederick Strand, to board *U88* as a prisoner. After distributing some basic necessities the U-boats motored away to the eastward, their diesel exhausts leaving brown trails in the still, cold air. Far below, the *Honomu*'s broken hull struck the ooze of the seabed, bounced, then gently settled, a steel sarcophagus for her cargo of tanks and nineteen of her crew.

At about the same time as the *Honomu* and *Daniel Morgan* were sunk during the mid-afternoon of 5 July, the Chief Officer of R. Chapman's 7,000-ton merchantman *Earlston* spotted what appeared to be a moving iceberg stalking the ship. Already running at full speed having evaded an aerial torpedo attack earlier, her crew were tense. Calling the master, Captain Stenwick, Mr H. Benson pointed out the disguised U-boat. In the clear weather through which the British steamer thrashed eastwards, the two men made out the white painted conning tower. Stenwick turned away, manned his stern gun and opened fire on their pursuer. Then he sent his radio officer to transmit a signal giving his position and the fact that he was 'in action with U-boat', and ordered all his firemen into the stoke-hold. The U-boat had increased to a speed superior to the tramp, but furious stoking allowed an extra knot to be coaxed out of the steamer's reciprocating engines and she slowed her attacker's rate of approach. Meanwhile on her poop the Maritime Royal Artillery gunners were in their stride, their shells plunging closer and closer to the U-boat which was finally forced to submerge and so lose her advantage of speed. The *Earlston* steamed on, safe – at least for the time being. Shortly afterwards the Ju88s found her, as did a trio of U-boats. For some time her gunners kept the bombers from landing a hit, but eventually a very close near miss exploded alongside the engine room. The whole ship shuddered, the engines were shifted on their mountings and multiple fractures occurred to the internal pipework. Mindful of the explosives in her holds Captain Stenwick ordered his crew to abandon ship. As the boats were lowered, the three U-boats surfaced, among them Siemon's *U334* which now fired several torpedoes at the *Earlston*. One struck No. 2 hold and the ship broke in two with a deafening roar. A large steam launch sent out to relieve the drifter *Chiltern* was flung into the Barents Sea; the rest of the cargo – Churchill tanks, ack-ack guns, lorries and munitions – plunged with the broken ship to the bottom. Only the barrage balloon lingered a moment, then it too vanished. Siemon approached the lifeboats and ordered the British ship's Norwegian master aboard. Stenwick protested that his duty lay with his crew but was coldly informed he had no option. The U-boats lay on the surface, congratulating each other until strafed by Ju88s mistakenly thinking them Allied submarines. A few days later Stenwick joined *Carlton*'s crew in Marlag-Milag Nord.

The He115 floatplanes of 906 Küstenfliegergruppe, which had initiated the rescue of the *Carlton*'s survivors, had been returning from a strike at the *Peter Kerr*, another American ship which had broken away from PQ17 to the southward. Seven of these aircraft had launched their twin torpedoes and all had missed as Captain Butler zigzagged and altered his engine speed in a successful evasive action which lasted two hours. At about 17.00, however, as the Heinkels flew off, four Junkers Ju88s attacked from high altitude, well out of range of the *Peter Kerr*. Three dozen bombs fell, a trio of which scored direct hits and others, near misses.

With her steering gear disabled and fires raging in her radio room and forward holds, she was taking water forward. The crew launched two lifeboats and abandoned ship as the fires spread remorselessly; they were pulling away when the *Peter Kerr* exploded.

The *Bolton Castle*, *Olopana*, *Washington* and *Paulus Potter* had maintained contact as they broke away to the north-east. Due to her age, the *Olopana* failed to keep up and dropped astern. The other three ships, British, American and Dutch, stayed together, for a strong friendship had formed between Captain Sissingh, master of the Dutch ship *Paulus Potter*, and Captain Pascoe of the *Bolton Castle*. At about 17.00, as units of KG30 found the *Peter Kerr*, a high-altitude Ju88 dived on the *Washington* which was already suffering from earlier near misses. Although the Junkers's bombs missed, she strafed the American ship before flying off. Half an hour later several Ju88s arrived and concentrated on the *Washington* so that her whole hull heaved out of the water with the simultaneous concussions. Almost at once the steering gear failed and the leaks increased. Her situation was hopeless. Captain Richter therefore ordered his crew to the boats before the 350 tons of TNT in her forward holds blew up.

The Ju88s now turned their attention on the *Bolton Castle* and the *Paulus Potter*; Pascoe knew his situation was equally bleak and had, in the interval between attacks, prepared all his boats. A bomb dropped through the hatch covers on No. 2 'tween deck where a stow of bombs counter-mined successively with a green flash and a roar 'like a giant roman candle'. The savage heat melted the hull, but the ship remained afloat long enough for her crew to man and lower her boats as, close by, near misses similarly disabled the *Paulus Potter*. The Junkers, of the third squadron of KG30 commanded by Hajo Herrmann, roared low over the milling lifeboats. They were in formation and their aircrews waved cheerfully as cameras rolled for the German newsreels. Finally they emptied their cannon shells into the smoking wrecks; then they flew off. Shortly afterwards *Bolton Castle* stood on end and sank, as did the *Washington*. *Paulus Potter* remained afloat, to be given her quietus by a U-boat.[12]

The survivors of these three ships, from which there had been no loss of life, might have been rescued by the *Olopana*, coming slowly up astern. She too had been attacked, but hurried preparations to abandon ship and the ignition of smoke floats persuaded the enemy into thinking themselves successful in firing the old tramp. Eager for blood worthier of their steel, they raced on, to encounter the Dutch, British and American ships that had left the *Olopana* astern.

To his astonishment, Captain Stone of the *Olopana* discovered none of the crews wanted to be rescued. Highly independent, the *Bolton Castle*'s boats struck out on a 400-mile voyage south to the Russian coast. Those of the *Paulus Potter* preferred to risk the hazards of ice and reach the nearer coast of Novaya Zemlya, as did the *Washington*'s, whose master boarded the British tramp, studied the chart and begged a boat compass. 'My crew felt safer in the lifeboats,' Captain Richter told Stone.

The order to scatter had rendered Commodore Dowding's presence on the *River Afton* somewhat superfluous. The ship's master, Captain Harold Charlton, took his ship north-east, also seeking shelter from the ice-edge where low fog banks lay. The ether was filled with the distress calls of the scattered merchantmen as they were picked off piecemeal. Charlton spotted a Ju88 and soon afterwards heard *Washington*'s last radio call. At about 17.00 the *River Afton* was hit by a torpedo. Again it was the engine room which took the impact and the ship was instantly disabled. Despite a degree of confusion, rescue attempts to get the wounded out of the engine room were mounted in which several men, including Chief Steward Percy Grey, distinguished themselves. The blast of the explosion had caused extensive damage, particularly in destroying two of the lifeboats. Men began to tumble into the after boat when a second torpedo struck the boiler room below; the men were either instantly killed or blown overboard into the icy sea. With only a small jolly-boat and Carley floats left, the remaining crew began to abandon ship while Charlton raced to his cabin to get the ship's papers and Dowding ditched the confidential books, though he hoped to save the ship. He was to be disappointed. The ship was sinking and was soon surrounded by swimming men, then Bielfeld's *U703* put a third torpedo into the *River Afton*.

As she sank, Dowding, his signals staff and the ship's gunners were swept overboard on the rafts. Charlton joined Chief Officer Longstaffe in the overloaded dinghy, which shortly afterwards capsized. Longstaffe, a 24-year-old engaged to be married, drowned in his heavy Arctic clothing. Captain Charlton and Lieutenant Cook, a naval transport officer on passage to Russia, clung to the dinghy and succeeded in righting it. Clambering in, Charlton used his briefcase, still secure round his neck, to bale. His ship's papers and £500 sterling drifted away on the calm sea. Other men got back to the dinghy and were painfully hauled aboard.

A stoker, clad only in dungarees and singlet, his skull burst and brain exposed, died while the Third Mate tried to warm his bare feet. Soon afterwards the Second Engineer died. He had been dragged from the engine room by Grey and his party minus a leg. The survivors' wet clothing began to freeze on them, but despite the differences of opinion that had characterized the shock of attack, there were no complaints, no demands. It seemed inevitable that they would soon join the score of their shipmates who were already dead.

Aboard the fleet oiler *Aldersdale* there was a feeling of fatalism by the afternoon of 5 July. They had been shadowed for hours and all hands awaited the inevitable. When, therefore, Captain Hobson's decision to head for Novaya Zemlya brought them within sight of other ships again, there was a slight comfort to be gained in the knowledge that they were not alone. At the same time wisps of cloud overhead gradually thickened and obscured the vulturine observers above. With the rescue ship *Zaafaran*, the *Ocean Freedom* and the minesweeper *Salamander*, the *Aldersdale* steamed east.

PQ17 was the first Russian convoy to include rescue ships, though *Zamalek* had set out with PQ6 as we have seen. Sadly, the order to scatter robbed them of much of their effectiveness, but they were to play a crucial role nevertheless. Rescue ships had been introduced following the outbreak of unrestricted submarine warfare which removed both the non-combatant status of merchant seamen and the custom that the open ocean was 'a place of safety' as defined in the old prize-laws. The Admiralty had initially been callous about losses among merchant seamen. In 1941, however, almost 9,000 were killed and both to harbour the nation's reserves and improve morale, several small coastal passenger ships with plenty of boats were requisitioned. Specially equipped, their 'tween decks were fitted with bunks and mess tables, for survivors did not like cabined confinement, and the sense of community after the trauma of being sunk was important to the restitution of morale; booms, nets and weighted baskets lowered from small cranes for recovering survivors lined their topsides with the boats, and they carried a surgeon from the RNVR with his own medical staff and operating facilities. Organizations such as the British Sailor's Society and the British War Relief Society of the United States donated clothes and comforts so that every rescued man should have a woollen jumper, socks and gloves, underclothes, trousers, a belt, a handkerchief, shoes, a raincoat or oilskin and a cap.

Apart from the effect it had on the spirits of merchant seamen, the provision of rescue ships released escorts from this humane duty which young escort commanders regarded as having a higher priority than did their distant masters. They also had Huff-Duff direction-finding equipment with which to assist convoy escorts to locate surfaced and transmitting U-boats and they bore a not inconsiderable armament which included a 12-pounder, Bofors and Oerlikons. Wearing grey paint and the blue ensign of naval auxiliaries they were, in the eyes of their enemies, targets like any other Allied ship.

Later in the war, corvette hulls were fitted out for the task, but the three rescue ships of PQ17 had already proved their worth during the earlier attacks on the convoy and now bore numbers of survivors from the *Navarino*, *William Hooper* and *Christopher Newport*. Ironically the *Zamalek* and *Zaafaran*, of some 1,500 GRT, had been built by the Germans for the Levant service of the Pharaonic Mail Line. Since being taken over in the spring of 1941, they had been placed under the management of the London-based General Steam Navigation Company. Though near deadly rivals, both their masters, Captain Owen Morris, a Welshman, who commanded *Zamalek*, and Captain Charles McGowan, a Scotsman, exemplified the small-ship mentality which was based on a thorough knowledge of ship-handling, absolute confidence in their crews and cool self-possession that had established their reputations long before they and their ships entered the Barents Sea.

It was not surprising that McGowan refused to keep company with Morris on the evening of 4 July. *Zamalek* not only needed a boiler clean and smoked abominably, she was also half a knot slower than his own ship. With his rival's smoke still sullying the horizon astern, it was the group of four ships which, on the afternoon of the following day, attracted the attention of four of KG30's quartering Junkers bombers. The first three planes aborted their attacks in the face of the extempore squadron's combined fire-power, but the fourth laid a stick of bombs across *Aldersdale*'s stern where, as a tanker, her engine room was located. She immediately took in water. With a part cargo of aviation spirit aboard, her engine shaken to a standstill and rescue near at hand, Captain Hobson had little choice but to abandon ship. Lieutenant Mottram brought *Salamander* close and evacuated the crew, but the *Aldersdale* doggedly refused to sink. Reassessments of the situation aboard *Salamander* persuaded Hobson and Mottram that they might be able to salvage the valuable cargo by towing the tanker, as Hobson had earlier sought to tow the *Christopher Newport*, but events in the near vicinity put paid to their deliberations. Mottram gave Hobson five minutes to decide whether he could restart the tanker's engines and *Aldersdale*'s Chief Engineer said this was impossible. Efforts to sink the oiler were farcical. At the first close-range shot *Salamander* shot away her own guard-rails, at the second the breech-block fell from her single 4-inch gun. Nor were depth-charges hurled under *Aldersdale*'s stern any more effective. She was finally left, still forlornly afloat.

What had drawn *Salamander* away from *Aldersdale* was the continuing attack on the other ships, away to the eastward, by the Ju88s. *Ocean Freedom* was to escape, but *Zaafaran* was not so lucky.

A Ju88 had straddled the rescue ship with devastating effect, disabling her engines, and McGowan quickly realized his position was hopeless. He began to abandon ship.

Miles astern to the north-west, Captain Morris had watched the attack in the clear visibility and, though hull down, saw McGowan's ship's masts assume a cockeyed angle. Then he saw the triangle of her forecastle rear briefly over the horizon and feared the worst. Morris immediately altered course to the south-east and called his radio operator. 'Tell that anti-aircraft ship we want anti-submarine protection to go and pick up survivors. If they refuse, quote the regulations at them!'

Morris's peremptory tone was in keeping with the general feeling of disgruntlement towards the navy as that 'black Sunday' drew on. To men of Morris's stamp, slavish obedience to the scatter order once it had so clearly failed to achieve its object was nothing short of stupid. He was not the only merchant seaman to wish for another Nelson as the death cries of ships filled the airwaves.

The anti-aircraft ship to which Morris referred was *Palomares* and Jauncey dispatched the *Britomart* to assist. Meanwhile Captain Morris had arrived and had begun to pick up both the *Zaafaran*'s crew and her unfortunate passengers. Eventually all but one MRA gunner were accounted for.[13]

Zamalek, *Ocean Freedom* and HMS *Britomart* now proceeded after *Palomares* and *Halcyon*; astern of them, having abandoned her attempt to sink the 8,000-ton *Aldersdale*, HMS *Salamander* strove to catch up.

Sensible of the opprobrium gathering round the Royal Navy, Captain Lawford of the other anti-aircraft cruiser, HMS *Pozarica*, had given Lieutenant Hall of HMS *Lotus* permission to turn back along the ice-edge. Remonstrations had occurred aboard her other accompanying corvettes, *Poppy* and *La Malouine*, but Lieutenant Boyd of the former lacked the seniority to challenge the decision, and Lieutenant Bidwell's *La Malouine* was short of fuel; most of this invective was aimed at the distant Lawford who had, as we have seen, agonized over his appalling dilemma.[14]

While the corvettes found their shackling to the *Pozarica* 'a sore point with us all', the other rescue ship, *Rathlin*, also remained under the ack-ack ship's guns, although she later failed to keep up. Lawford's squadron pressed on for Novaya Zemlya, sighting the American Liberty ship *Samuel Chase* the following morning and exchanging signals with her. Lawford was by now convinced that a German battle squadron was definitely at sea and, while giving the American permission to join up for a passage to the Matochkin Strait, he did not slacken speed. Soon afterwards the ships ran into fog.

Lieutenant Hall had been cheered when those aboard *La Malouine* heard he was turning back. HMS *Lotus* skirted the pack edge, sighted three anti-submarine trawlers and came across the still burning *Pan Kraft* inside the loose floes bordering the ice limit. Her largely Filipino crew were huddling in their boats in the open sea beyond. As Hall levelled his 4-inch gun to destroy the freighter, Captain Jacobson howled a warning: the *Pan Kraft* had 5,000 tons of TNT on board and they were about to fire at close range. Hall's crew gathered up the twenty-nine men from the two lifeboats and drew off. It was thus, afire and with empty boats bobbing nearby, that the *Olopana* came upon her in the small hours of 6 July. It was 'an unforgettable sight; behind the burning derelict the sun shone over a vast expanse of ice'.

The *Pan Kraft* burned for a further day, finally exploding at about 06.00 on 7 July, clearly heard by Lieutenant Gradwell and his group of ships still hiding in the ice several miles away. The ominous noise confirmed the wisdom of Gradwell's strategy; his ships lay doggo for a little longer, though already the first hints of a southerly breeze breaking up the calm and shunting the ice back to the north threatened their retreat.

Hastening after the others in her group, HMS *Lotus* was making her best speed to reach Lawford's rendezvous, the Matochkin Strait. Now, in the evening as the sun dipped towards the horizon, the refracted air caused extraordinary mirages and her lookouts sighted what seemed like tall columns of funnel smoke. Hall altered course to investigate and was further mystified when the smoke abruptly vanished. In the quick atmospheric changes that the Arctic produces, *Lotus* closed what were the two rafts and the jolly-boat of the *River Afton* through a dense sea-smoke, ghosting up to the survivors like a wraith. From aboard the corvette, the waving hats seemed like distant shell bursts, but finally it became clear that the smoke candles Commodore Dowding had set off from his raft and the waving hats were much closer than at first thought. After several freezing hours, the remainder of *River Afton*'s crew were rescued by the corvette.

The next day, 6 July 1942, proved to be quieter than its predecessor in the Barents Sea. Schmundt's U-boats had been withdrawn clear of the Rösselsprung operation and, thoroughly alarmed by the Admiralty's signals which now indicated the proximity of a German battle-fleet, the hapless merchant ships sped eastwards to whatever protection they might find in the Matochkin Strait. Last-ditch strategies were deliberated between Tovey and London: could the Home Fleet race east and at least threaten to cut off *Tirpitz* from her base? Could aircraft from *Victorious* hit her? Such strategies were as worthless as was the claim of the Russian submarine *K21* to have torpedoed *Tirpitz*, as worthless as the aborted Knight's Move itself. While the grey capital ships of Tovey's squadrons, joined now by Hamilton, turned through sleeting rain, head to wind, and laid a course for Scapa Flow, the frustrated predatory monsters under Schniewind's command returned to their polar moorings beneath the midnight sun, and command of the German submarines was handed back to Hubert Schmundt, Admiral Arctic. Aerial reconnaissance and the information gleaned from *Carlton*'s crew that PQ17 was destined for Archangel meant that the Konteradmiral could revise his dispositions, refuel and rearm his boats, and lay a fresh cordon of them across the approaches to the White Sea, while KG30, still operating from Banak, could continue to harry the remnants of the convoy.

Intelligence of the German raid did have one effect upon those with the code-books to understand it: it spread the sense of abandonment wider. Aboard *La Malouine*, still attending *Pozarica*, one of her officers wrote that they too felt they had been deserted. 'We will be slaughtered . . . sunk off Novaya Zemlya or sunk in the Barents Sea. *Pozarica* talks to Captain [of *La Malouine*] over loud hailer and leaves us with little doubt that the end has come. Everyone is becoming silent.'

In fact Novaya Zemlya had become, from purely practical considerations, the only place to make for, offering a degree of protection and, perhaps, support of some kind – other ships, the Russians – no one knew beyond the fact that, short-term objective though it might be, it was the straw desperate men had found to cling to. Indeed Matochkin Strait became known as Funk Creek, though in this self-deprecation lay a rekindling of resolve, the warming effect of seeing others in the same plight as oneself, a determination to assist each other, out of which was resuscitated the idea of convoy.

The geographical and strategic limitations of the Barents Sea as an area in which to scatter a convoy were quickly and savagely imposed. It was not merely self-preservation that attracted the ships to the Matochkin Strait; it was in fact the only practical way to carry out the Admiralty's confusing instructions.

Apart from Gradwell's group, the laggards in the north were strung out along the ice-edge. The *Alcoa Ranger*, the Liberty ship *John Witherspoon*, the CAM ship *Empire Tide*, the *Winston Salem*, *Bellingham*, *Hartlebury* and *Olopana* all headed east, running in and out of the fog banks and sea-smoke that swirled and fumed about the floes and growlers. Despite this, all seven ships were sighted by an FW Condor during the forenoon of the 5th. The Condor disdained to attack; instead her sighting prompted Schmundt to call in his most northerly U-boats. Twenty-four hours later, as the *John Witherspoon* ran out of fog, her lookouts spotted what they took to be a surfaced U-boat on a parallel course to the southward. Gunfire drove the submarine underwater, but at 16.30 a torpedo struck the Liberty ship, one of a spread of four fired by Reche from *U255*. As he surfaced alongside the lifeboats, filming the survivors and offering them cigarettes, water and cognac, he fired a fifth torpedo. The *John Witherspoon* broke in two and sank immediately, with the loss of one seaman. Having failed to detach the ship's master from among the wretched men huddling in the boats, Reche pointed out the direction of land and disappeared.

One ship which had not headed for Funk Creek was the *Pan Atlantic*. Instead her master, Captain Siebert, had increased speed and was making for Cape Kanin. At 12 knots he had a fair prospect of success, for most of the air attacks were occurring further north. Unknown to the Americans, Bohmann's *U88* and Bielfeld's *U703* were hot on their heels. To the frustration of the two U-boat commanders, after hours of pursuit through alternating clear visibility and fog banks, just as they were independently beginning their attacks at about 06.00 on the 6th, a single Ju88 dived on the *Pan Atlantic*. In addition to tanks, food, nickel and aluminium, the American ship was freighted with cordite. A bomb plunged into a forward hold and the cordite counter-mined, blowing the bows off the ship in an instant. Three minutes later she had sunk, with the loss of twenty-six men.

Another and more successful independent master was Captain Pavlov of the Russian tanker *Donbass*. Having rescued the crew of the *Daniel Morgan* whose gunners had voluntarily manned a forward ack-ack gun, his ship survived an air attack, the American gunners damaging the Ju88. Pavlov's tanker arrived at Molotovsk on 9 July, the Americans earning the approbation of a Soviet official.

At Jauncey's behest HMS *Britomart* was the first to round Cape Stolbovoi, Novaya Zemlya, and make contact with the Russians at the settlement of Lagerni, explaining with some difficulty that the ships now in the offing wanted only the haven of an anchorage. As a result, on the afternoon of 6 July, HMS *Palomares*, still towing *Norfolk*'s Walrus aircraft, the three minesweepers *Britomart*, *Halcyon* and *Salamander*, the crowded rescue ship *Zamalek* and a single merchant ship, the *Ocean Freedom*, dropped anchor. Jauncey called a conference and, on the advice of the Arctic expertise of the minesweeping officers, decided against breaking out east into the Kara Sea on account of ice. The *Norfolk*'s Walrus aircraft which, thanks to the calm weather, had remained docilely in tow, was refuelled and confirmed the impossibility of the idea.

Shortly afterwards *Pozarica*, *Poppy* and *La Malouine* arrived, and in the general relief a series of rather silly signals was exchanged, the upshot of which was that the ships anchored so that their guns could command the entrance to the strait. Lawford now joined Jauncey and the re-formation of the convoy was considered, despite their being somewhat short of customers and although the danger of surface attack had not, as far as the two acting captains knew, yet receded. Nevertheless, now that the two men were finally able to accept release from London's orders, they set about their task with energy. To remain in Funk Creek long enough to be blockaded by submarines or mines was unthinkable. Therefore, to the general relief of her officers and men, the corvette *La Malouine* was sent to render assistance to any merchantmen that might be found. She sailed that evening and in the succeeding hours contacted the *Hoosier*, *Benjamin Harrison*, *El Capitan* and *Samuel Chase* which struggled through deteriorating weather round Cape Stolbovoi and into the anchorage. Aboard the last-named, one man had now lost his reason and was transferred to the care of Surgeon McCullum aboard *Zamalek*. As the day drew to a close and the magnificent white slopes of the 'new land' glowed in the long Arctic twilight, other escorts arrived.

The three coal-burning and smoky trawlers *Northern Gem*, *Lord Middleton* and *Lord Austin* had kept their own company after the order to scatter. Proceeding along the ice-edge they had heard the many distress calls and had seen in the distance specks that were aircraft attacking their victims, which were hull down. Occasional palls of smoke rose and were dissipated; occasional dull and distant concussions rolled over the calm sea; overhead flew groups of German aircraft and the crews stood tensely at action stations, confidential books ready to be flung over the side, boats lowered to the rails and well-stocked with water and provisions. Men took personal precautions, pocketing photographs as talismans, slinging their pension books about their necks, but the aircraft had bigger fish to fry, and the three little ships went on unmolested. They sighted *Pan Kraft* and split up briefly as *Lord Austin* headed for the distant dots of her lifeboats. The other trawlers turned back from the shelter of the fog bank into which they had been running to avoid the aircraft still lingering about the freighter. They were closing the burning ship when *Lotus* appeared and warned them off with the news that the *Tirpitz* was at sea, advising them to proceed east at their best speed and overtaking them later as she strove to catch up with Lawford.

Lotus, her decks crowded with survivors, many of whom refused to discard their lifejackets, steamed into the anchorage off Lagerni to some well-merited cheers shortly before midnight. Like those who had arrived before them, all wanted only a few hours' blissful oblivion in sleep. The mental and physical exhaustion suffered by men kept at action or cruising stations without proper hot food or sleep in conditions of continual daylight cannot be over-emphasized. Add to this the strain of frequent fog and extreme cold and one begins to realize that the burdens of a sense of abandonment, hopelessness, uncertainty and enemy action were well-nigh intolerable. It is not a matter for wonderment that so many merchant ships were lost, but rather that *any* fought their way through.

At dawn on the 7th, with the rising Arctic sun warm on their faces, the crews of the three trawlers, *Lord Austin*, *Lord Middleton* and *Northern Gem*, joined their consorts at anchor. They were desperately short of bunkers and were relieved when *Ocean Freedom* later yielded a quantity of steam coal. Ironically all the escorts were now accounted for with the exception of *Dianella* (assigned to the cover of the two submarines *P614* and *P615*) and *Ayrshire*, now breaking out of the closing ice many miles to the west-north-west.

German reconnaissance aircraft failed to locate the ships sheltering in Matochkin Strait, still occupied as they were with lone merchantmen in the Barents Sea; they had, however, reported the derelict *Aldersdale*. Schmundt dismissed Navy Group North's 'technically impossible' idea of towing the British auxiliary in by submarine, but directed La Baume in *U355* to sink her. In the event she was finally torpedoed by Brandenburg in *U457* at about 07.00 on the 7th.

In the opinion of the German group commands, the operations against PQ17 had been highly successful. The Seekriegsleitung recorded that the convoy 'had been virtually wiped out . . . the submarines and air force have achieved what had been the intention of Operation Rösselsprung'. This may have mollified Raeder and helped convince the Führer that the Knight's Move had actually been a success, but it was Bohmann in *U88* who sounded the first note of dissent. He had been patrolling off Sukhoi Nos, north of Cape Stolbovoi, and suspected some ships had eluded the Luftwaffe and the Eisteufel wolf pack.

Not quite all; a frustrated young Günther La Baume in *U355*, having been cheated of success in the general carnage, came upon the 5,000-ton British tramp *Hartlebury* owned by Harrison's of London, hurrying along the shore of the southern island of Novaya Zemlya, off Moller Bay. *Hartlebury* still wore her owner's device upon her funnel and this swam into the lens of La Baume's attack periscope during the late afternoon of the 7th. Three torpedoes were dispatched and the ship was blown apart amid scenes of harrowing distress. Efforts to launch boats and rafts were hampered by the forward motion of the stricken ship and a panic among some of her crew. Amid a wild chaos of smashed or swamped boats, prematurely launched rafts and the deafening roar of the boilers venting steam, *Hartlebury*'s company abandoned ship.

The penultimate man to leave her was her master, Captain Stephenson, who had rammed a U-boat in an earlier convoy. He dived from the stern as his ship, her back broken, began her final plunge. In doing so he suffered a severe head wound, from which he afterwards died, the only master to be lost from PQ17 and the convoy's Vice-Commodore. Just as the ship began to go down, those watching from the water saw another figure, that of Second Officer Harold Spence. A few minutes earlier Spence had been scrambling down the lifeline into the only undamaged, though swamped, lifeboat as it dragged alongside the moving tramp by its painter. He had been about to step aboard when the painter was severed and the boat dropped astern. Spence climbed wearily back aboard and, as La Baume's fifth torpedo tore into the riven hull, he waved at his shipmates. It was the last they saw of him. He had been married shortly before the ship left Sunderland.

La Baume now surfaced near the Chief Officer's raft and asked the usual questions about the ship and her tonnage, took photographs as men on the casing covered the hapless survivors with machine guns, and told the survivors they were not far from land. They were ordered to hand over their captain, but he was not with them. They were then asked the standard question as to why they were helping Communists. Bread and schnapps were passed down, then *U355* 'cleared off, leaving us in such a state', wrote the Third Officer, Needham Forth, in the swamped lifeboat, 'it seemed one of the cruellest things possible'.[15]

The piercing cold and demoralization soon began to account for those that clung to the wreckage. The firemen who had come up from the heat of the stoke-hold in dungarees and singlets were among the first to die, but others had succumbed to nervous fatigue, battle weariness and strain, and had lost their powers of resistance. Within hours men had given up the ghost, their plight too desperate to sustain the slightest hope of relief, while many of those who did survive suffered barbarous mutilation as a result of frostbite and immersion foot. Of the score or so men who had left the ship in the swamped lifeboat, only four survived; of the fourteen of Radio Officer Fearnside's raft only five lived; while Chief Officer Gordon's nine men all survived, a can of whale oil massaged into their cold feet having done much to retard the otherwise inexorable progress of hypothermia. The sea, which had risen prior to the sinking, had subsided again and for two days Fearnside's raft drifted in mist and fog until they finally found themselves in sight of Novaya Zemlya and a large, grounded American ship, whose crew put out a boat and helped them ashore.

Meanwhile Gordon's raft had found the four survivors in the lifeboat. His men, being in better shape, boarded and baled it out and finally set some sail. A day after Fearnside, they too landed on Novaya Zemlya, set up camp under the boat's sail and lit a driftwood fire on the bleak foreshore. Their meagre emergency rations were supplemented by birds' eggs and Gordon led patrols to search for other survivors, one of which brought in a report of a stranded ship ten miles away. Thus the pitiful remnant of the Vice-Commodore's ship's company found shelter.

The ship in which they found sanctuary was the *Winston Salem* and the circumstances of her grounding must remain a matter of conjecture, though she closed the coast in fog. Nevertheless, she provided welcome refuge for the frost-bitten men drifting into Obsiedya Bay.

Like Bohmann, who was soon ordered back to base to refuel, Reche in *U255* was also freelancing on the coast of Novaya Zemlya, but was further south when he sighted the *Bellingham* and the *Rathlin*. The rescue ship, unable to keep up with Lawford's group, had fallen in with the American vessel and had not diverted to Matochkin Strait. Later the same day Surgeon Wilkins had performed an appendectomy on one of *Bellingham*'s men.

Reche fired two torpedoes, one of which missed and the other failed to detonate, though it dented the *Bellingham*'s shell plating and otherwise made its arrival known. Thus compelled to let the ships escape, a few moments later Reche caught sight of another steaming south on a steady course. A single torpedo blasted its way into a forward hold and water poured into the *Alcoa Ranger* as she blew off steam and lost way, settling slowly by the head. Short of torpedoes, *U255* surfaced, quizzed the escaping crew and then hastened the American freighter's end by pumping shells into her. Reche then motored southwards, unaware that he had been spotted by Captain Harvey of the CAM ship *Empire Tide*, some miles to the north.

Harvey and his officers also sighted other surfaced U-boats whose conning towers were, in the refracting Arctic air, given an occasional but fantastic prominence. He turned his ship short round and retreated, finally heading for Moller Bay, where he anchored and awaited relief.

Having resumed his northward patrol line Reche did in fact see the CAM ship, but he failed to maintain contact and lost her. Nevertheless, shortly before midnight, he caught sight of yet another vessel coasting south. This was the *Olopana* whose master, Captain Stone, had intended to put into a bay, anchor and rest his crew. The appearance of a shadower, the sight of extensive ice and a warning about minefields gave him second thoughts. Mustering his somewhat fractious crew he told them he was pressing on for the White Sea. Not until the small hours of the 8th did Reche manage to manœuvre *U255* ahead of the *Olopana*, acutely aware of his dwindling stock of torpedoes. At short range he aimed at the ageing freighter's funnel and for a moment thought he had fired another dud.

Stone's ship staggered under the blast and then slowly lost way. The starboard lifeboat was destroyed and the port one lowered too hastily, so that one fall ran slack and it bumped alongside, swamped. Three men in the engine room had been killed, a British gunner and an American seaman had been washed overboard by the explosion, and another man was missing; the remainder escaped on rafts as Reche surfaced and opened fire. Stone's reservist naval radio operator, Charles Schultz, earned the Master's commendation for getting off a distress signal, a fact which, when learned of by Reche, sent the U-boat commander scuttling away from his handiwork.

Having escaped Reche, the *Bellingham* and *Rathlin* continued southwards. Rising hopes of reaching their destination seemed dashed at about 02.30 on the morning of the 8th, when the bleary-eyed lookouts reported the approach of an FW Condor. Captain Mortensen of the *Bellingham* watched it circle and disappear into cloud astern, then it roared out of the cloud not, for once, homing others to a kill, but pressing its own attack. Both ships' machine guns opened up and succeeded in setting on fire the two outer engines. In a trice the aircraft was on fire and although the aircrew dropped their bombs and returned cannon fire, the former missed while the latter exploded a tank of ammonia on deck. Blast and fumes caused injuries among the *Bellingham*'s crew but it was the Condor that broke up as it crashed into the sea.

The *Bellingham*'s men were jubilant as Captain Banning dutifully turned *Rathlin* to close the floating wreckage and rescue the aircrew. As she drew alongside, her people saw the six men floating dead amid the wreckage. Both ships pulled away and continued south; they arrived safely at Archangel on the 9th, the same day that the Russian tanker *Donbass* arrived, one of her guns still manned by the armed guard from the *Daniel Morgan*.

On Tuesday, 7 July 1942, Commodore Dowding reinherited his kingdom: what was left of PQ17 was to be re-formed. It did not lack escorts. At a conference aboard *Palomares* the air was thick with rumour and conjecture. They were almost out of radio range and intelligence appreciation was impossible; Jauncey and Lawford were of the opinion that the anchorage could quickly turn from haven to trap. Several of the merchant Masters considered otherwise; they could wait for overwhelming naval support, while in the meantime the narrow strait and the massive anti-aircraft firepower they possessed were protection against aerial attack. In the event the naval officers carried the day and a radio message was transmitted to Archangel using the Russian radio station and passed to Captain Maund, the SBNO there.

Maund passed what must, in the circumstances, have seemed like good news to Rear-Admiral Bevan at Polyarnoe. Early the same day, the 7th, the corvette *Dianella* had arrived at Archangel after seeing the two submarines, *P614* and *P615*, to their patrol stations. At midnight, after refuelling, Lieutenant Rankin's ship left again, to search the Barents Sea for survivors. The Russians had no ships available and Crombie properly retained those minesweepers he still had in Russian waters for their prime purpose. All Bevan had to assist Rankin was the *Chiltern*. Meanwhile the rump of PQ17 had left Matochkin Strait.

It was 19.00 on a clear, frosty evening when *Lotus*, with Dowding aboard, led the ships out, picking up *La Malouine* from an anti-submarine patrol in the approaches. Shortly afterwards they ran into fog and the *Benjamin Harrison* returned to the anchorage. The rest of the ships pressed on, though straggling in the negligible visibility. The next day they met Schmundt's new cordon of U-boats. It was the worst of luck.

Admiral Arctic was playing his last card. The staff appraisal was that the operation was over and *U88* and *U355* were on their way back to base, short of fuel. But *U255* (Reche), *U703* (Bielfeld) and *U457* (Brandenburg) had been reinforced by the boats of Marks (*U376*), von Hymmen (*U408*) and Timm (*U251*). They reported an extensive ice-field lying athwart the entrance to the Gourlo, and Schmundt determined on a final sweep by the wolf pack up the coast of Novaya Zemlya, then west, along the ice-edge, mopping up any merchantmen that had so far escaped.

Coming south in the fog the Allied ships from Matochkin Strait had lost formation and were only loosely knit together, despite the radar of the escorts. The merchant ships remaining were now *Hoosier*, *Samuel Chase*, *Ocean Freedom* and *El Capitan*. At about 16.30, with a shrieking of whistles and sirens, an accompanying screech of ice on steel plating, and the thrashing of screws thrown into astern gear, they ground into the outlying floes of the ice-field barring their escape.

The ice broke up what was left of the 'convoy's' cohesion and for several hours the ships blundered about despite efforts by *Palomares* to locate them all by radio. *Zamalek* struck a submarine ice-ridge and remained fast for some hours before Morris worked her free, her forepeak leaking. Almost incredibly the Master and Mate of the *El Capitan* found themselves close to a boatload of nineteen survivors, huddling under an orange sail. They were from the Liberty ship *John Witherspoon*. In the early hours *Britomart*, *Lotus* and *Halcyon* broke out of the fog and ice, and sighted the *Samuel Chase* and *Ocean Freedom*, and the trawlers *Lord Middleton* and *Northern Gem*. *Lotus* also ran across and took aboard the two dozen survivors of the *Pan Atlantic*.

Separated, the two anti-aircraft cruisers, the freighters *El Capitan* and *Hoosier*, *Lord Austin*, *Poppy*, *Salamander*, *La*

Malouine and *Zamalek* also regained clear weather where the latter two executed a rescue that matched that carried out earlier by the Panamanian tramp. The balance of twenty-nine survivors also from the *John Witherspoon* were sighted by a vigilant look-out aboard the corvette and picked up. The two boats yielded up a mixed bag – men who fell asleep in odd corners, raided the wardroom drinks locker or gratefully pressed preciously preserved pornographic photographs on their rescuers. They had been in their two boats for three days and were severely frostbitten. Shortly afterwards, the temperature fell and freezing fog again settled itself over the sea, to persist for the remainder of the day.

About 11.00 on the 9th, Brandenburg reported he had sighted a small convoy and *U703*, *U408* and *U376* were homed on it during the afternoon and early evening. The latter was unsuccessfully depth-charged (possibly by *Lotus*) and an attack by von Hymmen failed. The group was that centred on *Palomares* and consisting of the merchant ships *El Capitan* and *Hoosier*, which had cleared the fog. It was forty to fifty miles ahead of the other ships and was now being trailed; no attempt was made to detach the corvettes to put *U255* down, because there was by now an acute shortage of fuel. Captain Morris suggested to Jauncey that they all re-enter the fog lying not far off, but was snubbed.[16]

The little convoy, first forced west by the ice and now steaming south-west, was, in fact, heading back towards occupied Norway and not long afterwards Reche reported to Schmundt that two shadowing Blohm and Voss aircraft were overhead. Conditions were excellent for air attack, with a light wind and, ironically, twenty miles of visibility, and continued to be fine, with the sun hanging low on the western horizon, as the first wave of KG30's two score Ju88s appeared. The alarms jangled on the ships and all able-bodied men, including survivors, joined in the defence, manning supply parties or relieving gun crews. With less than 150 miles to go, the proximity of Banak meant they would have to fight every inch of the way.

The Ju88s wheeled overhead like chiel-kites, then the first five moved in and others followed from differing directions, fragmenting the barrage and confusing the defenders who began expending their residual ammunition at a furious rate. Reche, surfaced astern, observed the fighting.

Three bombs exploded beside the 5,000-ton *Hoosier*, fracturing pipes and her shell plating: the ship rapidly lost way but fortunately remained on an even keel, sinking slowly. *Hoosier*'s boats were lowered and within minutes *La Malouine* was among them embarking the crew while *Poppy* circled, keeping *U255* at bay, as the 'convoy' and its tormentors drew away.

Ideas of towing the disabled freighter were short-lived. The presence of the U-boat, lack of fuel in the corvettes and a peremptory 'sink and rejoin' signal from *Palomares* caused Lieutenant Bidwell to abandon an attempt to salvage *Hoosier*. Instead he ordered his 4-inch gun to fire into the American ship while members of her crew milled miserably on deck. The two corvettes drew off, leaving *Hoosier* afloat but in flames. She was sunk several hours later by *U376*.

The attacks of KG30 came in waves and the ammunition stocks of the defenders were now dangerously depleted, particularly in *Palomares* and *Pozarica*. Jauncey radioed for Russian air cover, and five 'pusher'-engined flying boats of dubious identity attracted fire and turned away before they were recognized as Russians. No fighters were forthcoming, a mix-up several commentators thought 'almost deliberate'.

If one discounts the *Zamalek* which Morris wove in and out of the plunging bombs, there was only one merchant ship left among them, *El Capitan*, symbolic of the Allied effort dissipated in PQ17. The ship was Panamanian-registered, Captain Thevik was Norwegian, his mate British, and fifteen other nationalities made up the crew. She had, moreover, nineteen survivors of the *John Witherspoon* aboard. At about 02.00 on the 10th, near misses opened seams in her stern. Then at 04.00 a near miss on *Zamalek* cut loose the boat towing astern which started a panic among the Russians from the *Azerbaijan* who cut the lashings of a Carley float. It was swiftly surpressed by a burst of machine-gun fire from the bridge and the intervention of Chief Officer Macdonald, but the old ship's engines ground to a halt. With surfaced U-boats visible in the offing, Captain Morris signalled his chief engineer to bring the engine-room crew on deck as *Zamalek* lost way. Mercifully the Ju88s had drawn off, but so too had the convoy. Incredibly, no ship was sent back to help. Morris lost his Welsh temper and galvanized his men.[17] Among the survivors were several engineers, including *Zaafaran*'s, so, led by the two rescue-ship Chief Engineers Miller and Dawson and the Chief of the

Christopher Newport, the men re-entered the engine room with torches. Shattered light-bulbs were replaced, the fractured oil pipes bandaged and auxiliary generator restarted. In under an hour, capable of making 10 knots, *Zamalek* set out after the others, her strained rivets leaking water into the ship.

For two hours the 'convoy' enjoyed a respite, anticipating Soviet air cover as they neared the Russian coast. But the first lone plane to reappear proved to be a Ju88 and a stick of near misses finally disabled *El Capitan*. Cooling water intake valves were shattered and water poured into the boiler room, rising fast to the level of the fires; bunker oil pipes were fractured and fuel leaked from the settling and feed tanks; overside bilge discharge lines had been cracked and fires were starting from damaged circuits. Captain Thevik ordered the ship abandoned and the trawler *Lord Austin* ran alongside *El Capitan*'s boats and took in her crew together with the men from the *John Witherspoon*. The ship seemed destined for the bottom, but the rising water failed to reach the boiler fires before the fractured fuel pipes first cut off their supply of oil. *El Capitan* sat on the surface, slowly subsiding, until she too was finished off by *U251*. In her holds 7,500 tons of munitions, machinery and *matériel*, and on her decks eight tanks and four Boston bombers went to the bottom.

In the early hours of 10 July, as the remaining naval ships steamed south and closed the coast to anchor, *Zamalek* strove to catch up. Finally, off Iokanka, Captain Lawford slowed *Pozarica* and allowed *Zamalek* to run alongside. As she did so the entire company of the anti-aircraft cruiser lined their ship's side, lifted their caps and roared their appreciation. 'As the caps went up', Surgeon McBain recalled, 'and the sound floated across, all of us felt unexpectedly moved.' 'Choking with emotion', Captain Morris ordered his own 'grand' crew to respond. The ships dipped their tattered ensigns. It was not glorious, but it was at least gallant.

At 12.30 the ships off Iokanka weighed. The Russian destroyers *Gremyashchi* and *Grozni* joined and led the British warships into the Gourlo, but came no further; the battered squadron entered the White Sea and headed for the River Dvina. At 16.00 on 11 July 1942, as the *Zamalek* approached the quay to secure alongside at Archangel and join the *Bellingham*, *Donbass* and *Rathlin*, the insane seaman from the *Samuel Chase* jumped overboard and swam frantically ashore. Less eager to leave, the nervous Russians from the *Azerbaijan* were marched off under guard.[18]

The Russian destroyers do not appear to have put out to sea to accompany the second group of ships now receiving the attention of KG30 as they headed for Cape Kanin. The *Samuel Chase* and *Ocean Freedom* with *Lotus, Halcyon, Britomart, Lord Middleton* and *Northern Gem* were attacked by sixteen Ju88s from Banak reinforced by aircraft from Petsamo at 11.00 on the 11th. The attack lasted for an hour and a half and near misses brought the *Samuel Chase* to a standstill. The escort now split, *Britomart* and *Northern Gem* continuing to escort *Ocean Freedom*, while *Halcyon* took the American Liberty ship in tow and *Lord Middleton* provided anti-submarine cover. Both groups continued to fight off attacks and *Ocean Freedom* sustained damage from a savage near miss which fortunately failed to immobilize her. Having thought both vessels sunk, KG30 mounted a final attack during the late afternoon, but now, at last, Russian Hurricanes and Petlyakov fighters appeared and the Junkers bombers withdrew. *Hazard* and *Leda* also hove into sight and Russian minesweepers joined in the White Sea. Overhead a Stormovik bomber and a Hurricane fighter wheeled protectively and, as the pine-clad shores drew in, it began to rain. At long last the ships joined those already alongside, the trawlers at Maimska, the others further upstream. Tired men left their stations, almost too weary to turn in. The nights at Archangel, they found, offered a little brief but welcome darkness.

Reche had followed these last ships almost into the Gourlo but he had not pressed an attack and finally turned north, taking a wide sweep on his way back to base. The following day, the 13th, he sighted the derelict *Paulus Potter* and sent a boarding party which included his engineer to her with orders to investigate the possibility of salvaging the Dutch ship. The German submariners found the engine room full of water, but the mess-room tables were laid for a meal. They emptied the ship of available comestibles before returning to their U-boat. They also brought with them, according to Reche later, confidential papers which, though in a weighted box, had been forgotten on the bridge in the confusion. Filming the operation, Reche fired his last torpedo into the *Paulus Potter* and turned for home. Most of the other Eisteufel boats were already on their way. With the exception of Marks, Timm and von Hymmen's boats, their fuel was almost exhausted. The Nazi authorities broke the news of the 'massacre' of convoy PQ17 on

8 July, along with the news that Voronezh had fallen to German arms. The propaganda machine had a field-day.

In Moscow Rear-Admiral Miles had received copies of the signals scattering PQ17 and had been summoned to an interview with Admiral Alafusov, Vice-Chief of the Soviet Naval Staff, who was also aware of the order. Alafusov inveighed against the decision, for the Russians were already intercepting the first distress signals transmitted by the merchant ships, demanding a full explanation for his chief, Kuznetsov, who in his turn would report the facts to Stalin. Eventually Miles himself, armed with Pound's 'explanation', met Kuznetsov. The Russian newspaper *Pravda* had reported a successful attack on *Tirpitz* by the Russian submarine *K21*. Torpedoes had been fired, though they missed, and it may have been the subsequent reversal of course of the German battle-group that persuaded Kapitan 2 Ranga Lunin to claim his 'success'. Whatever the truth of the matter, Kuznetzov disputed the wisdom of dispersing the convoy: 'I hope we have not made a sad mistake.' Then he mellowed, commiserating with Miles that his superiors had placed him in an awkward situation. Miles confided to the record, in the language of the strained diplomat, 'I felt the dispersal had been premature.'

Marshal Stalin had no such sensibilities. On 16 August he bluntly asked Churchill, 'Has the British navy no sense of glory?'

In fact the Royal Navy on the spot had done its best to recover what it could – *Dianella* was at sea searching for survivors on the 8th – but two days later boatloads of exhausted men remained at sea, either adrift or under scraps of sail, while some had reached the dubious sanctuary of Novaya Zemlya by plying their oars.

'High courage' was, in the words of the Master of the *Silver Sword*, the quality demonstrated by Lieutenant Leo Gradwell and his anti-submarine trawler *Ayrshire*. Far to the north-north-west, at 21.00 on 6 July, Gradwell broke his 'mighty little ship' out of the ice in which it had been concealed with the *Ironclad, Troubadour* and *Silver Sword*. The four vessels crept eastward along the ice-edge in dangerously low visibility until the small hours of the 9th found them in a remote fiord in northern Novaya Zemlya where *Ayrshire* coaled from *Troubadour*. The group then coasted south and entered Matochkin Strait where both *Ironclad* and *Ayrshire* ran aground, the latter losing her asdic dome in the process, though both ships were got off without more serious consequences. Lieutenant Elsden made contact with the Russians at Lagerni and learned of the arrival and departure of the other convoy survivors. He also returned to the trawler with news of boatloads of survivors further south. Gradwell went off to investigate and returned with thirty-four men from three of the *Fairfield City*'s boats, most of whom were in a state of mental and physical collapse after their ordeal.

Penetrating beyond Lagerni, Gradwell was able to hand these men to the care of a primitive Russian hospital further east, and here he discovered, riding at anchor, the Liberty ship *Benjamin Harrison*. Sending news of his arrival to Archangel via the Russian radio station, Gradwell settled down to wait. He was pessimistic as to their overall chances.

Meanwhile, further south Captain Harvey's *Empire Tide* had taken refuge in Moller Bay. He too had made contact with Archangel, announcing his arrival and requesting urgent medical help for one of his gunners with a wounded thigh.

A few hours after *Dianella* had sailed on her quest, Captain Stone of the *Olopana* and his remaining nine men caught sight of the *Zamalek* through the mist, but the flares they set off were not seen from the rescue ship. Stone's men were kept relentlessly paddling their awkward raft east in an attempt to maintain circulation. That evening it began to rain. Later they saw two corvettes through the curtains of mist, but again were not themselves observed. Finally they made out North Gusini lighthouse and afterwards floundered ashore about 05.00 on 10 July. Breaking up their raft to make shelter and a fire, Stone sent out a patrol to the lighthouse. From the elevation of the unmanned light, the officers could see a beached ship which turned out to be the *Winston Salem*, also sheltering the *Hartlebury*'s survivors. Stone's men made a last trek to the stranded ship and, in the hours that followed, the combined ships' companies began building an encampment on shore. That afternoon a Russian Catalina buzzed the beach. She had just landed alongside the *Empire Tide*, thirty miles north, and evacuated the ship's wounded gunner for immediate medical attention. The Catalina's pilot, the Arctic aviator Captain I.P. Mazuruk, had, upon delivering the invalid to the hospital in Matochkin Strait, also spoken to Gradwell and told the young lieutenant there had been no great naval battle in the Barents Sea.

Much encouraged by this news, Gradwell reported to Archangel via Mazuruk the presence of one Panamanian and three American merchant ships whose masters were 'showing unmistakeable signs of strain'. He continued, 'I much doubt if I could persuade them to make a dash without . . . increased escort and . . . fighter protection . . . there has already been talk of scuttling ship . . . rather than go to what they, with their present escort, consider certain sinking.' Gradwell concluded that he would await a reply.[19]

In the succeeding days two Russian armed vessels arrived, the trawler *Kerov* and the ice-breaker *Murman*. Also steaming into the anchorage came the Russian tanker *Azerbaijan*, still showing the scars of the attack on her a week earlier.

The same day Mazuruk landed alongside the *Empire Tide*, another Catalina overflew the boat-load of survivors from the *Carlton* who had not been captured. To their disappointment it dropped them supplies but did not land, leaving them with the false impression that rescue was imminent. Aboard the boats of the *Bolton Castle* spirits were already low. A whale kept them company for several days as they pulled south, but the ceaseless rocking of the boat, the difficulties of keeping corned beef down with insufficient water, and the terrible cold all had a remorseless effect. One of the artillery gunners was in a state of collapse and the Master, Captain Pascoe, was very weak; he led his men in a prayer.

Mazuruk continued to fly up and down the coast, encountering another nine men from the *Olopana* and the deserted *Winston Salem* with its adjacent camp of survivors. The stranded ship's Master is alleged to have demanded a seat in the aircraft, claiming he had delivered his ship to a Soviet harbour. Attempts to tow the Liberty ship off using the Russian auxiliaries had failed and the Master appears to have been in a state of exhaustion. When Admiral Golovko heard Mazuruk's report he exploded: 'By harbour this shameless entrepreneur meant a deserted bay on an Arctic island . . . And these are our allies.' It was all most unfortunate.

Another raft from the *Olopana* had come ashore further south than Captain Stone's. Thirty men under the Chief Engineer were rescued by a small Russian coaster which took some of them to the hospital at Byelushka Bay, then picked up forty-one more survivors, chiefly from the *Alcoa Ranger*, and transferred them to the anchored *Empire Tide*. The coaster then encountered forty-three men from the *Washington* and twenty-eight from the *Paulus Potter* who had struggled through extreme privations of ice and bad weather to land on the northern coast of the 'new land'. Sustained by duck soup brewed in the boat-bailers, they had been coasting southwards when rescued on 15 July. These men, together with two more from the *Olopana* and fifteen from the *Hartlebury*, swelled Captain Harvey's complement to almost 130 men. Not only were facilities strained aboard the *Empire Tide*, so was the temper of the men. Their poor state of health and ragged nerves, and cultural differences between the various nationalities, were brewing trouble, so Harvey reported the state of affairs to the pilot of a British Catalina in the hope of some relief from Archangel. Meanwhile the Russian coaster removed more stores from the *Winston Salem* and, with great presence of mind, towed to Moller Bay a number of the abandoned boats she had discovered. These would come in useful, it was felt, in the final dash to the White Sea.

Those men in the worst condition were, after prodigious efforts, manhandled ashore to a small hospital at a polar station, from where the most severe cases of frostbite were flown out by Catalina on the 17th. The assembled masters also dispatched Captain Stone to plead for assistance from the British naval authorities. The appearance of a Junkers Ju88 at high altitude that evening was enough to convince some fifty men that the *Empire Tide* afforded no refuge, despite the fact that her Hurricane had actually been started up and prepared for launching – a fact which seemed to have persuaded the Ju88 not to loiter. These men, survivors from the *Olopana*, *Washington* and *Hartlebury*, set up camp ashore while those remaining in authority divided up the available stores and left them with a proportion of the boats, thanks to the forethought of the Russian coaster's master.

Nevertheless, despite this division of opinion, no disorder occurred, and with great ingenuity a conduit was fabricated to pipe fresh water from an inland stream to the beach, easing at least one of Harvey's problems.

Although the naval ships at Archangel could top up both fuel and water, their morale was equally low. Rumour became received 'truth' in the absence of fact. Attempts on the part of junior corvette officers to satisfy their curiosity as to what had happened were rebuffed by Maund's staff at Norway House, and while this may have been due to a prevailing ignorance, it was tactless and ill-received.

On arrival at Archangel, Captain Stone found that little liaison seemed to have taken place between the Russian and Anglo-American representatives. He met Maund and Frankel, the US naval attaché, who was disturbed to learn of the condition of the *Winston Salem*. Stone explained the situation in Moller Bay and the widespread perception that too little was being done to mop up the disaster. It was true enough, though Maund had sent out the first corvette to arrive.

Dianella's sweep lasted eight days and yielded sixty-one survivors from the *Empire Byron*. She reported a great deal of wreckage strewn about when she returned on the 16th. That evening, in army battledress and a plain officer's hat, Commodore Dowding boarded HMS *Poppy* and put to sea with *Lotus* and *La Malouine*. The corvettes' crews were pleased to be doing something useful, despite the heavy rain and strong wind, and *Lotus* and *La Malouine* ploughed north, swapping facetious signals concerning their lack of food.

By the time they arrived in Byelushka Bay on the 19th, the weather had moderated. They came across an abandoned raft, then espied nine survivors from *Olopana* huddled on the beach. Manœuvring closer inshore, *Poppy* damaged her asdic dome on a rock in the poorly charted bay. Later that day the two corvettes located the *Winston Salem* with her crew and the other survivors living nearby. A Russian trawler and a survey ship were still attempting to tow the freighter off.

Meanwhile Lieutenant Bidwell had taken *La Malouine* into Moller Bay and told Harvey to prepare to sail the next day. All the injured and hospitalized were brought back aboard the *Empire Tide* and even the reluctant shore-side campers were embarked, along with their boats. Bidwell then steamed north and, during the forenoon of 20 July, the three corvettes ran into Matochkin Strait and anchored. The sight of the camouflaged *Ayrshire*, four undamaged merchantmen and the bruised *Azerbaijan* among her fellow Russians, *Murman* and *Kerov*, was greeted with cheers.

After a conference, Dowding ordered Bidwell back to attend the *Empire Tide* before he took passage in the ice-breaker *Murman* and led out the remaining ships. All were united offshore early on 21 July but the wind had dropped and fog again closed in. On the 22nd *Pozarica*, *Dianella*, *Hazard*, *Leda* and the two Russians *Grozni* and *Gremyashchi* reinforced the escort and thus the

Azerbaijan, Silver Sword, Benjamin Harrison, Ironclad and *Troubadour* finally arrived at Archangel on 24 July 1942.

Only the *Winston Salem* remained outstanding. Her immobilized condition angered Frankel who flew up by Catalina to see what could be done. It is to the credit of those who had just survived a humiliating defeat that survivors from other ships made up a crew to bring her in, rather than have the Russians do it unassisted. Having lightened her by pumping fuel oil overboard, the Russian vessels succeeded in pulling her into deep water. She arrived at Archangel on the evening of 28 July 1942.

For the crews of the merchant ships rumours of delays to PQ18 meant a long wait for a passage west, turbulent behaviour and the demoralization noted in the previous chapter. Morale in the warships continued to be little better, with a degree of recrimination passing between some of the ships. The Russian port authorities put the discharge of the cargoes that *had* arrived in hand, so much so that even *Norfolk*'s Walrus, towed in by *Palomares*, was put on a flat-car, the Russians refusing to believe it was not part of the consignment.[20]

As for the Soviets, it was generally thought that, despite the presence of two Russian ships in the convoy, they did not believe that such a large convoy as was claimed had set out from Iceland. They were equally harsh towards those members of the *Azerbaijan*'s crew who had been left aboard *Zamalek*. These miserable wretches were marched off under military guard on arrival. Their fate can only be guessed at.

Admiral Miles came north to visit the hospitalized and to speak to the survivors, many of whom were in belligerent mood. Though, as we have seen, complaints were legion, some men thought the Russians had done their best, given the resources available to them and the hardships they themselves were enduring. After ten days in a boat one man remembered how he felt he had failed to help alleviate 'the great ordeal of the Russian people'.

Nevertheless, individual cases of extreme hardship were not yet over. The barbarous treatment of amputation for most frostbite cases had, in one instance, resulted in one young man losing all his limbs. Surgeon McBain of the *Zaafaran* recorded, 'I was fifteen minutes in the water . . . On boarding the raft, skin anaesthesia was complete to the neck. Joint sense was impaired and there was well-marked ischaemia [dead-white fingers and toes] . . . Massage and work at an oar restored sensation . . . [but] still showing traces after eight weeks'.[21]

Such were the privations endured by those who were quickly picked up. Others were at sea for days. Two of *Alcoa Ranger*'s boats had been rescued from Novaya Zemlya, a third made the mainland at Cape Kanin. The *Peter Kerr*'s boats had made a passage of 360 miles only to be intercepted by a suspicious Russian gunboat off Kildin Island, near the Kola Inlet. Twenty-six men from the *Earlston* discovered their boat had been rifled of stores and finally struggled ashore, half-demented, after a passage of over 400 miles. They found themselves near the North Cape, in German-occupied Norway. Their other boat had been picked up by a British escort, as had thirty-seven men from the *Honomu*. Both boats from the *Bolton Castle* pulled and sailed south over a similar distance to that of *Earlston*. Days blurred into one another, the eternal daylight confusing minds already bruised with the uncertainties of war, the trauma of sinking and the utter hopelessness of their situation; bodies assaulted by extreme cold and hunger. Finally they sighted the Murman coast and were rescued by Russian patrol craft.

Only the *Carlton*'s boat remained, destitute after the cheerful message dropped from the British Catalina on 10 July. After nine days, when the seventeen American survivors were near the end of their tether, *U376* ran alongside and Kapitänleutnant Marks gave them provisions, a chart, a compass and their position. They noted the food and gear were of US origin and learned that the U-boat had recently torpedoed the *Hoosier* from which they had first scavenged some luxuries. The same day, as the weather deteriorated, an engineer froze to death. Arguments flared and died, men became somnolent and fatalistic, utterly resigned to death. Then they sighted land and frantically began to fight a fierce tide. They were so weak that when a man and a boy came alongside and took them in tow, they were astonished at how easily they were dragged inshore. They had been nineteen days in a 32-foot boat and could not stand on their feet; they crawled ashore on the soil of occupied Norway. They too ended up in Stalag Marlag-Milag Nord.

The losses sustained by the Allies were enormous, amounting to twenty-four merchant ships, two-thirds of the convoy; eight totalling 48,218 tons sunk by U-boats, eight of 40,376 tons sunk by aircraft, eight of 54,093 tons damaged by aircraft and finished off by U-boats. In terms of lost *matériel*, 210 bombers, 430 tanks, 3,350 vehicles and a little under 100,000 tons of munitions, explosives and raw materials lay on the bed of the Barents Sea – all this for half a dozen German aircraft.

In London Ambassador Maisky pressed Eden for news of the next convoy and was angry when told the Admiralty would not send any more until the nights closed in again. All Eden and Churchill would do was to promise a meeting at which Maisky and the head of the Soviet military mission, Admiral Harlamov, could put their case. At the meeting, which included Eden, the First Lord, A.V. Alexander, and the First Sea Lord, Pound, Maisky reiterated his request to know the scheduled departure of PQ18. Pound said nothing could be done until better Russian air cover was arranged, whereupon Harlamov criticized the order to withdraw the cruisers from PQ17. Pound was furious, deeply resenting the Russian attitude and angrily admitting PQ17 was scattered by his personal order. Alexander attempted to smooth things over and Maisky purred, 'Even British admirals make mistakes.'[22]

In the Commons next day Emmanuel Shinwell MP asked the Financial Secretary to the Admiralty, George Hall, if he was 'aware that a recent convoy proceeding in a very important direction was denuded by Admiralty [of] protection . . . and that a large number of vessels were lost?' Hall remained seated and tight-lipped.

These were the first of a long series of inquests into what was, after all, nothing less than a huge and awesome blunder. In the unwise official British silence which followed, a silence which the reporter Godfrey Winn accurately warned the First Lord of the Admiralty would create mistrust on the part of the Americans and much mischief elsewhere, rumours circulated which sought to taint several officers, including poor Hamilton, with the whiff of reprehensible conduct. They were as unworthy as their origin was uncertain.[23] Tovey was so concerned that he boarded the USS *Wichita* after her arrival at Scapa Flow and addressed her company, apologizing for the circumstances which had led to so many losses among American merchant seamen.[24]

It was at least a manly act, to be expected of such a man, but no such consideration was afforded British merchant seafarers. When the majority of the PQ17 survivors arrived home in QP14 they were not allowed to disperse on arrival in Glasgow but were marched to St Andrew's Hall and addressed by Philip Noel-Baker, Under Secretary of State to the Ministry of War Transport. As a damage-limitation exercise this was an insult to the intelligence of weary men. 'We know what the convoy cost us. But I want to tell you that whatever the cost, it was well worth it.' Unsurprisingly, the Under-Secretary was howled down.

It has been suggested that the cost of PQ17 has been exaggerated, that the German offensive was in any case contained at Stalingrad (though at enormous cost). It has also been claimed that the loss of 153 Allied merchant seamen from 22 merchantmen was light compared to losses of 4,000 sustained in the preceding months by the Royal Navy from an equal number of warships. Such comparisons are as invidious as they are unworthy. Like can only be compared with like and this bald figure takes no account of the physical and mental scars of many others. Apart from the highly material fact that to have destroyed the *contents* of those humble freighters in combat would have cost the Germans dear, tragically, the reverberative effect on morale of the loss of those 153 men, augmented by the tales of the survivors, was more significant than the loss of the 4,000. War is full of such savage inequities.

'Looks like a bloody business,' Broome had shouted across to Dowding and Charlton. The rebounding irony was far greater than intended by Broome's well-meant, self-deprecating remark. Broome had anticipated a battle within a matter of hours, but the surviving merchant seamen remembered not that 'only' 153 of their comrades died in the catastrophe that followed the scattering of PQ17, but that not one naval sailor died in their defence.[25]

It was this that fuelled the ensuing bad feeling that spread like a viral infection and lasted long after the guns had fallen silent. American mercantile faith in the British navy was shaken and the Russian reaction was predictably uncompromising, but the most ulcerous wound was opened in the morale of the British Merchant Navy. The events of PQ17 were a catalyst, a culmination of the bitterness resulting from social divisions, injustices, real and imagined, of misunderstanding, mistrust and mutual ignorance.

Sir Dudley Pound's fateful and wrong decision, compounded in its effect by an injudicious amendment, was contrary to what every thinking sailor knew in his bones: that a convoy *always* stuck together. The threat of surface warships had been met by scattering in the early days of the war when only AMCs like the *Jervis Bay* guarded them and they had the wide Atlantic to lose themselves in. PQ17 was a different operation; PQ17 was ostensibly covered not only by the First Cruiser Squadron, but also by the Home Fleet in the offing, the battleship *Duke of York*, the aircraft-carrier *Victorious* and all the might, dominion and power of the King's ships.

14

'An extremely hazardous undertaking'

THE FIRST STEP taken to repair some of the damage after PQ17 was to send the destroyers *Marne, Martin, Middleton* and *Blankney* directly to Archangel loaded with ammunition and new gun-barrels, particularly for the *Palomares* and *Pozarica*. These had as passengers the interpreters mentioned in Chapter 12; they arrived on 24 July. A second fast force, consisting of the American cruiser *Tuscaloosa*, the destroyers *Rodman* and *Emmons*, and HMS *Onslaught* sailed from Glasgow on 13 August with RAF ground crew, stores and equipment which were to precede the dispatch of Hampden bombers to Russia. They also carried the demountable hospital and medical unit which, as we have seen, the Russians rejected (though they did not scruple to accept the medical stores). It was later shamefully returned to Britain aboard QP14. The three American ships plus the British destroyers *Marne, Martin* and *Onslaught* sailed from Russia on 24 August with the first fortunate survivors of PQ17.

Later that day the three British destroyers were detached as a consequence of Ultra intelligence and made a sweep to the south. Off Bear Island the next day they intercepted the German minelayer *Ulm* engaged on Operation Zar, the laying of mines off Cape Zhelania in the wake of the *Admiral Scheer*, then returning from Operation Wunderland described earlier. While *Marne* and *Martin* shelled the *Ulm*, Commander Selby of HMS *Onslaught* made a torpedo attack, his third torpedo striking the *Ulm*'s mine hold. The resulting explosion was horrendous, yet incredibly Korvettenkapitän Biet, two officers and fifty-seven men survived and were picked up before the three destroyers rejoined the American ships.

There were other subsidiary German operations off the polar coast. Earlier, on 24 June, the Kola-based British minesweepers had lost HMS *Gossamer*, bombed by Stukas in the inlet with the loss of twenty-four men. Submarine minelaying associated with Operation Zar was carried out off the Matochkin and Yugor Straits and resulted in the loss of the Soviet patrol vessel *Musson*. Frustrated in her attempt to mop up anything more from PQ17, *U601* shelled the Russian polar station at Karmakuly, Novaya Zemlya, on 26 July, then sank the Russian merchantman *Krestyanin* off the Kostin Strait on 1 August.

Churchill was not only sensible of the very real fact that PQ17 was a defeat, he was equally aware of the damage done to Britain's reputation among her allies. But there was another principle now at stake: what had to be re-established was the *possibility* of achieving the objectives of the northern supply route, of bolstering the morale of the Allied seamen, particularly the Americans, and of removing from the fleet itself the feeling of shame which permeated the lower deck. While the Admiralty placed an embargo on further PQ convoys during the period of continuous daylight with Churchill's concurrence, and pending the outcome of operations in the Mediterranean, as early as 15 July Churchill was already once more belligerently instructing Pound to fight another large convoy through with heavy and integrated naval support. If a fleet action resulted, 'so much the better'.

The First Sea Lord was lukewarm; there were practical difficulties, not least the lack of Russian facilities if any large warships were damaged, and the fleet aircraft-carriers envisaged by Churchill were simply not available. Nevertheless, four photo-reconnaissance Spitfires, No. 210 Catalina Squadron and Nos. 144 and 255 (RAAF) Squadrons of Hampden bombers were flown to North Russia in an attempt to provide an anti-ship strike force over the Barents Sea. Unfortunately several of the Hampdens were shot down by both the Germans and the Russians in what turned out to be something of a shambles. One, lost over Norway, carried papers relevant to the defence of PQ18 and QP14, details of which were thus made known to the enemy.

Armed with this information the German High Command prepared to attack PQ18 with the Luftwaffe and U-boats, and

QP14 with the *Panzerschiff Scheer*, and the cruisers *Hipper* and *Köln* which, with a swarm of destroyers, moved north to Altenfiord on 1 September.

For his part, recalling the success of PQ16, Admiral Tovey was preparing a strong 'fighting destroyer escort', which would stick to convoy defence, but could be deployed independently of the close escort, if circumstances warranted. From this concept stemmed subsequent British successes in the Arctic, though its architect was to have been superseded before it bore fruit. After the unhappy experience of PQ17 Tovey also decided to retain his flagship, the repaired *King George V*, at her buoy in Scapa Flow, in direct telephonic communication with London, and deploy the units of the Home Fleet under his Vice-Admiral, Fraser, in the battleship *Anson*. The fleet was without the *Victorious*, detained by a refit after resupplying Malta, and the American Task Force, which was required in the Pacific.

Meanwhile the merchant ships once again destined for Russia after the post-PQ17 hiatus had been assembling at Loch Ewe, on the north-west corner of Scotland. This change of departure port would, it was hoped, confuse the enemy, though Russian merchant ships were already at Hvalfiordur and would have to join on passage. This total of forty Allied merchantmen were to become the heart of a massive operation which, for the first time, would incorporate its own local air cover with the inclusion of an 'escort-carrier', HMS *Avenger* (Commander A.P. Colthurst). This was a light, unarmoured aircraft-carrier based on a merchant ship's hull built in the United States. She was armed with three Swordfish anti-submarine aircraft fitted with radar, and six operational Sea Hurricanes of 883 Squadron, Fleet Air Arm. *Avenger* would have her own dedicated close escort of the Hunts *Wheatland* and *Wilton*. This trio of ships would need freedom of manœuvre, since *Avenger* would have to turn into the wind to enable her aircraft to fly off and land.

The fighting destroyer escort (FDE) was placed under the command of Rear-Admiral Robert Burnett who flew his flag in HMS *Scylla*, a light cruiser fitted with eight high-angle 4.5-inch open breeched guns – in short, a genuine anti-aircraft cruiser, though known in the Service as the 'Toothless Terror'. It was her first commission.[1]

The subordinate destroyers were divided into Force A, which comprised *Onslow* (Captain(D) H.T. Armstrong, Senior Officer),

Onslaught, *Opportune*, *Offa*, *Ashanti*, *Eskimo*, *Somali* and *Tartar*; and Force B, *Milne* (Captain(D) I.M.R. Campbell, Senior Officer), *Marne*, *Martin*, *Meteor*, *Faulknor*, *Fury*, *Impulsive* and *Intrepid*. Before sailing from Scapa Flow the participating destroyers of the FDE were visited by the Prime Minister in an effort to improve morale.

An attempt to 'explain' the reasons for scattering PQ17 to the participating destroyers had been made to the destroyers' crews on their return to Scapa Flow by Rear-Admiral Burnett. It was not a success. One of Burnett's nicknames, 'Bullshit Bob', cannot have helped.

Because of the reliance of Burnett's destroyers on frequent fuelling, a third group, Force P, consisting of the fleet oilers *Blue Ranger* and *Oligarch*, together with the destroyers *Cowdray*, *Oakley*, *Windsor* and *Worcester*, was sent ahead to Lowe Sound, Spitzbergen, as an advanced fuelling facility, while the tankers *Gray Ranger* (repaired after her encounter with ice in July) and *Black Ranger* formed Force Q, part of PQ18. The movements of these were to be co-ordinated with a simultaneous operation then occurring concerned with the re-supply of the Norwegian garrison of Spitzbergen, and thus their tracking was somewhat complex.

The idea of the fighting destroyer escort was to cover both PQ and QP convoys through the most dangerous sector of the passage. The fuelling of these ships was therefore essential since they would be under way for a longer period than was customary and operating at high speed as circumstances demanded. Among the measures to conserve fuel, Burnett had given orders that no U-boat hunt was to exceed ninety minutes, an indication of the crucial nature of fuel rationing. Moreover, the seasonal retreat of the ice reached its most northerly limit during the early autumn and permitted the convoys to make considerable northing, a fact which would add to the length of the passage for Burnett's ships. One advantage of the delay in the dispatch of PQ18 was that it afforded an opportunity for proper contingency planning to take place, though none of this was explained to the merchant ships, in particular the Americans, who found the waiting interminable.

So did the enemy. Sightings of Allied ship movements during August which were thought to be the next PQ convoy proved false, but the Germans took advantage of the delay and the Luftwaffe made preparations in the mistaken belief that it was their attacks on PQ17 which had prompted the scattering of the merchant ships. Such was the over-confidence of the German pilots that they had strafed their own U-boats and had grossly exaggerated their 'kills'. Indeed in his report, Generaloberst Stumpff, commander of the 5 Luftflotte, had claimed a British cruiser sunk.

Notwithstanding Stumpff's claim, a formidable array of aircraft prepared to attack PQ18 from northern Norway. Forty-two Heinkel He111H-6 torpedo-bombers of KG26 were joined by thirty-five Junkers Ju88A-17s of KG26, the faster Ju88 modification capable of carrying torpedoes, which had been flown up from France. These aircraft were, of course, supported by the long-range Condors and Blohm and Voss flying boats though not by fighters, which did not possess the range to cover the bombers. They were, however, bolstered by the Ju88 bombers of KG30 and this combination allowed the Luftwaffe to employ a tactic known as the Golden Zange, or Golden Comb, a conjoint low-level airborne torpedo attack which was supported by diversionary medium-level and dive-bombing. By this tactic it was hoped to fragment a convoy's defences and enable the torpedo-bombers, who at low altitude would duck under the surveillance radar, to press home a devastating and overwhelming onslaught.

Intelligence had revealed that an aircraft-carrier would accompany the convoy and Goering insisted that 'the attack against the aircraft-carrier must be so violent that this threat is removed'. Despite this, German aircraft tended always to seek out merchant ships, knowing that in doing so they were aiming for the most significant targets. A victory over PQ18, the young pilots were told, would help their comrades in the Wehrmacht, easing the conquest of the Caucasus and the capture of Stalingrad by depriving the Red Army of its sinews.

PQ18's close escort was under the command of Commander A.B. Russell aboard HM Destroyer *Malcolm*, supported by the elderly *Achates*, the anti-aircraft ships *Ulster Queen* and *Alynbank*, the corvettes *Bergamot*, *Bluebell*, *Bryony* and *Camellia*, the minesweepers *Gleaner*, *Harrier* and *Sharpshooter*, and the submarines *P614* and *P615*. Four anti-submarine trawlers were in attendance and within the convoy were the rescue ship *Copeland*, three motor minesweepers of American origin transferring to the Red Navy and under orders to operate as rescue ships, Force

1. HM Anti-submarine trawler *Northern Gem* at anchor with her crew painting her pendant numbers. Her false bow-wave gives an impression of motion and her bow and joggled plating betray her German Building

2. Matilda tanks being loaded for PQ2 in October 1941

3. HMS *Douglas*. A destroyer flotilla-leader built in 1918 and converted for long-range escort work. Her 286P radar 'had a hand-rotated aerial, useless when the weather froze'

4. HMS *Leda*, one of the Halcyon-class minesweepers which did yeoman service in Arctic waters. *Leda* was sunk by *U435* when escorting QP14

5. HMS *Alynbank*. A tramp-ship converted to become an anti-aircraft 'cruiser'. She ended her life as a breakwater, scuttled off Arromanches in Operation Overlord

6. Junkers Ju88 over HMS *Nigeria*, 1 May 1942

7. 'In intense cold, at 22.00 on 1 May 1942, six Ju88s suddenly appeared and dropped bombs in a "ragged and very poorly executed attack". . .' *London* seen from *Nigeria*, PQ15

8. It was predominantly young men who manned these convoys. Typical was this 18-year-old Radio Officer. He was 15 when he first went to sea

9. Icing on the cruiser HMS *Nigeria*

10. *Empire Tide*: A Catapult Armed Merchantman (CAM ship) at the assembly anchorage, Iceland. The aircraft is a Hurricane

11. The Canadian-Pacific liner *Empress of Canada* and the Russian destroyer *Grozni* at Archangel, September 1941, after withdrawing Russian miners from Spitzbergen in Operation Gauntlet

12. A typical pre-war fleet destroyer, HMS *Fury*

13. Crew members of *Northern Gem* pose in front of the rescue ship *Zamalek*

14. A convoy proceeding through ice

15. The *Empire Purcell* on fire shortly before exploding. PQ16, 27 May 1942

16. Arctic gloom: midnight in mid-summer or midday in mid-winter? Such twilight conditions proved disorientating and exhausting

17. Churchill and Tovey aboard HMS *King George V*

18. The end of the American cargo ship *Mary Luckenbach*, 14 September 1942, during PQ18. A lone steward survived the explosion of her cargo of ammunition

19. A near miss: PQ18. HMS *Eskimo* in the foreground with the Hunt-class HMS *Wheatland*'s stern just visible clear of the bomb blast

20. HMS *Ashanti* standing by the torpedoed *Somali* prior to taking her in tow

21. A German Eckholdt-class destroyer off the polar coast

22. Destroyers in line ahead leaving Seidisfiord, *Echo* with *Eclipse*

23. Typical of her class, this Flower-type corvette, HMS *Bluebell*, was torpedoed on 17 February 1945 by *U711*. She blew up with fearful loss of life

24. HMS *Mermaid*, Black Swan-class sloop typical of the later escorts built for the Royal Navy between 1942 and 1945

25. Duty lookouts on watch, HM Cruiser *Nigeria*

26. Forecastle of a cruiser shower A and B 6-inch gun turrets, HMS *Nigeria*

27. A tanker and Empire-type cargo ship of JW53 steaming through Arctic 'sea-smoke'

28. Off Iceland an American freighter is framed by HMS *Duke of York* and the USS *Washington*

29. Golovko and Fraser aboard *Duke of York*, 16 December 1943

30. *Scharnhorst*

31. The escort carrier *Nairana* and an American Liberty ship in heavy weather, RA64

32. HMS *Tracker*: a typical escort carrier. Known as flat-tops, their merchant origins are clear below the flight-deck level. A pair of 'Stringbags' with folded wings are parked at the forward end

33. Swordfish torpedo-bomber landing on an escort carrier. Note the arrester hook just forward of the tail wheel and the arrester wires lying athwart the deck

34. *U288* under attack by aircraft from the escort carriers *Tracker* and *Activity* on 3 April 1944 during passage of JW58

Q and the tanker *Athel Templar*, on her way to relieve the *Hopemount*.

In addition to aerial reconnaissance the submarines *Tribune*, *Tigris* and *P34* patrolled off first Narvik and later North Cape, being reinforced by the *Unique*, *Unreal*, *P456*, *P540*, *P2210* and the Free French minelaying boat *Rubis*.

PQ18 left Loch Ewe on 2 September with a local escort and was in trouble almost at once. Bad weather broke up the formation and began what for Commodore Boddam-Whetham was to be a nightmare. 'The Americans in particular', he reported, 'pay but scant attention to signals, know little of the importance of good station-keeping and do not as yet know anything about convoy work'. What they did know was based on the rumours following PQ17 which were unfavourable to the Royal Navy. The largely inexperienced American mercantile marine had yet to acquire the battle-hardiness that would come in the succeeding months; it was not their fault, but it was not helpful to the convoy Commodore and made the handling of such a large and mixed convoy a difficult matter.

However, there was considerable inexperience in the escort too, as it struggled north from Scapa Flow. *Scylla* was new and unblooded; *Avenger* was equally new and not only pioneering naval aviation from a small deck in high latitudes, but also coping with unfamiliar equipment – on passage to the rendezvous off Iceland her engines failed due to dirty fuel and she lost one Sea Hurricane overboard in heavy seas. The passage was 'an absolute nightmare', one of *Avenger*'s seamen remembered, 'in the hangar the aircraft were secured at wing tips and tail with steel ropes which were completely useless, in a matter of minutes they all broke loose and were smashing into one another and the sides of the hangar'. Keeping their feet with difficulty the crew were relashing their planes with ropes when the sound of rolling and crashing in the lift well alerted them to the fact that a quantity of 500-pound bombs were also tumbling about, all fused. 'We finally secured the bombs by laying down duffle coats with rope ties and when a bomb rolled over the coats we secured them with the ties. God only knows how we did it, but we did!'

Although the weather caused havoc, it did not stop the convoy being spotted and reported by Teichert in *U456*. There were several submarine alarms on this first leg, but counter-attacks kept any U-boats at a distance. It was, therefore, the morning of the 7th before PQ18 rounded the south-west corner of Iceland at Reykjanes and the various complicated rendezvous arrangements were expedited. The local escort was sent in to Hvalfiordur; the close escort, including the anti-aircraft ships, together with the Russian merchantmen, joined up, and the whole vast mass of ships set out up the west coast of Iceland for the final rendezvous with Burnett. PQ18 was sighted the next day by an FW200 Condor, but heavy overcast then hid the convoy.

In addition to the rescue ships and tankers already mentioned, PQ18 incorporated a CAM ship, the *Empire Morn*, with her Hurricane, a further ten British ships, twenty American vessels, six Russians and three Panamanians. It was now covered by the close escort under Acting Commander Russell.[2]

Avenger and her Hunts were at Seidisfiord on 5 September when an FW200 dropped a stick of bombs close to her. Although German intelligence thought her the elderly *Argus*, the presence of a carrier was confirmed to the enemy. Burnett and his destroyers arrived later the same day, having also seen a Condor overhead. Guzzling fuel, Burnett's squadron, consisting of Forces A and B (with the exception of *Offa*, which joined on the 13th), *Avenger* and her Hunts, did not sail until 20.30 on the 8th. *Scylla* led them to their stations round the convoy twenty-four hours later; the delay had been due to the breakdown of the aircraft-carrier. PQ18 had not only been spotted by Condors, it had also continued to suffer a series of submarine alarms.

There were other cruisers in the offing: *London*, *Norfolk* and *Suffolk* in one group supporting PQ18 west of Bear Island, and *Cumberland* and *Sheffield* with the destroyers *Eclipse*, *Amazon*, *Bulldog*, *Echo* and *Venomous* off Spitzbergen, which would be engaged in resupplying the Norwegian meteorological station at Barentsburg in the knowledge that the Luftwaffe were busy with PQ18.

Distant cover was given to the convoy by Sir Bruce Fraser in *Anson*, with the *Duke of York*, the cruiser *Jamaica* and the destroyers *Bramham*, *Keppel*, *Mackay* and *Montrose*. Fraser's force operated from Seidisfiord up towards Jan Mayen and was not continuously at sea due to the deployment of destroyers to the FDE. In light of the value of Tovey's squadron during PQ17 and the fact that the Commander-in-Chief found it more efficient to exercise control from his mooring in Scapa Flow, the value of the squadron of capital ships as 'distant cover' is open to question. The dubious value of his employment was not to be lost on Sir Bruce Fraser when he succeeded Tovey as Commander-in-Chief, Home Fleet.

Strong winds kicked up a lumpy sea and poor visibility dominated 10 September. Rain gave way to fog and the destroyers in the outer screen criss-crossed the convoy's wake investigating asdic contacts. The ships wallowed north; it was typical Western Ocean weather. At the same time, many miles to the eastward, the submarines *Tribune* and *Tigris* both made unsuccessful attempts to torpedo heavy German units moving north. These were in fact the *Scheer*, *Hipper* and *Köln*, though the pocket-battleship was mistaken for the *Tirpitz*.

The following day was as gloomy and overcast as its predecessor, though the rain squalls gave way to snow. Station-keeping in the convoy remained poor and Commodore Boddam-Whetham, flying his broad pendant in the *Temple Arch*, was driven to chastise his flock. He also warned them that enemy action was certain within a day or so: 'Ships should keep closed up to two cables and be prepared to help with mass fire'.

Meanwhile Rear-Admiral Burnett left the convoy at 11.40 in *Scylla*, taking with him the *Marne*, *Martin*, *Meteor*, *Milne* and *Intrepid* to refuel and leaving Captain Scott-Moncrieff in HMS *Faulknor* in command. The 'M' class of the 3rd Flotilla were the most potent of his destroyers because, although they did not possess a main armament of dual-purpose guns, their late mark 4.7-inch weapons could elevate to 50° and they carried a formidable array of torpedo tubes. Most of the remaining destroyers had poor anti-aircraft armament with the exception of *Opportune* which though a new ship had old, but high-elevating 4-inch guns. It was for this rèason that Burnett led them off to Spitzbergen to bunker before the convoy underwent its first air assault. These men-of-war entered Bell Sound on the following evening, passed HMS *Windsor*, anchored as guardship, and sought out the *Oligarch* and *Blue Ranger* lying in Axelfiord with pumps and hoses at the ready. They sailed at 04.00 on Sunday, 13 September, but by then PQ18 had suffered its first casualties.

As Burnett's force raced ahead towards Spitzbergen, the 12th had dawned under a low overcast, but with a moderate north-westerly breeze and clear visibility to the horizon, revealing the convoy to a Blohm and Voss BV138 which dropped out of the cloud. *Avenger* flew off four Sea Hurricanes, but to their humiliation they failed to dispatch the shadower, which evaded them in the overcast. This was not entirely their own fault. Not only was the Sea Hurricane a rather makeshift adaptation of the famous fighter, whose airframe proved too weak for heavy deck landings, but it was also armed only with machine guns, not cannon, and like the light machine guns of many of the merchant ships, its projectiles were simply not heavy enough to penetrate the enemy aircraft.[3]

As the day wore on, Huff-Duff bearings indicated the presence of U-boats, and there were frequent alarms and excursions, with the outer screen of destroyers dropping depth-charges as percussive accompaniment to a rising tension within the convoy.

Then, at 21.00, as the *Faulknor* crossed ahead of the convoy, her asdic located a firm echo. Scott-Moncrieff attacked six minutes later and was in the act of turning to deliver a second pattern of depth-charges when his acoustic gear picked up the horrible eructations of a U-boat breaking up. The stink of oil hung in the air and in the twilight a silver-grey slick spread on the surface of the sea, the only tombstone of Bohmann's *U88*.

Avenger's slow Swordfish were on anti-submarine patrol by 04.00 next morning, Sunday, 13 September 1942, playing cat and mouse with a Blohm and Voss flying boat and a Ju88 reconnaissance plane. *Avenger* then flew off her Hurricanes, but again they were unable to hurt the shadowing Germans who vanished in the cloud and withdrew until the hue and cry had subsided. The only advantage gained from this aerial activity was that a number of Swordfish attacks kept the U-boats down, but at about 09.00 *U589* torpedoed the Russian freighter *Stalingrad* in the outer starboard column. She sank rapidly, her only casualty a still-born baby delivered of a woman on board who went into sudden labour.

As the Liberty ship *Oliver Ellsworth* hauled out of line to avoid the sinking Russian ship ahead of her, the U-boat fired a second torpedo. Struck in her after holds, she too began to founder as the whole of PQ18 wheeled in a clumsy attempt to foil the attackers, while the nearest escorts rushed in, in what proved a fruitless attempt to counter-attack. Fortunately the prompt arrival on the scene of the anti-submarine trawler *St Kenan*, the *Copeland*, the motor minesweepers and HMS *Sharpshooter* ensured that the survivors from both ships were promptly recovered.

Reports now came in from the Swordfish patrols that the enemy flying boats were dropping mines ahead of the convoy. Once again the Hurricane sorties failed to destroy these aircraft and the convoy altered course to avoid the floating menace while the Swordfish, endeavouring to attack surfaced U-boats in the distance, were themselves driven off by the heavily armed and protected Blohm and Voss BV138 flying boats.

During the early afternoon *Sharpshooter* caught a brief glimpse of a conning tower but, even when reinforced by *Tartar*, the two ships were unable to echo-locate the U-boat. A similar escape was achieved when *Onslaught* pursued a contact inside the screen and drove it off, but the northern horizon was now jagged with the silhouettes of HMS *Scylla* and the refuelled destroyers racing south from Spitzbergen to intercept PQ18 as it steamed east, about 150 miles north-west of Bear Island. It was 14.30 as, with flamboyant panache, the ships of the 3rd Destroyer Flotilla took up their stations.

This was not to be the last occasion on which Rear-Admiral Burnett's sense of timing proved impeccable, for hardly had his destroyers swung on to a parallel course to the convoy and reduced their speed to conform to the plodding merchant ships, than Ju88s made a high-level bombing attack through breaks in the cloud-cover. Hurricane fighters were launched to drive them off, but the lightly armed Mark I machines were unable to score any hits and had landed to rearm when, at 15.40, reports came in of enemy air formations being picked up by the long-range radar plots of *Scylla, Avenger, Ulster Queen* and *Alynbank*.

At sixty miles range the cathode ray tubes were aglow with waves of incoming aircraft. This was to be the triumphant Luftwaffe's hammer-blow against PQ18: the Golden Comb. At the time the sky was overcast, the cloud at about 3,000 feet. There was a fresh breeze, a moderate sea and the occasional snow or sleet shower to limit visibility intermittently.

A score of Ju88s from KG30 carried out the high-level diversionary bombing which, though ineffective in hitting targets, caused a degree of disruption in the order of the convoy as intended. They were followed by the torpedo-bombers of KG26, twenty-eight He111s in two waves, followed by eighteen Ju88s from Bardufoss. A further seventeen Ju88s of KG30 were also in support from Banak. To avoid delays, the incoming torpedo-bombers were met by one of the shadowing Ju88s, of which up to nine had been circling the convoy with the BV138, and led in directly to the attack. In the event this scheme faltered in the drizzle, but only for a few minutes, and then the mass of aircraft came into view. 'They rose up on the horizon, black and repulsive, and they extended far on either side of our view', wrote Sub-Lieutenant Hughes, watching from *Scylla*'s after gunnery director. 'They came in low on the starboard bow of the convoy and seemed to fill the whole horizon.' Another witness recalled, 'They swept in, thirty or forty of them, about twenty feet above sea-level, disregarding completely the escort screen. It was the merchant ships they were after, and the merchant ships they meant to get.'

Burnett had given specific orders that neither of the anti-aircraft ships was to leave its station, with the consequence that Captain Adam of the *Ulster Queen* was unable to contribute to the defence, since the attack came from the starboard side and he was on the port. Moreover, the outer screen of destroyers closed in on the convoy when under air attack, though the experience of American destroyers in the defence of PQ17 was that maximum effect was obtained by their standing off and breaking up the formations as they went overhead. Finally, although the handful of Sea Hurricanes available to Colthurst was inadequate to oppose such an onslaught, the badly demoralized aircrew were on deck rearming when the attack came and played little part in it. 'At the end of this unfortunate day,' Colthurst was to write with rueful candour, 'I realised that my operation of the ship and her fighters had been very wrong.'

For Boddam-Whetham, the moment had come to take the avoiding action he and his staff had planned. The contingency plan for massed torpedo attack was a simple 45° alteration of course, either to port or starboard using the appropriate international sound signal backed up by a single flag hoist. Its efficacy relied upon good lookouts, prompt response and co-ordinated repetition of the signal down the columns. In the event the Commodore made his port-turn signal, but the ninth and tenth columns failed to respond. Nor was it mere American inexperience which was to blame; the sheer size and variety of PQ18 militated against the manœuvre in such circumstances. Tragically it was the outer starboard ships which failed to execute it and who were about to bear the brunt of the attack, with horrifying results.

The leading Heinkels 'kept in rigid line abreast . . . like some strange things from another world', so low that even the despised

4.7-inch guns of the destroyers were in action. But so was almost every other gun in the convoy, so that 'a pall of smoke hung like a curtain out on the starboard flank . . . criss-crossed by the bright red tracers and punctuated by the flashes of the shell bursts. The place was an absolute inferno', as the swarm of torpedo bombers thundered into the attack, dividing as they passed *Scylla*.

The combined gunfire was prodigious, but most was wild, the product of excitable and undisciplined gunners, to which the subsequent exaggerated claims bore similar testimony. Ships on the unengaged and distant wing of the convoy joined in the barrage to little effect, beyond showering their comrades on the engaged side with spent bullets and shells. In this and in all subsequent attacks, the rapid low-level approach of the enemy attracted gunfire which did considerable damage to neighbouring ships, shooting holes in lifeboats and wounding armed guards and DEMS gunners exposed on the upper decks. As one American armed guard ensign wrote, 'Although my men did well, it was the first time they had ever fired . . . at a target! Actual combat is the best experience, but it seems a poor place to train men.'

As the German planes flew in close they attracted the fire of 'the smaller weapons too, few of them could have come through without damage of some sort, but they were undeterred. Each one, as it got into position, dropped two torpedoes, banked, and swept off astern, fast, wicked-looking monoplanes, a few on fire.' Several of these aircraft pressed their attack 'with suicidal daring, [and] flew in amongst the ships, dropping their torpedoes at very close range'.

One flew so close that the torpedo failed to hit the water, but dropped through No. 2 hatch of the *Wacosta* and exploded inside her hull. The ship had been slowing down, her engines disabled by the terrible explosion of the ship immediately ahead. Leading the ninth column, the *Empire Stevenson* 'was suddenly enveloped in a tower of flame and smoke' which, when it cleared, left only 'an oily slick on the water'. Another witness recalled this ship as being 'pulverised in a tremendous explosion that left no trace of her'. Yet another remembered the lack of noise: 'There wasn't a tremendous lot of noise, just a huge column of smoke and dull, red flame, lighting up the whole sky for a few seconds and then silence. Everyone seemed momentarily stunned or fascinated, watching the smoke billow upwards. Of the ship, not a trace remained.' This was the dreadful penalty of carrying explosives. While no one survived from her, all the crew of the *Wacosta* were rescued.

Similarly loaded with tanks and war materials, the *Macbeth*, second ship in the tenth column, succumbed to two torpedoes, while the *Oregonian* ahead of her capsized rapidly after three torpedoes stove in her whole starboard side. Only twenty-seven of her fifty-five man crew were rescued by the *St Kenan*, many of them in a fearful condition having swallowed oil and been immersed in the freezing sea.

Macbeth's crew were rescued by *Offa*, whose commanding officer, Lieutenant-Commander R.A. Ewing, ran her alongside the Panamanian freighter. Though the destroyer lost a number of guard-rails and stanchions, and despite the ice-encrusted state of her decks, the merchant seamen 'leapt like cats onto her'. *Macbeth*'s polyglot complement was typical and emphasizes the extraordinary composition of these convoyed ships. The ship's Master came from Liverpool, her Chief Officer was a Norwegian and the rest of the crew were from Belgium, Canada, Denmark, France, Spain, South America and the United States. They integrated themselves with *Offa*'s somewhat startled company, forming back-up and ammunition supply parties. They also provided extra lookouts and cleaned the destroyer's overcrowded mess-decks. The Master had escaped with his ship's imprest and insisted on paying his men's mess expenses when they were finally landed at Scapa Flow.[4]

Torpedoes had also hit the *Sukhona* and the *Afrikander*, a Panamanian ship chartered to the United States Maritime Commission. Both were abandoned as they sank, their crews being efficiently picked up by the small vessels of the close escort. With the exception of the *Mary Luckenbach* the outer two columns of PQ18 had been annihilated.

Nor was that all. Leading an inner port column, *Empire Beaumont* was set on fire after a torpedo struck in the only hold not containing explosives. The ship was successfully abandoned. Less fortunate were the crew of the *John Penn*. The three men on duty in the engine room were killed when two torpedoes exploded in their midst. The Liberty ship was actually sent to the bottom with gunfire from the escorts, for there was no question of salvaging her.[5]

Amid the confusion, the roaring of the aircraft engines, the high-level bombs exploding, the ships sounding their sirens as they dodged their unfortunate neighbours, the venting of steam, the chatter of ineffectual machine guns whose bullets ricocheted off the incoming aircraft, the boom of heavier guns and the explosions of fused shells, the *Copeland*, the trawlers and the motor minesweepers picked up the merchant sailors from their rafts, boats and the freezing sea. Several observers saw periscopes inside the columns of ships, and at least one claimed that a merchant ship was sunk by a U-boat's torpedo. Though the high-level bombs hit nothing, there were some unnerving near misses; the *Exford* suffered one close enough to shake the ship throughout her entire length.

Whatever the details, the sharp fact emerges that eight ships had been lost in under fifteen minutes. And despite the claims of the Allied gunners, German losses amounted to only five aircraft.

The next attack was, by comparison, a half-hearted affair by Heinkel floatplanes of the Kriegsmarine which hovered outside the range of the guns, then came in in two groups which were driven off without loss. One He115 was attacked by four of *Avenger*'s Sea Hurricanes of 802 Squadron but escaped after shooting down 802's leader, Lieutenant E.W. Taylor. Shortly afterwards *Faulknor* reported aircraft dropping mines ahead of the convoy and a bold alteration of course was made to port until 20.15 when the proper course was resumed. By 20.30 it was almost dark. A dozen He115s from Billefiord approached from the south-west. Once again the ships put up a barrage and drove off the aircraft. One plummeted into the sea alongside *Opportune* and another was shot down in flames. While the British destroyer rescued the crew of the first, that of the latter was picked up by *U405* as she trailed the convoy.

The success of the earlier, massed attack led to some radical rethinking. The Sea Hurricanes had failed to destroy the shadowers and had wasted their ammunition, so that when the first bombers appeared they could do no more than make feint attacks. As a consequence when the main low-level torpedo offensive arrived, the Sea Hurricanes were on deck and useless. It was clear to Colthurst and his flying staff that they must maintain constant air patrols and a plan was worked out in which the Sea Hurricanes spent no more than twenty-five minutes airborne then landed to rearm and refuel. Thus a number were kept aloft and, while they were never able to inflict significant losses on an enemy capable of comparable speed and incomparably better armed, they were able to break up the bomber formations' cohesion.

Burnett had also restricted the potential of his anti-aircraft ships by forbidding them to leave station and move out to intercept an attack in order to break up enemy formations as American destroyers had done defending PQ17. Captain Adam of the *Ulster Queen* determined to disobey this order and subsequently did so to good effect.

The following day, the 14th, began with another loss for the convoy. Returning to station from an asdic contact, HMS *Impulsive* had obtained a second echo and had begun a run in to depth-charge it when, at 03.30, the U-boat fired at the target she had been stalking, the tanker *Athel Templar*. *Impulsive* then lost contact as Korvettenkapitän Brandenburg dived *U457* under the convoy amid the noise of the propeller races.

Hit in the engine room, the tanker's cargo did not explode, but the fire soon made it impossible for her crew to do more than disconsolately abandon ship. They were picked up by *Copeland* and *Offa*, one of whose after depth-charge men, James Green, jumped into the icy sea in an abortive attempt to rescue a drowning boy. He was only recovered and revived with difficulty after his exertions.

The known proximity of other U-boats discouraged attempts to try and salvage *Athel Templar*, and the minesweeper *Harrier* was ordered to sink the 9,000-ton ship and her cargo of fuel oil. The tanker was left astern, to burn for some hours before she sank, when the fire was quenched by the cold grey waters of the Barents Sea.

HMS *Avenger* flew off her first Swordfish on anti-submarine patrol at daylight. At 09.40 the duty 'Stringbag' reported a surfaced submarine six miles out on the starboard bow of the convoy, marking the spot with a smoke float though driven off by one of the shadowing Ju88 reconnaissance planes. Seeing this through his periscope, Horrer brought *U589* back to the surface to continue recharging his batteries. *Onslow* was sent out to locate the float and sighted the U-boat which promptly crash-dived, but at 10.50 *Onslow*'s asdic had a firm echo at 1,900 yards. Captain Armstrong closed rapidly, dropped a shallow pattern of charges and then saturated the area. Oil and air bubbled to the surface, but

Armstrong was not satisfied and persisted, aware of the armoury of tricks resorted to by U-boat commanders to deceive their hunters. At last there was a loud underwater explosion and great gobbets of air, upwellings of oil, wooden crates and cabbages appeared on the surface. Armstrong made a ninth run, after which nothing could be detected. It was 13.07 when *Onslow* put on speed to rejoin the convoy; she had just six depth-charges left. The mood aboard was inconclusive and grim as they sped past the wreckage of a German bomber with its four crew squatting on top and left them astern. Far below, *U589* sought her grave on the seabed; Horrer and his company had joined those 'still at sea'.

The grim game of tip and run between the German observation aircraft and the *Avenger*'s Swordfish persisted. As the Stringbags headed out to search for U-boats, the Ju88s and BV138s closed in to intimidate the Swordfish which, in turn, promptly fell back on the convoy, drawing the interlopers on to the gunfire of the nearest escort in the outer screen. The shadowers would then sheer off, and the cycle would repeat itself. One of these dauntless biplanes, its pilot and observer exposed in their open cockpits to the full rigour of the Arctic air, reported to her flight controller a swarm of aircraft flying at wave-top height to avoid detection by the convoy's radar. These, Ju88 torpedo-bombers of KG26, were specifically targeted at *Avenger*. It was 12.37 when the alarms jangled aboard the escort-carrier.

Again the attackers divided to frustrate attempts to evade torpedoes by altering course, but *Avenger* had her Sea Hurricanes aloft and she increased speed, passed through the convoy and out ahead on the port bow, turning under full helm to run back down its left flank, her attendant destroyers, *Wilton* and *Wheatland*, spewing a curtain of lead into the air behind her.

It was now that Captain Adam disobeyed his orders and, with Nelsonic *élan*, left his paralysing defensive station and took *Ulster Queen* to meet the attack. *Scylla* also drew ahead and *Achates* dropped the oil hose by which she was fuelling alongside *Blue Ranger*. As the *Avenger* turned on to her reciprocal course, Boddam-Whetham wheeled the convoy in a 45° turn. These measures partially broke up the concentration of the German attack as some of the torpedo-bearing Ju88s veered after *Avenger*. The others, faced with the barrage, released their torpedoes prematurely, some of which cartwheeled and somersaulted alarmingly. No ships were hit, and KG26 had lost eleven aircraft by

12.45 when their more conventionally armed comrades of KG30 resumed dive-bombing from 2,000 feet. These attacks lasted from 12.50 until 14.10 and were harried by Sea Hurricanes and gunfire from the convoy when the cloud-breaks permitted. One German plane was shot down and, although no ships were hit, once again near misses – including one on *Avenger* and others on *Eskimo* and *Tartar* – were alarming enough.

At 14.05 twenty-two He111s and eighteen Ju88 torpedo-bombers under Klumper and Bloedorn flew in from Bardufoss. These aircraft had made a wide sweep and attacked from ahead in the light of earlier reports that *Avenger* was in an advanced station. Instead they found *Scylla*'s ack-ack guns ready for them and four Sea Hurricanes on their tails.

The carrier had launched these Sea Hurricanes earlier on airborne patrol and these quickly climbed and worked round behind the Germans as the Kampfgeschwader came into the attack. They now dived and followed the torpedo-bombers, impervious to the fact that they were flying into the convoy's flak and pouring their lightweight fire into the enemy.

Klumper sighted *Avenger* as he closed in and his planes peeled, sweeping down the starboard flank of the convoy where their dark silhouettes made good targets for the trigger-happy defenders. Three of the Hurricanes were shot down by 'friendly fire' as they strafed the bombers, though fortunately all three pilots were promptly picked up by *Faulknor*, *Wheatland* and *Tartar*.

Due to the intensity of the barrage, only a handful of the German aircraft were able to manœuvre into a position where they could release their torpedoes against *Avenger*, but Colthurst combed their tracks successfully. Others flew past without dropping torpedoes, while many had let go at random. Only one ship was hit as the tracks whirred down the columns, but that with an awe-inspiring effect. 'The *Mary Luckenbach* blew up with the most tremendous explosion,' wrote Adam of the *Ulster Queen*, 'sending a vast column of fire and smoke many thousands of feet high, which carried an enemy aircraft with it.' Horace Bell, Chief Radio Operator aboard the *Copeland*, saw the whole thing. The leading plane

> came in to about three hundred yards . . . before dropping his torpedoes and then swept on . . . As he passed, the gunner raked him fore and aft and bright tongues of flame flickered from his star-

> board engine. He dipped, recovered, dipped again and seemed just about to crash, when his torpedoes reached their mark and the ship simply vanished into thin air. As for the plane, it broke up into small pieces.[6]

The *Mary Luckenbach* had been the last survivor of the ill-fated ninth and tenth columns.

> In the stupefying moments of silence and inactivity that followed, we watched as an enormous column of smoke billowed upwards, slow, thick, black and ugly – no flame this time, just smoke, up and up till it reached the clouds. Gradually, from the over-hanging top, there drifted down dust, like a shower of rain, and that was all.

Closer to, the effect had even greater impact. 'It is impossible to put into words the force of the explosion or the amount of debris to hit the ship,' reported Lieutenant Billings of the armed guard aboard the *Nathaniel Greene*. Indeed, such was its concussive effect upon the hull of the American ship that 'abandon ship stations' was sounded, the engines stopped and at least one raft was thrown overboard by the crew in the confident belief that they themselves had been torpedoed. As the *Nathaniel Greene* dropped back, HMS *Onslaught* ranged up alongside and evacuated two gunners badly wounded by debris, whereupon Captain Vickers, receiving negative reports of serious damage, rang on his engines and reassured his crew while he regained his station.

The torpedo-bombers drew off, leaving one of the five shot down wallowing between the passing columns of merchant ships which opened fire on its hapless crew huddled on the wing; one by one they fell off into the sea. A further nine aircraft were so severely damaged that they were later declared unserviceable, though the claims from the convoy were understandably greater.

Now the high excitement of the torpedo attack was again replaced by opportunist high-level and shallow dive-bombing by KG30's Ju88s, mainly aimed at the escorts. It persisted for over an hour until, at 15.30, the Junkers climbed into the clouds and droned away, leaving their long-range cousins hovering on the horizon.

The impressive speed with which the destroyers had recovered the ditched Hurricane pilots, combined with the vigour and success of their interceptions (the Fleet Air Arm claimed five certain and three probable kills), put *Avenger*'s company in renewed heart. Colthurst felt his ship's performance, and in particular the radar-controlled fighter direction, had improved greatly in twenty-four hours.

The evening, as PQ18 passed Hope Island, was spent transferring survivors from the smaller escorts to *Scylla* and the Home Fleet destroyers, 209 aboard the cruiser, 234 among the destroyers. By this humanitarian measure Burnett avoided several hundred men languishing in Russia. About 550 survivors were now distributed among the convoy. HMS *Martin* removed the fit Britons and Americans from the *Copeland* for direct return to Iceland, leaving ninety-six aboard the rescue ship, eighty-seven of whom were Russian, two Czech, six British and two American cot-cases. Some of the Russians had been in bad shape: 'Two at least had not a stitch of clothing on and one poor devil was almost out of his mind. His wife and child were in his ship when it was hit, the infant was lost, but his wife survived with her ribs crushed and after being in the icy water for quite a time.'

On the same day, reports had been received that the *Tirpitz* was missing from her moorings in Altenfiord. Twenty-three of the serviceable Hampden torpedo-bombers recently flown to Russia were scrambled at 05.00 and flew out on a reconnaissance in force with the intention of attacking the German battleship if she was at sea. They saw nothing and returned to Vaenga at 15.00, for *Tirpitz* was not at sea, merely in an adjacent fiord on a training operation.

For PQ18, 15 September dawned with a calm grey sea under lowering grey cloud at 3,000 feet which was broken in places. The wind freshened during the day with rain, sleet and snow showers. Throughout the night and during the forenoon, Huff-Duff intercepts betrayed the continuing presence of U-boats in the offing, and at first light Swordfish were airborne from *Avenger*. By 08.00 the shadowers were back, though it was after noon before the first incoming bombers were detected. Sea Hurricanes were scrambled: combined with anti-aircraft gunfire from the ships through the rents in the clouds they rendered the three-hour attack both desultory and ineffective.

Monitoring of the German air frequency, 5610 khz, revealed the extent of the pilots' disillusion at the continuing size of the convoy. In the end, the presence of the Sea Hurricanes overhead compelled the demoralized Germans to circle impotently out of range, while some satisfaction was derived from *Ulster Queen*'s radar-controlled gunnery which shot down a Ju88 in thick cloud. At 16.46, the last bomber withdrew, leaving only the shadowers. By now the weather had worsened, though this did not lessen the U-boat alarms which had gone on all day and had kept the escorts as busy as had the Junkers. In the early afternoon, distant smoke sent Commander Power's *Opportune* south-east to investigate. The smoke, feared to be from surface warships, proved to be the diesel exhaust of two surfaced U-boats distorted by refraction. *Opportune*'s inopportune arrival broke up their conference with a few salvoes from her forward guns as she raced towards them before they crash-dived. One of the U-boats counter-attacked and an over-protective Blohm and Voss BV138 intervened, only to be driven off, but *Opportune* was neither hit nor able to locate either of the submarines. At 15.45 she rejoined the convoy.

In the deteriorating weather of the evening, *Meteor* dropped back to the oiler to refuel and was regaining station when she sighted a suspicious object which she attacked with depth-charges. This was but one of the many and continuous alarms occupying the outer screen. Four and a half hours later, at 03.00 the next morning, Korvettenkapitän Brandenburg had ducked *U457* under the leading line abreast of Scott-Moncrieff's destroyers and had positioned himself to fire a spread salvo when HMS *Impulsive*, stationed inside the outer screen, on the port wing, picked up the U-boat on her asdic. Lieutenant-Commander Roper pressed an immediate attack, turned and then lost contact in the thrashing propeller noises of the passing convoy. Roper wove his destroyer between the merchantmen and emerged in growing daylight at its rear, finding air bubbles and oil in the estimated position of his original attack. The air was thick with the stench of the oil and Roper modestly claimed a 'possible kill'. He had in fact sunk *U457*.

Shortly after daylight, *Avenger*'s weary Swordfish crews were relieved of the duty of anti-submarine patrol by Russian-based RAF Catalinas and at 09.00 the convoy altered course to the south and ran into a mist blowing up on the rising wind. At 10.40 *Opportune* and *Offa* attacked another contact which escaped by the deceptive device known as a *Pillenwerfer*, a release of compressed air which gave an asdic response identical to that of a submarine and acted as an effective decoy. They broke off their unsuccessful hunt at 13.00.

During the afternoon Burnett exchanged signals with the homeward-bound QP14 which would shortly pass them.

He and Boddam-Whetham had already exchanged farewell signals. As a former destroyer officer, the Commodore was deeply appreciative of the Rear-Admiral's support. Burnett responded with a Biblical quotation from the book of Isaiah: 'When thou passest through the waters, I will be with thee . . .'

It was all very civilized naval hyperbole, but Burnett was now to transfer his allegiance to Commodore Dowding's unhappy veterans of PQ17. With *Scylla*, he took not only his destroyers, but also *Avenger* and her two Hunts, the *Alynbank* and the submarines *P614* and *P615*. These left PQ18 in groups, in an attempt to deceive enemy reconnaissance.

Commander Russell in *Malcolm* was now left with the gallant but aged *Achates*, *Ulster Queen* and the corvettes, minesweepers and anti-submarine trawlers of the close escort. PQ18 ploughed steadily south in a near south-easterly gale accompanied by mist and rain.[7]

The U-boat alarms continued and at one point mines were seen floating through the convoy. Anything floating received fire from the gunners aboard the merchant ships and this proved deadly to inquisitive seals as well as several men, deck fittings and cargo.

During the forenoon watch on the 17th the Russian destroyers *Gremyashchi* and *Sokrushitelni* joined to augment the anti-aircraft defence and twenty hours later the escort was further reinforced by the *Kuibishev* and *Uritski*. This proved timely, for at 06.00 on 18 September 1942 the lookouts sighted Cape Kanin and the Luftwaffe made a further attack. Only a dozen He111s were now available to KG26 and these made a low-level run from astern while Ju88s of KG30 carried out complementary bombing. *Ulster Queen* turned broadside and with *Gremyashchi* and *Sharpshooter* put up a splash barrage, so low was the attack. The Heinkels 'swept in, skimming the water, divided just astern of us [aboard *Copeland*] and roared past on either side, dropping their fish as they went by. We could see them [the torpedoes] leaping clean out of the water like tarpon before settling down on their course.' Fortunately only one ship, the States Steamship Company's *Kentucky*, was struck on the starboard side below the bridge. The blast threw the tarpaulins and hatchboards of No. 2 hatch into the air and demolished the port bridge wing; fire broke out as circuits were wrecked and water rushed into the ship. The engines were stopped and the order given to abandon her. Despite the weather, the boats were launched and the survivors quickly picked up by the three little motor minesweepers, trawlers and *Sharpshooter*. As the convoy drew away, Adam of *Ulster Queen* transmitted a request to Archangel for tugs from Iokanka while *Sharpshooter* and *Cape Mariato* stood by. The former was manœuvring alongside to lodge a salvage party on board and preparing to pass a tow, when a lone Ju88 dropped two bombs into the *Kentucky*. These exploded aft, causing blast damage to *Sharpshooter* and starting further fires. The stricken ship now attracted more bombers, so Lieutenant Mottram pulled *Sharpshooter* astern, ordering *Cape Mariato* to stand off while she put a few rounds into the burning ship. The two small warships then drew away under the cover of their own barrage to rejoin PQ18 where the torpedo attacks were still in progress.

Russian air support was not forthcoming and the *Empire Morn* launched its Hurricane, PQ18's remaining airborne defence, at 11.50. Flying Officer Burr attracted the fire of his allies 'from the moment [he] was launched until . . . out of range; and there was no way to stop the imbeciles'. He also had difficulty avoiding the wires of the barrage balloons being flown by the merchantmen. Gaining height Burr dived on a formation of torpedo-bombers roaring up astern, expending his ammunition and setting one on fire. Again there were no hits and by late morning the attack had faltered; the Germans had lost three planes and one was badly damaged.

Rather than ditch and lose his plane, Burr asked his fighter direction officer for a course and sped off. Having fired the recognition signal over Archangel he landed with near-empty fuel tanks at Keg Ostrov airfield at 14.45.

Near misses from the bombers had shaken many of the ships in these last attacks and it was afterwards thought that a large number of the torpedoes dropped were duds, a problem which had beset some batches of these weapons on both sides. But the violence of the attack had its effect. The *Empire Tristram* suffered the embarrassment of ditching her confidential books and lowering a boat before her master, Captain W.H. Miller, realized little was wrong, recovered his boat and proceeded. The wild gunfire had, yet again, wounded a gunner and holed several aircraft which were deck cargo aboard the *Patrick Henry*, while the Master of the *William Moultrie* requested a safer station. Boddam-Whetham, tongue in cheek, told her to exchange with the British tramp *Goolistan*, recalling, 'I informed Master of *William Moultrie*, however, that the only difference I could see between 4,000 tons TNT and 2,000 tons was a fractional part of a second should she be hit.'

Thus ended the torpedo attacks of KG26. They were never again to be executed with such vigour or by such determined pilots, for shortly afterwards the Kampfgeschwader was redeployed to the Mediterranean, whence it had come. In fact the enemy were never afterwards to exploit the advantages conferred by aerial torpedoes which were, as the experience of PQ18 demonstrated, far from ineffective in accounting for ten of the thirteen ships destroyed. The Luftwaffe lost forty-four aircraft, thirty-eight of which were torpedo-bombers. It was a high price, but not as high as if German troops had had to destroy the contents of those thirteen merchantmen in the field.

Russian participation ensured that the battle off Cape Kanin was to be enshrined as a great Allied victory and Admiral Golovko was to contrast it with the débâcle of PQ17 which was said to be 'the fault of the Allies who abandoned the ships to their fate without forewarning' the Russians. 'This time, when we were able to take timely steps to secure the safety of the convoy in our operational zone, everything went differently.' The Admiral's criticism of the Royal Navy was implicit; the self-aggrandizement of the Soviet contribution embarrassing:

> The results of the September convoy PQ18 . . . confirm once more that given resolute action by covering forces . . . the enemy's surface ships can be neutralised, while the attacks of U-boats and aircraft can be repulsed – and with heavy loss to the enemy – by a correctly organized order of battle.[8]

There is no doubt that the addition of the four Russian destroyers was significant, and the appearance of Petlyakov fighters deterred the Ju88s from further interference, but the Admiral's claims were patronizingly extravagant. Equally instrumental in preventing further attacks that afternoon was the continuing worsening of the weather.

At 16.20 the incoming convoy met the local escort of HMS *Britomart*, *Salamander*, *Halcyon* and *Hazard*. Arrangements were concluded to lead the convoy in in two columns in the face of oncoming darkness and a strong ebb tide. To conduct the convoy through the shallows and over the Dvina Bar required the activation of light beacons and these were not operated; nor did all the pilot boats put out in the face of the wind. The ships of PQ18 were now to face the oldest enemy of all, a gale, and one from the north-west: they were thus compelled to anchor on a lee shore.

The hours of darkness were a final ordeal. Ships dragged their anchors or parted their cables. Some got under weigh and succeeded in clawing a little offshore and heaving to. The trawlers *St Kenan* and *Cape Argona* struggled slowly to windward, burning their last few tons of coal. *Harrier*'s anchor dragged and when she weighed and hove to, her steering gear failed, so she spent the next eleven hours under the wearisome control of her cumbersome hand-steering gear. A pilot ventured out and boarded the *Exford*, which had lost both anchors. Others made a run for the estuary.

On the morning of the 20th, four of these ships, *Exford*, *Campfire*, *Sahale* and *Lafayette*, were fast aground. So too was the trawler *Daneman*, and the shallower drafted corvette *Bergamot* tried to get a tow line aboard but only succeeded in losing her asdic dome. Her sister ship *Bluebell* came to her assistance and finally threw a line across by Costen gun, but failed to shift the trawler and finally abandoned the attempt.[9]

Aboard *Campfire* the Master sounded the general alarm and ordered the hands to abandon ship on the grounds of safety, for she was full of explosives, and the fact that the ship was indefensible. In appalling conditions the boats were lowered and all were got ashore to Modyugski Island. The armed guard commander, Ensign Rooker, had protested against the order and telephoned Commander Frankel at Archangel from the island's light-house. Frankel agreed he should reboard the ship, which he did on the morning of the 21st, when the weather had moderated, together with the Master, who had been the last to leave his ship, some volunteers and Frankel himself.

During the whole of the 20th, the ships endured as best they could. As the wind began to drop, a dozen Junkers bombers appeared at 15.40 through the heavy scud to deliver a long, but unsuccessful attack. Several near misses again thoroughly shook the *Exford*.

Early the next morning pilots came out and the ships passed the bar and steamed upstream to the waiting quays. The *Copeland* tied up to the Krasnaya Quay and disembarked her Russian guests. As she left, a woman survivor said, 'I thank you, Captain Hartley, your officers and men of this ship for your good fight and your kindness to me. Good luck to you and your country.'

Most of the escorts were piloted upstream to the Vorosenski and Krasny quays, *Bryony* by a female pilot and *Harrier* by the Master of the *Stalingrad*, a survivor on board. *Britomart*, *Ulster Queen* and a Russian destroyer remained at the bar to protect the stranded merchantmen which, at 15.45, sustained a bombing attack by two Ju88s. This achieved nothing beyond shaking up the ships with near misses and further stretching the nerves of exhausted men. At dusk Captain Adam took his ship across the bar, arriving at Archangel as the entire river suffered a heavy bombing raid. Quite incredibly the bombers missed the heavily laden ships and the quays, concentrating on the town.

In the succeeding days the heavy lift ships *Empire Bard* and *Empire Elgar* were sent alongside the ships stranded on the bar together with lighters to tranship cargo and lighten them. Attended by the Soviet salvage vessel *Schval* and a Colonel Petrov, they were all floated free by the 27th. The *Daneman* proved less tractable, but she too was eventually refloated, to follow her fellows upstream to the trawler-berth at Maimska.

A month later the discharge of the ships was completed and the famous banquet and meeting referred to in a previous chapter were held. During the banquet 'a spontaneous and whole-hearted reception' was given to the convoy Commodore, Rear-Admiral Boddam-Whetham. The Rear-Admiral, however, was exhausted by the strain of the last weeks and was declared sick. As almost his last act he commended the Master and Chief Engineer of *Temple Arch* for their support.[10]

So ended PQ18; something of a Pyrrhic victory for the Allies, but a victory nonetheless, in marked contrast to its predecessor. To Churchill's gratification it had restored the principle underlying these Arctic convoys, that of possibility. The magnitude of the combined escort and covering forces was nothing less than that of a fleet, a veritable mass of naval shipping to see forty merchant ships safely through to their destination, evidence enough of the vital necessity of those merchant ships and their crews. And while less than polite comments as to the gun-happiness and inexpertise of the American merchant marine were justified, it was only by acquiring such experience that the seamen of the United States would mature into the staunch allies they subsequently became.

There were flaws in the naval arrangements, too. *Avenger*'s unprepared state, though quickly rectified, could not make up for the weakness of her fighter arm, either in fire-power or numbers, a fact which Admiral Tovey was quick to point out. Nor could Admiral Fraser manœuvre freely, deprived as he was of so many destroyers committed to the convoy.

But there was one hopeful sign, a gratifying antidote to the depression following PQ17, an arresting of rot in morale. One American reported:

> Upon arriving in Archangel I heard one seaman exclaim, 'If I ever hear anyone knock the Limey navy, I'll knock his block off!' (A sentiment shared by all the men on my ship.) The . . . courageous job done by our British escort has instilled in our men . . . a deep respect for the British navy. As a result of a common experience relations between American and British seamen and officers were the most cordial I had ever seen.

It had not always been thus.

Perhaps more important was the reaction of the Germans to the British escort. The Luftwaffe had deceived itself by its own optimistic belief in earlier debriefing reports. Consequently it lost its customary *élan*:

> It was found that not only was it impossible to approach the carrier to launch an effective attack on account of fighters, but that a wide screen of warships made the launching of torpedoes against the inner merchant vessels an extremely hazardous undertaking.[11]

It had not always been thus, either.

15

'For eighteen days there was no let-up'

IN THREE GROUPS, one of which had been subjected to an unsuccessful attack by a U-boat, Rear-Admiral Burnett's ships had all joined QP14 by 03.00 on 17 September 1942. They were a welcome sight to the 141 survivors of PQ17, most of whom were accommodated aboard the *Alcoa Banner, Empire Tide, Harmatris, Minotaur, Ocean Freedom* and *West Nilus,* after their tedious and demoralizing sojourn in Russia. Among the returning merchantmen were the battered remnants of PQ17, plus a few others whose late discharge had prevented them leaving in earlier QP convoys. Commodore Dowding was aboard the *Ocean Voice,* and *Rathlin* and *Zamalek* were attached as rescue ships.[1]

QP14 had been led out of the Dvina on 13 September by the minesweepers *Britomart, Halcyon, Hazard* and *Salamander* which then detached, leaving Captain J.F.H. Crombie of HMS *Bramble* in command of the remaining escorts. These were the minesweepers *Leda* and *Seagull,* the two Hunts *Blankney* and *Middleton,* the anti-aircraft ships *Palomares* and *Pozarica,* the corvettes *Lotus, Poppy, Dianella* and *La Malouine,* and the anti-submarine trawlers *Ayrshire, Lord Middleton, Lord Austin* and *Northern Gem.*

Scylla, Avenger, the seventeen destroyers, two submarines and the anti-aircraft ship *Alynbank* of Burnett's force took station in accordance with the reduced size of the homeward convoy.[2]

By the time of the rendezvous QP14 had been reduced by two ships, the *Troubadour* and *Winston Salem,* which had straggled during the night of the 15th/16th; a Swordfish search flown off the next morning failed to locate either.

Aboard *Avenger* the ship's company had toiled to repair the damaged aircraft and had achieved a total of thirteen operational Sea Hurricanes, compared with a dozen on the outward passage. An advantage of the escort carrier's merchant origin meant that the *Avenger* was able to carry spare, unassembled aircraft in her holds and could thus make up the loss of her four machines and add a small bonus. Burnett conveyed his admiration to Colthurst, signalling, with a degree of typical facetiousness, 'You are a good father to your children,' to which Colthurst replied realistically: 'The nursery door is now closed.' However, the three original Stringbags remained airworthy. Their crews had endured, and continued to cope with, dreadful conditions in their open cockpits, and signs of the toll this was taking on the young men were already evident. On the day they located the homeward ships the temperature was extremely low, with snow-laden clouds and frequent squalls which persisted the following morning. The ships made several alterations of course to avoid icebergs.

Since the Luftwaffe was concentrating on PQ18, only shadowers appeared to harass QP14. These aircraft used the low cloud to edge up astern of the convoy until their brief appearance attracted gunfire; as the day wore on the weather thickened and they lost contact. By the afternoon of the 18th the convoy was passing Hope Island when a Catalina approached and, as a result of poor liaison between the naval authorities at Archangel and the base at Gryaznaya, gave the wrong recognition signal. Burnett was irritated by this want of attention, and seems to have been disinclined to believe the pilot's report of surfaced U-boats ahead of the convoy. In an attempt to keep the greatest distance between QP14 and Banak, he decided to round Spitzbergen's South Cape and coast north-west towards Bell Sound. To some extent he was influenced by the fact that he had to pick up the tanker *Oligarch* from her anchorage there to keep his destroyers fuelled, and accordingly the *Impulsive* and *Fury* were sent on ahead to collect her. Towards the evening, after the departure of the destroyers, a patrolling Swordfish sighted a partially surfaced U-boat trailing twenty miles astern of the convoy and dropped two depth-charges without apparent effect.

The next morning *Offa* was sent out to investigate mastheads seen above the horizon to the north-east. Such were the deceptive distortions of refraction that it was an anxious moment for the Rear-Admiral. 'Our thoughts turned to the anchorage at

Altenfiord,' he afterwards wrote, but *Offa* found no German capital ship, only the straggler *Winston Salem* which had been creeping along the ice-edge alone. The American ship was shepherded back to the fold as a German shadower located the convoy and began transmitting homing signals. It was just 06.00 on the 19th.

In an attempt to throw the wolves off his scent, Rear-Admiral Burnett deployed a number of his destroyers across the rear of the convoy while he made the alteration of course to the north-west round the South Cape of Spitzbergen. The destroyers then continued on the westward course for six miles before racing back to their stations round QP14.

The first U-boat alarm, however, came not from the convoy, but from a lone ship sixty-odd miles away to the south-east. This was the missing *Troubadour* and a Swordfish was flown off at 13.00 to cover her until *Onslaught* arrived. It was clear to Commander Selby that several U-boats were in the vicinity and by judicious use of the occasional depth-charge and the probing beam of a searchlight, these were kept at bay while every means possible was used to persuade *Troubadour* to make better speed. In the end darkness covered the truant freighter and her escort which made for the shelter of Bell Sound to join what was left of Force P, the tanker *Blue Ranger* and three destroyers. Here *Onslaught* bunkered and, in due course, she and the errant *Troubadour* returned to the United Kingdom with Force P.[3]

In the meantime QP14 had reached the rendezvous off the east coast of Spitzbergen, where *Impulsive* and *Fury* rejoined, bringing with them the tanker *Oligarch* and her guardship, the elderly *Worcester*. The latter replaced *Onslaught* in the screen as the outer destroyers commenced a long night investigating a constant stream of asdic contacts. At 05.20 on the 20th, the minesweeper *Leda*, bringing up the rear of the convoy, was hit by two torpedoes from von Strelow's *U435*. Like her sister *Gossamer*, the minesweeper had proved an invaluable asset to the Arctic convoy route and even now the tough little warship took over an hour to sink, succoured by rescue ships. Commander Wynne-Edwards, eighty-six of his crew and two merchant navy officers were picked up and ultimately accommodated aboard the *Seagull*, *Rathlin* and *Zamalek*, though sadly six afterwards died of wounds or hypothermia.

As more U-boats gathered, *Avenger*'s Swordfish maintained

their patrols, one sighting a submarine, which at first disdained to dive until bombed, then depth-charging it as it slid beneath the surface. Two destroyers responded to the aircraft's alarm and as the Swordfish flew in towards QP14 and sighted yet another, it diverted the destroyers to this latest target, but again the enemy escaped.

Meanwhile *Ashanti* was seeking a further U-boat seen to have dived in the distance. The destroyer raced off at full speed and her lookouts were rewarded with a brief glimpse of a periscope a mile away. Commander Onslow conned *Ashanti* down the line of bearing, pressing home his assault with a series of lobbed depth-charge patterns which appeared to be successful. Air and oil bubbled up to the surface and the asdic operators reported a heavy explosion followed by dramatic loss of contact. The sanguine expectations of *Ashanti*'s company were not subsequently confirmed.

Shortly before they were due to detach, Rear-Admiral Burnett had instructed his own submarines, *P614* and *P615*, to counter-attack, assigning *Opportune* to cover them as they dropped astern of the convoy to ambush the trailing Germans amid the snow squalls.

About 15.00, the two submarines having divided and submerged, Lieutenant D.J. Beckley of *P614* caught sight of a surfaced U-boat and fired a salvo at von Hymmen's *U408*, half a mile away. One of these torpedoes was seen by the German lookouts and an astonished von Hymmen crash-dived his boat. He escaped as the British torpedoes exploded, the detonator of one functioning prematurely and counter-mining the other. Lieutenant Newstead's submarine achieved nothing, and both boats then proceeded independently to Shetland, arriving on the 24th and 25th respectively.

The initiative was now to pass to the German submarines. At about 17.45, torpedoes from *U255*, commanded by the tenacious Reche, struck another survivor from PQ17, the *Silver Sword*, steaming in the rear of the convoy. She burst into flames and her company only escaped with difficulty. She was later shelled to destruction by HMS *Worcester*.

As twilight approached, Colthurst signalled Burnett that his Swordfish crews were reaching the end of their physical endurance. Burnett, uniquely suited to so active an Arctic command as one of the navy's foremost physical fitness experts, was not the man to disregard such a warning. Enormous difficulties had been experienced in operating Swordfish from *Avenger*'s 440 feet of flight-deck, since her speed of 16 knots gave little help unless she was steaming into a strong wind. Not only was the Stringbag obsolete, so were the methods used by its young crews to signal submarine sightings, particularly to the outer escorts. Nevertheless, her aircrews had done yeoman service and the greatest contribution *Avenger* made during the passage of Operation EV, the code-name for the naval support of PQ18 and QP14, was that of pioneer.

Burnett realized that both *Avenger* and *Scylla* had now ceased to be assets and, being vulnerable to submarine attack, were rapidly becoming liabilities. Accordingly, at 18.30 he ordered the destroyer *Milne* to come alongside. Captain Campbell ranged his ship up on the cruiser's port quarter, both ships lifting in the swell, their companies lining the rails, 'muffled in a variety of garments, and looking much as Willem Barents's men must have looked three and a half centuries before, when then, as now, cold and survival dictated the apparel'. Burnett sat himself in a sling, passing some jocular remarks before indicating he was ready. He was then hoisted up by the *Scylla*'s amidships aircraft and boat crane, and swung out over the water rushing between the two ships, where their mingled washes boiled and seethed, while *Scylla*'s bosun's mates sent the thin wails of their pipes into the bitter Arctic air. As the Real-Admiral was lowered on to *Milne*'s iron deck, those of the destroyer piped their welcome and Burnett's flag was hoisted to her masthead.[4]

A little later the cruiser and escort carrier detached, attended by the faithful *Wheatland* and *Wilton*, and augmented by *Fury*. On the homeward passage, to keep the survivors amused, a variety show was organized called the 'Shirkers' Gaytime', parodying a popular radio show hosted by various factories engaged in war production. One of its vocalists was a black seaman who came from the *Mary Luckenbach*. How had he survived? his new shipmates wanted to know, for he was the only person to endure the terrible explosion which had destroyed his ship. He explained he had been on deck taking the Master a cup of coffee when the *Mary Luckenbach* was hit. Then, 'Whoom! I find myself half a mile down the convoy!'

Disaster struck QP14 almost immediately after the departure of the cruiser and the carrier; HMS *Somali*, stationed on the convoy's port wing, was hit by a torpedo from Bielfeld's *U703*. As *Eskimo* and *Intrepid* began a frustratingly futile counter-attack in which they were unable to obtain a contact, *Opportune* and *Lord Middleton* manœuvred to take off survivors. Mercifully the sea remained slight. Having seen the bulk of his men safely off the ship, Lieutenant-Commander Maud signalled that *Somali* might be saved if towed, and Burnett directed Commander Onslow in the *Ashanti* to render her sister ship whatever assistance was possible.[5]

While the battered merchantmen of PQ18 embarked their pilots and crossed the Dvina Bar on the morning of 21 September, Huff-Duff intercepts betrayed the continuing presence of at least three U-boats trailing QP14. These were now joined by two BV138 flying boats. With a substantial number of destroyers attending *Somali* far astern, the convoy was once more vulnerable in an area where it had expected air cover from Shetland-based Catalinas. Burnett had doubled back in *Milne* to investigate the progress of the tow, but failed to locate the group of ships until he broke radio silence and found them to be a further forty miles away. Realizing the futility of his action, the Rear-Admiral prudently turned back for the convoy and was rewarded by the sight of a surfaced U-boat astern of QP14. To his irritation, the enemy boat dived and escaped.

A Catalina had made a brief appearance over the convoy and had then vanished in the cumulus, and it was not until late morning that the aircraft from 330 Squadron reappeared. In making a sweep round the convoy's perimeter the pilot spotted *U378* and was simultaneously seen by the German lookouts. Kapitänleutnant Zetsche ordered his anti-aircraft guns to open fire, scoring hits on the Catalina's fuel tanks. Losing fuel, the Catalina, *Z-Zebra*, dived on the U-boat as she began to submerge and dropped four depth-charges. The flying boat herself was forced to touch down, her aircrew were picked up by the *Marne*'s whaler and the aircraft was destroyed.

In the early afternoon, promising asdic contacts prompted attacks by *Bramble* and *Worcester*, but again the escorts were frustrated by the release of a *Pillenwerfer* and achieved nothing beyond intimidation. Somewhat disappointing anti-submarine operations seem to have characterized the activities of the fighting destroyer escort. Their inconclusive nature was, at the time, blithely attributed to the differing density layers in the sea which hampered sonic propagation. They did nevertheless inflict damage on five U-boats.[6]

At 05.30 on the next morning, the 22nd, Burnett handed command over to Scott-Moncrieff and *Milne* proceeded to Seidisfiord, leaving eleven destroyers and nine smaller escorts flung in a cordon round the convoy. An hour later, when QP14 was centred on an approximate position of latitude 71°N, longitude 011°W, Strelow's *U435* penetrated this screen and achieved a triple success, sinking within a few moments the *Bellingham*, the *Ocean Voice* and the oiler *Gray Ranger*. Once again Commodore Dowding and his staff found themselves in the icy water, to be picked up by the minesweeper *Seagull*; there were no losses, but it was a bitter blow and conceded that the advantage still lay with the predator. Dowding declined to move on to another merchant ship and handed over to his Vice-Commodore, Captain Walker, who, in *Ocean Freedom*, was aboard almost the last surviving ship of PQ17 now that the *Bellingham* had also been sunk.

Alarmed by this multiple disaster, Scott-Moncrieff closed up the screen, ordering *Middleton* and *Impulsive* to sweep the flanks and *Worcester* to zigzag across the rear during the night. A further U-boat sighting during the afternoon proved to be the last and, although depth-charges were dropped at regular intervals, no further attacks materialized.

By the next day, the 23rd, Catalina patrols were overhead. The rescue ships *Rathlin* and *Zamalek* were sent in to Seidisfiord for victuals, accompanied by *Onslow, Offa* and *Worcester* which were now short of fuel, and *Marne,* which had to land the crew of Catalina *Z-Zebra,* based at Akureyri. The duty watchkeepers of QP14 sighted Langanaes at 17.20 and, bypassing Iceland, headed south for Cape Wrath in deteriorating weather, with a gale coming on to blow from the north-east.

Astern of the convoy, meanwhile, Catalina *U-Uncle* of 210 Squadron was in action with a trailing U-boat. Flight-Sergeant J.W. Semmens had taken off from Sullom Voe shortly before midnight and sighted QP14 at 06.00. Running back over the convoy's track in thickening weather he shortly afterwards saw *U253* less than a mile away. As the U-boat crash-dived Semmens swept overhead, dropping to wave-top height and releasing six depth-charges into the swirl of white water marking *U253*. The detonation caused an upwelling in which the U-boat was blown back to the surface where she wallowed momentarily before submerging again. The Catalina climbed and then banked sharply, her aircrew staring back at the heaving surface of the sea. *U253* suddenly reappeared on her beam-ends, then her snout dipped and her stern lifted, slowly tilting until almost vertical, where she hung for a second before plunging to her doom.

The gale which buffeted QP14 through the 24th backed to the north and the light merchant ships had trouble keeping station in the re-formed convoy as they yawed, rolled and scended in the following sea. Once again the *Winston Salem* caused problems. She dropped out of column as her Acting Master hove her to and she was left astern, head to sea. An anxious and hard-pressed Scott-Moncrieff was obliged to turn the *Martin* back to stand by her. By the 25th the wind had dropped, leaving the convoy to struggle southwards in a heavy swell; during the day the two rescue ships and three destroyers, detached to Seidisfiord, returned. On the 26th, *Bramble* and *Seagull* left for Scapa Flow, followed by *Middleton, Blankney, Oligarch* and *Black Ranger*; finally, as QP14 hove in sight of Cape Wrath, Scott-Moncrieff's *Faulknor* led the Home Fleet destroyers east to Orkney in their wake. Russell in *Malcolm* saw the convoy safely into Loch Ewe later the same day and the straggler *Winston Salem* followed.[7]

The gale which had overtaken QP14 off Iceland on 23 September had swept out of the north-east quarter where, off Jan Mayen Island, the Tribal-class destroyer *Ashanti* had her sister ship HMS *Somali* in tow. Round them were clustered the destroyers *Eskimo, Intrepid* and *Opportune* and the anti-submarine trawler *Lord Middleton*.

At 19.00 on 20 September 1942, *Somali*'s lookouts had spotted the deadly torpedo fired from Kapitänleutnant Bielfeld's *U703*. Lieutenant-Commander Maud, who had been in the act of leaving the bridge but was held back by some intuitive instinct, leapt to the compass platform and ordered the helm thrown hard over to port in an attempt to comb the weapon's track. Alas, his evasive action came too late. The torpedo pierced the thin shell plating of her port side. The explosion in the engine room almost broke the ship's back; she whipped from end to end and the roar of escaping steam filled the air. Suddenly, the destroyer listed to starboard. This and the loss of power now dominated the senses of *Somali*'s crew as they struggled to determine the extent of the damage. It was considerable: the whole port side from turn of bilge to deck was breached and the long, slender hull was subject to torsion. The only flooded spaces, however, were the engine room, one boiler room and the gearing compartment. While the bulkheads took the strain, the damage-control parties worked with a will to drive, or tom, shores into place and caulk minor leaks with softwood wedges, rags and anything else which came to hand.

The cost in human terms to *Somali*'s company had been five killed and four wounded, and Maud decided to evacuate all but about eighty men with whom he hoped to save the ship, wounded though she was. The rest were taken off by the *Lord Middleton*, an operation facilitated by the slight sea. Consulting with Onslow, Maud resolved to connect a tow. The forecastle party aboard *Somali* unshackled an anchor cable, while the quarterdeck men aboard *Ashanti* roused out their 4-inch diameter steel towing hawser. Having manœuvred close to the motionless *Somali*, Onslow ordered a light line thrown across by Costen gun and to this was bent a heavier messenger by which *Ashanti*'s hawser was hauled over and shackled on to the *Somali*'s cable end. This was then veered, to render the catenary thus formed between the two ships capable of absorbing a certain amount of stress, but to his regret, Onslow realized this had been excessive. *Somali* began a violent yawing astern of *Ashanti*.

Gingerly moving ahead, with reports coming from First Lieutenant Bailly on the quarterdeck, Onslow managed to adjust speed to get a steady strain. Although this forward motion increased the leaking aboard *Somali*, an auxiliary diesel generator was coaxed into life and electric light and a submersible electric pump were brought into use. The destroyer's hull was now protesting in a series of ominous creaks and tremors. *Lord Middleton* remained alongside and loose items of heavy gear about the upper decks were quickly transferred to reduce topweight, to such effect that *Ashanti*'s motor launch soon took additional men aboard to assist. By jettisoning further stores and movable fittings (authorized vandalism which considerably lightened the spirits of *Somali*'s crew), the strain on the now twisted hull was eased, and the covey of ships crept south.

During the evening the generator failed and then the tow parted. Fortunately the calm sea enabled this to be swiftly reconnected, shots of chain being paid out from *Ashanti*'s stern. Able to make 5 knots, the *Somali* still yawed. It then occurred to Onslow and his officers that if power could be passed over then both pumps and steering engines might be coaxed back to life aboard *Somali*. Accordingly, a quantity of electric wire was garnered from the three destroyers maintaining an anti-submarine screen round the towed and towing.

Richard Onslow was now seriously concerned about *Ashanti*'s lack of fuel, when with almost dramatic timing, Force P hove over the horizon astern. After a flurry of signals, the *Blue Ranger* steamed into the group and began fuelling *Eskimo* and *Opportune*.

The makeshift cable had now been made up. Lieutenant Lewin led a party in *Ashanti*'s boat, working for four hours, arms immersed in the freezing sea, to secure a pair of wires at intervals to the towing hawser and chain, only to find it failed to work due to a short. The whole thing had to be recovered, overhauled and resecured. Eventually, however, a reel of new cable was discovered in one of *Somali*'s stores and this sufficed to restore power to *Somali*. A telephone link was also established.

Soon speed had been increased to 6 knots and, with the weather continuing fine throughout the 22nd, Onslow had high hopes of bringing his sister ship in. It was now *Ashanti*'s turn to fuel. With great skill the *Blue Ranger*'s master slowed ahead of *Ashanti*, and ran a line and hose down to her which her forecastle party grappled first time. 'We presented', wrote Richard Onslow, 'the somewhat unusual sight of three ships towing in line ahead while oiling was in progress.'

But after Force P had detached for Iceland their luck ran out; on the following day a swell rolled out of the north-east and the wind began to strengthen. By nightfall a full gale was blowing. Onslow had edged west to obtain some shelter from the ice-edge, now less than twenty miles away, but at about 01.00 the gale increased immeasurably with the component of a freezing katabatic wind off the *nunataks* of Greenland. Sleet and snow now cut the visibility and a short sea made any prospects of taking off *Somali*'s crew increasingly dangerous. Moreover, the severely weakened hull could not stand the incessant bending moments now affecting it, while the sea washed in and out of the frightful hole in her side, aggravating her condition.

By the early morning of the 24th, as wind and sea increased in violence, Maud was compelled to have all the remaining hands mustered on the upper deck. As *Somali*'s hull worked in the seaway the iron deck was alternately compressed and then stretched and it became clear that so grievously mauled a ship could not suffer thus indefinitely.

And then, for the waiting Maud, the inevitable happened in the blackest hour of the night. Above the scream of the wind came the sinister screech of rending steel. Assaulted by a heavy sea, and with a final heave, *Somali* broke her back. Simultaneously the tow parted, leaving bow and stern sections wallowing in the tumultuous darkness, surrounded by the dim and sudden glow of breaking waves. Below Maud's feet the tremor of collapsing bulkheads told him the worst: the bow section was being invaded by the sea and both sections began to rear almost vertically. The Carley floats and cork-nets were flung overboard and Maud ordered his remaining men to save themselves. The water was icy and the will to live quickly evaporated as hypothermia struck. Men from the after section took to their own rafts and drifted in the vast and terrible sea.

The sheltering after party aboard *Ashanti* realized the tow had parted, reported it to the bridge and began to slip the tow which, in accordance with the laws of perversity, chose this moment to jam. Once his screws were clear, Commander Onslow put his ship about and with *Lord Middleton* began to search for any survivors. *Ashanti* loomed above the cluster of rafts and began the business of hauling frozen and near-lifeless men aboard. Many were swept away, or trapped and drowned below *Ashanti*'s bilge keel. Many died on the destroyer's deck, frozen to the very marrow. One of the last to be dragged on board and respond to treatment was Lieutenant-Commander Colin Maud; he was among a mere thirty-five who escaped. Forty-seven perished as the *Somali*'s two halves sank after an almost epic tow of 420 miles in 80 hours.

Onslow and his attending consorts hung about until daylight in the forlorn hope of finding more, then shaped a course for Scapa Flow. They had at least the satisfaction of having done their utmost.

Rear-Admiral Burnett was uncertain as to the effectiveness of Operation EV: 'I do not know how far this operation may be considered to have been a success.' He was aware that had the enemy sunk all the oilers, had the aerial and submarine attacks been better co-ordinated, or if the escorts' ammunition had run out or the weather not allowed his destroyers to refuel, 'it must have been a tragic failure'.

But despite the serious losses, the risk had been worth the running. In the reservist-manned corvettes and anti-submarine trawlers the dashing hither and thither of the destroyers had often hitherto excited impolite comment. To the men in the smaller, less glamorous warships, a constant shortage of fuel meant not inconvenience but a night or two quietly alongside an oiler, and they envied the destroyer crews their comparative luxury. It was considered an unjustified perquisite of the 'real navy' and confirmation of the reservists' perception of themselves as operating in the second rank. Operation EV ended that misperception: 'For eighteen days there was no let-up,' reported Burnett to the Commander-in-Chief. When there were no air attacks in progress, the destroyers were engaged in 'countless anti-submarine hunts, counter-attacks and investigations, continuous zig-zagging in formation, moving positions . . . to fill gaps of others away chasing contacts, and, during lulls, topping up with oil or running alongside to take on or transfer survivors'.[8]

There was little doubt that despite losses, Admiral Tovey's concept of the 'Fighting Destroyer Escort' had proved its value under Burnett's able leadership.

16

'A tough blow for the Russians'

THE SEASON NOW closing upon the polar seas was the most propitious for the passage of convoys: the diminishing hours of daylight, the final eclipse of the sun by the rim of the world and the brief twilit noon which characterizes the Arctic mid-winter gave Allied shipping its best chance of running the gauntlet unseen. In the ports of North Russia the merchant ships remaining from PQ18 were now discharged and awaiting escort back to the west, while the inexorable industrial output of Great Britain and, more significantly, the United States of America had already filled the assembly anchorages with forty freighters awaiting convoy as PQ19.

In the event no such convoy sailed. Another of Stalin's demands was to be met, though in a way that found no favour with the Soviet dictator: a second front was to be opened, not in Europe, but in North Africa. In defiance of Russian pressure and American reservations, the northern convoys were suspended. In October of 1942 General Montgomery's Eighth Army had defeated Erwin Rommel's Afrika Korps at El Alamein. As the second week of November dawned, Operation Torch, the largest amphibious military undertaking in history, landed Allied troops in Vichy French North Africa. Their objective was to be the hammer to Montgomery's anvil: Rommel's Germans were to be crushed. Over 100,000 men, largely Americans under General Eisenhower, were convoyed in over 500 vessels. Protecting these merchantmen meant the withdrawal of much of the British Home Fleet from northern waters.

Worried about the effect this operation would have upon

the crucial battle then raging around Stalingrad, President Roosevelt wanted PQ19 to sail, but was dissuaded from this resolution by the counter-argument that it would delay Torch by three weeks. He then urged that the convoy be divided into three and sailed with smaller escorts. Churchill told Roosevelt this was unrealistic and that Stalin had to be informed no further convoys would be sailed until January 1943. It would, replied the American President, 'be a tough blow for the Russians'. The news was passed to Russia at the autumnal equinox: the sun had passed to the southern hemisphere and the approaching northern winter was to be of unparalleled severity.

The British and Russian alliance was strained in the wake of PQ17. '[Russian] naval experts consider[ed] the reasons put forward by the British naval experts to justify the cessation of convoys to the northern ports of the U.S.S.R. wholly unconvincing.'[1]

Stalin now reiterated these complaints along with the customary traducing and belittling of the British naval effort. Needless to say, whatever the merits of Russian naval expertise, and it was by no means contemptible, it did not extend to a continuous series of major fleet operations with a ratio of warship to merchant ship per convoy rapidly approaching 1:1. Churchill was stung by Stalin's attitude, long afterwards recalling the fact that during the first year of this 'thankless task', despite the overwhelming industrial might of the United States, Great Britain had contributed from its strained resources by far the greater number of aircraft and tanks. He thus repudiated critics who considered the British effort lukewarm. 'We gave our heart's blood resolutely to our valiant, suffering ally.'[2]

With this, at least, there was scarcely a merchant seafarer of any rank who would have disagreed.

There were plenty, however, who disagreed with the final compromise to this hiatus in the convoys – the running of single ships through to Russia, code-named Operation FB. In the mood prevailing after PQ17, undispelled by the Pyrrhic success of PQ18, the rumours and gossip which spread among red-ensign crews were full of the increasing perfidy of those who, from the ivory towers of Downing Street, the Admiralty and the Ministry of War Transport, dreamed up the scheme which was designed to maintain the illusion of continued supply to the Russian ally. It is unnecessary to stress the ridicule with which it was met by the Russian High Command, yet ironically, it appears that it was Russian insistence on the return of their own ships that initiated it, and not the duplicity and untrustworthiness popularly attributed to Churchill, the callous disregard of the naval mandarins, or the alleged inhumanity of a certain shipowner serving his country within the safety of the Ministry of War Transport.

There seems to be little doubt that Churchill, pragmatic politician that he was, saw no reason not to jump on so convenient a bandwagon in so bleak an hour. He was equally well aware of the extremity to which the Russians were being driven and the pivotal nature of the fight for Stalingrad. Nonetheless, once the idea was mooted, it gained impetus and one British shipowner was moved to stump up a bonus of the then considerable sum of £100 per officer and £50 per rating, cash in advance, for those who volunteered to participate. Thus was Operation FB born.

In the break between PQ17 and PQ18 the Russians had requested that two of their merchant ships then lying at anchor off Iceland be sent independently to Archangel. The *Friedrich Engels* sailed on 11 August, the *Belomorcanal* the following day. Both ships arrived safely. Such success, it was thought, could be repeated, an opinion of specious validity. In the case of Operation FB, the merchant ships' lack of speed would be compensated for by the Arctic darkness.

Aware of the risks, Churchill disingenuously cabled Roosevelt in early October that the vessels would all be British ships, 'for which the crews will have to volunteer, the dangers being terrible, and their sole hope if sunk far from help being Arctic clothing and *such heating arrangements as can be placed in the lifeboats* [my italics].' This assumption was crass, as was the assertion that no American vessels would be used.

Between 29 October and 2 November 1942, at approximately twelve-hour intervals, alternating British and American merchant ships with an additional Russian vessel set out alone, sailing roughly 200 miles apart. They were individually routed, and such protection as there was consisted of submarine patrols north of Bear Island and a line of trawlers disposed along the general track. *Cape Palliser, Northern Pride, Northern Spray* and *St Elstan* were dispatched from Iceland; *Cape Argona, Cape Mariato* and *St Kenan* from Murmansk. This absurd expedient was reminiscent of the cruiser patrols sent to 'protect' trade routes during the First

World War and which proved quite useless. It is, however, easy to write off the endurance and fortitude of those little ships' crews in the knowledge that their efforts were not only futile, but actually contributed to what followed. It seems the enemy were alerted to the fact that something was afoot when the *Northern Spray* made an unsuccessful attack on a U-boat.

'These independent sailings', the official historian afterwards commented, betraying a degree of misgiving, 'were more successful than some people had expected.' What those expectations actually were is not clear, but in the light of events, with an attrition rate in the laden eastbound ships of 50 per cent, they must have been dismal in the extreme.

In fact three ships, the British tramps *Briarwood* and *Daldorch*, and the American Liberty ship *John H.B. Latrobe* were recalled because of what happened to those ahead of them. On 2 November the *Empire Gilbert* was sunk by *U586* (Esch) off Iceland and two days later the Junkers Ju88s of KG30 bombed and sank the Russian vessel *Dekabrist*. They also damaged the *William Clark* and later the same day this American Liberty ship was finally sunk by a torpedo fired by Kapitänleutnant Herbschleb in *U354*.

The balance was somewhat redressed the following day, the 5th, when Catalina *H-Hotel*, patrolling north of Iceland, located and sank von Hymmen's *U408*; but on the 6th, Oberleutnant Benker, commanding *U625*, torpedoed the *Empire Sky* with the loss of her crew of forty-one men.

Five merchantmen, the British *Empire Galliard* and *Empire Scott*, and the American Liberty ships *Richard H. Alvey*, *John Walker* and *Hugh Williamson* got through unscathed. Five Soviet vessels sent west-bound during the same period reached Iceland and these were followed by others, totalling twenty-two in the period up to 24 January 1943.

The Soviet tanker *Donbass* was not so fortunate.

Between 24 and 28 September 1942, the heavy cruiser *Admiral Hipper*, flying the flag of Konteradmiral Miesel, accompanied by the destroyers *Richard Beitzen*, *Z23*, *Z28*, *Z29* and *Z30*, carried out Operation Zarin, the laying of a minefield off the west coast of northern Novaya Zemlya. The *Hipper* (Kapitän Hartmann) sortied again on receipt of intelligence from U-boats and KG30 that lone Allied merchant ships were attempting the passage of the Barents Sea. This time flying Kummetz's flag, the heavy cruiser was escorted by the *Richard Beitzen*, the *Friedrich*

Eckholdt, *Z27* and *Z30*. Two days out, on 7 November, the *Donbass* and the auxiliary escort *Musson* were engaged and sunk by Z27.[3]

Of the thirteen laden vessels sent from Iceland, three had turned back and four had been sunk by the enemy. For the SS *Chulmleigh* was reserved the worst fate of all.

Built by Pickergill's of Sunderland in 1938 and owned by the self-made Lord Glanely of St Fagans, Cardiff, she was a traditional British tramp steamer of 5,445 tons. In addition to her ship's company she bore a mixed complement of eighteen gunners, part DEMS ratings, part MRA soldiers, to man the after 4-inch, a Bofors, four Oerlikons and two Marlin machine guns, plus the usual rockets. Loaded at Philadelphia she had joined a transatlantic convoy at Halifax, Nova Scotia, detached off Iceland and proceeded to Hvalfiordur for the assembly anchorage of PQ19.

The *Chulmleigh* was 35-year-old Captain D.M. Williams's first command and she was routed north of Jan Mayen, then thirty miles south of Spitzbergen before swinging south towards the White Sea, a passage of 2,500 miles in darkness or crepuscular gloom. The naval officers briefing Williams and the other masters offered their sympathy at the coming ordeal and urged speed, not only as a defensive measure, but because ice was already forming in the Gourlo. In fact the weather proved difficult from the outset. Overcast skies, haze and snowstorms deprived Williams and his officers of astronomical fixes and the *Chulmleigh* was run on dead reckoning to her alter-course position off Jan Mayen, which it was estimated she had reached shortly after midnight on 3 November. An azimuth taken of a star during a brief break in the scud had revealed the standard magnetic compass to be as much as 8° in error, unsurprising in those high latitudes, but further compromising navigation and constantly compounding the errors in dead reckoning. That night the Radio Officer reported distress traffic which, Williams knew, came from other FB ships. At 01.00 on the 5th, the *Chulmleigh* received an Admiralty signal to head north until she reached the 77th parallel before turning east for Spitzbergen. This was an instruction which Williams could only obey in spirit. Uncertain of his position, it aggravated the danger he was already in and he delayed his compliance for four hours in the hope of obtaining a fix.

Six hours later, at 11.00, the cloud broke and instead of a star, a German BV138 loomed out of the murk. Although the cloud cover shut in again almost at once, the fear of aerial attack now added to Williams's worries and spread to the crew. This circumstance and the noon plot, which indicated the *Chulmleigh*'s latitude as 77°N, persuaded Williams to alter to the south-eastwards. The total darkness of mid-afternoon brought the additional cover of heavy snow. Now, however, a southerly wind sprang up, and with it a swell which presaged a gale. Williams was consumed by the growing anxiety that she would fail to clear Spitzbergen. However, at midnight, the Master considered his ship was clear of the South Cape and hauled the *Chulmleigh*'s head to the east.

Remarkably the *Chulmleigh* was only twenty miles out in her reckoning, but it was twenty miles north, and half an hour after midnight she ran aground on a reef off Spitzbergen's South Cape, driving over the rocks so that when she stopped, her stern was fast, her bow wallowing in the deeper water beyond. It was the worst kind of misfortune; at any moment she might break her back and the strain of their ordeal now affected the crew when Williams ordered them into the boats as a precaution. The Third Mate's boat was carelessly lowered, a fall running away and throwing the two men of the lowering detail into the sea which now surged up and down the tramp's side as the swell steepened and broke upon the reef. Fortunately the other three boats got away without damage, taking with them the redistributed crew of Third Mate Clark. Meanwhile Williams destroyed the confidential books, having given orders that the Mate, Mr Ernest Fenn, and Second Engineer, Mr Middlemiss, were to remain aboard.

It was at this juncture that the cries of the two ditched seamen reached Williams. He ran down to the main deck and located them in the beam of his torch. The nearest lifeboat's crew experienced difficulty returning alongside, but eventually Williams scrambled aboard himself and, with the help of the Boatswain and an apprentice, hauled the first of the freezing men from the water. He was revived with difficulty. The boat had meanwhile closed the second man only to find him already dead.

Williams reboarded his ship, but was in an exhausted condition. It was some time before he was able to recover himself. However, at 02.30 he ordered the boats back alongside and persuaded some firemen to reboard and assist Middlemiss in raising steam. The attempt to drive the *Chulmleigh* off the reef failed and, despite the obvious advantages of shelter conferred by the ship herself, he knew it was futile to try and get the crew aboard again. At 04.00 a message was transmitted on the Admiralty frequency reporting that the *Chulmleigh* was being abandoned, then Williams left his ship.

The boats remained close to the wreck until a little daylight leached into the interminable darkness and enabled them to find an exit from the encircling reef. As they passed into the rougher waters of the open sea beyond, five Junkers Ju88s flew in and bombed the helpless vessel, ignoring the escaping boats. As these pulled away, a twist of black smoke rose from the *Chulmleigh*.

The inhospitable cliffs of southern Spitzbergen were interrupted 150 miles to the northwards by the inlet of Icefiord where lay the mining settlement of Barentsburg and it was for this that sail was hoisted. The smallest of the three boats began to drop astern almost immediately, so her crew were transferred into the other two. Twenty-eight men were now in Williams's boat, twenty-nine in Fenn's, and darkness soon separated them. Williams's boat made good northing until the wind failed and becalmed it throughout most of the 7th. Then, on the 8th, the gale arrived, forcing them to stream their sea-anchor and heave to. The steep seas occasionally broke into the boat and Williams had to bully his men to fight the overwhelming euphoria that preceded death and was usually an irresistible symptom of hypothermia. Frozen and demoralized they awaited the grey dawn. When it came they discovered to their horror that they had lost sight of the coast. Williams ordered the engine started and headed east. Fortunately he had nursed the small stock of fuel for such an emergency and after two hours sighted both Spitzbergen and the other lifeboat.

The two boats ran alongside and the meeting immediately put new heart into everyone. Fenn and Williams decided the Master's boat should go on ahead, using sails and power, to raise the alarm. During the hours of darkness, however, the wind rose again and the temperature dropped. Spray froze on the sails and the gunwhales of the boat while the bilge-water was only kept liquid and baleable by the dwindling heat of human bodies. It was bitterly cold and in the early hours of the 10th Chief Steward Islwyn Davies, aged 30, died. They slid the cold body overboard.

Estimating his proximity to Icefiord in the twilit day, Williams restarted his engine and brought the boat within sight of Prince Charles Foreland beyond which lay the fiord and Barentsburg. Minutes later the engine died, taking with it the hopes of his crew, now badly affected by the death of Davies and all suffering from frostbite. Williams himself was by now in a state of collapse and the donkeyman had begun to rave. As the Master slid into unconsciousness, the mantle of command fell upon 20-year-old Third Mate David Clark whose hands and feet were frostbitten.

Shortly before noon on the 11th, Clark ordered sail rehoisted, hoping to regain sight of the Foreland which had been lost overnight. The order took an age to carry out, so badly affected were the men by cold, hunger and thirst. The agility of their minds was dulled, absorbed only by the desire either to drink or to sleep, their muscles were uncoordinated and weakened by lack of food and the extreme cold, and their breath froze in their beards. Their chilled blood flowed ever slower in feet and fingers and the very act of trying to grasp halliards produced either total ineptitude or excruciating agony, but in the end it was done, and Clark headed east.

When they sighted land, Clark resolved to get his men ashore and a fire lit as soon as possible, for he knew their endurance was almost at an end. However, attempts to run inshore were frustrated by outlying reefs and then the wind freshened again as the pitiless darkness descended. An air of desperation now prevailed. Clark was determined to cheat death and with all the confidence he could muster he ordered the sails down and the oars shipped in an attempt to find a way through the rocks. His resolve was rewarded by the distant glitter of the lights of Barentsburg.

At about 03.00 on the 12th, in a confusion of tumbling seas and clumsy rowing, Clark's boat rode over a reef upon the back of a swell and wallowed briefly before it was tossed ashore. Men and gear tumbled in helpless confusion, unaware of the damage being done to their nerveless extremities. The conscious disentangled themselves and dragged the unconscious over the shingle. Three dead were left in the shallows. Incredibly, twenty yards from the survivors loomed a row of wooden huts, temporary summer dwellings of itinerant seal-hunters. The living collapsed inside and, free of the wind, instantly fell asleep.

Next morning Clark made the discovery that one of the huts contained a stove and a supply of tinned food and coffee. Within an hour morale had begun to lift as more stores were found and were added to what remained of their lifeboat rations. Warmth from a plentiful supply of driftwood revived hopes but caused agonies in thawing flesh, and the onset of gangrene produced a foul stench in the hut. Frostbite and immersion foot affected them all, Clark particularly badly, though Williams began to recover and reassert his authority. Nevertheless, during the succeeding four days, thirteen men died of gangrenous septicaemia.

The burial party was made up of the fittest men, four MRA gunners who also undertook foraging. It was one of these men, Richard Peyer, who, with Third Mate Clark, set out to reach Barentsburg. Twice these two men made the attempt, and twice they were forced to return due to the awful terrain and the extreme weather. It was now December, blizzards raged outside almost continuously, giving way periodically to calm, frozen silence accompanied by the brilliant exhibition of the aurora. Only a brief dull greyness betrayed the passing of another noon, and a diet of biscuit, corned beef and Horlicks tablets could not stem inevitable lassitude and decline. Captain Williams did his best to maintain spirits, aware that lack of hope was by now a greater danger than lack of food. He encouraged exercise and modest local exploration which produced a small quantity of whale blubber. The discovery of a lighthouse turned to disappointment when it was found to be disused and empty. A third attempt to reach Barentsburg by Peyer and Gunner Burnett also failed, but on their return another hut was found containing corned beef and cocoa. Towards Christmas, however, almost all had run out and only hot water remained to sustain the survivors.

It was now Williams who was to be moved by desperation. With the toughest gunner, a small former Liverpool docker named Reginald Whiteside, he set off himself to get help. Within hours they had been beaten back: the terrain was impassable without skis, the conditions unendurable without proper Arctic clothing. The men of the *Chulmleigh* were reduced to eating the oil in which the whale blubber had been preserved. It was a stinking, unappetizing mess which men with no hope of surviving now declined to eat and which only added to the foul stench of decaying flesh.

Another man died on Christmas Eve. Williams knew he had strength only for one final attempt to get help. His obligations to his men and to Fenn's boat, whose fate, unbeknown to the captain, was already sealed, weighed heavily upon him. Peyer and Whiteside remained the fittest men and with them Williams set out again for the settlement, only to fail.

On 2 January 1943, Whiteside left the hut to get fuel. Only nine men remained alive, their stinking limbs discharging pus. All were very near the end. There was no food and they were now burning the wood of the neighbouring huts. A few moments later Whiteside re-entered the hut, flinging the door wide and babbling dementedly. Williams thought he had lost his mind or that the marauding polar bears seen in the vicinity were drawn towards the stench of the encampment.

Peering into the twilight, Williams saw two white-clothed figures skiing towards them; they were Norwegian soldiers on routine patrol who emptied their packs to resupply the Britons and, taking with them Whiteside and Burnett, went to get help.

Early on the 3rd two sledges arrived and immediately took off Clark and Boatswain Hardy, a doctor remaining with the others until more sledges arrived on the 4th. The entire party arrived at Barentsburg and were hospitalized that evening. The settlement was only twelve miles from their camp, but their ordeal of fifty-three days was over.

Clark did not live, but the survivors remained at Barentsburg for four months until the British cruisers *Bermuda* and *Cumberland* entered Icefiord to replenish the Norwegian garrison and embarked them. Captain Williams and his eight surviving men landed at Thurso on 15 June.

As for the *Chulmleigh*, she was bombed a second time by the Luftwaffe and torpedoed by Benker in *U625*. Blown apart, her rusting ribs and plates remain off Spitzbergen's South Cape. Most of her crew had perished in the foolhardy attempt to run single ships through to Russia and their bones, like those of their ship, lie still upon that bleak and terrible coast. The bonus put up by Mr Bilmeir had proved of little use to them, nor had they discovered any 'heating arrangements' in their lifeboats, but all had done their duty.[4]

Shortly before the dispatch of the single merchant ships, the cruiser *Argonaut* and the destroyers *Intrepid* and *Obdurate* were sent to Archangel on 13 October with the medical unit previously rejected by the Russians. This provided much-needed support for the wounded and exposed Allied seamen landed in North Russia, but its dispatch had been attended by protracted negotiations with Molotov, which Churchill described as 'a good example of how official jargon can be used to destroy any kind of human contact, or even thought itself'. The ships were sighted by German aircraft, but not molested. On the return passage, these ships withdrew the aircrews and ground support staff from what remained of the two squadrons of Royal Air Force Hampden bombers and photo-reconnaissance Spitfires at Vaenga, which were turned over to the Russians.

The Allied landings in North Africa had called south reinforcements of aircraft from the runways of Banak, Bardufoss and Kirkenes. Taking advantage of this, it remained for the Allied naval command to retrieve as many empty ships as possible from North Russia before the White Sea was closed to navigation. Convoy QP15 therefore sailed on 17 November. It consisted of fourteen American, eight British, one Panamanian and seven Russian vessels, ten more ships than Tovey thought sensible, such was the shortage of tonnage in American ports. The Commodore, Captain W.C. Meek, was embarked in *Temple Arch* and the rescue ship *Copeland* was in attendance. The American freighters *Ironclad* and *Meanticut* dropped out, one having failed to sail, the other running aground, and although they were both readied later, they were too late to overhaul the convoy and remained at Archangel.[5]

Also left behind was the rescue ship *Rathlin*. She had damaged her rudder when she touched the ground at Molotovsk and in the following summer she was trimmed down by the head, her stern raised and a repair platform built under her counter.

Covering QP15 and fit again after his illness, Rear-Admiral Hamilton cruised west of Bear Island in *London*, with *Suffolk* and the destroyers *Obdurate, Onslaught* and *Forester* in company. As a deterrent to the cruisers *Hipper* and *Köln* and four enemy destroyers at Altenfiord, the British submarines *P216* and *P312*, the Free French *Junon* and the Norwegian *Uredd* maintained their watch on the Norwegian coast.

Convoy QP15 was seen clear of the White Sea by the local escort of four minesweepers, the *Britomart, Halcyon, Hazard* and *Sharpshooter*. Their sister ship *Salamander* joined the ocean escort which comprised the corvettes *Bergamot, Bluebell, Bryony* and *Camellia*. The Russian destroyers *Baku* and *Sokrushitelni* kept company as usual, then detached on the 20th. The senior officer of the escort was to have been Captain Scott-Moncrieff in the *Faulknor*, who with the destroyers *Intrepid, Icarus* and *Impulsive* was intended to provide initial cover from Kola. Being short of fuel these detached on the 26th. HMS *Echo* put in a brief appearance between the 20th and 22nd when the Hunts *Ledbury* and *Middleton* were to have joined, *Oakley* and the fleet destroyers *Musketeer* and *Orwell* following the next day, releasing Scott-Moncrieff's ships. In fact neither of the two destroyer forces succeeded in making contact with the convoy, such was the state of the weather.

The first of a succession of gales struck QP15 on 20 November, scattering the ships and causing a fuel crisis in the close escorts as they tried to maintain contact in the continuous gloom. *Ulster Queen* was compelled to leave the convoy to refuel on the 24th, as were the corvettes *Bluebell* and *Camellia*. The scattered merchant ships struggled on, battered by heavy head seas, pitching and rolling in their light condition, their plight only marginally better than the sopping misery of the smaller escorts, the little corvettes and the *Salamander*, whose entire superstructures were swept intermittently by green seas and continuously by spray which froze in the air and rattled with the force of buckshot on steel, splinter matting and the human faces exposed to it. Upper decks were lethal and ice-encrusted, though the westerly winds were warm, in so far as comparative temperatures in the Barents Sea in November could be so described.

German decrypts had alerted the enemy to the passage of QP15 and eight U-boats had been ordered to intercept east of Bear Island. Routed north of the island, an Admiralty signal flashed to Meek ordered the convoy diverted to the south to avoid the lurking wolfpack. Many of the merchantmen failed to receive this information while others did, and complied. Ironically, of these, two, the British steamer *Goolistan*, owned by Common Brothers of Newcastle, and the Russian freighter *Kuznetz Lesov* were lost on the 23rd. The British ship was torpedoed by Benker's *U625* with the loss of all forty-two hands; the Russian with similar losses by *U601* (Grau). The remaining merchant ships, one officer remembered, 'just plugged on in heavy seas, as one black day followed a blacker and more depressing night. In the end . . . we sighted Iceland.'

The convoy arrived in fragments, was rounded up and escorted onwards to Loch Ewe in two groups, the first reaching the shelter of the Scottish inlet on 30 November, the second on 3 December.

Although the weather had caused disruption to QP15, it had also restrained the enemy who, in the absence of aerial reconnaissance, were reluctant to sail the *Admiral Hipper* and her squadron. Just as the Allies benefited from the diversion of Luftwaffe squadrons to the Mediterranean, so the Germans had intended capitalizing on the reduced strength of the Home Fleet. But although the heavy cruiser might have sailed, the weather was thought too bad for destroyers and the operation was therefore cancelled. No such considerations were entertained by the Western Allies.

Although British destroyers were at sea, it was the Russians who were to prove the accuracy of the German assessment for, in addition to the *Kuznetz Lesov*, the Russians suffered further frightful losses.

On 20 December 1942, QP15 had been approaching 30°E, the meridian at which Russian support terminated, when the first gale overwhelmed and scattered the convoy. The destroyers *Baku* and *Sokrushitelni* detached and turned back for their base in mountainous seas which ranged up on their starboard quarters. Rolling and scending, the low after decks of their slender hulls were continuously swept by seas, setting up tortuous stresses which began to split welds. The *Baku* developed serious leaks in her bow and boiler room, while heavy seas falling aboard actually washed away parts of her superstructure. The Soviet destroyer struggled gallantly south as the cracks in her shell-plating worsened, and finally reached the Kola Inlet without loss.

The *Sokrushitelni* was not so fortunate. As she turned and ran before the gale she was pooped by a heavy sea. Hundreds of tons of water broke over her iron deck and poured below, loading the hull with innumerable stresses and deluging the engine and boiler rooms so that she soon lost power and wallowed vulnerably in the heavy sea now running dangerously high. With *Baku* disabled and engaged in saving herself, Admiral Golovko dispatched the *Kuibishev*, *Razumny* and *Uritski* to her assistance. For two days the Soviet destroyer languished, her hull gradually twisting itself in two; then, on the 22nd, the stern tore away and both halves of the *Sokrushitelni* began to founder. In atrocious conditions the three destroyers sent to help succeeded in rescuing 187 men from the sinking wreckage.

Thus ended the last of the PQ–QP series of convoys. Far from depriving the Red Army of its muscle, as the young Luftwaffe pilots had confidently hoped, PQ18 like the majority of its forebears was to help it to counter-attack the Wehrmacht. In the coming winter of 1942/3 the Russians were to annihilate von Paulus's Sixth Army at Stalingrad and to regain the ground lost to the Germans during their offensive of the late summer.

The last convoys of 1942 were, for security reasons, to be designated JW51 and RA51. As Captain Williams and his surviving crew languished on Spitzbergen, the Kriegsmarine prepared to play its feared card and assault a convoy in the Barents Sea with heavy surface forces. This was to bring on a battle far less bloody than that for Stalingrad, but one of decisive importance in the maritime campaign being fought for command of the Arctic Ocean.

17

'Only destroyers'

WHILE QP15 BATTERED its way westwards, Grossadmiral Erich Raeder conferred with his Führer. As ever, Hitler was obsessed with the possibility of an Allied invasion of Norway under cover of the wintry gloom which robbed him of his long-range aerial 'eyes'. He therefore instructed his naval chief to maintain not less than twenty-three operational U-boats in the Arctic Ocean to guard against this and to keep up the pressure on the Allied convoys in the wake of the withdrawal of the Luftwaffe squadrons. Fearing incursions from Iceland, he further ordered an appreciation drawn up for a German invasion of the island using specially built transport submarines! This fantastical scheme was countered by Raeder's sober report of the propulsion problems of the *Tirpitz*, and the continuing shortage of boiler oil. The *Panzerschiff Lützow* and the cruiser *Prinz Eugen* were ready for transfer from the Baltic to Narvik, but in view of available fuel reserves only the *Lützow* was ordered north.

Meanwhile discussions had been taking place between Admiral Tovey and the Admiralty. By mid-December 1942 the fighting in North Africa had established Allied superiority, and units of the Royal Navy's Home Fleet were returning to Scapa Flow. The Battle of the Atlantic was approaching its crisis and, most significantly, the Red Army was poised for a winter offensive which would relieve Stalingrad and result in the surrender of Feld-Marschal von Paulus and 300,000 men of the Wehrmacht. It was time for the Arctic convoys to resume and take advantage of the remaining months of the polar winter.

Admiral Tovey recommended small, lightly escorted convoys.

He was overruled by London which insisted on large convoys covered by cruisers. These, again contrary to the Commander-in-Chief's advice and on the express insistence of the First Sea Lord, were to maintain contact with the convoys until well to the eastward. Admiral Tovey's opinion did win a compromise, however, which proved successful. The experience of PQ17 and Operation FB had clearly shown the extreme vulnerability of single merchant ships or small groups to U-boat attack, while that of QP15 had demonstrated the difficulties inherent in herding a large convoy through the gloom and bad weather to be expected in the Arctic winter. PQ19 therefore fragmented into two parts, which sailed as convoys JW51A and JW51B.

The first of these left from the new assembly point of Loch Ewe on 15 December 1942 under a retired rear-admiral, C.E. Turle, sailing as Commodore in the SS *Briarwood*. It consisted of sixteen ships, including the oiler *Oligarch* which carried fuel for the escorts and a part cargo for Russia. Significantly, there was no rescue ship attached to JW51A.[1]

The close escort comprised the corvettes *Oxlip* and *Honeysuckle*, the minesweeper *Seagull* and the anti-submarine trawlers *Lady Madeleine* and *Northern Wave*. The Hunts *Blankney*, *Chiddingfold* and *Ledbury* accompanied the convoy until breaking away on the 18th off Iceland, when the fighting destroyer escort (FDE) under Scott-Moncrieff in *Faulknor* joined from Seidisfiord in company with *Boadicea*, *Echo*, *Eclipse*, *Fury* and *Inglefield*. The Home Fleet provided the usual heavy distant cover with Tovey's flag in *King George V* (Captain P.J. Mack), supported by the cruiser *Berwick* and the destroyers *Quadrant*, *Raider* and *Musketeer*.

Cruiser support was given by Rear-Admiral Burnett in *Sheffield* (Captain A.W. Clarke) and *Jamaica*, screened by *Beagle*, *Matchless* and *Opportune*. Burnett's squadron was known as Force R and remained west of the convoy until it passed Bear Island, then closed JW51A to refuel the destroyers from *Oligarch* and transfer them to the FDE, whereupon *Sheffield* and *Jamaica* stood on to the south and east, arriving in the Kola Inlet a day ahead of the convoy which came in safely on Christmas Day. On arrival the destroyers and the oiler *Oligarch* prepared to return as escort to the westbound RA51 due to depart five days later. There was an air attack on Christmas Eve, but the expected naval sortie failed to materialize. *Tirpitz*, *Lützow*, *Hipper*,

Köln and *Nürnberg* were known to be in northern waters, though not all were operational.

Convoy JW51B sailed from Loch Ewe on 22 December, seven days after its predecessor, with the same three Hunts as for JW51A. These left off Iceland. The close escort was commanded from Loch Ewe by Commander H.T. Rust in the minesweeper *Bramble*, supported by the corvettes *Hyderabad* and *Rhododendron*, and the trawlers *Vizalma* and *Northern Gem*.

The commander of the destroyer escort, Captain R. St. V. Sherbrooke, who had recently relieved Captain Armstrong in *Onslow*, attended the pre-sailing conference at Loch Ewe while the remainder of his detachment of the 17th Destroyer Flotilla proceeded from Scapa Flow to oil at Seidisfiord. In addition to the 'O' class ships, he also had under his command the elderly *Achates* and *Bulldog* which joined at Seidisfiord from Greenock.

Prior to departure, the contrast between Sherbrooke, a tall, handsome and austere man, and the extrovert 'Beaky' Armstrong had impressed the former's juniors. His orders were spare and, as befitted an officer named after Earl St Vincent, a model of brevity. Sherbrooke anticipated surface attack and, in the event of this occurring, ordered his own flotilla, the 17th, to form immediate line ahead on the threatened side, while *Achates* and *Bulldog* were to lay smoke between the enemy and the convoy. The merchant ships meanwhile were to turn away from the enemy and thereafter adjust their course to keep the enemy astern, with *Bramble*, the corvettes and the trawlers reforming a close escort.

This plan was also explained to the merchant masters before *Onslow* left to make a fast solo passage to refuel at Seidisfiord. *Onslow*, and *Achates* and *Bulldog* coming up astern, made heavy weather of the passage in a Force 10 storm. Both the older ships were damaged, the *Bulldog* so badly that she was forced to turn back while *Achates* effected repairs to her rigging in Iceland. The other destroyers of the 17th Flotilla anchored in the fiord had a bad time of it too, snubbing at their cables in an anchorage renowned for its poor holding ground and sudden, violent katabatic squalls.

Meanwhile, the convoy wallowed its way northwards in the storm with 'pouring rain and the wind dead astern', according to the Commodore's yeoman aboard *Empire Archer*, 'which blew the thick black funnel smoke all over the bridge and made us all look like chimney sweeps'.

JW51B was located by German air reconnaissance on Christmas Eve and then shadowed by Kapitänleutnant Herbschleb in *U354*. As the wind dropped, so did the temperature. The Arctic night, reported Herbschleb, brought 'a bright yellow moon which showed up the ships of the convoy'. On Christmas Day 1942, Sherbrooke's six destroyers, *Onslow, Obedient, Obdurate, Oribi, Orwell* and *Achates*, joined at the rendezvous 150 miles east of Iceland and Sherbrooke relieved Rust as senior officer. He also retained the three Hunts to round up stragglers, conserving the fuel of his fleet destroyers.

In the light of subsequent events, Sherbrooke's dispositions are of some importance: at the conclusion of the day the convoy was closed up in four columns with the *Onslow* ahead of Commodore Melhuish, whose pendant flew in the *Empire Archer*; *Orwell* and *Oribi* formed the port flank screen, *Obedient* and *Obdurate* the starboard; *Achates, Rhododendron, Northern Gem* and *Vizalma* brought up the rear as both anti-submarine cover and rescue ships; and *Bramble* and *Hyderabad*, both of which possessed good radar sets, were sent ahead on either bow as pickets. During the day a long-range Liberator and a Catalina overflew the convoy and Sherbrooke was able to pass his position to London without breaking radio silence.[2]

Two other forces were to sail in support of JW51B. Force R, Burnett's cruisers *Sheffield* and *Jamaica* with *Matchless* and *Opportune*, left Kola on the 27th, while Vice-Admiral Sir Bruce Fraser (VA2) in the battleship *Anson*, with the cruiser *Cumberland* and the destroyers *Forester, Icarus* and *Impulsive*, plus the Hunts *Blankney* and *Chiddingfold* which had brought JW51B from Loch Ewe, sailed from Akureyri.

Unaware of the presence of Herbschleb's U-boat, JW51B passed Jan Mayen and was half-way to Bear Island when the next depression caught up with the convoy. Storm-force north-westerly winds drove a heavy sea upon the ships' port beams, causing them to roll. Curtains of rain and snow swept from horizon to horizon, cutting visibility to nil. Ice formed on decks and upper-works, the gloom of the Arctic winter depressing the parties sent to clear it. Below, the customary ingress of water in the escorts slopped about the messdecks churning up a soup of odds and ends, items of clothing and broken crockery, while the bulkheads and deckheads streamed with condensation. Mephitic air and the violent motion combined to add vomit to the mess. Len Matthews, Commodore's yeoman in the comparative comfort of the *Empire Archer*, recorded the merchant ship's 'water pipes frozen. Unable to wash, unable to sleep, unable to keep warm. Inside bulkheads covered with ice.'

With their excessive deck cargoes the merchant ships were rolling almost as violently as the destroyers. In every wheelhouse, helmsmen fought to keep their charges within 20° of the course. On the open bridges, lookouts tried to focus their eyes on their adjacent consorts and avoid the affliction of snow blindness which almost closed the eyes due to swelling in the frozen facial tissues.

In the confusion, *Oribi*'s gyro compass and radar failed and she lost touch with the convoy. Magnetic compasses being notoriously inaccurate in such high latitudes, Commander McBeath, after vainly casting about for the convoy, was driven to the desperate expedient of steaming south until he had located land and then coasting east along the Norwegian and Murman littoral until, on 31 December, he entered the Kola Inlet. *Oribi*'s separation deprived Sherbrooke of his only other ship armed, as was *Onslow*, with 4.7-inch guns; the remaining 'O boats' mounted the older, vintage 4-inch type. In addition to *Oribi*, five merchant ships also from the port side of JW51B lost touch, as did the *Vizalma*, which had been assiduously keeping station on one of them. The American *Jefferson Myers* had hove to in order to secure her deck cargo of bombers which was threatening to break loose from its lashings. That of the *Daldorch* did break loose and her master also hove to, thereby probably misleading the remainder of the port column including the *Calobre* and *Chester Valley* which the hapless trawler had been following.

As the light improved and a slight moderation in the weather enabled Sherbrooke to re-form his remaining nine ships, he dispatched Rust to search for the stragglers, using *Bramble*'s superior radar. It was the last the British were to see of this little ship.

Evening passed into 'a night as black as a lion's throat'. A near collision between *Onslow* and *Orwell* gave Sherbrooke what he later considered to be the worst moment in his life, deprived as he was of *Oribi* and *Bulldog*. With hindsight he realized that the loss of either his own ship or Austen's *Orwell* would have resulted in disaster.

On the 29th, with JW51B 150 miles south-west of Bear Island

and well astern of her dead reckoning, three of the missing merchantmen returned to the fold, leaving *Vizalma* and *Chester Valley* in company to the north of the convoy and *Bramble* still searching for the fifth, the *Jefferson Myers*.

Burnett's cruisers had left Kola on the 27th and steamed west as far as the 11th meridian, overlapping the north-east extremity of the battle-fleet's patrol line and only about thirty miles from JW51B at noon on the 29th. Force R then swung to the eastwards, running ahead of the convoy to reach the meridian of Kola at 18.00 on the 30th, when JW51B was some ninety miles south-east of Bear Island. Burnett then turned north-west again, intending to cross the convoy route and take station parallel to, and fifty miles north of JW51B, but fifty miles astern, thus keeping his vulnerable cruisers clear of any shadowing U-boats, though poised to intervene if needed. His reason for going north of the convoy route rather than remaining south, and thus closer to the likely threat, was to avoid aerial detection and keep the advantage of the gloom. Throughout this period Burnett had no actual verification of the convoy's position.[3]

That morning Herbschleb, still in contact despite the weather, had transmitted to Dönitz at L'Orient, repeated to Narvik, the intelligence that the convoy was 'weakly escorted', giving its position and the misinformation that as well as destroyers a light cruiser was in attendance. *U354* then worked ahead of the convoy and was preparing to make a torpedo attack when she was picked up on *Obdurate*'s asdic. Lieutenant-Commander Sclater, sighting the U-boat surfaced in the dark, ran in to ram her. The U-boat dived and avoided collision.

Sending *Obedient* to Sclater's support, Sherbrooke filled the gap in the screen with his own ship and left the two destroyers to their hunt. After the alloted two hours, Kinloch of the *Obedient* signalled their lack of success and the two ships returned to their stations.

Relieved, Herbschleb surfaced and signalled his escape and the convoy details, adding: 'Weather very good and I am pursuing.' By now he was no longer alone.

Operation Regenbogen, or Operation Rainbow, was contingent upon the conditions Herbschleb reported. Despite their success against Operation FB, the hiatus in the Arctic convoys had sorely tried the Germans' patience. The patrolling U-boat crews, in particular, endured conditions as dreadful as those aboard the smaller Allied escorts, while the frustrated officers aboard the heavy ships and destroyers, the 'chained dogs' of the fiords, chafed to emulate the success of operations against PQ17 and PQ18.

Following Raeder's conference with Hitler of 19 November, *Lützow* (Kapitän Stange) was now in Altenfiord and had joined Vizeadmiral Kummetz in *Hipper* (Kapitän Hartmann), whose orders to destroy the convoy only awaited some favourable spur such as Herbschleb now provided. Kummetz was, of course, to avoid action with superior forces and not waste time in rescues, but he was also to attempt the capture of a few officers and a ship if possible. On completion, *Lützow* was to implement Operation Aurora, a break-out into the Atlantic.

At 18.00 on the 30th *Hipper* and *Lützow*, escorted by the destroyers *Friedrich Eckholdt*, *Richard Beitzen*, *Theodor Riedel*, *Z29*, *Z30* and *Z31*, slipped through the Leads, avoided the cordon of Allied submarines and put to sea, heading north-east. Almost immediately Kummetz received a signal from Vizeadmiral Klüber at Narvik which further enjoined him to exercise restraint if he confronted an enemy of comparable strength, since it was not thought desirable to submit the heavy ships to excessive risk.[4]

Once again, a German admiral had been constrained by his superiors ashore. At midnight Kummetz received a further update from Herbschleb and the news that *U626* had joined *U354*. He also learned that two British cruisers had left Kola on the 27th.

Operation Regenbogen had been carefully prepared and depended on the hours of twilight around noon, for German gunnery still relied upon optical control. It was mid-winter and on the parallel of latitude along which JW51B was approximately steering, 73°N, the sun never rose within the limits of 'civil twilight' (when a newspaper might be read); but, from about 08.00 to 15.00, it was less than 12° below the horizon and produced that condition known astronomically as 'nautical twilight'.

Kummetz intended to divide his force and attack from two sides. *Hipper* therefore steered to work north of the convoy, *Lützow* to the south. The heavy ships opened out to seventy-five miles with the destroyers deployed between them on a wide front in line abreast. As the attack developed they would split into two groups to support the cruiser and pocket-battleship. It was an excellent plan and, given Sherbrooke's scheme of defence and his power, one that was set fair to succeed; Kummetz's only real worry was the torpedoes of the British destroyers but, with the calmer weather, his own light forces ought to be able to out-gun their enemy.

With the fate of von Paulus's Sixth Army in the balance before Stalingrad, the obligation laid upon Kummetz was to do his utmost. The previous afternoon Raeder had signalled Vizeadmiral Kranke, his liaison officer at headquarters, that he had given Kummetz orders to execute an attack on an eastbound convoy. Hitler gave his approval and said he wished to be kept fully informed.

Kummetz divided his force at 02.30, maintaining contact by short-wave radio. At 07.15 the *Hipper*'s lookouts spotted the convoy and the heavy cruiser slowed and even turned west for a while to avoid betraying her presence until the light improved, leaving the *Friedrich Eckholdt*, *Richard Beitzen* and *Z29* to keep in touch while the other destroyers closed up on the *Lützow*. As the darkness of the night imperceptibly gave way to a crepuscular murk, Kummetz had every reason to be satisfied.

The Arctic dawn broke to a freezing morning with a heavy frost and all the ships covered with a thick mantle of ice. The wind had dropped and the sea state had moderated, leaving a heavy residual swell. Both the icing and the swell were to hamper the operations of the destroyers. Except where snow squalls shut it in, visibility was quite good, up to ten miles to the south, less to the north where, forty-five miles away from the cluster of JW51B, *Vizalma* and *Chester Valley* steamed east. Burnett's cruisers lay between these two stragglers and the convoy, thirty miles north of JW51B. Somewhere about a dozen miles north-east, *Bramble* was still searching for the straggling *Jefferson Myers*. She, however, was miles away. None of these groups was precisely certain of the position of the others, all being beyond radar range.

At about 08.30 on New Year's Eve, the German destroyers led by the *Friedrich Eckholdt* (Bachmann) held the key to the coming events, for they were in touch with JW51B, whose escorts were unaware of their presence. Curiously, they were to play almost no part in the battle. At this time *Hipper* was about twenty miles north-west of the convoy, still heading west under easy revolutions. *Lützow* was some fifty miles south-east and beginning to close.

At 08.20 *Hyderabad*'s radar picked up a suspicious echo astern, thought at first to be the missing straggler and then Russian destroyers coming to reinforce the escort. This false assumption resulted in no report being made, but *Obdurate*'s lookouts now saw first two, then three, enemy destroyers and alerted *Onslow*. Sherbrooke ordered Sclater to investigate and, as *Obdurate* swung round from her station on the starboard after flank of the convoy, the enemy turned away to the north-west, falling back towards *Hipper*. At 09.30, at a range of 4.5 miles, they opened fire on the inquisitive *Obdurate*. Sclater immediately reversed course as Sherbrooke, seeing the distant gun-flashes in the gloom, turned *Onslow* west and called up *Orwell*, *Obedient* and *Obdurate* to join him. *Achates* and the other escorts were ordered to make smoke across the rear of the convoy in accordance with Sherbrooke's battle-plan.

A moment or two later Kummetz ordered the *Theodor Riedel*, *Z30* and *Z31* to join *Lützow*, and the *Hipper* to turn east and rejoin her destroyers prior to making a descent on the convoy. As the heavy cruiser swung round she betrayed her identification in silhouette to Sherbrooke, now intently studying his enemy as *Onslow* raced back through the convoy, burying her bow in the swell as she drove along, her forward guns' crews fighting to keep the ice off their weapons.

Kapitän Hartmann held his fire, thinking the approaching destroyers might be his own, until *Achates* began to lay smoke. At 09.40 Kummetz signalled Narvik that he was engaging the convoy and *Hipper*'s guns fired at *Achates*, but to no effect.

Simultaneously Sherbrooke broke silence to report the presence of the enemy and alert Burnett. *Onslow*, with *Obedient* astern, returned radar-controlled fire at a range of six miles, and swung to run parallel to the *Hipper* as she edged north, drawing her three destroyers about her. This surprising reaction persuaded Sherbrooke that Kummetz feared his ships' torpedoes, an accurate perception that was skilfully exploited as the two sides skirmished in the semi-darkness to the north-west of the convoy. Intermittent smoke was emitted by *Hipper* and snow squalls further confused the situation.

At about 10.00, seeing Sherbrooke's destroyers between his charges and the enemy, with *Achates*, *Rhododendron* and *Northern Gem* spewing smoke across his wake, Commodore Melhuish turned JW51B south-east. By this time *Obedient* had worked round to join Sherbrooke and *Obdurate* was coming up fast from the west. Uncertain of the position of the *Friedrich Eckholdt*, *Richard Beitzen* and *Z29* which had already joined Kummetz, Sherbrooke retained *Orwell* in support and sent *Obdurate* and *Obedient* (Kinloch) back to cover the convoy. As they did so they too joined the smoke-laying operation.

So far Sherbrooke's tactics had proved both effective and, by their very simplicity, adaptable in the detachment of Sclater and Kinloch. As Sherbrooke and his flotilla staff officer, Lieutenant-Commander Tom Marchant, watched their two sisters belching smoke, they learned 'with acclamation' that Rear-Admiral Burnett's Force R was approaching from the north. To their joy, *Hipper* altered course to the north, and thus towards the approaching Burnett.

For his part, Burnett, erroneously believing the convoy was north of him, had began to steam away at 08.30, misled by radar contacts to the north-north-west. However, these were identified as Lieutenant Anglebeck's *Vizalma* and *Chester Valley*, and the cruisers swung back south-east a few minutes after 09.00. Twenty minutes later Burnett's lookouts spotted the dull flashes of gunfire to the south, though the Rear-Admiral delayed before closing, a hesitation possibly excused by the slowness of human reactions in the Arctic, but also because his primary responsibility was to protect the convoy and he was still confused as to its position. Were the *Vizalma* and the *Chester Valley* a part of the convoy to the north and the gun-flashes an isolated engagement to the south? On the other hand, due to misplotting, the speed of the straggling ships had initially been thought to be high, suggesting they were far from plodding merchantmen. In the prevailing twilight, doubts clouded the Rear-Admiral's mind. Burnett can be forgiven his hesitation; he had the spectre of Hamilton's alleged 'misjudgement' to compound his worries.

Shortly before 10.00 he formed his resolve: tardy or not, Force R now sped south, in time-honoured tradition: towards the sound of the guns.

So far, *Hipper*'s gunnery had been unimpressive, and Kummetz's tactic of drawing off the British destroyers had been foiled by Sherbrooke's counter-move in splitting his own force. What Sherbrooke did not know was that Kummetz was awaiting *Lützow* from the southward and that at this time, about 10.15, Stange's *Panzerschiff* with the *Theodor Riedel, Z30* and *Z31* were only about eight miles south of the convoy and on a collision course. As if divining this, for they could have had no accurate knowledge, Kummetz and Hartmann suddenly altered *Hipper*'s posture and she turned back to engage *Onslow* and *Orwell*. The German cruiser soon found the *Onslow*'s range and four heavy-calibre shells hit her, disabling A- and B-guns and wrecking the bridge, the main aerials and both radar scanners. The funnel was split apart and the engine room holed. Fires were started in the forward superstructure and messdecks below; the torpedomen's mess was flooding fast and the carnage was considerable. Forty men were dead or wounded; Petty Officer Cook, mortally wounded with both legs blown off, dragged himself along an alleyway complaining they would only give him 'bloody aspirins' in the sick bay and that he would rather have his daily ration of rum.

Sherbrooke himself had been severely wounded in the face where shrapnel had dislodged his left eye, but he remained on the bridge while his ship's company fought the fires and plugged shot holes. Bereft of his means of communication and losing speed, Sherbrooke handed over command of the flotilla to Lieutenant-Commander Kinloch in *Obedient* who, by an irony, was promoted Commander on that very day.

Austen in *Orwell* led the *Onslow* south and made smoke to add to that from the wounded ship's fires. Shells rained about both destroyers, then a snow squall masked the *Hipper* and she swung away. Meanwhile, aboard *Onslow*, Sherbrooke had turned the ship over to Marchant and was taken below by Surgeon-Lieutenant Holland.

A brief hiatus now ensued as *Hipper* and Force R unwittingly drew closer. The British cruisers were steaming south at 31 knots.

Onslow, now capable of making 20 knots, closed the convoy, on the port quarter of which lay *Achates* still making smoke and on *her* port quarter lay *Orwell, Obdurate* and *Obedient*. At this point *Rhododendron*, also astern of the convoy, reported smoke coming from a large vessel heading north-east and seen beyond the mass of the convoy, a report that Kinloch doubted, being unconfirmed by nearer vessels. He continued to maintain his station between *Hipper*'s last known position and the convoy, while covering *Onslow*'s retirement. The large vessel was, in fact,

Lützow, accompanied by her destroyers. *Hyderabad* also seems to have spotted the *Panzerschiff* and her screen less than two miles away, but this went unreported. Stange's detachment cut across the head of the convoy, but such was the visibility in a sudden snow squall that he stood on and awaited an improvement, thus discarding the advantage of complete surprise.

Hyderabad also received a signal from *Bramble*, coming in from the east. Commander Rust reported a cruiser ahead of him. It was *Hipper* turning north and she opened fire on the small minesweeper, her guns stabbing the gloom with savage brilliance. Leaving the *Friedrich Eckholdt* to administer the *coup de grâce* to the hapless *Bramble*, Kummetz now swung *Hipper* south again, intending to re-engage the British destroyers stationed on the port flank of JW51B.

At 11.00 *Obedient* reported a cruiser to the east and Kinloch led round towards her and made smoke. The enemy, which was in fact *Lützow*, appeared to open fire, but no fall of shot was observed. The flashes came from *Hipper* lying on the same line of bearing but beyond the *Lützow* and firing to the eastward. Her target may have been either the unfortunate *Bramble* trying to escape south, for her precise fate is unknown, or the *Friedrich Eckholdt* returning from sinking the minesweeper and wrongly identified in the gloom. Whatever the truth, Stange's missed opportunity had lost the advantage of a pincer attack and resulted in both groups of German ships being on the same, eastern, side of the convoy. They were there, however, in overwhelming force.

As *Lützow* continued south-east and opened up the bearing, she exposed the advancing *Hipper* which now shifted target to *Achates*. Apart from making smoke, the destroyer's crew had continued the standard routines of ice chipping and training tubes and turrets every fifteen minutes to avoid them freezing up. At 11.15 the *Achates* was clearing her own smoke-screen in order to join *Onslow* with the convoy as Kinloch had ordered. A few minutes later she received shell hits forward which destroyed the bridge and killed B-gun's crew. The ammunition lockers also exploded and rendered B-gun useless. Men aft recalled that a fire seemed to be raging forward of the bridge as they were fallen out from their action stations to help with the removal of the wounded and damage control.

Achates's young captain, Lieutenant-Commander A.H.T.

Johns, was killed with forty of his ship's company and the command devolved upon Lieutenant Peyton-Jones. Aware that he could not fulfil his orders, Peyton-Jones disregarded them and continued to make smoke, despite another shell having entered the boiler room, for almost miraculously, the little ship 'still had plenty of way on'.

Repair parties were hard at work plugging leaks and getting emergency lighting rigged when the ship began to list to port. High-explosive shells now burst above *Achates* and shrapnel rained down on the decks, driving many of the men under cover, filling both whalers full of holes and increasing the tasks of the first-aid parties. 'One rating', George Barker recalled, 'had a piece of [shrapnel] sticking out of his head.' Then a shell came through the ship's side and exploded in the transmitting station. 'One chap . . . said he couldn't move his legs. He lost consciousness and died as we were getting him free from the debris and we saw that both his legs had been taken off. It was a shambles, with bits of bodies all over the place. If the ship hadn't sunk we would have had to hose it all away . . .'

As *Hipper* shelled *Achates*, Kinloch led his three destroyers towards her. JW51B, which had swung back towards a more easterly course at 10.51 as, unbeknown to it, *Lützow* crossed close ahead, now resumed a southerly course and a little later swung south-west as the action developed astern. Kinloch therefore kept his trio of ships between the convoy and *Hipper*. The German cruiser now opened fire on *Obedient* and turned north-west, again intimidated by the British torpedoes. Kinloch followed, maintaining his threat on a parallel course. At about 11.30, having been straddled and with *Obedient*'s aerials shot away, the three destroyers ran back across the stern of the convoy, for reasons shortly to become clear, and afterwards resumed a heading of north-west.

Attempts to save the elderly *Achates* were in vain. She was fast losing steam and was settling by the head, with the deck canted steeply to port. Finally she slowed to a stop. Peyton-Jones called for immediate assistance. As the order to abandon ship was passed, so were some 'liberated' bottles of wardroom whisky.

The *Northern Gem* had been ordered to tow her and the trawlermen had hardly ranged their wire on deck than the word came down from Lieutenant Aisthorpe to abandon the task: the destroyer was sinking.[5]

As *Northern Gem* drew alongside, *Achates* fell over on her side. Men, some in lifejackets, walked down her starboard plating as it came horizontal; then she capsized, her torpedo mounting 'just dropped off with a terrific splash' and she wallowed bottom up, her crew either on her upturned hull, scrambling aboard Carley floats or in the sea. A moment later, 'the screws came out of the water, went up in the air . . . until the ship was absolutely upright in the water – and then she was gone'.

Swimmers and paddlers made for the *Northern Gem*. As the trawlermen flung scrambling nets over the side they heard the fortified survivors in the Carley rafts singing 'Roll out the barrel!' Others, struggling in the icy water, made desperately for the nets hanging from the *Northern Gem*.

'I was so numb,' remembered George Charlton:

> I waited for the swell to take me up the net and then I just [pushed] my arms and legs through the mesh and I was left hanging there until two ratings came down over the side and pulled me aboard, with a third helping me up by the hair . . . I flopped on the deck . . . and then the numbness started wearing off and the cold hit me. I have never before or since felt anything like the pain that wracked my body . . .

The trawler's deckhands, descending the nets to help, 'could only stand it for three or four minutes', entwining their legs in the rope to leave hands free and being completely immersed as the trawler rolled. Barker found that

> the hands couldn't do what the brain told them to do . . . Some of the wounded had managed to get to the *Gem*'s side and we tried to get them up first but after a while it was each man for himself. I had a line thrown over me and thankfully didn't do anything other than take two turns round my forearm and stick the end in my mouth . . . I was twenty-two at the time.

In the *Northern Gem*'s boiler-warmed belly, a 40-year-old Ordinary Seaman named Eric Mayer moved among the wounded, doing what he could. 'All the *Gem*'s crew were heroes,' a survivor stated. Mayer was no exception. His medical knowledge was largely derived from being married to a nurse and counting a few doctors among his peacetime friends. He did his best, but it was clear Aisthorpe needed more experienced assistance.

Barker, Charlton and their shipmates had hardly been taken below when a terrific explosion shook the *Northern Gem* as the sinking destroyer's depth-charges detonated below the trawler. Shortly afterwards she increased speed and headed back towards the convoy. It was almost dark, but as the *Gem*'s crew passed the shattered *Onslow* they could see her forecastle party toiling to rig a heavy collision mat over the bow to contain a leak.

At this point in the action Stange finally brought *Lützow* on a westward heading. Then Burnett swept out of the north on the wings of Nemesis. Forewarned by radar, lookouts aboard *Sheffield* saw *Hipper* seven miles away as she swung broadside on to her north-westerly course. Burnett altered his own course and, under starboard helm, *Sheffield* led *Jamaica* round parallel and opened fire, with her consort's forward turrets in support. The British cruisers shot off four salvoes before *Hipper* responded, made smoke and turned to starboard in a round turn which culminated in her making off to the south-west. She had been badly hit and her speed was consequently reduced to 28 knots.

Taken completely by surprise by the British flashless cordite, Kummetz was caught between Kinloch's torpedo-bearing destroyers and this unknown enemy. He had just identified the position of the *Lützow* and discovered her to be on the same side of the convoy as himself; after a propitious start, his plan was ruined. At 11.37 he ordered the action broken off and all units to retire west.

The British ships had conformed to the German cruiser's round turn, but found their target briefly obscured by her own smoke. Two German destroyers then appeared in the confusion, one of them the *Friedrich Eckholdt* trying to rejoin the Admiral and mistaking *Sheffield* for *Hipper*. The British cruiser swung towards her, intending at first to ram, an order which was 'thankfully quickly cancelled', one of A-gun's crew remembered, for few of the ratings in A-turret knew what was expected of them or 'what the consequences might have been'.

Disdaining the *Friedrich Eckholdt*'s torpedo potential, *Sheffield* swept past her at point-blank range, the full-calibre guns depressed at an elevation never previously attempted, firing into the enemy destroyer with 'all guns down to pom-poms' and destroying her in minutes.[6]

Jamaica meanwhile drove off the second destroyer, the *Richard Beitzen*, but refrained from firing into the blazing shambles of the *Friedrich Eckholdt* as Captain Storey followed Burnett's flag.

While Kummetz ordered the action broken off and headed west, some five miles to the south-east, the *Lützow*'s twin triple 11-inch turrets swung menacingly round on her port beam and she finally fired at the convoy. At 11.42, shell splinters struck the American freighter *Calobre* eight miles away, but no one was hurt.

Fearing worse, Melhuish brought JW51B on to a south-south-westerly course. One of the destroyers accompanying the *Lützow* also fired, but to even less effect. It was at this point that *Obedient*, *Obdurate* and *Orwell* quartered the rear of the convoy and made smoke before heading north-west again as the dim shapes of the German ships headed in that direction. The British destroyers were now under Sclater's command since the loss of *Obedient*'s aerials.

Deprived of a target by the smoke, the pocket-battleship ceased fire, but shortly before noon, despite Kummetz repeating his signal to retire at 11.48, the *Lützow* opened up again on *Obdurate* at the head of the British line. The destroyers returned fire, but at 12.02 they broke off the action as *Obdurate* suffered a near miss, and the German ships thereafter drew away from the convoy. Sclater led the destroyers south in search of it. It was only 12.40, but already the dim light was waning.

As the German ships withdrew, Force R followed, catching a brief sight of *Hipper*, distant some twelve miles. At 12.23 two enemy destroyers were seen broadside on five miles away and in a good position for launching torpedoes. Burnett altered course towards them and prepared to open fire just as a larger ship, the *Lützow*, loomed up beyond them, upon which the cruisers shifted target and engaged. *Lützow* and then *Hipper* returned shots, the fire of the former falling short but that of the latter very accurate. Burnett altered course to stop Kummetz working round on the other bow and dividing his own force. The Germans continued to withdraw to the westward at 28 knots, fire ceased at 12.36 and the British radar operators tracked them until 14.00 when contact was lost. These men had been working their primitive equipment in exposed positions for several hours and were exhausted. They could not be relieved by *Jamaica*'s sets because the blast from the cruiser's own guns had shattered them.

Believing, quite erroneously, that the cruiser *Nürnberg*, which was known to have been in the Altenfiord with the other heavy units, was in the vicinity, Burnett now cruised to the south, still uncertain of the exact whereabouts of the convoy.

Aboard the German ships the sense of having been outclassed prevailed. Although the intervention of the British cruisers had been timely, it was the constant threat of the British destroyers' torpedoes, which never actually materialized, which had decisively robbed the Germans of the advantage they had possessed. They retired to Altenfiord demoralized. 'As we withdrew,' the *Lützow*'s War Diary recorded, 'the unsatisfactory feeling reigned that in spite of the general position, which was favourable at first, we had not succeeded in scoring any successes . . . The sad truth remains that the *Friedrich Eckholdt* was lost.'

The convoy proceeded unmolested. While the warships had fought off the enemy, Melhuish had handled his own command with coolness and initiative, helped in part by its reduced size. The irreproachable conduct of JW51B, composed largely of American ships, was in marked contrast to the indiscipline of earlier convoys. Commodore Melhuish, aboard *Empire Archer*, had used strings of coloured lights to signal his intended manœuvres, the convoy executing the order when the streamers were extinguished. He had also had more personal problems; at the beginning of the action he had dropped his glasses and trodden on them, thereafter relying on the reports of his yeoman, Matthews. In addition, on the 29th, a disturbance had broken out among the *Empire Archer*'s firemen after a group of them had broached a consignment of rum intended for the Kola-based minesweepers. In the ensuing violence two men were knifed. This fight occurred simultaneously with the threatened break adrift of a railway locomotive which, among a deck cargo of eight heavy tanks, had parted some of its lashings. The drunken firemen were suppressed by the ship's master, Captain Maughan, and his officers. Desperate for merchant seamen, the MOWT had inconsiderately offered a bonus of £100 to these ne'er-do-wells and recruited them from Scotland's notorious Barlinnie Gaol.

After an anxious night of uncertainty as to whether the German ships were still in the vicinity or not, New Year's Day found the convoy licking its wounds and enduring another gale. During the day Aisthorpe was ordered to attempt to transfer *Obdurate*'s doctor and, taking the helm himself, he worked *Northern Gem* skilfully up on the destroyer's port quarter in a rough sea. For a few moments the two ships ranged together, anxious parties watching and waiting their moment on both ships. Sclater kept his ship on a steady heading and, choosing his moment, Aisthorpe nudged the *Northern Gem* into the *Obdurate*'s side. Surgeon-Lieutenant Hood 'heaved his bag over and then jumped'. Within minutes, the diminutive messdeck was converted into an operating theatre, with Lieutenant Peyton-Jones acting as anaesthetist, both men literally braced in their positions by helpers in order to leave their hands free, so violent was the motion of the little ship. Hood was loud in his praise of Mayer.

On the afternoon of the 2nd the minesweepers *Harrier* and *Seagull* together with two Russian destroyers from Kola met the convoy. The former reinforced the escort and led the main body of JW51B into Kola where it arrived next day, though final berthing was further delayed by dense fog. The Commodore and the remainder, covered by the Soviet warships, pressed on to the White Sea, pushing through ice on the 6th and finally reaching Ekonomiya on the 7th.

Through the good offices of the female pilot who had assisted *Empire Archer* alongside, the services of a Russian army doctor were obtained for the injured firemen, one of whom had now developed pneumonia. By sledge and van, through deep snow, the Commodore's yeoman accompanied the casualty to a Red Army field hospital. 'At one point we had to wait . . . and I shall never forget seeing an army unit moving up to the line – like Napoleon's retreat from Moscow, led by a man on a poor old horse, a battalion of boys shuffling along with rags on their feet with snow six feet high on either side.' The fireman eventually recovered and Matthews was subsequently mentioned in dispatches.[7]

Thus ended 'The Battle of the Barents Sea', which had taken place in the vicinity of latitude 73° 30′N, longitude 030° 00′E, about 230 miles to the north-west of the Kola Inlet. It was not quite the end of convoy JW51B, for the *Jefferson Myers* was still at sea, having lost contact when she hove to.

This merchant ship had been attacked in a coastal convoy which lost five ships to E-boats as she made passage from London, where she had dry-docked, to Hull where she was to load. Proceeding then to Methil, she finally reached Loch Ewe. After her separation from JW51B she had secured her cargo and, when the weather abated, headed for Murmansk, seeing distant flashes to the north-east during the battle. On 2 January 1943 a plane circled her which, from its lack of aggression, the Master thought to be Russian. As it flew off to the south, he followed, being by now uncertain of his own position. Later, two more aircraft appeared, but before they pressed an attack a Russian destroyer arrived, opened fire on the aircraft and escorted the *Jefferson Myers* into the White Sea where she required the assistance of an ice-breaker before reaching Molotovsk on the 6th. She afterwards left for Murmansk.

Having seen off Kummetz's squadron, Force R turned south-east to cover JW51B until 03.00 on 1 January 1943. Burnett then turned north and west to catch up with and theoretically cover RA51, to the southward, though just how effective this was will be discussed later. By now short of fuel he ran on ahead, arriving at Seidisfiord on the 4th.

Convoy RA51 had sailed from Kola on 30 December and consisted of fourteen ships, five American, four British and five Russian under Commodore Turle in *Empire Scott*. Among the merchant ships was the tanker *Hopemount* finally returning from her long period in the Arctic. One Soviet ship, the *Okhta*, straggled and proceeded to Iceland alone, while the remainder arrived at Loch Ewe on 11 January. They were escorted by the destroyers *Faulknor* (Scott-Moncrieff), *Fury*, *Echo*, *Eclipse*, *Inglefield* and *Beagle*; the trawlers *Cape Argona*, *Cape Mariato*, *St Kenan* and *Daneman*; and the minesweeper *Gleaner*. Scott-Moncrieff's destroyers left off Iceland and were relieved by the Hunts *Blankney* and *Ledbury*, the fleet destroyer *Montrose* and the old LRE *Worcester*.

Burnett's cover of this convoy was purely notional, for in fact it passed well south of the usual track, being 150 miles south-east of the battle raging round JW51B. Afterwards, a witness aboard the tanker *Hopemount* recalled seeing the Norwegian coast, 'so close that I could see the white mountain tops'. The feeling of being decoys was inescapable. In fact, Hamilton in HMS *Kent*, with *Berwick* in support, had also been sent to cover RA51 while Tovey himself in *King George V*, with another battleship, a cruiser and six destroyers, had put to sea on the 31st. Their attempt to nail the German ships was in vain; *Hipper* and *Lützow* retreated to the Altenfiord, as we have seen, and *Nürnberg* had never sailed.

Only HM Submarine *Graph* sighted the beaten enemy which straggled into the shelter of the fiords on New Year's Day. Tovey and Hamilton's forces cruised east of Jan Mayen until noon of the 3rd and then headed for Scapa Flow. RA51 finally arrived at Loch Ewe on 11 January 1943.[8]

The following day in Russia the badly wounded Sherbrooke learned he had been awarded the Victoria Cross. Typically Sherbrooke wrote to his ship's company expressing his sentiment that it belonged to them all. Terribly mutilated, he was much later the recipient of plastic surgery.[9]

Others commended were the dead Johns, his first lieutenant, Peyton-Jones, and the ship's company of *Achates*. Skipper-Lieutenant Aisthorpe was praised for his 'courageous and seaman-like handling of the *Northern Gem*', which resulted in the rescue of eighty-one of the destroyer's crew.

In its summary of the action, the British Admiralty pointed out that although the initiative lay with the attacking enemy, it subsequently carried out this role defensively. Its destroyers hardly made any mark at all, whereas the British, whose task was wholly defensive, acted with aggressive tenacity. However, at no time did Sherbrooke and his successors forget their primary duty to defend the convoy.

The supremely gallant action of the destroyers did much to restore confidence in the Royal Navy among both American and British merchant seafarers. The loss of *Achates* was keenly felt by men who sailed under the red ensign, while that of *Bramble* was genuinely mourned, for she and her company had become well-known and much liked.[10]

In Germany a false impression of success had been created by a signal from the shadowing Herbschleb in *U354*. At 11.45 the watching U-boat commander had transmitted a signal that 'According to our observation the battle has reached its climax. I see nothing but red.'

This Wagnerian hyperbole was forwarded somewhat jubilantly by Klüber at Narvik to Hitler. The Führer thereafter waited impatiently for further news, confidently expecting to hear of a German victory. But Kummetz maintained strict radio silence during his retreat and Hitler waited in vain. He therefore first learned of the Barents Sea action from a report carried by the British Broadcasting Corporation and monitored in Germany. He was furious and broke into a towering rage.

Kummetz was also angry that his actions were to be judged against such an irresponsible and false assumption. Speaking on the telephone from his mooring at Altenfiord to Vizeadmiral Klüber at Narvik, Kummetz said, 'It takes a long time to overcome a well-disciplined close-range escorting force, even when they are only destroyers . . . it is seldom possible to reach the ships in convoy before having destroyed the close-escort force.'

Schniewind's appreciation pulled no punches, condemning the High Command's attempt to limit risk by shackling its commanders afloat and recommending its withdrawal. Raeder, summoned on New Year's Day to explain all, found the Führer's temper unabated and heard with horror Hitler's opinion that 'the ships are utterly useless . . . idly lying about and lacking any desire to get into action. This means the passing of the High Seas Fleet; it is now my irrevocable resolve [to remove the guns of the heavy ships for shore defence].' Appalled, a disillusioned Grossadmiral Raeder resigned. He was succeeded by Karl Dönitz.

As for the Kriegsmarine's heavy units, they were not scrapped nor were they disarmed, though the *Hipper* had fought her last action. Hitler's threat was never quite carried out, though it hung over the demoralized fleet, reducing them once again to the status of 'chained dogs'. Even under the submarine enthusiast Dönitz, however, the German navy was capable of one last action; and, for the Allies, it was still a fleet in being, poised to emerge again from its lair and maul an Arctic convoy with the mighty *Tirpitz* in its van.

18

'Dangerous work in hazardous circumstances'

CAPTAIN SHERBROOKE AND the other severely wounded men were rushed home aboard *Obdurate* and *Obedient*, leaving Kola on 11 January and arriving at Scapa Flow on the 15th. Two days later convoy JW52 sailed from Loch Ewe and was routed east of the Faeroe Islands. The corvettes *Lotus* and *Starwort*, the minesweeper *Britomart* and trawlers *Northern Pride* and *St Elstan* saw the convoy to its destination as 'through escort', with the Hunts *Ledbury*, *Blankney*, and *Middleton* forming the western local escort until the destroyers arrived. What had ceased to be called the FDE and had become known as the 'ocean escort' relieved the Hunts on the 21st to the east of Iceland. Led by Commander W.H. Selby in *Onslaught*, the supporting destroyers were *Offa*, *Matchless*, *Musketeer*, *Bulldog*, *Beagle* and the Polish *Piorun*. Rear-Admiral Hamilton flew his flag aboard *Kent* which, with *Bermuda* and *Glasgow*, provided cruiser cover from the 10th meridian east to Kola; British and Soviet submarines operated along the enemy coast and distant heavy cover was provided by Sir Bruce Fraser in *Anson*, one cruiser and nine destroyers.[1]

The convoy Commodore, aboard *Empire Clarion*, was a retired vice-admiral, Sir Malcolm Goldsmith. Once again, no rescue ship was available, operations in the North Atlantic demanding their presence elsewhere, but the *Oligarch* again supported the escorts with fuel and extra depth-charges. Four American, one Panamanian and eight other British ships, most of them by now veterans of the run, made up the convoy.[2]

The voyage was blessed with fair weather and made good time, so much so that the *Empire Baffin* and *Atlantic* failed to keep up and had to turn back. Enemy air reconnaissance spotted Fraser's ships and the convoy on the 23rd. As JW52 approached Bear Island the next day, four He115 torpedo-bombers of Küstenfliegergruppe 406 made an abortive attack, losing half their force to Allied gunfire. Dönitz's U-boats were less easy to drive off, but as they gathered round chattering on the surface they revealed their presence and position to the listening Huff-Duff operators. The convoy's size and the experience of its participants made a series of evasive alterations of course highly successful. These, combined with aggressive counter-attacking sallies by 'Bluenose Joe' Selby's destroyers, 'kept the enemies' heads down', though they confused Hamilton and his cruisers, who were never quite sure where the convoy was. On one occasion, thinking he was forty miles on the convoy's port bow, Hamilton found himself just twenty miles astern, 'in the hornet's nest which swarms [with U-boats] astern of any shadowed convoy and which is the obvious place to avoid'.

Outclassed by the destroyers, the U-boats failed to make any kills and JW52 arrived intact in the Kola Inlet on 27 January, the local eastern escort being provided by five Soviet destroyers.

One U-boat had been successful the previous day: Herbschleb in *U354* had torpedoed the Soviet steamer *Krasny Partizan* as she made a solo independent westward passage. A series of these had been ordered by the Russian authorities and, like Operation FB, they suffered heavily. While the *Bureya* and *Leonid Krasin* reached Iceland and the *Andre Marti* and *Mossovet* made Russia safely, Kapitänleutnant Reche in *U255* sank the Soviet ice-breaker *Malygin* on the day JW52 arrived off Kola, and the steamer *Ufa* two days later as she made a dash for Iceland.

Delays in discharging had prevented the sailing of RA52 under the cover of naval ships deployed for JW52, and even by the end of January only eleven merchant ships were ready to leave under Commodore Melhuish in *Daldorch*. These had an exceptionally large escort: all the destroyers which had just arrived with JW52, *Icarus* and *Forester* which had come on to Kola after screening the distant cover for JW51B, plus the damaged *Onslow*. The close escort was similarly composed of an amalgamation of corvettes, minesweepers and trawlers which had formerly operated separately.[3] Hamilton's covering squadron and distant heavy units were as for the outward convoy, though with a different screen.[4]

Oberleutnant Benker's patrolling *U625* reported and unsuccessfully attacked RA52 on 1 February, and several boats thereafter probed the defences, but it was the 3rd before the experienced Reche foiled the tiring escorts, some of which had been in the Arctic for a month with crews badly in need of proper rest. *U255* torpedoed the American freighter *Greylock*, but all hands were rescued by the prompt arrival of the *Harrier*, *Oxlip* and the trawlers.[5]

Various destroyers detached during the passage (the battered *Onslow* on the 2nd), the majority leaving off Iceland on the 5th. *Honeysuckle* and *Seagull* detached to fuel at Iceland for two days but rejoined on the 8th, and a local escort of *Blankney*, *Middleton* and *Vivacious* accompanied the convoy safely to Loch Ewe where the weary merchantmen anchored late on 8 February 1943.

The same day RA52 anchored in Loch Ewe, Karl Dönitz, a committed Nazi, relieved Raeder. Though giving priority to the U-boat campaign, in the following weeks Dönitz not only succeeded in winning a reprieve for the surface units of the Kriegsmarine but also got his liaison officer, Kranke, to persuade Hitler of the wisdom of freeing the hands of the flag-officer on the spot, should a surface action be fought in the future. Furthermore, at a naval conference at the end of February, contemplating the recapture of Stalingrad and the surrender of von Paulus and the Sixth Army, Dönitz pressed the point that it was of paramount importance for the Kriegsmarine to do all in its power to destroy the Allied northern supply route. A 'fairly powerful' force could be composed of *Tirpitz* and *Lützow* if reinforced by *Scharnhorst*, then in the Baltic. Hitler's response was intemperate, but in the end he grudgingly consented.

It was now delays in loading which interfered with the convoy schedule. Despite deferments, JW53 remained five ships short when it left Loch Ewe on the 15th. Three additional merchantmen sailed on the 16th under the escort of *Matchless*, *Musketeer* and *Bryony*, but heavy weather compelled them to turn back as their deck cargoes threatened to go overboard.[6]

Nevertheless, the convoy was large enough and, with the rapidly increasing hours of daylight in the Barents Sea, demanded a strong escort force comparable to that of PQ18. Sailing under the through escort of *Jason*, *Bergamot*, *Poppy* and *Lord Austin*, with

Bluebell and *Camellia* joining from Iceland on the 20th, JW53 had a local escort of three destroyers, two minesweepers, two corvettes and a trawler between Scotland and Iceland, where these were replaced by the destroyers of the ocean escort, thirteen of them led by Captain (D) I.M.R. Campbell in *Milne*. Campbell's second was Scott-Moncrieff in *Faulknor* with *Boadicea, Inglefield, Orwell, Opportune, Obedient* and *Obdurate*. *Eclipse, Fury, Impulsive, Intrepid* and the Polish *Orkan* joined two days later with HM Cruiser *Scylla*, under the command of Captain I.A.P. MacIntyre as senior officer. It was intended that an escort carrier would join but, as will be seen, this proved impossible.

In support, Rear-Admiral Burnett cruised in *Belfast* with *Sheffield* and *Cumberland*. Distant heavy cover was provided by the Commander-in-Chief in *King George V*, with *Howe, Norfolk* and the destroyers *Icarus, Meteor, Musketeer, Offa, Onslaught* and the Pole, *Piorun*.

Storm-force winds and heavy seas hampered JW53 from the start; as already mentioned, three late merchantmen were forced back, one requiring the escort of *Matchless* to Scapa. In this early stage of the passage, Commander Lewis of the minesweeper *Jason* was in charge of the escort and earned Tovey's praise for his achievement in keeping even a semblance of order in the confusion. For two days conditions were extremely bad and several of the ships suffered damage. Most were hove to, the merchant ships to preserve their deck cargoes, the destroyers to preserve themselves, and several of the former were compelled to retreat to Loch Ewe to avoid the loss of precious war supplies.

Aboard the British merchant ships the radio officers kept watch on the bridge until the actions of the enemy ended radio silence. Employed as signallers, one recalled the difficulty of signalling to a corvette as both ships rolled and pitched, frustrating the aim of the Aldis lamp.

Incredibly, it was the cruiser *Sheffield* which sustained the most dramatic damage. With her forward guns trained off the bow, a heavy sea tore off the armour plate atop her A-turret and flung it overboard. Her place was taken by *Norfolk*, but there was no replacement escort carrier. HMS *Dasher* had been badly battered and with her dedicated escorts *Blankney* and *Ledbury* took no further part in this convoy, or indeed the war. Sent to the Clyde for repairs, she was working up prior to returning to service when an explosion of aircraft fuel set her on fire: in five terrible minutes she was all but destroyed, becoming a total loss.

Finally the weather moderated, whereupon the rounded-up convoy made good progress, unhampered by pancake ice and the frequent squalls of snow and sleet that periodically shrouded it. The ice limit being at its southerly extremity, JW53 was forced towards the Norwegian coast. When still west of Bear Island it was located by enemy air patrols on the 23rd and thereafter daily, homing the U-boats in on the 24th.

But this was no longer 1942. The overwhelming size of the escort, the Huff-Duff intercepts and the dash and fury of the destroyers, helped by a ready supply of fuel from the *British Governor* acting as escort oiler, prevented the U-boats from pressing any attack, though both Reche in *U255* and Queck in *U622* tried. Moreover, neither of the two bombing strikes by twenty-one Ju88s of KG30 on the 25th and 26th made any impression beyond shaking one ship, the *Dover Hill*, with a near miss, such was the fury of the defensive barrage. Joined the same day by the Soviet destroyers *Gromki, Grozni, Kuibishev, Uritski* and *Uragan*, and later by the British minesweeper *Britomart*, convoy JW53 won through, fifteen ships reaching the Kola Inlet on 27 February 1943, the other seven entering the White Sea on 2 March with the *Uritski* in company and Russian ice-breakers attending them to their berths at Molotovsk.

Sadly, Murmansk was no safe haven. On the 27th and 28th the ships lying at anchor in the Kola Inlet were dive-bombed by Stukas and three of them damaged. The Luftwaffe continually bombed and strafed Murmansk, Messerschmitt Me109s and Focke-Wulf FW190s operating in conjunction with the Ju88s, or in small groups, making short and vicious attacks. The armed guard ensign of the Liberty ship *Thomas Hartley* recorded the exhaustion that affected both him and his men after incessant air raids throughout March and early April during which they had contributed to the defences of the Russian port.

Of most significance for the ships were the Junkers Ju88s of KG30. One raid on 6 March resulted in the *Empire Kinsman* suffering extensive damage to her port bridge wing and wheelhouse. On the 13th, KG30 sank the *Ocean Freedom* as she lay at Murmansk working cargo.

Sir Malcolm Goldsmith, Commodore of the returning RA53, left the Kola Inlet on 1 March 1943, his broad pendant flying in *Temple Arch*. Escorted by *Scylla* and the thirteen destroyers from JW53 (supported by the oiler *Oligarch*, the corvettes *Poppy*, *Starwort*, *Lotus* and *Bergamot*, and the trawlers *St Elstan* and *Northern Pride*), the thirty westbound merchantmen carried seventy-nine passengers distributed among them. These were more survivors from the Barents Sea action and Russian naval personnel travelling to collect new ships for the Northern Fleet. The cruisers and distant cover were almost identical to that for the outward JW53.[7]

On the 2nd, Kapitänleutnant Reche made contact, but *U255* had to trail the convoy for three days before he was able to seize an opportunity. During this time a dozen Ju88s of KG30 made an ineffective bombing raid which quailed in the face of a furious barrage put up by both the men-of-war and the merchantmen. Then Reche launched a torpedo, sinking the 5,000-ton *Executive*, before manœuvring and firing a second which struck the Liberty ship *Richard Bland* and penetrated her No. 1 hold without exploding. To Reche's annoyance, the ship resumed her voyage. Reche continued to shadow as the convoy passed Bear Island and shortly afterwards ran into a gale.

Two of the Liberty ships were soon in severe difficulties. On the 7th the *J.L.M. Curry* started to break up, her deck, bulwark and shell welds fracturing under the stresses of rolling and pitching. The following day, in latitude 74° 44′N, longitude 000° 24′E, she began to founder and was safely abandoned, one of the escorts speeding her on her way with a few shells.

The second Liberty ship in difficulties, the *John H.B. Latrobe*, suffered a breakdown and wallowed helplessly in the swell until Commander 'Johnnie' Lee-Barber got a tow-line aboard and dragged her into Seidisfiord behind HMS *Opportune*, a feat of seamanship which Tovey described as 'an excellent piece of work'.[8]

During the gale, the freighter *Puerto Rican* had straggled. As the weather moderated on the 9th she was encountered by *U586* (von der Esch) and promptly sunk, with the loss of her company. The persistent Reche was still in touch on the 10th when the convoy was thirty-five miles north-east of Langanaes. He now made a second attack on the *Richard Bland* and this time his torpedo blew the ship in two. He was still denied complete success, however, for although the stern section sank, the bow was taken in tow by the naval tug *Horsa*. However, the tug got into difficulties and was wrecked near Akureyri and the remains of the Liberty ship were blown ashore and beached.

Bad weather was also affecting the Norwegian coast, and under its cover the German battleship *Scharnhorst* slipped out of the Baltic and ran north to join the *Tirpitz*, *Lützow* and *Nürnberg* at Narvik. Leaving the latter to return to German waters, the three heavy capital ships reached Altenfiord on 20 March 1943 where their presence dominated Tovey's thoughts and continued to tie down the Home Fleet. Tovey once again advised the Admiralty not to press the northern convoys through the summer, but in the end events dictated their suspension as the crisis in the Battle of the Atlantic demanded every available escort be withdrawn to that vast battlefield, leaving only a handful of destroyers at Scapa in support of the Home Fleet.

As the struggle for domination of the Atlantic raged through April and May, a break-out of the German heavy ships became increasingly possible. Their reinforcement of the wolfpacks would tip the balance in the Axis' favour, so cruiser patrols in the Denmark Strait and in the Iceland–Faeroes–Shetland gaps were reinstated. To counter this possibility and to reinforce the British Home Fleet, the United States Navy formed Task Force 22 at Portland naval base in Maine. Fortunately the German ships remained shackled to their moorings during those critical spring weeks and by May the crisis had passed; Dönitz temporarily withdrew his U-boats. Though he had not yet lost the battle, he had lost the initiative: from now on in the Atlantic, it was the Allies who dominated, having established command of the air above that querulous ocean. The same had yet to be achieved in the Arctic.

As the fate of the principal Allied supply route hung in the balance, Dönitz unwisely depleted his wolfpacks in the Atlantic by dispatching several eastwards into the Kara Sea on minelaying operations off Port Dikson. These were designed to frustrate the annual Russian supply convoys which moved across the top of the world during the brief Siberian summer. Between mid-June and early July the ice-breakers *Krassin*, *Mikoyan*, and *Fedor Litke* attended the White Sea squadron under Rear-Admiral Kucherov who commanded the destroyers *Uritski* and *Kuibishev*, the patrol ships *SKR28* and *SKR30*, and the British minesweepers *Britomart* and *Jason*, proof, if proof were necessary, of the adaptability of these mundane little ships. A second convoy was forced through by the ice-breakers *Admiral Lazarev* and *Montcalm* under the command of Kapitan 1 Ranga Kolchin in the *Baku*, with *Gremyashchi*, *Gromki*, *Uritski*, *SKR28* and *SKR30*.

These operations were finally concluded in mid-November when the ice-breakers returned to the White Sea from Tiksi Bay accompanied by a strong Russian destroyer flotilla under Kucherov. As the force approached the Gourlo it claimed to have carried out highly successful anti-submarine operations, but these seem to have been exaggerated as few, if any, U-boats were in the area. No British units took part in this later phase.

The German minefields claimed several Soviet ships, as did the U-boats themselves, while Russian minesweeping operations made extensive use of the motor minesweepers delivered from Britain and America.

Numerous fierce air and sea actions were fought between Soviet and German units off the polar coast and the Fisherman's Peninsula, mainly associated with the interception of Axis coastal traffic, and though they were largely inconclusive, considerable losses were sustained on both sides, particularly by mines.

Almost as soon as Dönitz inherited supreme command of the Kriegsmarine, he carried out a reorganization of the naval command structure which amalgamated the Flag Officer Northern Waters (Narvik) with Group North. Thus the flag-officer commanding the battleships at Altenfiord, Kummetz, now came under the orders of Schniewind at Kiel. Furthermore, having won a reprieve for the surface fleet, Dönitz needed both to prove their value to Hitler and to raise the morale of their crews. After a summer of idleness, the three capital ships and two destroyer flotillas were ordered to prepare for sea and embark the 349th Grenadier Regiment. On 6 September Kummetz took the *Tirpitz* (Meyer) and *Scharnhorst* (Hüffmeier) to sea on Operation Zitronella. Supported by Kapitän Johannesson's 4th, Kapitän Wolff's 5th and Kapitän Kothe's 6th Flotillas, they sped north towards Spitzbergen. At 03.00 on the 8th *Scharnhorst* with Wolff's and Kothe's destroyers detached to land their troops in Advent Bay. Kummetz took *Tirpitz* on with the 4th Flotilla to Barentsburg where, after a brief barrage, coastal guns, coal tips, supply dumps, water reserves and the electricity generating facilities were blown up. The defenders got a message out and the British Home Fleet left Scapa Flow in response, but it was too late: by the 9th the raiders had returned to Altenfiord.[9]

Five weeks later, however, the USS *Tuscaloosa* with one American and four British destroyers landed Free Norwegian troops on the island to re-establish the base at Barentsburg.

There had been two significant changes in the British naval command corresponding to those in the German. On 10 September Sir Dudley Pound was relieved as First Sea Lord by Sir Andrew Cunningham, a fighting admiral of wide experience. Pound's physical collapse had been as tragic as it had been complete. In constant pain from an arthritic hip, he had suffered a stroke and was almost paralysed. The view that Churchill could and should have retired him earlier is inescapable; as it was, Pound dragged himself to Churchill's room while the two were in Washington and said he could not go on. Brought home in HMS *Renown* he suffered a second, crippling stroke on the passage and died on Trafalgar Day, 21 October 1943. Whatever his shortcomings, and they were many, Pound had stuck to his post in the best tradition of his service. That this had been for too long was no fault of his.

The previous year, Cunningham had been asked to relieve Sir John Tovey. Characteristically he had replied, 'If Tovey drops dead on his bridge I will certainly relieve him. Otherwise not.' In fact Sir John, at loggerheads with Churchill, had preceded Pound out of office, having been relieved by his VA2, Sir Bruce Fraser, on 8 May 1943. Tovey was consigned to the backwater of the Nore, the price of his forthright integrity. An almost forgotten figure, his contribution had been great: he was, in many ways, the architect of the Arctic victory his successor would inherit.

Vice-Admiral Sir Bruce Fraser shared Tovey's view that summer convoys were too dangerous. In fact the destruction of von Paulus in February had eased the imperative and absolute urgency that had existed the previous summer. Kind, sensitive and courteous, Fraser was a bachelor dedicated to a service he loved with an almost spiritual devotion. A natural conciliator, he combined dignity and authority with an easy manner, allowing him equally to cross the Royal Navy's formidable social barriers and to admonish the recalcitrant with devastating effect. Keen on ship visits, he maintained close touch with lower-deck feeling and generated a warmth of loyalty comparable in its way with that inspired by Nelson. He had declined the First Sea Lord's place in favour of Cunningham, whose independence Churchill feared, with the memorable phrase that while he believed he himself had the confidence of the ships he commanded, 'Cunningham has that of the whole Navy.'

Fraser's apprehensions of the power of the German 'fleet in being' resulted in Operation Source. This was an attack on the three capital ships in Altenfiord made by midget submarines on 22 September 1943. Towed across the North Sea by six of their larger sisters, the tiny submersibles *X5*, *X6*, *X7*, *X8*, *X9* and *X10* were manned offshore and sent in to penetrate the German defences and lay ground mines below the enemy. *X5* sank, *X8* and *X9* were lost on the way, and *X10* suffered a breakdown and had to return. Only *X6* (Lieutenant Cameron) and *X7* (Lieutenant Place) succeeded in this hazardous mission, reaching their target, passing beneath the *Tirpitz*'s anti-torpedo nets and laying their mines. The resulting explosions rendered the German battleship *hors de combat* until March 1944.[10]

Alarmed by this incursion, the German High Command ordered the *Lützow* south the following day. Escorted by four destroyers she headed for the Baltic. Located by British aircraft, the strike force of Beaufighters and Avengers sent against her failed to find her and she escaped, reaching Gotenhafen on 1 October.

Only the *Scharnhorst*, which had been temporarily absent from her moorings on a gunnery exercise when *Tirpitz* was attacked, now remained operational in Altenfiord.

The suspension of the Arctic convoys during the summer of 1943 had left a handful of escorts and a larger number of merchant ships in the ports of North Russia. The men of the latter referred to themselves as 'the forgotten convoy', and even in the summer their fate was unenviable. The constant alarms wore them out, and when moved to the safer ports and anchorages of the White Sea and the Dvina they were enervated by boredom and the petty, but very real irritation of Russian restrictions. No amount of regattas and jolly japes could rid them of the polar cafard which with the consumption of their stores brewed discontent and frustration. Occasional serious lapses of discipline, particularly among the polyglot merchant seamen, gave the Russians some grounds for their own complaints.

The dangers of the Kola Inlet had not diminished. By April the elderly steamship *Dover Hill* had discharged her cargo of fighters, guns, lorries, tanks, lubricating oil, shells and high explosives, and was lying at anchor in Misukovo Road near the tanker *British Governor*. The BP tanker, which had doubled on the outward voyage as a fleet oiler, was regularly lightened by Russian coastal tankers, but was holding a reserve of 1,200 tons of fuel for the next batch of incoming escorts – whenever that might be. Other ships of JW53 were either still discharging, were anchored, or were engaged in Russian coastal trading, like the American tanker *Beaconhill* which endured eight months of this dull traffic.

On Sunday, 4 April 1943, a high-level attack was made on the Kola Inlet by Ju88s which then appeared to have been driven off. In fact the planes had released their bombs, and sticks straddled both the *British Governor* and the *Dover Hill*. The tanker was badly shaken, with damage to her plating forward and splits in way of Nos. 6 and 7 tanks, but the *Dover Hill* received a direct hit, the bomb piercing the deck and disappearing below without detonating.

As there were no naval bomb-disposal experts in the port, the SBNO told the *Dover Hill*'s master that there was little he could do. He would have to exercise that great defensive measure always alloted the Merchant Navy in time of war: improvization. The naval authorities did, however, order the minesweeper *Jason* to lay off on the merchantman's quarter and render assistance if the bomb exploded!

The Master mustered the crew and called for volunteers to join him in digging the bomb out of a coal bunker, where it had lodged. There were eighteen offers and, with shovels from the stoke-hold, these men began the task of emptying the bunker to expose the bomb.

By this time the Russian authorities had learned of the problem and offered an officer to remove the detonator if the bomb could be brought out. Ten feet down, the fins of what appeared to be a half-ton bomb gleamed faintly in the lamp-light. Then they slipped from sight as the German planes came back and the ship shook to the explosions of more bombs and the concussion of her own anti-aircraft Bofors and Oerlikons. Understandably, tension rose among the working party as they resumed their task. For two days and two nights they hoisted bucketfuls of coal out of the filthy bunker, digging over twenty feet into the stow until at last they were able to lower a tackle and drop a strop over the hideous thing. Finally the bomb lay on deck where, with a hammer and punch, a Russian named Panin indelicately defused it. To the inexpressible relief of the crew the ordnance was dumped overboard. In October 1943, the *London Gazette* bore a notice that five merchant naval officers had been awarded the OBE and fourteen seamen the King's Commendation for brave conduct. The citation read 'For dangerous work in hazardous circumstances'.

The *Dover Hill* afterwards moved from Kola to Ekonomiya on the Dvina where she remained until 18 July when she was ordered to the White Sea port of Molotovsk. There she stayed until November, when she started for home.[11]

Another ship which suffered bomb-damage was the *Llandaff* which was engaged in coastal trade and received a shaking on 24 July 1943, when she was twenty miles north-east of Kildin Island, off the entrance to the Kola Inlet. She, too, was to survive, for already the equinox had passed and the days were shortening perceptibly in the land on 'the edge of the earth'.

It was to be November before the convoys resumed, and in preparation Operations Holder and FR took place. The first was the running of HM Destroyer *Onslaught* and the Royal Canadian destroyers *Huron* and *Iroquois* through to Kola between 1 and 11 October with ammunition for the waiting escorts *Britomart* and *Jason*. Operation FR was the passage of an escort group sent during the last week in October 1943 to bring back the accumulated merchantmen – the relieving force, in fact, for 'the forgotten convoy' and the weary naval personnel stationed in North Russia. Nine destroyers, the Norwegian corvette *Eglantine* and HM minesweepers *Harrier* and *Seagull* were accompanied by five small, Russian-manned coastal minesweepers and five launches sent to reinforce the Russian Northern Fleet.

Holder was covered by the cruiser *London* and the destroyer *Impulsive*. For the first time in a year, American warships too were in the Arctic for FR, the USS *Augusta* accompanying HMS *London* and the Hunt *Middleton* in the covering force.

The dozen readied merchantmen of RA54A had been assembled during the summer at Archangel and left on 1 November under Commodore Cox aboard *Empire Galliard*.[12]

The nine destroyers sent out in Operation FR were *Milne*

(Captain Campbell, Senior Officer), *Mahratta, Matchless, Musketeer, Savage, Saumarez, Scorpion, Scourge* and *Westcott.* The latter, with *Harrier* and *Seagull,* went on to the White Sea and joined the Russian local escort of the *Gromki* and *Kuibishev.* The destroyers refuelled from the *British Governor* at Kola. Then, together with *Eglantine,* and joined by the re-ammunitioned *Jason* and *Britomart* and the tanker herself, they all sailed to join convoy RA54A coming from the eastward.

Burnett in *Belfast* with *Kent* and *Norfolk* covered the route between the Greenwich and the 32nd meridians and was supported by Fraser's new VA2, Vice-Admiral Sir Henry Moore, flying his flag in the battleship *Anson* with the cruiser *Jamaica,* the British destroyers *Onslow* and *Venus,* the American *Capps* and *Hobson,* and the Royal Norwegian Navy's *Stord.* Moore also had under his command the aircraft-carrier *Formidable,* an important increase in British naval strength in the north since the departure of *Victorious* months earlier.

Dense fog and mist, frustrating though they were to ships in close company, concealed RA54A from the enemy and all arrived safely at Loch Ewe, shepherded in by a local escort of *Halcyon, Brissenden* and *Middleton* who had relieved the destroyers of the ocean escort off Iceland.

Next morning, 15 November, nine months to the day after JW53, convoy JW54A steamed through the boom at Loch Ewe and headed out into the Minch, deeply laden with military stores for the Soviet Union.

19

'An inconvenient, extreme and costly exertion'

THE SAILING OF JW54A marked a new phase in the maritime war in the Arctic. From the autumn of 1943, Allied victory, though by no means certain, was now probable. The crisis in the Atlantic had passed and the triumphs in North Africa had been followed by the invasion of Italy. Operations in the Mediterranean had drawn off German aircraft from the Eastern and polar fronts, and the Red Army's victories over the Wehrmacht at Kursk, Orel and Kharkov had been supported by a vastly enlarged Soviet airforce. After a series of conferences between Churchill and Roosevelt, the first moves in the planning of Operation Overlord were put in train. The invasion of Occupied Europe from the English Channel would far surpass Torch in its magnitude and complexity, and what the world now knows as D-Day would cause the Arctic convoys to be suspended once more.

Unfortunately, the accord between London and Moscow was in disarray. The underlying cause of this souring had been the hiatus in the convoys, despite efforts to increase supplies via the Persian Gulf and, from America, through Vladivostok. But the Soviet attitude had deteriorated by degrees over points of detail. Churchill, aware of the delicate morale among the participants, had again pressed the Russians for better facilities for the wounded and the 170 British personnel stationed in North Russia, all but 20 of whom were long overdue a relief. Prior to the resumption of Arctic operations, Churchill reiterated his demands, determined to use the opportunity to improve conditions in North Russia. He particularly insisted that the Soviet authorities lift the petty restrictions that hampered the local liaison necessary to the smooth organization of convoys. These were imposed by ignorant Red Army soldiers, indoctrinated to a perverse perception of Westerners as allies only under duress. The numerous petty formalities, the passes and visas, the plethora of guards and the prohibition of movement, all tried the patience of the naval staff who had daily to deal with them.

Churchill's requests were wholly reasonable and indeed had little purpose but to improve the efficiency of the machinery of supply, yet Stalin disdained to reply for a fortnight. On 12 October 1943 Churchill prompted the British Ambassador in Moscow, Sir Archibald Clark Kerr, to press for an answer, as the lack of a response was holding things up. The destroyers of Operation FR were under sailing orders and distributed among its ships were 150 naval personnel destined to relieve those in North Russia.

Stalin's reply arrived the next day. It had been delayed in part by his summoning Admiral Golovko to Moscow for consultation. The reply was not to Churchill's liking and the correspondence between the two men betrays their deep mutual mistrust. To be fair, both were driven by pragmatic reasons. On the one hand, Churchill could never guarantee the Arctic convoys on either a scheduled or a contents-intact basis, subject as they were to the vicissitudes of war, nor could he countenance their interfering with British commitments elsewhere. On the other hand, it was a measure of Russia's dependence on Western armaments that the flow of *matériel* should be uninterrupted, for as Stalin said, 'the Northern route is the shortest way which permits delivery . . . within the shortest period to the Soviet-German front'. There were other reasons, all cogent given Stalin's perspective, the most important being that a shortfall in expectations could ruin Soviet military planning. In his refutation of Churchill's claimed restrictions on British personnel, however, the Soviet leader was unequivocally offensive. Much of this may be attributed to misrepresentations by a defensive Golovko, but over this dialogue can be discerned the advancing shadow of the Cold War.

Churchill refused to reply and handed the matter over to Anthony Eden, the Foreign Secretary, just then arriving for consultations in Moscow. Stalin's response, Churchill commiserated with Roosevelt, was 'not exactly all one might hope from a gentleman for whose sake we are to make an inconvenient, extreme and costly exertion'. While he waited for Eden to produce results, Churchill interviewed Gousev, Maisky's replacement in London.

Handing back Stalin's message he was otherwise conciliatory, but to influence the Soviet leader, Churchill delayed the sailing of Operation FR, without which the convoys could not resume.

The crucial meeting between Eden and Stalin took place on the day that Pound died, and hinged on Stalin relinquishing his hitherto absurd insistence that the dispatch of the convoys should not be thought of as an absolute obligation, but as something that should and would be done as the fortunes of war permitted. Eden persuaded Stalin that the British did not regard the supply of armaments as an act of charity, to be given or withdrawn at will. As to the difficulties regarding personnel, the debate over the number of signal staff in North Russia, the alleged superior attitude of British naval officers and the disruption caused by merchant seamen, these were to be discussed by Eden with Molotov in Moscow.

One such instance involved the bosun and cook of the *Dover Hill*, during the ship's wait at Ekonomiya. The former was returning to his ship the worse for drink when a Russian pointed out that he should be smoking in one of the booths provided by the side of the wooden road rather than outside, where greater risk of fire existed. The bosun obliged, but was less happy when the Russian followed him inside and began accusing Great Britain of failing her ally by not opening a second front. Finishing his cigarette, the bosun stood up and laid the man out. He resumed his walk but was soon accosted by two Russian militiamen who attempted to arrest him. The ship's cook then arrived, whereupon a fight ensued. Finally both bosun and cook were overpowered and subsequently sentenced to seven and four years' imprisonment respectively: the bosun's interlocutor had been a Communist Party official.

The outrage this draconian decision provoked had its echoes in Downing Street. Churchill personally intervened and the affair became something of a *cause célèbre* – its resolution, in fact, a precondition for the resumption of the convoys.

Months later, when the *Dover Hill* lay in Molotovsk, both bosun and cook were returned to their ship without a word of explanation. Almost simultaneously, as we have seen, Operation FR was given the green light, RA54A was brought home and the cycle of convoy departures got under way again.

With the escorts returning to northern waters came, in due course, steady reinforcements. Both convoy and escorting force were to grow in size in the coming months, until the passage of each was to become a fleet operation. Local air superiority, so desirable after PQ18, was to be achieved in incredibly difficult conditions, and the more challenging task of defeating the U-boats would be tackled with overwhelming resources, for new breeds of warship were now available.

The escort carrier was to play a full part in supporting the merchantmen, and American warplanes were gradually to replace the makeshift Sea Hurricanes, though the old Swordfish was to continue as a gallant and potent anti-submarine weapon. The Luftwaffe, however, was never to be the threat it had been in 1942, even when torpedo-bombers returned to Arctic skies.

More important still, the frigate was about to enter service together with an improved version of the Flower-class corvette, both more efficient anti-submarine escorts with better anti-aircraft armament than the converted trawlers and co-opted fleet destroyers. Eventually, teams of anti-submarine ships which acted as independent 'support groups' were to make their appearance in the Barents Sea when they could be spared from the Western Ocean that had bred them. They were dedicated to the sole purpose of hunting U-boats.

For the U-boat was to be the prime and most deadly enemy to the last, and, as Dönitz withdrew them from the Atlantic, they were to make their final, aggressive stand in the Arctic. Here, particularly in the approaches to the Kola Inlet and the White Sea, where the Gulf Stream finally gives up its incursion into the polar ocean, 'layering' occurs. This stratification of water density that refracts or reflects sonar waves, gave the U-boats sufficient cover to frustrate their would-be hunters and permitted them their last savage kills. In short, the Arctic convoy route was to remain bloody to the bitter end.

The Allies had been able to win the Battle of the Atlantic because they could build merchant ships faster than the Germans could sink them, and this was almost entirely due to the fantastic output of the American shipyards building the Liberty ships. From JW54A onwards, the composition of the Arctic convoys became increasingly American. The elderly British veterans of the run were gradually withdrawn. Participating British ships were largely new tonnage, Forts and Sams to join the Empires and Oceans. A scattering of Dutch and Norwegians continued in company with American-owned, flag of convenience-registered Panamanians, but there were no more Russians. At this period one is conscious of a vast shift in gear from the extempore and makeshift, and from the black-humoured cameraderie of a relatively small number of men, to the less personal, more methodical and mechanical atmosphere of total war. The Arcadia Conference of January 1942 had declared the Allied aim of defeating Germany as a priority. The Casablanca Conference of January 1943 determined to force Germany to unconditional surrender, and the whole mood of the Grand Coalition was dedicated to this purpose.

Notwithstanding the huge access of material strength now at the disposal of the Western Allies, the Germans were far from beaten. Having been withdrawn from the Atlantic in May, the U-boats returned in the autumn with two important improvements, the *schnorkel* which enabled a submarine to use her diesel engines when at periscope depth, and the T-5 acoustic torpedo, code-named the Gnat by the Allies. This was a significant counter-attacking device, for it sought the noise of a ship's propeller and was most effective against the high revving screws of questing warships. Thus the relative immunity that anti-submarine escorts had enjoyed hitherto abruptly vanished; they, and not the lumbering, vulnerable merchantmen, were now Dönitz's prime targets.

In neutralizing this menace, the support groups proved particularly effective for they had developed a technique known as 'creeping', the stealthy hunting of a U-boat by a co-ordinated group with one frigate pinning down the position of the targeted U-boat and directing others to make slow, acoustically 'silent' approaches. Pioneered by Captain Walker's Second Support Group, the method caught on whenever ships could operate in force and as the rising numbers of escorts and increased availability of fuel removed the limitations placed upon counter-attacking escorts. It was against this background that the maritime war in the Arctic entered its penultimate phase.

Commodore B.B. Grant hoisted his pendant in the *Fort Yukon* and led the nineteen ships of JW54A out of the Minch in seven columns on 15 November 1943. In their ranks were the rescue ship *Copeland*, the Panamanian tanker *Norlys* operating as a fleet oiler, three patrol boats and two motor minesweepers for the Russian Northern Fleet, all five American-built under Lease-Lend terms. A through escort of the destroyers *Inconstant* and

Whitehall, the minesweeper *Hussar* and the corvette *Heather* were accompanied to Iceland by *Brissenden, Termagant* and *Burza* (Polish). At the rendezvous these were relieved by HM destroyers *Impulsive, Onslaught, Orwell* and the repaired *Onslow*, together with the Canadian destroyers HMCS *Haida, Huron* and *Iroquois*.

The Royal Canadian Navy had expanded enormously and, with the United States increasingly committed to the war in the Pacific against the Japanese, had come to play a very important role in the Battle of the Atlantic and, to a lesser extent, in the Arctic.

Aboard HMS *Onslow*, the senior officer, J.A. McCoy, had replaced the wounded Sherbrooke as Captain (D) of the 17th Destroyer Flotilla. *Obedient* joined but had to return to Seidisfiord with engine defects. Distant cover was equally 'mixed' in character, HMS *Anson* being supported by the USS *Tuscaloosa* and the US destroyers *Corry, Fitch, Forrest* and *Hobson*. *Kent, Bermuda* and *Jamaica*, under Rear-Admiral Palliser, Hamilton's successor, cruised between the Greenwich and 30th easterly meridians. At this eastern point four Soviet destroyers joined, taking the White Sea portion of the convoy on with *Hussar*, while Palliser's ships ran ahead to Vaenga and the minesweeper *Seagull* joined the Russians for the last two days of the operation.

Mist and cloud had completely obscured the ships from enemy detection and the bulk of JW54A lumbered into the Kola Inlet on 24 November, the White Sea section arriving on the 26th. On its arrival the latter's escort turned about and, augmented by the trawler *Lord Austin*, escorted the returning convoy RA54B. Having fuelled at Vaenga from *Norlys*, the eastward ocean escort, with the exception of *Hussar* which had come out to relieve *Harrier* and exchanged with her, became the westward escort for RA54B. They were accompanied by the rescue ship *Copeland* and the oiler *Norlys*.

Frustrating delays in unloading ensured that only a handful of the waiting merchantmen were ready to join the return convoy. Although witnesses at this time spoke of the pace with which tanks in particular were discharged and driven off at frantic speed, the more prosaic, less easily handled sinews of war often left the yawning holds of the merchant ships with agonizing slowness. All too frequently, munitions and equipment were left on the quay, and often the cargo shifted out of the previous occupants of the berth still lay where it had been dumped weeks earlier. It was as demoralizing a spectacle as the poor wretches who were pressed to unload it and who begged or stole anything they could to eat. Occasionally these unfortunates would pilfer cargo if it seemed worthwhile. A bale from a consignment of American long johns split open as it was lifted from the hold of the *Henry Villard*. Searched at the end of the shift, one docker was found to have stuffed a pair inside his clothes and was promptly shot.[2]

To move some ships west, the Master of the *Empire Scott*, which had borne Commodore Leir outward in JW53, sailed as Commodore of RA54B. With him went the Panamanian tanker *Artigas*, the American freighter *Bering*, the British steamships *Atlantic*, the damaged *Dover Hill* and *Llandaff*, the Norwegian *Marathon* and the Dutchman, *Pieter de Hoogh*.

Palliser's flagship, HMS *Kent*, shipped fifty-four tons of gold bullion in part payment for war supplies, and proceeded to sea as cover, while Vice-Admiral Moore in the battleship *Anson*, with *Belfast* and five British destroyers, provided distant support. In the prevailing bad weather these were scattered for four days and one, *Matchless*, was compelled to turn back after sustaining storm damage.[3]

However, the gales, thick weather and Arctic winter again provided the overcast scud, low visibility and darkness that seamen had come to regard as a boon, hiding them from the airborne eyes of the enemy, and RA54B passed safely through the boom at Loch Ewe on 9 December.

Even before JW54A had rounded Kildin Island inwards for Murmansk, JW54B was at sea, escorted to Iceland by *Middleton*, *Saladin*, *Skate* and the little minesweeper *Speedwell*. Her sister ship *Halcyon* remained as through escort together with the destroyer *Beagle* and the corvettes *Dianella*, *Poppy* and *Rhododendron*, these being joined off Langanaes by the destroyers *Saumarez*, *Savage*, *Scorpion*, *Scourge*, *Hardy*, *Venus*, *Vigilant* and the Norwegian *Stord*. JW54B and RA54B were simultaneously covered by Palliser and Moore and both subject to the same bad weather.

The merchantmen of JW54B plunged their way through the grey Barents Sea, their decks humped by their tarpaulin-covered cargoes of tanks and aircraft. The smaller escorts were even livelier. Accretions of ice built up as the spray froze on cold steel, and were chipped away by slithering working parties. The Arctic gloom was relieved by the brief hours of twilit day and the 'absolutely breathtaking', almost numinous beauty of the aurora borealis. Aboard His Norwegian Majesty's Ship *Stord*, a British S-class fleet destroyer built at John Samuel White's on the Isle of Wight, her Norwegian crew marvelled at her sea-keeping qualities. She 'slipped like a shark through the waves', recalled one, whose regard for his captain was equally complimentary. Lieutenant-Commander Skule Storeheil was 'a truly great officer and seaman' who had, when his crew were drafted into the *Stord* from the *St Albans*, volunteered to revert in rank from Commander.[4]

Watching from the bridge of *Daldorch*, Commodore Dennison kept his six columns in formation. It was bitterly cold and snow showers caused drifts to form on deck, so that his MRA and DEMS gunners were alternately digging out their gun pits or traversing and elevating their guns, an exercise that had to be carried out frequently to avoid their freezing up. This was more than a routine precaution, as his gunners well knew, for they, though not the merchant seamen, had had the benefit of a briefing at Loch Ewe. Mustered ashore, all the merchant ships' gunners had been marched under naval escort to a large Nissen hut and addressed by naval officers. The gist of the briefing was that they 'were in a convoy to Russia and would be sailing fairly close to the Norwegian coast – the object being to draw out the *Scharnhorst*'. They were then marched back to their boats, their guards making them feel rather like prisoners, evidence of the secrecy of the imparted information.[5]

It is not difficult to imagine how this news was received aboard by the merchant seamen from whom it was impossible to keep such scuttlebutt. It was a common belief among them that they were being used as bait, an opinion current a year earlier in the homeward-bound RA51, and which lost nothing as time passed and circumstances changed. Given all their experience of the naval establishment, and their self-perception as underdogs and victims of a careless bureaucracy, it was both plausible and credible. To what extent the British Admiralty actively pursued this policy of setting bait, it is now difficult to say with absolute certainty. The departure of *Lützow* and the incapacity of *Tirpitz* were certainly known in London, the Royal Navy had a tradition of seeking an enemy, and circumstances were hardly likely to be more propitious.

In late June 1943, the new Commander-in-Chief, Sir Bruce Fraser, had expressed the view that the Soviet Union was no longer so dependent upon the Arctic supply route, those via the Pacific and Persian Gulf being adequate. The resumption of the convoys could therefore have only one real purpose, to 'enable the German surface forces to be brought successfully to action'. While this may well have been the private desire of many naval officers, the continuing use of the northern route owed much to political considerations and the maintenance of British credibility which made its abandonment impossible. Nevertheless, in naval circles the temptation to entice *Scharnhorst* out and strike her must have been well nigh irresistible and second only to the conviction that the Germans would hardly waste the dark nights and thick weather. Moreover, the overriding principle of the safe and timely arrival of the convoy need not suffer if the supporting operation was properly and carefully conducted.

There were equally pressing political as well as material reasons for the Germans to act aggressively. Interdicting the Arctic convoys would aggravate already strained relations between Stalin and the Western leaders, and it was inconceivable that Hitler would let such an opportunity pass.

In fact British naval planners overestimated the effectiveness of German radar at this time, wrongly believing it to be nearly as advanced as their own. They were not wrong in their strategic thinking, however. It was simply that with JW54B they were premature.

Commodore Dennison was thus a relieved man when, on 2 December, in poor visibility he watched the Murmansk section break away in some confusion towards Kildin Island and into Kola. Fortunately, he had had no need of the rescue ship *Rathlin*, for like the others that month the convoy was unscathed, though not completely undetected.[6]

The escort remained close by until the 4th when the White Sea section, led by the *Daldorch*, was safely delivered into the hands of ice-breakers which smashed the ice up to the berths at Ekonomiya. Lieutenant-Commander Murch's *Beagle* and the corvettes thereafter proceeded to Polyarnoe, where the rest were refuelling from the *San Adolfo*. This British tanker, owned by the Eagle Oil Company, had acted as fleet oiler with JW54B and now topped up *Saumarez*, *Stord* and their sisters before the eight destroyers, lacking a homeward convoy, made an independent passage to Scapa Flow.

The lack of German interest in the first of the new convoys concerned Admiral Fraser. Persuaded that the only possible reason could be lack of reconnaissance, he considered that with the Arctic winter darkness, intervention was increasingly likely and that convoy JW55A, which left Loch Ewe on 12 December, was at risk. Part of that perceived risk arguably lay in its function as a decoy.

The convoy itself was composed of nine American and ten British merchantmen, including the tanker *San Ambrosio*, acting as oiler to the escorts. This balance argues strongly in favour of there being an element of provocation in its passage. Fraser's staff had alloted the usual local eastern escort, the elderly LRE *Westcott*, the minesweeper *Speedwell* and the corvette *Acanthus* being accompanied to Iceland by the minesweepers *Harrier* and *Cockatrice*. Here Captain Ian Campbell in *Milne* joined from Seidisfiord with *Ashanti, Matchless, Meteor, Musketeer, Opportune, Virago* and the Canadian destroyer *Athabaskan*. Cruiser cover was provided by *Belfast, Norfolk* and *Sheffield* under the command of Burnett, now promoted Vice-Admiral.[7]

When Fraser learned that JW55A had been sighted by an aircraft, he ordered the Home Fleet to sea in anticipation of the *Scharnhorst* emerging. This did not happen, and thus it was that his flagship, HMS *Duke of York* (Captain the Honourable G.H.E. Russell), the cruiser *Jamaica*, and their screen of *Savage, Scorpion, Saumarez* and *Stord* steamed right through to Kola, arriving on 16 December 1943, four days ahead of the convoy.

Once there, Fraser made a virtue of necessity and called upon Golovko, whom he both charmed and flummoxed: 'I still do not grasp for what purpose the Commander-in-Chief of the British Home Fleet should have decided to visit us at the height of the polar night season.' Perhaps solely to see for himself; at any rate, Fraser caught the Russian off guard and with his instinctive sensitivity to the other man's predicament did much in two days to thaw some of the Russian resistance to full co-operation with the Royal Navy.[8]

His squadron's departure on the 18th took Golovko even more by surprise than had his arrival, but Fraser was anxious to be at sea on the departure of the next convoy. As JW55A approached the Murman coast, he was already dashing west to Akureyri to refuel. JW55A had in fact been seen by *U636* which, with *U277, U387* and *U354*, had been sent out to intercept it west of Bear Island, but the sighting, on 18 December, was too late to enable the pack to catch up. Three Russian destroyers joined with *Harrier* as local escort on the 20th while the Murmansk-bound section headed for Kola, taking the White Sea ships eastward. The former berthed that day, the latter on the 22nd.

The U-boats that had been searching for JW55A had also been out after JW54B and one, *U307*, had sighted escorting destroyers on 28 November. She had been part of the Eisenbart wolfpack which lost contact so that the British authorities were misled into thinking these convoys had been unobserved.[9]

In fact the Germans were well aware of the resumption of the convoys and among the officers of the Seekriegsleitung the opinion was that the superiority of British radar made a surface attack, almost certainly the equivalent of a night action at this season, a most hazardous undertaking. The experiences of the Barents Sea action were too fresh in their minds to encourage risking the *Scharnhorst*.

Dönitz, anxious to justify his hard-won preservation of the surface fleet, thought otherwise. He cannot have been insensible to the fact that the outcome of the action with Sherbrooke's destroyers should have been very different.

20

'We're going alongside the bastard!'

ON 21 DECEMBER 1943 the huge grey shape of HMS *Duke of York* loomed through a thick mist and, in company with a cruiser and four destroyers, entered Akureyri fiord at full speed: Admiral Fraser had great confidence in his radar and he was in the devil of a hurry. On his way from Kola he had received two Ultra decrypts, both indicating that the *Scharnhorst* was on short notice for steam. As the flagship and *Jamaica, Saumarez, Savage, Scorpion* and *Stord* guzzled oil next day, the Commander-in-Chief summoned his captains and announced his intentions. The run to Vaenga had given all the ships in company the opportunity to exercise, and Fraser had not wasted it, having practised night tactics. He now outlined his plan which relied on an initial limitation of speed to 15 knots to conserve fuel. If and when a general action ensued, the cruiser *Jamaica* was to remain in support of the flagship, and the destroyers were to divide into two subdivisions and mount a torpedo attack. Fire would be opened with star-shells at seven miles' range.

Less radiophobic than Tovey, Fraser believed in the benefits of swift, plain-language communication via TBS, and this too was practised while the council of war was in progress. It ended with the prophetic *Make to Admiralty* Scharnhorst *sunk*.

On the 22nd, the same day the eastern portion of JW55A arrived in the White Sea, the westbound RA55A left Kola escorted home by Campbell's eight destroyers, with *Beagle, Westcott,* the corvettes *Acanthus, Dianella* and *Poppy,* and the minesweeper *Speedwell.* It was due to pass the cross-over point with the next outward convoy, JW55B, off Bear Island on Christmas Day.

Convoy JW55B had left Loch Ewe on the 20th with a local escort of the corvettes *Borage* and *Wallflower* and the minesweepers *Hydra* and *Hound*. Commander Majendie's support group, consisting of the elderly LRE conversions *Wanderer, Wrestler* and *Whitehall,* also joined with the close escort of the corvettes *Honeysuckle* and *Oxlip* and the minesweeper *Gleaner*.

The convoy ran through fine weather. Aboard *Wanderer* the watch were cleaning guns when an Ordinary Seaman 'servicing an Oerlikon, slipped and fell over the side'. Despite the fact that the seaboat was away in quick time and had the young man inboard and in the doctor's hands within seven minutes, the cold had killed him at once.

Off Iceland Captain McCoy joined in *Onslow* with *Onslaught, Orwell, Impulsive, Scourge* and the Canadian Tribals, *Huron, Haida* and *Iroquois*. The convoy was located from the air on the 22nd and ineffectually attacked by Ju88s on the 23rd. By Christmas Eve JW55B was being continuously shadowed but it had successfully evaded the Eisenbart wolfpack the day before when escorts had detected the presence of two U-boats and discouraged them with depth-charges. This was all they could achieve in the heavy sea, due to the under-hull aeration caused by the movement of the ships. By the late afternoon the trailing aircraft had also vanished. At this time Vice-Admiral Burnett's covering squadron of three cruisers, *Belfast, Sheffield* and *Norfolk,* sailed to the west from Vaenga.

Still at Akureyri, early on Thursday, 23 December 1943, Fraser received further Ultra decrypts revealing that the enemy knew of the sailing of JW55B and that U-boats had been ordered to close in. A second decrypt informed the Commander-in-Chief that *Scharnhorst* had been put on three hours' notice to sail. Consumed by the desire to be on the move, Fraser wanted not an inch of ullage in his squadron's fuel tanks and so the ships topped up their bunkers. While this was in progress, he and Captain Russell went for a walk ashore where, in the lights of the little town, Icelanders were happily skating. Offshore, on the black waters of the fiord, the squadron, now to be known as Force Two, lay in darkness. Back on board and mindful of the portentous moment, Fraser 'asked the [marine] band to come up on deck and play Christmas carols; and really, it almost brought tears to your eyes'.

At 23.00 that night, led by the four destroyers in box formation, *Duke of York* preceded *Jamaica* to sea. Beyond the shelter of the fiord the darkness engulfed them, and the plaintive echoes of the marine bandsmen gave way to the dreary howl of the Arctic wind.

Dönitz had obtained Hitler's sanction to attack a Russia-bound convoy on 19 December and although the meteorological data-gathering aircraft that spotted JW55B on the 22nd gave an inaccurate report, suggesting it was composed of troopships bent on the much-feared invasion of Norway, it was soon realized that it was nothing more than an ordinary munitions convoy and offered a reasonable target. *U601* and *U716* of the Eisenbart group made contact on Christmas Eve, but were driven off by the escorts despite the firing of a Gnat which failed to hit its target. The continuous air shadowing of that day ended at about 16.00 in the gloom. Following events from Kiel, Schniewind was not optimistic but awaited Dönitz's reaction. In the meantime Kummetz had reported sick and had been temporarily relieved by Konteradmiral 'Achmed' Bey, an experienced destroyer officer who had led successful mining raids on the east coast of England. Conditioned by experience, Bey was sceptical of the *Scharnhorst*'s chances, passionately advocating the aggressive use of destroyers. On Christmas Day Bey and his staff were ordered to leave *Tirpitz* and transfer the Admiral's flag to *Scharnhorst*.

In the freezing early hours of Christmas Eve 1943, as Force Two plunged and scended to the north-east with a stern gale, Fraser ordered Lieutenant-Commander E.W. Walmsley to take HMS *Saumarez* fifteen miles to the south-east and then make a dummy attack. The weather was appalling, but the practice given the radar operators and the confidence that suffused the whole squadron as a consequence of this blind operation were worth the suffering of the poor ship's company of *Saumarez*. As the exercise progressed further, Ultra decrypts told of enemy ship movements in Altenfiord. With Burnett, whose cruisers Fraser had denominated as Force One, still 400 miles to the east of JW55B, the Commander-in-Chief realized that if *Scharnhorst* struck to the west of Bear Island, the Germans would meet little opposition. He therefore broke radio silence, ordered Captain McCoy to reverse the convoy's course for three hours during the late twilight, and increased the speed of Force One to 19 knots.

On that Christmas Day, the westbound RA55A passed Bear Island. This convoy had left Kola on the 22nd and consisted of twenty-one ships including the *Rathlin*, repaired after her grounding had damaged her rudder. One ship had turned back. This convoy was now ordered by Fraser to alter to the north-westwards to clear the area and relinquish most of its fleet destroyers to reinforce JW55B. Accordingly, at 02.00 *Musketeer* (Commander R.L Fisher, Senior Officer), *Opportune* (Commander J. Lee-Barber), *Matchless* (Lieutenant-Commander W.S. Shaw) and *Virago* (Lieutenant-Commander A.J.R. White) bore away in the darkness.

The convoy continued under the cover of *Ashanti*, *Beagle*, *Westcott*, *Athabaskan*, *Seagull*, *Dianella*, *Poppy* and the Norwegian-manned *Acanthus*. On Boxing Day, in latitude 75°N and longitude 005° 30′W, RA55A swung to the west and passed out of the area. Later, turning south, it ran into heavy weather which dispersed the ships. However, it remained unmolested by the enemy and most of the vessels arrived at Loch Ewe on New Year's Day, 1944.[1]

On *Onslow*'s uncomfortable open bridge, Captain McCoy had had a less than happy Christmas as he approached Bear Island. He had lost part of Majendie's support group, which had returned to Western Approaches Command's base at Londonderry. Having reported his position to the SBNO North Russia the day before, the dismal darkness of Christmas morning found McCoy's flotilla and convoy JW55B approaching an alter-course position with its units spread disastrously widely in the gale that was now backing into the south, evidence of another depression following the one just past.

Signalling those vessels in close company to slow down, he waited for the stragglers to come in. Shortly after noon, McCoy received Fraser's signal to turn to the west and called up the *Fort Kullyspell*. Commodore M.W.S. Boucher, a retired rear-admiral, agreed with McCoy that the order was impractical in the conditions prevailing, but that continuing a slow speed of advance would partially meet the Commander-in-Chief's requirements. As the convoy gradually regained its cohesion, *Matchless*, *Musketeer*, *Opportune* and *Virago* arrived from RA55A.[2]

Schniewind and his staff at Kiel had prepared a sortie planned to take place at first light. The *Scharnhorst* was not to be committed unless circumstances were wholly favourable. The destroyers were to attack alone if necessary, allowing Bey two options which, given his style of leadership, might have achieved at least part of his objective.

Group North had kept *Scharnhorst* and her destroyers on short notice pending a decision from Dönitz who now arrived back in Berlin from Paris and appraised the situation. Fraser's signals concerning the detachment of RA55A's destroyers and JW55B's reversal of course had been intercepted, but misunderstood. Classed as 'doubtful' they failed to alert Dönitz to Fraser's presence. Moreover, the long-maintained British practice of keeping the heavy distant cover well to the westward argued the continuation of such a policy by an enemy wedded to tradition. Dönitz does not seem to have regarded as significant Fraser's dash to Kola. Perhaps he thought it a political gambit, rather than a naval operation. At all events, the last known position of JW55B indicated the time for interception was fast approaching.

Despite the heavy weather, Oberleutnant Hansen in *U601* was still trailing JW55B. His report that the wind was now south at Force 7 with thick weather and rain persuaded Schniewind to postpone any thoughts of a sortie until the visibility improved, a view which found no favour with Dönitz.

The Grossadmiral now supplemented Schniewind's planned orders with a conflicting view on the use of the destroyers; more significant, however, was the almost inevitable caveat: 'You may use your judgement when to break off action. You must disengage if a superior enemy force is encountered.' On the face of it, it was a reasonable order, but in fact it limited Bey, as others had been before him, and left him compromised. In the uncertainty of war, especially in the Arctic winter, he had almost no chance of success against a determined enemy unless he acted with extraordinary resolution.

But Bey was an active commander and shortly before 19.00 on Christmas evening, he ordered Kapitän Hintze to call his men to stations. The signal to proceed was flashed to Johannesson's 4th Destroyer Flotilla. *Z29, Z30, Z33, Z34* and *Z38* weighed and steamed down the narrow, steep-sided gullet of Altenfiord. Astern of them came the great lean grey shape of the *Scharnhorst*, as majestic as the mountains beneath whose cloud-shrouded peaks she moved.

When the German squadron cleared the land and headed due north out of its lee at 25 knots, the destroyers began their languid, unstable roll. A few hours later Bey received a radio report indicating no surface force was within fifty miles of JW55B. It was old, aerial intelligence that had been delayed. Later, Bey transmitted to Kiel the information that the weather would hamper the operating ability of his destroyers.

No Christmas dinners had been eaten aboard the *Duke of York*. The motion of the ship was unpleasant and the day passed in that claustrophobic stuffiness familiar to seamen in vessels working in a heavy seaway. Besides, the sense of anticipation was so keenly felt throughout the flagship that sleep, a sailor's one sure consolation, was also impossible. Running before the prevailing weather, the low hull of the battleship was continually wave-swept. Oerlikons mounted on the bows were swept overboard and water poured into the messdeck below through the empty rivet holes. The great quadruple A-turret was letting water through the mantlets guarding the gun apertures, and icy water poured down the interior of the barbette, reaching the shell room below. On the destroyers conditions were unimaginable; only the squadron's relatively slow speed allowed them to keep up.

The dreary hours ticked past. Frozen lookouts stared out over a black and heaving sea, streaked with grey spume, to the obscurity of the horizon. The air was filled with the roar and shriek of the wind and the hiss of breaking waves running alongside the labouring ships. Mastheads gyrated against a sky clouded by scud which, it seemed, was raked by their trucks. Funnel smoke added to the murk and, in the idiosyncratic turbulence possessed by every ship, sent its sulphurous stench in random waves over the signals staff wedged in odd corners of the after bridge. Below, operators peered at the radar screens beyond the blips of sea-clutter, identifying their own ships and seeking beyond for the first sign of the enemy. Officers stared at the plots in the dimmed red light of the chart and plotting rooms, endlessly fussing over the accuracy of their dead reckoning; asdic operators plied their tedious but essential trade and duty-gun crews shivered at their cruising stations. In the boiler and engine rooms, heated and toiling men maintained steam and tended boilers and turbines, while in cabins and messdecks, the off-duty watch tried to sleep, gave up and read, or played cards.

Thus Christmas Day merged imperceptibly with Boxing Day.

On his admiral's bridge, Fraser and his staff analysed the stream of signals now coming in from the Admiralty, all based on Ultra decrypts. At 01.30 a message timed ten hours earlier revealed that the *Admiral commanding Northern waters informed Battle Group and Admiral Polar Coast 'Codeword Epilepsy 1700/25 December'*. This portended the beginning of an operation. Then, at 02.17, followed the long-awaited confirmation: *Emergency SCHARNHORST probably sailed 1800/25 December*. And, hard on its heels, *A patrol vessel presumably in the Altenfiord area was informed at 1715 that SCHARNHORST would pass outward bound from 1800/25 December*.

As the officers and ratings due on duty at 04.00 arrived at their stations to take over the morning watch, Admiral Fraser was handed another signal chit which read: *Admiralty appreciate that SCHARNHORST is now at sea*. It was, the Fleet Wireless Officer, Commander Dawnay, recorded, 'the moment for which the heavy ship covering force for the North Russian convoys had waited for so long'.

For Fraser there was little feeling of imminent fulfilment, only a gnawing anxiety that events might miscarry. He did not know of McCoy's failure to turn JW55B about, but he did worry that the distance of Force Two from the convoy was too great to prevent the German battle group from mauling it. He ordered an increase of speed to 24 knots and then again broke radio silence, transmitting a request for McCoy and Burnett to report their positions, simultaneously revealing his own. The advantage Fraser derived from this action outweighed the risk; in fact the Germans made no use of their intercepts of this traffic.

Convoy JW55B was at that time fifty miles south of Bear Island, steering east-north-east at 8 knots. A little south of due east, at a distance of 150 miles from it, Burnett's Force One was headed roughly south-west, steaming at 18 knots, it being the Vice-Admiral's intention to be within 30 miles of the convoy four hours later when, at 08.17, nautical twilight leached a little light into the sky.

Relative to the convoy then, the Commander-in-Chief's Force Two remained 350 miles to the south-west, steering east-north-east at 24 knots, too late to intercept the enemy battle group before it reached the convoy, but able to place itself between the *Scharnhorst* and her base. Realizing McCoy had not turned round, and to delay the enemy's interception, Fraser now ordered JW55B to turn north.

Bey's battle group, intending interception of JW55B on the meridian of the North Cape, was steaming due north, 100 miles south-east of the convoy, but only 90 miles south-west of Burnett's cruisers.

'The stage was well set,' Fraser later wrote in his Report of Proceedings, 'except that if the *Scharnhorst* attacked . . . and immediately retired, I was not sufficiently close to cut her off.' This conveys a misleading impression of precise control. In fact the lonely personal pronoun is eloquent both of the enormity of the burden Fraser bore, and of the risk he ran.

Concerned about the proximity of the ice-edge just north of Bear Island and the danger of the convoy being pinned against it under *Scharnhorst*'s guns, Fraser ordered a second alteration of course at 06.28, seeking to bring JW55B on to a course of north-east. None of these signals were either passed on or acted upon speedily. The vagaries of radio propagation in the Arctic combined with the difficulties, particularly besetting McCoy, in retransmitting them to all the ships and then executing them. Burnett's position report did not reach Fraser until 05.46, and McCoy had only just cajoled JW55B on to a northern course when Fraser ordered the second alteration back to north-eastward. Control of the developing situation was not, therefore, as precise as hindsight may suggest.

Bey was worried too, and was about to be confronted by real problems. He had been the recipient of another signal from Dönitz in reply to his own report of the severity of the weather and its effect upon his labouring destroyers. The Grossadmiral wanted Bey to attack the convoy with *Scharnhorst* alone if conditions did not allow Johannesson's flotilla to keep up. This was directly contrary to Bey's own opinion, though Dönitz added consolingly, 'decision rests with Admiral commanding', presumably in an attempt to limit his earlier hedging. Bey was now misled by a U-boat report from *U716* (Dunkelberg) which, with *U601*, had clung on to the convoy's flanks and had failed to detect the northerly diversion of its quarry. Having reached the position in which he expected to find JW55B, Bey had ordered Hintze to broadcast to the crew Dönitz's message of exhortation: a successful attack on JW55B would relieve their comrades in the Wehrmacht defending the Eastern front. After delivering this, Hintze sent his men to action stations.

The Germans' expectations were dashed: they discovered

nothing beyond the swirl of snow squalls and were as frustrated by the darkness as McCoy, chivvying his charges not far away. Bey therefore swung south-west, advanced his destroyers ten miles and spread them in line abreast, each five miles apart. The consequence of this was that the northernmost German destroyer and the southernmost picket of the convoy passed each other at about 09.40 on opposite courses some fifteen miles apart. In the gloom of the polar day it might have been a hundred, but by then events had occurred elsewhere.

As the next depression moved in with characteristic Arctic swiftness, the wind veered again to the south-west, building up a head sea over the earlier swell. The German destroyers were labouring heavily, encrusted with accumulations of ice, their optical gunnery control instruments blinded by frost and snow. Bey was compelled to order a reduction of speed to 12 and then 10 knots. This obliged her screen, but made the *Scharnhorst* vulnerable to submarine attack. Bey therefore ordered Hintze to alter course to the northward. This move was the first leg of a zigzag across the rear of the destroyers, but it brought the German battleship on to a converging course with Vice-Admiral Burnett's Force One.

Led by Burnett's flag in *Belfast* (Captain F.R. Parham), *Norfolk* (Captain D.K. Bain) and *Sheffield* (Captain C.T. Addis) were approaching from the east. Shortly before dawn their companies had conformed to routine and gone to action stations, a fortuitous coincidence because within minutes first *Norfolk* and then *Belfast* picked up on their Type 273 surface surveillance radars echoes of a lone ship, seventeen miles to the west-north-west, almost exactly midway between Force One and JW55B.

Forty-five minutes later, at 09.21, the lookouts aboard *Sheffield* saw a slightly jagged hump of intenser darkness breaking the indistinct horizon seven miles away on the port beam. Captain Addis flashed 'enemy in sight' to the flagship and Burnett ordered Parham to open fire with star-shell. *Belfast*'s 6-inch guns failed to find the range and the flares burst short, hanging in the sky above an empty sea, but at 09.29 Burnett ordered Force One to open fire with main armament.

Scharnhorst had just turned on to the southward leg of her zigzag when sighted. Burnett ordered a small alteration to port to close the range, but firing over the port quarter made it impossible for all three cruisers to engage fully and the 6-inch guns of *Belfast* and *Sheffield*, which did bear, achieved nothing. HMS *Norfolk*, using radar control, succeeded in firing six broadsides, hitting the enemy with three 8-inch shells and destroying the *Scharnhorst*'s port high-angle gunnery director and her main radar aerial, as well as causing minor internal damage. A fourth, unexploded shell penetrated the upper deck.

Far ahead of *Scharnhorst*, her destroyers had had an embarrassing encounter with one of their own flotilla which had got out of station and was sighted regaining it on an opposite course. This circumstance, radioed to Hintze, was understood to mean they had made contact with an enemy unit. Before the error of this assumption was clear, the battleship was transmitting a reciprocal message that she too had been engaged by enemy cruisers. From the German destroyers the slowly descending star-shell flares could be seen astern. It was the last Johannesson and his officers saw of their flagship.

As the shell landed, *Scharnhorst* increased speed to 30 knots, made smoke and turned south-east, rapidly opening the range. Burnett's ships ceased fire at 09.40 but followed round until 10.00 when the Vice-Admiral, realizing his cruisers were incapable of getting within range of the speeding battleship in the prevailing sea conditions, disengaged, turned north-west and fell back towards JW55B. Burnett was quite correct in his conviction that Bey would try and work round to get at the convoy from the north. Aboard *Scharnhorst* her company were being told just that, with the added information that the destroyers would attack from the south. To implement this, Bey now ordered Johannesson's destroyers to put about and steam north-east, hoping thereby to trap both Burnett and the convoy, intimidating the British cruisers with the threat of torpedoes and guns which almost matched their own in calibre, while the battleship annihilated the merchantmen at will.

Alerted by Burnett's reports, Fraser had again instructed McCoy to signal the Commodore of the convoy to bring his ships on to a northerly heading. He also ordered the four destroyers received as reinforcements from RA55A, *Matchless*, *Musketeer*, *Opportune* and *Virago*, to reinforce Burnett's cruisers just as McCoy himself asked the Vice-Admiral if his ships could be of any assistance. This simultaneity of thought was characteristic of British naval officers – the product of a long tradition based on Nelson's famous statement that 'no captain could do very wrong if he laid his ship alongside that of an enemy'. Mutual support was a fundamental tenet of the Royal Navy.[3]

At about the time the junction of Fisher's destroyers and Burnett's cruisers was made, Fraser, still worried about the ice-edge, ordered JW55B to resume a north-easterly course and, an hour later, left the matter to McCoy's discretion. At noon on 26 December 1943, convoy JW55B therefore altered course to the south-east. It had hardly steadied on its new heading when *Belfast*'s radar operators picked up the enemy again. In her two-hour respite, *Scharnhorst* had raced in an arc forty miles to the north. By disengaging at 10.00 in defence of the convoy, Burnett's instinct had proved flawless, taking Force One along the chord, to a position about ten miles east of JW55B.[4]

Having made some adjustments to his destroyers' dispositions and the squadron's speed due to the difficulties caused by the high sea still running, Burnett was about to conform with the convoy's alteration to the south-east when contact with the enemy was again made. Aware that the convoy's new course was opening the distance, Force One, its four destroyers flung out ahead of the three cruisers, stood on to the east-north-east, rapidly closing the range from an initial fifteen miles.

Abruptly out of the gloom at 12.20 on the starboard bow of the British cruisers loomed the German battleship heading south-west. Immediately Burnett ordered his ships to open fire and his destroyers to attack with torpedoes. A moment later *Belfast*'s star-shells burst above the *Scharnhorst*.

Seeing the destroyers pitching towards him and fearing their torpedoes, Kapitän Hintze opened fire and turned away under a series of violent helm movements, which shortened the range to four and a half miles, finally steadying on a course of east-south-east. His gun layers concentrated upon *Norfolk*, the easiest target, for she was not using flashless cordite charges, and the yellow brilliants of her salvoes enabled her range to be quickly established.

The German salvoes soon engulfed the British cruiser; she was hit by an 11-inch shell which disabled X-turret, and both her main radar sets were knocked out of action. One officer and six men were killed, and a further five severely wounded. Near misses showered *Sheffield* with splinters as *Scharnhorst* increased speed and drew away on a course of south-east. At 12.41 she vanished in her own smoke and the Arctic murk.

Such had been the speed of Hintze's reaction to their appearance, and so bad the state of the sea, that Fisher's destroyers had been unable to manœuvre into a position to fire their torpedoes. Nor had the cruisers fared much better, only one unexploded shell landing on the retreating battleship's quarterdeck. Both destroyers and cruisers now clung to the enemy in a long 28-knot chase to the south-south-east, maintaining contact by radar. At first converging on JW55B, such was the *Scharnhorst*'s speed that by 14.00, although across the line of the convoy's advance, the German battleship was thirty miles ahead of it, the three cruisers fine on her port quarter, the four destroyers fine to starboard. She was now opening her distance from the convoy in an attempt to return to Altenfiord.

Vice-Admiral Burnett was anxious not to dissuade her from this line of retreat, and, running across the seas, his smaller destroyers could keep up. He would continue to shadow; with luck the *Scharnhorst* would come under the guns of HMS *Duke of York*.

The Commander-in-Chief was a far from happy man. The euphoria which had spread upon the report that Force One was in sight of the enemy ended abruptly when Burnett signalled that he had *lost touch with enemy who was steering north. Am closing convoy*. Its arrival coincided with the appearance of a Blohm and Voss BV138 flying boat which droned on the horizon. Its presence and Burnett's apparent 'failure' seemed to have ruined all chances of surprise, for it was inconceivable the *Duke of York*'s presence would not be reported.

In fact the BV138's report of 'one big and several smaller ships' failed to raise any suspicions and, though forwarded to Bey, was too garbled to influence him. Ignorant of this almost incredible disregard, Fraser's depression was understandable: he had gambled on high stakes, risked humiliation and now seemed about to get his come-uppance.

At 10.58 he replied somewhat peevishly to Burnett: *Unless touch can be regained by some unit, there is no chance of my finding enemy*. The receipt of this signal might have shaken a less convinced man than Bullshit Bob; when he learned of the emergence of *Scharnhorst*, he is reputed to have remarked, 'I have prayed for this moment.' Now he stood on, maintaining his defensive posture.

Fraser was less sure, and with some reason. *Scharnhorst* did not have to have as her objective JW55B; there were convoys aplenty in the Atlantic and a break-out to the west would threaten the fast passenger liners then being used to ferry American and Canadian troops to England in preparation for Operation Overlord. The loss of one of those troopships to the *Scharnhorst*'s guns was unimaginable.

At 11.57, with a heavy heart, Fraser ordered his signals staff to send to the ships of Force Two, *Course is to be altered in succession to 260° ships turning to starboard*. In the heavy stern sea the destroyers could not execute this manœuvre with the precision of an exercise. It was a matter of individual judgement. To avoid broaching, each captain must decide the moment most suiting his own ship. *Duke of York* and *Jamaica* reduced speed to 18 knots and waited for their screen to comply, adding, *Mean line of advance from now is to be 250° until further orders*. Force Two turned away and headed back to the west-south-west.

The news was received throughout the squadron with a dismay only slightly less than that which had greeted the sloppy mess of 'pork swilling in fannies full of greasy sludge' served to the men at their action stations. The motion of the ships changed to pitching. The destroyers, already short of fuel, pounded into the heavy seas, one minute with their bows pointing at the sky, the next with their sterns flung high, the propellers cavitating and shaking their frail hulls. Weighed by her armour plate, the *Duke of York* slammed through the waves, swept from end to end by green water. Her low bow, built to facilitate the forward firing of her massive quadruple A-turret, was now a liability. A mood of total gloom matched that of the day itself.

Then, quite suddenly, everything changed. Fraser was handed a signal and in 'an electrifying moment', his eyes alight, called out, 'Turn 'em round again!' Burnett had regained contact with the enemy. It was just after noon.

It was also just after noon when Johannesson's destroyers converged on the position where Bey, having reversed their track, had indicated they would intercept the Allied convoy. In fact, JW55B had just steadied on its final south-easterly course and had they delayed, the convoy, with only McCoy's destroyers and the through escort protecting it, would have been delivered on to the German guns. But Bey now committed Johannesson further west, misled by shadowing U-boat reports. As it was, their closest approach to JW55B was only eight miles. But the moment passed and, at 14.18 when he himself was committed to a return to Altenfiord, Bey ordered the 4th Flotilla back to base.

The *Duke of York, Jamaica* and the destroyers of Force Two pressed on to the east-north-east, a calmer Fraser sitting on his bridge smoking his pipe and receiving a succession of position reports from Burnett which, passed on to the chart room, confirmed that matters were finally moving steadily to a climax. At 15.30 all watertight doors and armoured hatches were closed. As the distance between the chief protagonists diminished, a mounting sense of tension gripped the men at their action stations. It was bitterly cold and already dark.

And then, at 16.17 on that black and icy night, there appeared on the radar screen aboard Fraser's flagship a bright point of light that glowed with renewed brilliance every time the trace of the Type 273's scanner raked the distant *Scharnhorst*. The enemy ship bore north-north-east, distant twenty-five and a half miles. She was zigzagging on a mean course of south-south-east at 27 knots. Shortly afterwards a trailing cluster of smaller echoes revealed Force One.

At 16.32 the *Scharnhorst* was located by the *Duke of York*'s Type 284 fire-control radar eleven miles away. Flag-Captain Russell pointed out to Fraser that the enemy was within the range of their 14-inch guns. Fraser, with a cool aplomb, aware that he was making history, declined until the range closed further. He did, however, order his destroyers to prepare for a torpedo attack, though forbidding them to do so until permitted by his orders. On the port bow *Saumarez* and *Savage*, and on the starboard bow *Stord* and *Scorpion* blinked their acknowledgement. It was the one mistake the Commander-in-Chief made.

At 16.50, with both battleships rapidly converging and now less than seven miles apart, Fraser altered course to starboard to open the firing arcs of all the guns of both the flagship and *Jamaica* astern. The gun's crews were stood to and the three huge turrets swung on the line of bearing indicated by the director; the guns were loaded with armour-piercing shells and full charges. There then followed a period of tense silence broken only by the hiss of hydraulics as the layers and trainers elevated and rotated the guns in conformity with their pointers and receivers.

Then at last Fraser told Burnett to fire star-shell over the enemy. This proved ineffectual, only a grey and rolling waste of water appearing in the binoculars of the Admiral's watching staff.

It was time for Fraser to throw off the mask. The 5.25-inch guns of the *Duke of York*'s port secondary battery fired four star-shells which exploded and hung above and behind the *Scharnhorst*, descending slowly and throwing the beautiful ship into a brief, haunting silhouette, 'like a great silver ghost' – 'of enormous length . . . it was a gunnery officer's dream come true'. Her gun turrets, aligned fore and aft, betrayed the extent of her surprise.

It was 16.51 when the firing gongs jangled in the turrets and the *Duke of York* opened fire, not with the alternate guns of a salvo, but with the thunderous concussion of a full broadside. Ten 14-inch guns, each of whose recoil was the equivalent of 400 tons, stabbed the Arctic night. The huge battleship shuddered with reaction. Astern of them *Jamaica* followed suit. The tracer bands soared up into the blackness and then descended. It took a full fifteen seconds for the shells to cover the 6.8-mile range at a speed of 1,800 miles per hour.

At such short range the flat trajectories lacked the plunging effect that would ensure armour penetration, but the watching officers saw the brief green glows on *Scharnhorst*'s hull that indicated hits by the radar-controlled broadsides. Her forward turret was wrecked but, as she emerged from the wall of water thrown up by the exploding shells around her, 'her turrets wore a different aspect'.

Hintze swung away to the north, turning on Burnett who hurriedly conformed, unaware of the damage to *Scharnhorst*'s forward turret and worried over a report just received that *Sheffield* had had to reduce speed due to stripped gearing on one shaft. *Come ON!* he signalled Captain Addis impatiently. Fraser, too, followed round in hot pursuit, while Burnett's remaining two cruisers opened fire, inhibiting Bey and compelling him to order Hintze to turn east. *Scharnhorst* made off, swinging from time to time to allow her B-turret to fire on her tormentors from whom, due to her superior speed, she drew slowly away.

It was now just after 17.00 and Fraser's destroyers were attempting to overhaul the German and reach a position from which they could loose their torpedoes. Meanwhile the German gunners had steadied and put two shells between the British flagship's masts, neither of which exploded. More straddled the chasing ships as *Jamaica* edged out on the flagship's port quarter and the *Duke of York* was eased over to starboard to keep her quadruple after turret bearing. The effects of muzzle blast inflicted a number of wounds upon herself, scorching Fraser's barge and sending searing heat down ventilation trunkings amidships.

While the main armament pounded away, the secondary battery sent star-shell over the target: at 17.13, Fraser finally ordered Walmsley in *Saumarez* and Meyrick in *Savage* to launch torpedoes, but the opportunity had passed. The wildly rolling and pitching destroyers had no chance of delivering their weapons, though they gallantly stuck to the chase. Fraser was confronted by the distinct possibility that speed alone might yet save the *Scharnhorst*. To be outrun now was the worst humiliation Fraser could imagine, for he had been Comptroller of the Navy when the much-criticized King George V class of battleship had been designed.

Four knots faster than her pursuer and infinitely more weatherly, the lighter *Scharnhorst* now dropped first Burnett's cruisers and then *Jamaica* out of range astern. It had become a duel between the heavy guns of the two battleships. While the *Duke of York* fell astern, however, she still possessed the advantages of radar-controlled fire and unexploited range, up to eighteen miles, for although the higher muzzle velocity of *Scharnhorst*'s guns could range for twenty-five miles and the *Duke of York*'s for only twenty, the German ship possessed neither radar control nor her full armament. She was capable of throwing a weight of metal of a mere two tons against the British flagship's broadside of seven, though in the wild, windswept darkness even this seemed small enough at the time. Only three hits had been observed and although one of these had started a fire amidships, the German fire-parties had soon controlled and extinguished it. Moreover, the gunnery radar had failed due to the formidable concussion of the full-calibre guns smashing valves. This reduced the British to visual gun control which was hampered by a trailing veil of smoke, drifting languidly on the following wind behind the fleeing *Scharnhorst* and which lay by a fluke along the direct line-of-sight of the chasing British.

But all was far from well aboard the *Scharnhorst*. She had lost speed, first to near misses and then to the explosion of a 14-inch shell in her starboard boiler room. Her speed had fallen to 10 knots and, although swift cross connection of her steam supply enabled her quickly to work back up to 22 knots, she had sacrificed a vital part of her lead. An increasingly apprehensive Bey transmitted a defiant signal to Berlin: *We shall fight to the last shell, SCHARNHORST ever onwards*!

Despite this her guns fell silent at 18.20 as she opened the range to eleven miles. Four minutes later, the order to cease firing on the British ships stopped the exertions of the sweating gun crews aboard *Duke of York* and *Jamaica*; they had fired fifty-two broadsides, but 'the resultant despondency was profound'.

For Fraser there now occurred the second black period of the day. He turned the *Duke of York* away to port in the forlorn hope of inducing *Scharnhorst* to follow and move closer to her base at Altenfiord, but neither Bey nor Hintze fell for the ruse and Fraser was constrained to signal Burnett, *I see little hope of catching* Scharnhorst *and am proceeding to support convoy*. The ironic memory of his reaction to a similar signal from Burnett some eight hours earlier cannot have escaped him.

But Fraser had reckoned without his destroyers. Frustrated by the Commander-in-Chief's earlier restriction, they had gained somewhat in the appalling conditions as the *Scharnhorst* had slowed. As the fire of the heavy guns died away, *Savage* and *Saumarez* ranged up astern of the battleship and then opened their bearing on her port quarter, coming under fire from the *Scharnhorst*'s secondary and anti-aircraft armament. The British destroyers' guns were firing star-shell over the enemy, and while these blinded their colleagues in *Stord* and *Scorpion* on the *Scharnhorst*'s starboard side they also obscured the approach of these two ships. The Germans spotted them when less than two miles away at about 18.50. To the men on the destroyers' iron decks, swinging the torpedo tubes at their enemy, it seemed that the *Scharnhorst* loomed above them.

'We're going alongside the bastard!' a seaman aboard *Scorpion* was heard to exclaim.

But at that moment Hintze heard the proximity of the enemy reported and threw the helm hard a-starboard to comb the track of any torpedoes. Swift adjustment of the tubes enabled *Stord* and *Scorpion* to fire, launching sixteen torpedoes at 18.52, though only one hit the battleship as she swung to steam past on a reciprocal course. The two destroyers then withdrew under fire.

The *Scharnhorst*'s alteration of course gave Meyrick and Walmsley their chance. They in turn swung away, north-east to the enemy's south-west, but in the moment of crossing, beam to beam, with a hiss of compressed air, torpedoes shot from the midships tubes of *Savage* and *Saumarez* at almost point-blank range. Of the dozen launched, two struck home, wrecking a second boiler room and distorting a propeller shaft. As the destroyers escaped to the north-east, though not without damage, *Scharnhorst*'s speed again fell to 10 knots.

On receiving the news that the destroyers were attacking with torpedoes, Fraser cheered up. He had just learned that the gunnery radar had been repaired and then, seeing Bey turn his flagship south-west, altered his own course to port, with *Jamaica* following in his wake, to a heading of north-east. Both ships reopened fire, the *Duke of York* mixing star-shell among the armour-piercing. Immediately both British ships found their target and Fraser led them round to a southerly heading, slowly passing the German battleship as she swung back to the north and then round to the south again, pounding the *Scharnhorst* with a succession of hits. As the British flagship skirted to the southward and then finally to the east on a heading of north-east, *Jamaica* detached, swinging first to starboard and then to port, bringing her torpedo mountings on each side to bear on the great grey ship. The German battleship slowed to a stop and her last main turret fell silent. She was in her death throes, awaiting the *coup de grâce*.

Burnett now approached from the north, engaging with *Belfast* and *Norfolk* until, at 19.18, he swung his cruisers to starboard, exposing their port tubes from which the bright, silvery gleam of the torpedoes flashed in the gunfire before sliding into the water. He also unleashed his four destroyers. They divided into two, *Matchless* and *Musketeer* opening for the enemy's port side, where her bilge was exposed, and *Virago* and *Opportune* making for the starboard. *Matchless* had been damaged amidships by a green sea which destroyed her voice pipes and the torpedo crews missed the order to fire, but the others struck at the mortally wounded and heavily listing *Scharnhorst*. Steam and smoke rose from her, the flames of myriad fires flickering intermittently through the gloom.

On her decks her company were mustered among the dead and the wounded. Above them on the bridge Kapitän Fritz Julius Hintze raised his megaphone. 'Don't go overboard to starboard, my friends.Go over from the port side, and slide from the rail into the water. Don't forget to inflate your lifejackets. And now, one after the other, over the rail.'

The *Scharnhorst* rolled heavily and still crept through the water, though almost on her beam ends. Breaking waves flicked spray over her angled mastheads above which the orange glow of the British star-shells gleamed through the snow and hail squalls. About her she drew a dense pall of smoke.

As the shells and torpedoes from the three cruisers slammed into her and the ring of gunfire deluged her decks with spray and splinters from near misses, in the plotting room of the *Duke of York*, four miles away, a mood of calm prevailed. The officers 'controlling the destiny of some eighteen hundred souls . . . gave the impression that they were able to make time wait for them', wrote a witness. 'The question I have sometimes asked myself, and heard others ask, as to why boys were taken away from home at so young an age to be trained for the Royal Navy, was answered then.'

At the radar screen Lieutenant Cox reported the *Scharnhorst*'s echo fading, inferring the enemy was sinking, but Fraser could not bring himself to believe it, and sharply instructed Cox to retune the set.

The smoke hanging over the scene, even in the wind-whipped darkness, prevented a single observer in any of the British ships from seeing the *Scharnhorst* finally founder. Only a dull under-water explosion reported by some of them marked her going.

Still unable to accept what had happened Fraser, showing signs of the strain he had so long borne, sent a series of frantic signals to his ships demanding confirmation. It was over half an hour before *Belfast* replied. Still firing star-shell, Burnett's flagship passed through the pathetic debris; oil and a raft of frozen and traumatized survivors were almost all there was left of the Kriegsmarine's proudest ship. Burnett signalled, *Satisfied SCHARNHORST sunk*.

With her, unseen in the freezing, spray-sodden night, went Bey and Hintze and 1,765 officers and ratings. *Scorpion* recovered 30 survivors, *Matchless* 6. There was little jubilation among the victors. The remoteness of modern war left no room for hate; there was only the satisfaction of achievement to ease the bone-weariness. 'It had been a long day's night.'[5]

Fraser now ordered that the Admiralty be informed of his victory. His signals officer had difficulty contacting a British station, finally transmitting through Iceland the two words, *SCHARNHORST sunk*. The Admiralty's three-word reply arrived at 21.53: *Grand. Well done*. Fraser then spoke somewhat awkwardly to Burnett over the TBS. He was worried about his destroyers' fuel state. 'I'm off to Russia, Bob, follow me when you can . . .'

The combined squadrons of Fraser and Burnett arrived in the Kola Inlet during the 27th to the congratulations of the SBNO North Russia and Admiral Golovko. The Russian Admiral had brought his destroyers to a state of readiness at Polyarnoe, alerted the Russian airforce and sent his submarines to patrol the approaches to Altenfiord in case the *Scharnhorst* had escaped Fraser.[6]

Meanwhile JW55B had continued to be shadowed by remnants of the Eisenbart wolfpack until they were sent to search for survivors on the 27th. On that day McCoy brought the ten merchantmen of JW55B bound for Murmansk into Kola with the ocean escort and steamed past the warships anchored at Vaenga. Two days later the remainder, with the through escort, arrived in the White Sea.

Fraser's action, known to history as the Battle of the North Cape, had not only destroyed the *Scharnhorst*, it had also ensured the safe and timely arrival of the convoy.

Fraser's ships took on 10,000 tons of fuel oil before they were ready to sail, at 18.00 on 28 December. The handful of German survivors were transferred to the flagship and *Saumarez* patched up the damage from her close quarters engagement.

On New Year's Eve, *Duke of York*, *Jamaica* and Fisher's and Meyrick's two destroyer flotillas entered Scapa Flow through the Hoxa gate. Led by the flagship and flying their battle ensigns they passed anchored units of the Home Fleet whose companies manned their sides and cheered the victorious ships to their anchorages.

Fraser, soon to be knighted, received a stream of congratulatory telegrams from the King and Churchill among others, while the crews of the battered warships sat down to a belated tot of rum and their postponed Christmas dinners. Commander Thomas, Master of the Fleet, was sent south by air with Fraser's victorious dispatch. In the bad weather, his pilot failed to locate Hendon and landed at Hornchurch. Thomas finally reached the Admiralty for his interview with the First Sea Lord by a Royal Air Force three-ton lorry. This was not to Cunningham's liking and Thomas's reception was frosty; full of the drama of the hour, Cunningham ridiculously had arranged for Thomas to ride in on horseback.

Four centuries earlier, Shakespeare had written of 'a tide in the affairs of men that, taken at the flood, leads on to fortune'. Fraser caught that flood-tide, in the full knowledge that it was almost high water for his beloved Service. It was, however, his personal fortune to command the victorious squadrons in the last action between battleships. Like Nelson and Jervis before him, he took as the title of the peerage later conferred upon him after service in the Pacific the location of the battle he had fought as Commander-in-Chief of the British Home Fleet, becoming Lord Fraser of North Cape. Like Nelson, too, he had been unconventional, dispensing with radio silence when a greater advantage could be gained by breaking it. In this he showed the genius of his judgement. Of his inspirational qualities much might be said; indeed he was ably supported by Sir Robert Burnett who, with a sense of the dramatic, had on more than one occasion in the bleak Barents Sea arrived on the field of battle at a critical moment.

Admiral Fraser was a man who made his own luck, unlike Tovey before him for whom the tide was slack. It was not beyond Fraser to make use of the Arctic convoys as bait, but neither would he maintain a cover so remote as to be ineffective. Deeply affected by the tragedy of PQ17 which he had distantly witnessed as VA2, Fraser was determined to restore the confidence of Allied merchant seafarers in the British Royal Navy. That he was too late to be wholly successful was not his fault; the facts and falsehoods had spread swiftly over half the globe. In the aftermath of the disaster Tovey had restored the shaken morale of the Home Fleet; Fraser's task was more difficult. It could only be done by that essential ingredient of leadership: example.

This he had shown by total commitment, and thus he had dared to dice his reputation upon his chance of destroying the *Scharnhorst*; and thus he won his great gamble.[7]

21

'They never let me down'

TO HIS CHAGRIN, Captain McCoy, though closely associated with the chief object of *Scharnhorst*'s sortie, had seen little of the action; he was also to be allowed little rest, for on New Year's Eve his seven refuelled destroyers were once again under way with the two LREs *Whitehall* and *Wrestler* and the corvettes *Oxlip* and *Honeysuckle*, all of which had brought out JW55B. With the addition of *Rhododendron*, left from the outward escort of JW54B, McCoy now prepared to take RA55B home. It was only a small convoy of eight ships and was seen clear of the Murman coast by the minesweepers *Halcyon*, *Hussar* and *Speedwell*. During the passage several U-boats were detected and driven off, and though *U957* fired a Gnat torpedo at her tormentor it failed to find its target. McCoy's four British and three Canadian destroyers detached off Iceland, relieved by the minesweepers *Orestes* and *Ready*. Commodore Dennison, a retired Royal Naval captain, broke with precedent and made the passage in the American Liberty ship *Thomas Kearns* which led the eight merchant ships in through the boom at Loch Ewe on 8 January 1944.[1]

The new year was to see a dramatic increase in German submarine activity in the Barents Sea, a greater concentration of effort to halt the flow of supplies via the Arctic route in a futile attempt to arrest the threat to the Fatherland from the Red Army on the eastern front. In 1942, five U-boats had been destroyed by the defenders of the PQ convoys, in 1943 only one. The final sixteen months of the war were to account for a further twenty-five, evidence of a more intense struggle which offered no respite to the Allied seamen, whatever the fortunes of war elsewhere.[2]

When convoy JW56A left Loch Ewe on 12 January, followed by JW56B on the 22nd, they were to find an efficient wolfpack lying in wait. They were also to encounter bad weather.

Commodore Whitehorn aboard the United States Liberty ship *Penelope Barker* led twenty laden merchantmen, including the British tanker *San Adolfo*, out of Loch Ewe and headed north. The corvettes *Borage, Wallflower, Poppy* and *Dianella* gathered on the flanks, with the sloop *Cygnet* and the minesweepers *Orestes* and *Ready* in local attendance. HM destroyers *Inconstant* and *Savage* with H Nor. MS *Stord* also joined, and JW56A made for the rendezvous with the ocean escort off Iceland. As the convoy approached the Faeroes conditions deteriorated until its cohesion was threatened by the onset of exceptionally heavy weather. By the 15th, Whitehorn was receiving reports of damage to ships and cargoes as his convoy disintegrated; the escorts, too, were faring badly, so all ships were given permission to run for shelter, to reassemble at Akureyri.

The battered merchantmen straggled into Eyja fiord throughout the 18th and flashed reports of their condition to an anxious Whitehorn who now transferred into *Fort Bellingham*. The quickly built Liberty ships were the most vulnerable to the onslaught of heavy weather, their welded hulls rigid to the point of overstressing. Five of them, *Charles Bulfinch, Jefferson Davis, John A. Quitman, Joseph N. Nicollet* and *Nathaniel Alexander*, were left behind to repair damage when, on the 21st, JW56A resumed its passage with a newly constituted escort.[3]

Of the four corvettes, two had returned to Loch Ewe on the 18th and only *Poppy* and *Dianella* continued, though the two minesweepers assisted until JW56A was clear of Iceland. The destroyer force was led by Captain Robson in *Hardy*, with *Inconstant, Obdurate, Offa, Savage, Venus, Virago* and *Stord*. There was no heavy cover, but Vice-Admiral Palliser was in command of the cruiser squadron in *Kent*, with *Bermuda* in company; a third cruiser, *Berwick*, had turned back with defects, but later caught up towards the end of the operation, for Palliser's force had also to cover the next convoy, JW56B, which left Loch Ewe on the day following the departure of JW56A from Akureyri.

The Germans were alerted to the plight of JW56A thanks to the report of an agent at Akureyri. Kapitän Peters, in tactical charge of the Norwegian-based U-boats, dispatched the six-strong Isegrim wolfpack to intercept in the vicinity of Bear Island, reinforcing them with two from Hammerfest, *U314* and *U716*, both of which had been part of the Eisenbart pack sent to search for survivors from *Scharnhorst*. All of these boats carried the acoustic homing T-5 torpedo, known to the British as the Gnat.

Meanwhile, JW56B had left with a local escort of two corvettes, *Rhododendron* and *Honeysuckle*, two minesweepers, *Onyx* and *Hydra*, and the LRE *Wrestler*, all of which had departed the convoy by the 25th, leaving a through escort of the LREs *Whitehall* and *Westcott*, the sloop *Cygnet*, the corvette *Oxlip* and the minesweeper *Seagull*. The convoy had steamed out of Loch Ewe seventeen strong, but the *Henry Lomb* had suffered engine problems and returned to Scotland. The ocean escort of destroyers came up on the 26th under Captain Campbell in *Milne*, with *Mahratta*, *Musketeer*, *Opportune*, *Scourge* and *Huron*.[4]

Although German air reconnaissance had not sighted either convoy, the Isegrim U-boats were in touch in the darkness of the late afternoon of the 25th, concentrating for an attack which was to take as its targets both the escorts and the merchantmen. That night they closed on the advancing convoy. Robson's escorts were hard-pressed and in some cases inexperienced. Evading sonic detection by remaining surfaced, the U-boats caused some confusion to the Huff-Duff monitors, but their chatter had alerted the defenders and a mêlée ensued in which *U965*, *U601*, *U360*, *U425*, *U737*, *U278* and *U314* fired a total of ten Gnat torpedoes against the escorts and *U278*, *U360*, *U716* and *U957* used conventional torpedoes against the merchant ships. The Gnats, though they almost all missed their targets, nevertheless detonated as they passed through their victims' wakes. The resulting explosions, heard by the listening submariners, undoubtedly contributed to the exaggerated claims of a victory over this convoy which were broadcast to the German people. As the action began, Captain Robson of *Hardy* ordered *Obdurate* to render assistance to *Penelope Barker* which had reported having on board a seaman suffering from acute appendicitis. Sclater laid his destroyer alongside the dangling pilot ladder flung over the cargo ship's side. Once again it was Surgeon-Lieutenant Hood, the man who had leapt aboard *Northern Gem* during Sherbrooke's action, who came to the succour of the sick man.

As Hood began work, Oberleutnant Franze in *U278* fired at the

American Liberty ship, which fell out of line shortly afterwards, followed by the Commodore's *Fort Bellingham*, hit by a torpedo from Becker's *U360*. The *Penelope Barker* began to sink quickly, with heavy loss of life. Hood made his patient, Harold Hazard, as comfortable as possible in a Carley raft and he was later picked up, but Hood himself did not survive. Meanwhile *Fort Bellingham* struggled on and began to regain station.

Having completed his mercy mission, Commander Sclater's *Obdurate* had counter-attacked *U360* but, launching a Gnat which missed the destroyer, Becker ran deep, evading the rapidly approaching ship.

Two hours later a torpedo from Oberleutnant Schaar's *U957* slammed into the Commodore's ailing ship with a terrifying explosion. The *Fort Bellingham* heeled rapidly, slowed to a stop and began to settle. As she sank and the convoy drew ahead, Schaar surfaced, approached her boats and took prisoner several of the survivors.

Meanwhile other U-boats were still surfaced and *Obdurate*'s radar operators had located Becker again. Sclater swung his ship and ran down the bearing. Once again *U360* loosed a Gnat and this time Becker achieved at least partial success. The torpedo destroyed the *Obdurate*'s starboard screw and damaged the adjacent shell, making the destroyer unmanageable for a while. Lieutenant-Commander Argles of *Vigilant*, overhearing *Obdurate* report her plight, volunteered to stand by, but Robson, conscious of the pressure on the escort, refused permission. *Obdurate* was left astern, while her crew, under the direction of Lieutenant Henry Hewlitt RNVR and the engineering lieutenant, Lieutenant Densham, isolated the flooded compartments, shored bulkheads, hammered softwood plugs into the worst leaks and ran salvage suction lines from the emergency pumps. Four hours later *Obdurate* rejoined the convoy by steaming on one screw.

By this time, the morning of the 26th, JW56A had sustained its last loss, the *Andrew G. Curtin*, torpedoed by *U716*. The Liberty ship sank quickly, her survivors being rescued by *Inconstant*.

The next day, as JW56A approached the Murman coast, the Soviet destroyers *Gremyashchi*, *Grozni*, *Razyarenny* and *Razumny* arrived, fresh from a combined operation commanded by Golovko in person against Axis shipping along the polar coast. The convoy entered the Kola Inlet on the 28th, the merchant ships dispersing to their berths or the anchorages, Robson's destroyers to fuel in haste. Learning of the loss of the three freighters, Admiral Fraser had ordered the returning RA56A postponed and Campbell's following ocean escort of JW56B reinforced by Robson's, sending also HMS *Meteor* from Scapa Flow. Leaving behind the damaged *Obdurate*, Robson's eight British and Norwegian destroyers left the same day and met up with the incoming convoy on 29 January. Captain Campbell's ships were being hard-pressed and he was moved to remark that it was 'with infinite relief that Captain Robson in the *Hardy* arrived with six other destroyers from Kola in support'.

Located by enemy aircraft five days out of Loch Ewe, Campbell had routed his charges well north but, in the Bear Island passage, convoy JW56B had run into a wolfpack reconstituted by Peters from the reinforced Isegrim group. This pack, aptly named Werwolf, contained no less than fifteen U-boats.

On the gloomy morning of the 29th, Mohs in *U956* transmitted a homing signal when he gained contact with JW56B, but at about noon, as he manœuvred for an attack, he was located and driven off three times by escorts at whom he ineffectually fired Gnats. Overnight all the boats sought an opening as the augmented screen fought back in defence of the sixteen merchantmen. *U737*, *U601*, *U957*, *U278*, *U472*, *U425* and *U313* fired a total of twelve Gnats, one of which, from *U278* (Franze), homed on HMS *Hardy* and blew her stern off. Despite the engagement then in progress, Commander Richardson coolly laid *Venus* alongside the damaged flotilla leader and evacuated her crew, afterwards hastening her end with a torpedo.

Luckier were Campbell himself, in *Milne*, and Storeheil in *Stord*, the one just missed by Kapitänleutnant Brasack in *U737*, the other likewise attacked by Schaar with his British prisoners on board *U957*. The Gnats exploded disconcertingly in the destroyers' wakes. Meanwhile, *U313*, *U965* and *U425*, having jockeyed for position, made futile attacks on the merchant ships.

Then out on the starboard advanced flank of the convoy at 19.17, *Meteor*'s lookouts spotted torpedo tracks, dull white smears in the gloom, as her asdic operators gained a contact. Combing the tracks, Lieutenant-Commander Jewitt reported his situation and Campbell ordered the adjacent elderly and much-modified *Whitehall* to her assistance. Twenty minutes later *Whitehall* made and then quickly lost contact, while *Meteor* pressed on in the darkness. At 20.00 *Whitehall*'s radar picked up a new echo three miles south of *Meteor* and her asdic operators heard the noise of torpedoes being fired: the quarry appeared to be attempting a surface retreat, so Jewitt and Lieutenant-Commander Cowell in *Whitehall* continued south in pursuit.

Kapitänleutnant Basse in *U314*, aware of their approach and the fact that, being destroyers, he could not outrun them on the surface, fired his stern tubes and then submerged. As the U-boat dived, *Whitehall* regained contact and informed *Meteor*, whereupon both ships dropped depth-charges. Neither Jewitt nor Cowell were convinced they had been successsful, even after combing the area for four hours. Their quarry, they assumed, had escaped their questing sonar beams, hidden by a layer of denser water. Breaking off their hunt at midnight, they headed back for the convoy, signalling their results as 'inconclusive'.

In fact they had sunk *U314*. She had been built at Flenderwerft's Lübeck yard, a Type VIIC boat commanded by Kapitänleutnant Georg-Wilhelm Basse who, because he had trained in 1936, the year of the Berlin Olympics, bore the Olympic rings on his conning tower. His submarine had been in commission just six weeks.

Although harried and subjected to continuing Gnat attacks, JW56B suffered no further material damage and entered the Kola Inlet on 1 February.

Due to the postponement of convoy RA56A, the ships of JW56B were now ready to return to the west. Fraser ordered them amalgamated into one large convoy of thirty-nine merchant vessels, protected by the already united escorts of JW56A and B. To replace *Obdurate* and *Hardy*, the Commander-in-Chief sent the destroyers *Verulam*, *Swift* and *Obedient* eastwards to meet RA56 on the 6th, withdrawing HMS *Virago* to the west independently with the survivors and wounded. *Obdurate* herself, having been patched up with Russian help consisting largely of female and adolescent labour, joined the body of the convoy and limped home on her one screw.

The combined convoy, RA56, sailed on 3 February. Shortly afterwards two ships, *Empire Pickwick* and *Philip Livingston*, turned back with engine problems. *Gleaner* and *Seagull* cleared the channel and *Halcyon*, *Hussar* and *Speedwell* accompanied until the 10th, when they broke away, returning to Britain after their long sojourn in Arctic waters. *Whitehall*, *Westcott*, *Cygnet* and the corvettes *Dianella*, *Oxlip*, *Poppy* and *Rhododendron* formed the close escort, with Campbell's thirteen destroyers as the outer screen. The destroyers departed on 9 February when the western local escort of corvettes and minesweepers arrived to shepherd the returning merchantmen into Loch Ewe on 11 February.[5]

German aerial reconnaissance had located the mass of ships on 5 February and the Werwolf pack was manœuvred to lie in wait. But as a result of an incorrectly reported (or plotted) reciprocal course it was thought that the westbound convoy was going the other way, an embarrassing slip which caused the eight U-boats to miss their target entirely. The Luftwaffe revenged itself on the 10th, however, bombing the Bowring tanker *El Grillo* as she lay at anchor in Seidisfiord 'on Admiralty service' as a fleet oiler.

The growing hours of daylight and the increased possibility of German air attack, combined with the effectiveness of this large convoy and its equally large escort, were to persuade Fraser to implement a change of policy and revert to the sailing of very large convoys. Two factors had changed somewhat since the experiences of PQ17 and 18; there were more escorts of all classes, and the composition of the convoys themselves had altered. This latter factor was significant in that almost all the merchantmen were war-built tonnage with an improved anti-aircraft capability of their own. The only disadvantage was the fact that the vast increase in American merchant shipping had watered down much hard-gained experience. But this was also true of some escorts, many undergoing changes of command during the spring of 1944 as experienced officers were withdrawn to prepare for roles in Operation Overlord.

Nevertheless, Fraser was undaunted by this drain on his manpower. He knew the number of his ships would be drastically reduced by May and was determined to force through as many cargoes of munitions to the Soviet armed forces as was possible. For their part, the Russians had, in January 1943, driven the Germans from the gates of Leningrad and were now advancing on northern Estonia. On the central and southern fronts the Germans were being pushed back from Kiev and across the Polish border. Support to maintain the momentum of this gigantic Soviet advance was therefore crucial.

In order to achieve this, Fraser arranged for every Arctic convoy to be reinforced by at least one escort aircraft-carrier. Due to Allied ascendancy in the Western Ocean and the availability of long-range aircraft overflying the Atlantic, the Western Approaches Command could relinquish some of its 'Woolworth-carriers' for Arctic service.

When convoy JW57 left Loch Ewe on 20 February 1944 it consisted of forty freighters, two tankers doubling as oilers and the rescue ship *Copeland*, all under Commodore Binks aboard the *Fort Romaine*. In addition there were three Russian-manned coastal minesweepers and three patrol craft being delivered to their new owners.[6]

The close escort was provided by the customary workhorses, the corvettes *Bluebell, Camellia, Lotus* and *Rhododendron*, and a local escort of two corvettes, *Burdock* and *Dianella*. Also joining were two Western Approaches support groups, one under Commander Tyson in HMS *Keppel* with *Beagle, Boadicea* and *Walker* which arrived at Loch Ewe; the second under Commander Majendie with two frigates, the American-built Captain-class *Byron*, the River-class *Strule* and the LREs *Wanderer* and *Watchman* made a rendezvous after refuelling in the Faeroes. The minesweepers *Hydra, Loyalty, Orestes* and *Rattlesnake* accompanied JW57 north for two days, when the ocean escort joined.

This was formidable; taking station within the convoy came two significant ships, the anti-aircraft cruiser *Black Prince* (Captain D.M. Lees), sister to *Scylla* and flagship of Vice-Admiral I.C. Glennie, and the escort carrier HMS *Chaser* (Captain H.V.P. McClintock). The *Chaser* carried eleven radar-equipped Swordfish for anti-submarine detection, and eleven American Grumann Wildcats, small, stubby fighters with a strong airframe capable of sustaining the tremendous shock inherent in deck landings. Their main limitation was their speed which proved insufficient to catch the Junkers Ju88 reconnaissance aircraft. With the carriers came Captain Campbell in *Milne* leading over a dozen destroyers, including *Impulsive, Mahratta, Matchless, Meteor, Obedient, Offa, Onslaught, Oribi, Savage, Serapis, Swift, Verulam* and *Vigilant*. Once again in the offing, Palliser's cruiser force operated in support.

The day after the ocean escort joined, first a reconnoitring Ju88 and shortly afterwards an FW200 Condor flew over the convoy and circled it for ten hours. Next day, 24 February, a Condor reappeared. *Chaser* flew off her Wildcats and it was thought that they had driven the Condor off; in fact it maintained distant contact.

Determined not to risk a humiliating repeat of the previous fiasco, accurate reports from these aircraft ensured that two wolfpacks were assembled athwart the convoy's line of advance. The Werwolf and Hartmut groups were already at sea and were now brought up by the Condor. First to approach were *U425*, *U601*, *U739* and *U713* of the Werwolf pack.[7]

They were almost immediately detected by a Swordfish patrol, whereupon Commander Tyson's *Keppel* attacked and dispatched *U713* with depth-charges. Lieutenant-Commander Whinney in *Wanderer* had been eavesdropping on the aircraft reporting radio frequency and immediately swung his elderly destroyer on to the bearing of the sighting and increased speed. Glennie restrained his eagerness as *Wanderer* was not on the outer screen, but Whinney confessed the order left him 'speechless with fury'.

During the following day, the 25th, a long-range Catalina from 210 Squadron of the RAF flew above the convoy and attacked the trailing *U601*, diving on and sinking Hansen's boat. But the Germans continued to probe the screen, keeping submerged or trimmed down using their *schnorkels* during the brief hours of daylight when *Chaser*'s Swordfish were aloft, then surfacing and drawing ahead, constantly trying to induce the destroyers to work up to full speed in endless quest and pursuit, to create the underwater 'noise' that favoured the use of T-5 torpedoes.

On *Wanderer's* bridge there was a certain amount of criticism of the night screen dispositions signalled from *Black Prince*. In the prevailing rough, following sea the convoy was thought to be even more vulnerable than usual from a stern attack, for only two Home Fleet destroyers covered this sector, and they had been alloted arcs to sweep with their radars. 'This', wrote Whinney afterwards, 'was unusual, even for those comparatively enlightened days.' Loyally assuming that 'the Admiral knows more than we do', Whinney suppressed his own and his officers' misgivings. The escorts blooded in the long struggle in the Atlantic considered their own expertise somewhat condescendingly received by the newer 'crack' destroyers of the Home Fleet. But these animadversions were to prove justified. On the night of the 25th Whinney heard a voice call up the flagship on TBS radio telephone and announce, 'Have been hit by torpedo aft and am stopped,' followed shortly afterwards, in an increasingly anguished tone which was harrowing to hear, by 'Have been hit amidships by second torpedo.'

U990 (Kapitänleutnant Nordheimer) had fired at the M-class destroyer *Mahratta*. In the prevailing darkness Lieutenant-Commander Drought and all but seventeen of his men died in the freezing waters, despite the fact that *Impulsive* and another destroyer were quickly on the scene to pick up survivors. In the extreme cold, *Wanderer*'s antique guns were the only weapons in the escorts available to illuminate the dolorous scene with star-shell. The LRE's commanding officer, Bob Whinney, a maverick officer whose criticisms of the Royal Navy's shortcomings in anti-submarine warfare had begun in 1936 and who had been at school and at Dartmouth with Drought, regarded the failure to send an escort back after the U-boat with a 'rasping anguish'. Two days later *Wanderer* and the other three members of her support group detached and returned to the Faeroes for fuel, enduring a severe gale on their passage.[8]

During the succeeding two days Condors and reconnaissance Ju88s maintained surveillance of the convoy, and the wolfpacks clung to its flanks firing several more Gnats at the destroyer escort but without results. At 11.30 on the 28th the convoy divided off Kildin Island, the eight American Liberty ships bound for the White Sea taking a Russian escort as the remainder steamed into the Kola Inlet towards Vaenga Road and Murmansk. The White Sea portion picked up pilots at 12.45 next day and in line ahead made slow progress through thick ice. Assisted by two ice-breakers it took three days and five hours to smash 176 miles through to Molotovsk.

Much was made of the success of this convoy. It was described as the biggest sent to Russia, and had been accompanied by several war correspondents who, in the parlance of the time, were 'with the Home Fleet in Northern Waters'. In an article which was not published until late May, Admiral Glennie was widely quoted as paying tribute to the young pilots of HMS *Chaser* who manned the Swordfish. 'They never let me down once,' Glennie was reported to have said, 'they were so frozen after their flights that they had to be lifted out of the cockpits when they had landed . . .'

Careful censoring and clever editing telescoped the events of JW57 with the homeward RA57 which followed, omitting the loss of an American merchant ship, though admitting that of *Mahratta* which had been officially announced on 18 March. Typical of a wartime 'dispatch', the article had a contrived immediacy, spoke of young men 'blasting their way through to Russia', and then described a U-boat hunt that in fact properly belonged to the homeward run. Whatever its faults, however, the article had no need to employ journalistic licence to describe the conditions. They were awful, and the brunt of them had been taken by the very young Swordfish pilots.

Convoy RA57 assembled and sailed from the Kola Inlet on 2 March 1944.[9] *Black Prince* and *Chaser* again took up their alloted positions within the body of the merchant ships; the close through escort was formed from the same six minesweepers and corvettes which had brought out JW57, with Tyson's support group, *Keppel, Beagle, Walker* and *Boadicea.*[10]

The ocean escort was again Captain Campbell's baker's dozen of destroyers. The prospects that faced them as they headed out astern of the local escort of minesweepers were far from encouraging. Frustrated in their previous two attempts, Peters's boat-commanders had congregated off the Murman coast. The Soviet navy, however, having been particularly active against enemy traffic, in addition to aircraft, sent destroyers, minesweepers and submarine chasers out against four boats of the Boreas wolfpack, *U703, U315, U472* and *U739*. A further eight from the same pack were on their way as RA57 eluded them all by a diversion to the east, though the heavy lift ship *Empire Bard,* which had done yeoman service in the discharge of tanks, had to turn back to Murmansk.[11]

Clear of the land, the wretched ships were once more swept by snow- and sleet-laden gales and were soon pitching and rolling in heavy seas, conditions in which it was for two days impossible to operate *Chaser*'s aircraft. When the weather cleared up on 4 March, the convoy was immediately reported by airborne reconnaissance and the Boreas group quickly homed in. During the night Oberleutnant Mangold launched an abortive Gnat attack from *U739* on HMS *Swift*.

Next morning Swordfish *B-Bravo* of the Fleet Air Arm's No. 816 Squadron was patrolling over the convoy, piloted by 20-year-old Sub-Lieutenant P.J. Beresford RNVR who had with him an observer and a tail gunner, Leading Airman John Beech. It was a bitterly cold morning with a high overcast. While sweeping around the outer screen, Beech spotted a surfaced U-boat about nine miles away and Beresford attacked at once. The surprised Germans began 'belting away . . . with 44 mm flak'; it was the first time Beresford had seen a U-boat but he pressed home his attack, disregarding the flak, 'let fly' with two bombs and 'got two hits on the hull'. As he pulled out of the dive, tracer shells were flashing round the Stringbag. Beresford's observer, Sub-Lieutenant Laing, noted oil leaking from the U-boat, which was von Forstner's *U472*, and that the submarine was weaving erratically. Seizing the Aldis lamp he flashed a terse 'Submarine' to the nearest destroyer. Commander the Honourable A. Pleydell-Bouverie, who had recently relieved 'Bluenose Joe' Selby in command of *Onslaught*, altered course and increased speed. At four and a half miles the destroyer opened fire with her 4.7-inch main armament, engaging with smaller calibre weapons as she drew closer. *U472* was already sinking, her crew abandoning ship. Damaged by Beresford's bombs and shelled by *Onslaught*, von Forstner had scuttled her.

Pleydell-Bouverie stopped his ship and watched as her crew scrambled out of the conning tower and on to the casing. The bright spots of their lifejackets broke the uniform grey of the scene as the German seamen slid into small rubber dinghies. *Onslaught*'s crew flung scrambling nets over the side, picking up as many survivors as they could in the appalling cold. They were pulled inboard looking like 'sodden paper, frozen stiff. Altogether we saved twenty-seven men,' Pleydell-Bouverie was reported as saying, 'I was surprised at their appearance. They were not tough-looking seamen, but long-haired, ascetic types, aged about twenty-five.' The last to leave the submarine in a small boat of his own was her commander.

Freiherr von Forstner climbed unaided over *Onslaught*'s rail and defused his hostile reception by acknowledging the destroyer's quarterdeck with a punctilious naval salute. He thanked the First Lieutenant for stopping to rescue his men, two of whom later died despite the attentions of Surgeon-Lieutenant Miller and his sick-berth attendants. Accepting that First Lieutenant Wickham had no Nazi colours, von Forstner expressed his satisfaction that they should be buried beneath their enemy's white ensign. *Onslaught* was briefly slowed, and the German sailors, supported by Y-gun's crew and the depth-charge parties at their stations, slipped the bodies overboard.

Later the same day Brünner in *U703* was able to evade *Milne*, at which he fired a salvo of T-5 torpedoes, missing Campbell's ship but deceiving the British defence and placing himself in a position to fire into the *Empire Tourist* which soon afterwards sank.

Keeping their distance and skilfully making use of cloud cover to elude the *Chaser*'s patrolling fighters, the Luftwaffe reconnaissance planes kept in touch with the convoy which continued to be shadowed by the U-boats. Compelled to run on the surface to keep up, the gloom afforded them some cover and four worked up close enough to attempt to disable destroyers of the outer screen, but firings from *U278, U288, U959* and *U673* failed.

Pitching heavily in the swell, conditions aboard the escort carrier were far from favourable. Spray froze on the steelwork and snow squalls swept the flight deck which had to be cleared of ice by working parties before the first glimmer of grey dawn thrust its way into the Arctic murk. Thereafter steam hoses, brooms and shovels cleared the exposed, windswept deck of the 'flat-top', which hauled clear of the convoy with her attendant escorts. The aircraft handling parties readied the Swordfish coming up from the hangar deck on the after lift, wings folded, pushing them aft where the aircrew came up from the ready-room. The racket of firing Pegasus engines competed with the steady whine of the wind in the aerials strung from the 'island', the only protuberance marring the horizontal lines of the squat and ugly camouflaged ship. From here the Commander (F) co-ordinated flight-deck operations with the Captain. At the ready signal from the deck landing control officer, the signalmen hoisted a white flag superimposed with a red diamond and the carrier turned into the wind. A moment later the flight-deck men dodged out of the way, the removed chocks trailing on their lanyards behind them, and the first two biplanes trundled down the deck and lifted awkwardly into the sky, on the lookout for the enemy. Every one of *Chaser*'s Swordfish 'saw at least one U-boat', reported the squadron's leader, Lieutenant-Commander F.C. Nottingham.

Once airborne the cold was intense, affecting the bodies of both men and machines. It was not unusual for tail wheels to break away on landing, so brittle had the metal become. Exposure to such conditions often had equally damaging effects on the young men themselves. The observers and gunners in their exposed rear cockpits felt the cold most, 'looking . . . like two children in a pram,' wrote a member of the flight-deck crew. 'We wore as much clothing as we could, but there is a limit to what you can get in a cockpit,' recalled a Swordfish pilot.

Nevertheless, the Fleet Air Arm's No. 816 Squadron succeeded in accounting for two more U-boats in the following days, helped by a pallid sunshine now lighting the Barents Sea which burned off the sea-smoke. Sighting a U-boat on the starboard bow of the convoy, Sub-Lieutenant Mason's Swordfish *F-Foxtrot* attacked out of the low sun. Ice encrustations impeded the defensive fire of the U-boat's crew, and the Swordfish's bombs and rockets forced the U-boat to scuttle. A second plane, *X-X-ray*, hit another U-boat and these two turned out to be *U366* and *U973*. Both *Oribi* and *Boadicea* recovered survivors and all the destroyers were sporadically engaged in the investigation of either asdic or radar contacts, as a consequence of which other U-boats were believed damaged.

Trailed desultorily by aircraft and U-boats, RA57 escaped further interference. On the 7th some of Campbell's destroyers broke away to refuel and more left the following day when the ocean minesweepers *Hydra, Orestes, Onyx, Loyalty* and *Ready* joined. The convoy finally steamed into Loch Ewe on 10 March 1944.

Convoy JW58, which followed, was a huge naval operation in its own right, a response by the Western Allies to the continuing advance of the Red Army which had now cleared the Germans out of the Ukraine and was approaching the Crimea and the Carpathians, and driving into Poland.

A close escort of elderly destroyers (*Westcott, Wrestler* and *Whitehall*) and corvettes (*Bluebell, Honeysuckle* and *Lotus*) accompanied the armada of merchantmen from Loch Ewe, departing on 27 March, and a local escort of three minesweepers and two corvettes kept company as far as the Iceland/Faeroes rendezvous where an enormous concentration of shipping met.[12]

The main ocean escort was commanded by Vice-Admiral Dalrymple-Hamilton in the cruiser *Diadem* (Captain E.G.A. Clifford), with two escort carriers, *Activity* (Captain Willoughby) and *Tracker* (Acting Captain Huntley), the former carrying three Swordfish and seven Wildcats, the latter seven Wildcats and a dozen Avengers. The destroyer screen was provided by *Impulsive, Inconstant, Obedient, Offa, Opportune, Onslow, Oribi, Orwell, Saumarez, Serapis, Scorpion* and *Stord*. A second cruiser, USS *Milwaukee*, was on her way to Russia to be delivered to the Soviet Northern Fleet, while one frigate and two minesweepers destined for the Royal Navy escorted the American freighters *John T. Holt, William S. Thayer* and *Eloy Alfaro* directly to the rendezvous before detaching, though the last-named subsequently returned to Iceland.

Further to this force, Western Approaches sent two support groups, Tyson's (*Keppel, Beagle, Boadicea* and *Walker*) and the highly successful Second Support Group of Bird-class sloops under Captain 'Johnnie' Walker in *Starling*, with *Magpie, Wild Goose, Whimbrel* and *Wren*. To see these ships arriving was, in the words of *Opportune's* Lieutenant-Commander Lee-Barber, 'a great moment'.

Nor was the Commander-in-Chief absent. Fraser and the Admiralty had, for some time, been increasingly anxious about the condition of the *Tirpitz*. There were indications that repairs had rendered her seaworthy again and so Operation Tungsten was planned to coincide with the passage of JW58. Naval aircraft from the fleet aircraft-carriers *Victorious* and *Furious* and the escort carriers *Emperor*, *Searcher* and *Pursuer*, with *Fencer* providing fighter cover, were accompanied by Vice-Admiral Sir Henry Moore in the battleship *Anson*. Moore's task-force sailed from Scapa Flow on 31 March, returning on 6 April. Fraser, his flag flying in *Duke of York*, with three cruisers and a cloud of destroyers provided cover for both operations.

Aboard *Chaser* during JW57 had been a number of RAF ground crews and photo-reconnaissance experts. At the beginning of March three photo-reconnaissance Spitfires and a Catalina flew to North Russia where the SBNO, Rear-Admiral Archer, organized facilities to enable the Spitfires to overfly Altenfiord. Having obtained satisfactorily developed plates these were flown back to Britain in the Catalina, to assist in the planning of the raid.

Despite the Fleet Air Arm pilots pressing home their attacks on the *Tirpitz*, she was not immobilized and a second attempt later in the month was frustrated by bad weather. Widespread casualties and a degree of damage were inflicted, but the armoured heart of the great ship remained intact. Nevertheless, she had been rendered at least temporarily inoperative and the experience proved the need for heavier bombs to pierce her steel carapace. Convoy JW58 had better luck.

Before leaving Scapa, Captain Walker, among the other senior destroyer officers, had attended a briefing during the course of which the importance was stressed of ensuring that the USS *Milwaukee* was safely delivered to Polyarnoe. The American cruiser was part of a deal struck with Stalin to recompense Russia for her failure to receive any of the Italian warships surrendered at the time of Italy's capitulation. It is suggested by Walker's biographer that it was this imperative that had influenced the Admiralty in sending Walker to escort JW58.

On 29 March 1944, Captain Walker's almost faultless instinct led HMS *Starling* to make contact with a U-boat. The asdic contact was picked up a mile on the starboard bow and hurried patterns of depth-charges were thrown, set to explode at between 50 and 100 metres. There was a thunderous underwater explosion followed by an eruption of oil, debris and human remains. *Starling* had almost stumbled across a new U-boat on passage to her Atlantic patrol area from her Norwegian base. 'She was that rare thing,' Walker said afterwards, 'a genuine mug.' It seems unlikely that anyone aboard *U961* knew what had happened.

The first casualty in the convoy occurred that day when Ordinary Seaman Coston fell overboard from *Tracker*'s flight deck where an Avenger, returning from an anti-U-boat patrol, landed heavily and askew. Although the ship was stopped and a seaboat launched, the young man had vanished in the icy water.

Next day, in the rapidly increasing hours of daylight, the expected shadower arrived, a long-range Ju88 from Fern Aufklärungs Gruppe 22 which was set upon and shot down by Wildcats from *Activity*. On the 31st, Wildcats from both carriers had even greater success, dispatching no less than three of the hated FW200 Condors which had proved too strong for the Sea Hurricanes deployed against them during PQ18. The three aircraft were from KG40 and were not the end of the tally for the young pilots of the Fleet Air Arm. They finished the day's flying with a ready-room debrief loud with triumphant laughter.

On Saturday, 1 April 1944, Avenger *L-Lima* from *Tracker* flown by Sub-Lieutenant Ballentyne made a depth-charge attack on a surfaced submarine, but the charges failed to disengage from the underbelly of the aircraft and the U-boat dived. Returning to *Tracker*, Ballentyne released the depth-charges and was satisfied that three had gone as he made his approach. But, as the carrier rose and fell, he made a bad landing at full power, ramming his engine into the 'round down', the curved after end of the flight deck. The Avenger burst into flames. On the deck below, the *Tracker*'s own depth-charges were hurriedly jettisoned and the emergency hose parties approached, apprehensive of Ballentyne's last charge exploding. One wing of the aircraft lay across an after Bofors gun, and the ammunition in the ready-use locker and the aircraft itself began detonating. Ballentyne fell out of his machine on to the end of the hangar deck below, his clothes on fire. Demented by pain, the poor man finally collapsed dead as others tried to douse the flames consuming him.

For fifteen minutes the fireball raged on *Tracker*'s stern, watched by all the ships in the convoy, but Ballentyne must have dumped all four of his depth-charges, for no explosion resulted and in the end the fire was extinguished and the wreckage heaved overboard.[13]

At 19.32 that evening one fighter from each carrier attacked and destroyed a huge Blohm and Voss BV138. This aircraft was only marginally less detested than the Condor by veterans of the run who had watched them on many occasions droning impregnably on the horizon, impervious to lightweight attack. The death of this 'flying clog' was followed on the 2nd by the downing of another Ju88 from FAGr 124, the last aerial kill.

It was not the end of flying operations for *Activity* and *Tracker*, however. Homed in by the aircraft, no less than three wolfpacks were now closing on the convoy, the Thor, Blitz and Hammer groups, the last after being reinforced from Norway.[14]

On the same day the BV138 was shot down, Avenger *H-Hotel* of 846 Squadron embarked in *Tracker* made a rocket attack on La Baume's surfaced *U355* and damaged her sufficiently to enable Lieutenant-Commander Murch to bring up *Beagle* and administer the *coup de grâce*.

Next day was the anniversary of Nelson's action at Copenhagen and a Sunday like 2 April 1801; flying began early, at 02.00, such was the rapid transition from the total gloom of winter to the white nights of high summer. The Avengers were airborne on their long-ranging patrols which kept the enemy submerged and deprived them of their surfaced superiority of speed. But for the pilots and observers, flying through snow squalls could render indistinct the dark shapes of ships below. One such over-zealous Avenger dived on a shocked Commander Tyson, who was outraged that *Keppel* should be taken for a U-boat. The same day a Wildcat, flown by Lieutenant Lucy, crashed into the sea. Struggling clear Lucy managed to get into his dinghy from which, an hour and a half later, he was rescued, hypothermic and barely alive after paddling with his bare hands. To end the day, however, Tyson's *Keppel* depth-charged and sank Kapitänleutnant Becker in *U360*.

Early on the 3rd the final action of the convoy took place when a dawn air patrol located *U288*. Oberleutnant Meyer's after conning-tower gunners opened fire on the approaching Swordfish from *Activity*'s 819 Squadron and shot her down. Her sister Stringbag, *C-Charlie*, called up assistance and Avenger *G-Golf* and Wildcat *Y-Yankee* from *Tracker* soon combined forces to depth-charge Meyer back to the surface and finally sink him and his boat.

That day Kapitan 1 Ranga Kolchin arrived in command of a Soviet destroyer flotilla consisting of *Razyarenny*, *Razumny*, *Gremyashchi*, *Kuibishev*, four minesweepers and four submarine chasers, a suitable escort for the USS *Milwaukee* which was soon to become the Russian cruiser *Murmansk*. Having seen the mass of merchant ships and men-of-war into the Kola Inlet, Kolchin's force escorted nine freighters to the White Sea.

Despite the Admiralty's secondment of Walker's crack Second Support Group, it was largely the aircraft of the two carriers that underwrote the delivery of the *Milwaukee* and the success of the operation. *Tracker*'s aircraft, for instance, flew 132 sorties in 139 flying hours, a commendable performance for young and largely reservist men.[15]

One last anecdote remains to be told of JW58 and concerns a Communist-inspired seaman aboard HM Sloop *Whimbrel* who attempted to desert to the workers' paradise on a Carley raft. Having thrown the raft overboard he paddled happily away, full of anticipation though forgetting to slip the painter. Word of his escape passed quickly to the messdecks and the wardroom which was entertaining a Russian pilot and colleagues from *Starling*. As the Stalinist sympathizer paddled unknowingly off, his shipmates quietly pulled him back by the painter, until he gently bumped the ship's side, and looked up. History does not relate either his reaction or his punishment.[16]

Apart from one straggler, the *Gilbert Stuart* which turned back to Iceland, the convoy arrived intact, forty American, largely Liberty ships, one Norwegian, the tanker *Noreg* acting as oiler to the fleet, and nine British ships, one of them the redoubtable rescue ship *Rathlin*.[17]

The success of this convoy should not diminish the determination of the enemy. Between midnight on the 1st and the evening of the 3rd, the U-boat commanders made repeated attacks with their T-5 acoustic torpedoes, between them loosing at least seventeen of these weapons, some of them near misses and most exploding in the destroyers' wakes. In response the Royal Navy dropped countless depth-charges, the reverberations of which, hammering on the sides of the ships' hulls, kept many of the seamen of both sides from sound sleep.[18]

Before the departure of convoy RA58, *Tracker* and her fellows had two days' rest and recuperation at Vaenga, the smaller escorts filled their fuel tanks from the *British Valour*, and the carriers took on board some of the American sailors from the *Milwaukee*. The cruiser *Diadem* with the two carriers formed a central column, *British Valour* acted as oiler and *Rathlin* was convoy rescue ship. The escorting destroyers, sloops and corvettes were the same as those for JW58 and the convoy of thirty-six merchantmen, under Commodore Binks in *Fort Romaine*, left Kola on 7 April 1944.[19]

To attack RA58 the Germans deployed two wolfpacks, the Donner and Keil groups,[20] but the decimation of the air reconnaissance aircraft by the outward convoy had persuaded the Luftwaffe command to restrict their surveillance to night radar searches. Thus it was the 9th before contact was made, and the U-boats homed in for an attack the following night. Combat air patrols flown by Swordfish and Avengers from *Activity* and *Tracker* seriously hampered the U-boats and while two manœuvred and delivered Gnat attacks on the outer escorts, these failed. Just after midnight on 11 April, aircraft relocated RA58, but by then neither of the two wolfpacks were in a position to attack, having been left too far astern, and the convoy proceeded on a voyage the American passengers declared was 'like a holiday'.

Perhaps it was for those with no official duties, but for the flight-deck handling parties and the aircrews, the asdic operators, plotting teams, lookouts, gunners and depth-charge parties, it was business as usual with a bitter and severe frost to contend with. *Tracker*'s Captain Huntley praised 'the splendid work done by the [carrier's] maintenance ratings, whose interest, enthusiasm and hard work made possible a high standard of serviceability'. These men, labouring on the hangar deck below the flat-top's flight deck, repaired, refuelled and rearmed a constant stream of aircraft.

Unmolested, RA58 arrived at Loch Ewe on 14 April 1944.

Having delivered the stipulated convoy quota for the spring of

1944 in JW58, and with the projected invasion of Occupied France drawing nearer, the convoys were again suspended. Almost every ship in the Home Fleet was allocated a task in Operation Neptune, the naval component of Overlord, and few were available for Arctic tasks. It was, however, desirable to recover all possible empty merchant ships in order that they could be reloaded in the United States and readied for the later resumption of the convoys, for nothing must now stop the onslaught of the combined Allies on both the eastern and the new western fronts.

A naval force was therefore dispatched to form a strong escort for the huge accumulation of empty merchant ships in the anchorages and alongside the wharves of Russian ports. *Diadem*, now flying the flag of Rear-Admiral Roderick McGrigor, accompanied by the escort carriers *Activity* and *Fencer* (Acting Captain W.W.R. Bentinck), was screened by Tyson's Eighth Support Group (*Keppel*, *Walker*, *Beagle*, *Boadicea*, *Westcott*, *Inconstant*, *Whitehall* and *Wrestler*); Campbell's 3rd Destroyer Flotilla (*Milne*, *Marne*, *Matchless*, *Meteor*, *Musketeer*, *Ulysses*, *Verulam* and *Virago*); and the Sixth (Canadian) Support Group (*Cape Breton*, *Grou*, *Outremont* and *Wakesiu* with the gallant little *Lotus*).

A special personnel transport, the *Nea Hellas*, sailed with the force to provide accommodation for numerous Americans remaining from the *Milwaukee* and Russian officers and ratings due to travel to Britain to form the crews of a number of additional ships being handed over to the Russians in compensation for units of Mussolini's navy. Shortly after sailing, the *Nea Hellas* developed engine trouble and had to turn back. This necessitated a great deal of hurried reorganization by Rear-Admiral Archer's staff to redistribute 2,500 American and Russian sailors among the waiting merchantmen and the expected warships which arrived safely on 23 April.

While the homeward convoy was mustered, Vice-Admiral Moore led another Fleet Air Arm raid on the Norwegian coast. Designed to hit *Tirpitz*, it was frustrated by bad weather and eventually struck at German coastal shipping, destroying three ships with the loss of an equivalent number of planes from the six carriers involved.

Under the escort of *Gremyashchi* and *Gromki*, the minesweeper *T119* and five patrol ships of the Pogranitchni Storoshevoi, the Coastal Patrol, sixteen freighters arrived from

White Sea ports on 27 April to join RA59, which now consisted of forty-three merchantmen under Commodore J.O. Dunn aboard *Fort Yukon*.[21]

This enormous convoy sailed from Kola and formed up off Kildin Island on 28 April. An eastern escort of *Razyarenny*, *Grozni* and *Kuibishev*, the minesweepers *T112*, *T114* and *T119*, and five submarine chasers provided a Soviet component to the fleet, for over 150 Russian sailors were accommodated in the 'tween decks of most of the Liberty ships and a score or so of officers aboard each British and Canadian destroyer. The Russians, shortly to take over a British battleship, ten destroyers and five submarines, were commanded by Admiral Levchenko who, with his staff, was accommodated aboard *Fencer*, and they became interested spectators of the flying operations that followed.

These were to be hampered by extremely hazardous conditions with a heavy mantle of snow covering the carriers' flight decks. Nevertheless, the anti-submarine patrols began as soon as the deck handling parties had turned to and cleared the snow. The Germans located the convoy by airborne radar before midnight on the 28th and the waiting U-boats of the enlarged Donner and Keil packs, frustrated by their previous failure, deployed eagerly and began persistently to probe the defences. Towards midnight on the 30th, having fired between them innumerable torpedoes and been counter-attacked by the destroyers so that the night was riven by the crump of depth-charges and exploding Gnats, Oberleutnant Lange in *U711* fired a spread of conventional weapons and hit the Liberty ship *William S. Thayer*. With 116 passengers, the ship settled quickly and only 43 souls were rescued, by *Whitehall* and *Walker*.[22]

Vengeance was swift. On 1 May 1944, despite further abortive Gnat attacks on escorts by *U278*, *U307* and *U959*, Swordfish *C-Charlie* of 842 Squadron embarked in *Fencer* sank *U277*. The next day Swordfish *B-Bravo* from the same squadron sank both *U959* and *U674*. These losses did not deter the zealous young U-boat commanders who continued to press attacks. Caught on the surface in *U278*, Kapitänleutnant Franze defended himself against two Swordfish and a Wildcat, shooting down the latter before diving and escaping undamaged. It was the last attack; RA59 steadily drew away from the wolfpacks to steam unopposed towards Cape Wrath where, on 6 May 1944, the convoy divided, one section passing through the boom across Loch Ewe, the other heading for the Clyde to anchor on the Tail o' the Bank the next day.

Summing up this concluding convoy of the season, Admiral Fraser wrote in his dispatch, 'taken as a whole the campaign can be claimed as a success. A large volume of supplies has reached Russia . . . and the enemy has sustained far greater losses . . . than he has inflicted . . .' If this was true of the maritime war, it was an understatement of the conflict raging on the eastern front. The Red Army had by now cleared the Ukraine and the Crimea, and had penetrated deep into Poland and Romania.

22

'Allies, or just two nations?'

THE INVASION OF Occupied France began on D-Day, 6 June 1944, and involved almost the entire Home Fleet in the succeeding days. Several veterans of the Kola run, such as the former anti-aircraft 'cruiser' and ex-Bank Line tramp *Alynbank* and the *Dover Hill*, were scuttled off the Normandy coast to make a vast artificial harbour at Arromanches into which the reinforcements, *matériel* and supplies for the invading American, British, Canadian and Free French armies poured.

It was not until the middle of August that the success of the invasion and the closing in of the Arctic night enabled Russia-bound convoys to resume. Admiral Sir Bruce Fraser having been appointed to command the Royal Navy in the Far East for the final campaign against Japan, these now came under the direction of the new Commander-in-Chief, Sir Henry Moore, who, as Vice-Chief of the Naval Staff, had made the fatal amendment to Pound's signal for PQ17 and, as VA2, had led the raids on *Tirpitz* and Bodo. Moore was confronted by a renewed threat from the German battleship which, with five destroyers, lay at Altenfiord in a seaworthy state.

The Fleet Air Arm's series of raids on *Tirpitz* had failed largely because of the inadequacy of bombs and aircraft, but their persistence had been clear evidence to Dönitz of the threat this single puissant warship posed to the Arctic sea route, a point of view he had pressed on Hitler in April, obtaining the Führer's sanction to continue repairing her. Dönitz had also pointed out the immense advantage the British had seized by providing fighter cover for the convoys, and the success with which carrier-borne aircraft had thwarted both aerial reconnaissance and submarine attacks. These carriers, he had continued, were themselves vulnerable to aircraft and considerable success might yet be enjoyed by German arms if the Luftwaffe again deployed torpedo-bombers in northern Norway. Pressed on other fronts, Goering was unwilling to comply, but Dönitz had shrewdly exploited Hitler's mood and the Reichsmarschall reluctantly agreed to see what he could do.

The effectiveness of aerial torpedo attacks had been demonstrated during the passage of PQ18, but the Germans had mercifully failed to exploit this, due to demands elsewhere. Had they capitalized on it, the outcome of the Arctic campaign might have been very different. Even so, lukewarm and long delayed though Goering's acquiescence was, it was sufficient to maintain pressure on the Arctic convoys during the final months of the war.

The Germans had taken advantage of the summer's lull in Allied Arctic operations. Between 30 and 31 May 1944 Kapitän Johannesson's 4th Destroyer Flotilla (*Z29*, *Z31*, *Z33*, *Z34* and *Z38*) made a sweep between the North Cape and Bear Island, repeating this on 30 June and 1 July. More significant, the same flotilla accompanied the *Tirpitz* to sea on 31 July for two days of exercises in the Barents Sea, while on 5 August wolfpacks departed for a deep penetration into the Kara Sea to attack the Siberian summer convoys, destroy radio stations and lay mines in the Pechora Strait.

It seems incredible that Johannesson's destroyers missed Captain I.M.R. Campbell's 3rd Destroyer Flotilla which was retained in northern waters to prevent Norwegian-based U-boats making passage to the North Atlantic. At the end of May, Campbell's *Milne* sank *U289* of the Trutz group and a fast voyage with mail, ammunition and essential supplies was made by *Matchless*, *Meteor* and *Musketeer*, sailing on 29 June and arriving at Polyarnoe on 3 July. They departed next day, missing Johannesson's ships which had dodged back into Altenfiord, and returned to Scapa Flow on the 8th.

Nor had the Russians been idle, having launched a series of combined operations against German commercial traffic along the vital Axis supply-line of nickel from Petsamo.

On 15 August 1944, convoy JW59 left Loch Ewe. It consisted of three tankers, *British Promise*, *Lucullus* and the Norwegian *Herbrand*, the last two acting as oilers, the rescue ship *Rathlin*, and thirteen other British ships of which nine, like all eighteen Americans, were Liberty ships. The Commodore, G.H. Creswell, took passage in one of these, the *Samtredy*.[1]

The convoy was joined by eleven American-built and Russian-manned submarine chasers, which sheltered within its columns. In fact the whole disposition and conduct of JW59 reflected many changes. Rear-Admiral Dalrymple-Hamilton shifted his flag into the escort carrier *Vindex* which with *Striker* and the cruiser *Jamaica* occupied stations within the enormous spread of ships, with freedom of manœuvre for the two carriers to fly off and land their aircraft. *Vindex* operated twelve Swordfish and *Striker* a dozen Avengers and half a dozen Wildcats. The close escort was composed of the corvettes *Bluebell*, *Camellia*, *Charlock*, *Honeysuckle* and *Oxlip* with the sloop *Cygnet*, the new frigate *Loch Dunvegan* and the old LRE *Whitehall*. Tyson's new support group was split with the frigates *Mermaid* and *Peacock* ten miles out on the left rear flank of the convoy, and *Keppel* and *Kite* on the right, ready to attack trailing U-boats when spotted from the air. Ahead of the convoy were spread Campbell's destroyers, *Caprice*, *Milne*, *Marne*, *Meteor* and *Musketeer*, which joined from Scapa with Levchenko's Russian squadron. This was made up of the former British battleship *Royal Sovereign*, now the *Archangelsk*, and eight of the original fifty four-stack ex-American destroyers switched to the Royal Navy as part of the Lease-Lend agreement. The battleship, which took station within the convoy, had been dubbed by the British the 'Regal Rouble'.[2]

To counter the enemy's T-5 acoustic torpedo, British warships had begun to use a towed device, known as a 'foxer', which trailed in a ship's wake and, by making an induced noise, deflected the Gnat, causing it to detonate astern. This, and frequent alterations of course and speed, known as 'step-aside procedure', made the Gnat a much less successful weapon than at first feared. However, these counter-measures were not always effective and did bring with them a loss of acuity of the asdic equipment which at speed led to loss of contact with an echo.

At 08.20 on 20 August 1944, with the convoy east of Jan Mayen, a reconnoitring Ju88 located JW59. Twenty-two hours later *U344* of the five-strong Trutz wolfpack was in its vicinity. Kapitänleutnant Pietsch's first attacks with T-5s against the escorts failed, but a conventional spread salvo hit Lieutenant-Commander A.N.G. Campbell's *Kite*. The frigate sank rapidly, only nine men being saved by *Keppel*, though *Mermaid* crossed the rear of the convoy to assist and counter-attack. She was allowed only a brief search before Dalrymple-Hamilton recalled her.[3]

In the succeeding two days, air patrols from *Vindex* and *Striker* combined with attacks by a Russian Catalina to inhibit the remainder of the pack from keeping up, and on 22nd Swordfish *C-Charlie* from *Vindex*'s 825 Squadron bombed and sank Sthamer's *U354*. Undeterred, the enemy formed a new line east of the convoy's position, with *U703* and *U344* from Norway and *U365* and *U711* approaching from their foray into the Kara Sea.

As these dispositions were being taken up, Admiral Moore's synchronized attack on the *Tirpitz* took place between 20 and 29 August 1944. The air sorties were first frustrated by the weather and then disrupted by anti-aircraft fire and fighter defence, despite the fact that 247 were flown during Operation Goodwood. Moreover, the carriers were detected by *U354* on her way to intercept JW59. Sthamer, her commander, attacked and sank the frigate HMS *Bickerton* and badly damaged the escort carrier *Nabob*. Her Avengers, operating from her listing deck, drove off Sthamer's boat but *Nabob* was not afterwards repaired. Sthamer's triumph was to be short-lived, for that day was, as we have seen, to be *U354*'s last.[4]

During 23 August 1944, the activity of the air patrols and escorts forced the waiting U-boats to lose touch. But coming up from the east and his foray into the Kara Sea, Lange in *U711* made contact and fired T-5s at the *Archangelsk* and the *Zharki* which, with the other Russian ships, had detached from and drawn ahead of the convoy. Lange was deprived of success by the premature detonation of his torpedoes.

Only two U-boats were now in a position to attack, *U344* (Pietsch) and *U394* (Borger). Kapitänleutnant Pietsch in *U344* used radio bearings of tactical chit-chat between the escorts to con the duo to an advantageous point ahead of the convoy. These boats were reported by one of *Vindex*'s patrolling Swordfish at 23.00 as being fifty-six miles distant. As a consequence, *Keppel, Peacock* and *Mermaid*, all of which had been moved up from the rear in anticipation, were sent off to hunt them, reinforced by *Loch Dunvegan* from the close escort.

The two U-boats now betrayed themselves by broadcasting, though they dived on the approach of the British destroyers. However, HMS *Keppel* gained asdic contact at 02.07, towards the end of the six hours of twilight which in late August passed for nightfall. Keeping Lieutenant-Commander Stannard's *Peacock* in company, Tyson sent *Mermaid* (Lieutenant-Commander J.P. Mosse) and *Loch Dunvegan* (Commander E. Wheeler RNR) to locate the second U-boat.

Mosse was swallowing cocoa at 03.51 when 'suddenly *PING!* – the sound I had been waiting to hear for five years! We took immediate anti-Gnat precautions just in time. Ninety seconds later a Gnat exploded close astern, followed a minute later by another . . .'

Tracking their quarry proved difficult for sonic conditions were poor, and a depth-charge attack launched after half an hour 'was not a very good one'. Both ships' operators lost contact as Pietsch took *U344* deep. It was now full daylight and a sense of depression gripped the hunters. Then at 04.50 the crew of X-gun aboard the *Mermaid* saw a conning tower briefly surface astern. Mosse immediately increased speed at this report and swung round, regaining contact half a mile on the port beam, turning away to increase the range preparatory to a deliberate attack, but maintaining contact and streaming a foxer. Pietsch released two *Pillenwerfers* which failed to fool *Mermaid*'s asdic team, led by Sub-Lieutenant Gauntlett. Depth-charges were then dropped, Mosse gauging that the U-boat had gone deep, and the foxer was cut away with an axe because, with the U-boat astern, the risk to his sloop was considerable since a T-5 would home directly on his propellers. A smudge of diesel oil appeared and the smell of it was like perfume to the British.

At 05.55 *Loch Dunvegan* launched a Squid attack, the mortar firing ahead of the frigate, 'but to the extreme frustration of . . . Commander Wheeler, her asdic set broke down and remained almost continuously out of action'. At 06.21 *Mermaid*'s 'third attack was considered the best of the day. The depth of the U-boat was . . . 600 feet.' The explosion 'started a leak in the U-boat's tanks which exuded diesel oil steadily for the next twelve hours and eventually covered an area five miles long and one mile wide'.

Receiving this information, Rear-Admiral Dalrymple-Hamilton now ordered Mosse to rejoin the convoy, but Mosse was eager for evidence of a 'kill' because, as he later wrote,

> [the] depth of water was hardly sufficient to burst the hull if he was lying on the bottom.

> There began a tug of war between a senior officer who was concerned for our safety in the event of attack by enemy surface forces or aircraft, and an anti-submarine officer who was not going to let go of his first U-boat. It was a dog with a bone situation.

Mosse prevaricated, unwilling to disappoint his able asdic team who, in the depressing period when contact had been lost, had been given confidence by the plotting team. He made more attacks and signalled *Vindex* he was still in contact and would 'stay here until I kill him'. His time limit was extended twice when *Keppel* and *Peacock* joined, having lost contact with their own quarry. The deadline was extended twice more, but in the end Mosse signalled, *Have left U-boat still gushing oil and probably severely damaged in position 72°49′ North 030°41′ East . . . He has been submerged since 0450*. This message was timed at 14.18. The hunt had lasted twelve hours, though in fact the U-boat and her crew had long given up the ghost in circumstances the horror of which can only be guessed at. Tyson's ships rejoined the convoy. Afterwards, at the Admiralty, Mosse's persistence earned warm praise: Admiral Edelsten minuted his report, 'A grand story of pertinacity . . . There is no moss on Mosse.'

Borger's *U394* had been driven off and only Lange in *U711* now remained ahead of the convoy after his abortive attack on Admiral Levchenko. He fired torpedoes at the advancing destroyer screen and a Soviet submarine which appeared as JW59 approached the Murman coast, but this attack too failed, and he broke away as convoy JW59 entered Kola on 25 August 1944, a detachment for the White Sea arriving two days later.

> The escorts bunkered from the tanker at Vaenga where Mosse enjoyed a cup of coffee with her master. He couldn't wait to get away, recalled Mosse, and told 'dismal stories of sailors who were picked up drunk ashore, and were thrown into jail. He was giving a few days sanctuary to one who had just been released after fifteen months incarceration.'
>
> *Mermaid* afterwards went alongside at Polyarnoe, where the 'austere barracks were dotted about haphazard and the roads rough and unmade. The whole place seemed to be wired for sound, and loudspeakers fixed on poles and rooftops blazed forth distorted music, news and propaganda.'

The officers were

> invited to visit the Hall of Culture . . . a moth-eaten opera-house [with] a musty smell of incense and powder, and we sat on a jaded old plush sofa and gazed at a whole row of Stalins on the wall. The play we had been expecting never started . . . Although we had, not without some difficulty, brought them a battleship, some ex-US destroyers and a vast quantity of supplies, we lay alongside the naval base for three days and not a single courtesy call was paid. Were we allies or just two nations fighting a common foe?

Mosse might well have asked.[5]

Convoy RA59A sailed on 28 August and consisted of the two oilers *Herbrand* and *Lucullus* which had quickly discharged their fuel oil, five ships from JW58, the *Barbara Frietchie*, *Empire Prowess*, *Fort Vercheres*, *Lacklan* and *W.R. Grace*, and the two heavy lift ships *Empire Bard* and *Empire Elgar*. It was a small convoy for such a large escort, the same that had brought out JW59, and was unmolested, though numerous U-boat sightings were reported by the patrolling aircraft.

The only real contact with the enemy occurred at 06.20 on 2 September when Swordfish *A-Able* patrolling from *Vindex* sighted a U-boat on the surface recharging her batteries. Tyson's support group was sent in quest. At about 09.00 the four ships, *Keppel*, *Peacock*, *Mermaid* and *Whitehall*, reached the smoke marker above which the Swordfish maintained watch and began a systematic search. During the course of it, at 11.17, lookouts aboard *Keppel* spotted a periscope upon which all ships were then ordered by Tyson to concentrate. At 11.51 *Mermaid* gained a contact and proceeded to attack, lobbing depth-charges at the U-boat which was estimated to have dived to 300 feet; she repeated this at 12.49 and 13.29, after which contact was lost.

For three-quarters of an hour all ships lost contact and then, quite suddenly at 15.00, both *Mermaid* and *Peacock* received asdic responses and *Peacock* drove in to launch depth-charges. But these took time to sink and a deep U-boat could evade them by deductions made from the received asdic pulses and propeller noise. It was precisely to counter this tactic that Walker and his anti-submarine officer Michael Impey had devised the 'creeping attack', and at 16.14 all four of Tyson's ships manœuvred to deliver one.

All streamed foxers were recovered and *Mermaid* assumed the central position with *Keppel* a short distance to port and *Whitehall* to starboard, all three dousing their asdics and slowing to seven knots. *Peacock*, astern of this line, maintained asdic contact and directed the movements of the three warships ahead of her. When the operators in *Peacock* estimated the group were over the enemy, an attack was made. At 17.16 *Keppel* threw twenty-two depth-charges to port, *Whitehall* the same to starboard, while *Mermaid* rolled eighteen over the stern, thus catching the U-boat in a cross-fire of charges set to detonate at between 350 and 900 feet. At 18.13, as *Mermaid*'s asdic regained contact, there were three underwater explosions and, although Mosse pressed a last attack, it was 'probably unnecessary . . . after which bubbles and wreckage came to the surface, and *Peacock* recovered some positive evidence of destruction which her doctor classified as blood group four'. It was the recoverable remains of *U394* commanded by Kapitänleutnant Wolfgang Borger which had imploded under the assault of multiple explosions.

Thereafter the convoy proceeded uneventfully, arriving at Loch Ewe on 6 September 1944.[6]

The next convoy to depart, JW60, left Loch Ewe on 15 September under Commodore J. Smith aboard the *Empire Celia*. With the exception of the British tankers *Lucerna*, *Neritina* and *British Patience*, the Norwegian tanker *Noreg*, the British freighter *Samaritan* and the rescue ship *Zamalek*, the remaining two dozen Liberty ships were all American.[7]

The escort was commanded by Rear-Admiral McGrigor flying his flag in the escort carrier *Campania* (Acting Captain K.A. Short) with *Striker* (Captain W.P. Carne) and the anti-aircraft cruiser *Diadem*. The carriers disposed between them two dozen Swordfish, fourteen Wildcats and three Fulmars. The escorting destroyers were *Milne*, *Meteor*, *Marne*, *Musketeer*, *Saumarez*, *Scorpion*, *Venus*, *Virago*, *Volage*, *Verulam*, and the Canadians *Algonquin* and *Sioux*. The close escort was provided by the sloop *Cygnet*, the destroyers *Keppel*, *Bulldog* and *Whitehall*, and the new corvettes *Allington Castle* and *Bamborough Castle*.

Because of the threat of the *Tirpitz* the Commander-in-Chief sent the battleship *Rodney* (Captain the Honourable R.O. Fitzroy) to take station within the columns of this convoy from where her nine huge 16-inch guns could, if required, inflict damage on the enemy. She had fired these in a practice shoot coming through the Minch to join the merchant ships but they proved unnecessary for, on the day the convoy left Loch Ewe, the *Tirpitz* had been badly hit by the RAF.

Prior to the raid on *Tirpitz* it had been decided to arrange for the release of a squadron of Lancaster heavy bombers from the Supreme Allied Command, under General Eisenhower. This accomplished, co-operation with the Russians was the next step, for it was intended that the aircraft, having completed their mission, would then fly on from the North Cape area and land in Russia for fuel. However, the weather proved bad and it was decided to reverse the operation, the Lancasters flying to and then operating from Russia. Armed with five-ton 'Tallboy' bombs, the Lancasters took off under Group Captain C. McMullen. They landed in such poor weather on the primitive runways of Yagodnik that six were damaged. Moreover, further delays were experienced in refuelling which inexplicably took two days, but on the 15th they took off again.

Warned of their approach, the Germans released a most effective smoke-screen, so that only one direct hit was achieved on the *Tirpitz*, with two near misses causing a degree of damage, though a ferry, the *Kehrwieder*, was sunk. This was a disappointment to McMullen, who withdrew to Yagodnik before returning to Britain. However, the German High Command was intending to abandon the Altenfiord base and this, combined with the damage to *Tirpitz*, led to her being moved south to Tromsö where she was anchored in shallow water on 16 October.

With the surface threat greatly reduced, convoy JW60 steamed to the north of Bear Island. The weather was calm, possessed of an ethereal stillness, with extensive fog patches. The sea, though dotted with ice floes, was as 'flat as a fluke'. So benign were the conditions that good progress was made and the convoy was undetected by German aircraft or any of the seven U-boats of the Grimm wolfpack lying in wait, arriving safely off Kildin Island on the 23rd. Here the convoy divided, the White Sea section going on under Soviet escort to berth on the 25th.

At Vaenga, Rear-Admiral McGrigor shifted his flag to *Rodney* to entertain Admiral Golovko. The battleship possessed a magnificent chapel, known as 'the cathedral of the fleet', with oak panelling and stained glass. When shown this the Russian Admiral demonstrated not only the excellence of his English but also a knowledge of theology, which surprised *Rodney*'s chaplain, Gordon Taylor. However, this hospitality did not prevent the ship's company from being disappointed in having a football match, to which they had been looking forward, cancelled at short notice. The rebuff was a reminder, once again, that the alliance was fragile to the point of illusion.

Had the men in the ships lying at Vaenga known of the events then taking place around Warsaw, they might have been less surprised, for Marshal Stalin had commited an act of the grossest cynicism designed to reduce a people to vassal status by destroying its heart. Minsk, Vilnius and Lvov had all been captured by the Red Army, and the advance on Warsaw, the Polish capital, had seemed inexorable. In August 1944 the Polish Home Army rose against its German oppressors, expecting imminent support from the approaching Russians. But the Red Army halted and remained inert while the gallant Poles fought forlornly for two months until, with 200,000 dead, they capitulated to the ruthless Germans on 2 October.

The Russians were increasingly confident of victory everywhere and Golovko, in particular, had been pursuing an aggressive policy along the coast of occupied Norway. Earlier in October, his Northern Fleet had supported an offensive by Colonel-General Shcherbakov's 14th Soviet Army, by landing naval infantry units in the rear of the German line and disrupting its supplies. In the wake of the Tehran Conference of October 1944 and with Warsaw in ruins, it was clear that, while Roosevelt had thought he had the measure of Stalin and had marginalized Churchill, the American President had been deceived.

The thirty merchant ships of RA60 were the returning vessels from JW59, the oiler *Noreg* from JW60, plus the two rescue ships *Rathlin* and *Zamalek*, all under the direction of Commodore Creswell in *Samtredy*. During the night of the 27/28 September 1944 they steamed out of the Kola Inlet and began forming up.

The escorts taking up station were identical to those of JW60. HMS *Rodney* steamed in the centre of the convoy, astern of the *Samtredy* and ahead of *Campania* and *Tracker*, with the *Diadem* on her starboard beam.

Against RA60, the Grimm pack was still on station and the Zorn group was on its way to intercept, bringing the total to a dozen U-boats. But the routeing of the convoy avoided both, though on the 29th, it having overrun *U310*, her commander seized the advantage thus thrust upon him and fired several Gnats at the escorts, all of which exploded harmlessly. Oberleutnant Ley was not to be entirely disappointed, however, for conventional salvoes fired into the convoy caused the almost simultaneous sinking of the Liberty ships *Edward H. Crockett* and *Samsuva*. The swift and efficient intervention of the *Zamalek* and *Rathlin* minimized the loss of life, which was confined to the luckless engineering staff on duty below.

The following day, when the convoy was well to the north-west of Hammerfest, a patrolling Swordfish from the flagship *Campania* attacked and sank *U921* which was probably returning to her Norwegian base from an Atlantic patrol.[8] Thereafter the convoy's passage proceeded uneventfully, the carriers, *Rodney*, *Diadem* and the destroyers detaching for Scapa two days before the merchantmen, and the close escort arrived at Loch Ewe on 5 October.

On their return to Liverpool from RA59A, Mosse and Stannard had both reported to the Commander-in-Chief of the Western Approaches, Admiral Max Horton, and delivered the gruesome glass jar of mortal remains of 'blood group four'. Horton turned away with a shudder. In the course of a brief leave while *Mermaid* underwent a boiler clean, Mosse reported to Captain Howard-Johnston, Director of the Anti-U-boat Division, who 'was particularly keen to have a report on asdic operating conditions in Northern Waters'. Mosse explained that though the effects of 'layering' were frustrating and produced fainter echoes than the more homogeneous waters in the North Atlantic, conditions were 'quite acceptable to well trained and experienced A/S teams, though extra concentration was needed'.

Mosse's report was timely, for among the Naval Staff it was thought that the dispatch of Western Approaches groups on U-boat hunting forays in support of Arctic convoys was largely a waste of time 'because they never had any hope of getting results with the asdic'.

In view of the final months of the Arctic campaign, Mosse's visit might be seen as pivotal.

Though Grossadmiral Dönitz had persuaded his Führer to sanction an increase in torpedo-bombers flying from Norway, Goering did not immediately comply. However, with the Battle of the Atlantic lost and the French Biscay ports falling to the Western

Allies, Dönitz pulled his submarines back to Norway where they continued to operate vigorously in the Barents Sea. It was a defiant, Wagnerian stand against increasing and remorseless odds with all the undertones of *Götterdämmerung*. It was not to be without its successes.

Doubts as to the efficiency of asdic in the Barents Sea led to the Commander-in-Chief alloting a three-strong carrier force to JW61, which sailed on 20 October 1944. These aircraft-carriers also had a subsidiary purpose – the destruction of the enemy's submarines known to be concentrating in the area, a practical demonstration of the dictum that the best form of defence is attack.

The convoy, which consisted of twenty-seven merchant ships, the rescue ship *Syrian Prince*, the oilers *Noreg* and *Laurelwood* and six American-built submarine chasers destined for Golovko's Northern Fleet, was equally heavily supported by anti-submarine forces.[9]

The core of this task-force were *Vindex* (flagship of Dalrymple-Hamilton), *Nairana* and *Tracker*, together with the cruiser *Dido*, which occupied the rear central columns of the convoy where they could steer into the wind for flying operations without disrupting the formation ahead. The cruiser's purpose was to operate with the 17th Destroyer Flotilla in the event of a surface attack, and to provide anti-aircraft fire for the carriers if torpedo-bombers broke through their own air defences. Between them the carriers mustered twenty-three Swordfish, sixteen Wildcats and eleven Avengers.

Close escort from Loch Ewe was provided by the Western Approaches Third and Eighth Escort Groups led by *Walker* with the sloops *Lapwing* and *Lark* and the corvettes *Camellia*, *Oxlip* and *Rhododendron*. The main ocean escort comprised the carriers and cruiser attended by the 17th Destroyer Flotilla under its new senior officer, Captain Browning in *Onslow*, with *Obedient*, *Offa*, *Opportune*, *Oribi* and *Orwell*, together with two more Escort Groups, the Fifteenth (the frigates *Inglis*, *Lawson*, *Loring*, *Louis*, *Mounsey* and *Narborough*) and the Twenty-first (*Conn* (Lieutenant-Commander R. Hart, Senior Officer), *Byron*, *Deane*, *Fitzroy*, *Redmill* and *Rupert*).[10]

Ranged against this formidable force was an equally large wolfpack of nineteen boats, code-named Panther.[11]

The weather turned bad almost immediately, gale-force winds causing the carriers to pitch heavily which made flying difficult.

The obsolete Swordfish, with their low speed, were landing at an airspeed of no more than 30 knots. Although the wind later moderated, it left a heavy residual swell which even on a cruiser caused considerable discomfort. Aboard *Dido*, 'with her great narrow length, high top-weight and shallow draught', Lieutenant Bunn RNR had a most uncomfortable time in the quartering swell:

> there were some nights when sleep was almost impossible without a hammock. Every mealtime as I juggled with plates in the chart-house, I could be heard cursing when the inevitable happened and all my food went spinning off the table with me in hot pursuit . . . The shambles was indescribable . . . the biggest roll recorded was only 37° for all that, and did not compare impressively with the frigates' 57°. The air temperature was not cold, averaging 5 ° Celsius, but the sky was perpetually cloudy so that obtaining sights was quite a science but fortunately no fog was encountered . . . The days grew very brief as our latitude increased, the shortest period between sunrise and sunset being slightly under six hours. The Northern Lights were brilliant on some nights and their peculiarly wispy patterns were fascinating.

As JW61 moved along the 73rd parallel east of Bear Island on 26 October, Huff-Duff operators picked up the noise of chattering U-boats. The airborne air patrols were directed to investigate and the support groups, already operating up to 100 miles clear of the main body, were dispatched ahead to intercept. An increasing number of U-boats were now fitted with the *schnorkel*, allowing them to run trimmed down to periscope depth on their diesel engines. As the frigates drew ahead, *Tracker* turned into the wind and flew off her strike-force of two Avengers and two Wildcats which were manned and in instant readiness. Sub-Lieutenant Brewer located one enemy boat which dived, avoiding the 'Oscar' acoustic depth-charge he dropped.

The German concentration lay at the end of the convoy route, as the ships turned south-south-west and lost their freedom of manœuvre in the approaches to the Kola Inlet; this area was increasingly to be the battlefield in the coming months.

For two days, between 26 and 27 October, the commanders of *U956*, *U995*, *U1163*, *U365* and *U295* repeatedly attempted to destroy the frigates with T-5s, but the foxers and step-aside procedures foiled them. For their part, the frigate commanders reported poor asdic conditions, though this was a matter of some dispute.[12]

Although the escort failed to sink any U-boats, the convoy was safely delivered to the rendezvous, where waiting Russian destroyers took the White Sea contingent further east. This arrived on the 30th, the Murmansk section having berthed on the 28th. Here, Captain Hastie of the *Rathlin* was called upon for the first time since leaving Loch Ewe, when his doctor was required to attend a seaman with an injured finger.

It snowed while the ships lay in Vaenga Bay and a whaler race was cancelled when the wind fell light and a blizzard came on. A Russian choir performed movingly on *Tracker*'s hangar deck and relations were once again amicable enough. While the warships waited for the homeward RA convoy to assemble, the Third and Fifteenth Escort Groups were sent to sea to hunt for U-boats and prevent a concentration gathering in ambush for the emerging ships. One of these, HMS *Mounsey*, was torpedoed by a Gnat from *U295* (Wieboldt), but was able to limp back to Polyarnoe, though a dozen men were killed or wounded. The rest of the escorts awaited the emergence of the homeward convoy, keeping the enemy guessing.

At daylight, on Thursday, 2 November 1944, the merchant ships forming RA61 steamed to sea, preceded by the escorts and followed by the carriers and *Dido*. The cruiser had loaded six and a half tons of gold bullion, in boxes labelled 'furs', which fooled no one. The merchant ships were those that had come out with JW60 plus the rescue ship *Syrian Prince* and the oilers *Laurelwood* and *Noreg* from JW61, and the Liberty ship *F.T. Frelinghuysen* from JW59. The Commodore, Rear-Admiral Boucher, sailed in the American Liberty ship *Edward A. Savoy* and the whole convoy was thirty-three strong. The feeder convoy from the White Sea had been escorted by Russian destroyers and all ships had taken station by 15.30, as darkness fell.

Dalrymple-Hamilton held to a north-easterly course until midnight when, in latitude 71°30′N, longitude 030°30′E, he was clear of the estimated position of the Panther boats. He then swung north, and six hours later west-north-west. The carriers flew constant air patrols which sighted several U-boats in the distance, but none closed or were attacked. A late landing after dark on the 3rd cost *Vindex* a Swordfish which crashed into the sea: though escorts were soon on the scene, the observer was lost.

RA61 finally turned west at 02.00 on the 4th when in latitude 72°30′N, longitude 031°30′E. *Tracker* had a Swordfish damaged on landing and engaged in some night operations, though light winds prevented her flying off her heavily loaded Avengers and she had to hand over her patrol duty to *Nairana*'s Swordfish.

The contrary easterly set of the current sweeping up the Norwegian coast combined with a heavy swell to slow down the lightly laden merchant ships. Until the convoy turned south-west ninety miles north of the North Cape at 17.15 that night, progress was tediously slow. Three hours earlier several frigates had been detached to assist the high-speed convoy JW61A then passing some distance away (see below).

All Saturday, 4 November, and Sunday, 5 November, the ships were within 100 miles of the Norwegian fiords, in one of which the *Tirpitz* lurked. No one aboard the ships was unaware of this fact.

Then the barometer dropped ominously to 970 millibars, though the weather remained calm. Navigation was easier than on the outward passage with less cloud and a moon that did not set at all above the 68th parallel.

On Tuesday, the 7th, a second Swordfish from *Vindex* developed engine trouble and belly-flopped into the sea, though her aircrew were rescued by a destroyer. And then the weather broke and the foretold northerly gale was upon them. The ships began to work in a heavy beam sea. During a severe roll at 11.30 next day, an Avenger slid off the *Vindex*'s flight deck, taking a man with it into the sea.

The convoy then altered course to pass east of the Faeroes. There the Twenty-first Escort Group detached to proceed to Londonderry and the *Byron* put in to land her commanding officer who was suffering from acute appendicitis. The carrier group also departed for Scapa Flow. For the officers and ratings of those stalwart little ships, the corvettes, this was something of a relief. 'The presence of an admiral', one corvette commander recalled ruefully, 'made things rather "pusser".'

The bulk of the convoy plodded on through the wild seas thrown up by the northerly gale and entered either Loch Ewe on 9 November, or the Clyde the next day. A postscript was written to this convoy by a flanking British submarine, HMS *Venturer*. Operating off the Norwegian coast, she made an underwater attack on *U771*, returning unsuccessfully from the Murman coast, and sank the U-boat.

During the operations connected with the passage of JW61 and RA61, another small and highly emotive convoy, JW61A, had made a fast, unobtrusive passage from Liverpool to Murmansk, leaving the Mersey on 31 October 1944 with a local escort of the Canadian-manned River-class frigate *Nene*, the destroyers *Westcott* and *Beagle* and the sloop *Cygnet*. The convoy consisted of only two passenger liners, the Canadian-Pacific liner *Empress of Australia* and Cunard's *Scythia*, both of whom carried some 11,000 incarcerated 'Russian collaborators'. Many of them were Ukrainians and all of them had been captured serving in the Wehrmacht, a large number as gunners, during the invasion of Normandy. Churchill had just returned from an 'extremely cordial' dialogue with Stalin and the decision to repatriate these unfortunates preceded the discord which emerged after Yalta. Stalin's insistence that these men were returned ranks with his halting of the Red Army before the gates of Warsaw as an example of the Soviet leader's wickedness; that it was sanctioned was a manifestation of the uncontrollable amorality of war, for JW61A was the least creditable convoy in a saga of otherwise honourable endeavour.

The local escort of the two fast liners was relieved on 2 November by the cruiser *Berwick* (Captain N.V. Grace), the escort carrier *Campania* and the destroyers *Cambrian*, *Caprice*, *Cassandra*, *Saumarez*, *Scourge* and *Serapis*. Leaving on the 3rd, the destroyers *Savage* and *Scorpion* embarked a party of Norwegian soldiers, an advanced guard of those aboard *Berwick* whose flight had been cancelled due to bad weather. The separate passage of the two destroyers, whose arrival coincided with that of the fast convoy, was ironically code-named Operation Freeman.

Berwick had taken on board a large contingent of Norwegian troops to join the Red Army as it finally drove the enemy back from the Murmansk front and crossed into Norway. The presence of the Norwegians was to assert the integrity of the territory and the authority of the government-in-exile. All were disembarked on arrival on 6 November, but British guards and the crews of the two liners were forbidden permission to land, nor were Rear-Admiral Archer's staff allowed to make contact with the ships as the wretched Ukrainians were 'repatriated'.

All eight destroyers, with *Berwick* and *Campania*, accompanied the two liners on their return passage to the Clyde, made between 11 and 17 November, and which constituted convoy RA61A. These two voyages were covered by an escort group, consisting of the frigates *Duckworth*, *Berry*, *Cooke*, *Domett*, *Essington* and

Rowley, which remained at sea after the return of RA61 upon the flank of which it had been sent out.

Three days after the arrival of RA61, on 12 November, a special force of twenty-eight Lancaster bombers finally eliminated the mighty *Tirpitz*. Anchored near Tromsö south of Haakoy Island, she was theoretically protected by elaborate smoke-screening devices and fighters from nearby Bardufoss. Owing to 'a whole series of unhappy coincidences and failures', as Admiral Ciliax admitted, these failed to materialize and the first strikes were unimpeded by smoke. Several hits by Tallboy bombs opened *Tirpitz*'s port side and, despite counter-flooding, she listed, suffered an internal explosion and then capsized. About a thousand men were drowned in her, eighty-five escaping through a hole afterwards cut in her hull. This single ship had, simply by her almost passive existence, succeeded in exerting a huge strategical influence, though inflicting little damage on her enemies. In fact the *Tirpitz* had fired her guns in anger only once, at the defenceless installations on Spitzbergen, in September 1943.

Thus it was that the thirty-strong convoy JW62 sailed from Loch Ewe on 29 November without the threat of a heavy surface attack. Under an unusual commodore, Captain Ullring of the Royal Norwegian Navy aboard the *Fort Boise*, JW62 consisted of two British escort oilers, *Lucullus* and *Laurelwood*, a British tanker and the rescue ship *Rathlin*, with six other British and twenty American Liberty ships.[13]

The convoy was accompanied by the Eighth Escort Group (the destroyers *Keppel*, *Beagle*, *Bulldog* and *Westcott*) and the Twentieth Escort Group (the sloops *Cygnet*, *Lapwing* and *Lark*, and the corvettes *Allington Castle* and *Bamborough Castle*), to which were attached the Norwegian-manned *Tunsberg Castle* and *Eglantine* for transfer to Polyarnoe.

Once again Rear-Admiral McGrigor hoisted his flag in a carrier, HMS *Campania*, which, with the *Nairana* and the cruiser *Bellona*, adopted the same dispositions as for the preceding convoy. This force arrived with part of the 7th and the whole of the 17th Destroyer Flotillas (*Caesar*, *Cambrian*, *Caprice*, *Cassandra*, *Onslow*, *Obedient*, *Offa*, *Onslaught*, *Oribi* and *Orwell*), plus the frigates *Tavy*, *Bahamas*, *Tortola*, *Somaliland* and *Loch Alvie*. Also present were the Canadian Ninth Escort Group, the frigates *Monnow*, *Nene*, *Port Colborne*, *St John* and *Stormont*, all of whom had joined by 1 December.

German aircraft knew of the sailing of JW62 four days earlier. Two wolfpacks were assembled, the first, ten boats of the Stock group, was sent to intercept close west of Bear Island, while the second, the seven-strong Grube pack, waited in the Kola approaches.[14] The Stock pack failed to make contact and was hastily withdrawn, crossing the Barents Sea to close up on the other boats while the convoy wheeled east and then south. Meanwhile the waiting Grube boats attacked Russian coastal convoys, sinking the steamer *Proletari* and a veteran of earlier PQ convoys, the *Revolutsioner*. Then, as the incoming JW62 approached, they turned their attention to the British and American merchant ships.

Although aerial reconnaissance from the carriers had sighted U-boats, the hunting support groups had failed to make contact as their quarry withdrew to the south-east. However, the air and surface activity, reinforced by the small submarine chasers and patrol ships of the Soviet Northern Fleet succeeded in thwarting the dogged attempts of several U-boat commanders to break through, and the convoy split off Kildin Island unharmed, the merchant ships bound for Murmansk berthing on 7 December, the White Sea contingent two days later.

Soviet contact with the waiting U-boats necessitated another 'clearing operation' of the approaches before the departure of the westbound convoy. The British and Canadian ships sailed on the 9th, in company with a Soviet destroyer flotilla commanded by Kontr Admiral Fokin and made up of the *Baku*, *Gremyashchi*, *Razumny*, *Derzhki*, *Doblestny* and *Zhivuchi*. The waiting U-boats counter-attacked with Gnats which failed to find their targets. In the mêlée, the last-named Russian destroyer claimed to have rammed *U387*, though whether she was sunk thus or by depth-charges from *Bamborough Castle* is uncertain. The combined operation had its desired effect, however, and when convoy RA62 sailed the following day, only *U365* was in touch.

With the exception of the escort oilers *Laurelwood* and *Lucullus*, and the rescue ship *Rathlin*, the returning twenty-six ships were all from JW61. The Commodore, his staff and all escorts transferred from the convoy just arrived and the ships steamed north with the comforting drone of aircraft overhead.

Oberleutnant Todenhagen in *U365* trailed, and on 10th fired an abortive salvo at the *San Venancio*. But on the next day he manœuvred into a favourable position to fire again, and blew the bows off HMS *Cassandra* (Lieutenant-Commander G.C. Leslie), a new C-class destroyer, killing several men. The badly mauled ship was towed back into Kola by Russian tugs under Soviet protection, while the U-boat, hunted by vengeful escorts, was driven off, though she escaped and remained in touch with the convoy.

Throughout the passage the cold was intense and the weather poor. Night patrols were flown by the radar-equipped Swordfish and several made bad landings, while others missed the small, pitching flight decks altogether. HMS *Onslaught*, stationed astern of the *Nairana* as what had irreverently become known as 'the gash boat', attempted one rescue in the frozen darkness, Pleydell-Bouverie stopping his ship directly upwind of the tiny red lights attached to the ditched aircrews' Mae West lifejackets. Despite the efforts of X-gun's crew, and the depth-charge party, they only succeeded in recovering the pilot, the observer and gunner being swept away in the darkness. In the next two days Pleydell-Bouverie had better luck, but only by using a searchlight as he manœuvred upwind of the floundering aircrews, and thus betraying his position.

On 13 December 1944, in the vicinity of Bear Island, Todenhagen made another approach, but this time patrolling units of 813 Squadron embarked in *Campania* spotted him and the Fleet Air Arm avenged the *Cassandra*'s dead. Swordfish *L-Lima* and *Q-Quebec* bombed and sank *U365*. Later that day the convoy was attacked by air, nine Junkers Ju88 torpedo-bombers of KG26 making an unwelcome appearance. Their presence marked a belated response by the Luftwaffe to Dönitz's appeal to Hitler that spring and was a foretaste of things to come, although on this occasion two were shot down by the squadron's fighters.

One danger that beset the accompanying escort groups in their hunt for U-boats was that they were often operating miles off the convoy route in concert with the carriers' aircraft. On one such mission the next day, the Norwegian corvette *Tunsberg Castle* ran into a mine barrage off her native but still hostile coast. She was blown apart and sank with tragically heavy loss of life.

The only other event of note was the sudden sickness of the captain of the frigate *Tortola*, who, like the commanding officer of the *Byron*, was suffering from acute appendicitis. It was a reminder of how young these men were, and that they could muster a sense of humour – the group's senior officer, the captain of HMS *Tavy*, reported: 'Operation not immediately necessary. HMS *Tavy*'s gyro had also developed an internal complaint, but was operated on successfully and by midnight was running correctly.'

23

'We are having a bad time with the U-boats'

AT THE END of 1944 the First Sea Lord, Admiral Sir Andrew Cunningham, admitted that recent German submarine successes were causing the Admiralty concern. The widespread provision of *schnorkel* breathing pipes on the standard Type VII and XI U-boats and the appearance of more sophisticated Type XXI and XXIII units had dramatically reduced the effectiveness of Allied air superiority. The trimmed down submarines now transmitted their undisciplined radio-telephone chatter over a much shorter range, often cheating the listening Huff-Duff operators of early and precise information of their positions and concentrations. Furthermore the T-5/Gnat acoustic torpedo, though not infallible, was causing a worrying number of casualties among the escorts.

In his catalogue of mounting difficulties, A.B.C., as he was known, added the ominous words 'the asdic is failing us'. This, as mentioned in the previous chapter, was a debate current at the time. The countermeasures adopted to foil the acoustic torpedo, chiefly noisy decoy devices, undoubtedly robbed the asdic of some of its potential, but Walker's 'creeping attack' had circumvented the problem, though it was not possible without sufficient escorts and, it has to be said, did not much appeal to the more dashing destroyer commanders. There was also the widespread belief that excessive 'layering' occurred in the Barents Sea; this is only a half-truth though it certainly affected the early asdic sets fitted in destroyers, corvettes and anti-submarine trawlers. However, later sets fitted to the newer River- and Loch-class frigates and the Castle-class corvettes were much improved. Today, the Barents Sea presents no problems to modern sonar and, as Lieutenant-Commander Mosse's report to the Admiralty suggested, in 1944 the deficiency was, at least in part, attributable to lack of practice on the part of some operators.

However, there was one area in which 'layering' did play an important part, most certainly thwarting Allied underwater detection gear, and that was in the Kola approaches. As Lieutenant Bunn's narrative of his westwards passage in HMS *Dido*, cited in the previous chapter, indicates, a strong easterly current runs along the coast of Norway – the residual North Atlantic Drift, itself a remnant of the Gulf Stream and the means by which Murmansk is accessible all year. But off Kola it is defeated by the cold Arctic current moving west out of the Kara Sea and here it gives shelter almost as impervious as a brick wall. The Germans were to make full use of this tactical advantage.

The thirty-nine merchantmen of JW63 left Loch Ewe on 30 December 1944. One ship, the *Adolph Ochs*, returned to Iceland because of engine defects, but the convoy proceeded undetected by the enemy, despite the deployment of the Stier wolfpack, four boats of which lay athwart the Bear Island passage and three off the Kola Inlet.[1]

Commander Tyson, with the destroyers *Keppel*, *Walker* and *Westcott*, the sloops *Cygnet*, *Lapwing* and *Lark*, and the corvettes *Allington Castle*, *Alnwick Castle* and *Bamborough Castle*, formed the close escort. On New Year's Day, Rear-Admiral Dalrymple-Hamilton in *Vindex* joined from Scapa with *Diadem* in company, together with the British destroyers *Myngs*, *Savage*, *Scourge*, *Scorpion*, *Serapis*, *Zambesi* and *Zebra*, the Canadian *Algonquin* and *Sioux*, and the Norwegian *Stord*. Because the passage would be made in continuous darkness, *Vindex* again embarked 825 Squadron, which was trained in night flying and whose ageing Hurricanes had just been replaced with seven Wildcats, to augment the twelve radar-equipped Swordfish.

On 3 January 1945, surface surveillance radar picked up a distant echo approaching. Two Wildcats sent to intercept failed to find the enemy aeroplane in the murky gloom and cloud, though it closed in to within six miles of the convoy. Returning to *Vindex*, the Wildcats were fired upon by jumpy anti-aircraft gunners in *Scorpion* and indignantly protested, though fortunately aim was poor and no damage was done. As JW63 approached Bear Island the Swordfish patrols were flown round the convoy. One aircraft crashed on landing on the 5th: two days later the visibility closed in and all flying stopped. That day the Russian escorts arrived to detach those merchantmen bound for the White Sea. Fog and heavy snowstorms persisted, obscuring the rest of the ships from the three waiting U-boats. They arrived at Kola on 8 January, a day before the White Sea detachment.

Two days later the thirty-one ballasted ships of RA63 were forming up off Kildin Island when the first U-boat reports began to be received and the escorts dropped random depth-charges to prohibit a closer approach. It says much for the confidence of the Commodore, Rear-Admiral Boucher in the tanker *British Respect*, that he felt able to order an eight-point, right-angled alteration of course with his flock hardly settled down.[2] This done, and with *Vindex*'s aircraft already aloft, the convoy drew away from the dismal coast in the darkness, rolling to a distantly generated swell and with the fog still hanging about. As one of the carrier's planes landed, it missed the arrester wires and smashed into the crash barrier, taking five hours to repair and render serviceable again. Out on the perimeter, the destroyers hunted like inquisitive dogs, sniffing out the asdic contacts and firing deterrent depth-charges. By the evening the forecast gale had materialized. All the ships began rolling heavily on their northerly heading, the beam wind playing on the wings of *Vindex*'s parked aircraft so that they lifted first one wheel and then the other.

Next day, 12 January, the convoy's speed was reduced to allow stragglers to regain station. The moderation in the weather that followed on the 13th was swiftly displaced by a second full gale on the 14th, which swept heavy seas and dense curtains of snow over the wildly rolling ships. Minor injuries were caused to personnel as they struggled to get about, and the ballast of the Liberty ship *Amasa Delano* shifted so that she lolled, taking up a semi-permanent list. The Commodore ordered the convoy hauled round to the south-westwards to ease her plight. After some hours of pumping bunkers and water ballast in her double-bottoms, a hazardous and desperate expedient in heavy weather with the effects of free surfaces to worry about, she regained both the vertical and her station.

On 15 January 1945 the weather moderated. Swordfish patrols were flown off to investigate distant submarine contacts but returned having located nothing as the weather again deteriorated.

They were hardly landed on *Vindex* when the wind rapidly freshened to storm force. The meteorological report forwarded from Iceland now promised winds of hurricane force, 65 knots and over.

The convoy began to disintegrate, each ship fending desperately for herself. The British tanker *Longwood* suffered a power failure as her auxiliary generators failed, then one of her boiler furnace linings collapsed, she lost steam pressure and was reduced to hand-steering. The American freighter *John Gibbon* developed a defective condenser and also fell astern with an escort detailed to stand by her. Abruptly, at about 19.00, the shriek of the wind changed to a great booming roar. In the blackness, the sea gradually lost its high, crested ridges with the descent of tumbling seas circumscribing each ship's visible horizon. Instead the force of the storm simply tore the whole surface of the ocean and flung it into the air so that it became difficult to breath. Water was everywhere, cascading across the *Vindex*'s flight deck where the wind speed reached 80 knots.

By 21.00 the convoy was hove to, though it had lost all cohesion and consisted of a great flock of ships, aboard each of which untold havoc was being wreaked. *Vindex* rolled 38° and tables in her messdecks sheared off. Water leaked below through ventilation trunkings while stools, broken crockery, mess kids and personal effects slopped under the swaying hammocks which offered her unhappy company their only refuge. In the carrier's wardroom, the piano broke adrift, rolling back and forth until secured by some enterprising music-lovers, while tool boxes and items of gear crashed across the hangar deck in which the lashed aircraft trembled and twitched, their air-sensitive wings affected by the tremendous variations in pressure caused by the resonance of the mighty wind outside.

This state of affairs lasted for two days by which time a strange smell permeated the carrier, caused by massive breakages in the spirit room. Leaking rum ran into adjacent alleyways and was eagerly cleaned up by volunteers until they discovered that it had become tainted, having dissolved the red lead in the deck paint.

All the destroyers had suffered superficial damage and the cruiser *Diadem* had her hawse-pipes set in and her boats torn from their davits. The convoy itself was scattered all over the Norwegian Sea. It was ordered to reform at Thorshavn in the Faeroes and by 20 January had reunited, proceeding on towards

Scotland the same day. Dalrymple-Hamilton's carrier group pressed on for Scapa, flying off No. 825 Squadron to Machrihanish before putting to sea for a boiler clean and refit at Greenock on the Clyde. Here the merchantmen, with *Keppel, Westcott* and *Walker*, arrived on the 23rd, having put in to Loch Ewe on the 21st. Only the *Fort Highfield* had been left in Thorshavn, patching up collision damage, though she afterwards went to Kirkwall and then the Clyde.

While convoy RA63 was enduring the onslaught of hurricane-force winds, the Red Army launched its last great offensive of the war, from Warsaw to Berlin.

The weather was to dominate the next pair of convoys, but so too was the enemy, for at last Goering had acceded to Dönitz's plea for torpedo-bombers, and the opposition to the passage of convoy JW64 was to be fierce.[3]

As an economy measure, the base at Loch Ewe was shut down and the convoy sailed from an assembly anchorage at the Tail o' the Bank in the Clyde estuary late on 3 February 1945. The close escort was composed of the Seventh Escort Group under Commander A.H. Thorold in *Cygnet*, with *Lark* and *Whitehall*, and the all-corvette Eighth Escort Group, *Bamborough Castle, Alnwick Castle, Rhododendron* and *Bluebell*. In the body of the convoy was located the diminutive Royal Norwegian Naval trawler *Oksoy*. Steaming through the Minch these headed up towards the Shetlands where, on the 5th, they were joined by the fleet oiler *Black Ranger* escorted by the destroyer *Serapis* and the corvette *Denbigh Castle*.[4]

Next morning, at 08.30, when well north-east of the Faeroes, the ocean escort arrived from Scapa Flow, Rear-Admiral McGrigor flying his flag in the escort carrier *Campania*, with her twelve Swordfish, four Wildcats and one Fairey Fulmar, and supported by the *Nairana*, with fourteen Swordfish and six Wildcats, the anti-aircraft cruiser *Bellona* and the enlarged 17th Destroyer Flotilla under Captain Browning in *Onslow*, with *Onslaught, Opportune, Orwell, Sioux, Zambesi, Zest* and *Zealous*. HMS *Zebra* also joined but was shortly afterwards detached with defects. At about the same time a routine German meteorological flight detected the convoy.

The report soon produced a Ju88 shadower which was engaged by two Wildcats flown off from *Campania*. One, piloted by

Sub-Lieutenant Smyth, was shot down and although the Junkers had, by 17.30, suffered the same fate, the convoy was thereafter continuously shadowed.

Thus warned, McGrigor kept his destroyers in an outer defensive ring with the close escort forming an inner ring, night cruising stations which the Rear-Admiral retained next morning when, shortly after the resumption of shadowing, a group of torpedo-bombers was detected approaching at 07.45. These were immediately engaged by the combined anti-aircraft fire of the convoy. The gunners of the *Denbigh Castle* (Lieutenant-Commander Butcher RNVR) succeeded in shooting one down and McGrigor executed a right-angled turn to starboard as a second wave came in, thus frustrating the Germans from quickly reaching their most favourable position to mount an attack, the rear of the convoy.

Nevertheless, the next incursion developed from both quarters of the mass of ships, with a dozen aircraft flying in from the north-west and south-west, though they did not press home their attacks, being deterred by the circling Wildcats. Bad light kept both defenders and attackers at a mutually respectful distance, but the Wildcats fired into a Junkers Ju88 shadower, setting it on fire and causing it to crash into the sea. Meanwhile the convoy resumed its north-easterly track.

During the 8th the convoy was distantly circled by Ju88s transmitting homing signals, but the only flight against them, flown off that evening, was unsuccessful due to the darkness and poor radio communications. The lone and antique Fulmar, intended for night-flying, crashed on landing. Beyond repair it had to be unceremoniously ditched.

At the first glimmer of twilight, McGrigor flew off his anti-submarine patrols. Intelligence indicated the usual mustering of U-boats in the Bear Island passage towards which, at 09.00, the convoy altered course to head east. In fact, despite the presence of the Rasmus wolfpack, nothing was sighted. Engaging the more persistent and accessible shadowers proved the only action of a day which was ended by deteriorating weather and the grounding of the aircraft. Analysis of the Huff-Duff intercepts seemed to indicate that JW64 had skirted round to the northwards of the wolfpack, which is indeed what had occurred.

McGrigor's force had been luckier than it knew. On the 7th no less than forty-eight Ju88 bombers of KG26 had set off to locate JW64, but had failed to do so in force and had been compelled to return to their base. On the 10th, however, things were different. The day began with the appearance of shadowers at 03.40 when, about 120 miles south of Bear Island, the convoy was no more than 250 miles from Bardufoss, steaming under a total overcast with dull light, five miles visibility and frequent snow showers which dramatically and suddenly reduced this to virtually nothing.

At 10.00 an aircraft flying in from the south was, as a result of corrupt radio traffic from Polyarnoe, thought to be Russian. Fortunately, alert lookouts aboard HMCS *Sioux* recognized the plane as a Junkers Ju88 and immediately opened fire. Their response prompted the other escorts, though not before the aeroplane had loosed a torpedo which went wide. This premature and unsupported attack warned the warships, which fanned out to their air-defence stations just in time to receive the main force which now swept in low on the advanced right flank of the escort, a station occupied by *Whitehall*, with the sloop *Lark* on her port beam. The formations sent against JW64 were fourteen bombers of the second, and eighteen torpedo-bombers of the third squadrons of KG26.

Three aircraft made straight for *Whitehall*. Cowell's ancient LRE 'sent one away damaged, shot down the second, shared the third with the *Lark*, and successfully avoided all torpedoes'. McGrigor concluded his subsequent report with the comment that this was 'fine work by a veteran with a close-range armament of only two Oerlikons each side'. Lieutenant-Commander Gower's *Orwell* was also credited with a Junkers, while hits were claimed by *Onslow*, *Cygnet* and *Sioux*. The Wildcats from *Nairana* were airborne on patrol and engaged the enemy aircraft at some peril to themselves, so intense was the fire of the escorts.

McGrigor and Commodore Ullring now instituted a series of course alterations to enable *Campania* to fly off her Wildcats. The enemy air formations had fragmented to exploit weaknesses in the defence and to divide the defensive fire and fighters. Attacks were made from several directions simultaneously and the merchant ships were hard put to comb the torpedo tracks in time to avoid hits, though several exploded in their wakes. Much of this defensive manœuvring was made possible by the cool reporting of torpedo tracks by the lookouts aboard the outer escorts.

Far less cool was the response from the predominantly American merchant ships, whose fire 'showed a quite inexcusable lack of . . . discipline even taking into account the bad visibility, low cloud and the pace of events. There is', McGrigor reported scathingly, 'little resemblance between a Ju88 and a Wildcat, and none with a Swordfish.'

Pleydell-Bouverie's *Onslaught* shot down one Ju88, fighters registered damage and the combined fire of several ships fatally struck another bomber. In fact five aircraft failed to return to Bardufoss, but damage was also inflicted by so-called 'friendly fire' on the British fighters, some of which had taken punishment, as they prepared to land on their carriers, despite reiterated warnings broadcast in plain language over the TBS system. There was an understandable failure on the part of the young Fleet Air Arm pilots to comprehend this reaction on the part of their allies.

Shortly after 11.00, some forty hectic minutes later, there was a brief lull, then a final attack at about 11.30, before the bloodied enemy withdrew. Excepting damage, only one British aircraft had been shot down, though its pilot was picked up.

Thereafter, the Luftwaffe made no further appearance, though constant air patrols were kept aloft whenever the weather permitted. This proved a foul mixture of bitter cold with icing and frequent heavy snow showers which kept the visibility low and in which the *Oksoy* straggled.

Having missed the outward convoy off Bear Island the Rasmus pack cruising there was withdrawn and sent to reinforce the U-boats in the Kola approaches. As the convoy divided on the 12th, detaching the Archangel portion which was met by a Russian escort and supported by *Lark*, *Lapwing* and *Alnwick Castle*, the U-boats moved in.

It was wild, squally and dark as the merchantmen steamed into the inlet. The Commodore's *Fort Crevecoeur* and the *Aruna S. Abell* fouled one another in a minor collision. Among the last of the warships to follow the main body of the convoy and ocean escort was the new Castle-class corvette, *Denbigh Castle*. Her asdic operators were exhausted after days of boring and repetitive sweeping but made contact with a U-boat. Notwithstanding this, half an hour into the ominous 13 February, Oberleutnant Falke in *U992* fired his torpedoes into her.[5]

Enormous efforts were made to save her by her company, and Lieutenant Walker brought *Bluebell* alongside and passed a towline; all might have been well had the ingress of water been stemmed, for the *Bluebell* made good progress and was later relieved by the Russian tug *Burevestnik*, but the corvette was filling rapidly. As a last resort, she was beached in order to save her. Alas, she did not settle properly, the weather made her roll so that the water already in her caused her to fall on her side and she became an unsalvagable wreck, still visible today at the eastern entrance to the inlet.

The following day, 14 February 1945, a Russian feeder convoy coming in from the White Sea under Russian escort was attacked by the relocated Rasmus boats in the same position. Oberleutnant Westphalen's *U968* sank the Norwegian tanker *Norfjell,* and Kapitänleutnant Lange in *U711* torpedoed the *Horace Gray*. The Liberty ship had loaded potash as a homeward cargo at Molotovsk and did not sink immediately, though abandoned. She was reboarded, taken in tow by a Russian tug and towed to Tyuva Bay where she was beached and afterwards declared a total loss. Another veteran bound to join the returning RA64, the Norwegian freighter *Idefjord,* had been sent to Kirkenes, now liberated by the Red Army, and was located by *U995* on 9 February. The torpedoes fired at her fortunately missed and she later arrived to join the westbound convoy.

At Polyarnoe, the British naval authorities were alerted to the fact that a force of Germans was attacking Norwegians on the island of Sørøy, so Captain Allison in *Zambesi* was dispatched with *Zealous*, *Zest* and *Sioux* to evacuate 500 men, women and children.

In addition to this complication, solved by distributing these unfortunate refugees as passengers in the ships of the assembling convoy, McGrigor and Archer were considering the problem of forcing the exit of the Kola Inlet. This was being most efficiently blockaded by the Rasmus boats, one of which was working right in the entrance, while the remainder clustered along the first forty miles of the convoy route. Russian daytime reconnaissance flights and small-craft patrols kept up a spate of intelligence reports but, to quote Roderick McGrigor, 'Russian counter-measures were . . . quite ineffective. There was no night flying, no hunting groups, and no thought on their part of taking the offensive against the U-boats so handily placed.'

The Russians did agree, however, to co-operate at the time of sailing by providing heavy air support and supplying escorts and salvage tugs to follow and pick up any torpedoed ships. As for the British, McGrigor ordered all available escorts to sea the day before the convoy's departure. Led by Commander Thorold in *Cygnet, Lapwing, Bamborough Castle, Lark* and *Alnwick Castle* sailed at dusk on 16 February, closed up at action stations. In the resulting asdic sweep the latter two ships located and sank *U425* in the small hours of the 17th.

Meanwhile, McGrigor's main force followed Thorold's sloops and corvettes to sea and shortly before 08.00 the first merchant ships of RA64 emerged to form up off Toros Island.[6] They were slow in taking up their stations, and the delay allowed the enemy to close in again. At 10.24 Westphalen fired a Gnat from *U968* at HMS *Lark* as she carried out asdic sweeps ahead of the convoy. This time the weapon was devastatingly effective and, with a shattering explosion, the sloop's stern was blown off. Commander Lambton's crew fought valiantly to keep their ship afloat, while Thorold's group were detached by McGrigor to stand by her and render assistance.

A Russian tug arrived and began to tow her back towards Polyarnoe at 17.40, but it was clear her wound was mortal. Having handed her over to the Soviet naval authorities Thorold left them to salvage her and swung *Cygnet* after the convoy. HMS *Lark* was finally beached and part of her crew were taken off by the small, shallow-draught Soviet submarine chaser *MO434*, which ran alongside. In the succeeding days, British naval working parties withdrew the most sensitive gear and machinery aboard and turned her hulk over to the Russians, though they left her where she lay.

Meanwhile, *Cygnet, Lapwing, Alnwick Castle* and *Bamborough Castle* made to catch up. Rear-Admiral McGrigor's detachment of these four escorts to attend *Lark* had seriously weakened the defences of RA64, which had suffered its next blow within two hours of the strike against the British sloop.

By noon the convoy had almost formed up. However, Oberleutnant Westphalen had avoided detection by virtue of the extreme effects of 'layering' in the water, and now accounted for the American Liberty ship *Thomas Scott*, the crew of which abandoned ship, leaving their vessel 'floating on an even keel with little sign of damage, in a calm sea surrounded by escorts'. Her crew and forty-one Norwegian refugees from Sørøy were picked up by *Onslaught*.

Rear-Admiral McGrigor's report was uncomplimentary, for he

considered that the ship, though empty of all but ballast, might have been saved. This conclusion was also precipitate: the highly subdivided hulls of two warships had been so damaged as to resist the efforts of their large and energetic crews and submit to the overwhelming influx of the sea. There was very little the much smaller crew aboard a Liberty ship could do when their ship had been blown in two and only her deck plates held her forward and after holds together. Efforts were made by the Russian destroyer *Zhestki* to tow her in, but the strain was too much and she broke in two and sank.

The convoy had now to steam east-north-east for about three hours before it would be clear of the area of U-boat infestation. All the merchantmen were in column with the short-handed screen on station. Shortly before 15.00 the flag signals soared up the halliards aboard Commodore Ullring's *Samaritan* and the Rear-Admiral's *Campania* for the major alteration of course to the northward. At their downward, jerked descent, the mass of ships turned obediently due north.

Now that the U-boat alarms had ceased and the grim, grey line of the Russian coast had dropped astern, the escorts went from action to cruising stations. Despite the lack of Commander Thorold's escort group, an air of relaxation pervaded the ships. Aboard *Onslow*, one of her telegraphists took a moment to pause and admire the lumbering collection of ships.

His eye lit upon HMS *Bluebell*, a stubby contrast to his own famous destroyer whose very funnel, upon the warm plates of which he now leaned his back, had been wrecked by *Hipper*'s shells. *Bluebell* had few glorious battle-honours to her name, if one discounted the long, hard slog of the great maritime war across the Western Ocean and the present struggle for mastery of the Barents Sea. The telegraphist was chiefly thinking of a man aboard her whom he had heard on the TBS earlier that day and with whom he had done basic training at HMS *Royal Arthur*, the *nom de guerre* of a holiday camp at Skegness.

> I watched *Bluebell* rolling gently about half a mile on our starboard beam and pictured him in the minuscule wireless office. Suddenly his ship disintegrated before my eyes and seconds later came a muffled explosion. We raced to the spot but few crew members survived, just driftwood and the reek of oil. This . . . was awe-inspiring, reminding us that even though we might relax for a moment, death was at any time just a second or two away.[7]

With the exception of one man, Petty Officer Albert Holmes who was picked up by *Zest*, Lieutenant Walker and his entire crew were lost to a torpedo from Lange's *U711*. The vengeful hunt that followed yielded a brief and single contact at 18.30, but after that, nothing. *U711* had simply disappeared. With *U286, U716, U307, U968* and *U992*, she was already speeding north-west towards Bear Island, along the chord of an arc by which the slow convoy would, sometime afterwards, re-encounter them.

Thorold's four ships caught up with the convoy early the next morning, 18 February, as it swung to the west-north-west. The air patrols searched a grey and empty sea which, towards noon, began to show the white streaks of spume and a mounting swell that presaged a gale. By 18.00 the aircraft were landed on and struck down into the hangar decks as the wind freshened from a near to a full gale and continued to increase until, by midnight, airspeeds of 60 knots, almost hurricane force, were registering on the carriers' anemometers.

The empty and ballasted merchantmen were soon lurching all over the sea and the story of RA63 repeated itself; by morning the convoy was widely scattered, to the alarm of senior officers, for now a shadower put in a brief appearance, and they knew they were detected. There was, however, little that could be done until the following day when, after a moderation around midnight, the grey light of dawn saw the destroyers sent off to round up the merchantmen. Steaming as fast as their captains dared in the heavy seas, their rolling iron decks awash, the crews stuffed into their forecastles, spaces approximating two double-decker buses which now climbed towards the sky and then dropped into the troughs of the sea with a gut-wrenching lurch, their lookouts stared in expectation at the indistinct horizon. Some, like HMS *Zambesi*, steamed over 1,000 miles at 'the highest possible speed' to round up just nine of the straggling merchantmen, but gradually the convoy was drawn together again and by mid-morning twenty-nine merchant vessels were in company, with two more coming up astern and only two still straggling.

As the ships reassembled and steered due west, they found the enemy shadowers already droning on the horizon, keeping an intermittent watch from distances of twenty to twenty-five miles. A torpedo attack seemed imminent, since the first reconnaissance aircraft had been on the scene as early as 04.20. Shortly after 10.00

the first of forty Ju88s were seen approaching from the south-west. They crossed ahead of the convoy and McGrigor altered course to the south-west as they swung round and made their approach, being joined by even more planes, all from KG26. The flagship had only one fighter serviceable and as a consequence it was *Nairana* that flew off interceptors. The sea remained rough and the wind strong, with the escort carrier heaving and tossing wildly.

However, the conditions failed to favour the attackers either, and though several pressed home their approach runs and loosed torpedoes these were seen to skip out of the waves and failed to find targets, many exploding spontaneously. This saved one of the stragglers which was the target of a determined assault. The anti-aircraft barrage was again a deterrent, and some aircraft were hit, 'probables' being claimed by several ships with 'positives' from *Onslow* and *Zealous*. In fact, the greatest damage was inflicted by the Wildcats and six enemy aircraft were lost at no cost to the convoy.

Once again, despite forceful warnings made at the masters' conference before departure, the returning Wildcats were fired upon by some of the ships in convoy as they made their approaches to land on *Nairana*. Landing was feat enough without the complications of 'friendly fire', for the carrier's deck was pitching heavily and the head wind speed was 50 knots. Three British aircraft were compelled to ditch, their crews ably rescued in very difficult conditions by Commander Ryder VC who had succeeded Lee-Barber in command of *Opportune*. Simultaneous ditchings resulted in Ryder slipping his whaler and leaving the crew to rescue the aircrew of a Swordfish while he worked *Opportune* across the wake of the carriers to pick up the second. Having done so he swung round to recover the whaler but, to his horror, discovered that the boat was missing and lost in heavy seas and heavier snow. For half an hour nothing was heard from the boat until *Orwell* reported a small radar echo and conned *Opportune* towards it. There, to the infinite relief of the anxious men on *Opportune*'s bridge, the whaler lay waiting for them. After the immensely difficult job of picking up a pulling boat in rough seas, Surgeon-Lieutenant Hartigan succeeded in resuscitating two airmen suffering from hypothermia.[8]

By noon, however, the attacks were over and the Luftwaffe pilots were barrelling back to their Norwegian bases where they claimed to have sunk or damaged two cruisers, two destroyers and at least eight cargo ships. In response to this debrief, *U307, U716* and *U286* were ordered on a fruitless search of the area to sink damaged vessels. It was the closest the U-boats were to get to RA64. The convoy, meanwhile, having passed Bear Island, turned on to the long, south-westward leg; it was almost complete, with only the *Crosby S. Noyes* and the *Henry Bacon* now straggling. It had, moreover, been reinforced by the destroyers *Savage, Scourge* and *Zebra*, sent up by the Commander-in-Chief to make up for the earlier losses, and with this access in strength, at noon on the 21st, McGrigor felt able to detach the ailing *Whitehall* which was experiencing problems with her boiler feed water.

For the rest of that day and the next, shadowing aircraft were seen and Huff-Duff bearings revealed the presence of U-boats not far away. Conditions remained very poor, with the wind still at gale- and near gale-force from the south-west, rolling a heavy head sea and swell at the bucking ships. As McGrigor reported of his charges, 'these constant gales . . . caused much difficulty . . . Engine trouble, defective steering, ice-chipped propellers, shifting cargoes and splitting decks [in the Liberty ships were] very real reasons for dropping astern and at times stopping.' Two of the cargo ships were reduced to steering with blocks and tackles rigged upon their rudder stocks, a task which in practical terms is almost impossible in a gale and enables a vessel to do no more than heave to.

But things were to become far worse as 22 February wore on. While some of the better-found merchantmen stuck loyally to the Commodore on a south-south-easterly course, heading away from the worst of the sea, others hove to, including McGrigor's flagship, the *Campania*, which fell out of station after two tremendous rolls of 45° each way had reduced everything below decks to a shambles. The wind now backed into the west and rose to 70–80 knots.

The terrible weather did not stop the German reconnaissance aircraft, one of which appeared over the scattered convoy at 05.15 on the 23rd, but as the morning drew on a moderation enabled *Campania* to set a course south-east to rejoin the convoy forty miles away. To his relief McGrigor found a score of merchantmen and a considerable portion of the escorts in a group, and the expected torpedo-bombers failed to find the convoy.

By noon, with the wind dropping to a mere 55 knots, the convoy's course had been hauled to the south-west to gain some offing from the Norwegian coast. By 17.00 all except two ships had been accounted for. The *Crosby S. Noyes* was not heard of for some time, but the *Henry Bacon* had sent in a plain-language message over TBS that she was under attack by about nineteen torpedo-bombers, suffering alone the onslaught intended for RA64. She was soon foundering, but a radio bearing on her transmission allowed a patrol of two Wildcats, flown off from *Nairana*'s still madly gyrating deck, to locate her shortly before she sank. Quite incredibly, her company had managed to lower boats and Rear-Admiral McGrigor, aware that she bore Norwegian refugees from Sørøy, immediately sent Captain Allison in *Zambesi*, with *Zest* and *Opportune*, to the rescue. Arriving on the desolate scene, the three destroyers came upon the boats which contained only a handful of the Liberty ship's crew, but all sixty-five Norwegians. Their debriefing revealed that the majority of the *Henry Bacon*'s thirty-five strong crew had sacrificed their lives to give up places in the boats. This Liberty ship occupies a further footnote in history: she was the last vessel to be sunk by German aircraft in the Second World War.

For two more days the storm raged with wind speeds gusting above hurricane force and RA64's speed of advance a mere 3½ knots. Most of the ships were having problems of one sort or another and the hard-worked escorts, particularly *Bellona* and the destroyers, were running very short of fuel. Rear-Admiral McGrigor began to send them in detachments to refuel in the Faeroes. At Thorshavn those of the refugees accommodated aboard the destroyers were landed; the children had made themselves very popular with the sailors.

On the evening of the 23rd the *Myngs*, *Scorpion* and *Cavalier* arrived and two were sent to escort the worst damaged merchant ships directly to the Faeroes. By the night of the 25/26 February 1945 the wind had veered to the north-west, allowing the convoy to double its speed, though it afterwards backed again.

On the afternoon of 26 February, when off the Faeroes and with refuelled destroyers rejoining, McGrigor with the carriers, cruiser and most of the remaining destroyers proceeded to Scapa Flow. Command of the escort devolved to Commander Jessel in *Zealous*. Next morning, as RA64 passed west of the Shetlands, a report was received from the *Crosby S. Noyes*; she was 300 miles astern of the convoy, but safe. On the 28th the battered and storm-tossed ships put into Loch Ewe briefly before pushing on to the Clyde where they arrived on 1 March.

During the worst of the storms, on the evening of 22 February, the barograph aboard HMS *Opportune* had registered 950 millibars. The conditions weathered by RA64 were accounted to be the worst endured in the entire North Atlantic theatre. Such a sea-state had prevented any refuelling of the destroyers at sea and their lack of bunkers had caused additional concern as to their stability in such extreme weather. On their arrival, all the destroyers reported serious defects and a dozen required refits and dry-dockings.

Such weather, unusual though it was, served as a timely reminder of the seaman's perennial and most dispassionate enemy. As for the Germans, they were to continue to harry the remaining convoys, the chief danger now being the U-boats congregating in the approaches to Kola, which the Russians, with a fine sense of procrastination, gibbed at attacking, an odd decision given their resources and their undisputed valour elsewhere.

It is perhaps not cynical, in the light of subsequent events, to see in Soviet supineness an attitude of indifference to losses sustained by the Western Allies at this late and irreversible stage in the war against Germany. Nor was such an attitude confined to one side. Royal Navy crews escorting convoys and approaching Murmansk were told not to fraternize with the native Russians since 'after the war we might have to "take them on"', thought by the hearer, a 'hostilities only' rating, to be 'a rather paranoid response'.

Odd examples of war weariness beset some British warships too. It is alleged that aboard one destroyer two ratings complained to their first lieutenant of the eviction of a man with a broken arm from a sick-bay berth in favour of a fit officer. The First Lieutenant dismissed 'this complaint perfunctorily . . . with what Hamlet describes as "the insolence of office"'. As an example of this kind of attitude, the complainant records, 'it was by no means the last'. Whether or not this incident was isolated, the messdecks of every ship in the British fleet were seething with the prospect of a General Election and the anticipation of a new, more equitable and juster postwar world.

24

The true glory

THE LAST CONVOYS to Russia sailed in the spring of 1945, later than planned due to hull damage to the destroyers which had accompanied RA64. Twenty-six ships formed JW65 and left the Clyde on 11 March under Commodore Meek in *Fort Boise*. They included the Norwegian ship *Idefjord*, loaded with relief supplies for Kirkenes.[1]

Before their departure, Sir Henry Moore had urged the sweeping of a new channel through the minefields off the Kola Inlet. Although JW65 was routed so as to swing wide of the airfields at Banak and Bardufoss, it was prohibited from using this new channel in order not to betray it to the enemy and so reserve it for the exit of RA65.

The close escort of the eastward convoy consisted of the newly constituted Seventh Escort Group, comprising the sloop *Lapwing* (Commander Hulton, Senior Officer) and the corvettes *Alnwick Castle, Bamborough Castle, Lancaster Castle, Allington Castle, Oxlip, Camellia* and *Honeysuckle*; and the destroyers *Stord* and *Myngs*, whose Captain Cazalet nominally commanded the 23rd Destroyer Flotilla. Clear of Cape Wrath, Rear-Admiral Dalrymple-Hamilton, flying his flag in *Campania* and with the anti-aircraft cruiser *Diadem*, six destroyers and an additional corvette, took station. Finally, on the 15th, the escort carrier *Trumpeter* (Captain K.S. Colquhoun) joined with the destroyers *Savage* and *Scourge*. On arrival, the second carrier sent a recognition flight of an Avenger, a Wildcat and a Swordfish over the merchantmen in an attempt to prevent any of the disgraceful incidents that had occurred in the previous convoy.[2]

Despite the fact that the Red Army were almost at the gates of Berlin, the Germans persisted in their attacks on the Arctic convoys to the bitter end, maintaining pressure on their defence which was, in turn, met by an equally relentless doggedness.

The German *B-Dienst* bureau detected the convoy was at sea by radio intercepts, though aerial reconnaissance had failed to locate it, and the Hagen wolfpack were sent out against it, the six U-boats being *U307*, *U312*, *U363*, *U968*, *U997* and *U716*. Lange's *U711* later put to sea to reinforce these boats in the Bear Island passage.

U995 was already operating off the Kola Inlet, attacking any feeder convoys, and had sunk the Soviet submarine chaser *BO223* on 3 March. She was now reinforced by *U992* and *U313* and the three submarines awaited the approach of JW65.

Huff-Duff bearings and sightings by the carriers' air patrols had already detected the enemy's presence off Bear Island, but destroyers sent out to hunt aerial sightings failed to make contact. Nor were the U-boats able to grapple with the convoy in time to attack, so they were withdrawn to join their comrades lurking off Kildin Island. In the sanguine hope of relatively easy pickings, they were deployed in two lines athwart the convoy track.

The convoy itself proceeded unremarkably, the air patrols being divided between night flying from *Campania* and day flying from *Trumpeter*. Until 20 March, the only thing of general interest had been a vast area of the curiously rounded floes known as 'pancake ice'. But on that morning, in dense snow showers and squalls which grounded the airborne patrols and halted the Russian fighter cover, the convoy was sighted by Oberleutnant Hess in *U995*, who promptly torpedoed and sank the American Liberty ship *Horace Bushnell* before JW65 cleared the first line of the redeployed wolfpack.

Three hours later, at about noon, the second line were in contact. Swordfish patrols were airborne but this did not deter the enemy. *U716* fired at, and missed, an escort, but Westphalen once again made his sinister mark in *U968*. Attacking with Kapitänleutnant Schweiger in *U313*, he struck *Lapwing* and shortly afterwards a second American Liberty ship, the *Thomas Donaldson*, both of which sank. Only sixty officers and ratings were saved from the British sloop.

The convoy reached Murmansk and the escorts anchored at Vaenga or berthed at Polyarnoe on the 21st, refuelling for the departure of RA65 two days later. Shortly before the assembled convoy weighed, the five corvettes began harrying U-boat contacts in the entrance to the inlet while four fleet destroyers steamed at speed along the old, eastward channel firing star-shell in the darkness and dropping random patterns of deterrent depth-charges.

Aboard the *Fort Crevecoeur*, Commodore Meek in concert with Dalrymple-Hamilton then got the merchantmen under way and proceeded outwards through the newly swept channel. It was a ruse which achieved complete success. The enemy were utterly deceived, despite there being nine U-boats lying in wait. Two, *U313* and *U968*, sighted or heard the convoy, but failed to make contact at this or any other time in the passage. Nor did German aerial searches fare any better. RA65 picked up some ships from the White Sea and, making passage in good weather, arrived off Kirkwall on 31 March where it dispensed with the carrier force and divided, both parts arriving on 1 April 1945, the one in Belfast Lough, the other in the River Clyde.[3]

Convoy JW66 was destined to be the last wartime, though not the last, convoy to Northern Russia. Composed of twenty-seven ships under Commodore Sir Roy Gill in *Samaritan*, it left the Tail o' the Bank on 16 April with a close escort of the sloop *Cygnet* and the corvettes *Alnwick Castle*, *Bamborough Castle*, *Farnham Castle*, *Honeysuckle*, *Lotus*, *Oxlip* and *Rhododendron*, shortly afterwards joined by the 19th Escort Group, comprising the frigates *Loch Insh*, *Loch Shin*, *Cotton*, *Goodall* and *Anguilla*. On the 18th Rear-Admiral Cunninghame-Graham, flying his flag in the escort carrier *Vindex* and with a second carrier, HMS *Premier*, and the anti-aircraft cruiser *Bellona* in company, joined with nine destroyers.[4]

Next day, as the convoy drew away from friendly waters, sixteen American-supplied but Russian-manned submarine chasers joined, while all ships, merchant and naval, fired their armaments and the convoy exercised at turning. During the passage, the fleet oiler *Blue Ranger* appears to have detached, perhaps as a reserve fuelling point for the ships of Operation Trammel (see below), but apparently without escort. The carriers maintained flying patrols round the clock, working the alternating day and night duty which had now become an established routine. The weather was cold and thick and the usual icing problems were encountered, but there was no sign of the enemy.

Once again the *B-Dienst* service had picked up the convoy's radio traffic. The Faust pack of six boats was sent to intercept west of Bear Island, but to no avail. The U-boats were again pulled back to concentrate in the Kola approaches, and here they scored their last successes. St George's Day, 23 April, was one of strong winds, rough seas, a heavy swell and snow showers, as JW66 headed towards Kildin Island, receiving reports of U-boats in the area.

The Germans were aware that whilst they had had the initiative in the final forty miles of coastal approach to the Kola Inlet, they were in danger of losing it as a result of the swamping techniques of random and intense depth-charging employed increasingly by the British and Russians. However, the fact that even this saturation depth-charging rarely resulted in the loss of a U-boat gave some comfort, and they continued to cram the area. The British naval authorities in Russia were well aware of their presence and now sought to counter it before the arrival of JW66.

The solution was to be the laying of a tethered minefield, deep enough to allow the safe passage of surface vessels, but set to trap prowling U-boats. Russian approval was sought and, after the customary delay, granted; Sir Henry Moore's staff allocated to the task the fast minelayer *Apollo* and the destroyers *Obedient*, *Opportune* and *Orwell*, all of which were fitted for minelaying. HMS *Dido* was sent to give anti-aircraft cover and this squadron sailed from Scapa Flow on 17 April to lay the minefield ahead of JW66 on the night of the 21st/22nd in what was code-named Operation Trammel. Arriving at Kola to refuel at noon on the 21st the ships were not ready to sail until late on the 22nd, so poorly was the operation co-ordinated. However, the Nineteenth Escort Group were sent ahead of the approaching convoy to assist and keep the U-boats away, while the Russians provided air cover. At a depth of ten fathoms, 276 mines were laid without mishap in six lines between Syet Navolok and Kildin Island. On completion, the squadron returned to the Kola Inlet, topped up with fuel and departed for Scapa on 23rd, arriving on the 26th. The thirsty *Apollo* refuelled again from an oiler at Thorshavn in the Faeroes, and then steamed directly to Milford Haven.

The Allies had not, however, been having it all their own way. A Russian coastal convoy bound from Petsamo to Kola was escorted by the destroyers *Karl Liebknecht*, *Zhestki*, *Derzhki* and *Dostoiny* with a swarm of submarine chasers and patrol craft, supported by a Free Norwegian escort group led by *Eglantine* with the trawlers *Karmöy, Jelöy* and *Tromöy*. *U997* (Lehman) sank the Soviet steamer *Onega* and damaged the Norwegian *Idefjord*, a veteran of Arctic convoys, which had delivered relief stores to her homeland. Taken under tow, she later sank, her thirty-four survivors ultimately returning to Britain aboard the rescue ship *Copeland*. Other U-boats fired T-5s which the escorts succeeded in avoiding or deceiving.

After the White Sea portion of JW66 had detached under Russian escort to arrive on the 28th, Cunninghame-Graham sent the Nineteenth Escort Group to drop depth-charges ahead of the convoy. On its flanks the Castle-class corvettes deployed their forward-firing Squid mortars and lobbed salvoes of charges to deter the enemy, for the layering effects rendered the asdic more or less useless. However, even this terrible barrage only inflicted minor damage on one U-boat. More concern seems to have been caused aboard the British Liberty ship *Samaritan* where Commodore Gill expressed grave misgivings about the concussive effect on the frail hull of his vessel and the 500 tons of TNT and cordite reposing in No. 1 hold.

With the Nineteenth Escort Group and the destroyers ahead, and the Russian submarine chasers nipping erratically about the convoy, the enemy was kept at bay. A new gadget, the sonobuoy, a remote transmitting device dropped from the air, was used to listen for U-boats as both Russian and British aircraft from the two carriers standing offshore provided additional cover.

This concentration of effort saw JW66 brought safely into the inlet on the 25th despite the best endeavours of the persistent Lange in *U711* who penetrated the defences but failed to find any opening to exploit. As he extricated his submarine, the merchantmen dispersed to their anchorages or berths, conscious perhaps that they had made their last passage in wartime.

While fuelling and awaiting the assembly of RA66, the escorts, corvettes and destroyers mustered their best voices and gave a concert at the Red Navy club at Polyarnoe to celebrate the junction of the British and Russian armies in Germany. The war seemed all but over.

Convoy RA66 consisted largely of ships from JW65. Commodore Gill and his staff transferred to *Fort Yukon* and the twenty-six merchantmen left with the escort of JW66 on the evening of

29 April. The Nineteenth Escort Group's frigates again preceded the convoy with the Seventh Escort Group's corvettes following suit. Fourteen U-boats lay in wait beyond the minefield for this last encounter which became a mêlée. Westphalen in *U968* narrowly missed *Alnwick Castle* with a Gnat and both the Canadian destroyers *Iroquois* and *Haida* similarly escaped torpedoes fired from *U427* which was subsequently counter-attacked and subjected to a long and harrowing chase with literally hundreds of depth-charge explosions being counted by the German crew. Supporting Russian submarine chasers latched on to *U313* but both of these boats ultimately evaded serious retribution.[5]

The Nineteenth Escort Group located *U307* which was sunk by depth-charges from *Loch Shin* on the 29th, then Westphalen achieved the dubious honour of the last sinking on a Russian convoy and the final Royal Naval loss in the European theatre of war, torpedoing the American-built Captain-class frigate *Goodall* (Lieutenant-Commander J.V. Fulton RNVR). Lieutenant-Commander Wright RNR ran HMS *Honeysuckle* alongside to take off her crew, whereupon the *Goodall* exploded, damaging the little corvette with the tremendous concussion. *Honeysuckle* drew off and as *Goodall* listed badly, *Farnham Castle* picked up a few survivors, and *Anguilla* put an end to her agony. Despite the courageous action of Wright, *Goodall* sank with heavy loss of life.

In the early hours of the following morning the boot was to be on the other foot, for the frigates *Loch Insh*, *Loch Shin*, *Cotton* and *Anguilla* attacked and sank *U286* (Dietrich). Wolfpack and convoy then drew apart, the former never to regain contact. Unknown to either party, Adolf Hitler was to die by his own hand in his bunker in Berlin later that same day, his successor as leader of the German Reich, Grossadmiral Karl Dönitz.

As for convoy RA66, it was to steam unmolested, in 'exemplary' order, through the Barents and Norwegian Seas and round Cloch Point, heading for the Tail o' the Bank on VE Day, 8 May 1945. The war in Europe was over.

In the closing weeks of the war, as the Allies converged from east and west to discover in the death-camps the full infamy of the Nazi regime, several U-boats were sunk in the waters of the Arctic Ocean by patrolling long-range Liberators. Allied air superiority also put an end to the capital ships of the Kriegsmarine which had exerted so baleful an influence on the Arctic convoys. In a heavy bombing raid on Kiel on 9 April, Lancasters had sunk *U1131* and seriously damaged the cruisers *Admiral Hipper* and *Emden*; and exploding near misses caused the *Admiral Scheer* to capsize. The following day, two torpedo-boats were bombed and sunk, while at Königsberg the cruiser *Seydlitz*, undergoing conversion to an aircraft-carrier, was scuttled to avoid her falling into Russian hands. On the 12th, HM Submarine *Tapir* sank *U486* off the Norwegian coast and on the 16th, Lancasters bombed and sank the *Lützow* at her berth at Swinemunde. As the Reich collapsed, German sailors finished the Allies' work for them. On 3 May, the day after the Russians entered Berlin, the grounded *Lützow* and the *Hipper* were blown up by their crews. The damaged *Gneisenau* and the uncompleted aircraft-carrier *Graf Zeppelin* fell into Russian hands at Gdynia and Stettin. The cruisers *Prinz Eugen* and *Nürnberg* were at Copenhagen and surrendered to a Royal Naval squadron of two cruisers and four destroyers, and were afterwards escorted to Wilhelmshaven. The *Leipzig* also fell into British hands in Denmark and was finally sunk in the North Sea by the Royal Navy in 1946.

But the surrender of Germany 'meant for the naval forces not an easing up, but a greatly increased activity,' Admiral Burrough wrote, alluding to the opening up of ports, the clearing of mines, the supply of Allied forces and of civilian communities disrupted by occupation, plus the job of rounding up German units, chief among these being the submarine arm of the Kriegsmarine.

Because of the unpredictability of the crews of the U-boats still at sea, among whom numerous Nazis could be counted, it was decided to continue the convoy system for several weeks following the end of hostilities. The technical advances made in the design of the later marques of U-boat had constituted a very real threat up to the last day of the war and the margin of victory was technically narrow. Over a dozen of the new Type XXI boats were already in commission with ninety-one others working up or training crews, a prodigious number given the extensive bombing of the construction sites and the aerial mining of the Baltic. In these late stages of the war, their crews can have had only one object in view, the most effective disruption of the final Allied effort, of which the most accessible targets were those off the Norwegian and polar coasts.

In a broadcast on the afternoon of 4 May, Dönitz instructed his commanding officers to cease hostilities and return to their bases.

Three days later, 7 May 1945, when the unconditional surrender of Germany was signed at General Eisenhower's HQ at Rheims, only ten of the forty-five U-boats known to be at sea had obeyed. At noon on 8 May, VE Day and the day on which Germany surrendered to the USSR at Karlshorst, RA66 entered the Clyde. The British Admiralty transmitted a message that by order of the German High Command all U-boats were to surface at once, report their positions and proceed to specified ports. The order was not obeyed promptly. That night, the first six proceeded towards their bases submerged. Nine boats did not surrender until the 9th, followed by a further nine on the 10th. Thereafter the toll mounted. Some, however, refused to obey, two were scuttled off Lisbon, one was run aground off the Dutch coast and a further two, *U530* from the east coast of the United States and *U977* from Kiel, made for the River Plate where they were interned by the Argentine authorities.[6]

The designated mustering point for U-boats operating in the western North Atlantic, North and Barents Seas was Loch Eriboll on the Scottish mainland south of the Orkneys. Here Captain M.J. Evans, who had received the first surrender, that of *U1009*, commanded a special reception force of escorts drawn from Western Approaches. It was in this atmosphere of instability and uncertainty that convoy JW67 left the Clyde on 12 May. Aboard *Empire Prowess*, Commodore Sutcliffe led to sea under perfect wartime discipline twenty-six Allied merchantmen flying the ensigns of the United States, Great Britain and Norway. The latter were loaded with relief supplies for the newly liberated areas of polar Norway.[7]

Captain Browning, Rupert Sherbrooke's successor in *Onslow*, commanded the escort, having with him the escort carrier *Queen* (Acting Captain K.J. D'Arcy) and the *Obdurate* of his own 17th Destroyer Flotilla which was merged with the Fourth Escort Group, the frigates *Bentinck*, *Bazeley*, *Byard*, *Pasley* and *Drury*, together with the Canadian Ninth Escort Group, the *Matane*, *Monnow*, *St Pierre*, *Nene* and *Loch Alvie*.

A considerable number of German submarines had been operating from Norwegian bases and these began surrendering in substantial numbers to a handful of young British escort commanders who relished the task, enhanced as it was by the warmth of their welcome in Norwegian ports. Ironically it was also aided at Bergen by a German officer with previous experience, who had surrendered at Harwich in 1918. Eventually escort groups were sent over to shepherd the German submarines back to Britain, but the first fifteen were brought across the North Sea by the Ninth Escort Group. Commander Skinner RCNR in HMCS *Monnow* and his Canadian frigates had been detached from JW67 for the purpose.

To cover the convoy, air patrols were flown from HMS *Queen*, but the passage of JW67 was blissfully uneventful and it arrived in the Kola Inlet on 20 May, the day after Skinner led the surrendered U-boats into Loch Eriboll.

It only remained for Captain Browning's escort group to bring back the discharged ships from earlier convoys, all but a score of which were ready to sail as RA67 on 23 May 1945 under Commodore Sutcliffe embarked in the aptly named British Liberty ship *Samaritan*.[8]

Many of the men-o'-war of all classes which had at some time in the preceding four years taken part in the escort of convoys to North Russia now undertook duties connected with liberating occupied countries and rounding up the surrendering Germans. For them there were to be memories of rapturous welcomes and the satisfaction of seeing, at last, the beaten enemy against whom they had toiled for so long. Perhaps most poignant was the task of His Norwegian Majesty's ship *Stord*. British-built but Norwegian-manned, her commanding officer, Skule Storeheil, had voluntarily reverted in rank and kept his company together and now served under a British admiral for the last time. Rear-Admiral McGrigor hoisted his flag aboard the cruiser *Devonshire* and with *Stord* and three British destroyers escorted the cruiser *Norfolk* from Rosyth on 5 June 1945. Aboard the *Norfolk* were King Haakon and members of his family who had escaped the invading Germans five years earlier in McGrigor's flagship. The squadron entered Oslo fiord to a tumultuous welcome.

But for the men leaving Russia in convoy RA67 there were only memories of unused cargoes lining the quays, and the hostility or indifference of Soviet officialdom.

The convoy arrived in the Clyde estuary on 30 May 1945. Every ship had her navigation lights burning, as did the shoreline of Gourock and Greenock, of Helensburgh and Dumbarton, and the great wen of Glasgow beyond.

* * *

There were fifteen ships left discharging in Russian ports which made independent passages to the west during June, July and August. About a third were British, the remainder American. A further five were turned over to the Russians, while a few last cargoes were shipped to the Soviet Union under the terms of the Lease-Lend agreement, the final American voyage being made in December 1945 by the *Caesar Rodney*. The Liberty ship loaded a mixed general cargo at Philadelphia which included machine tools, lathes, milling machines and diesel generating sets – the machinery necessary to set up a factory for the manufacture of vehicle tyres. 'Tween decks were filled with foodstuffs and clothing collected from relief agencies for the alleviation of the terrible hardships endured by the Russian people.[9]

On her decks the ship bore 5 steam locomotives, almost 2,000 of which had been shipped to Russia during the course of the war to repair the damage to the country's infrastructure and economy. Her passage marked almost the end of a collaboration which, despite the waste, inefficiency and disruption of war, had worked well enough but which was soon to degenerate into a hostility which would last for forty-five years and sometimes come perilously close to open hostilities. For some the euphoria of victory never came: on the afternoon of 12 April President Roosevelt had died at Warm Springs, Georgia. For others victory was bittersweet: before RA67 anchored at the Tail o' the Bank, Winston Churchill's coalition government had resigned after the British electorate had rejected his further leadership. As for Great Britain herself, her economy was ruined, her imperial power was at an end and her people were exhausted.

Others had benefitted from the war: as the new American President, Harry Truman, busied himself with the final defeat of Japan and introduced the world to the atomic age, Stalin declared war on Japan, emerging as the true victor. He had succeeded in outwitting the sick Roosevelt and marginalizing Churchill in their orchestration of the closing stages of the war: his Red Army dominated Eastern Europe and his centralized version of Communism was soon to root out and supplant any emergent democracies there.

The extent to which the thousands of tons of war materials shipped to the Soviet Union between 1941 and 1945 contributed to this pre-eminence is impossible to quantify. At the height of the Cold War it was contended even by Western historians that the whole of this effort had been trifling, and ultimately of little consequence.

When Captain Denny entertained General MacFarlane aboard his cruiser HMS *Kenya* after the passage of PQ12, he asked MacFarlane what, in his opinion, was the material contribution made by the cargoes of the early PQ convoys. MacFarlane, who had visited Moscow to present British decorations to Soviet airmen, said the aid in the Arctic convoys was 'a mere drop compared with what Russia was now producing'. But MacFarlane thought Stalin a good chap and his evidence for this strongly expressed opinion is suspect. Undoubtedly quantities of *matériel* were wasted, left to rot on docksides and in sidings, victims of a Russian inability to organize. Likewise aircraft were damaged by careless handling, for Russian maintenance was notoriously poor, and a broken-down machine was more likely to be abandoned than repaired. But poor stowage in British ports and heavy weather had also been wasteful. It is equally incontestable that the British Matilda and Valentine tanks were vastly inferior machines to native-built Russian armour, especially the T-34 tank, but to state that the best they achieved was to relieve Soviet units for active fronts is a perverted assertion. Certainly the majority of tanks delivered in 1942 and 1943 were light tanks, and these were not what was required by the Red Army at the time.

Similar criticisms of the aircraft supplied are less easy to justify. That the early convoys were defended by one obsolescent Mark 1 Hurricane, for instance, when the holds of their merchantmen were crammed with Mark 22 machines, speaks for itself. Other detractors have suggested that the vast quantities of explosives shipped to Russian ports were a prodigal excess since Russia was capable of massive production of explosives herself. Nor was Stalin's Soviet Union a country to admit, as Britain has, that without the supply of guns and butter from the United States of America, she could never have survived.

In point of fact, between October 1941 and March 1946, Britain shipped to the Union of Soviet Socialist Republics war material to the value of £308 million and raw materials, foodstuffs, plant and medical supplies worth £120 million.

War material comprised: 5,218 tanks (1,388 made in Canada); 7,411 aircraft (3,129 made in America); 4,932 anti-tank guns; 4,000 rifles and machine guns; 4,338 radio sets; 2,000 field telephones; 1,803 radar sets; 473 million projectiles; 9 torpedo craft; 4 submarines; 14 minesweepers; 10 destroyers; and a battleship. All this went by the Arctic route.

Between March 1941 and December 1945, the United States of America contributed to Russia: 14,795 aircraft; 7,537 tanks; 51,503 jeeps; 35,170 motor bicycles; 8,700 tractors; 375,883 trucks and lorries; 8,218 anti-aircraft guns; 131,633 sub-machine guns; 345,735 tons of explosives; 1,981 locomotives; 11,155 railway wagons and trucks; 540,000 tons of steel rails; in excess of 1 million miles of telephone cable; food shipments to the value of $1,312 million; 2,670,000 tons of petrol; 842,000 tons of chemicals; 3,786,000 tyres; 49,000 tons of leather; and 15 million pairs of boots. The total value of the above is said to be $11,260,343,603.

Approximately one quarter of this was shipped via the Arctic route, a further quarter via the Persian Gulf and half via the Pacific. The overall tonnage for the Arctic route was 3,964,231 tons out of a global total of 16,366,747.

Of all these consignments the least glamorous were probably the most valuable: the anti-aircraft and field guns, the small arms and ammunition, the radio and radar sets, the field telephones, lorries and personnel carriers, the tyres and locomotives, the quantities of raw materials and chemicals, the two and a half million tons of petrol and forty-nine thousand tons of leather. The supply of no less than fifteen million pairs of boots or four and a half million tons of canned food are statistics that speak for themselves. There seems little doubt now that these were appreciated and that while the latter fed the Soviet war industry, the former allowed the Red Army to sustain its advance with an almost exponential vigour.

Doubt as to the real worth of the convoys was expressed at the time by Field-Marshal Lord Alanbrooke, who considered that the tanks and aircraft could have been better employed elsewhere, that in shipping them at all, but especially by the northern route, heavy losses of vital tonnage were incurred and that in return the Soviet authorities heaped abuse and ill-informed criticism upon British conduct of the convoys.[10]

But although there is a case for arguing a difference of opinion as to priority, evidence exists to affirm the essential nature of Western supplies to Soviet arms. A later defector, Victor Kravchenko, whose wartime position was uniquely involved with Soviet procurement and who 'came to know more intimately than the high-ranking generals and admirals how valuable American lease-lend weapons, material and machinery were in achieving victory', wrote of his country's failure to prepare adequately for its confrontation with Nazi Germany. 'Without the great influx of American aeroplanes . . . motor transport [and] a thousand other things we lacked, what would have been the fate of Soviet resistance?'

Aware of postwar doubts, Kravchenko concluded, 'Americans may have some doubts about this, but not the Soviet leaders, for them it is a fact. God knows we paid them back in full – in Russian lives – for Allied help, but that does not alter the fact itself.'[11]

Whilst the Russian authorities did erect memorials to the Allied dead, it remains the abiding opinion of many who survived that men of both the naval and merchant ships who died in Arctic convoys did so in vain, that the baleful influence of Stalin was as evil as that of Hitler and that the game scarcely proved worth the candle. It is an extreme view, but one to be respected. Postwar revelations have demonstrated that Stalin's insistence that the Arctic route achieved the quickest delivery was a sophism, far outweighed by his fear of Anglo-American hegemony in Mesopotamia if the Persian Gulf route was favoured. Is it possible that this insistence was also motivated by a Machiavellian desire to exhaust the British Royal Navy? Certainly it never recovered, as Great Britain never recovered, and the Arctic campaign was its own last unique victory.

Nor, in the opinion of many, was adequate tribute paid to the men of the campaign by Britain or America. Since it was almost entirely a British naval operation, it was to a large extent ignored in subsequent American perceptions, to the resentment of many former American merchant seafarers and personnel of the armed guards. Amongst the British themselves, the fact that the Arctic convoy route was never conceded independent campaign status and granted a medal rankles among both Royal Naval and mercantile veterans to the point of extreme bitterness. It seems that as the 'Iron Curtain' of Churchill's inimitable phrase settled over Europe, British governments, confronted with their own country's postwar problems and inadequacies, could not admit to having helped create the monster behind it.

Yet since the Berlin Wall was torn down in 1989, marking the end of the Cold War, there have been greater contacts between Russia and the West. The Russians have issued medals to claimants in Britain and the United States, and the return of veterans to Murmansk and Archangel has shown that shore-going sailors, even if superannuated, may still prove good ambassadors.

Moreover, the warmth that many old hands recognized lay beneath the façade the Russians had been compelled to maintain, was but part of the Russian character.

Indeed, it had struck one young Fleet Air Arm officer after a concert given in the hangar deck of an escort carrier, when some of the participants withdrew to the wardroom. He afterwards wrote,

> One vignette of the evening remains in my mind: a surging crowd round the piano, people standing on chairs and tables to see better, a small, bald, bespectacled professor of music accompanying, and one of the girls, a handsome, dark woman with a superb figure, singing a Russian love song . . . At 11 pm they left amid demonstrations of pleasure . . . A gay, delightful, and somehow rather unreal evening.

Amid such memories lie more sober thoughts. For others the ordeal left ineradicable scars – the excoriating cold, the fear and the proximity of untimely and senseless death mixed with the sheer degradation of life in a small, weather-battered warship to kindle a lifelong abhorrence of war which subsequently spurred an active and lifelong repudiation.

The Arctic convoys formed the last great campaign waged by the Royal Navy. It was a campaign based on unsound principles, beyond that of sustaining an ally who was hard-pressed, and though its success owed much to luck, this went hand in hand with courage and sheer, persistent doggedness. That the enemy failed to exploit the great advantages geography conferred upon him does nothing to diminish either the achievement of the objective itself, or the fortitude of those who accomplished it.

Though the majority of the participating merchant ships were American, or American-owned, a large proportion were British. In the years since 1945, the mercantile fleets of both nations have been in decline and are now almost non-existent. For many years the United States government maintained numerous war-built ships in 'reserve fleets', but like their British counterparts, American merchant seamen went home to be seen as 'bums and hobos'.

There has been no policy at all in support of maintaining a British merchant fleet. Successive governments have abandoned the seafaring community, yet the greatest lesson of the Second

World War was that supply by sea is vital. Naval histories concentrate upon naval affairs, yet the contribution of merchant shipping and its seamen is often overlooked, its ships anonymous, its seamen forgotten. A convoy's heart is its mercantile core, justifying the very existence of a fleet, but merchant ships are ordinary things, and like all ordinary things are not noticed, even in their absence. They do not conspicuously cover themselves with glory, except perhaps as Sir Francis Drake conceived of any great enterprise: 'that it was not the beginning, but the continuing thereof until it be thoroughly finished, which yieldeth the true glory'.

That much was true of every ship which made the Kola run, and while only about a quarter of the total shipments made to Russia went via the Arctic route, it was at the cost of 18 men-of-war and 1,944 souls. As for those commonplace merchant vessels, 87 were lost, 6 when sailing independently and 5 when in Russian ports, at a cost of 829 lives. For the Germans, the toll was probably similar: 1 battleship, 3 destroyers and 32 U-boats, whose crews almost all perished, plus numerous aircraft, are to be set against Allied losses.

None of these figures mean much in the appalling tolls rung up throughout the world during the 1930s and 1940s; but they can be put in perspective with a single salient statistic: the Arctic passage was the most lethal of all convoy routes and casualties among Allied merchant seamen were proportionately higher than among any of the armed services.

Ivan Maisky, Stalin's ambassador in London for much of the war, called these Russian convoys 'a northern saga of heroism, bravery and endurance' and spoke of the memory of them living for ever, and of their being 'one of the most striking expressions of collaboration between Allied governments without which our common victory would have been impossible'.

It was rhetoric, of course, to be expected of a politician in that heady honeymoon moment. Memories fade and great institutions disappear. Achievements of the past are diminished by time and traduced by historians.

Of all battlefields, the sea retains no trace of what has passed upon its surface, nor of those who claimed its mastery, for such things are ephemeral, part of humanity's conceit. Yet it was done and, for that alone, should not be forgotten.

CONVOY QP1

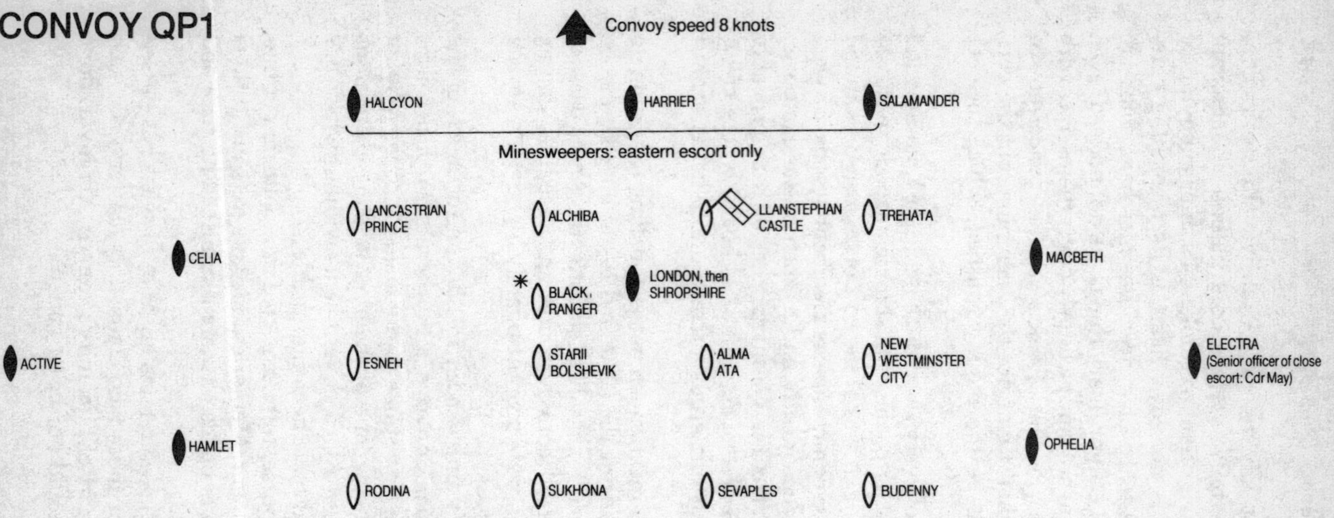

Note: QP1 received a simple escort of two, later three, destroyers with four armed trawlers of the 73rd Anti-submarine Group, plus a covering cruiser and an eastern escort of three Kola-based minesweepers. These detached as soon as the convoy cleared Russian waters.

* The oiler *Black Ranger* and destroyer *Anthony* joined later.

CONVOY PQ17

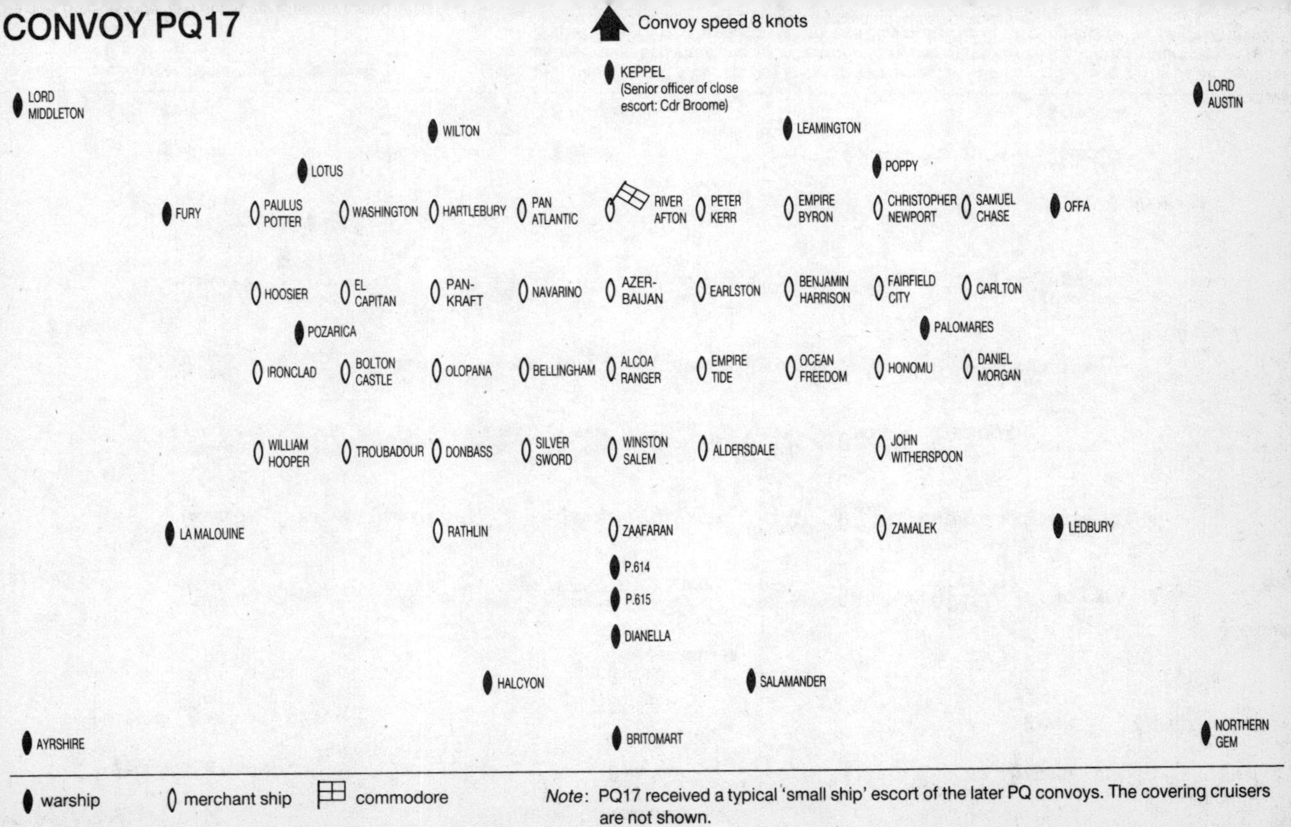

Convoy speed 8 knots

KEPPEL
(Senior officer of close
escort: Cdr Broome)

LORD MIDDLETON
LORD AUSTIN

WILTON
LEAMINGTON

LOTUS
POPPY

FURY
PAULUS POTTER
WASHINGTON
HARTLEBURY
PAN ATLANTIC
RIVER AFTON
PETER KERR
EMPIRE BYRON
CHRISTOPHER NEWPORT
SAMUEL CHASE
OFFA

HOOSIER
EL CAPITAN
PAN-KRAFT
NAVARINO
AZER-BAIJAN
EARLSTON
BENJAMIN HARRISON
FAIRFIELD CITY
CARLTON

POZARICA
PALOMARES

IRONCLAD
BOLTON CASTLE
OLOPANA
BELLINGHAM
ALCOA RANGER
EMPIRE TIDE
OCEAN FREEDOM
HONOMU
DANIEL MORGAN

WILLIAM HOOPER
TROUBADOUR
DONBASS
SILVER SWORD
WINSTON SALEM
ALDERSDALE
JOHN WITHERSPOON

LA MALOUINE
RATHLIN
ZAAFARAN
ZAMALEK
LEDBURY

P.614
P.615
DIANELLA

HALCYON
SALAMANDER

AYRSHIRE
BRITOMART
NORTHERN GEM

warship
merchant ship
commodore

Note: PQ17 received a typical 'small ship' escort of the later PQ convoys. The covering cruisers are not shown.

CONVOY PQ18

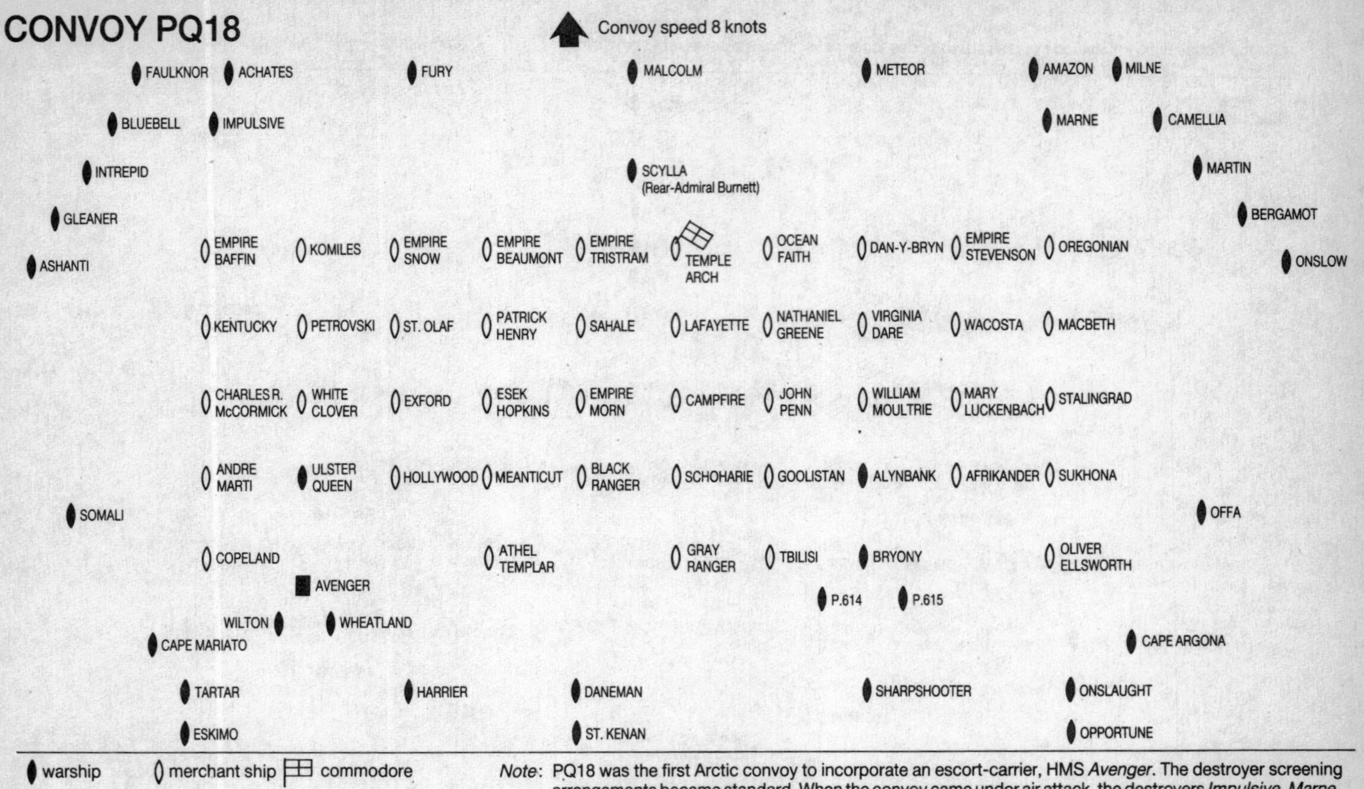

Convoy speed 8 knots

FAULKNOR ACHATES FURY MALCOLM METEOR AMAZON MILNE

BLUEBELL IMPULSIVE MARNE CAMELLIA

INTREPID SCYLLA (Rear-Admiral Burnett) MARTIN

GLEANER BERGAMOT

ASHANTI ONSLOW

EMPIRE BAFFIN | KOMILES | EMPIRE SNOW | EMPIRE BEAUMONT | EMPIRE TRISTRAM | TEMPLE ARCH | OCEAN FAITH | DAN-Y-BRYN | EMPIRE STEVENSON | OREGONIAN

KENTUCKY | PETROVSKI | ST. OLAF | PATRICK HENRY | SAHALE | LAFAYETTE | NATHANIEL GREENE | VIRGINIA DARE | WACOSTA | MACBETH

CHARLES R. McCORMICK | WHITE CLOVER | EXFORD | ESEK HOPKINS | EMPIRE MORN | CAMPFIRE | JOHN PENN | WILLIAM MOULTRIE | MARY LUCKENBACH | STALINGRAD

ANDRE MARTI | ULSTER QUEEN | HOLLYWOOD | MEANTICUT | BLACK RANGER | SCHOHARIE | GOOLISTAN | ALYNBANK | AFRIKANDER | SUKHONA

SOMALI OFFA

COPELAND | ATHEL TEMPLAR | GRAY RANGER | TBILISI | BRYONY | OLIVER ELLSWORTH

AVENGER P.614 P.615

WILTON WHEATLAND

CAPE MARIATO CAPE ARGONA

TARTAR HARRIER DANEMAN SHARPSHOOTER ONSLAUGHT

ESKIMO ST. KENAN OPPORTUNE

warship | merchant ship | commodore

Note: PQ18 was the first Arctic convoy to incorporate an escort-carrier, HMS *Avenger*. The destroyer screening arrangements became standard. When the convoy came under air attack, the destroyers *Impulsive*, *Marne*, *Somali*, *Offa*, *Tartar*, *Onslaught*, *Meteor* and *Fury* closed up to the perimeter of the merchant ships.

CONVOY JW65

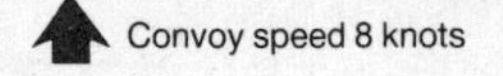

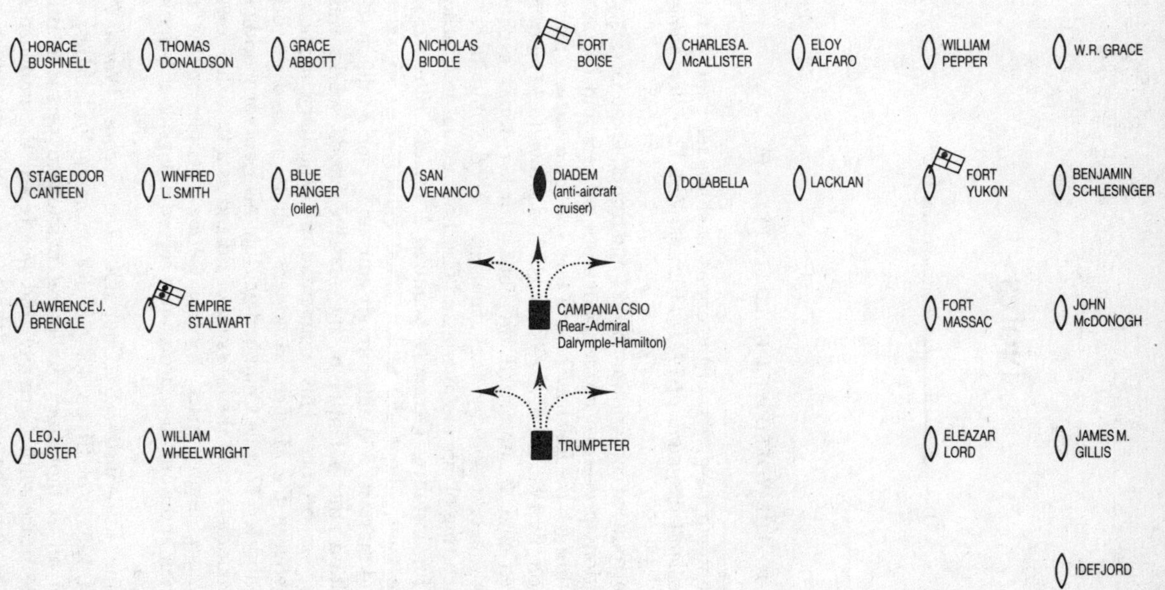

Note: JW65 with the outer screen omitted, showing the disposition of later JW convoys incorporating the escort-carriers' 'box' allowing them freedom of manoeuvre for their aircraft to take off and land on head to wind.

Notes

CHAPTER 1: 'THE WORLD WILL HOLD ITS BREATH'

1. For a contemporary view of the opposing sides, see Paul Muratoff, *The Russian Campaigns of 1941–43*, trans. W.E.D. Allen, Penguin, 1944.
2. Hitler introduced conscription in 1935 and from then on German war preparations proceeded apace. Numerous officers and NCOs had passed through the Reichswehr and they formed a nucleus for rapid expansion. By 1938 the new Wehrmacht had grown to 34 infantry, 6 armoured and 2 motorized divisions. Further rapid expansion followed, accelerated by the acquisition of the munitions and manufacturing plants of Austria and Czechoslovakia. In Czechoslovakia, for instance, Germany acquired 1 million rifles, 158,000 machine guns, about 450 tanks, 1,500 military cars, 3,000 field guns and mortars, 500 anti-aircraft guns and some 3 million shells. In addition, the potential of the massive Skoda works was of immense importance. This augmentation of military might took place between the Munich crisis, when Hitler assured the British Prime Minister, Neville Chamberlain, that his fears for world peace were groundless, and the invasion of Poland as a first step towards *Lebensraum*, 'living space' for the German peoples in the east. Hungarian and Romanian army units served alongside the Germans in Russia.
3. According to Winston S. Churchill, *The Second World War*, Penguin, 1985, Vol. III, pp. 43–9, Hitler's intimate, Rudolf Hess, who flew on an extraordinary unilateral mission to persuade Britain to make peace with Germany, did not reveal the imminence of Barbarossa when he arrived in Britain in May 1941, though he spoke of Hitler's 'hatred of Soviet Russia, his lust to destroy Bolshevism, his

admiration for Britain and his earnest wish to be friends with the British Empire . . .'

4. Churchill, *The Second World War*, Vol. III, p. 344.
5. In addition to Britain's native resources, Churchill could call upon help from Canada (whose navy expanded rapidly and played a major role in the Battle of the Atlantic), South Africa, Australia and New Zealand as well as Free French, Dutch, Polish and Norwegian contingents, all of whom made maritime as well as military contributions. Belgians also fought with distinction in the Battle of the Atlantic, and Greeks, Chinese, Indians, Sudanese and Somalis were among the diverse nations who manned Allied merchant ships. As will be seen, the Norwegian merchant fleet was of particular importance.

CHAPTER 2: TO THE EDGE OF THE EARTH

1. Admiral Golovko's fleet, comprising a handful of destroyers, some elderly, some modern, fifteen submarines, an assortment of patrol craft, torpedo boats and two minesweepers, was to prove of limited support to the British. Lower-deck opinion tended to be scathing, though genuinely fulsome in its praise of other aspects of the Russian character. Correspondents tended to regard the Red Navy's contribution as typically 'Soviet', distinguishing it from the fellow suffering of Russians themselves. Nevertheless, as will be seen, valuable contributions were made by individual units of the Soviet Navy.

   Captain Denny of HMS *Kenya* considered the Russian destroyers to be 'singularly ineffective . . . I understand that anything approaching fourteen days at sea per month was considered an intolerable strain.' Later, Rear-Admiral Burrough found incomprehensible the erratic discipline of two of them operating in support of PQ11. His Russian liaison officer thought the behaviour of their captains would make Golovko 'very angry'. This behaviour was in contrast to earlier experience, however, when Burrough operated with two of them under his command in December 1941 in a raid on the polar coast (see Ch. 4). They later gave creditable support and earned a measure of appreciation initially denied them.

   At Archangel the White Sea fleet under Rear-Admiral Stepanov (whose head, according to one rear-admiral's account 'was innocent of a single hair') was an even more motley collection of ships, though its numerical strength reached 100. It consisted of merchant auxiliaries, ice-breakers and fishing boats, and failed to render the expected assistance to British escorts.
2. I am indebted to the late Lieutenant-Commander Peter Kemp OBE

RN, whose wartime work in Operational Intelligence brought him into contact with Pound, for an informed opinion of the First Sea Lord's character. He was 'unique among admirals in believing the navy belonged to the nation, not its flag-officers. He visited Operational Intelligence daily, usually about 01.00. His successor, Cunningham, never bothered.'

3. For details of this and aid to Russia, see Churchill, *The Second World War*, Penguin, 1985, Vol. III, Chs. XXIV and XXV.
4. *London* brought back a corporal of the Royal Military Police, captured at Calais and lately a prisoner of the Russians. James Allan had escaped from a prison camp in Poland into Russia where he was arrested and thrown into the Lubyanka on suspicion of being a spy. Barbarossa had resulted in his release. He was quietly given the Distinguished Conduct Medal, but without a citation, so as not to upset Russian sensibilities. This small act of placation was the first in a long series, in which British pride was swallowed for the common good.
5. For an authoritative sociological study of the British merchant seaman at war, together with associated propaganda and a realistic assessment of mercantile practice, see Tony Lane, *The Merchant Seaman's War*, Manchester University Press, 1990. The author's own service at sea and numerous conversations with war veterans of all ranks have proved particularly revealing.
6. The Royal Naval Reserve (RNR), being from the Merchant Navy, were said to be seamen but not gentlemen and wore interlaced braid; the Royal Naval Volunteer Reserve (RNVR) were thought gentlemen but not seamen and wore wavy braid. The Royal Navy (RN) proper were considered gentlemen *and* seamen. The Merchant Navy, on the other hand, were neither gentlemen nor seamen! A more disparaging description of the Merchant Navy once current was that it was 'the pickings of the prisons officered by the sweepings of the public schools'. This was a generalization as inaccurate as it was unjust, but pigeon-holed the status of the Merchant Navy in the minds of certain of the community. It was deeply resented throughout, and long after, the war.
7. See Captain J. Broome RN, *The Convoy is to Scatter*, William Kimber, 1972. Broome nevertheless persists in calling the masters of merchant ships 'skipper'. See also Rear-Admiral Sir Kenelm Creighton, *Convoy Commodore*, Futura, 1976. Creighton also offers this telling evidence against the British shipowner: 'There were many disgracefully unseaworthy ships at sea flying the red ensign. Any merchant ship that managed to . . . assemble with a convoy was automatically covered by government insurance . . . Certain unscrupulous British shipowners whose consciences did not boggle

at the idea of gambling with the lives of seamen, were despicable enough to send ships not up to the standard needed to battle against the fury of the gales that haunt the Western Ocean in winter, ships that were not fit to be anywhere but in a breaker's yard.'

8. L.A. Sawyer and W.H. Mitchell, *The Liberty Ships*, 2nd ed., Lloyds, 1985; and Björn Landstrom, *The Ship*, Allen and Unwin, 1961. The Liberty ships were remarkable for their longevity, many of them being lengthened after the war and employed tramping until well into the 1960s. If they had a defect it was in their 'stiffness', excessive and very uncomfortable positive stability. This was frequently countered by ballast carried in their 'tween decks which led to a number of serious incidents where ships 'lolled' dangerously when solid ballast was not used. Post-war differences between the American and British governments concerning the continuing operation of *Sams* eventually led to their 'return' and repurchase by individual owners at around £137,000 each, expensive for war-built tonnage, but desperately needed by British shipowners whose fleets had been decimated. The later and superior class of utility-built ships, the *Victories*, faster with steam turbines, enjoyed a similar post-war history.
9. Correspondence with A. Johnsen of H. Nor. M.S *Stord*. 'There was no organized evacuation, we just grabbed what we could of fuel and provisions and cleared off . . . as for myself I did not have any family alive, so I did not bother at all, as long as I was fed and paid I was content. I went to sea when I was 14, so I did not know anything else . . . At the finish of the Norwegian campaign we had lost every sixth man of our Navy . . .' These losses mounted to 'every fourth man by 1943'. *Stord* was a fleet destroyer. Hunt-class destroyers and Flower-class corvettes (*Potentilla* and *Eglantine* served in the Arctic), as well as smaller craft such as minesweepers and MTBs, were manned by Norwegians.

Chapter 3: Undertaking the impossible

1. For a succinct and objective analysis of British naval ship design and its shortcomings, see E.H.H. Archibald, *The Fighting Ship in the Royal Navy, 897–1984*, Blandford Press, 1984.
2. It was pointed out in Parliament after the war, when the value of capital ships was being debated by the Labour-led government, that at the height of the Battle of the Atlantic when convoys were operating with wholly inadequate escorts, 'never less than a dozen' fleet destroyers were 'swinging round their moorings' at Scapa Flow, ready to attend the movements of the Home Fleet's capital ships (*Hansard*, Navy Estimates debate, 18 March 1947).

3. For a serving officer's critical view of the Admiralty's anti-submarine policies, see Captain R. Whinney DSC ■■ RN, *The U-boat War*, Arrow Books, 1986. See also Richard Humble, *The Rise and Fall of the British Navy*, Macdonald, 1986; John Terraine, *Business in Great Waters: The U-boat Wars, 1916*–1945, Leo Cooper, 1989; and Corelli Barnett, *Engage the Enemy More Closely*, Hodder and Stoughton, 1991. The anti-submarine training establishment at Portland was minimal, run by largely passed-over officers of little seniority. Anti-submarine warfare was considered the Cinderella of the service. Even career fleet destroyer commanders of the Home Fleet, the self-styled *élite*, did not take the matter very seriously, a pride which was to be humbled by the greater efficiency of the less glamorous Western Approaches escorts which were largely manned by reservists and hostilities-only personnel. This discrepancy showed up on Arctic convoys where units from both forces were deployed side by side.

   The effectiveness of asdic was most limited by these temperature and density differences in the approaches to the Kola Inlet. Elsewhere it was less inhibiting than at first thought and the Barents Sea today proves no problem to modern sonar.
4. For an accessible account of pre-war German naval developments, see Edward P. Von der Porten, *The German Navy in World War Two*, Pan Books, 1969, which has the merit of Dönitz's endorsement by way of a foreword. See also Cajus Bekker, *Hitler's Naval War*, Macdonald and Jane's, 1974.
5. Bonar Law, the then Chancellor of the Exchequer, made a tactless speech in the Commons in 1917 at the very crisis of the war on trade, boasting of profits made from compensation paid him for losses of ships in which he had an interest. Sir William Burrell amassed his art collection from the sale of his fleet during the acute post-war shortage of tonnage. 'It was bad economically', said one commentator, 'and still worse from the social and political standpoint that any section of the community should reap so rich a harvest from the common peril.' See Ronald Hope, *A New History of British Shipping*, John Murray, 1990, Ch. 10.
6. These were known to the Germans as the Deutschland class of *Panzerschiffe*, or armoured ships. Three of them had been built under the limitations of the Washington Treaty of 1922 which, apart from producing these revolutionary ships, encouraged the innovative qualities of German naval architecture already seen at Jutland. Hitler, nervous of the loss of prestige if a ship so called was sunk, ordered the class ship renamed as the *Lützow*. After the sinking of the *Graf Spee* in 1939, only the *Lützow* and the *Admiral Scheer* remained.
7. Apart from deficiencies in British torpedo design and the deployment

of a vast number of ships in the hunt for *Bismarck*, the German battleship quickly outgunned the battlecruiser *Hood* which blew up with enormous loss of life. As the darling of the Royal Navy, the *Hood*'s loss was a blow to British prestige *and* morale. Nor did the destruction of the battlecruiser *Repulse* and the new battleship *Prince of Wales* by Japanese aircraft in December offer much comfort. The latter had previously been mauled by *Bismarck*. With the *Royal Oak* sunk at her moorings in Scapa Flow by Günther Prien in *U47*, the British became nervous about preserving their capital ships.

8. Fegen was awarded a posthumous Victoria Cross. Further major successes were scored by German surface ships, both raiders and heavy fleet units, in the spring of 1941. They were not sustained, and *Scharnhorst* and *Gneisenau* ended their cruises at Brest where they were joined by the *Prinz Eugen* after her break-out with *Bismarck*. The latter was sunk in May and the ships in Brest subjected to bombing by the Royal Air Force.

Chapter 4: 'Now there is no end to our troubles'

1. For assessments of Tovey see Ludovic Kennedy, *Pursuit*, Collins, 1974; Gordon Taylor, *The Sea Chaplains*, Oxford Illustrated Press, 1978; and Martin Stephen, *The Fighting Admirals*, Leo Cooper, 1991. Tovey's expressed opinions are to be found in Roskill's *The War at Sea*, HMSO, 1954–61, and in Admiral Schofield's *The Arctic Convoys*, Macdonald and Jane's, 1977, and *The Russian Convoys*, Batsford, 1964.
2. On 25 June 1941 the *Nigeria* with three destroyers had played a vital part in assisting the British to regain access to German encrypted signals. After a short chase of the German weather-reporting trawler *Lauenburg* off Jan Mayen, a boarding party from HMS *Tartar* seized the Enigma codes before the scuttled ship sank. In order not to arouse German suspicions as to British knowledge of Enigma signals traffic, the force sailed in wide line abreast to give the impression that the encounter was 'accidental'. When the *Lauenburg* was boarded, the trawler's Enigma operators plunged the June codes into water which rapidly destroyed their blotting-paper constituency. The boarders nevertheless seized the July codes from their secure stowage and thus fulfilled the purpose of their raid.
3. Admiral Tovey was not the only senior officer to realize the vital need for long-range aerial reconnaissance and airborne anti-submarine patrols, nor to resent the priority given to Bomber Command's demands for aircraft for the bombing offensive against Germany. There seems little doubt today that the tide would have turned in

favour of the Allies in the Atlantic earlier than it did had this view found favour with Churchill.

4. As late as May 1944 German intelligence was worried by the presence of Andrew Milne's British 4th Army, an almost entirely bogus force, camped on the east coast of Scotland, anticipating that the feared Allied invasion might strike not at France or the Low Countries but at Norway. Consequently 17 divisions remained between Kristiansand and Tromsö during that fateful summer (see Richard Collier, *The War that Stalin Won*, Hamish Hamilton, 1983, p. 63).

   Hitler's concern for Norway was partly due to the fact that vital Swedish iron ore reached Germany via the railway terminating at the Norwegian port of Narvik.
5. This apparent vindication of the big-gun theorists was entirely due to the fact that the *Glorious* was not flying combat air patrols and had therefore deprived herself of her airborne eyes. This was largely due to the overcrowding of her flight deck as she withdrew RAF aircraft as well as her own in the aftermath of the Norwegian fiasco. She was sighted and engaged at extremely long range. Her escorting destroyers behaved with the customary suicidal gallantry.
6. For first-hand accounts of PQ6 and QP4, together with details of Murmansk in this and subsequent chapters, I am indebted to Lieutenant-Commander F.W.W. Lewes RN, then a midshipman aboard HMS *Edinburgh*, and Able Seaman I. Priscott, of the *Explorer*.
7. One of Golovko's 'troubles' was to be the Panamanian tanker *El Oceano* which was chartered to the Russians during the winter. When, in February 1942, she was coasting towards Murmansk to join a homeward convoy, she broke away from her escort in the darkness and made directly for Iceland. Such erratic behaviour caused equal anxiety to the Rear-Admiral at Murmansk.

CHAPTER 5: 'A MATTER OF THE HIGHEST URGENCY'

1. QP4 consisted of the British ships *Briarwood, Cape Race, Dan-y-Bryn, El Mirlo, San Ambrosio* (tanker), *Trehata, Wanstead* (commodore), *Cape Corso, Eulima, Trekieve*, the Panamanian-flagged *El Capitan* and *Cocle*, and the Russian ship *Sukhova*.
2. It was customary to refer to the ship in which the Commodore was embarked as 'the' Commodore, and I have adopted this convention. Similarly when the masculine gender is used with a ship's name, it refers to the officer or master commanding that ship. The ship itself is always referred to as 'she,' *never* 'it', as has now become the fashion. (Curiously the Kriegsmarine called the *Admiral Scheer* '*der*

Scheer', whereas other German warships took the feminine *'die'*.) A commodore's presence is always denoted by a broad pendant, in the case of convoy commodores a white flag with a blue St George's cross.

3. It was only later discovered that the second torpedo fired by Hackländer had failed to explode. Chronic defects affected the torpedoes of both sides in the early years of the war. Hackländer's *U454* was to fight a duel with a Coastal Command Sunderland in the Bay of Biscay in August 1943. Both the U-boat and the Sunderland were lost, though Hackländer and a dozen of his men were later rescued by the Royal Navy. The other two boats of the Ulan pack were *U134* and *U584*, the first of which had already sunk the *Waziristan*.
4. See Frank Pearce, *The Ship that Torpedoed Herself*, Baron Jay Ltd, 1975, Ch. 3.
5. I am greatly indebted to Captain C.W. Leadbetter RNR and to Bob Ruegg in whose excellent unpublished history of HM Corvette *Oxlip*, Captain Leadbetter's remarks are quoted, for these observations on PQ11 and those on QP8 in the following chapter.
6. It has become conventional British practice to class these two ships as battlecruisers simply because their superior speed defied British classification as battleships, but this is in fact what they were, though less potent than the heavier *Bismarck* or *Tirpitz*.
7. Cajus Bekker, *Hitler's Naval War*, trans. Frank Ziegler, Macdonald and Jane's, 1974, p. 215.
8. The 'Channel Dash' was not quite the surprise to the British that it is sometimes thought to have been, though German efforts to confuse British defences were certainly thorough. Nevertheless, the Ultra decrypters at Bletchley Park, who had penetrated the German Enigma codes, warned of the likelihood of such a break-out and certain measures were taken in anticipation of its occurrence.
9. Though subject to the incessant ministrations of dockyard workers, the *Gneisenau* was towed from Kiel to Gotenhafen, never put to sea again and was scuttled in March 1945 to avoid her falling into the hands of the advancing Russians. The *Prinz Eugen* survived to be used as a target for post-war atomic bomb tests in the Pacific.
10. Winston Churchill, *The Second World War*, Penguin, 1985, Vol. IV, p. 98.
11. See Roskill, *The War at Sea*, HMSO, 1957, Vol. 2, Ch. 5, for this and subsequent chapters. Also *Naval Staff History (Second World War)*, Battle Summary No. 22, Arctic Convoys 1941–1945; and R. Ruegg and A. Hague, *Convoys to Russia, 1941–45*, World Ship Society, 1992.

Chapter 6: 'Ideal weather for carrier aircraft'

1. In total twenty destroyers were at sea during the passage of QP8 and PQ12 giving distant cover: *Ashanti, Bedouin, Echo, Eclipse, Faulknor, Fury, Grove, Icarus, Inconstant, Intrepid, Javelin, Lancaster, Ledbury, Lookout, Onslow, Punjabi, Tartar, Verdun, Wells* and *Woolston*.
2. Position estimated by *Kenya* as 72° 09′N 010° 34′E.
3. C. Bekker, *Hitler's Naval War*, Macdonald and Jane's, 1974, p. 261 *et seq*.
4. The *Tirpitz*'s own aircraft encountered two of the searching Albacores twenty-five miles astern of the battleship but, when she met some Swordfish later, she had expended all her ammunition.
5. *Uredd* was a Norwegian naval submarine commanded by Lieutenant R.O. Rören, R. Nor. N., and *Junon*, a Free French vessel commanded by Captaine de frégate Querville DSC. The C-in-C Submarines, Admiral Max Horton, had not yet taken over the Western Approaches Command from Admiral Noble and, as an ex-First World War submariner, understood the frustrations of the kind of watch-and-ward operation his vessels were engaged upon so close to an enemy-held coast.

Chapter 7: 'Baptism of fire'

1. Under the terms of the Anglo-Russian Trade Agreement of August 1941, Britain granted Russia five years credit of £10 million at 3.5 per cent because Russia wanted far more in the way of war materials from Britain than vice versa.
2. Admiral Tovey was afterwards critical of this as he was of the Admiralty's routeing of the convoy to the eastward. His attitude to radio silence was in marked contrast to that of his successor, Admiral Fraser.
3. The Blohm and Voss aircraft reported by the Second Officer of the SS *Induna* as having been sighted on the afternoon of 26 March and engaged by the group then in company, was seen to have been hit and disappeared in a snowstorm. Indications are that she may have been lost.

   The 'western' group centred on the oiler *Scottish American* had, prior to their junction with HMS *Eclipse*, also been overflown by a German aeroplane. For this and subsequent details of HMS *Trinidad*'s ordeal, see Frank Pearce, *The Ship that Torpedoed Herself*, Baron Jay Ltd, 1975.
4. The *Hipper*'s exasperated captain, Wilhelm Meisel, stated, 'If we are

to achieve anything at all, the crippling fuel shortage must be ended forthwith' (C. Bekker, *Hitler's Naval War*, Macdonald and Jane's, 1974, p. 265).

5. A rather confused account of this part of PQ13 by S.C. Whitehead exists in J. Lennox Kerr (ed.), *Touching the Adventures of Merchantmen*, Harrap, 1953. However, I am indebted to W. Sergeant, son-in-law of Captain Stein, for clarification of the subsequent ordeal of the *Empire Starlight*.
6. The detached Commodore in *River Afton* was, incidentally, astern and to the north of this latter group, having swung north towards the original convoy route prior to turning south for the Murman coast.
7. TBS – 'Talk Between Ships' – was an early short-range VHF (Very High Frequency) system and was used once the enemy had located a convoy for inter-ship communication and tactical control. It was still supplemented by the traditional, though largely superseded system of flag signals which, whilst slow, made it clear what a particular escort was doing. The other rapid inter-ship system was, of course, morse by signal projector, but in the poor visibility so often prevalent in the Arctic, it was useless unless ships were in sight of one another; even in clear weather, escorts on opposite sides of a large convoy rarely were.
8. These men appear to have been destined to be amongst the growing numbers of British personnel stationed in Russia in an attempt to improve the turn-around facilities for both naval and merchant ships. See Ch. 9.
9. The fate of the whale-catcher *Sulla*, which failed to make port, is somewhat uncertain. *Sulla* was probably sunk on 1 April by *U436* (Seibicke). *Sumba* suffered badly from icing but the exertions of her crew ensured she arrived at Polyarnoe. Icing was certainly the cause of *Shera*'s loss described in the previous chapter. See John H. Harland, *Catchers and Corvettes: The Steam Whalecatcher in Peace and War, 1860–1960*, Jean Boudriot Publications, 1992, p. 53, and correspondence with the author. Confusion also exists in the names of some of the participating merchant ships, possibly a result of wartime typographical and phonetic errors. Similarly, some resolution of the attacking U-boats was required, and I have followed J. Rohwer and G. Hummelchen, *Chronology of the War at Sea*, 1939–45, Greenhill Books, revised ed., 1992.

Chapter 8: 'Just a Process of Attrition'

1. Several correspondents indicated this feeling and I have alluded to it in an earlier chapter. See also Tony Lane, *The Merchant Seaman's*

War, Manchester University Press, 1990, p. 18 *et seq*. It varied in strength from a mild disappointment combined with an attempt to see the RN point of view, to an angry and deeply felt resentment and sensation of abandonment. Some held strong views, but asked that their names were withheld. The extreme conditions of the Arctic and the common knowledge that the early escorting forces were insignificant engendered an expectation that all-out efforts should be made to cover these convoys, particularly in the season of growing daylight. It is clear from subsequent events that the Admiralty themselves finally came to this conclusion. It is interesting that a number of RNVR officers and 'hostilities only' ratings who owed only an expedient and temporary loyalty to the Royal Navy offered the same opinion. It should, however, be emphasized that the crews of the escorts felt equally exposed.

2. The elderly, ex-American *Newmarket*, one of the fifty 'four-stack' destroyer escorts supplied under the Lease-Lend arrangements of 1941, did not join due to condenser trouble. The *Beverley* was another; they were renamed the 'Town' class when under the white ensign.
3. I am indebted to the Chief Officer of the SS *Hopemount* for much information concerning PQ14. See also Ch. 11.
4. See *Merchantmen at War*, HMSO, 1944. After PQ14 Captain Lawrence was seconded for special Admiralty duties.
5. This incident is not mentioned in the official British histories, though the fact that the cruiser several times took up defensive positions outside the screen is recorded. It was clearly and memorably witnessed from the *Hopemount* and is confirmed from German records.
6. It became the practice, if required, to run warships directly through to make up escorts to replace losses or damage. In this instance *Liverpool*, *Punjabi* and *Marne* had been sent to reinforce the homeward escort and replace the dry-docked *Trinidad*. This is one further instance of the complexities of the overall operation and of the drain on resources made at a time when the Royal Navy was suffering unprecedented losses worldwide.
7. S.C. Whitehead, 'The SS *Empire Starlight*' in J. Lennox Kerr (ed.), *Touching the Adventures of Merchantmen in the Second World War*, George Harrap, 1953. See also Ch. 7, note 4.
8. S. Roskill, *The War at Sea*, HMSO, 1957. Vol. II, p. 128.

Chapter 9: 'It is beginning to ask too much . . .'

1. R. Ransome-Wallis, *Two Red Stripes – A Naval Surgeon at War*, Ian Allan, 1973, p. 77.

2. Sir Archibald Hurd (ed.), *Britain's Merchant Navy*, Odhams, 1943, p. 104.
3. The *Zebulon B. Vance* was launched only hours before the Japanese attacked Pearl Harbor. In November 1943, on conversion to a hospital ship, she was renamed but she reverted to her original name, that of a Confederate Congressman and Colonel in the Civil War, on alteration to a passenger transport. In this role she carried war brides and military dependants after which she was mothballed in the US Army reserve fleet, and scrapped in Italy in 1970. The *Francis Scott Key*, already an Arctic veteran, survived as a cargo carrier until 1967.
4. Report of Rear-Admiral H.M. Burrough CB DSO RN, Rear-Admiral 10th Cruiser Squadron (CS10). PQ15 was in position 73°17′N 008°25′E. A witness in *Nigeria* claims the aircraft for his own ship's guns.
5. *Seagull*, built in 1937, was the first all-welded ship in the Royal Navy. The Norwegian *St Albans* was another Town class (see Ch. 8, note 2). An account of the incident occurs in the New London, Connecticut, *Evening Day*, 21 October 1957, and I am indebted to its author, George Parnell of the *Jastrzab*, for this and other details; also my thanks to Frank Kismul of *St Albans* and Len Matthews. Commanding Officers' reports are in ADM 199/721, p. 99 *et seq*. In the enquiry *Jastrzab*'s navigating officer stated he had not had a sight for five days.
6. More sophisticated modern sets can discriminate between 'hard' and persistent echoes and the random response from the adjacent sea surface.
7. 'Huff-Duff' was the slang for HF-DF, high frequency direction finding, whereby a radio bearing of an enemy transmission could be obtained from a ship fitted with the appropriate equipment. Many escorts and rescue ships were so fitted and two or three bearings could pinpoint the transmitting source, thus updating the tactical plot. The Germans' reliance on both homing signals and copious and imprudent quantities of radio chit-chat made them vulnerable to sudden and often unexpected counter-attack. Huff-Duff should not be confused with RDF, which is now a synonymous term but was then the accepted secret name of radar.
8. This aerial torpedo attack has been recorded as being made by Heinkel He115 seaplanes (B. Schofield, *Arctic Convoys*, Macdonald and Jane's, 1977, p. 36), whereas Captain Lawrence recalls torpedo-armed Ju88s, one of which lingered to shadow, which is more likely to have been the case given the vulnerability of the slow He115s and the recent location of the modified Ju88s in Norway. This theory seems to be confirmed by Rohwer and Hummelchen (*Chronology of*

the War at Sea, 2nd revised ed., Greenhill Books, 1992) who mention these aircraft as being from KG26.

9. The *Hermann Schoemann* mounted five 5-inch guns and the two Narviks each had five 5.9-inch guns, an overwhelming force when pitted against *Beverley*'s three 4-inch guns (only two of which could be broadside-fired simultaneously), and the two 4.7-inch guns of the three other destroyers, all of which had lost after guns in favour of anti-submarine weaponry.
10. Three detonations were heard by the destroyers and *U378* (Hoschatt) which was in the area. It seems probable that the *Tsiolkovsky* was sunk by the destroyers. Perhaps other torpedoes struck the ice. German observers saw this happen to one British torpedo (C. Bekker, *Hitler's Naval War*, Macdonald, 1974, p. 267).
11. I am greatly indebted to Bob Ruegg, editor and compiler of *From Archangel to Alexandria on His Majesty's Service: The Story of HMS* Oxlip, and to the corvette's first lieutenant and later commanding officer, Captain C.W. Leadbetter RNR, for information on this and subsequent convoys.
12. See F. Pearce, *Running the Gauntlet*, Fontana, 1989, Ch. 7, an anecdotal account based on eyewitness reports.
13. The *Rubin* was a small vessel of the Pogranitchni Storoshevoi, or Coastal Patrol, mounting one 4-inch and two AA guns with a minelaying and minesweeping capability.
14. See Bekker, *Hitler's Naval War*, p. 269.
15. In both world wars the Germans tended to favour blowing up their disabled ships, in marked contrast to the British tradition of trying to save a ship or fighting her to the finish. Hitler's rhetoric was often full of exhortations to fight to the last man. Nowhere but in the unwritten rules of engagement does it appear in the British canon of conduct in time of war. Although *Z24* was firing her guns until the very last moment of finally securing alongside the *Hermann Schoemann*, the distractions necessary to conduct this manœuvre would have seriously reduced her effective capacity to fight. It is difficult to imagine a British crew cheering the disappearance of their ship (*Trinidad*'s last moment was accompanied by no such outburst). Certainly the action had denied capture by the enemy, but little else; she was most certainly lost to the Kriegsmarine. It is probable that the German habit of spending so much time in port never inculcated that *esprit de corps* fundamental to the underpinning of a lethal naval tradition and which was a contrast to the sea-time essential to the maintenance of British sea-power.
16. Destroyers, like minesweepers, were usually grouped in flotillas though the exigencies of the Service rarely enabled them to remain together. Though commonly individually commanded by officers of

junior or middle rank, the senior officer afloat was often a captain, known as Captain (D). Eaton was the Captain (D) of the 6th Destroyer Flotilla composed of Tribal-class ships operating with the Home Fleet and based on Scapa. The administrative commander of the fleet destroyers at Scapa was the Rear-Admiral commanding Destroyers, or RAD, at this time Robert Burnett. Because of the breaking up of these units I have not troubled the reader over-much with these details.

17. The official position given for *Trinidad*'s sinking is 73°35′N 022°53′E. It was remarkable that so cumulatively damaged a vessel as HMS *Trinidad* should have survived as long as she did, manœuvring at a considerable speed while under a punishing attack. The repairs effected at Rosta had stood up well, given their 'jury' nature, and attest to the versatility, ingenuity and skill of those responsible.

CHAPTER 10: 'SUCCESS WAS BEYOND EXPECTATION'

1. The British merchant ships consisted of *Empire Lawrence* (CAM ship), *Empire Baffin, Lowther Castle, Empire Selwyn, Ocean Voice, Atlantic, Empire Elgar* (heavy lift ship) and *Empire Purcell*. American ships were *Alcoa Banner, Richard Henry Lee, City of Omaha, Nemaha, Heffron, City of Joliet, Minotaur, Steel Worker, Mauna Kea, West Nilus, Massmar, Alamar, Carlton, John Randolph, Hybert, American Press, American Robin, Syros, Michigan* and *Mormacsul*. The Russian contingent comprised *Arcos, Chernyshevski, Revolutsioner, Shchors* and *Starii Bolshevik*. There were two Panamanian-registered vessels, the *Michigan* and the *Exterminator*, and a Dutch ship, the *Pieter de Hoogh*, formerly the *Empire Halley* (see PQ7B).
2. *Hyderabad* was a Flower-class corvette originally named *Nettle*, but was renamed in honour of the Nizam of Hyderabad who had made a large donation to British war funds.
3. Details from the report of the CO, *Hyderabad*.
4. Some accounts 'credit' the *Carlton* with this mistake; others mention fire from two American ships having hit Hay's Hurricane. In his report to the Admiralty Trade Division, the *Empire Lawrence*'s Second Officer, Mr N.S. Hulse, the ship's senior surviving deck officer, stated that the 'American ship astern of us opened fire on him, not realising that he was a British plane but they did not hit him'. In the order of sailing this was the *Alcoa Banner*. *Carlton* was the third ship astern of the *Empire Lawrence*. Hulse goes on to say that Hay 'again circled the convoy and came up on our beam and baled out.

Using our R[adio] T[elephone] we told the destroyer escort [*Volunteer*] and she picked the pilot up.' In addition to the gallant Hay, the CAM ship bore a second pilot, Macpherson, a Canadian.

5. The Admiralty's Confidential Battle Summary No. 22 states that this was only attack of the day. The Trade Division debriefs suggest quite otherwise, that the attacks began in the early morning and lasted all day. During the six-day battle Captain Stuy, Master of the Dutch freighter *Pieter de Hoogh*, reported that his ship, typically armed with a 4-inch gun, a 12-pounder, two Oerlikons and four twin Marlin machine guns, had loosed off 2,400 rounds of ammunition from the Oerlikons and 10,000 from the Marlins. He claimed two aircraft shot down. 'The entire crew stood by their guns night and day never relaxing for a single moment, sustenance being brought to them at their stations.' Stuy had on board British DEMS gunners and his own crew had had the benefit of a two-day (!) training course at Cardiff. (Debriefs from *Pieter de Hoogh*, *Lowther Castle*, *Empire Selwyn*, *Empire Purcell*, *Empire Elgar* and *Empire Lawrence*.)
6. See R. Ransome-Wallis, *Two Red Stripes: A Surgeon at War*, Ian Allan, 1973.
7. CO's report on the escort of PQ16 by HMS *Hyderabad*.
8. Commander R.G. Onslow, a regular officer, won four Distinguished Service Orders during the course of the war, three of them in five months.
9. Notwithstanding this success 32,400 tons of cargo had been lost including 147 tanks, 770 vehicles and 80 aircraft.

Chapter 11: 'It is not enough'

I am indebted to a large number of people for background detail of conditions in North Russia. Several did not wish to make their names known, but emphasized certain points about the conditions they found at Molotovsk, Murmansk or Archangel. As might be expected, there was a wide variety of experience which I have endeavoured to reflect in this chapter. Attitudes to the Russians were highly subjective. There was every shade of opinion from disgust through irritation and resignation to sympathy. Political orientation, location and circumstances all played an inevitable part in the formation of opinion. A distinction also has to be made between those whose contacts were 'official', and those who met the ordinary Soviet citizens with whom relations were consequently less formal.

1. See Ch. 15.
2. See Richard Collier, *The War that Stalin Won*, Hamish Hamilton, 1983, p. 78. Churchill was well aware of Stalin's desire to capitalize

on victory after the war. It was his fate to relinquish power to Roosevelt and the United States of America. By the Teheran Conference, Roosevelt, who had more or less dismissed Churchill, the British and their Empire as lacking any further influence, thought he had the measure of Stalin. In this he was utterly deceived.

3. See Ch. 4. Later, as the *Tirpitz* was moved north to Altenfiord, three photo-reconnaissance Spitfires, fitted with long-range fuel tanks, arrived at Gryaznaya to overfly the German capital ship regularly. Their films were sent back in a lone Catalina whose precarious flights looped into the far north, over the ice-cap itself, to avoid interception from the Luftwaffe.
4. The black-market rates were 0.25 litres of vodka = 30 roubles; 20 cigarettes = 40 roubles. The official rate was about 48 roubles to the pound sterling.
5. Several of these little ships which served so gallantly in North Russian waters did not survive the war. On 27 August 1944, by a tragic error, RAF Typhoons sank *Britomart* and *Hussar* and so damaged *Salamander* that she became a constructive total loss.
6. A slightly different version of this story is given in Harry Ludlam and Paul Lund, *PQ17: Convoy to Hell*, New English Library, 1968, new ed. 1978, where Stepanov's exhortation is said to have been to the whole ship's company of *Pozarica*. The substance of the Russian Admiral's message is, however, almost identical.

Chapter 12: 'A Serious Fleet Operation'

The historiography of Convoy PQ17 is, to a degree, as fascinating as the events themselves. In dealing with this episode I have been conscious that although the general facts are by now well-known, it remains a highly emotive issue for many of those who took part, as well as for those who lost relatives in PQ17. Traditionally the historian, in reacting to the paradox of human response to war, has too often erred on the side of glory: *dulce et decorum est pro patria mori*. But this, as Wilfred Owen pointed out, is an old lie, and war's scars are also part of the paradox, more personal and lasting than any ill-defined abstraction. Often ineradicable and requiring courage and fortitude to bear, such memories can burden those whose lives have been affected. Some wanted to forget, and shut doors in my face; others, whether they conceived themselves to be mere victims or actually victimized by events, though free in their reminiscences and opinions, wished to remain anonymous. Again I discovered a breadth of opinion, views which ranged from the apologists who claimed that PQ17's losses had no obvious material effect upon the course of the war, through tolerant understanding of men who recognized the risks and inherent uncertainties of war, to those whose sense of betrayal remained, poignant and unmodified by the passage of time. It was this legacy of emotion that I felt obligated to record alongside the bare facts, for this too is the stuff of history.

As for the facts themselves, no two accounts agree precisely, but I have drawn heavily on four books in particular: David Irving, *The Destruction of Convoy PQ17*, Granada, revised ed. 1985; Captain Jack Broome, *The Convoy is to Scatter*, Kimber, 1972; Paul Lund and Harry Ludlam, *PQ17: Convoy to Hell*, NEL, new ed. 1978; and Godfrey Winn, *PQ17, The Story of a Ship*, Hutchinson, collected ed. 1953. Other points of local detail have come from Kerslake, interviews, letters and several manuscript accounts in my possession.

1. Hitler's 41st War Directive which also announced the Blau offensive.
2. Operation Harpoon depleted the Home Fleet by two cruisers and eight destroyers, one of which was lost in the Mediterranean, between 4 and 24 June 1942.
3. The alleged quotation of Tovey's used as the title for the next chapter is given in several books, most notably by Martin Stephen, *The Fighting Admirals*, and Cajus Bekker, *Hitler's Naval War*. There is no evidence to suggest he used this expression directly to Pound, since his conversations with the First Sea Lord were private. It seems, however, that he may have made this remark on learning of Pound's intention to scatter a convoy in the Barents Sea if it came under heavy surface attack.

   Extracts from Tovey's dispatches for the period were made public in a supplement to the *London Gazette*, 17 October 1950, largely due to increasing public demand to counter the many rumours which PQ17 had spawned. Upon its issue Tovey, besieged by journalists, is alleged to have said, 'There are a great many things that I could say. But perhaps I had better not.' The true facts only finally came to light in 1957 when Stephen Roskill's second volume of his officially commissioned *The War at Sea* revealed them. By then, of course, the damage had been done.

   Pound's remarks about the millstone were made to Admiral King of the United States Navy in May 1942.
4. Quoted in David Irving, *The Destruction of Convoy PQ17*, Granada, 1985, p. 46.
5. HM destroyers *Ashanti, Blankney, Escapade, Faulknor, Marne, Martin, Middleton, Onslaught, Onslow* and *Wheatland*, and the USS *Mayrant* and *Rhind*.
6. See Captain J. Broome, *The Convoy is to Scatter*, Kimber, 1972. This is the substance of paragraph (k) of the Admiralty's Instructions of 27 June 1942 and is in keeping with what Stephen Roskill calls 'the primary duty of the convoy escorts', namely that 'it is one of the

strongest traditions in the Royal Navy that *no purposes whatsoever* [my italics] can supersede that of ensuring the safe and timely arrival of a convoy'.

7. QP13's returning merchantmen were: Russian, *Alma Ata, Komiles, Rodina, Starii Bolshevik, Archangelsk, Budenny, Kuzbass* and *Petrovski*; Panamanian, *Capira, Exterminator, Michigan* and *Mount Evans*; American, *American Robin, City of Omaha, Hegira, Hybert, Lancaster, Mauna Key, Mormacrey, Nemaha, Massmar, Richard Henry Lee, Yaka, John Randolph, Heffron* and *American Press*; Dutch, *Pieter de Hoogh*; and British, *Atlantic, Chulmleigh, Empire Mavis, Empire Selwyn, Empire Baffin, Empire Meteor, Empire Stevenson* and *St Clears*.
8. This sweep is mentioned in Ivor Saul, *Camera in Convoy*, Ellisons' Editions, 1987.
9. Broome wrote an account of his escort of PQ17 prior to his book *The Convoy is to Scatter*, which is to be found in John Winton's anthology, *Freedom's Battle: The War at Sea, 1939–45*, Vol. 1, entitled 'I am ready and willing to go back', pp. 241–7. He was understandably concerned about the mixed force under his command and had had a conference with his commanding officers aboard *Keppel*. He had also attended the convoy conference at Hvalfiordur and another aboard *London* back at Seidisfiord. Hamilton presided at the last two. Correspondence with the author confirms exercises being held on passage to Iceland. It is clear that Broome, though unhappy about the abrupt transfer of ships from Western Approaches to Iceland, had done all in his power to mitigate its effects and had deliberately formulated a plan, based on the classic use of destroyer tactics, later to be brilliantly exploited by Captain Sherbrooke in Arctic waters (see Chapter 17). Broome's main concern was that these exercises had only been carried out with the destroyers which left Lough Foyle a day later (24 June) rather than with the corvettes, rescue ships and the two anti-aircraft 'cruisers' which had left the day before. The latter had come up from Milford Haven where they had been employed on coastal convoys; the corvettes and rescue ships were lately from the North Atlantic.
10. The ranks of PQ17 from port to starboard were made up of merchant ships as follows. First: *Paulus Potter* (Dutch), *Washington, Hartlebury* (Vice-Commodore), *Pan Atlantic* (all American), *River Afton* (British: Commodore), *Peter Kerr* (American), *Empire Byron* (British), *Christopher Newport* and *Samuel Chase* (both American). Second: *Hoosier* (American), *El Capitan* (Panamanian), *Pankraft* (American), *Navarino* (British), *Azerbaijan* (Russian), *Earlston* (British), *Benjamin Harrison, Fairfield City* and *Carlton* (all American). Third: *Ironclad* (American),

Bolton Castle (British), *Olopana, Bellingham* and *Alcoa Ranger* (all American), *Empire Tide* (British, CAM ship), *Ocean Freedom* (British), *Honomu* and *Daniel Morgan* (both American). Fourth: *William Hooper* (American), *Troubadour* (Panamanian), *Donbass* (Russian), *Silver Sword* and *Winston Salem* (both American), *Aldersdale* (British fleet oiler), *John Witherspoon* (American). The rear rank was made up of the three rescue ships, *Rathlin, Zaafaran* and *Zamalek*.

11. Force Q, from an account of an officer aboard *Douglas*, did not return immediately to Iceland, but in fact steamed on a triangular course 'day after day' amid loose ice to the north-east of Jan Mayen and refuelled Home Fleet destroyers.
12. Quoted in B. Schofield and L. Martyn, *The Rescue Ships*, Blackwood, 1968.
13. Tovey's dispatch is in the Supplement to *The London Gazette*, Friday, 13 October 1950. This was the first intimation given to the public of the now notorious débâcle of PQ17. The choice of date is, to a seaman, significant.
14. The circumstances of the recovery of *Azerbaijan*'s people was recounted by G. Quantock of *Zamalek*, who witnessed the incident.
15. Latitude 75° 40′N, longitude 027° 25′E.

CHAPTER 13: 'SHEER BLOODY MURDER'

1. Quoted in an article by Richard Whitehead, *Daily Mail*, 18 February 1970, about the PQ17 libel trial. This was an action brought by Captain Broome against David Irving and his publishers.
2. Pound's perception was such that he made a remark to the effect that had the positions been reversed, he would have succeeded in stopping convoys to North Russia. The Admiralty maintained a silence over these events until the issue of a special supplement to the *London Gazette*, published on Tuesday, 17 October 1950. When, at that time, journalists pressed Admiral Tovey, he suggested there was more that he could say on the subject, but that he would maintain a discreet silence. Churchill, in *The Second World War*, claims to have known nothing about the details of the scatter order, though even Roskill, the official naval historian, points out (*The War at Sea*, Vol. II, page 144) that he was present at a cabinet meeting on 1 August 1942 when Pound explained the situation, stating the belief that German battleships were at sea and that he took responsibility for the fatal signal.
3. In the PQ17 libel trial Admiral Frewen, then Hamilton's navigating officer aboard HMS *London*, was asked if the sequence of messages was received in such a way that the 'scatter' signal could have been

construed as a correction to the 'disperse' order. He emphatically denied this possibility under the circumstances.

4. See Vice-Admiral J. Hayes, *Face the Music: A Sailor's Story*, Pentland Press, 1991.
5. Among the Royal Navy's lower-deck members, whose perceptions of the realities of life are often underestimated, HMS *London* became unkindly known as 'the Wop flagship'. See note 7.
6. Quoted in P. Lund and H. Ludlam, *PQ17: Convoy to Hell*, and G.G. Connell, *Arctic Destroyers*. Admiral O'Brien said at the PQ17 libel trial in 1970, 'You had the dreaful feeling that this was the sort of thing the navy did not do. You were ashamed and you were hurt.'
7. Returning to Scapa Flow, poor Hamilton, acutely aware of the effect on morale, took the unprecedented step of clearing the lower deck and explaining to his entire crew the rationale behind the PQ convoys and the reasoning, as he then understood it, behind what had gone wrong with PQ17. The mood aboard *London* has been described as 'near mutinous' and 'shameful.'
8. Considerable distress in both the smaller warships left with the convoy and many of the merchant ships was caused by this apparent self-preservation of the anti-aircraft cruisers. See note 16.
9. See note 16.
10. Not only were the Liberty ships mass-produced, but to a degree so were their hastily composed crews. An unsurprising lack of steadiness, evidence of which surfaced in the uncertain conditions then prevailing in the Barents Sea, was much commented on by the battle-hardened veterans of British merchantmen. However, Lieutenant John G. Sexton of the *Samuel Chase*'s armed guard was disparaging about both the British escort's anti-aircraft capability and his own guns. See Justin F. Gleichauf, *Unsung Sailors*, Naval Institute Press, Annapolis, 1990, p. 204, and Irving, p. 207 *et seq*.
11. Just as the Royal Navy acquired an unjustified reputation for 'running away' in the aftermath of PQ17, so did the United States mercantile marine for abandoning their ships, 'surrendering' and so forth. These stories were still current when the author first went to sea eighteen years after the events described. See Irving, p. 208, *et seq*.
12. Reche's *U255* on 11 July.
13. See Irving, *The Destruction of PQ17*, p. 235. Also see Schofield and Martyn, *The Rescue Ships*. McGowan and his Chief Engineer both received the DSC. McGowan, who was also awarded Lloyd's Medal, was lost with all hands from the rescue ship *St Sunniva* in the Atlantic the following January. See note 18.
14. Lieutenant Carradus's diary is extensively quoted by Irving and is eloquent on this point, but see note 18.

15. See Irving, *The Destruction of PQ17*, p. 286 *et seq*. As Vice-Commodore, *Hartlebury* had additional signals staff aboard.
16. It is easy to condemn both Jauncey and Lawford for some of their decisions and actions subsequent to the scatter order on the evening of 4 July. However, in fairness, it should be pointed out that to some extent the Admiralty had further hamstrung them. On the evening of the 6th, London had transmitted a signal to 'any escorts favourably placed . . . to endeavour to pick up survivors . . . [those] who find themselves in touch with several merchant vessels are to form them into a group and escort them to Iokanka . . . escorts short of fuel to proceed direct to Archangel . . . be refuelled and sailed to round up merchant vessels and escort them . . . ' It was very much a case of shutting the stable door after the horse had bolted and, whilst clearly well-meant, actually compromised any freedom of action on the part of Jauncey and Lawford by adding, '*Pozarica* and *Palomares* are not to take risks in rescue operations and are to proceed without delay to Archangel.' Morris's snub understandably rankled, and was just a fragment of the 'them and us' mentality alluded to earlier in this book, which found its voice in PQ17 and subsequently passed in full measure into the embittered folklore of the British Merchant Navy.
17. See Irving, *The Destruction of PQ17*, p. 324. Captain Morris's tempestuous character undoubtedly saw his ship and her passengers through their ordeal.
18. Captains Morris, Banning (*Rathlin*), Walker (*Ocean Freedom*) and Harvey (*Empire Tide*) were awarded Distinguished Service Orders for PQ17, the first time this military order was made to merchant officers. As for the gallant *Zamalek*, she ended her life as a blockship in the Suez Canal, sunk by the Egyptians in 1956. During the return of *Zamalek* in QP14, Surgeon McBain operated on a number of the survivors from the *John Witherspoon* whose frostbitten limbs had been amputated in Russia so badly that they suffered from gangrene and had bones protruding from the wounds. With help from volunteers among her crew McBain debrided the wounds and refashioned the stumps.
19. Gradwell earned high praise for his conduct. He is almost unique in receiving the praise of Admiral Golovko. He too was awarded the DSC and afterwards became a well-known London magistrate.
20. Irving, *The Destruction of PQ17*, p. 360, states that the crews of *Pozarica* and *Palomares* were barely speaking to each other. When the Walrus crew finally returned to HMS *Norfolk*, the lower deck was cleared and they were cheered aboard.
21. Quoted in Schofield and Martyn, *The Rescue Ships*. See this also for problems on board these vessels caused by survivors.

22. Irving, *The Destruction of PQ17*, p. 368 *et seq*.
23. A.V. Alexander was the Labour politician who served as the First (Civil) Lord of the Admiralty in Churchill's wartime coalition government. He was not always privy to the most secret deliberations of the Admiralty. He suppressed Winn's manuscript about PQ17 which later became a bestseller. Alexander also boarded *Keppel* some time after PQ17 in a morale-boosting exercise and Broome had an unsatisfactory interview which he describes in his book, *The Convoy is to Scatter*.
24. See Gleichauf, *Unsung Sailors*, p. 207.
25. A personal memoir of these events lies before me as I write. It points out in strong and emotional language that not a single naval ship was lost in the defence of PQ17. It was the breaching of this unwritten 'covenant' between the two services that caused the trouble, and the departure of the destroyers which sparked it, for they, among all the Royal Navy's proud traditions, personified, and again and again elsewhere exemplified, the notion of self-sacrifice in the face of odds. This feeling was clearly shared among naval crews and, as noted, the authorities took some pains to offset it.

Chapter 14: 'An Extremely Hazardous Undertaking'

1. Burnett had been Rear-Admiral (Destroyers). He replaced Hamilton because the latter was suffering from appendicitis.
2. The merchant ships of PQ18 were: American, *Campfire, Charles R. McCormick, Esek Hopkins, Exford, Hollywood, John Penn, Kentucky, Lafayette, Mary Luckenbach, Meanticut, Nathaniel Greene, Oliver Ellsworth, Oregonian, Patrick Henry, Sahale, St Olaf, Schoharie, Virginia Dare, Wacosta* and *William Moultrie*; British, *Dan-y-Bryn, Empire Baffin, Empire Beaumont, Empire Morn, Empire Snow, Empire Stevenson, Empire Tristram, Goolistan, Ocean Faith* and *Temple Arch* (Commodore); Panamanian, *Afrikander, White Clover* and *Macbeth*; Russian, *Andre Marti, Komiles, Petrovski, Stalingrad, Sukhona* and *Tbilisi*.
3. The British had shamefully neglected naval aviation between the wars and the Sea Hurricane was never more than an extempore measure.
4. G.G. Connell, *Arctic Destroyers*, William Kimber, 1982, p. 97.
5. Admiral Golovko was contemptuous of the practice of sinking merchant ships while they still floated. Though, as we have seen, damaged merchantmen *were* salvaged, individual circumstances dictated the chances of carrying out an operation which is difficult

at the best of times. Nevertheless, much Soviet propaganda was made of this form of alleged 'cowardice'.

6. The report of Proceedings from HMS *Ulster Queen* is quoted, as are several other first-hand witness accounts, in Peter C. Smith, *Arctic Victory, The Story of PQ18*, William Kimber, 1974. Horace Bell's impressions are from L. Martyn and B. Schofield, *The Rescue Ships*, William Blackwood, 1968.
7. The trawlers were *St Kenan, Cape Argona, Cape Mariato* and *Daneman*; the motor minesweepers which had done yeoman service as rescue tenders were *MMS90, MMS203* and *MMS212*.
8. See A. Golovko, *With the Red Fleet*, Putnam, 1965, p. 180. See also note 6. Golovko's jaundiced view of Allied naval conduct is so subjectively unbalanced that it serves best as an example of a genre. Unfortunately, it masks the very real contribution made by the Russians in such areas as extempore repair (*vide Hopemount*) and in the salvage of the grounded merchantmen on the Dvina Bar.
9. According to another account *Bergomot* succeeded in pulling *Daneman* off the shoal.
10. These officers were Captain Lamont and Mr Curry, both of whom already held decorations. Boddam-Whetham later returned to active service and died alone in sad circumstances at Gibraltar in July 1943.
11. Air Ministry Pamphlet No. 248, 'The Rise and Fall of the German Air Force'.

CHAPTER 15: 'FOR EIGHTEEN DAYS THERE WAS NO LET-UP'

1. The accompanying ships which left the Dvina were: American, *Bellingham, Benjamin Harrison, Deer Lodge, Samuel Chase, Silver Sword* and *Winston Salem*; British oilers, *Black Ranger* and *Gray Ranger*; Panamanian, *Troubadour*; and Polish, *Tobruk*. The Master of the *Winston Salem* had suffered a nervous breakdown and was sent home sick.
2. The destroyers were *Ashanti, Eskimo, Somali, Tartar, Faulknor, Fury, Impulsive, Intrepid, Marne, Meteor, Milne, Offa, Onslaught, Onslow* and *Opportune*, with *Wheatland* and *Wilton* attached to *Avenger*.
3. The three destroyers were *Oakley, Cowdray* and *Windsor*.
4. Rear-Admiral Burnett was a 'springer', a physical training specialist who had been the Royal Navy's sabre champion. Though no great intellectual, he was tough, fit and eminently suited to his Arctic command. Generally popular, being known as either 'Bullshit Bob' or 'Uncle Bob', he possessed a fighting instinct which, as we shall see in subsequent chapters, made him a leading figure in the maritime war

in the Arctic. A short section of archive film remains showing part of this transfer. See *Hazards of the Russian Convoys*, Naval Video Time Capsules, 1992.

5. *Somali* was under the temporary command of Lieutenant-Commander C.D. Maud, whose destroyer *Icarus* was refitting, and in the absence of Captain J.W.M. Eaton who was ill. Details of *Ashanti*'s tow are from Onslow's own account published in an anthology, Peter Smith (ed.), *Destroyer Action*, William Kimber, 1984, p. 162 *et seq*.
6. The damaged boats were: *U251*, *U255*, *U403*, *U405* and *U255*.
7. *Winston Salem* had perhaps the most chequered career in the saga of PQ17 and QP14. One other survivor, the American *Ironclad*, had been left behind in Archangel. She was later damaged by bombs and eventually broken up in Russia after being sold to the Russians and renamed *Marina Raskova*.
8. See S. Kerslake, *Coxswain in the Northern Convoys*, William Kimber, 1984, for an elaboration of the 'hostilities only' and 'reservists' opinion.

Chapter 16: 'A Tough Blow for the Russians'

1. Stalin to Churchill, 23 July 1942, quoted in Winston S. Churchill, *The Second World War*, p. 241.
2. Ibid., p. 244.
3. The other Russian ships which arrived safely were the *Aldan*, *Azerbaijan*, *Chernyshevsk*, *Dvina*, *Elna II* (having been transferred from British to Russian ownership, this ship afterwards plied the Pacific, supplying the Soviet Union via Vladivostok), *Kara*, *Komsomolets Arctiki*, *Krasnoe Znamya*, *Kuzbass*, *Mironych*, *Mossovet*, *Msta*, *Ob*, *Okhta*, *Osmussaar*, *Sakko*, *Sheksna*, *Shilka*, *Soroka*, *Uritski*, *Vanzetti* and *Vetluga*.
4. Captain Daniel Morley Williams was awarded the OBE, Richard Peyer, Reginald Whiteside and James Burnett the BEM. A curious footnote to add as an example of the difficulties of traversing Spitzbergen at this season is given by the fact that the free Norwegian garrison, who acted as a meteorological station, were joined at this time by a German one landed from *U212* and *U586*. Both operated for some time in mutual ignorance of the other's presence.
5. The other ships of QP15 were: American, *Charles R. McCormick*, *Esek Hopkins*, *Exford*, *Hollywood*, *Lafayette*, *Nathaniel Greene*, *Patrick Henry*, *Sahale*, *St Olaf*, *Schoharie*, *Virginia Dare* and *William Moultrie*; British, *Dan-y-Bryn*, *Empire Baffin*, *Empire Morn* (CAM ship), *Empire Snow*, *Empire Tristram*, *Goolistan* and *Ocean Faith*; Panamanian, *White Clover*; and Russian, *Andre Marti*,

Belomorcanal, *Friedrich Engels*, *Komiles*, *Kuznetz Lesov* and *Tbilisi*. In the event *Ironclad* remained in Russia; see Ch. 24, note 9.

6. The heavy armaments of both the Russian and German destroyers made them particularly vulnerable in heavy weather. Both navies adopted designs that required extensive upper-works which conferred superior fire-power when compared with British destroyers but sacrificed stability with low freeboards and small metacentric heights. Welding techniques, though no longer in their infancy, were far from the sophisticated standards later achieved.

Chapter 17: 'Only destroyers'

I am indebted to George Barker, George Charlton, Sid Kerslake, Len Matthews, Charles Owen and H.A. Twiddy, among others, for material used in this chapter. A detailed account of the battle is given in Dudley Pope, *73 North*, Secker & Warburg, 1988. I must also thank Mrs Rosemary Sherbrooke for her kindness and generosity in supplying details concerning her husband and also PQ17.

1. The remaining ships of JW51A were: American, *Beauregard*, *Dynastic*, *Gateway City*, *Greylock*, *J.L.M. Curry*, *Oremar*, *Richard Bassett*, *Richard Bland*, *West Gotomska* and *Windrush*; British, *Empire Meteor* and *San Cipriano* (tanker); and Panamanian, *El Almirante* and *El Oceano*.
2. The remaining ships of JW51B were: American, *Chester Valley*, *Executive*, *Jefferson Myers*, *John H.B. Latrobe*, *Puerto Rican*, *Ralph Waldo Emerson*, *Vermont* and *Yorkmar*; British, *Daldorch*, *Dover Hill*, *Empire Emerald* (tanker) and *Pontfield*; and Panamanian, *Ballot* and *Calobre*.
3. Rear-Admiral Burnett's Report of Proceedings. Just how significant this was will be seen.
4. The Allied submarines were *Seadog*, *Unruly*, *Trespasser* and *Graph*, the latter a captured U-boat commissioned into the Royal Navy.
5. Skipper-Lieutenant H.C. Aisthorpe RNR had replaced Lieutenant Mullender.
6. Commanded by Fregattenkapitän Bachmann, the *Friedrich Eckholdt* flew the pendant of the senior officer of the German 5th Destroyer Flotilla, Kapitän sur Zee Schemmel.
7. Correspondence and conversations with L. Matthews, Commodore's Yeoman, *Empire Archer*. Commodore Melhuish was uniquely awarded the Order of Kutusov by the Russians for his services.
8. The returning ships of RA51 were: American, *Campfire*, *Hugh*

Williamson, John Walker, Meanticut and *Richard H. Alvey*; British, *Empire Galliard, Empire Scott, Hopemount* and the fleet oiler *Oligarch*; Russian, *Belorussia, Kotlin, Revolutsioner, Volga* and the *Okhta* which straggled.

9. When he learned of Sherbrooke's condition, Admiral Tovey personally telephoned his wife and warned her. It was her determination that ensured he received plastic surgery, then still in its infancy. Ironically Sherbrooke had complained of eye trouble in the Arctic after seeing service in the brilliant sunlight of Sierra Leone. Earlier in the war he had distinguished himself as the captain of HM Destroyer *Cossack* by bringing her across the North Sea stern first after the second Battle of Narvik. According to his widow, Sherbrooke never regarded his action in the Barents Sea as 'heroic'. 'He thought he was simply doing his job.'
10. The officers and crews of the minesweepers operating on the Russian convoys were, by virtue of their specialist role, almost all regulars. Their chosen skill consigned them to the least glamorous (and some would contend, most despised) arm of the naval service. It is, perhaps, no coincidence that, particularly among the officer corps of Merchant Navy veterans, this class of ship and their crews drew warm admiration.

Chapter 18: 'Dangerous work in hazardous circumstances'

1. *Sheffield, Echo, Eclipse, Faulknor, Inglefield, Montrose, Queenborough, Raider* and *Orkan*.
2. Other vessels in JW52 were; American, *Gulfwing* (tanker), *Cornelius Harnett, Delsud* and *Nicholas Gilman*; British, *Atlantic, Dan-y-Bryn, Empire Baffin, Empire Snow, Empire Portia, Empire Tristram, Ocean Faith* and *Temple Arch*; and Panamanian, *El Oriente*.
3. The other merchantmen of RA52 were: American, *Beauregard, Dynastic, Gateway City, Greylock* and *Windrush*; British, *Briarwood* and *Empire Meteor*; and Panamanian, *El Almirante* and *El Oceano*. The close escort consisted of: corvettes *Honeysuckle, Hyderabad, Rhododendron* and *Oxlip*; minesweepers *Harrier* and *Seagull*; and trawlers *Lady Madeleine, Northern Gem, Northern Wave* and *Vizalma*.
4. *Inglefield, Oribi, Obedient* and the Polish *Orkan*.
5. The Soviet submarines had also been successful, interdicting a German minelaying operation on the polar coast and sinking a patrol boat and transport steamer. On 20 January the Soviet destroyers

Baku and *Razumny* had indecisively engaged the German minelayer *Skagerrak* and some smaller craft off Syltefiord. Soviet coastal naval operations were more frequent than is generally appreciated in the West, which has been easily influenced by an accepted view deriving from that 'unconscious superiority' of the Royal Navy, that the Russian naval service was not particularly effective at this time.

6. Records for this convoy have not survived and I am indebted to David Craig and James Mitchell for unscrambling a confusing situation and supplying the missing details. The Commodore of JW53 was Rear-Admiral E.W. Leir (Ret'd.) in *Empire Scott*. Other ships were: American, *Beaconhill* (tanker), *Bering, City of Omaha, Francis Scott Key, Israel Putnam, James Bowie,** *John Laurance,** *Joseph E. Johnston,** *Mobile City* and *Thomas Hartley*; British, *Atlantic, British Governor* (tanker), *Dover Hill, Empire Baffin,** *Empire Fortune,** *Empire Galliard, Empire Kinsman, Explorer,** *Llandaff* and *Ocean Freedom*; Dutch, *Pieter de Hoogh*; Norwegian, *Marathon* (tanker); Panamanian, *Artigas* and *Norlys*; Polish, *Tobruk*; and Russian, *Tblisi* and *Petrovski*. The six ships marked with an asterisk all returned to Loch Ewe due to weather damage. None afterwards seem to have reached Russia by the northern route. Since the Arctic convoys were suspended during the summer of 1943, they were probably routed to Basra, via the Cape. The *Norlys* appears to have been destined originally for JW53, but subsequently sailed with JW54A as a fleet oiler.
7. Apart from the convoy commodore and fleet oiler, the other ships of RA53 were: American, *Chester Valley, Cornelius Harnett, Delsud, Executive, Gulfwing, J.L.M. Curry, Jefferson Myers, John H.B. Latrobe, Nicholas Gilman, Oremar, Puerto Rican, Ralph Waldo Emerson, Richard Bassett, Richard Bland, Vermont, West Gotomska* and *Yorkmar*; British, *Dan-y-Bryn, Empire Archer, Empire Clarion, Empire Emerald, Empire Snow, Empire Tristram, Ocean Faith* and *San Cipriano*; Panamanian, *Calobre* and *El Oriente*; and Russian, *Mossovet*.
8. The *John H.B. Latrobe* survived in the American Reserve fleet until 1969.
9. The German destroyers engaged in Operation Zitronella were: *Z27, Z29, Z30, Z31, Z33, Erich Steinbrinck, Karl Galster, Theodor Riedel* and *Hans Lody*.
10. Cameron, a reservist, and Plaice were both captured but survived and were awarded the Victoria Cross.
11. The *Dover Hill* had been building on the River Tyne as the *Maenwen*, a typical Cardiff-registered trampship, but was acquired by the Clan Line and completed as the *Clan Macvicar*, later being sold on to the Dover Hill Steamship Company. On her return from

Russia she was taken over by the MOWT and ended her life as a blockship scuttled off Arromanches on 9 June 1944 to form part of the artificial harbour used for the invasion of Normandy.

12. In addition to the Commodore, RA54A consisted of: American, *Beaconhill, City of Omaha, Francis Scott Key, Israel Putnam, Mobile City* and *Thomas Hartley*; British, *Empire Fortune, Empire Kinsman, Empire Portia* and *Pontfield*; and Polish, *Tobruk*.

Chapter 19: 'An inconvenient, extreme and costly exertion'

1. The rest of convoy JW54A were: American, *Daniel Drake, Edmund Fanning, Gilbert Stuart, Henry Villard, James Gordon Bennett, James Smith, Park Holland, Thomas Sim Lee* and *William Windom*; British, *Empire Carpenter, Empire Nigel, Empire Celia, Junecrest, Ocean Verity* and *Ocean Vanity*; and Dutch, *Mijdrecht*.
2. Justin F. Gleichauf, *Unsung Sailors: The Naval Armed Guard in World War II*, Naval Institute Press, p. 212.
3. *Bermuda*, with *Ashanti, Matchless, Musketeer* and *Oribi*, had relieved the *Tuscaloosa* and Moore's ships worked out of Akureyri on Iceland's north coast. *Tuscaloosa*, the aircraft-carrier *Ranger* and United States destroyers had participated in the Home Fleet's October raid on shipping in Norwegian waters.
4. Correspondence with Arne Johnsen.
5. I am indebted to E.G. Robson for his manuscript account of JW54B.
6. Other ships in JW54B were: American, *Arthur L. Perry, Eugene Field, John Fitch, Horace Gray, Thomas Kearns* and *William L. Marcy*; and British, *Empire Lionel, Empire Stalwart, Fort Columbia, Fort McMurray, Fort Poplar* and *Ocean Strength*. The Kola portion detached, but orders were not passed to the *Fort McMurray* and *Ocean Strength* which were sent back later when the mistake was discovered. As the *Fort McMurray* approached the Kola Inlet, Captain Henderson, her master, described the guba. 'A narrow tapering stretch of placid water lying straight ahead bounded closely by dark, high, snow capped cliffs gleamed brightly under the stars and streaming light from the Aurora Borealis and about equidistant on either side towering above, were the powerful flashing lights on the stark headlands guarding the entrance'. In fact the two delayed ships overhauled their detached convoy-mates and, as intended, led the Murmansk portion of JW54B into port.
7. Other ships in JW55A were: American, *Collins P. Huntington, Daniel Willard, George Weems, James A. Farrell, James Woodrow, Lewis*

Emery Jr, Philip Livingston, Thomas Scott and the wonderfully named *Stage Door Canteen*; and British, *Empire Archer, Empire Pickwick, Fort Astoria, Fort Hall* (Commodore), *Fort Missanabie, Fort Thompson, Lapland, Lucerna* and *Thistledale*. Two small motor minesweepers destined for the Soviet Northern Fleet accompanied the convoy.

8. Stories about Fraser are legion, but one which illustrates his unconventionality occurred in the summer of 1943. Thoroughly irritated by telephone calls from the First Sea Lord's office, Fraser declared he must take the flagship to sea away from the 'telephone buoy'. When asked by his staff where they should go, Fraser replied, 'To Glasgow. There I can inspect the Wrens.' Unbeknown to Arseni Golovko, he had, as a young officer, been a prisoner of the Bolsheviks at Baku, on the Caspian Sea, during the civil war.

   Fraser's sensitivity was remarkable. His lack of xenophobia enabled him to perceive the eclipse of the Royal Navy as the world's most powerful navy by its burgeoning American partner, and made him the ideal man for Britain's last major fleet deployment in the Pacific where he worked brilliantly with the Americans.
9. German authorities state that *U307* was driven off by a depth-charge attack, though whether this was a deliberate or a random defensive drop by one of the escorts, I have not been able to discover. The other boats in this group were *U277, U354, U360, U387, U636* and *U713*.

Chapter 20: 'We're going alongside the bastard!'

1. Convoy RA55A consisted of the following merchantmen: American, *Arthur L. Perry, Daniel Drake, Edmund Fanning, Gilbert Stuart, Henry Villard, James Smith, Park Holland, Thomas Sim Lee, William L. Marcy* and *William Windom* (the *Thomas Kearns* turned back with defects); British, *Empire Carpenter, Empire Celia, Empire Nigel, Fort McMurray, Fort Yukon* (Commodore Grant), *Junecrest, Ocean Strength, Ocean Vanity, Ocean Verity*, the tanker *San Adolfo* which acted as escort oiler, and *Rathlin*.
2. In addition to the Commodore, Convoy JW55B consisted of the following: American, *Bernard N. Baker, Brockholst Livingston, Cardinal Gibbons, Harold L. Winslow, John J. Abel, John Vining, John Wanamaker, Thomas U. Walter* and *Will Rogers*; British, *British Statesman* (tanker), *Fort Nakasley, Fort Vercheres, Ocean Gypsy, Ocean Messenger, Ocean Pride, Ocean Valour* and *Ocean Viceroy*. The Panamanian tanker *Norlys* was oiler.
3. The tenet of mutual support, on a large or small scale, almost always achieved its objective, a local superiority of force ensuring victory. It

was ironic that it was this principle which Commander Broome was misled into applying when he went to Hamilton's support in the 'defence' of PQ17. Only in the development of the *Rüdeltaktik*, or wolfpack, did the Kriegsmarine ever emulate it. The desertion by German destroyers of their capital ships in both the Barents Sea and North Cape actions is significant in this context.

4. Burnett's achievement in thus twice engaging a superior enemy has received less attention than it deserves, though he received a knighthood for his services.
5. Lieutenant (afterwards Admiral of the Fleet, Sir Henry) Leach, quoted in John Winton, *Death of the* Scharnhorst, Granada, 1980. The position of the *Scharnhorst*'s sinking was estimated as latitude 72°16'N, longitude 028°41'E.
6. *L20*, *S102* and *K21*. In the flanking operation, an attack by the British submarine *Seadog* had sunk a large freighter on the Norwegian coast. One Free Dutch and six Russian submarines had also been engaged in operations on the polar coast, as had Russian light surface forces.
7. Fraser had shown a great interest in crew welfare from his days as a gunnery lieutenant in the First World War. He had successively commanded a cruiser and a carrier. As Director of Naval Ordnance he had helped develop the rather unsuccessful quadruple turrets and 5.25-inch guns of the 'K-G-Fives', these also being fitted to the Didos, like *Scylla*. Promoted Rear-Admiral in 1938, he had been Chief of Staff to Pound in the Mediterranean and at the end of the Munich scare wrote a very perceptive paper anticipating war with Germany, Italy and Japan. In 1939 he became Third Sea Lord and Comptroller under Pound. In charge of procurement, he oversaw production of the Flower-class corvettes and the Hunt-class escort destroyers. He was also instrumental in introducing degaussing, the magnetic 'wiping' of naval and merchant ships to neutralize their magnetic fields. He worked well with Churchill, though he stood up to him. See Richard Humble, *Fraser of North Cape*, Routledge & Kegan Paul, 1983. For his later work in the Pacific, see John Winton, *The Forgotten Fleet*, Michael Joseph, 1969; reprinted Douglas Boyd Books, 1989.

CHAPTER 21: 'THEY NEVER LET ME DOWN'

1. Other ships of RA55B were: American, *James Gordon Bennett*; and British, *Daldorch*, *Lucerna*, *Empire Stalwart*, *Fort Columbia*, *Fort Poplar* and the tanker *San Ambrosio* which fuelled the escorts on passage as she had done at Vaenga.
2. A further two were sunk by the Russians in the Kara Sea and seven in the Arctic Ocean unassociated with the passage of convoys.

3. The ships of JW56A were now: American, *Andrew G. Curtin, Charles Scribner, Edwin L. Drake, Penelope Barker, Richard H. Alvey, Thorstein Veblen, William Tyler Page* and *Woodbridge N. Ferris*, all of which were Liberty ships; British, *Empire Ploughman, Fort Bellingham* (now Commodore), *Fort Slave* and the tankers *San Cirilo* and *San Adolfo*, the latter of which was escort oiler; Dutch, *Aert van der Neer*; and the Norwegian tanker *Noreg*.
4. Convoy JW56B finally consisted of: American Liberty ships, *Abner Nash, Albert C. Ritchie, Charles A. McAllister, Edward L. Grant, Henry Bacon, Henry Wyncoop, John H.B. Latrobe, John Lafarge, Paul Hamilton Hayne, Robert Lowry, Samuel McIntyre, Willard Hall* and *Winfred L. Smith*; and British, *Empire Tourist, Fort Crevecoeur* (Commodore Mayall) and *Fort Norfolk*. All were war-built tonnage and there was no oiler. The 'sloop' *Cygnet* was a 'Black Swan' class sloop, a pre-war type of escort of which there were far too few. Particularly able anti-submarine vessels, they were extensively used in the independent 'support groups'. Walker's famous Second Support Group was entirely composed of these ships. The term 'sloop' was replaced by that of 'frigate'.
5. Campbell's destroyers were *Huron* (Canadian), *Inconstant, Mahratta, Meteor, Milne, Musketeer, Scourge, Offa, Opportune, Venus, Vigilant, Savage* and *Stord* (Norwegian). The merchant ships of RA56 were: American, *Brockholst Livingston, Cardinal Gibbons, Collis P. Huntington, Daniel Willard, Eugene Field, George Weems, Harold L. Winslow, Horace Gray, James A. Farrel, James Woodrow, John J. Abel, John Vining, John Wanamaker, Lewis Emery Jr, Stage Door Canteen, Thomas Scott, Thomas U. Walter* and *Will Rogers*; British, *British Statesman* (tanker), *Empire Archer, Empire Lionel, Fort Astoria, Fort Hall, Fort Kullyspell, Fort Missanabie, Fort Nakasley, Fort Thompson, Fort Vercheres, Ocean Gypsy, Ocean Messenger, Ocean Pride, Ocean Valour, Ocean Viceroy* and *Thistledale*; and the Norwegian *Noreg* and Panamanian *Norlys*, both fleet oilers.
6. The ships of JW57 were: American, *Alexander White,* Byron Darnton,* Caesar Rodney,* Charles Bulfinch,* Charles M. Schwab,* Edward Sparrow,* Henry B. Brown,* Henry Lomb,* Jefferson Davis,* John A. Donald,* John A. Quitman,* John Langdon, John Rutledge,* John Sharp Williams,* John Stevenson,* John W. Powell,* John Woolman,* Joshua W. Alexander,* Lord Delaware,* Louis D. Brandeis,* Marie M. Meloney,* Nathan Towson,* Nathaniel Alexander,* Richard M. Johnson,* Philip F. Thomas,* Robert J. Collier,* Robert Eden,† Stevenson Taylor,* Thomas Hartley,* William H. Webb;** British, *British Valour* (tanker),* *Daphnella,* Empire Carpenter, Empire Celia,* Empire Nigel, Fort*

Brule,† *Fort Romaine,** *Fort McMurray,** *Lucerna,** *Ocean Strength,** and *San Ambrosio (tanker)*; and Dutch, *Mijdrecht.** Ships marked with an asterisk returned with convoy RA58, those with a dagger RA59.

7. The Werwolf pack consisted of *U312, U313, U362,* U425, *U601, U674, U739, U713, U956* and *U990*, and the Hartmut group, *U472 U315, U673* and *U366*.
8. See R. Whinney, *The U-Boat Peril,* Arrow Books, 1989, Ch. 11, p. 153 *et seq*. My thanks also to Captain Dennis Foster.
9. The ships of RA57 were: American, *Abner Nash, Albert C. Ritchie, Bernard N. Baker, Charles A. McAllister, Charles Scribner, Edwin L. Drake, Edward L. Grant, Henry Bacon, Henry Wyncoop, John H.B. Latrobe, John La Farge, Paul Hamilton Hayne, Philip Livingston, Richard H. Alvey, Robert Lowry, Samuel McIntyre, Thorstein Veblen, Willard Hall, William Tyler Page, Winfred Smith* and *Woodbridge N. Ferris*; and British, *Empire Bard, Empire Pickwick, Empire Ploughman, Empire Tourist, Fort Norfolk, Fort Crevecoeur* (Commodore Mayall), *Fort Slave, San Ambrosio* (tanker), *San Adolfo* (tanker) and *San Cirilo* (tanker). The last three were all escort oilers. It is not certain whether the rescue ship *Copeland* sailed with RA57 or 58, though there is no apparent reason for her delaying in Russia. The Dutch ship *Aert van der Neer* was also part of this convoy.
10. Lieutenant-Commander F.W. Hawkins, the commanding officer of *Boadicea*, was an interesting example of his type. Trained as a deck officer in the Merchant Navy, he had served as seaman aboard the Finnish barque *Loch Linnhe*, and as an officer in the Khedival Mail Line and the Royal Naval Reserve. In 1938 selected officers were offered regular commissions in the Royal Navy, and Lieutenant Hawkins was one such officer who, on the outbreak of war, rose to command a destroyer. Hawkins and *Boadicea* were lost off Portland Bill when an aerial torpedo blew the ship up, nine days after D-Day. Hawkins was a keen photographer, and I am indebted to his son for several of the plates.
11. The remaining boats in the Boreas group were: *U361, U959, U278, U973, U366, U673, U288* and *U354*.
12. Local escorts were *Rattlesnake, Onyx, Orestes, Rhododendron* and *Starwort*.
13. The Grumann Wildcat was officially known to the Royal Navy as the Martlet, the Avenger as the Tarpon, but these Anglicizations never really caught on and have been disregarded.
14. The U-boat groups were: Thor, *U278, U312, U313* and *U674*; Blitz, *U277, U355, U711* and *U956*; and Hammer, *U288, U315, U354* and *U968*. *En route* were: *U716, U739, U360, U361* and *U990*.

15. Having, like cruisers, large bunker capacity, escort carriers frequently fuelled sloops, destroyers and corvettes. *Tracker* was built on a standard C-3 American merchant ship hull designed for mass-production. *Activity* was taken over on the stocks where she was building as a cargo liner for Alfred Holt's Glen and Shire Line. After the war her flight deck was removed and she was finally completed as the twin-screw motor vessel *Breconshire* which traded on Holt's Far East service until the late 1960s. Details of the carriers' part in JW58 are largely from notes by the late D.J.W. Woodman of HMS *Tracker*.
16. See Terence Robertson, *Walker, RN*, Pan Books, 1966.
17. The remaining ships of JW58 were: American, *Andrew Carnegie,*† *Arunah S. Abell,*† *Barbara Frietchie, Benjamin H. Latrobe, Benjamin Schlesinger, Charles Gordon Curtis, Charles Henderson,*† *Edward P. Alexander,*† *Francis Scott Key,*† *Francis Vigo,*† *George Gale,*† *George M. Cohan,*† *George T. Angell,*† *Grace Abbott,*† *Hawkins Fudske,*† *Henry Villard,*† *James Smith,*† *John B. Lennon,*† *John Carver,*† *John Davenport,*† *John McDonogh,*† *John T. Holt,*† *Joseph N. Nicolet,*† *Joshua Thomas,*† *Joyce Kilmer,*† *Julien Poydras,*† *Morris Hilquit,*† *Nicholas Biddle,*† *Pierre S. Dupont,*† *Thomas Sim Lee,*† *Townsend Harris,*† *W.R. Grace, William D Byron,*† *William Matson,*† *William McKinley,*† *William Moultrie,*† *William Pepper*† and *William S. Thayer;*† and British, *Dolabella,*† *Lacklan, Empire Prowess, Fort Columbia,*† *Fort Hall,*† *Fort Kullyspell,*† *Fort Vercheres* and *Fort Yukon.*† Ships marked with a dagger returned with RA59.
18. See Chapter 22 for the methods used to combat the acoustic torpedo.
19. For ships in RA58 see those marked with an asterisk in note 6.
20. These groups were composed of: *U313, U636, U703, U277, U361, U362, U711, U716, U347* and *U990*.
21. For ships in RA59 see those marked with a dagger in notes 6 and 17. There was also the *Noreg* from JW58 acting as fleet oiler and *Lapland* from JW55A.
22. HMS *Walker* went alongside the American ship and evacuated about 50 Russians going to take over HMS *Royal Sovereign*. They cleaned up the messdecks, to the delight of *Walker*'s crew.

CHAPTER 22: 'ALLIES, OR JUST TWO NATIONS?'

1. The remaining ships of JW59 were: American, *Charles Dauray, Charles A. McAllister, Clark Howell, David B. Johnson, Edward H. Crockett, Edward L. Grant, Elijah Kellogg, F.T. Frelinghuysen, Frank Gilbreth, John La Farge, Jose Marti, Josephine Shaw Lowell,*

Leo J. Duster, Oakley Wood, Silas Weir Mitchell, Thomas Donaldson, Thomas H. Sumner and *Warren Delano*; and British, *Empire Buttress, Fort Glenora, Nacella, Samannan, Samcalia, Samconstant, Samgara, Samidway, Samloyal, Samlyth* and *Samsuva.*

2. Ten were finally transferred: these were the *Doblestny** (ex-HMS *Roxborough*, USS *Foote*), *Dostoiny** (ex-H. Nor MS *St Albans*, USS *Thomas*), *Derzhki** (ex-HMS *Chelsea*, USS *Crowninshield*), *Dyeatelni** (ex-HMS *Churchill*, USS *Herndon*), *Druzhny* (ex-HMS *Lincoln*, USS *Yarnall*), *Zharki** (ex-HMS *Brighton*, USS *Cowell*), *Zhyuchi** (ex-HMS *Leamington*, USS *Twiggs*), *Zhivuchi** (ex-HMS *Richmond*, USS *Fairfax*) and *Zhestki** (ex-HMS *Georgetown*, USS *Maddox*). Those marked with an asterisk accompanied the *Archangelsk.*

   Two of these, the *Dostoiny* and *Zhestki*, with several of the motor minesweepers supplied from America took part in the operations in the Siberian seas. Some of the latter were lost to U-boats and *T116* sank *U362*.

   Between 26 July and 4 August 1944 the four submarines handed over to the Soviet Union made passage from Dundee towards Murmansk. One, alas, failed to arrive. The *V1* (ex-HMS *Sunfish*), commanded by Kapitan 2 Ranga Fisanovich, was sunk by a patrolling Liberator, *V-Victor* of 86 Squadron RAF, by a tragic mistake. The other boats were: *V2* (Kapitan 1 Ranga Tripolski, ex-HMS *Unbroken*), *V3* (Kapitan 3 Ranga Kabo, ex-HMS *Unison*) and *V4* (Kapitan 3 Ranga Iosseliani, ex-HMS *Ursula*).

   Admiral Golovko was most disparaging about the addition of a battleship and cruiser to the Northern Fleet, dubbing them both 'steamers' and complaining that the *Milwaukee/Murmansk* was particularly obsolescent. He was more enthusiastic about the light craft which, it has to be said, the Russians employed vigorously in the North East Passage and along the polar coast.

3. The other boats in the Trutz group were *U363, U668, U394* and *U997.*

4. Some sources reverse the order in which *U344* and *U354* were sunk and their numbers are so close as to suggest clerical errors. However, I have followed the British Admiralty's Particulars of Destruction, published by HMSO in 1946, and the advice of Commander J.P. Mosse, C.O. of HMS *Mermaid*. *Bickerton*'s survivors were picked up by *Vigilant* which finished off the frigate.

5. I am indebted to Commander J.P. Mosse RN for permission to use papers in his possession relating to the operations of HMS *Mermaid* during the passage of JW59. He and some of his crew were afterwards decorated for their success. Stannard of the

Peacock was a holder of the Victoria Cross. Ironically, HMS *Mermaid* was afterwards sold to West Germany and renamed *Scharnhorst*.

6. Further Soviet attacks were made on shipping near Kirkenes between the 17th and the end of August when submarines and torpedo-boats achieved mixed results.
7. The American ships of JW60 were: *Adolph S. Ochs, Arunah S. Abell, Cardinal Gibbons, Daniel Willard, David Stone, Dexter W. Fellows, Edward A. Savoy, Edward E. Spafford, Francis Scott Key, Frederic A. Kummer, Frederick W. Taylor, George T. Angell, Hawkins Fudske, Henry Lomb, John J. Abel, John Vining, John Woolman, Joshua Thomas, Julius Olsen, Lewis Emery Jr, Nathaniel Alexander, Raymond B. Stevens, Richard M. Johnson* and *Thomas U. Walter*.

   Simultaneous with the running of this convoy, the cruiser *Jamaica* and destroyers *Orwell* and *Obedient* were sent to Spitzbergen to replenish the Free Norwegian garrison there.
8. The U-boats of the two groups were: *U293, U310, U315, U363, U365, U387, U636, U668, U965, U968, U992* and *U995*. The same day *U703* was lost to a mine off Iceland.
9. The merchant ships of JW61 were: American, *Abner Nash, Andrew W. Preston, Benjamin Schlesinger, Collis P. Huntington, Donald W. Bain, Eleazar Lord, Eloy Alfaro, Harold L. Winslow, Henry Adams, James M. Gillis, John Sharp Williams, Joyce Kilmer, Keith Palmer, Lawrence J. Brengle, Nicholas Biddle, Park Benjamin, Stage Door Canteen, William Pepper, William Wheelwright* and *Winfred L. Smith*; British, *Dolabella, Fort Crevecoeur* (Commodore Boucher), *Fort Romaine, Fort Yukon, Lapland* and *San Venancio* (tanker); and Norwegian, *Marathon*.
10. All these were Captain-class diesel or turbo-electric frigates supplied by the United States as part of the Lease-Lend agreement.
11. These were *U293, U295, U310, U315, U363, U365, U387, U425, U636, U668, U737, U771, U956, U965, U968, U992, U995, U997* and *U1163*.
12. In the Admiralty papers relating to Lieutenant-Commander Mosse's debriefing, a note in Admiral Edelsten's hand expresses the implication that the persistence of *Mermaid*'s captain should be emulated elsewhere and it is clear that Western Approaches escorts were trained to a very high degree of anti-submarine efficiency. Home Fleet destroyers spent more time training against aircraft and surface ships, and their anti-submarine expertise suffered accordingly. However, see R. Whinney, *The U-Boat Peril*, Arrow, 1989, p. 155, for a claim of the overall superiority of the Western Approaches escorts!

13. The remaining unnamed ships of JW62 were: American, *Amasa Delano, Andrew Turnbull, August Belmont, Barbara Frietchie, Cecil N. Bean, Edward N. Hurley, John Gibbon, Linn Boyd, Nelson W. Aldrich, Owen Wister, Robert Lowry, Renald Fernald, Stanton H. King, Stephen Leacock, Stevenson Taylor, U.S.O., W.R. Grace, William H. Wilmer, William Tyler Page* and *Woodbridge N. Ferris*; and British, *British Respect* (tanker), *Empire Garrick, Empire Stalwart, Fort Highfield, Fort Island, Fort Massac* and *Longwood*. *Fort Massac* today lies a wreck in the approaches to Harwich.
14. The Stock group comprised: *U313, U315, U293, U363, U299, U365, U286, U318, U995* and *U992*. The Grube boats were: *U295, U1163, U387, U997, U668, U310* and *U965*.

CHAPTER 23: 'WE ARE HAVING A BAD TIME WITH THE U-BOATS'

1. JW63 consisted of the following ships: American, *Alanson B. Houghton,* Benjamin H. Hill,* Bernard N. Baker, Caesar Rodney,* Charles M. Schwab,* Charles Scribner,* Crosby S. Noyes,* Edmund Fanning,* Francis C. Harrington,* George H. Pendleton,* Henry Bacon,* Henry Villard,* Henry Wyncoop,* Horace Gray, J.D. Yeager,* James Kerney,* John A. Quitman,* John Ireland,* John La Farge,* Jose Marti,* Joshua W. Alexander,* Lebaron Russell Briggs,* Paul H. Harwood,* Philip F. Thomas,* R. Ney McNeely,* Silas Weir Mitchell,* Thomas Scott** and *Warren Delano**; British, *Blue Ranger* (fleet oiler), *British Promise** (tanker), *Empire Archer,* Empire Celia,* Lacklan* (tanker), *Nacella** (tanker), *Samaritan** (Commodore Boucher) and *Laurelwood* (escort oiler); and Norwegian, *Idefjord* and *Norfjell* (tanker). Ships marked with an asterisk returned with convoy RA64.
2. RA63 consisted of: American, *Amasa Delano, Andrew Turnbull, August Belmont, Barbara Frietchie, Bernard N. Baker, Cecil N. Bean, Edward N. Hurley, John Gibbon, Linn Boyd, Nelson W. Aldrich, Owen Wister, Renald Fernald, Robert Lowry, Stanton H. King, Stephen Leacock, Stevenson Taylor, U.S.O., W.R. Grace, William H. Willmer, William Tyler Page* and *Woodbridge N. Ferris*; and British, *Blue Ranger* (fleet oiler), *British Respect* (tanker), *Empire Garrick, Empire Stalwart* (escort oiler), *Fort Boise, Fort Highfield, Fort Massac, Fort Island, Lacklan* (escort oiler), and *Longwood* (escort oiler).
3. JW64 consisted of: American, *Adolph S. Ochs,* Arunah S. Abell,* Ben F., Dixon,* Byron Darnton,† Daniel Willard,* Edwin L.*

*Drake,** *F.T. Frelinghuysen,** *Francis Scott Key,** *George Steers,** *Harold L. Winslow,** *Hawkins Fudske,** *Henry Lomb,*† *John J. Abel,** *John Wanamaker,** *Joyce Kilmer,** *Lewis Emery Jr,** *Nathan Towson,** *Marie M. Meloney,** *Townsend Harris** and *Willard Hall*†; British, *British Merit** (tanker), *Black Ranger*† (fleet oiler), *Empire Flint,** *Fort Crevecoeur** (Commodore Ullrig R. Nor. N.), *Fort Vercheres,** *Lucerna** (escort oiler) and *Neritina** (tanker); and Norwegian, *Skiensfjord.** Those ships shown with an asterisk returned with convoy RA65, those with a dagger, RA66.

4. The term fleet oiler has been used throughout to indicate tankers built for naval service as what are now called Royal Fleet Auxiliaries. Oilers/escort oilers were standard merchant tankers allocated to the fuelling of escorts. The stern refuelling method was used in the Arctic and could be quickly adopted by merchant-type ships. The beam method, now a standard NATO technique, was adopted by Fraser's British Pacific Fleet in emulation of the American Navy and proved far superior, allowing multiple replenishment.
5. The Rasmus boats initially off Bear Island were: *U286, U307, U425, U636, U711, U716, U739* and *U968*; and off Kola: *U293, U318, U992* and *U995*. Evidence of the asdic-operators' exhaustion from correspondence with the author.
6. Ships of RA64 are marked with an asterisk in note 1. Also in RA64 were the fleet oiler *Black Ranger, Idefjord* and *Paul H. Harwood*.
7. I am indebted to Derek Wellman for permission to quote this extract. See Morris Brodie (ed.), *A World Worth Fighting for; Ex Services Campaign for a Non-nuclear World*, Gooday Publishers, 1990, pp. 27–30.
8. Many of the extremely young Fleet Air Arm pilots suffered not only the effects of extreme cold, but also nervous problems which in some squadrons approached epidemic proportions. The ordeal of handling aircraft in such appalling conditions and the technical difficulties of operating from small and lively flight decks was bad enough, but to suffer persistent gunfire from one's own side must have been intolerable.

Chapter 24: The True Glory

1. Ships of JW65 were: American, *Benjamin Schlesinger,** *Charles A. McAllister,** *Eleazar Lord,** *Grace Abbott,** *Horace Bushnell, James M. Gillis,** *John McDonogh,** *Lawrence J. Brengle,** *Leo J. Duster,** *Nicholas Biddle,** *Stage Door Canteen,** *Thomas Donaldson, W.R. Grace,** *William Pepper,** *William Wheelwright** and *Winfred L. Smith**; British, *Blue Ranger** (fleet oiler), *Dolabella,** *Empire*

*Stalwart,** *Fort Boise** (Commodore), *Fort Yukon,** *Fort Massac,** *Lacklan* (escort oiler) and *San Venancio** (tanker); and Norwegian, *Idefjord*. Ships marked with an asterisk returned with convoy RA66.

2. Unnamed escorts were *Onslaught, Orwell, Opportune, Scorpion, Zambesi, Sioux* and *Farnham Castle*.
3. For the ships in this convoy see Chapter 23, note 3, to which must be added the fleet oiler *Blue Ranger* and escort oiler *Lacklan*.
4. The ships of JW66 were: American, *Albert C. Ritchie,** *August Belmont,** *Benjamin H. Hill,** *Cecil N. Bean,** *David B. Johnson,** *John Gibbon,** *Joshua Thomas,** *Keith Palmer,** *Linn Boyd,** *Lord Delaware,** *Nelson W. Aldrich,** *Owen Wister,** *Park Benjamin,** *Renald Fernald,** *William D. Byron,** *Stevenson Taylor,** *William Tyler Page** and *Woodbridge N. Ferris**; British, *Black Ranger* (fleet oiler), *Blue Ranger* (fleet oiler), *British Respect** (tanker), *Copeland* (rescue ship), *Empire Garrick,** *Laurelwood** (escort oiler), *Samaritan** (Commodore); and Norwegian, *Kong Haakon VII* and *Kronprinsen.** Ships marked with an asterisk returned with convoy RA67. The destroyers arriving with the carriers from Scapa were: *Offa, Zealous, Zephyr, Zest* and *Zodiac*; the Canadians *Haida, Huron* and *Iroquois*; and the Norwegian *Stord*.
5. For the ships of RA66, see Chapter 23, note 3, and also above, note 1. The waiting U-boats were: *U278, U286, U307, U312, U313, U318, U363, U427, U481, U711, U716, U968, U992* and *U997*. *Black Ranger* and the *Eloy Alfaro* were also in RA66.
6. Using her *schnorkel, U977* afterwards made the longest underwater passage then achieved by a submarine.
7. The ships of JW57 were: American, *Adolph S. Ochs, Alanson B. Houghton, Barbara Frietchie, Bernard N. Baker, Caesar Rodney, Cardinal Gibbons, Charles Bulfinch, Edward N. Hurley, George H. Pendleton, George Weems, Henry Wyncoop, John Ireland, Julien Poydras, Joshua W. Alexander, Philip F. Thomas, Robert J. Collier, Samuel McIntyre* and *Thomas Sim Lee*; British, *British Promise* (tanker), *Empire Emerald, Empire Prowess* (Commodore), *Fort Highfield* and the rescue ship *Rathlin*; and Norwegian, *Ivaran* and *Egero* (escort oiler). With the exception of *Rathlin* and *Egero* these vessels made independent passages after discharging in Russian ports.
8. For the ships of RA67 see note 4 above, plus the rescue ship *Rathlin* and escort oiler *Egero*.
9. This was in fact not quite the last sailing. British cargoes did not cease until March 1946. The ships left in Russia were: *Charles Gordon Curtis* which became the *Sergei Kirov*; *Panama City*, the *Novgorod*; *Empire Carpenter*, the *Dikson*; *Empire Nigel*, the *Archangelsk*; and *Ironclad*, the *Marina Raskova*.

10. See Alexander Werth, *Russia at War*, Barrie Rockliff, 1964, pp. 623 and 627; Arthur Bryant, *The Turn of the Tide*, p. 374; and Alan Clark, *Barbarossa*, Hutchinson, 1965, pp. 172–4.
11. See Victor Kravchenko, *I Chose Freedom*, Robert Hale, 1953, p. 193. I am most grateful to Paul Kemp for drawing this reference to my attention. Recent Russian publications are equally gracious and I am most grateful to Richard Kindersley for the loan of, and Vladimir Rakov for translating excerpts from two books about the Arctic convoys in Russian, both published in 1991 in Archangel: R. Gorchakov (ed.), *The Brotherhood of the Northern Convoys, 1941–1945*, and M.N. Suprun (ed.), *The Northern Convoys*.

Sources and bibliography

UNPUBLISHED MATERIAL

As I have mentioned in the Preface, I have discovered a number of inconsistencies during the writing of this book. These chiefly concern the names of merchant ships, wartime clerks not always being conscientious. This is particularly true of foreign ships and is aggravated by the idiosyncratic transliteration of Russian names. American ships' names were sometimes spelt incorrectly or inaccurately: whilst no one can argue with *Stage Door Canteen*, sloppy copying renders *Makawao* into *Wakawao* in one convoy list, for instance. Given the strain of convoy work, it is perhaps not surprising that these sorts of errors were also occasionally made in Commodores' Reports.

Records of Arctic convoys are held in the Public Records Office, Kew. The Admiralty File ADM199, Piece 2492, which concerns the War Diaries of the British Naval Mission to Moscow, remains closed.

Otherwise details of convoys are covered in the following Admiralty Files:

Dervish	ADM199/72
PQ1–PQ8	ADM199/72 and ADM237/160
PQ9	ADM237/161
PQ10	ADM199/72 and ADM237/174
PQ11	ADM199/72, ADM237/162 and ADM237/165
PQ12	ADM237/163
PQ13	ADM199/1709 and ADM237/164
PQ14	ADM199/721 and 1709, ADM237/165 and 177, and ADM1/12414 and 12425
PQ15	ADM199/721 and 1887, ADM237/166 and ADM1/17291

PQ16	ADM237/167 and 176
PQ17	ADM237/168
PQ18	ADM199/758 and 1709, and ADM237/169
JW51A	ADM199/620
JW51B	ADM199/73 and ADM1/14220
JW52	ADM199/73
JW53	ADM199/73
JW54A	ADM199/74
JW54B	ADM199/77 and ADM217/109
JW55A	ADM199/77
JW55B	ADM199/77, 913 and 914
JW56A	ADM199/77, 1491, 2027 and 2061
JW56B	ADM199/77 and 2027
JW57	ADM217/62 and 86
JW58	ADM217/18 and 111
JW59	ADM199/2061 and ADM217/113
JW60	No records kept
JW61	ADM217/310 and 647
JW62	ADM199/602 and 2061, and ADM217/114, 532 and 651
JW63	ADM199/602
JW64 and 65	ADM199/77, ADM 237/182 and 183, and ADM217/533
JW66	ADM199/1339 and ADM 217/69
JW67	ADM199/1339, ADM237/236, ADM199/1709 and ADM1/17628
QP1 to QP8	ADM199/72
QP9	ADM199/72 and 237/161
QP10	ADM199/1490, 2003 and 2059, and ADM237/174
QP11	ADM199/721 and 1709, ADM237/165 and ADM1/12414
QP12	ADM199/721 and 757, and ADM237/175
QP13	ADM237/176
QP14	ADM199/721, 757, 758 and 1709, and ADM237/177
QP15	ADM199/721 and ADM237/166
RA51	ADM199/73 and ADM237/178
RA52	ADM199/73 and 1403B, and ADM237/178
RA53	ADM199/73
RA54A	ADM199/77 and ADM1/15427
RA54B	ADM199/77 and 1035, and ADM1/15427
RA55A	ADM199/77 and ADM217/109
RA55B	ADM199/77
RA56	ADM199/77, 1491, 2027 and 2061, and ADM217/415
RA57	ADM237/179

RA58	ADM237/180 and ADM217/19, 62, 111 and 189
RA59	ADM199/1491, 1709, 2031 and 2061
RA59A	ADM237/181
RA60	ADM217/43 and 113
RA61	ADM217/319 and 647
RA61A	ADM217/291
RA62	ADM199/602, 1013 and 2061, and ADM217/651, 114 and 532
RA63	ADM199/602
RA64	ADM199/524 and 777, and ADM237/182
RA65	ADM199/777, ADM237/183 and ADM217/533
RA66	ADM199/1339 and ADM217/69
RA67	ADM199/1339 and ADM217/236

The Naval Staff Histories No. 22 (Arctic Convoys 1941–1945) and No. 24 (The Sinking of the *Scharnhorst*) are held in the PRO as files ADM234/369 and ADM234/342 respectively.

Submarine patrols associated with PQ convoy: ADM199/1887
Attacks on the *Admiral Tirpitz*: ADM234/345–350
Interception of German surface ships, 1941–2: ADM199/620
Submarine attacks on British warships: ADM199/160
Survivors' Reports: ADM199/2130–2148
Rescue Ships: ADM199/2149–2155
DEMS: ADM199/2168
Allied warships transferred to Russia: ADM199/1333 and 1334
Convoy Commodores: ADM199/8
Military co-operation with Russia, 1942: ADM199/604
Russo-British relations, 1943–4: ADM199/605, 606

Books

The following were among the books consulted:

General Background

Churchill, Winston S., *The Second World War*, Penguin, 1985
Clarke, Alan, *Barbarossa*, Heinemann, 1966
Collier, R., *The War that Stalin Won*, Hamish Hamilton, 1983
Hitler, Adolf, *Hitler's War Directives, 1939–45*, Pan Books, 1966
Humble, R., *The Rise and Fall of the British Navy*, Queen Anne's Press, 1986

Kennedy, P., *The Rise and Fall of British Naval Mastery*, 3rd ed., Fontana, 1991
Lewin, R., *Ultra Goes to War*, Hutchinson, 1978
Muratoff, P., *The Russian Campaigns of 1941–43*, Penguin, 1944
——*The Russian Campaigns of 1944–45*, Penguin, 1946
Reader's Digest, *The World at Arms*, 1989
Ruegg, R., *From Archangel to Alexandria on His Majesty's Service: The Story of HMS* Oxlip, privately circulated typescript
Seaton, A., *The Russo-German War, 1941–45*, Presidio Press, 1971
Werth, A., *The Year of Stalingrad*, Hamish Hamilton, 1946
——*Russia at War*, Rockliff, 1964

Naval Background

Archibald, E.H.H., *The Fighting Ship in the Royal Navy*, Blandford, 1984
Bacon, R. (ed.), *Britain's Glorious Navy*, Odhams, 1944
Barnett, C., *Engage the Enemy More Closely*, Hodder & Stoughton, 1991
Bekker, C., *Hitler's Naval War*, Macdonald, 1974
Busch, F-O., *The Drama of the* Scharnhorst, Hale, 1991
Creighton, K., *Convoy Commodore*, Futura, 1976
James, Sir W., *The British Navies in the Second World War*, Longman's Green, 1947.
Jane's Fighting Ships of World War Two, Bracken, 1991
Jones, G., *Defeat of the Wolf Packs*, Kimber 1986
Kemp, P., *Victory at Sea*, Muller, 1957
——*H.M. Destroyers*, Herbert Jenkins, 1956
Kennedy, L., *Pursuit*, Collins, 1974
Lenton, H.T., *British Escort Ships*, Macdonald and Jane's, 1974
Piekalkiewicz, J., *Sea War, 1939–45*, Blandford, 1985
——*Air War*, Blandford, 1985
Porten, E.P., *The German Navy in World War Two*, Pan, 1964
Rohwer, J., and Hummelchen, G., *Chronology of the War at Sea*, 2nd revised ed., Greenhill Books, 1992
Roskill, S., *The War at Sea*, HMSO, 1961
Smith, G., *The War at Sea, Royal and Dominion Navy Action in WW2*, Ian Allan, 1989
Stern, R., *U-Boats of World War Two* (Warships Illustrated No. 13), Arms and Armour Press, 1988
Tarrant, V.G., *King George V Class Battleships*, Arms and Armour Press, 1991
Taylor, G., *The Sea Chaplains*, Oxford Illustrated Press, 1978
Terraine, J., *The U-Boat Wars, 1914–1945*, Leo Cooper, 1989

Till, G., *Air Power and the Royal Navy*, Jane's, 1979
Tute, W., *The True Glory*, Macdonald, 1983
Whinney, R., *The U-Boat Peril*, Arrow, 1986
Whitley, M.J., *Destroyer! German Destroyers in World War Two*, Arms and Armour Press, 1983

Merchant Naval Background

Edwards, B., *The Merchant Navy Goes to War*, Hale, 1990
Gleichauf, Justin F., *Unsung Sailors*, Naval Institute Press, Annapolis, 1990
Harland, J., *Catchers and Corvettes: The Steam Whalecatcher in Peace and War*, Jean Boudriot, 1992
Hay, D., *War under the Red Ensign*, Jane's, 1982
Hope, R., *A New History of British Shipping*, John Murray, 1990
Hope, S., *Ocean Odyssey*, Eyre and Spottiswoode, 1944
Hurd, A. (ed.), *Britain's Merchant Navy*, Odhams, 1944
Lane, T., *The Merchant Seaman's War*, Manchester University Press, 1990
Lennox Kerr, J., *Touching the Adventures of Merchantmen*, Harrap, 1953
Rutter, O., *Red Ensign: A History of Convoy*, Hale, 1942
Sawyer, L., and Mitchell, W., *The Liberty Ships*, 2nd ed., Lloyds of London Press, 1985
Schofield, B., and Martyn, L., *The Rescue Ships*, Blackwood, 1968
Sclader, J., *The Red Duster at War*, Kimber, 1988
Thomas, D.A., *The Atlantic Star*, W.H. Allen, 1990
Young, J.M., *Britain's Sea War*, Patrick Stephens, 1989

Operations in the Arctic

Broome, Captain J., *The Convoy is to Scatter*, Kimber, 1972
Campbell, I., and MacIntyre, D., *The Kola Run*, Pan Books, 1958
Connell, G.G., *Arctic Destroyers (The 17th Flotilla)*, Kimber, 1982
Irving, D., *The Destruction of PQ17*, revised ed., Granada, 1985
Kemp, P., *The Russian Convoys* (Warships Illustrated No. 9) Arms and Armour Press, 1987
Lund, P., and Ludlam, H., *PQ17 - Convoy to Hell*, New English Library, 1969
Moore, J., *Escort Carrier*, Hutchinson, 1944
Ommaney, F., *Flat Top: The Story of an Escort Carrier*, Longmans Green, 1945
Pearce, F., *The Ship that Torpedoed Herself*, Baron Jay, 1975
——*Running the Gauntlet: The Battles for the Barents Sea*, Fontana, 1989

Pope, D., *73 North*, Alison Press, 1988 (reissue)
Ruegg, R., and Hague, A., *Convoys to Russia*, World Ship Society, 1992
Schofield, Vice-Admiral B.B., *The Arctic Convoys*, Macdonald and Jane's, 1977
——*The Russian Convoys*, Batsford, 1964
Smith, P.C., *Arctic Victory, The Story of Convoy PQ18*, Kimber, 1975
Winton, J., *The Death of the* Scharnhorst, Granada, 1980
Woodman, D., *HMS* Tracker *and the Attacker-Class Escort Carriers*, Friends of the Fleet Air Arm Museum, 1987

Personal

Hayes, Vice-Admiral J., *Face the Music: A Sailor's Story*, Pentland Press, 1991
Kerslake, S., *Coxswain in the Northern Convoys*, Kimber, 1984
Mallalieu, J.M.W., *Very Ordinary Seaman*, Granada, 1962
Popham, H., *Sea Flight*, Kimber, 1954
Ransome-Wallis, R., *Two Red Stripes: A Naval Surgeon at War*, Ian Allan, 1973
Saul, I., *Camera in Convoy*, Ellison's Editions, 1987
Smith, Roland, *Naval Time Capsule Videos, The Hazards of Russian Convoys*
Wellman, D., *A World Worth Fighting for*, Gooday, 1990
Winn, G., *PQ17: Story of a Ship*, Hutchinson, 1953
Winton, J. (ed.), *Freedom's Battle, Vol. 1: The War at Sea 1935–45*, Hutchinson, 1984

Biography

Humble, R., *Fraser of North Cape*, Routledge and Kegan Paul, 1983
Stephen, M., *The Fighting Admirals*, Leo Cooper, 1991

The Soviet Navy

Golovko, A., *With the Red Fleet*, Putnam, 1965
Mitchell, M., *The Red Fleet and the Royal Navy*, Hodder and Stoughton, 1942
Woodward, D., *The Russians at Sea*, Kimber, 1965

MISCELLANEOUS

Blackwood's Magazine, July 1945, article by Hugh Popham
Hansard, 18 March 1947, Navy Estimates Debate
HMSO, 'Merchantmen at War', 1944

HMSO, Supplement to the *London Gazette* of Friday, 13 October 1950, 'Convoys to North Russia'

HMSO, *German, Italian and Japanese U-Boat Casualties during the War*, 1946

The Listener, February 1945. Article by Howard French

The Northern Light, Official Journal of the North Russia Club, miscellaneous editions

Acknowledgements

I AM ACUTELY aware of the enormity of my own presumption in attempting a work of this nature. I was not even a distant witness to the events described in these pages, though an uncle served, and I share a birth date with the arrival of a homeward convoy! Beyond those tenuous and insubstantial connections, I can claim only deep admiration and the fascination of a seafarer for the endeavours of his predecessors.

I am therefore conscious of the great debt I owe to so many people. The help and kindness I have received have been almost overwhelming, and I have been spurred on at bleak moments by the constant urging of many who insisted the story was worth the telling. I hope I have not disappointed their expectations nor that their letters and telephone calls, the time they gave me, and their hospitality, have been misplaced.

I must record a special debt of gratitude to Charles Owen, whose service in the Arctic was the initial inspiration for this book and whose guidance and encouragement have been much appreciated; also to Admiral of the Fleet Lord Lewin for his foreword, his recollections and his reading of my typescript. Former Commodore's Yeoman Len Matthews also ploughed doggedly through an early draft, assisted with research and made many helpful suggestions, while his wife indulged us with a splendid dinner. Maurice Irvin must also be singled out for special mention for providing me with a great deal of material. Sadly, two more of those who were of particular help, Peter Kemp and Bob Whinney, have died before publication. Mrs Whinney was kind enough to pass on my late queries.

My thanks also go to the following for supplying me with information, diaries, recollections or photographs, or for permitting me to invade their privacy and interview them: E.R. Allan, Steve Attwater, L. Bainborough, G. Barclay, Roy Barclay, W. Beacham, Bill Bowen-Davies, L. Bradley, Canon P.J.M. Bryan, Captain Dennis Bunn, G. Charlton, Eldred Clark, W.H.H. Coates, R.A. Cobb, J.C. Coles, David B. Craig, Arnold Crossley, F.R. Crozier, A.F. Dickson, Jeff Dines, Cyril Elles, Captain David Evans, Captain Farquarson-Roberts, Captain D. Foster, Alfred W. Fowler, Richard Frampton, H. George, Canon Peter Gillingham, L. Gorham, Lord Greenway, Arthur Hague, Dr John R. Harland, John Hawkins, J. Hay, E. Hayes, C. Holder, A. Johnsen, Mrs M.M. Keeble, the late Charlie Keen, Sid Kerslake, Richard Kindersley, Frank Kismul, Captain Charles Leadbetter, Rear-Admiral John Lee-Barber, Professor Harold Levine, Fred Lewes, Canon P. Llewellyn, G.W. Long, L.J. Lynch, David MacNeill, John McFarquar, Kenneth Mason, Frank Metson, James S.G. Mitchell, Commander J.P. Mosse, Captain Arthur Nunn, Kevin O'Donoghue, David Page, Captain George Parnell, Maurice Passingham, Dr Hans Otto Pelser, Hugh Popham, Ian Priscott, George Quantock, Vladimir Rakov, Tom Reville, C.V. Reynolds, H. Richards, M.S. Richards, H.R. Robinson, E.G. Robson, Dr Jurgen Rohwer, Bob Ruegg, A. Russell, Captain George Salvesen, Mrs Rosemary Sherbrooke, Mrs Ann Shirley, A. Smith, R. Smith, P. Spicer, G. Stacey, S. Stevans, R.D. Squires, Rev. Gordon Taylor, H. Taylor, J. Taylor, H.A. Thomas, R.H. Towersey, Captain J.A. Tuttle, H.A. Twiddy, A.J. Waine, C. Walker, G.P. Ward, E. Wares, Commander D.W. Waters, D. Wellman, Captain John Wells, I. Wheble, Mrs Whinney, Roy Wilkinson, R.F. Williams, W.W. Williams, Alex Wood, Bill Wood and George Woodman.

For specific help in finding additional illustrations I must thank Paul Kemp of the Imperial War Museum for his kindness and help, notwithstanding the fact that we found ourselves rivals of a sort, and I acknowledge with thanks the Trustees of the Imperial War Museum for the use of material from their photographic archives.

Further illustrations are reproduced courtesy of the Fleet Air Arm Museum whose staff were most helpful.

For permission to quote material, I would like to thank the following: Winston S. Churchill, *The Second World War*, Messrs. Cassell and the Estate of Winston S. Churchill; Victor

Kravchenko, *I Chose Freedom*, Messrs. Robert Hale; Captain J. Broome, *The Convoy is to Scatter*, A.M. Heath & Co.; Robert Hughes, *Flagship to Murmansk*, Futura; and G.S. Connell, *Arctic Destroyers*, and Rear-Admiral Sir Kenelm Creighton, *Convoy Commodore*, both originally published by William Kimber, now an imprint of Harper Collins; and Sir John Hayes, *Face the Music*, Pentland Press.

I must also thank the Director and Staff of the Directoraat General Scheepvart En Maritieine Zaken, Riswijk, The Netherlands; Mrs C. Freeman of the General Register and Record Office of Shipping and Seamen, Cardiff; and the staff of the Public Records Office at Kew.

Additional corrections to this edition have been provided by John Annett, George Brown, Nigel Bryant, Bruce Burgess, Harry Carter, John Culverwell, Peter S. Dawson, G.D. Fletcher, Captain Dennis Foster, Alex Farrer, Vice-Admiral Sir John Hayes, Captain James Henderson, Adrian Hughes, W.A. Haskell, F.A. Howorth, Captain Peter King, A. Laylee, W. Lea, P.G. Mallett, Captain Arthur R. Moore, Bill Looker, Jack Neale, P. Oastler, John Roberts, F. Saunders, Dick Squires, John Sweeney, A. Taylor, Captain Maurice Usherwood and Morley F. Wheeler.

To my publisher John R. Murray I owe a great measure of gratitude not only for his enthusiastic support throughout the project, but also for supplying Lieutenant Law's personal diary of PQ17. My editor, Gail Pirkis, has been magnificent in a multitude of ways and while all opinions expressed in these pages are my own, the finished product owes much to her diligence. Warmest thanks are also due to my agent, Barbara Levy, and my wife Christine whose support has been, as ever, unfailing.

Index

Note: Ranks and titles are generally the highest mentioned in the text. Individual ships are listed under the heading **Ships**; individual **Convoys**, **Submarines** and **U-boats** under those headings. Only ships mentioned in the main text are indexed.